SALEM HEALTH

ADDICTIONS & SUBSTANCE ABUSE

SALEM HEALTH

ADDICTIONS & SUBSTANCE ABUSE

Volume 2

Editor
Robin Kamienny Montvilo, RN, PhD

SALEM PRESS
A DIVISION OF EBSCO PUBLISHING
Ipswich, Massachusetts   Hackensack, New Jersey

Note to Readers

The material presented in *Salem Health: Addictions and Substance Abuse* is intended for broad informational and educational purposes. Readers who suspect that they or someone they know has any disorder, disease, or condition described in this set should contact a physician without delay. This set should not be used as a substitute for professional medical diagnosis. Readers who are undergoing or about to undergo any treatment or procedure described in this set should refer to their physicians and other health care providers for guidance concerning preparation and possible effects. This set is not to be considered definitive on the covered topics, and readers should remember that the field of health care is characterized by a diversity of medical opinions and constant expansion in knowledge and understanding.

Library of Congress Cataloging-in-Publication Data

Addictions and substance abuse / editor, Robin Kamienny Montvilo.
  p. cm. – (Salem health)
 Includes bibliographical references and index.
  ISBN 978-1-58765-959-1 (set) – ISBN 978-1-58765-960-7 (volume 1) – ISBN 978-1-58765-961-4 (volume 2) – ISBN 978-1-58765-963-8 (ebook set) 1. Substance abuse–Treatment–United States. 2. Drug abuse–Treatment–United States. 3. Alcoholism–Treatment–United States. 4. Cognitive therapy. I. Montvilo, Robin Kamienny.
  RC563.A356 2012
  362.29–dc23
                    2012020279

Contents

Complete List of Contents
Volume 1

Volume 2

M

Marijuana

CATEGORY: Substances

ALSO KNOWN AS: Cannabis; dope; ganja; grass; hashish; hemp; mary jane; pot; smoke; weed

DEFINITION: Marijuana consists of the dried, shredded leaves and flowers of the hemp plant *Cannabis sativa*. Its psychoactive effects derive from a substance in the resin of the plant, called delta-9-tetraydrocannabinol (also known as THC).

STATUS: Illegal in the United States and other countries

CLASSIFICATION: Schedule I controlled substance

SOURCE: *Cannabis sativa* is a hardy annual that grows wild in almost every climactic region and condition. In hot, dry climates, the plant produces much more of the resin containing THC, the active ingredient of marijuana.

TRANSMISSION ROUTE: Ingested nasally by smoking; ingested orally

HISTORY OF USE

Marijuana is the world's most widely used and oldest illegal drug. Archeological evidence dates its cultivation to 8,000 BCE in China, where its fibers were used to make textiles and later paper. (The type of marijuana used for such purposes is more fibrous and is called hemp.) Beginning in the first century BCE, marijuana also was used for its psychoactive effects. Marijuana also then began to be used for medicinal purposes, a use that has pervaded its history and is a significant feature of its contemporary status.

In India, the psychoactive effects of marijuana were known at least since the second millennium BCE. The Vedas state it was originally given by the god Shiva because it "releases us from anxiety." Marijuana also was an important aspect of the practice of Tantric sex. The Persians, the Scythians, and especially the Arabs, also used marijuana for its psychoactive effects, but most cultures familiar with the plant knew it only for the quality of its fibers for rope and clothing.

Throughout European history, the economic value of marijuana continued to be its prevailing use, though medieval magicians, witches, and sorcerers used it for its psychoactive powers. Mainstream Europeans learned of such effects only when, in the seventeenth and eighteenth centuries, they colonized Asia, particularly India. By the nineteenth century, marijuana was used by leading artists and writers, especially in France and most famously at the Paris Hashish Club.

In the United States, interest in marijuana's psychoactive properties increased in the mid-nineteenth century, especially with the 1857 publication of Fitz Hugh Ludlow's *The Hasheesh Eater*. Popular magazines and books included stories of its use, and marijuana was available at local pharmacies. By the end of that century, some of the most prominent psychologists in the United States also studied the drug through personal use. Even so, by the twentieth century, marijuana was largely limited to upper-class intellectuals. Most Americans did not know anything about marijuana; their drugs of choice were opium, morphine, cocaine, and alcohol.

Racism against Chinese immigrants seen as taking jobs from Americans, combined with a desire to build commercial interests in China, led the US Congress to pass the Harrison Act in 1914, which imposed recordkeeping and taxation requirements on the sale of opium. Morphine and cocaine, other previously popular narcotic drugs, which by this time had come to be seen as having problematic addictive properties, also were included in this bill. Marijuana was included as well, simply because it was considered another narcotic, though it had no similar reputation for addiction. Five years later, the adoption of the Eighteenth Amendment to the US Constitution prohibited alcohol and began an era in which federal power had authority over matters of morality, cast in the light of the intensifying class warfare of the age, as minorities and the working class fought for labor rights.

Marijuana was primarily used by Mexican immigrants in the Western United States, immigrants who had been welcomed for the inexpensive labor they supplied. They were then blamed for job losses as agribusiness reduced farm workforces during the 1910s and 1920s. During those decades every Western state passed laws to make marijuana illegal. Its criminalization was supported by alleged links between marijuana use and laziness, promiscuity, mental illness, and violence, all of which were based on the apparently greater incidence of such symptoms in the minority populations who tended to use marijuana.

As the Great Depression accelerated job losses during the 1930s, the rhetoric of violence-prone minorities fueled by marijuana next targeted African Americans in major cities. Led by Harry Anslinger, the director of the new Federal Bureau of Narcotics, public advocacy for marijuana's criminalization as a "killer weed" convinced Congress in 1937 to prohibit its possession with the Marijuana Tax Act. Subsequent legislation, in 1951 and 1956, increased penalties.

In the 1960s, marijuana use increased dramatically and became the focus of the intense controversy that has continued to structure the national debate into the present. Marijuana, used especially by college-age youth disaffected by the dominant culture, became an expression of the youth rebellion of the times for those on both sides of that cultural divide. US president Richard M. Nixon's "war on drugs" was his attempt to curtail the rebellion. As middle-class youths became subject to arrest and incarceration, the justification for marijuana's criminalization came into question. Even as strictures against its use were increased in 1968 and 1970, presidential commissions in 1962, 1963, 1967, and 1972 concluded that the claims against marijuana were exaggerated or false.

Trends in marijuana use have continued at high levels. Statistics for twelfth graders who have used marijuana show a peak of more than 60 percent by the late 1970s, declining to a low just under 40 percent in the early 1990s and an uneven rise since then. In 2009, the National Institute on Drug Abuse

A Colombian police officer checks part of the five tons of marijuana that were seized on the road between Palmira and Andalucia in Cali, Colombia, February 27, 2012. Marijuana is one of the most commonly encountered forms of illicit drugs and easily produced in nearly every region of the world. (Christian Escobar Mora/EPA/Landov)

reported that 28.5 million Americans age twelve years and older had used marijuana at least once in the year prior. A World Health Organization (WHO) survey in 2008 found that 42 percent of the US population, more than 100 million people, had used marijuana at least once, the highest rate in WHO's seventeen-country study.

EFFECTS AND POTENTIAL RISKS

Marijuana is a mild intoxicant, with aspects of both a stimulant and a tranquilizer. When smoked, the effects of marijuana begin in minutes and can last for a couple of hours; the maximum intensity occurs within the first hour. These effects, colloquially known as getting high, vary considerably according to the potency, the dosage, the setting, and the person's experience and attitude.

Positive short-term experiential effects include feelings of light-hearted well-being and euphoria; increased sensory sensitivity and appreciation; and greater awareness, creativity, insight, and sense of humor. Negative effects include difficulty with concentration, short-term memory, and motor performance skills; and feeling anxious, tense, socially awkward, and paranoid. At high dosages, new users may experience disorientation and panic, which account for most of the emergency room visits associated with marijuana use.

Longer-term experiential effects are more speculative. Many users report that insights remained significant and even life-changing. Negative effects also have been proposed, including amotivational syndrome and an increased tendency to later use other, more dangerous drugs (the "gateway drug" theory). These claims continue to be asserted but have failed to withstand rigorous research, which has repeatedly disproved them.

Short-term physical effects include dilated blood vessels and increased heart rate. No damaging effects on the body have been found from occasional use of marijuana. Several such effects have been asserted, most prominently chromosomal damage, lung damage, brain damage, and depressed immune response. None of these claims has withstood further scrutiny.

Research findings on long term effects of heavy marijuana use are highly varied. First, some studies have found a correlation with psychotic or affective mental health outcomes. Whether this correlational link implicates a causal one is hotly debated, but the possibility persists that marijuana use may exacerbate pre-existing mental disorders. Second, marijuana smoke contains a number of carcinogens that can be irritants to the lungs. Third, studies on animals also indicate that the cannabinoids in marijuana may accumulate on the brain for days afterward, and it is assumed that larger and more frequent use would result in a longer period of such accumulation.

Marijuana does not cause physical dependence and so has almost no addictive potential, though claims to the contrary are asserted on the basis of long-term usage patterns. Withdrawal symptoms are rare, but after prolonged heavy use may include general unease, insomnia, lethargy, boredom, a reduced experience of pleasure, and a desire to continue use. Based on studies of acute toxicity in animals, it has been determined that a lethal dose of marijuana would be roughly five thousand times a normal dose, impossible to ingest by the usual means. No human deaths from marijuana use have been documented.

Christopher M. Aanstoos, PhD

FURTHER READING

Booth, Martin. *Cannabis: A History.* New York: Macmillan, 2005. A detailed and balanced history of marijuana, including its current controversies.

"Deglamorizing Cannabis (Editorial)." *The Lancet* 346 (1995). The famous editorial in which the prestigious British journal of medicine concluded that smoking marijuana is not harmful to health.

Earleywine, Mitch. *Understanding Marijuana.* New York: Oxford UP, 2002. A careful analysis of the scientific evidence of the short- and long-term effects of casual and heavy marijuana use.

Grinspoon, Lester. *Marijuana Reconsidered.* 2nd ed. San Francisco: Quick American Archives, 1994. Deeply researched study of the effects of marijuana by a prominent psychiatrist often called upon to provide expert testimony.

Iverson, Lester. *The Science of Marijuana.* 2nd ed. New York: Oxford UP, 2008. Detailed examination of scientific studies.

Zimmer, Lynn, and John Morgan. *Marijuana Myths, Marijuana Facts.* New York: Lindesmith Center, 1997. A comprehensive and objective overview of the scientific evidence, particularly with respect to the more exaggerated claims.

See also: Gateway drugs; Hashish; Medical marijuana;
Pipes and hookahs; Psychosis and substance abuse

Marriage/partnership and alcoholism

CATEGORY: Psychological issues and behaviors

DEFINITION: Alcoholism commonly affects marriages and other domestic partnerships. Partners are at risk for developing serious physical and emotional problems. Most literature has focused on men in relationships because alcohol abuse is far more common among men, although statistics show that alcohol abuse by women is increasing. It is estimated that one-half of all divorces in the United States occur in families in which at least one person has abused alcohol.

INTRODUCTION

In the early 1930s, social workers in state hospitals reported their observations of the wives of alcoholic men, describing the wives as having anxiety, depression, and psychosomatic symptoms. The social workers suggested that such psychological symptoms were not caused by living with a chronic alcoholic; instead, the women who displayed such symptoms were using their marriages to alcoholic men to resolve their own neurotic conflicts. Furthermore, it was suggested that if the male alcoholic would decrease his drinking, the wife would suffer from the loss of a defense mechanism.

In the 1950s and 1960s, theory and treatment options shifted this view to one in which family members' symptoms were viewed as a normal process in a high-stress environment with care similar to that required for a chronically ill spouse or partner. Continued research has focused upon the interactive process between alcoholics and others in close relationship with them.

ALCOHOLIC SPOUSE/PARTNER RELATIONSHIPS

Addiction to alcohol is a relationship issue. Being married to or in a domestic partnership with an alcoholic places a strain on that relationship, causing the nonalcoholic partner to take on responsibilities that would not be expected in a nonalcoholic relationship. Studies find that marital or domestic relationships with alcoholics have a high degree of relationship dissatisfaction and that tension and verbal conflict are usually high.

A partner may assume a relational preoccupation that parallels the alcoholic's obsessive preoccupation with alcohol, trying to convince the alcoholic mate to discontinue drinking. When this process characterizes the relationship, the nonalcoholic partner needs encouragement to emotionally abstain from participating in the partner's alcoholic behavior.

RELATIONSHIP DYNAMICS

Couple interaction can be significantly affected by alcoholism and alcohol-related behaviors. Alcoholism requires energy, not for long-term growth but for maintaining short-term stability. The developmental milestones that would be expected in a relationship are identified instead as developmental distortions.

A negative cycle may occur in which the spouse becomes more fearful as the alcoholic increases alcohol use, and may then respond with a greater focus on getting the alcoholic to stop drinking. The alcoholic experiences this through feeling overscrutinized and pressured. The assumption, relative to the relationship conflict, is that if the drinking stops, the problems will stop. This attempt to manage the behavior of the other further deteriorates the relationship. Alcoholic behaviors become the primary factors in how the family system functions and is organized. In such cases, nonalcoholic partners may lose their sense of direction and identity as they attempt to survive in the high-stress environment and realize that their life has been structured around the alcoholic.

Under normal circumstances, a marital or domestic relationship exists to meet the basic needs of protection, shelter, and food of family members through a unified process. With heightened tension, such as when one partner is an alcoholic, changes occur in regulatory behaviors to ensure a relationship that accommodates the demands of alcoholism. If the partner of the alcoholic becomes anxious, the anxiety can escalate and spread to all family members. When this happens, the normal emotional connectedness that should be comforting becomes stressful. Eventually, family members begin to feel overwhelmed and out of control.

Family members who feel the greatest stress tend to accommodate others to alleviate familial tension. The person who accommodates the most, usually a spouse but sometimes a child, is attempting to absorb the anxiety present in others. This family member will become the most vulnerable to physical illness and depression, or even to alcoholism.

RELATIONSHIP VIOLENCE

Although excessive use of alcohol has been associated with spouse (mostly wife) abuse, no evidence has found a causal relationship between alcoholism and family violence. However, factors that add stress to the family are associated with marital and partner violence, and excessive use of alcohol is a stress-producing factor. Conflict between the couple over drinking patterns also increases the potential that violence will be used to manage conflict.

Undesired sexual relations (including rape) may be forced by a partner after drinking. Substantial research shows that physical and sexual aggression in men is intensified by alcohol. A partner who is normally not aggressive can become aggressive or even violent when drinking heavily.

A national study found that the more often a spouse or partner was drunk, the greater the likelihood that physical violence would be a part of the relationship. In cases of extreme drinking by one partner who was almost always drunk, the likelihood of violence dropped to a lower level.

INTERVENTION

Working with spouses and partners of alcoholics requires careful exploration. Many people have experienced

---

Denial

Denial is a defense mechanism used by all people to protect themselves from being consciously aware of knowledge that is emotionally threatening to them. Addicts and their families often use denial to avoid facing the reality of the addiction and its consequences. Denial is a process that can take many forms, ranging from simple to complex.

All people use denial to avoid being emotionally overwhelmed by something difficult or emotionally threatening. However, for addicts and their families, denial maintains an addiction by preventing the addict from consciously realizing and addressing the consequences and negative trajectory of his or her behavior. Denial also may impair an addict's judgment, prevent an addict from developing a desire to change, impair the addict's realistic self-perception, and increase the likelihood that an addict will engage in increasingly more self-destructive behaviors. For families and friends of addicts, denial may impair judgment, prevent them from dealing with the full emotional impact of a loved one's addictive behavior, or facilitate the continued use of enabling behavior.

---

relationships that are chaotic, unreliable, and emotionally confusing. Often the feelings of anger and resentment are not expressed for fear of exacerbating the alcoholic's drinking or hindering his or her recovery. There may be repressed desires and dreams for the future that the nonalcoholic partner does not voice, such as buying a house or having more time together.

If a couple seeks therapy, and if one partner is a substance abuser, it is likely that the use of alcohol or the impact of alcohol-related behaviors will not be the focus of the relationship problems. This is to be expected because it is estimated that only one in four persons who abuse alcohol will seek treatment for their drinking problems. If the therapist does not demonstrate sensitivity to how alcoholism affects relationships, the issue may never become a part of treatment. It is generally believed that a combination of approaches, which includes both couple therapy and self-help approaches for alcoholism, will be necessary. A therapist should always assume the responsibility of helping the couple understand how alcoholism affects their relationship. Also, the therapist should help the couple understand what precipitates excessive drinking or what leads to a relapse.

Communication by the nonalcoholic partner will sometimes include diagnostic labeling as an attempt to encourage a partner to seek help. Labels such as *being an alcoholic* or *being in denial* carry certain stigmas, and it is only reasonable that persons with self-confidence will reject such labels. Relationships may have an underlying dynamic that represents a power struggle and one person's attempt to assert control. A remark such as "Your problem is that you are in denial" may seem harmless when it is uttered, but tends to be perceived as judgmental.

Therapists in twelve-step programs usually focus on the processes that enable drinking. The goal is to help spouses or partners experience emotional insight and to identify enabling behaviors. Self-help support groups attempt to empower spouses and partners and to begin the process of establishing a meaningful and satisfying life, regardless of the partner's alcoholism.

The National Council on Alcoholism and Drug Dependence in New York City provides five guidelines for persons dealing with an alcoholic. The organization's advice is to recognize alcoholism as a disease, to learn as much as possible about alcoholism, to avoid becoming an enabler, to avoid home treatments, and to seek professional help for personal development.

Lillian J. Breckenridge

FURTHER READING

Ackerman, R. *Perfect Daughters: Adult Daughters of Alcoholics*. Deerfield Beach, FL: Health Communications, 2002. An interesting read for women who grew up with alcoholic parents to determine if they find the characteristics descriptive of themselves. Ackerman is a founding board member of the National Association for Children of Alcoholics.

Freeman, Shelley MacKay. *Paths to Recovery: Al-Anon's Steps, Traditions, and Concepts*. Virginia Beach, VA: Al-Anon, 1997. Author gives a thorough explanation of both the twelve steps and the twelve traditions of Al-Anon. Important reading for those who are thinking of connecting with Al-Anon.

Jay, Jeff, and Debra Jay. *Love First*. 2nd ed. Center City, MN: Hazelden, 2008. Discusses how families, friends, and professionals can focus on love as an approach to intervention for alcoholism. Provides tools for families and couples.

Watt, Toni Terling. "Marital and Cohabiting Relationships of Adult Children of Alcoholics." *Journal of Family Issues* 23 (2002): 246–65. Print. A critical review of the popular belief that children raised by alcoholic parents have difficulty establishing healthy and happy adult relationships of their own.

WEBSITES OF INTEREST

Families Anonymous
http://www.familiesanonymous.org

Nar-Anon Family Group Headquarters
http://www.nar-anon.org

Partnership at Drugfree.org
http://www.jointogether.org

See also: Families and substance abuse; Marriage/partnership and behavioral addictions; Marriage/partnership and substance abuse; Parenting and alcoholism

Marriage/partnership and behavioral addictions

CATEGORY: Psychological issues and behaviors
DEFINITION: Behavioral addictions, which include pathological gambling and sex addiction, affect not only the addict but also the addict's partner or spouse and other family members. Much like substance abusers, behavioral addicts often perpetuate their actions with manipulative and deceitful behavior much to the detriment of themselves and those close to them.

BEHAVIORAL ADDICTIONS AND RELATIONSHIPS
Behavioral addiction causes a person to lose control of the impulses that lead to negative actions. The most common behavioral addictions include gambling addiction and sex addiction. Less common but prevalent impulse control disorders include kleptomania and pyromania and addictions to food, computer and Internet use, shopping, and exercise.

Behavioral addictions are far less common than substance addictions. There remains a significant debate among mental health professionals as to whether such impulse control disorders should even be technically classified as addictions because they do not involve the consumption or use of a chemically addictive external stimulant.

Experts believe that as many as 6 percent of all American adults have some form of sex addiction. It also is believed that as many as two million Americans are pathological gamblers, meaning that they lie about the frequency of their gambling and place bets with little or no financial backing to cover the costs.

While all instances of addiction can have negative consequences on interpersonal, family, and professional relationships, few impulse control disorders are as corrosive to marriages, partnerships, and families as gambling addiction and sex addiction. Each of these disorders can have extreme effects on the foundations of trust and security. Like substance abusers, many behavioral addicts fail to see the negative ramifications of their actions on those closest to them until after severe damage has been done.

NEUROLOGICAL SIMILARITIES TO SUBSTANCE ABUSE

The neurological causes of behavioral addictions remain unknown to medical professionals and sociologists alike. A widely held theory states that behavioral addicts become hooked on the euphoria-producing chemicals in the brain that impulsive behaviors such as gambling produce. These patterns of addiction are similar to the neurological stimulation experienced by those under the influence of drugs.

SEX ADDICTION

Sex addiction is classified as the inability to control sexual thoughts, impulses, and behaviors. Exhibitionist and voyeuristic behavior are both symptomatic of sex addiction, as is sexual promiscuity. Some sex addicts habitually seek sexual gratification through sexual interactions with others, often including those outside their partnership. Other sex addicts require constant immersion in sexually explicit material such as pornography.

The proliferation of online sexual material makes Internet sex addiction one of the fastest growing segments of sex addiction. Because many sex addicts engage in inappropriate extramarital relationships,

violation of trust is the most frequent negative impact sex addiction can have on marriages and partnerships. An addict's preoccupation with sexual activity also can lead to the neglect of family, professional, and social responsibilities.

Much like substance abusers, sex addicts often distance themselves from those closest to them for reasons of both shame and defense of their addiction. Undisclosed promiscuity by sex addicts also may put them and their unknowing domestic partners or spouses at higher risk for sexually transmitted disease. Research has shown that sex addicts also respond to confrontation about their sexual activity through verbal and physical abuse of their partners. Children also are harmed by the consequences of sex addiction. Domestic stability and the safety and well-being of loved ones are often of little or no concern to those with a sex addiction.

While sex addiction often leads to the dissolution of domestic partnerships and marriages, research indicates that spousal support in the sex addiction recovery process can be helpful in eliminating such behaviors. Sex addiction treatment plans focus primarily on ceasing risky sexual behavior through close monitoring, examining the root causes of the desire for ritualistic sexual behavior, deconstructing the underlying motivations of sexual fantasies, and coping with the emotional despair and shame that often results from deviant or risky sexual behavior.

GAMBLING ADDICTION

Gambling addiction is classified as an obsessive preoccupation with betting money in hopes of achieving financial rewards in return, no matter how slim the odds. Compulsive gamblers partake in any number of gaming activities, from sports betting to casino gaming. Because legalized gambling has been one of the fastest growing industries in the United States since the mid-twentieth century, incidences of compulsive gambling have continued to rise.

Forty-seven of the fifty US states now allow some form of legalized gambling, while twenty-eight states now have casino gaming. Many state governments face severe financial burdens, expanding payrolls, and dilapidating infrastructures, making them unable to refuse the tax boon that the gaming industry provides to state budgets.

Whereas the majority of people gamble infrequently for pleasure, an expanding number of Americans views the slim odds of gambling as a reasonable path to financial stability. As part of their never-ending quest to increase profits and attract customers, many casinos now have theme parks, golf courses, and amusement rides, and many gaming cruises include stops at these attractions. The result is a family-centric gaming experience, where gambling no longer takes place away from spouses, partners, and children, but becomes a group experience. The concept of gambling to please one's partner or children ends up supporting gambling as a way to mask a lack of self-esteem and the daily stresses of raising a family. These circumstances, coupled with the neurological effects of gambling on the brain's pleasure centers, often lead to impulsive gambling.

Most compulsive gamblers participate in several avenues of gambling activity simultaneously. The proliferation of Internet-based sports betting allows bettors to place wagers on hundreds if not thousands of sporting events taking place all over the world from the comfort of home. Much as sex addiction shakes the foundations of interpersonal trust and intimacy, pathological gambling can jeopardize the financial stability of a marriage or domestic partnership, often without the knowledge of the gambler's partner.

Unlike substance abuse, which often involves years of abuse before the addict admits to having a problem, pathological gambling can swiftly snowball from a difficult-to-control compulsion to a ruinous problem in a matter of days, as compulsive gamblers seek that one final payoff. While certain financial peril may be the most obvious risk that the gambling addict poses to his or her partner and family, the downfall is not always swift. Many partners of gambling addicts learn to adapt to the behavioral addictions of their spouses, even to the point of enabling their partners' impulsive behaviors. The stresses of covering up a partner's compulsive gambling problem are often detrimental to the entire family.

Hiding the behavior of a compulsive gambler from family and friends only delays the consequences of the behavior. Attempting to control gambling through moderation is simply a way of supporting an addict's habit.

The rise in impulsive gambling has been paralleled with the founding of several nationwide advocacy programs designed to provide resources for intervention and treatment. Among these programs are the National Council on Problem Gambling and Gamblers Anonymous.

John Pritchard

FURTHER READING

Gadoua, Susan Pease. "So You're Married to An Addict: Is Divorce Inevitable?" 11 Sep. 2011. Web. 26 Apr. 2012. http://www.psychologytoday.com/blog/contemplating-divorce/201109/so-youre-married-addict-is-divorce-inevitable.

Laaser, Mark. *Healing the Wounds of Sexual Addiction.* Grand Rapids, MI: Zondervan, 2004.

Matta, William. *Relationship Sabotage: Unconscious Factors That Destroy Couples, Marriages, and Families.* New York: Praeger, 2006.

Wilson, Meg. *Hope after Betrayal: Healing When Sexual Addiction Invades Your Marriage.* Grand Rapids, MI: Kregel, 2007.

WEBSITES OF INTEREST

Elements Behavioral Health
http://www.elementsbehavioralhealth.com/addiction/how-sex-addiction-impacts-partners

Gamblers Anonymous
http://www.gamblersanonymous.org

National Council on Problem Gambling
http://www.ncpgambling.org

Sex Addicts Anonymous
http://saa-recovery.org

See also: Children and behavioral addictions; Families and behavioral addictions; Love and relationship addiction; Marriage/partnership and alcoholism; Marriage/partnership and substance abuse; Parenting and behavioral addictions

Marriage/partnership and substance abuse

CATEGORY: Psychological issues and behaviors

DEFINITION: Substance abuse often occurs within the context of marriages and domestic partnerships. One partner's substance abuse has a significant impact on the relationship, and a deteriorating relationship interacts with continued or exacerbated substance abuse. Spouses or partners may play a significant role in engaging substance abusers in treatment, assisting progress in treatment, and avoiding relapse. Treatment that includes spouses or partners can benefit the relationship, decrease substance abuse, and decrease intimate partner violence related to substance abuse.

RELATIONSHIPS AND SUBSTANCE ABUSE

According to researchers, relationships that include someone who is abusing substances are often characterized by poor communication patterns, relationship instability, high levels of partner violence, risky sexual behaviors, and poor adjustment of children who reside in the homes. These characteristics often lead to low overall relationship quality and low relationship satisfaction.

It is important to note that relationship discord and substance abuse or substance relapse are intertwined, so that each causes the other in a kind of vicious cycle. Partners often feel helpless and frustrated when a significant other is abusing substances and failing to respond to requests to decrease or eliminate use. The partners end up stuck between enabling and confronting reactions to the substance abuse. For instance, partners enable the abuse when they make excuses for the addict or when they try to avoid creating any problems that might trigger a substance abuse episode, leading the partner to "walk on eggshells" around the addict.

Sometimes partners will join Al-Anon family groups, self-help groups for the partners of addicts. Al-Anon is focused on helping the partner only and does not usually engage the addict in treatment. Also, the partner will sometimes become so injured or upset by the substance abuse that they become angry and confront the addict with a demand to change.

Many addicts have learned to pull back or walk away when confronted to avoid the problem; this is termed the *demand-withdraw* interaction, and it rarely engages the addict successfully in change. Alternatively, some addicts will promise change when confronted, but will quickly revert to old behaviors once the partner's anger has passed. This pattern of enabling or demanding change can go on for years before the partner seeks outside assistance.

ENCOURAGING TREATMENT

Partners can play a significant role in encouraging substance abusers to enter treatment, assisting in treatment progress, and helping the addict to avoid relapse. However, concerned significant others are often not included in treatment or they are included only in minor ways, such as participating in an occasional family night or a special session just before the conclusion of treatment.

It is notoriously difficult to engage substance abusers in treatment to change their addictive behavior. Research has shown that the majority of addicts who seek treatment were motivated by their partner or family member to do so. Intervention is one method used to engage addicts in treatment. It has received much media attention, but studies indicate that it is successful less than 25 percent of the time, primarily because many families cannot handle the high level of confrontation involved in the procedure and so decide not to do it.

The Community Reinforcement and Family Training (CRAFT) model is another approach that teaches significant others how to change their own behavior to motivate substance abusers to enter treatment. Jane Smith and Robert Meyers conducted research that indicates that CRAFT can successfully engage the substance abuser in treatment in 64 to 86 percent of cases. The CRAFT model was featured on a recent HBO television series on addiction.

Once in joint treatment, partners function as collaborators with the therapist because they can provide or withhold positive reinforcement from the addict to encourage decreased use. The partner can provide personal information about the addictive behavior that the addict may not recognize or think to share in treatment. Behavioral couples therapy works on the couple's relationship and the substance abuse behavior in tandem. It keeps the couple focused on the present and the future using weekly activities (such as "catch your partner doing something nice"), self-help group involvement, drug testing, and a "daily sobriety contract" in which the substance abuser directly commits to abstinence for the next twenty-four hours as a promise to the partner. This model has had great success in reducing substance abuse.

AVOIDING RELAPSE

One key aspect of couples treatment for substance abuse is the role the partner can play in helping the addict avoid relapse once he or she is clean and sober. Relapse prevention is recognized as an important aspect of substance abuse treatment because there is such a strong temptation to use again while in recovery. Partners can facilitate the identification of high-risk situations because they know from experience when the addict is tempted to use. Once the high-risk situation is identified, the partner can help the recovering addict plan coping responses that avoid relapse when the addict faces temptations. Finally, the partner can reinforce the addict's perception of his or her ability to manage challenges through compliments after successful management of temptation.

TREATMENT SUCCESS

Research has shown that spouses or partners can contribute in important ways to treatment success. More so than the standard individual treatment that includes only the substance abuser, couples treatment has demonstrated more positive treatment success, such as a reduced amount of substance use, increased periods of abstinence, decreased substance-related arrests and hospitalizations, and reduced violence toward partners.

A decrease in domestic violence is one important outcome of couples therapy for addiction. Substance abuse often lowers inhibitions and increases violent episodes. Domestic violence is approximately twice as frequent in substance-abuse-treatment populations as in the general population. Couples therapy that improves relationship dynamics and lowers substance abuse significantly decreases the rates of domestic violence.

Mark Stanton, PhD

FURTHER READING

Fals-Stewart, William, et al. "Behavioral Couples Therapy for Alcoholism and Drug Abuse." *The Wiley-Blackwell Handbook of Family Psychology.* Eds. James H. Bray and Mark Stanton. Malden, MA: Wiley, 2009. This chapter provides research information about the effects of behavioral couples therapy for substance abuse.

O'Farrell, Timothy J., and William Fals-Stewart. *Behavioral Couples Therapy for Alcoholism and Drug Abuse.* New York: Guilford, 2006. Provides information and forms for use with spouses and partners in couples therapy for substance abuse.

Smith, Jane E., and Robert J. Meyers. *Motivating Substance Abusers to Enter Treatment: Working with Family Members.* New York: Guilford, 2004. Discusses the CRAFT model of therapy.

Stanton, Mark. "Motivational Interviewing and the Social Context." *American Psychologist* 65 (2010): 297–98. Print. Argues for increased inclusion of spouses and family members in motivational interviewing for substance abuse.

---. "Relapse Prevention Needs More Emphasis on Interpersonal Factors." *American Psychologist* 60 (2005): 340–41. Print. Argues for greater recognition of the role of family members in theories about relapse prevention.

WEBSITES OF INTEREST

Al-Anon Family Groups
http://www.al-anon.alateen.org

Families Anonymous
http://www.familiesanonymous.org

Nar-Anon Family Groups
http://www.nar-anon.org

The Partnership at Drugfree.org
http://www.jointogether.org

See also: Families and substance abuse; Marriage/partnership and alcoholism; Marriage/partnership and behavioral addictions; Parenting and substance abuse

MDMA

CATEGORY: Substances

ALSO KNOWN AS: Adam; E; ecstasy; love drug; methylene dioxy methamphetamine; rave; X; XTC

DEFINITION: MDMA, or ecstasy, is a stimulant that is related to amphetamine and mescaline. It is considered a mind-altering drug that has properties similar to both amphetamines and hallucinogens.

STATUS: Illegal in the United States and worldwide

CLASSIFICATION: Schedule I controlled substance

SOURCE: A synthetic material with no natural sources; smuggled and illegally produced in underground laboratories

TRANSMISSION ROUTE: Ingested orally; snorted; smoked; injected intravenously or subcutaneously

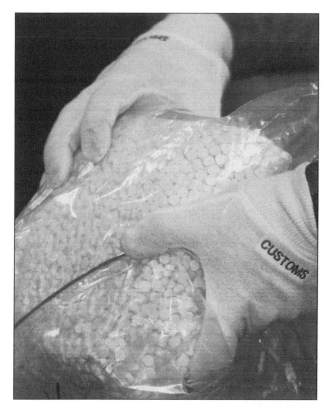

MDMA (ecstasy) tablets seized from Melbourne's water-front at the Australian Federal Police Headquarters April 15, 2005 in Melbourne, Australia. (Getty Images)

HISTORY OF USE

MDMA was first synthesized in Germany in 1912 for Merck Pharmaceuticals, which patented the substance in 1914. MDMA originally was intended to be an anticoagulant but was ineffective for that purpose. During World War I, however, the drug was taken as an appetite suppressant.

In the 1970s, attempts were made to use MDMA to facilitate psychotherapy. It was then that the drug was found to have hallucinogenic properties, which in 1985 led to its being declared an illegal substance. MDMA was classified as a schedule I controlled substance. Class I drugs are those that have a high potential for abuse and have no recognized medical value.

Because MDMA increases energy, endurance, and arousal, it became widely used in underground dance clubs in England in the 1980s because it allowed people to stay up and dance all night. These all-night events came to be called raves, and the drug itself became known as a club drug, party drug, or recreational drug. Its use in this manner spread to the United States around 1990. MDMA has remained popular in the club scene because it is both a hallucinogen and a psychoactive stimulant.

EFFECTS AND POTENTIAL RISKS

MDMA is derived from methamphetamine and differs from it chemically in only one way that makes it resemble the hallucinogen mescaline. As such, it has the characteristics of both a stimulant and a hallucinogen. Its action is explained mainly by its effects on the serotonin pathways in the body, since it affects serotonin reuptake.

Most of the short-term effects of ecstasy are attributable to the psychological changes from increased serotonin in the brain. These effects include feelings of pleasure, mood elevation, and heightened perception. Negative short-term effects include difficulty thinking clearly, agitation, and physical symptoms such as sweating, dry mouth, tachycardia (rapid heartbeat), fatigue, muscle spasms (especially jaw-clenching), and increased temperature.

Some ecstasy users engage in behavior known as "stacking," or taking multiple doses of ecstasy in one night. This may occur if the person wishes the positive effects of the drug to continue as they begin to wear off. Stacking can result in serious or even fatal physical problems. High blood pressure, extreme elevation of temperature, or cardiac arrhythmias may occur, sometimes resulting in death.

MDMA use often leads to aftereffects too, including depression, restlessness, and difficulty sleeping. Evidence shows that with long-term MDMA use, serotonin levels remain low in the brain, thus affecting brain function over time.

Robin Kamienny Montvilo, PhD

FURTHER READING

Baylen, Chelsea A., and Harold Rosenberg. "A Review of the Acute Subjective Effects of MDMA/Ecstasy." *Addiction* 101 (2006): 933–47. Print.

De la Torre, R., et al. "Non-Linear Pharmacokinetics of MDMA ('Ecstasy') in Humans." *British Journal of Clinical Pharmacology* 49.2 (2000): 104–09. Print.

Eisner, Bruce. *Ecstasy: The MDMA Story.* Berkeley, CA: Ronin, 1993.

Mills, Edward M., et al. "Uncoupling the Agony from the Ecstasy." *Nature* 426 (2003): 403–04. Print.

WEBSITES OF INTEREST
National Institute on Drug Abuse
http://www.drugabuse.gov/Infofacts/ecstasy.html

US Drug Enforcement Administration
http://www.deadiversion.usdoj.gov/drugs_concern/
   mdma/mdma.htm

See also: Club drugs; Hallucinogen abuse; Hallucinogens: Short- and long-term effects on the body; LSD; Mescaline; Mushrooms/psilocybin; PCP; Psychosis and substance abuse; Recreational drugs

---

Media and behavioral addictions

CATEGORY: Social issues
ALSO KNOWN AS: Media and compulsive behaviors; media and process addictions
DEFINITION: Behavioral addictions are complex mental disorders that stem from physiological, emotional, social, and mental factors. Research has shown that many behavioral addictions can be attributed to media and media technologies.

THE INFLUENCE OF MEDIA

Just as controversy continues over a link between video games and violent behavior, so too is society divided over the role of media in behavioral addictions. The only certainty is that Internet addictions did not exist before the invention of the Internet and television addictions did not exist before television.

An increasing number of health professionals believe that behavioral addictions are caused by a combination of social, physiological, mental, and emotional factors. Media is now implicated as a contributing factor and, in some cases, a primary influence. In response to such research, broadcast and print media have been using their roles as the purveyors of information, commentary, and entertainment to educate and shape public attitudes while opening up a national dialogue about behavioral addictions.

While the general public has been struggling with the definitions of sex addiction and other types of behavioral addictions, talk-show hosts have been featuring therapists discussing the behavior of celebrities, including professional golfer Tiger Woods and actor David Duchovny, who had checked into sex addiction rehabilitation clinics after their sexual behaviors became public knowledge. Popular news shows have been featuring neurobiologists and other scientists discussing the relationship of behavioral addictions to brain chemistry and the genetic link to addictions.

Television shows such as Lifetime's *Love Sick: Secrets of a Sex Addict* (2008) and Logo's reality show *Bad Sex* use sex addictions as fodder for entertainment while also enlightening viewers about twelve-step programs and other types of therapy. Memoirs, such as Ryan G. Van Cleave's *Unplugged: My Journey into the Dark World of Video Game Addiction* (2010) or Peach Friedman's *Diary of an Exercise Addict* (2009), and articles in *Time, Newsweek,* the *New York Times,* and other publications examine the personal costs of addiction and offer caution to readers who spend too much time jogging or playing computer games, for example. The result of all this attention has been increased awareness of the potentially devastating effects of behavioral addictions, while addictive behavior has been destigmatized.

However, the mass media's tendency to confuse mental health terminology or to overuse words, such as *addict,* has led to misunderstandings about behavioral addictions. For example, when journalists write about "dark chocolate addiction" or "golf addiction" they are referring not to clinical addictions but to activities or objects that give people enormous pleasure and might not be easily substituted. Such activities would become genuine eating or exercise addictions only when consuming dark chocolate or playing golf interferes with work or important relationships, or when the tolerance level changes so that more and more chocolate or golf is required to maintain the same level of pleasure, or when the activity is continued despite repeated or prolonged health issues caused by the activity, or when withdrawal causes emotional, physical, and mental harm.

Some of this confusion is directly related to the need to attract readers and viewers. Sensationalism, including sex addiction, sells. Hence, perhaps the most glaring misuse of the term *addict* came during the sensational coverage of sex scandals involving Jesse James, Woods, Eliot Spitzer, Dominique Strauss-Kahn, and others. Little consensus exists among journalists and the general public as to whether the behavior of these men constituted a sex addiction or represented immoral behavior. Also, their motives for checking into sex addiction rehab clinics raised additional questions.

IMAGES IN THE MEDIA

Numerous studies have shown that children and young adults in particular are especially vulnerable to what they see on television, read in print, and view on the Internet. The link between smoking and drinking alcohol and the promotion of those activities in the media was established decades ago, and government policies were established to keep young people from smoking and drinking.

Although not as much research has been conducted on the effect of media on behavioral addictions, the evidence has been pointing in the same direction. Despite research findings, the US Supreme Court lifted restrictions on gambling advertisements, and few policies are in place to limit other types of potentially influential media.

Just as an increase in anorexia nervosa has been linked to the pervasive portrayal of ultrathin women and slim, muscular men in advertising and film, so too is the increase in exercise addictions being linked to this objectification of men and women. While running, cycling, bodybuilding, and other sports are often started with good intentions, a person can become addicted to that sport if he or she begins to question how they appear and perform.

The constant attention given to the rich, beautiful, and famous is playing a role in shopping and gambling addictions. In addition, advertisements for credit cards can operate as powerful lures to a shopping addict in need of more money, while the proliferation of televised blackjack tournaments and lottery games, which often feature sexy, powerful players, can be influential among young adults and others who might be vulnerable to gambling addictions for other reasons. Young adults also are especially vulnerable to sexually oriented advertisements and to the depiction of sex in film and on television.

ADDICTIONS TO MEDIA AND MEDIA TECHNOLOGIES

Compulsive television watching, the first behavioral addiction to be identified in the age of modern technology, continues to be problematic. With the addition of cable and satellite, remote controls, home theaters, QVC, and the Home Shopping Network, compulsive shoppers can obtain instant gratification. Television addicts often become compulsive eaters too. DVD and video players have allowed closet pornography addicts to watch in their own homes, and now the availability of streaming video on the Internet provides pornography on demand.

The Internet has made many other addictions possible, including cybersex, computer gaming, social media, and online shopping. People who are already dealing with low self-esteem, anxiety, or depression are especially vulnerable to the anonymity offered by the Internet, to the opportunity to create an alternative persona, or to the sense of belonging or instant gratification offered by social media. Internet addictions are increasing at an alarming rate, especially among college-aged students and adult men, as smartphones and tablet computers make it easy and convenient to access email and websites everywhere and at any time.

Sally Driscoll, MLS

FURTHER READING

Bowen, Matthew W., and Marvin Firestone. "Pathological Use of Electronic Media: Case Studies and Commentary." *Psychiatric Quarterly* 82.3 (2011): 229–38. Print. Examines the latest research on Internet addictions and provides a historical overview of the mental disorder.

Clark, Neils, and P. Shavaun Scott. *Game Addiction: The Experience and the Effects.* Jefferson, NC: McFarland, 2009. Explores the seduction of computer games and how to curb an addiction.

Dill, Karen E. *How Fantasy Becomes Reality: Seeing through Media Influence.* New York: Oxford UP, 2009. An engaging discussion about the pervasiveness of media and its influence from childhood through adulthood.

Horvath, Cary W. "Measuring Television Addiction." *Journal of Broadcasting and Electronic Media* 48.3 (2004): 378–98. Print. Presents an overview of the history of television addiction research and a discussion about the underlying, related emotional and mental factors.

Johnson, Nicola F. *The Multiplicities of Internet Addiction: The Misrecognition of Leisure and Learning.* Aldershot, England: Ashgate, 2009. Compares and contrasts addiction with the normal use of the Internet.

King, Daniel, Paul Delfabbro, and Mark Griffiths. "The Convergence of Gambling and Digital Media: Implications for Gambling in Young People." *Journal of Gambling Studies* 16.2 (2009): 175–87.

Print. Examines the increased risk for gambling addictions among teenagers as online gambling opportunities converge with cellphones and other digital technologies.

Lee, Chris. "This Man Is Addicted to Sex." *Newsweek* 158.23 (2011): 48–55. Print. Examines how the media responded to the sexual exploits of Tiger Woods and other celebrities in relation to clinical sex addictions.

Ley, David J. *The Myth of Sex Addiction.* New York: Rowman, 2012. While presenting his case against the trend toward labeling immoral sexual behavior as addictions, this clinical psychologist also discusses the role of the media in this shift.

Rutledge, Pamela Brown. "Social Media Addiction: Engage Brain Before Believing." 22 May 2010. Web. 26 Apr. 2012. http://www.psychologytoday.com/blog/positively-media/201005/social-media-addiction-engage-brain-believing. This general interest article about social media addictions also serves as an introduction to media literacy and critical thinking.

WEBSITES OF INTEREST

American Psychological Association
http://www.apa.org/topics/addiction

Center for Media Literacy
http://www.medialit.org

Helpguide.org
http://www.helpguide.org/mental/internet_cybersex_addiction.htm

See also: Behavioral addictions: Overview; Crime and behavioral addictions; Media and smoking; Media and substance abuse

Media and smoking

CATEGORY: Social issues
DEFINITION: The depiction of smoking in film, television, and news programs powerfully shapes attitudes and beliefs about smoking. This depiction significantly affects individual decisions about whether or not to smoke.

SMOKING IN FILM

In 2009, a furor of public disapproval followed actor Sigourney Weaver's smoking scenes in the PG-13 rated blockbuster film *Avatar.* The smoking scenes involving the character Dr. Augustine were lambasted not only as illogical for portraying a smoking doctor but also as gratuitous, inasmuch as the scenes contributed nothing to the storyline. Director James Cameron responded to the criticism by saying that portraying Weaver as a smoking scientist revealed her as a conflicted and flawed character.

The American public takes for granted that smoking is likely in R-rated films, but it becomes increasingly difficult for directors to justify smoking scenes in films rated G, PG, or PG-13, given that minors make up the most likely audience for these films. In 2007, after decades of prompting by antismoking activists, the Motion Picture Association of America (MPAA) acquiesced and said that it would take into account during the ratings process all superfluous smoking scenes, those scenes deemed unnecessary in creating historical authenticity or in the telling of the film's narrative. Regardless, the MPAA is still criticized by parents and antismoking activists for not taking smoking in films and its negative influence on young people more seriously.

Although smoking had always been portrayed by Hollywood on screen to some degree, it was in the early 1940s, during World War II, that smoking in film experienced an explosion in popularity, which accelerated throughout the 1950s. With smoking's health risks still largely unknown by the public at the time, and with free cigarettes being distributed to US troops by the military, smoking came to be regarded more and more as an affordable luxury, hedonistic and provocative and sensually gratifying.

Women, newly representative of the American workforce, were depicted onscreen as seductive, liberated, sexual, and erotic smokers. Hollywood studios received compensation from tobacco companies for on-screen endorsements. Female stars such as Bette Davis, Joan Crawford, and Betty Grable exuded glamour and sex appeal while smoking on screen. Leading men such as Clark Gable, Humphrey Bogart, and Spencer Tracy personified masculinity as they smoked their way through scene after scene.

By the 1990s, however, some Hollywood stars, recognizing their responsibility as role models for young people, began to resist. Pierce Brosnan, for instance, who had smoked repeatedly as the character James Bond in previous films, vowed that he would never again smoke on screen playing that role; producers conceded, and Brosnan continued to play the role of James Bond, but newly smoke-free. This is significant because researchers have found a direct correlation between seeing tobacco use depicted in films and trying cigarettes among adolescents. Higher levels of exposure to smoking in films are associated with an increased likelihood of trying cigarettes, even when researchers controlled for age, school performance, gender, and the smoking habits of family members or friends.

SMOKING ON TELEVISION

Before the passage by the US Congress of the Public Health Cigarette Smoking Act in 1970, which banned all television and radio advertising of cigarettes, cigarette advertisements were a pervasive feature of American television programming. Winston, Camel, Marlboro, and Tareyton were just a few of the ubiquitous tobacco sponsors of television shows throughout the 1950s and 1960s.

For many years, the longest running Western on television, *Gunsmoke*, which was sponsored by Winston cigarettes, was introduced with the slogan "Winston tastes good, like a cigarette should." The Marlboro Man television advertising campaign, in particular, is often cited as the single most successful advertising campaign in history. At a time when Westerns like *Gunsmoke*, *Bonanza*, *Wagon Train*, and *The Rifleman* dominated television ratings, the image of the Marlboro Man, a cowboy figure from the Old West, resonated with the American public in a profound sense like no other image. Consequently, Marlboro cigarettes became the best-selling brand, not only in the United States but also in countries with consumers who connected with the cowboy archetype.

The two actors who portrayed the Marlboro Man, Wayne McLaren and David McLean, both developed cancer and died as a result of smoking. After being diagnosed with cancer, both men launched antismoking public-service campaigns, informing the public that their illness was directly attributable to smoking. After his death from lung cancer in 1995, McLean's family filed a wrongful death lawsuit against Philip Morris, the manufacturer and distributor of Marlboro cigarettes.

Commercials were the primary advertisers of cigarettes and smoking, but television shows did their part too. Ashtrays and cigarettes were omnipresent props on set, including those of talk shows and game shows. This type of advertising is now called product placement.

In the early 1960s, members of the most popular entertainment group, dubbed The Rat Pack, held a lit cigarette in one hand and a glass of alcohol in the other, while they sang, danced, joked, and acted their way to stardom. Frank Sinatra, Dean Martin, Sammy Davis Jr., Peter Lawford, and Joey Bishop were emblematic of their time. Almost ten years later, attitudes had changed little, as evidenced by the television show *Rowan and Martin's Laugh-In*. The show's hosts

---

Television and Youth Smoking

Because of the prevalence of smoking depicted on television, researchers conducted a study to determine if youths with greater exposure to television viewing were more apt to start smoking. These results were published in the journal *Pediatrics*.

Researchers from the Center for Child Health Outcomes at Children's Hospital and Health Center in San Diego, California, studied data on 592 youths (age ten to fifteen years) from the National Longitudinal Survey of Youth, Child Cohort. Specifically, researchers examined the association between television viewing in 1990 and smoking initiation from 1990 to 1992.

After controlling for baseline factors, researchers found an increasing association between the duration of TV viewing and the likelihood of starting smoking. Compared with children who watched less than two hours of TV per day, children who watched more than two to three hours of TV per day were 2 times more likely to begin smoking. Those who watched three to four hours of TV per day were 3.2 times more likely to begin smoking, those who watched four to five hours of TV per day were 5.2 times more likely to begin smoking, and those who watched five hours of TV per day were 6 times more likely to begin smoking.

The results of the study suggest that the more television that youths watch, the more likely they are to begin smoking. However, the study had major limitations because it did not consider the type of television programs the youths had been watching.

and characters each week held lit cigarettes and alcoholic beverages throughout the show.

With the advent of the cigarette brand Virginia Slims in 1968, whose slogan announced to women, "You've come a long way, baby," more and more women similarly were depicted on television as smokers. Smoking became a sign of female equality, liberation, and independence. After January 2, 1971, when cigarette advertising was banned on television and radio, Virginia Slims, Marlboro, and other brands were relegated primarily to print media and billboards.

Television, especially in later decades, began to provide a venue for public service and antismoking campaigns. Television and film stars, such as Yul Brynner and many others in the mid-1980s, made powerful and moving antismoking commercials for the American Cancer Society. Brynner, throughout his career, was seen on television either smoking or holding a cigarette. Shortly after his death from lung cancer, a commercial revealing a frail and ravaged Brynner urged American audiences to avoid smoking, attributing his premature death from lung cancer to cigarettes.

SMOKING AND THE NEWS MEDIA

The news media reports on issues of smoking and tobacco. Sometimes, the news media itself is the source of that news.

In 1995 the CBS newsmagazine show *60 Minutes* became a source of controversy after learning from Jeffrey Wigand, the vice president of research and development at Brown and Williamson tobacco company, that Brown and Williamson had consistently lied about the dangerous threats posed to health by tobacco and had deliberately deceived the public for decades. In April 2005, *ABC World News Tonight* anchor Peter Jennings announced on the air that he had been diagnosed with lung cancer. Viewers reacted with shock and disbelief. Jennings, who had smoked for years and then quit, confessed to his viewers that after the enormous stress of the terrorist attacks of September 11, 2001, he had been "weak" and had resumed smoking. Less than four months after making this revelation on air, Jennings died of lung cancer.

Jennings's story marked one of the latest in a long line of television journalists to succumb to the effects of smoking. For decades, news anchors read the news with cigarette in hand, as an ashtray rested conveniently near the microphone. Legendary journalist Edward R. Murrow, who was rarely seen without a cigarette, died in 1965 of lung cancer. NBC national news anchor Chet Huntley, also seen nightly smoking a cigarette while delivering the news, died of lung cancer in 1974. More recently, in 2007, television news anchor Tom Snyder, who also had appeared on television holding a cigarette, died of leukemia.

Mary E. Markland, MA

FURTHER READING

Egendorf, Laura. *Issues That Concern You: Smoking.* Farmington Hills, MI: Greenhaven, 2008. Examines the specific ways that Hollywood and the film industry inspire young people to smoke.

Hyde, Margaret, and John Setaro. *Smoking 101: An Overview for Teens.* Minneapolis, MN: Twenty-First Century, 2006. Discusses the commonplace policy of tobacco companies providing free cigarettes to Hollywood stars, and the lucrative endorsement contracts to stars who filmed tobacco commercials to be aired in foreign countries.

Lehu, Jean-Marc. *Branded Entertainment: Product Placement and Brand Strategy in the Entertainment Business.* London: Kogan, 2007. Analyzes the historical practice of product placement of branded tobacco products on television and in film, often as a way to fund production.

O'Reilly, Terry, and Mike Tennant. *The Age of Persuasion: How Marketing Ate Our Culture.* Berkeley, CA: Counterpoint, 2009. Discusses the Marlboro Man and Virginia Slims advertising campaigns as the most successful targeted advertising strategies in marketing history.

Rabinoff, Michael. *Ending the Tobacco Holocaust.* Santa Rosa, CA: Elite, 2007. Argues that the number-one determining influence on fourteen-year-old peer groups regarding smoking is the Hollywood film industry and actors who smoke on screen.

WEBSITES OF INTEREST

Action on Smoking and Health
http://www.ash.org

Americans for Nonsmokers' Rights
http://no-smoke.org

Campaign for Tobacco-Free Kids
http://www.tobaccofreekids.org

Smoke Free Movies
http://smokefreemovies.ucsf.edu

See also: Advertising for tobacco products; Media and behavioral addictions; Media and substance abuse; Smoking; Teens/young adults and smoking; Tobacco use disorder

Media and substance abuse

CATEGORY: Social issues

DEFINITION: Mass media has been used as a tool to inform the public of the dangers of substance abuse since the early twentieth century. Conversely, mass media has been studied since the 1970s as a potential influence of the cultural proliferation of substance abuse.

HISTORY OF MEDIA AND SUBSTANCE ABUSE

While much is known about the influences of genetics, psychosocial development, peer interactions, and communal surroundings in a person's decision to begin drug and alcohol abuse, little is known about the ability of media to contribute to or detract from these factors. Similarly, while media campaigns in both print and television have been utilized by local, state, and federal governments to highlight the dangers of drug and alcohol abuse, their effectiveness is difficult to define.

The 1936 film *Tell Your Children* is largely recognized as the first antidrug film in American cinema. Originally created as a propaganda-style production by a church group, the film depicted the dangers of marijuana use in overtly dramatic and exaggerated fashion to spread fear of the drug. The film did not gain a large viewership until its rerelease in 1971 as *Reefer Madness*, where the film's outrageous claims that marijuana induced insanity and homicidal tendencies were perceived as comical by modern audiences, transforming the film into a pro-marijuana piece by the National Organization for the Reform of Marijuana Laws (now called NORML).

The alteration of *Reefer Madness* from cautionary tale to hyperbolized farce in thirty-five years is representative of a long-standing trend in the relationship between substance abuse and media. Namely, that media in most forms is rarely capable of being produced with the speed at which the cultural perceptions and attitudes of drugs and alcohol fluctuate. The use of media as a tool against the abuse of drugs and alcohol always has been hampered by another historical disadvantage: Nearly all forms of major mass media, from music to film, television, and art, all originally portrayed substance abuse in a casual manner devoid of association with its potential danger.

As alluded to in an October 2010 study by the American Academy of Pediatrics, drug and alcohol abuse have been portrayed as normative behaviors in American culture in nearly all facets of media since the early twentieth century, depictions that may be the result of lax attitudes toward such portrayals. This tradition has made the challenge of creating effective antidrug media campaigns that much more difficult.

MEDIA AS A CAUSE OF SUBSTANCE ABUSE

The notion of media as an influential factor in the prevalence of substance abuse has been examined by sociologists since the 1970s. Media studies began to identify the frequency with which alcohol was depicted in television programming. This research found that alcohol use was predominantly portrayed as socially acceptable across the entertainment-television landscape, and that depictions of use were rarely portrayed negatively.

Hard drugs such as heroin and cocaine have rarely been portrayed glamorously in American media, and studies dating to 1974 began to decry the depiction of marijuana on television as a humorous, harmless escape or even a rite of passage. This notion of harmlessness has remained through contemporary American television series such as *That 70's Show*, a Fox situation comedy that aired from 1998 to 2006 and that regularly depicted scenes alluding to marijuana use by its main characters, all of whom are high school students.

A landmark 2012 study by Dartmouth College examined the influence of film on the predictors of adolescent alcohol consumption. A two-year survey sample revealed that 80 percent of the films watched by American teenagers depicted alcohol consumption, while 65 percent contained product placements for alcoholic beverages for advertising purposes. The study concluded that widespread exposure to cinematic depictions of substance abuse does act as a predictor for adolescent binge drinking and cigarette smoking.

Activist groups and civic organizations of all kinds have condemned a perception of pervasive themes like sexual promiscuity, rebellion, and violence since the beginnings of popular music. The prevalence of substance abuse in popular music also has been widely criticized. A 1999 report by the US Department of Health and Human Services indicated that of the one thousand most popular songs between the years 1996 and 1997 that were surveyed, more than one-quarter of those songs made reference to either alcohol or illicit drug use.

Perhaps no form of media is more responsible for persuasive messages aimed at promoting substance abuse as advertising media. According to the US Department of Justice, the alcohol industry spends close to $2 billion annually on television, radio, print, and outdoor advertisements, while figures for advertising expenditures for the tobacco industry are often three times that amount. These vast expenditures are likely reasons for the increase in youth exposure to alcohol advertising; ads increased by as much as 71 percent between 2001 and 2009, according to figures from the Johns Hopkins School of Public Health. While limited evidence has resulted in legislation and in voluntary advertising codes to restrict the advertisement of alcohol near such places as schools, it has remained difficult to extract the precise effect an increasing prevalence of alcohol advertising exposure has on society.

Contradictory research contends that no large-scale scientific evidence exists that concretely attributes the proliferation of alcohol- and substance abuse-related portrayals in advertising and mass media as a pathway to abuse. These findings marginalize the effect of such media, stating that they act merely as any other commercialized persuasive device, such as those for food, soft drinks, and cosmetics, aimed at the market of a particular group of consumers.

USE OF MEDIA TO PREVENT SUBSTANCE ABUSE

New rounds of criticism aimed at the film and music industries decrying their legacy of positively portraying drug, alcohol, and tobacco use have corresponded with a new immersion by anti-substance-abuse advocacy groups into contemporary forms of media such as social networking. Programs initiated by groups such as the National Youth Anti-Drug Media Campaign have created youth-centric websites like AbovetheInfluence.com and theAntiDrug.com to warn young people about the dangers of substance abuse. Other groups have produced public service announcements for television.

Similar sites such as the American Legacy Foundation's TheTruth.com attempt to tackle issues such as tobacco smoking with a rebellious flair, voicing not only the health dangers of tobacco use but also rage at the perceived duplicity of the tobacco industry. The site even sells clothing with antitobacco messages. Academic journals such as *Prevention Science* and the *American Journal of Public Health* have explicated the success of the National Youth Anti-Drug Media Campaign among young people.

The newly pervasive nature of custom-tailored media and social networking will solidify its already established arena in which both the ills and successes of society are portrayed. The prevailing belief among sociologists contends that until the values and goals of society place the education of the dangers of substance abuse at higher regard, their presence in media will not be abolished. Only through dismantling the misconceptions surrounding drinking, smoking, and drug use built by previous generations can substance abuse be regarded as negative and dangerous behaviors by popular culture as a whole.

John Pritchard

FURTHER READING

Ericson, Nels. "Substance Abuse: The Nation's Number One Health Problem." *OJJDP Fact Sheet* 17 (2001). Web. 27 Apr. 2012. https://www.ncjrs.gov/pdffiles1/ojjdp/fs200117.pdf.

Flay, Brian R., and Judith L. Sobel. "The Role of Mass Media in Preventing Adolescent Substance Abuse." *NIDA Research Monograph* 47 (1983): 5–35. Print.

Newman, Lori M., ed. *Does Advertising Promote Substance Abuse?* Detroit: Greenhaven, 2005.

Office of National Drug Control Policy. "Substance Use in Popular Music Videos." Jun. 2002. Web. 27 Apr. 2012. http://www.scenesmoking.org/research/SubstanceUseIinMusic.pdf.

Stoolmiller, Mike, et al. "Comparing Media and Family Predictors of Alcohol Use: A Cohort Study of US Adolescents." *BMJ Open* 2.1 (2012). Web. 27 Apr. 2012. http://bmjopen.bmj.com/content/2/1/e000543.full.

Strasburger, Victor C. "Children, Adolescents, Substance Abuse, and the Media." *Pediatrics* 126.4 (2010). Web. 27 Apr. 2012. http://pediatrics.aap-publications.org/content/126/4/791.full.

See also: Advertising for alcohol; Celebrities and substance abuse; Crime and substance abuse; Media and behavioral addictions; Media and smoking; Teens/young adults and alcohol abuse; Teens/young adults and drug abuse

Medical marijuana

CATEGORY: Social issues

ALSO KNOWN AS: Medical cannabis

DEFINITION: Marijuana, which is derived from the dried leaves and flowers of the herbal plant *Cannabis sativa*, is used illegally as a recreational drug but also legally when prescribed for medicinal and therapeutic uses.

MEDICAL AND THERAPEUTIC USES

Medical marijuana, cannabis, and its constituent cannabinoids, such as THC (delta-9 tetrahydrocannabinol), were used in China and India in 2700 BCE and then spread worldwide to treat pain, seizure, muscle spasm, poor appetite, nausea, insomnia, asthma, depression, and menstrual cramps. In 2000 BCE Egyptians used marijuana to treat sore eyes. The Greek doctor Galen prescribed marijuana for flatulence.

The Chinese in 200 CE used marijuana as an anesthetic. In twelfth-century Africa, marijuana (known as dagga) was used to treat snakebites, anthrax, dysentery, and malaria. Marijuana, which tends to dry out mucous membranes, was used in fifteenth-century India to treat congestion, and the juice of the marijuana seed was used for earaches.

In the eighteenth century in the United States, marijuana was used to treat sexually transmitted diseases and incontinence. A tincture of marijuana (marijuana soaked in alcohol) was used in the nineteenth century to improve appetite, sexual interest, mental disorders, gout, cholera, and hydrophobia. The British in the nineteenth century used marijuana to treat facial tics and the pain, nausea, and spasms associated with rabies and tetanus.

Beginning in the 1970s, marijuana was used around the world to treat glaucoma (high intraocular pressure). People who used other glaucoma treatments experienced headache and blurred vision and could develop a tolerance for conventional drugs. However, treating glaucoma with marijuana is of short duration because eye pressure increases after three to four hours.

Other medical and therapeutic uses of marijuana now include adrenal and airway diseases, adult attention deficit disorder, nausea associated with acquired immunodeficiency syndrome (AIDS), anorexia, anxiety, arthritis, bruxism (teeth grinding), bulimia, cancer (associated nausea and vomiting from chemotherapy), chronic fatigue, chronic pain, color blindness, constipation, depression, diabetes symptoms, diarrhea, epilepsy (seizures), genital herpes, hiccups, intestinal disorders, kidney problems, migraines (associated pain, nausea, and vomiting), obesity, phantom limb pain, post-traumatic stress disorder, schizophrenia, spasticity (uncontrollable muscle flexing, loss of fine motor functioning, and choking resulting from spinal cord injury, stroke, cerebral palsy, or multiple sclerosis), stuttering, tinnitus, tooth and gum pain, whiplash, and writer's cramp.

Persons with AIDS or cancer often lose lean body tissue through a process called wasting. Because marijuana is known to stimulate appetite, or "the munchies," it is often prescribed for persons needing to gain weight. However, the THC in marijuana increases levels of fat more so than lean tissue, which could lead to unhealthy weight gain in people with diabetes and in persons who are obese.

Other hazardous consequences of marijuana use that may outweigh any therapeutic benefits include paranoia, pneumonia, diarrhea, short-term problems with thinking and working memory, and a decrease in immune function. Smoked marijuana contains high levels of tar, twice as much as in tobacco cigarettes, thus leading to an increased risk of lung and throat damage. Also, marijuana may potentiate the effects of alcohol.

Marijuana users can experience withdrawal symptoms such as restlessness, anxiety, irritability, insomnia, muscle tremor, sweating, and changes in heart rate. Medicinal marijuana can be addictive too. (One in nine people become addicted, especially if marijuana is used for long periods of time.) A person who smokes marijuana for the first time may experience anxiety and panic attacks, and persons with bipolar disorder who smoke marijuana may notice increased mania and rapid cycling.

The correct dosing of marijuana can be difficult. Marijuana, in addition to being smoked, can be delivered in the following ways: through vaporizers, which may reduce harmful chemicals entering the lungs (takes effect within minutes and lasts for two to four hours); through topical applications, which are useful for reducing pain and inflammation; through nasal spray; through rectal suppository; sublingually (sprayed under the tongue); through lozenges; and through ingestion. The effects of marijuana take

longer (up to two hours) if ingested because the compounds have to be digested before entering the bloodstream. The effects can last four to eight hours. There have been no documented cases of fatal marijuana overdose.

Marinol (generic dronabinol) is a synthetic THC in pill form available by prescription. However, some say the medicinal effect of marijuana requires many compounds found in the plant, of which THC is only one. In addition, it might be difficult to swallow a pill if one is nauseous or vomiting, and the effects of Marinol do not appear rapidly. Furthermore, Marinol is expensive, and dosage is not as easy to modify as smoked marijuana.

THE LAW

Marijuana has been illegal in the United States since 1937. Before that date, marijuana was prescribed for many different conditions. The Marijuana Tax Act of 1937 required expensive taxes and paperwork and discouraged medicinal and recreational uses of the drug. The 1970 Comprehensive Drug Abuse

Medical marijuana facility in Colorado. (Bloomberg via Getty Images)

Prevention and Control Act classified marijuana as a schedule I controlled substance (along with heroin and LSD, or acid), which means it has no approved medical value, making it unavailable for medical use. In contrast, schedule II drugs have an accepted medical use.

According to California's Proposition 215 (the Compassionate Use Act of 1996), a person may use medical marijuana with a physician's recommendation. The law allows for marijuana cultivation and gives caregivers the right to buy marijuana for the patient. A patient must see a licensed physician to document a medical condition that merits the use of marijuana.

The US Department of Veterans Affairs (VA) allows veterans to use marijuana for medical reasons while still accessing government-sponsored health care. Veterans must obtain the marijuana from a state in which medical marijuana is legal; they cannot get the marijuana from the VA. Other states have made medical marijuana legal with their own guidelines. However, possession of marijuana, even for medicinal use, remains a federal offense.

Opponents of decriminalizing medical marijuana argue that its use will lead to recreational use, addiction, and increased crime. They also fear that marijuana is a gateway to harder drugs.

Elizabeth Marie McGhee Nelson, PhD

FURTHER READING

Bott, Carol S. *How-To Marijuana: A Step-by-Step to Medical Marijuana*. New York: iUniverse, 2007. Presents a case for the therapeutic use of marijuana.

Earleywine, Mitch. *Understanding Marijuana: A New Look at the Scientific Evidence*. New York: Oxford UP, 2002. Covers the history, use, effects, and social problems of medical marijuana.

Gonzalez, Raul, Eileen M. Martin, and Igor Grant. "Marijuana." *Neuropsychology and Substance Use*. Eds. Ari Kalechstein and Wilfred G. van Gorp. New York: Taylor, 2007.

Kane, Brigid. "Medical Marijuana: The Continuing Story." *Current Clinical Issues* 134.12 (2001): 1159–62. Print. Discusses the legislative issues regarding medical marijuana.

WEBSITES OF INTEREST

Center for Medicinal Cannabis Research
http://www.cmcr.ucsd.edu

ProCon.org
http://medicalmarijuana.procon.org

Veterans for Medical Cannabis Access
http://www.veteransformedicalmarijuana.org

See also: Decriminalization; Hashish; Legislation and substance abuse; Marijuana

---

Memory loss and substance abuse

CATEGORY: Psychological issues and behaviors
DEFINITION: Memory loss, and its effect on other brain functions, has long been associated with substance abuse, especially alcohol abuse. Memory loss is often used as an indicator of substance abuse for certain substances such as alcohol.

INTRODUCTION

All substances of abuse (with the possible exception of heroin) have been shown to create decreased activity in the areas of the brain responsible for short-term memory and attention while the drug is being used. The lasting effects of these drugs on memory functions vary with the type of substance being abused, the amounts of substance used, and the length of time the substance was used.

SUBSTANCES

Different substances affect various parts of the brain and impair cognition in distinct ways. Some substances reduce the brain's ability to focus attention, thus impairing the formation of memory. For example, amphetamine or methamphetamine affects one's working memory (ability to hold information in the mind to use while performing complex functions) while MDMA (ecstasy) users have difficulty "coding" information (linking or associating information to be able to recall and use it later) to keep in long-term memory.

One study found that MDMA use affects retrospective memory (remembering something immediately, and then continuing to remember it after a short time). In this study, MDMA users were read a story, asked to immediately recall it, and then asked to re-call it again after a short delay. Their ability to recall the story declined by 50 percent between the first and second time they were asked to recall it.

Those who use cocaine have impaired memory function, as do those who use cannabis (marijuana). In studies of chronic cocaine users, 57 percent of users reported significant memory problems. Genetically modified mice that were exposed to cocaine demonstrated that cocaine destroys a protein called PSD-95, which is linked to learning and long-term memory and thus is important in remembering people and places. In the mice, levels of this protein dropped 50 percent with cocaine use. Another study of amphetamine users reported that 28 percent of these users had problems with immediate and remote memory, even in younger users who had not used the drug for a long period of time.

ALCOHOL ABUSE

Alcohol has been studied more extensively than many other substances with regard to its use and its effects on memory loss. Even people who report drinking smaller amounts and who are thus considered to be social drinkers (rather than problem drinkers) have been shown to have decreased scores on memory tests.

Among alcoholics who enter treatment, up to 70 percent have impaired function when performing difficult memory tasks. This impaired function may only be recognizable when the person is asked to perform during tests of memory; often, people who drink alcohol have learned to function in a way that appears normal to others and possibly even to themselves.

Some researchers link the impaired neurologic functions of alcoholics, including impaired memory functions, to actual physical changes in their brains, which have shown reduced electrical activity and impaired blood flow. A disorder called Korsakoff's psychosis or Wernicke-Korsakoff syndrome that affects up to 10 percent of severe alcoholics is characterized by critical impairment in short-term memory; those affected are unable to remember new information for more than a few seconds and are thus unable to retain any information for short- or long-term use.

RECOVERY OF MEMORY FUNCTION

In recovering alcoholics, some memory function has been shown to return even with no intervention, improving for some as the length of abstinence increases. In others who are recovering, memory function improves with training and practice. However, in some recovering alcoholics, only minimal function is regained.

Possible pharmaceutical intervention is being investigated as a way to help affected persons regain cognitive function, including short- and long-term memory function. In some studies, memory impairment has been shown to be an obstacle in treatment for all types of substance abuse. Those who are recovering simply do not remember what instructions they have been given to try to overcome the abuse or to deal with cravings for the substance they have been abusing. Thus, memory impairment from substance abuse undermines a user's ability to overcome substance abuse.

Marianne M. Madsen, MS

FURTHER READING

Bechara, Antoine, and Eileen M. Martin. "Impaired Decision Making Related to Working Memory Deficits in Individuals with Substance Addictions." *Neuropsychology* 18.1 (2004): 152–62. Print. Examines the results of a study of persons who are dependent on substances to see whether they have impairment in their working memory and, if so, whether that impairment affects decision-making processes.

Becker, J. T., and J. H. Jaffe. "Impaired Memory for Treatment-Relevant Information in Inpatient Men Alcoholics." *Journal of Studies on Alcohol* 45.4. (1984): 339–43. Print. Describes how alcohol abuse can affect the recall of treatment information for those attempting to recover from substance abuse.

Lundqvist, Thomas. "Cognitive Consequences of Cannabis Use: Comparison with Abuse of Stimulants and Heroin with Regard to Attention, Memory, and Executive Functions." *Pharmacology, Biochemistry, and Behavior* 81.2 (2005): 319–30. Print. Compares and contrasts the loss of memory functions among several different types of commonly abused substances.

O'Malley, Stephanie, et al. "Neuropsychological Impairment in Chronic Cocaine Abusers." *American Journal of Drug and Alcohol Abuse* 18.2 (1992): 131–44. Print. Describes loss of brain function, including memory loss, in cocaine users.

WEBSITES OF INTEREST
BBC: The Memory Experience
http://www.bbc.co.uk/radio4/memory/understand/memory_drug_abuse.shtml

MedicineNet.com
http://www.medicinenet.com/memory_loss/symptoms.htm

Memory Loss and the Brain
http://www.memorylossonline.com/winter2007/alcohol_brain.html

National Institute on Alcohol Abuse and Alcoholism
http://www.niaaa.nih.gov

See also: Alcohol: Short- and long-term effects on the body; Brain changes with addiction; Hallucinogens: Short- and long-term effects on the body; Stimulants: Short- and long-term effects on the body; Symptoms of substance abuse

Men and behavioral addictions

CATEGORY: Psychological issues and behaviors
ALSO KNOWN AS: Compulsive behavior; process addictions; psychological addictions
DEFINITION: A behavior or activity becomes an addiction when it interferes with daily functioning; when it becomes harmful physically, emotionally, or psychologically; and when the person is unable to quit or resume the behavior or activity at a healthy level.

CAUSES

Neither scientists nor mental health experts know exactly what causes behavioral addictions, although the latest research does provide evidence for the possibility of a genetic role. A variant of the NRXN3 gene, previously linked to smoking, drug, and alcohol addictions, has also been linked to impulsivity in men.

This link does not mean the gene causes behavioral addictions, but it can set the stage for their development when combined with other social, psychological, cultural, and emotional factors. Men are at least twice as likely as women to become dependent on drugs and alcohol, increasing men's vulnerability to sex, gambling, and Internet addictions as well, as they share a high comorbidity rate.

In general, behavioral addictions among men have been increasing as society has changed. The proliferation of computer games, social networking sites, and pornography on the Internet make these activities prime targets for abuse. The growing availability of casinos and promotion of lotteries and sports betting have resulted in an increase in pathological gambling. The emphasis on physical attractiveness has resulted in more exercise addictions, while easy access to credit cards, especially among college-age youth, has led to more shopping addictions.

RISK FACTORS

Studies have shown that men between age sixteen and twenty-five represent the most vulnerable age group for many behavioral addictions, including Internet, gambling, computer gaming, shopping, sex, and exercise addictions, although an addiction can begin at any age. Also vulnerable are men with substance abuse addictions and men with depression, anxiety, perfectionism, low self-esteem, and poor social skills.

The greatest risk for an exercise addiction, usually bodybuilding or running, can be found among men who are borderline narcissistic or who have an eating disorder. At high risk for a gambling addiction are men who identify pathologically with wealth. Other risk factors include child abuse, often a factor in sex addictions, and chronic unemployment, a factor especially in computer gaming and Internet addictions. Men with physical disabilities might also be at a higher risk for any of the sedentary addictions, such as computer gaming or television watching.

SCREENING AND DIAGNOSIS

Guidelines for diagnosing pathological gambling are provided in the American Psychiatric Association's *Diagnostic and Statistical Manual of Mental Disorders*. A variety of screening tools are available to help with the diagnosis of other addictions. These tools include the running addiction scale, exercise dependence scale, Internet addiction diagnostic questionnaire, Internet addiction test, workaholism battery, compulsive buying scale, sexual addiction screening test, and online cognition scale.

In addition to conducting tests, the mental health professional usually conducts a physical exam of the client and, in some cases, talks to family members or obtains legal records for additional information. While a diagnosis is usually only made after a thorough examination, sometimes it depends on one criterion: the inability of the client to limit his behavior to within a normal, healthy range.

SYMPTOMS

As a person becomes addicted to a behavior or activity, the initial sense of pleasure or euphoria, similar to that induced by drugs or alcohol, often gives way to pain or a variety of negative thoughts and emotions. In some cases, the activity actually alters the chemistry of the body so that the person becomes both physically and psychologically dependent. When withdrawal is attempted, the addict may experience mood swings, insomnia, depression, headaches, and other physical or emotional symptoms.

Symptoms also may include the inability to perform satisfactorily at work or to maintain regular hours. Many addicts end up losing their jobs because of repeated absences or tardiness. Divorce, losing custody of children, and destroying friendships are also common among addicts.

Compulsive gamblers and shoppers usually end up with devastating financial problems. Exercise addicts often have prolonged pain and may have had multiple physical injuries or surgeries that would normally have convinced a nonaddict to stop the activity. Sexual addictions often result in sexually transmitted diseases and in unintended pregnancies. Internet and computer game addictions cause eating and sleep disorders, vision problems, headaches, and hygiene issues related to not bathing or using the toilet regularly. Suicide is prevalent among men with severe behavioral addictions, as the shame, guilt, financial problems, and other woes are often too difficult to handle.

TREATMENT AND THERAPY

Treatment for a behavioral addiction often involves many steps. There are no miracle medications. Finding the underlying cause of the problem is key to a successful treatment plan.

A behavioral addiction can sometimes be a symptom of, or exist alongside, a mental disorder or illness, such as depression, bipolar disorder, or an obsessive-compulsive disorder. In those cases, pharmacological intervention is the normal course and

would take precedence over treating the behavioral addiction. Psychotherapy will help uncover any repressed attitudes or child abuse that can be at the root of an addiction.

In many cases, the standard form of treatment is a twelve-step program similar to the model conceived by Alcoholics Anonymous or individual cognitive-behavior therapy (CBT) administered by a mental health expert. Family or couples therapy also is included when relevant.

CBT and the related twelve-step programs explore the negative or maladaptive thoughts, or cognitions, which are often the source of an addiction. For example, gambling addicts usually place an abnormally high value on personal wealth, whereas compulsive shoppers tend to believe their identities are closely associated with consumer goods. CBT will also confront the shame and denial often associated with addictions and help a man to ask for forgiveness from the people he has hurt. Most therapy programs also include an educational component to teach relevant skills, such as good nutrition or financial management.

PREVENTION

A man can prevent a behavior or activity from becoming an addiction by maintaining a healthy and balanced lifestyle and remaining vigilant when too much time, energy, or attention is focused on one particular activity. A balance between sedentary activities and sports, and between work and leisure, is important, as is nurturing happy, productive relationships and pursuing a fulfilling career.

Sally Driscoll, MLS

FURTHER READING

Benson, April Lane, ed. *I Shop, Therefore I Am: Compulsive Buying and the Search for Self.* Northvale, NJ: Aronson, 2000. This collection of essays examines buying and money disorders.

Clark, Neils, and P. Shavaun Scott. *Game Addiction: The Experience and the Effects.* Jefferson, NC: McFarland, 2009. Explores the seduction of computer games and offers self-help advice for addicts.

Grant, Jon E., et al. "Introduction to Behavioral Addictions." *American Journal of Drug and Alcohol Abuse* 36.5 (2010): 233–41. Print. Compares and contrasts behavioral addictions with impulse control disorders and substance addictions.

Hartston, Heidi. "The Case for Compulsive Shopping as an Addiction." *Journal of Psychoactive Drugs* 44.1 (2012): 64–67. Print. Discusses the factors associated with addictions and argues for recategorizing pathological gambling in the *Diagnostic and Statistical Manual of Mental Disorders* from an impulse control disorder to an addiction.

Kerr, John H., Koenraad J. Lindner, and Michelle Blaydon. *Exercise Dependence.* New York: Routledge, 2007. Written by clinical and sport psychologists, this book offers case histories, research, assessment, and treatment plans.

Lee, Chris. "This Man Is Addicted to Sex." *Newsweek* 158 (2011): 48–55. Print. The devastation and shame of a genuine sex addiction is contrasted with the sexual exploits of Tiger Woods and other celebrities.

Ley, David J. *The Myth of Sex Addiction.* New York: Rowman, 2012. A clinical psychologist cautions about the growing pressure to label some sex addictions as mental disorders rather than immoral or irresponsible behavior to be dealt with as personal failings.

Morgan, John F. *The Invisible Man: A Self-Help Guide for Men with Eating Disorders, Compulsive Exercise, and Bigorexia.* New York: Routledge, 2008. Argues that men with cating disorders and exercise addiction are stigmatized in society and are suffering silently.

Pappas, Stephanie. "Male Impulsivity and Addiction Linked to One Gene." 18 Nov. 2011. Web. 2 Apr. 2012. http://www.livescience.com/17095-men-impulsivity-addiction-gene.html. Presents the latest research on a genetic connection to behavioral addictions.

Skolnik, Sam. *High Stakes: The Rising Cost of America's Gambling Addiction.* Boston: Beacon, 2011. A journalist and former pathological gambler examines the social, political, and economic reasons for the increase in gambling addiction in the United States.

WEBSITES OF INTEREST

American Psychological Association
http://www.apa.org

National Institute of Mental Health
http://www.nimh.nih.gov/health/topics/depression/men-and-depression/depression-in-men.shtml

PubMed: "Pathological Gambling"
http://www.ncbi.nlm.nih.gov/pubmedhealth/PMH0002488

See also: Behavioral addictions: Overview; Gambling addiction; Gaming addiction; Gender and addiction; Impulse control disorders; Internet addiction; Media and behavioral addictions; Men and smoking; Men and substance abuse; Pornography addiction; Sex addiction; Work addiction

Men and smoking

CATEGORY: Social issues

DEFINITION: According to the American Cancer Society, 1 billion men worldwide are smokers. Tobacco-related illness is responsible for 8.8 percent of all global deaths and 4.2 percent of all health disabilities worldwide.

HISTORY OF SMOKING

Tobacco smoking is one of the most ancient, globally prevalent, and enduring practices in the history of substance abuse. Historians have found evidence of the activity dating to 500 BCE. In the annals of European and Western cultures, smoking has been a long established habit of boys and men especially. Not until the invention and swift proliferation of the cigarette at the turn of the twentieth century did tobacco smoking became prevalent among both men and women.

The practice of tobacco smoking has been perceived in many ways, including as religious custom and potential health benefit to herbal remedy, relaxant, and energy booster. Only relatively recently has medical evidence shown the dangers of tobacco smoking. This has led to monumental cultural changes that have placed restrictions on a practice that was an epidemic in American culture for more than a century.

It is now widely known and accepted that tobacco smoking causes damage to nearly every system of the body. Investigations into the numerous and varied health hazards of tobacco smoking have yielded evidence that illustrates how the practice affects men and women differently.

According to the Centers for Disease Control and Prevention (CDC), nearly 443,000 Americans die each year from smoking-related conditions and from the effects of secondhand smoke. This figure represents more fatalities than are caused by illegal drugs, alcohol, motor vehicle accidents, human immunodeficiency virus infection, suicides, and homicides combined. CDC data also indicate that smoking triples the risk of heart disease in middle-aged men and increases the risk of acquiring lung cancer more than twenty-two times that of nonsmokers.

Statistics from the American Lung Association (ALA) indicate that smoking among men decreased 11 percent between the years 1965 and 2009. ALA figures also indicate that more than 25 million American men still smoke, a number that represents 25.3 percent of the adult male population of the United States.

SMOKING: INTRODUCTION AND PREVALENCE

Research shows that men and women start smoking for different reasons. Even though smoking has been an acceptable behavior for both adult men and women in the United States for decades, the ritual is, because of cultural beliefs, societal attitudes, popular media, and advertising, still associated with masculinity and machismo. This is perhaps the underlying cause of the tendency of men to experiment with or start smoking in their teenage years: They attempt to model or construct a masculine image.

Research indicates that men begin smoking at an average age of sixteen years, whereas women do not usually start until the age of nineteen years. As with any experimentation with potentially abusive substances, peer pressure is a major reason boys and young men begin smoking in their teenage years. Many male youths do not want to appear averse to risk-taking, which can result in smoking for social support and affirmation. The acceptance and camaraderie young smokers receive from other young smokers can be more rewarding than tobacco itself. The process of obtaining and learning to use tobacco also can be construed as a risky and therefore thrilling prospect to many teenage boys.

Parental, familial, and communal influences also affect a boy's decision to begin smoking at a young age. Children whose parents smoke grow up to presume that the practice is acceptable if adult behavior; children of smokers also grow up to suffer negative effects from early exposure to secondhand smoke. Newer research on substance abuse also has revealed that nicotine addiction may be linked to genetic disposition. Having parents who smoke also can make boys erroneously skeptical of cultural attitudes, advertising, and public health information that tries to warn youths of the dangers of smoking.

SHORT-TERM HEALTH DANGERS

The long-term effects of tobacco smoking are widely known. However, tobacco smoking also causes an array of immediate psychological and health effects, even with occasional or sporadic

A man living at a halfway house smokes a cigarette. (Getty Images)

use. Many of these effects, which occur in both men and women, include increased stress levels from cellular manipulation to dopamine receptors. Abnormal tightening of airways results in shortness of breath and increased phlegm production that result in persistent bouts of coughing. All of these factors combine to decrease overall physical performance and well-being.

The damage a single cigarette or exposure to secondhand smoke causes to the cardiovascular system is also significant. Smoking dilates blood vessels, resulting in a reduction of blood supply throughout the body. In addition to an increased heart rate while ingesting smoke, smokers also have a higher resting heartbeat than do nonsmokers.

Smoking also can cause negative effects to a person's teeth, stomach, and digestive system. Changes in blood supply slow immune responses responsible for preventing periodontal infection. Excess mucous production in the lungs and stomach, a result of the body's attempt to cast out harmful toxins from smoke, also can lead to gastroesophageal reflux disease and peptic ulcers. Tobacco smoking also interferes with the body's absorption of key minerals, enzymes, and micronutrients such as vitamins A, C, and E, all of which are necessary to maintain health.

LONG-TERM HEALTH DANGERS

The body's short-term reaction to tobacco smoking and the litany of health complications surrounding even occasional exposure to or use of tobacco persist in habitual smokers. What results is a constant struggle by the body to return to a nonsmoking state, a struggle made more difficult because of the numerous degenerative effects of the toxins found in tobacco smoke.

In men, the restriction of blood vessels resulting from long-term use of or exposure to tobacco smoke can result in erectile dysfunction, sperm damage, and impotence. Newer evidence also suggests that long-term exposure to the toxic chemicals in tobacco smoke can result in genetic mutations to the sperm that increase the risk of birth defects and cancer in the future children of smokers.

While lung cancer and emphysema are the most widely known potentially fatal diseases associated with smoking, heart disease remains the leading cause of death among smokers in the United States. Furthermore, estimates predict that more than one billion people will die from tobacco use in the twenty-first century.

The widespread legislative and cultural changes in developed countries such as the United States have made the dangers of smoking more evident than any previous time. The new health campaigns and changing cultural attitudes toward tobacco smoking are perhaps the biggest reason that the percentage of male smokers older than age eighteen years in the United States has gone from 52 percent in 1965 to just 26 percent in 1999, according to the World Health Organization (WHO).

The tobacco epidemic, however, will continue to take its toll in such nations as China, where the health risks are less known and smoking remains a widely accepted practice among men. WHO estimates that more than 300 million Chinese men are smokers, a number of people equal to the entire population of the United States.

John Pritchard

FURTHER READING

American Lung Association. "Trends in Tobacco Use." Jul. 2011. Web. 30 Apr. 2012. http://www. lung.org/finding-cures/our-research/trend-reports/Tobacco-Trend-Report.pdf.

Gately, Iain. *Tobacco: A Cultural History of How an Exotic Plant Seduced Civilization.* New York: Grove, 2003.

Herrick, Charles. *100 Questions and Answers about How to Quit Smoking.* Sudbury, MA: Jones, 2009.

Rabinoff, Michael. *Ending the Tobacco Holocaust.* Fulton: Elite, 2010.

"Smoking's Immediate Effects on the Body." 17 Sep. 2009. Web. 30 Apr. 2012. http://www.tobaccofreekids.org/research/factsheets/pdf/0264. pdf.

Zang, Edith A., and Ernst L. Wynder. "Difference in Lung Cancer Risk Between Men and Women: Examination of the Evidence." *Journal of the National Cancer Institute* 88 (1996). Web. 30 Apr. 2012. http://jnci.oxfordjournals.org/content/88/3-4/183.abstract.

WEBSITES OF INTEREST

American Cancer Society
http://www.cancer.org

Centers for Disease Control and Prevention
http://www.cdc.gov/tobacco

Partnership for a Tobacco-Free Maine
http://www.tobaccofreemaine.org/channels/
   providers/gender_differences.php

World Health Organization
http://www.who.int/tobacco/en/atlas5.pdf

See also: Gender and addiction; Media and smoking; Men and behavioral addictions; Men and substance abuse; Smoking; Smoking: Short- and long-term effects on the body; Tobacco use disorder

---

Men and substance abuse

CATEGORY: Social issues

DEFINITION: Medical professionals have recorded the effects of substance abuse on men since alcohol addiction was defined in the mid-nineteenth century. Since the 1980s, experts have documented and compared the effects of substance abuse in men and women and have found that the risk factors that men face when abusing drugs and alcohol differ from those that women may experience. Also, the treatment men receive for substance abuse also differs when compared with treatment for women.

STATISTICS

Men are more likely than women to abuse drugs and alcohol. This has been a stable finding throughout many decades of research. A study by the National Household Survey on Drug Abuse (NHSDA) in 1997 showed that 8.5 percent of male participants admitted to using illicit substances, while only 4.5 percent of female participants responded similarly.

In that same survey, a higher number of men than women admitted to using cocaine and alcohol during a twelve-month period. Twenty-three percent of men surveyed said they regularly participated in binge drinking, while only 8 percent of women said the same. Finally, 8.7 percent of male and 2.1 percent of female participants admitted to frequent heavy drinking.

In 2010 the National Survey on Drug Use and Health (NSDUH) surveyed 67,500 people and discovered that previous findings received further support:

11.6 of male participants age twelve years and older said they had abused drugs or alcohol in the past year while only 5.9 percent of female participants said the same. The same survey found that in participants age twelve to seventeen years, a slightly higher percentage of females than males said they had become dependent on drugs or alcohol in the past year (7.7 percent to 6.9 percent). Analyzing responses from participants age eighteen years and older, however, produced findings that matched the history of all other surveys: 12.2 percent of men had identified themselves as dependent either on drugs or alcohol while only 5.8 percent of women had done the same.

Additionally, studies have shown that gay, bisexual, and transgender (GBT) men abuse drugs and alcohol more often than do heterosexual men and women. Also, GBT men are more likely to experiment with drugs and alcohol and are also more likely to continue using drugs and alcohol throughout their lives. Research has shown that this is often how GBT men respond to or cope with instances of homophobia, discrimination, or violence experienced because of their sexual orientation or gender expression.

Surveys also have found that men are more likely than women to start using drugs and alcohol earlier in their lives. Men also are more likely to continue using drugs and alcohol throughout their lives, often in larger doses than most women. The duration and frequency of use typically leads to the body's ability to tolerate small dosages. This means that most men will increase the amount of drugs or alcohol they consume so they can experience a better high. This behavior often leads to substance abuse and addiction. Men are more likely than women to overdose from illicit drug use but women are more likely to die from an overdose of prescription medications, such as antidepressants.

RISK FACTORS

People abuse drugs and alcohol for a variety of reasons. Many of these reasons—stress at work, social pressures, and escape from traumatic memories of the past—are shared between genders.

Women who abuse drugs and alcohol have been found to do so if they are in a mentally, physically, or sexually abusive relationship. Women also are more likely to abuse drugs and alcohol to calm anxiety, depression, post-traumatic stress, and eating disorders. Women tend to develop addictions to drugs or alcohol after having sought comfort in their drug of choice; that is, they wish to numb their feelings and avoid the effects of these situations.

Men, however, appear to turn to drugs and alcohol after they have experienced an unfortunate event, typically one that has occurred at their own hands. Men may drink alcohol or use drugs to avoid the consequences of their own aggressive or violent behaviors, for example.

Men who drink frequently and in large amounts are at a higher risk of developing heart disease, various types of cancers, and other health problems, such as human immunodeficiency virus infection. The additional risks of abusing drugs or alcohol include developing depression or anxiety, contemplating or committing suicide, and forming an addiction to the drug of choice. Men with substance abuse problems also are more likely to participate in risky sexual behaviors, such as having unprotected sex with multiple partners. In this case, men may unintentionally impregnate women they do not know or they may become infected with a sexually transmitted disease.

Men and women both risk developing problems at work if they form an addiction to drugs or alcohol; their need to use the substance may become so strong that they arrive at work drunk or high or may simply not show up for shifts to become drunk or high instead. This lack of dependability also may affect their relationships with friends and family members, as the substance abuser may forget plans or neglect responsibilities to acquire or take drugs.

Men also risk becoming aggressive and violent when they abuse drugs and alcohol. Though medical professionals have not proven a direct causal relationship between the use of drugs and alcohol and domestic violence, studies have consistently shown that the two factors are directly related. The US Department of Justice (DOJ) has reported that 61 percent of domestic violence offenders have drug and alcohol abuse problems. The DOJ also found that 50 percent of all spousal murders were committed while the offender was intoxicated.

Scientists, criminologists, and medical professionals cannot say, however, whether becoming intoxicated leads men to physically, verbally, or sexually abuse their spouses or children—or if the relationship works the other way. For example, is it possible that most men who abuse drugs and alcohol do so to deal with the guilt they feel after they acted violently or abusively toward their family? One thing all medical professionals agree on, though, is that substance abuse is never an excuse for violence. Men who are violent, and those who witness such violence, should not attempt to blame their behavior on the substance in question.

TREATMENT

Treating drug and alcohol abuse is difficult, regardless of the patient's gender. One of the most important tasks to complete while diagnosing a patient with a substance abuse problem or addiction is determining whether the abuse or addiction exists with another disease or disorder.

Many men who abuse drugs and alcohol may also have a conduct disorder or antisocial personality disorder. Attention deficit hyperactivity disorder is common in men who abuse cocaine. Although women have higher rates of anxiety and depressive disorders than men, both men and women are commonly diagnosed with depressive disorders when they also abuse drugs or alcohol.

In addition to diagnosing any personality disorders or mental illnesses that may be underlying causes or results of substance abuse, medical professionals also must determine whether the patient also needs treatment for aggressive behavior, domestic violence, or past cases of sexual, physical, or emotional abuse. When all underlying conditions are documented, medical professionals then decide how to best treat their patients. In an ideal world, one therapist or group would be able to address all the patient's issues. However, this is often not the case. A man who is both a drug addict and a domestic violence offender most likely needs to attend one session to talk about his violent behavior with domestic violence counselors and another session to discuss his substance use with drug and alcohol counselors. He may also need to visit another location to be treated for withdrawal symptoms.

In 2010, the NSDUH reported that of the 23.1 million people in the United States who needed treatment for illicit drug or alcohol use, 20.5 million of those persons did not get help. A mere 1.7 percent of people who needed assistance were able to get it. Another 3.3 percent felt they needed help dealing with their substance abuse issues but did not take any action, citing reasons such as a lack of health insurance, transportation, time, and finances. The remaining 95 percent did not feel they had a problem that needed to be treated.

The majority of the 1.7 percent surveyed who received treatment in 2010 were men. Women are often uncomfortable seeking treatment or admitting they have a substance abuse problem. When seeking treatment, they often do not wish to share their most intimate details in a group of both men and women. For this reason, women often seek women-only support groups or female therapists if they wish to receive help for their condition.

Another reason that keeps women from seeking treatment is child care. Most men do not have this problem, as they are typically not the primary child-care providers in their household. If women cannot find a caretaker, they may have to skip meetings and appointments. Men, in general, do not have the same childcare responsibilities and thus have fewer barriers to attending therapy and doctors' visits.

Nicole Frail

FURTHER READING

Brady, Kathleen T., and Carrie L. Randoll. "Gender Differences in Substance Use Disorders." *Addictive Disorders* 22.2 (1999): 241–52. Print.

Center for Substance Abuse Treatment. *Substance Abuse Treatment and Domestic Violence.* Rockville, MD: SAMHSA, 1997.

McCabe, Sean, James Cranford, and Brady West. "Trends in Prescription Drug Abuse and Dependence, Co-Occurrence with Other Substance Use Disorders, and Treatment Utilization: Results from Two National Surveys." *Addictive Behaviors* 33 (2008): 1297–1305. Print.

National Institute on Alcohol Abuse and Alcoholism. *Assessing Alcohol Problems: A Guide for Clinicians and Researchers.* 2nd ed. Washington, DC: DHHS, 2003.

Shelton, Michael. *Gay Men and Substance Abuse: A Basic Guide for Addicts and Those Who Care for Them.* Center City, MN: Hazelden, 2011.

US Department of Health and Human Services. *Results from the 2010 National Survey on Drug Use and Health: Summary of National Findings.* 2011. Web. 23 Apr. 2012. http://www.samhsa.gov/data/ NSDUH/2k10Results/Web/HTML/2k10Results. htm#7.1.

WEBSITES OF INTEREST

Centers for Disease Control and Prevention
http://www.cdc.gov

National Institute on Drug Abuse
http://drugabuse.gov

Substance Abuse and Mental Health Services Administration
http://www.samhsa.gov

See also: Families and substance abuse; Gender and addiction; Marriage/partnership and substance abuse; Media and substance abuse; Men and behavioral addictions; Men and smoking; Parenting and substance abuse; Substance abuse

Mental illness

CATEGORY: Psychological and behavioral issues
ALSO KNOWN AS: Comorbidity; co-occurrence; dual diagnosis
DEFINITION: Addiction often occurs, simultaneously or in sequence, with other psychopathological symptoms at a rate that exceeds chance. The phenomenon is called comorbidity. Each condition has the potential to influence the other's course, therapeutic responses, and prognoses, creating a complex clinical presentation.

ADDICTION AND OTHER MENTAL DISORDERS

Addiction can occur with another mental disorder. Roughly one-half of drug abusers and alcoholics have one or more other mental illnesses. Moreover, of all persons diagnosed with a psychiatric disease, almost one-half have a substance abuse disorder. The substance is most commonly alcohol, followed by marijuana and cocaine. Other commonly abused substances are prescription drugs such as tranquilizers and sleeping pills.

In 2002, approximately four million adults in the United States met the criteria for both a serious mental disorder and substance dependence or abuse the year before. The incidence of abuse is higher among males and those age eighteen to forty-four years. Any of the disorders identified by the American Psychiatric Association's *Diagnostic and Statistical Manual of Mental Disorders* (DSM-IV) can occur in conjunction with addiction. The dual diagnosis often includes depression, bipolar disorder, schizophrenia, attention deficit hyperactivity disorder (ADHD), generalized anxiety disorder, obsessive-compulsive disorder, post-traumatic stress disorder (PTSD), panic disorder, and antisocial personality disorder.

An impressive body of medical literature documents specific comorbid associations. Subjects with mood or anxiety disorders are two to four times more likely to have a substance use disorder compared with normal subjects. The same is true for people with an antisocial syndrome, such as antisocial personality or conduct disorder. Almost one-half of persons with schizophrenia also have a lifetime history of substance use disorders—a much higher percentage than the one seen in unaffected persons. Cannabis use disorders are prevalent among schizophrenic dual-diagnosis patients, particularly among young adults. In some studies, the rate of smoking in persons with schizophrenia reached 90 percent. The percentage of smokers is also much higher in persons diagnosed with depression, PTSD, and panic disorder, than it is in normal age-matched controls. Methamphetamine use co-occurs with psychiatric manifestations, including depression, suicidal thoughts, and psychosis.

The comorbid associations, however, do not stop at substance use disorders. Studies show that adolescents with Internet addiction have more ADHD symptoms, depression, social phobia, and hostility. Comorbidity of pathological Internet use and psychiatric disorders also is seen in other age groups. Exercise addiction displays a high comorbidity and has many symptoms in common with eating disorders and body image disorders.

Establishing a cause-and-effect relationship for the association of addiction and psychiatric illnesses remains difficult, even when one of these disease categories is diagnosed first. The psychiatric diagnosis often does not happen until symptoms have progressed to a specified level, in accordance with DSM-IV guidelines. Meanwhile, mild symptoms may prompt drug use, and vague recollections of when drug abuse started can generate inaccurate assessments of what occurred first.

The relationship between addiction and other psychiatric disorders is bidirectional. Several mechanisms probably contribute, to different extents, to how specific comorbidities manifest themselves. Because of the substantial economic and psychosocial burden associated with dual diagnosis, identifying the cause of co-occurrence constitutes a public health priority.

MENTAL DISORDERS AND ADDICTION

Physicians have long known that psychiatric symptoms such as insomnia, fatigue, depressed mood, and anxiety increase a person's likelihood of using drugs. It appears the affected person attempts to self-medicate with drugs, or to engage in other addictive behaviors, to obtain a pleasant feeling (via a neurotransmitter surge in the brain's reward system). This eases the suffering caused by the underlying illness. Repeated administration of these "remedies" puts the stressed and anhedonic person at risk for addiction, especially when not under adequate medical care.

According to the American Psychiatric Association, persons with schizophrenia use substances such as marijuana to mitigate negative symptoms and some of the adverse effects of antipsychotic medication. Several self-medication mechanisms have been proposed to explain the strong association between schizophrenia and smoking, but none has been confirmed. The use of tobacco products by persons with schizophrenia could alleviate disease symptoms and improve cognition. In addition, smoking behavior also may help patients cope with the social stigma of their disease.

Multiple studies have demonstrated an increased risk for drug use disorders in young persons with untreated ADHD. Some researchers suggest that only ADHD-affected persons with coexisting conduct disorders are vulnerable. Treatment of childhood ADHD with methylphenidate and amphetamines, although efficient in reducing the characteristic manifestations, has generated concern regarding the child's vulnerability to drug abuse later in life.

New types of addiction are making their way into the lives of psychiatric patients. A number of studies reported excessive online game-playing in persons with major depressive disorder. Depression, hostility, ADHD, and social phobia were found to predict the occurrence of Internet addiction in follow-up studies. Hostility and ADHD represented the most important predictors of Internet addiction in male and female adolescents, respectively.

MENTAL DISORDERS AND DRUGS OF ABUSE

Substances of abuse, and the expanding cycle of brain dysfunction they produce, can cause users to experience symptoms of mental illness in the absence of a previous psychiatric history. Ecstasy (MDMA) use, for example, causes long-term deficits in brain serotonin function, resulting in depression and anxiety. Psychosis occurs in stimulant abusers (for example, in the chronic phase of amphetamine use), apparently because of alterations in the dopamine system. Stimulants also cause anxiety, panic attacks, and sleep disorders.

Suicidal behavior is frequently observed among cocaine-dependent persons. Cocaine affects mood negatively, as indicated by the high frequency of dysphoria (unpleasant mood) in users. Brain imaging and post-mortem studies conducted in these subjects show reductions in dopamine receptors and in dopamine release. Dopamine is a key molecule in reward and motivational circuits; therefore, these reductions could lead to loss of interest and depressed mood. In persons with predisposing factors, this effect elevates the risk for suicide.

Elucidating the long-term impact of early drug exposure is an important area of comorbidity research. Chronic drug abuse by teenagers represents a major concern because, at this formative stage, it has a negative impact on socialization and cognitive development and can contribute to the generation of mental disorders. The connection between early drug exposure and psychopathology is, however, a complex one, because of potential genetic and environmental influences. One study, for example, shows that frequent marijuana use in adolescence increases the risk of psychosis in adulthood, but only in subjects with a certain gene variant.

OVERLAPPING CAUSES

Addiction and other psychiatric illnesses have overlapping causes that include genetic vulnerabilities, brain dysfunction, and early exposure to stress or trauma. Research is aimed at finding genes that favor the development of both addictive behavior and mental diseases, or increase the risk of comorbidity. Approximately one-half of a person's vulnerability to addiction is caused by genetics, mainly through complex relationships between genes and interactions with environmental factors.

Several regions of the human genome have been linked to an elevated risk of both substance use disorders and mental illness. One prominent example is the existence of genetic factors associated with a higher vulnerability to teenage drug dependence and conduct disorders. Pathological gambling shares genetic vulnerability factors with antisocial behaviors, alcohol dependence, and major depression.

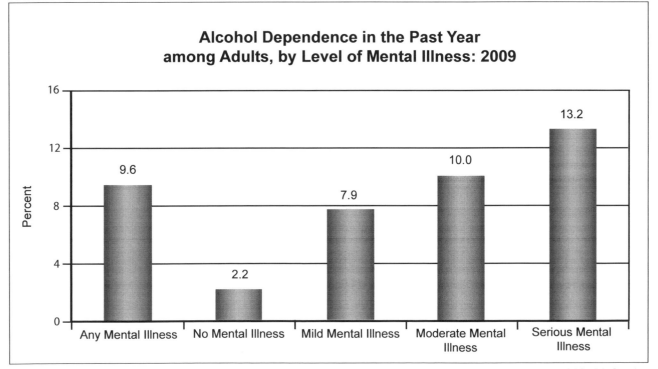

Source: National Survey on Drug Use and Health (NSDUH), sponsored by the Substance Abuse and Mental Health Services Administration (SAMHSA)

Pathological changes in certain brain areas and neurotransmitter systems underlie both substance use disorders and other mental illnesses. This led to the hypothesis that brain changes associated with one disease category may influence the other. Drug abuse may cause structural changes in the brain that render a person more prone to developing a psychiatric disorder. When a mental disorder develops first, it changes brain activity in a way that increases the propensity to abuse substances in an attempt to alleviate the unpleasant effects of the mental disorder or the medication used to treat it.

Dopaminergic and serotonergic dysfunctions lead to psychiatric disorders and increase the risk for addiction. Dopaminergic circuitry, for example, is altered both in addiction and in psychiatric disorders, such as depression and schizophrenia. The presence of these abnormalities may predispose a person to developing schizophrenia, increase the rewarding effects of substances like nicotine, and even diminish the person's ability to quit smoking. The drug clozapine is used to treat schizophrenia and acts on nicotine receptors, among others. It improves attention and memory in animal models of schizophrenia, and it reduces smoking in persons with schizophrenia. This observation further underscores the existence of common disorder mechanisms.

Psychosocial stress participates in the initiation and maintenance of addictive disorders and other psychiatric diseases, including depression and PTSD. Evidence suggests that the limbic-hypothalamic-pituitary-adrenal axis, which controls stress reactions, may be important in the development of depression and addictive disorders. Dopamine signaling has also been implicated in the way stress increases vulnerability to drug addiction. As stress is a risk factor for multiple mental disorders, these findings provide a possible link between the mechanisms underlying addiction and those of other psychiatric disorders.

DIAGNOSIS AND TREATMENT OF COMORBIDITY
The strikingly high rate of addiction and psychiatric illness co-occurrence calls for a thorough evaluation of patients and prompt, concurrent treatment of these disorders. Patients presenting with mental illnesses should receive screening for addictions, and substance abusers should undergo a comprehensive psychiatric evaluation. This approach will help patients with dual diagnosis, in which symptoms may be more severe and difficult to manage than in patients with only one disorder.

Substance abuse in persons with schizophrenia, for example, is associated with poorer clinical outcomes and contributes significantly to their morbidity and mortality. Skilled assistance and careful observation will also distinguish between the symptoms of intoxication or withdrawal and the often similar manifestations of comorbid mental disorders.

Health providers should be aware that the rates of addiction relapse are higher in people with psychiatric comorbidities. Smokers with depression, for example, have a more difficult time quitting and require more attempts to quit than do smokers without depression.

Targeted and early treatment can significantly reduce the increased risk of persons with mood disorders resorting to drugs and can reduce the development of severe mental illnesses in persons with addictive behaviors. In the United States, the care for patients with comorbidity poses several problems. The health system employs distinct channels for treating psychiatric disorders and addiction. Health practitioners' qualifications render each system better suited to dealing with one or the other of these disease categories. When faced with dual-diagnosis patients, substance-abuse treatment centers may be reluctant to use medications, even when needed to treat mental disorders. Some may not have employees qualified to prescribe and monitor medication. Consequently, when surveyed, patients with comorbidities report the lowest satisfaction with health care and the greatest prevalence of unmet need.

Patient population factors (such as social status, gender, and scope of insurance coverage) contribute to a deepening of the gap between the two closely related therapeutic fields. According to the National Institute on Drug Abuse, when suffering from both substance abuse and mental illness, women tend to seek help from mental health practitioners, whereas men prefer substance-abuse treatment channels. Epidemiological studies indicate that one-half of military veterans diagnosed with PTSD have a substance use disorder comorbidity, which creates a challenge for the health system. Urgent research efforts are needed to identify the best treatment strategies for addressing PTSD-substance abuse comorbidities and to explore possible distinct treatments for combat versus civilian PTSD.

A high percentage of detainees in prisons and jails have a psychiatric disorder associated with substance abuse or addiction. In these settings, co-morbidity treatment avenues are insufficient and improvements have a great potential to enhance public health and safety.

Despite these difficulties, progress in screening and treatment of comorbidities has been made in many settings. Research efforts aim to identify the best pharmacologic treatments that reduce cravings, while alleviating associated mental disorders. One successful approach concerns patients who receive atypical antipsychotic agents, especially clozapine: They smoke less and have an easier time quitting. Psychosocial strategies that show promise in treating comorbidity include cognitive-behavioral therapy, therapeutic communities, assertive community treatment, and integrated group therapy.

Mihaela Avramut, MD, PhD

FURTHER READING

Hesse, Morten. "Treating the Patient with Comorbidity." *Evidence-Based Addiction Treatment.* Ed. Peter M. Miller. Burlington, MA: Academic, 2009. Well-written chapter that discusses potential treatments for comorbidity through the lens of scientific evidence.

Kranzler, Henry R., and Joyce A. Tinsley, eds. *Dual Diagnosis and Psychiatric Treatment: Substance Abuse and Comorbid Disorders.* New York: Marcel Dekker, 2004. Good resource for health practitioners and dedicated students, detailing research on the epidemiology, genetics, and management of dually diagnosed patients.

Martin, Peter R. *Substance Abuse in the Mentally and Physically Disabled.* New York: Marcel Dekker, 2001. Reviews major studies on comorbidity and discusses treatment options.

Miller, Norman S., and Mark S. Gold, eds. *Addictive Disorders in Medical Populations.* Hoboken, NJ: Wiley, 2010. Written mainly for medical practitioners but a useful resource for all interested therapists, counselors, and families helping persons with comorbidities.

Thakkar, Vatsal G. *Addiction.* New York: Chelsea House, 2006. Summarizes a variety of addiction topics, including the relationship with mental illness.

Volkow, Nora D. "Substance Use Disorders in Schizophrenia: Clinical Implications of Comorbidity." *Schizophrenia Bulletin* 35 (2009): 469–72. Print. Article written by an authority in the field of addiction research.

WEBSITES OF INTEREST

National Alliance on Mental Illness
http://www.nami.org

National Institute on Drug Abuse
http://drugabuse.gov/researchreports/comorbidity/whyoccur.html

See also: Addiction; Anxiety; Bipolar disorder and addiction; Co-occurring disorders; Depression; Obsessive-compulsive disorder (OCD); Post-traumatic stress disorder and addiction; Psychosis and substance abuse; Schizophrenia and addiction; Suicide and addiction

---

Mescaline

CATEGORY: Substances
ALSO KNOWN AS: Buttons; cactus; mesc; peyote
DEFINITION: Mescaline is a naturally occurring psychedelic with mind-altering properties. It is structurally related to amphetamine but has mental effects similar to lysergic acid diethylamide (LSD).
STATUS: Illegal in the United States and worldwide
CLASSIFICATION: Schedule I controlled substance
SOURCE: Exists naturally in the mushroom-like crown or buttons of the peyote cactus, *Lophophora williamsii*, and can be produced synthetically
TRANSMISSION ROUTE: Chewed or swallowed, soaked in water and ingested as an intoxicating drink, or dried and ground into powder and smoked, or made into capsules and tablets

HISTORY OF USE

Mescaline, named after the Mescalero Apaches, is a classic psychedelic drug with a long history of use worldwide. It was first isolated from the peyote cactus by a German chemist named Arthur Heffter in 1897.

Mescaline-containing cacti were traditionally used by Native American tribes in religious ceremonies to treat physical and spiritual ailments, to alter states of consciousness, to generate mystical visions, and to induce spiritual cleansing through nausea and vomiting. In the early twentieth century the establishment of the Native American Church (NAC) legitimized the use of psychoactive cacti in ritual ceremonies.

In 1919, mescaline became one of the first natural hallucinogens to be produced synthetically. During the hippie movement in the 1960s and 1970s, the use of mescaline as a recreational drug became extensive because of its mind-expanding properties. Mescaline use has been illegal in the United States since the early 1970s, with the exception of use in NAC ritual ceremonies. Mescaline is a schedule I hallucinogen because of its high abuse potential and its lack of legitimate medical use.

EFFECTS AND POTENTIAL RISKS
Mescaline is most commonly known for its powerful psychotropic effects. Although its chemical structure does not resemble that of LSD, it acts similarly. Its hallucinogenic effects are caused by its binding to serotonin receptors in the brain and inducing numerous behavioral and perceptual changes.

Mescaline's short-term psychological effects are related to increased serotonin levels. Mescaline alters sensory, time, and space perceptions and thought processes and mood. It induces intense visual hallucinations of enhanced color and detail followed by euphoric dreamlike states, giving the illusion of having an out-of-body experience. Negative short-term physical effects include nausea, vomiting, sweating, dizziness, headache, anxiety, and tachycardia (rapid heartbeat).

Mescaline's hallucinogenic effects are known as trips. Users experience good trips resulting from pleasurable images or bad trips resulting from disturbing images. Some users experience a blending of the senses called synesthesia. Long-term use can potentially lead to mental health problems, including drug-induced psychosis and hallucinogen-persisting perception disorder known as flashbacks.

Rose Ciulla-Bohling, PhD

FURTHER READING
Brands, Bruna, Beth Sproule, and Joan Marshman. *Drugs and Drug Abuse.* Toronto: Addiction Research, 1998.

Cunningham, Nicola. "Hallucinogenic Plants of Abuse." *Emergency Medicine Australasia* 20.2 (2008): 167–74. Print.

Fantegrossi, William E., Kevin S. Murnane, and Chad J. Reissig. "The Behavioral Pharmacology of Hallucinogens." *Biochemical Pharmacology* 75.1 (2008): 17–33. Print.

WEBSITES OF INTEREST
National Institute on Drug Abuse
http://www.drugabuse.gov/Infofacts/
    hallucinogens.html

Native American Church
http://www.nativeamericanchurches.org

See also: Amphetamine abuse; Hallucinogen abuse; Hallucinogens: Short- and long-term effects on the body; LSD

Methadone

CATEGORY: Treatment
ALSO KNOWN AS: Dolophine; methadose
DEFINITION: Methadone is a schedule II medication used for the management of opioid dependence and withdrawal. Initial treatment is generally followed by the slow tapering of methadone at a timed interval, which is highly patient-specific. Additionally, methadone can be used for treating moderate to severe pain that is unresponsive to non-narcotic analgesics.

HISTORY OF USE
Methadone hydrochloride is a synthetic opioid with mu (μ) agonist properties. It was developed in the 1930s in Germany, and by the 1950s methadone began to be used by the US government, specifically the Public Health Service, in the treatment of opioid abstinence syndrome.

Methadone acts on the same brain receptor as heroin and other opioids, producing similar effects. For this reason, it is used to help bridge users from more hazardous drugs. In the treatment of addiction in the United States, methadone is used primarily for the treatment of heroin addicts. Persons who stop taking heroin without taking medication for withdrawal, such as methadone, naltrexone, or buprenorphine, can experience severe withdrawal symptoms. These symptoms include agitation, anxiety, sweating, and other flu-like symptoms, potentially leading to hospitalization.

When beginning therapy with methadone, those treated may experience common adverse effects, including constipation, dizziness, sedation, gastrointestinal distress (nausea and vomiting), and possibly itching, headache, and hypotension. More serious adverse reactions include cardiac and pulmonary complications and respiratory depression. Patients are monitored and undergo a complete medical history assessment to identify any significant medical conditions that may increase risks of developing complications from methadone.

OPIOID DETOXIFICATION

Methadone is used in opioid detoxification, in treating opioid addiction, and in maintaining treatment for opioid addiction. Methadone is available orally in 5 and 10 milligram (mg) tablets and as a solution and in suspension. Patient response to methadone is highly variable, in part because of its broad range of bioavailability, because of the time to peak plasma concentration, and because of the drug's half-life. Knowing methadone's half-life's variability is critical because respiratory depression, which occurs with methadone and other opioids as a class, generally lasts longer than pain control. Respiratory depression from methadone and other opioids can be severe and fatal.

Starting doses of methadone are generally between 20 and 30 mg and are gradually tapered until withdrawal symptoms are controlled. This taper usually occurs during the first week of treatment. The typical maintenance dose is 80 to 120 mg, once daily. However, it is not uncommon for higher doses to be required.

Treatment generally continues for one year or more, followed by a slow taper. Tapering off methadone requires dose reductions of less than 10 percent within ten to fourteen days, often requiring

A patient drinks his daily dose of methadone, a synthetic narcotic drug similar to morphine that is used in nartcotic detoxification and maintenance of heroin addictions. (Navesh Chitrakar/Reuters/Landov)

an extended period before a patient is completely weaned off the methadone.

Patients also generally require a combination of psychosocial and behavioral counseling to be successful at staying clean from opioids. During the first week of therapy, and until the medication and side effects are fully realized, patients are advised to avoid activities requiring mental alertness. Additionally, while being treated with methadone, patients should avoid ingesting other central nervous system depressants (including alcohol and other medications) and should avoid discontinuing the medication abruptly.

AUTHORIZED TREATMENT

Methadone used for the treatment of opioid dependence can be provided only by authorized opioid treatment programs (OTPs), which are certified by the federal Substance Abuse and Mental Health Services Administration. Providers must meet specific criteria, including board certification in addiction specialties, to legally prescribe methadone for opioid dependence treatment. However, if a patient on methadone is admitted as an inpatient for reasons other than opioid addiction, therapy can be continued with provider certification if it can be verified that the patient is receiving treatment at an OTP.

Allison C. Bennett, PharmD

FURTHER READING

Connock, M., et al. "Methadone and Buprenorphine for the Management of Opioid Dependence: A Systematic Review and Economic Evaluation." *Health Technology Assessment* 11.9 (2007). Print. A systematic review of clinical trials evaluating the effectiveness of both methadone and buprenorphine replacement therapy. Also includes information on cost effectiveness and total economic impact.

Gouldin, Winston, Daniel T. Kennedy, and Ralph E. Small. "Methadone: History and Recommendations for Use in Analgesia." *American Pain Society Bulletin* 10.5 (2000). Print. Brief history of methadone, followed by information on its use for pain control, including dosing and cost. Includes information on pharmacokinetics and equivalent dosing with other pain medications.

Nicholls, Lance, Lisa Bragaw, and Charles Ruetsch. "Opioid Dependence Treatment and Guidelines." *Journal of Managed Care Pharmacy* 16.1 (2010): S14–21. Print. Article begins by assessing a patient's readiness to quit opioids and continues with various treatment options. Includes information on methadone and other medications used to treat withdrawal, including buprenorphine, clonidine, and naltrexone. Compares methadone and buprenorphine replacement therapy.

WEBSITES OF INTEREST

"Addiction Science." National Institute on Drug Abuse
http://www.drugabuse.gov/related-topics/addiction-science

Substance Abuse and Mental Health Services Administration
http://www.samhsa.gov

See also: Addiction medications; Opioid abuse; Withdrawal

Methamphetamine

CATEGORY: Substances
ALSO KNOWN AS: Crank; crystal meth; meth; speed
DEFINITION: Methamphetamine is a psychostimulant in the phenoethylamine and amphetamine class of drugs. It is a white, odorless, bitter-tasting crystalline powder that is highly addictive. It is used medically to treat attention deficit hyperactivity disorder, exogenous obesity, and narcolepsy.
STATUS: Legal status varies depending on whether methamphetamine is approved for medical use. Legal but highly regulated in the United States and illegal in any form in Canada.
CLASSIFICATION: Schedule I drug in Canada, Hong Kong, the Netherlands and New Zealand. Schedule II drug in the United States because of its medicinal use. Class A drug in the United Kingdom.
SOURCE: Commonly synthesized in a laboratory, although it can be found naturally in the traditional Chinese herb Ephedra sinica, or ma huang. Illegal methamphetamine labs range from large-scale operations to small, one-room labs. Methamphetamine production also occurs at the microscale, in which meth is produced with no more than a soda bottle and ingredients found in a convenience store. Individual methamphetamine production

has become popular because the synthesis requires no special skills or instruments. Recipes for mixtures that include ingredients such as phosphorus from matches, pseudoephedrine from cold medicine, and iodine can be found on the Internet.

TRANSMISSION ROUTE: Ingestion; inhalation; insufflation (snorting); intravenous; suppository (anal and vaginal)

HISTORY OF USE

A Japanese scientist first synthesized methamphetamine in 1919. Along with amphetamines, methamphetamine was given to both Axis and Allied soldiers during World War II as performance aids and to counteract sleep deprivation. Illegal use of methamphetamine rose in the United States in the 1960s, originating in the Southwest. Methamphetamine was supplied by labs in Mexico and smuggled into the United States through US border states. By the 1980s, methamphetamine had become increasingly popular in the Midwest and in the southern states, partially because of the availability of fertilizer that could be used as an ingredient in methamphetamine production.

Although the National Institute on Drug Abuse reports that methamphetamine use among teenagers is in decline, studies show that there are between 15 and 16 million methamphetamine abusers worldwide, a number some experts say is second only to marijuana use. Admission rates to rehabilitation centers for methamphetamine addiction are higher in some states than for cocaine or even alcohol abuse.

One of the methods of coping with the rising methamphetamine problem has been a slow but progressive change in treating addicts. Prison officials, psychologists, and legislators have made changes in the prison system so that prisoners addicted to methamphetamine can safely go through detoxification and receive further treatment.

Treatment for methamphetamine addiction has become specialized. The matrix model includes cognitive-behavioral therapy, family education, positive reinforcement for behavior change and treatment compliance, and a twelve-step program. No ideal medication has been found for treatment, although some studies have examined the use of the tricyclic antidepressant imiprazine (Tofranil).

EFFECTS AND POTENTIAL RISKS

The physical effects of a methamphetamine high resemble those of the body in a fight-or-flight, hyperarousal response. Heart rate and blood pressure increases, and awareness is heightened with increased self-confidence.

Chronic methamphetamine use and methamphetamine overdose lead to extremely dangerous physical conditions, including myocardial infarction, cardiopulmonary arrest, seizures, hypoxic brain damage, hyperthermia, and intracranial bleeds. Psychiatric symptoms are extremely common and include insomnia, mood disorders, violent behavior, paranoia, and hallucinations.

Methamphetamine increases the release of and blocks the body's reuptake of dopamine, which increases the levels of dopamine in the brain. The inability of the brain to release the excess dopamine creates the user's rush or high. Chronic methamphetamine use leads to a change in the activity of the dopamine system, specifically a decrease in motor skills and impaired verbal learning skills. Chronic use also affects emotions, memory, and general cognitive abilities. Because methamphetamine is highly lipophilic, it enables a rapid and extensive transport across the

---

Meth Mouth

Meth mouth is a popular term for the extensive tooth decay and oral hygiene issues associated with heavy use of methamphetamine, a potent central nervous system stimulant. The acidic nature of methamphetamine may contribute to meth mouth, but the condition largely results from drug-induced changes that profoundly affect oral health.

These changes include decreased production of saliva, which fosters bacterial growth and tooth decay; repetitive jaw clenching and tooth grinding, which damages enamel and causes teeth to fracture; and frequent cravings for sugary, carbonated beverages, with extended periods of poor oral hygiene.

A common sign of meth mouth is extreme tooth decay, with stained, blackened, or rotting teeth that often cannot be salvaged. Often, the only remedy is tooth extraction, with full-mouth reconstruction or a dental prosthesis as treatment. The effects on the oral cavity include dry mouth, cracked teeth, and sore and bleeding gums.

blood-brain barrier. It is highly neurotoxic and can stay in the body's system for eight to thirteen hours.

Even after a methamphetamine user stops using the drug, the damage to his or her brain continues. There is evidence of impairment of the anterior cingulated cortex, the area of the brain that influences cognitive functions and emotions and regulates behavior. The drug disables the ability to choose between healthy and unhealthy behaviors. Enhanced cortical gray matter volume also declines with age, leading to an accelerated rate of mental functioning, primarily because of a reduction in the number of neurons rather than shrinkage of gray matter. Methamphetamine users are at a greater risk for degenerative or cognitive diseases, and persons who are comorbid with depression are at a higher risk for dementia.

Methamphetamine use also increases the risk of transmission of the human immunodeficiency virus (HIV) and the hepatitis virus. Shared-needle use and higher risk sexual behavior increase the chances that a user will be infected with a sexually transmitted disease. Methamphetamine users who are HIV positive tend to suffer more neuronal injury and cognitive impairment.

A common physical trait of a chronic methamphetamine user is poor oral hygiene, or meth mouth. Methamphetamine use can cause a decrease in saliva output, leading to chronic dry mouth. Users will often drink large amounts of sugary carbonated soft drinks, which leads to severe dental decay. Many methamphetamine users also may grind or clench their teeth, causing tooth fractures.

S. M. Willis, MS, MA

FURTHER READING

Nakama, Helena, et al. "Methamphetamine Users Show Greater Than Normal Age-Related Cortical Gray Matter Loss." *Addiction* 106.8 (2011): 1474–83. Print. A cross-sectional study that suggests that methamphetamine users suffer a decline in cognitive health at earlier ages than those who do not use methamphetamine.

Padilla, Ricardo, and Andre V. Ritter. "Meth Mouth: Methamphetamine and Oral Health." *Journal of Esthetic and Restorative Dentistry* 20.2 (2008): 148–49. Print. Examines the occurrence of meth mouth.

Schep, Leo, Robin J. Slaughter, and D. Michael G. Beasley. "The Clinical Toxicology of Methamphetamine." *Clinical Toxicology* 48 (2010): 675–84. Print.

An overview of the biochemical mechanisms of methamphetamine on the brain and an extensive list of toxicokinetics and clinical features of methamphetamine abuse.

WEBSITES OF INTEREST

Drug Information Portal. National Library of Medicine
http://druginfo.nlm.nih.gov/drugportal

National Institute on Drug Abuse
http://www.drugabuse.gov/drugs-abuse/
    methamphetamine

See also: Dopamine and addiction; HIV/AIDS and substance abuse; Meth labs; Psychosis and substance abuse; Stimulant abuse; Stimulants: Short- and long-term effects on the body

Meth labs

CATEGORY: Social issues

DEFINITION: A meth lab, or laboratory, is a clandestine location for producing the drug methamphetamine. Meth labs can range from high-scale labs in industrial warehouses to individually operated labs in homes to rolling meth labs in the back of a car. In common usage, meth lab refers to small labs found in sheds, garages, hotel rooms, recreational vehicles, and trailers that produce enough methamphetamine for personal use and a limited amount to sell.

HISTORY

Methamphetamine, also known as meth, crystal meth, or ice, is a psychostimulant that provides a temporary feeling of euphoria and energy. There is a legal form of methamphetamine that is prescribed for attention deficit disorder and narcolepsy; this too is abused. Crystal meth is much cheaper to obtain and easy to make.

Laws passed in 1983 prohibited the sale and possession of meth and prohibited the possession and use of meth-producing equipment. Before this time, meth production was primarily located in California, mostly because of ties with Mexican meth labs. By 1989, the US government restricted over-the-counter sales of the cold medicines Sudafed and Contac, drugs whose ingredients, pseudoephedrine and ephedrine, were being used to manufacture meth, most often in home labs. This law, however, led to a noticeable rise, and not a reduction, in the number of meth labs around the United States, including in the Midwest and the South. These two regions offer something especially attractive to meth production: anhydrous fertilizer.

THE PRODUCTION OF METH

Meth production is not complicated, but it is extremely dangerous. Several "recipes" are freely available online, and many of the ingredients are easily found in one's kitchen and at local drug stores. A batch can be made in something as simple as an empty two-liter soda bottle.

Meth production includes different combinations and different chemical reactions. Some are more popular, given the availability of certain chemicals, such a fertilizer (anhydrous ammonia), but all techniques are dangerous. The most common technique is called red, white, and blue and involves the use of red phosphorus, pseudoephedrine or ephedrine (from cold tablets), and iodine. The reaction with the red phosphorus produces an odor that is not only toxic but also extremely foul. The odor has been described as that of rotting fish, dirty diapers, and human corpses. Another popular production method is Birch reduction (or Nagai method), which uses metallic lithium from lithium batteries. This method is highly flammable.

One relatively new style of making methamphetamine, called shake and bake, has become increasingly popular because it requires only a few cold tablets. The meth can be made anywhere, and it produces enough of the drug to provide a few "hits." Shake and bake also is known as the one-pot method, in which household chemicals are added to a two-liter soda bottle. The result is an extremely dangerous and highly flammable liquid. If oxygen gets in the bottle or if the bottle is not shaken correctly, the bottle's contents can explode. The discarded bottles, filled with a brownish sludge, also can be dangerous and poisonous.

This photo shows a room where a fire caused by a meth lab in the room killed one person and injured six others. (AP Photo)

ENVIRONMENTAL AND SOCIAL EFFECTS

The drug meth has devastating physical effects on its users, and meth labs can be extremely dangerous for other reasons. First, the chemicals used to synthesize meth give off noxious fumes, causing inhalation injuries and contact burns to the "cooker," the person in charge of the chemical reactions that produce meth. Second, the combinations of chemicals can lead to explosions. Finally, these chemicals create a toxic environment.

A property that has been used as a meth lab is no longer fit for human inhabitation. Toxic chemicals become embedded in the walls, floors, and ceiling. Safety experts insist that it is better to tear such a property down than to try to clean it. After teardown, the property requires a complete and thorough safety check that includes the surrounding area.

Meth labs also pose a special danger for law enforcement. Many labs are booby trapped with explosives or more primitive traps using sharp objects. These traps often remain after a meth lab has been abandoned. The main danger is chemical inhalation and burns due to explosion. Cleanup requires the use of hazardous materials gear.

Social services agencies report that children are most at risk from meth labs. It is common that both parents are cookers or, at minimum, users, leaving children without any proper care. One common scenario is poisoning, caused by an unsupervised child eating or drinking inside the meth lab.

S. M. Willis, MS, MA

FURTHER READING

Hammon, Tracy L., and Susan Griffin. "Support for Selection of Methamphetamine Cleanup Standard in Colorado." *Regulatory Toxicology and Pharmacology* 48 (2007): 102–14. Print. Attempts a cost analysis on what it would take to make a former meth lab into a safe residence.

Hunt, Dana E. "Methamphetamine Abuse: Challenges for Law Enforcement and Communities." *NIJ Journal* no. 254 (2006). Web. 12 Mar. 2012. http://www.nij.gov/journals/254/methamphetamine_abuse.html. Discusses the specific dangers in approaching suspected meth labs, including chemical inhalants and fire hazards. Describes what a suspected meth lab might look like.

Santos, Ariel P., et al. "Methamphetamine Laboratory Explosions: A New and Emerging Burn Injury." *Journal of Burn Care and Rehabilitation* 26 (2005): 228–32. Print. A detailed description of how a patient burned in a meth lab explosion needs extreme care.

WEBSITES OF INTEREST

Crystal Meth Anonymous
http://www.crystalmeth.org

National Institute on Drug Abuse
http://www.drugabuse.gov

See also: Law enforcement and drugs; Methamphetamine; Psychosis and substance abuse

Military and substance abuse

CATEGORY: Social issues

DEFINITION: The use of alcohol and drugs among military personnel, especially those coping with combat-related trauma, is generally understood among mental health professionals as a way for service members to self-medicate. Although alcohol and drugs may bring short-term relief from the emotional and physical pain of deployment, the long-term consequences pose a threat to military morale and to the quality of life for service members and their families. The prevalence of alcohol and drug use in the military necessitates the development and implementation of best practices and programs for supporting the emotional state of service members to prevent them from turning to alcohol and drug use as a stress-coping mechanism.

ALCOHOL AND DRUGS

Mental health disorders are strongly linked to substance abuse. Post-traumatic stress disorder (PTSD) is a medically diagnosed anxiety disorder and believed to be common and underdiagnosed among military personnel, especially those who have been in combat. A person with PTSD continually relives in his or her mind a highly traumatic event. This manifests itself in an involuntary flood of thoughts related to the trauma. It includes nightmares, an adrenaline rush, and spikes of anxiety when visual or audible reminders of the experience appear.

Many who have PTSD placate symptoms with alcohol and drugs such as marijuana and prescription pain killers. These drugs slow brain activity and reduce chronic anxiety during the substance high.

The authors of the book *After the War Zone* (2008) recommend that military personnel experiencing PTSD and substance abuse disorders be treated for both conditions at the same time. Explaining the common parallel occurrence of both, the authors write that

> Some say that substance abuse needs to be dealt with before you can deal with PTSD symptoms. Some say that you need to get treatment for PTSD before you can deal with the substance abuse. Since it's really difficult to disentangle these two conditions, we strongly urge that you seek treatment for both at the same time.

PTSD and substance abuse disorders are underdiagnosed among military service members. PTSD and substance abuse carry a heavy stigma in the military; the inclusion of such conditions as part of one's official record often means that the service member may not be able to pursue a career in, for example, defense or law enforcement after military service. Therefore, both disorders are believed to be highly underreported by service members and their supervisors. Until PTSD and substance abuse disorders are addressed in a way that does not lead to stigmatization, service members will likely continue to self-medicate.

The danger in self-medicating is that the method (drinking alcohol or taking drugs) used for short-term relief of the emotional pain inevitably worsens emotional conditions later. The release of dopamine in the brain triggered by alcohol or drugs results in impairment of emotion-regulation in the brain, once the high wears off.

According to National Institute on Drug Abuse (NIDA) director Nora D. Volkow, "Demographic factors and the military's unique organizational structures, culture, and experiences contribute to service members' overall high prevalence of smoking and binge drinking and low prevalence of illicit substance abuse, when compared with civilian rates." According to NIDA studies, tobacco use is 50 percent higher among active military personnel than the general civilian population. Among military personnel, smoking is another 50 percent greater among those who have been deployed. According to NIDA, one in four veterans of Operation Enduring Freedom and Operation Iraqi Freedom, and who were in combat, presented symptoms of a mental or cognitive disorder and one is six veterans of these two missions showed signs of PTSD.

ALCOHOL AND DRUG USE POLICY

In 2001, the US Army revised Army Regulation 600-85, which changed the name of the Alcohol and Drug Abuse Prevention and Control Program to the Army Substance Abuse Program (ASAP). The regulation also changed the requirements and process for the administrative separation of soldiers using drugs or alcohol illegally. The regulation also prescribed random drug-testing and deployment restrictions on soldiers undergoing rehabilitation for substance abuse. The new policy, however, conflicted with existing separations regulations for active enlisted personnel, so commanders were directed to use the latter as their policy for confronting drug and alcohol use among their subordinates.

While the new ASAP regulation directed commanders to initiate separation for first-time offense, the legacy policy on enlisted separations allowed for more leniency. Coupled with modern military living-arrangements designed to allot soldiers more privacy, this conflict and confusion in regulations makes standardized enforcement more difficult.

In 2009, an *Army Times* article brought to light the consequences of commander discretion trumping ASAP regulation. An investigation led by Army vice chief of staff, General Peter Chiarelli, found that among all soldiers who tested positive for illegal drug use, only 70 percent were referred to ASAP for treatment. The most common illegal drug found through urine tests was marijuana, followed by cocaine, LSD, methamphetamine, heroin, and illicitly used prescription drugs. Brigadier General Colleen McGuire found that among 1,000 soldiers who tested positive for drug use, 372 were repeat offenders and none had been sent to treatment.

Major General Anthony Cucolo, who reviews substance abuse cases for the Army, said that alcohol use is the most prevalent substance-abuse concern. Commander rejection of a standard separation policy, given the urgent need for retaining soldiers during wartime, compounds the substance-abuse issue and generates a need for case-by-case analysis of each offender's need for treatment and level of readiness to serve.

TREATMENT

According to a 2010 article in the journal *Addiction Professional*, increasingly, more veterans are seeking treatment at the community level rather than through the US Department of Veterans Affairs (VA). There remains a degree of distrust in relying on the government to treat drug and alcohol abuse. Any diagnosis or treatment given through the VA will show up on the service member's record.

Knowing that military personnel are more inclined to seek help outside the military structure, the VA is seeking to partner with community resources. Treatment strategies include twelve-step therapies, "stop, think, act" impulse-control programs, and "soldiers helping soldiers" programs, in which soldiers are trained to help their peers in dealing with combat-related stress. According to a June 2010 poll by *Addiction Professional*, more than 90 percent of respondents felt that there is a shortage of community-based assistance for returning veterans, many citing the lack of PTSD treatment.

INTERVENTION AND REHABILITATION OUTLOOK

Mental health and military experts agree that more investigation is needed into how to better support military personnel emotionally during and after deployment. Though recognition of depression, anxiety disorders, and substance abuse is pervasive, more needs to be understood about wartime stress on military personnel and their families, so that techniques for early intervention and treatment can be developed.

In July of 2010, the US National Institutes of Health announced the approval of $6 million in federal funding to support research by institutions in eleven states specializing in substance abuse among military personnel, veterans, and their families. NIDA partnered with the VA to award the grants earmarked for investigating the links between deployment and combat-related trauma to the prevalence of substance abuse, mainly among veterans returning from the wars in Iraq and Afghanistan.

Melissa Walsh

FURTHER READING

"Army Substance Abuse Program." *Army Lawyer* (Sept., 2002): 51–53. Print.

Cavallaro, Gina. "Army Cracks Down as Drug, Alcohol Cases Rise." *Army Times*, 8 Jun. 2009.

Enos, Gary A. "Doing Whatever It Takes: Treatment Programs Try to Employ a Full Arsenal to Meet the Complex Needs of Veterans." *Addiction Professional* 8.4 (2010): 16. Print.

Slone, Laurie B., and Matthew J. Friedman. *After the War Zone: A Practical Guide for Returning Troops and Their Families.* Cambridge, MA: DaCapo, 2008.

"Studies on Combat-Related Substance Use and Abuse to Be Funded by NIH and VA." *Defense and Aerospace Week* (15 Sep. 2010): 142. Print.

Volkow, Nora D. "Substance Abuse among Troops, Veterans, and Their Families." *NIDA Notes* 22.5 (2009). Web. 26 Mar. 2012. http://www.drugabuse.gov/news-events/nida-notes/2009/11/substance-abuse-among-troops-veterans-their-families.

WEBSITES OF INTEREST

American Council for Drug Education
http://www.acde.org

National Institute on Drug Abuse
http://drugabuse.gov

NotAlone.com
http://www.notalone.com

Substance Abuse and Mental Health Services Administration
http://www.samhsa.gov/militaryfamilies

See also: Mental illness; Post-traumatic stress disorder and addiction; Substance abuse; Veterans and addiction

Minnesota model

CATEGORY: Treatment

DEFINITION: The Minnesota model is a multiprofessional model of drug treatment based on the principles of Alcoholics Anonymous and on cognitive-behavioral therapy.

BACKGROUND AND TREATMENT PHILOSOPHY

The Minnesota model (MM) was established in 1948 as a new form of drug treatment. The first MM residential program, known as Pioneer House, was established in an old warehouse in Minnesota and was modeled after the principles of Alcoholics Anonymous (AA). The treatment centers Hazelden and Willmar State Hospital, both in Minnesota, adopted a similar model in 1949 and 1950, respectively. Collectively, these three programs constitute the origins of MM. Pioneer House is now the Hazelden Center for Youth and Families. MM was initially designed as a residential treatment program, although outpatient variants of the model exist today and the model itself is amenable to variety of delivery settings.

The principles and philosophy of AA and the disease concept of addiction, a central element of AA, are essential parts of the MM treatment philosophy. The disease concept of addiction views addicts as having an incurable or chronic disease. Addicts are believed to be biologically different from nonaddicts. They are not blamed for their addiction, but they are considered responsible for facing their disease. The program emphasizes that addicts can change their beliefs, behaviors, and lifestyles and can become well, but only through complete abstinence from all chemical substances.

The typical residential stay ranges from three to six weeks, with a common twenty-eight-day program of inpatient treatment and lifelong aftercare, primarily through AA, to manage the disease. Aftercare may also include family counseling and extended care. The residential treatment program comprises many dimensions of care, including individual counseling, group therapy, family counseling, working the AA twelve-step program, attendance at AA or Narcotics Anonymous meetings, daily reflection and readings (usually of AA's "big book"), and lectures.

MM-based programs are staffed by different professionals, a central feature of the model's multiprofessional and comprehensive approach to treatment, and include nurses, clergy, professional social workers, psychologists, and counselors. Counselors are recovering addicts themselves and have trained through the residential program.

The client is treated as a whole person with professional attention devoted to the mind, body, and spirit, a focus sometimes referred to as the physical-psychological-spiritual model of treatment. Clients are treated with dignity by staff and other residents. Although there are no standard guidelines as to what a treatment center must do to officially claim the MM concept, the common elements discussed here make up a typical program of treatment. The Betty Ford Center and Hazelden are among the larger and more recognizable residential treatment programs based on MM today.

MM is similar to concept houses and therapeutic communities in their emphasis on mutual aid, the peer community, and treating the whole person. The heavy emphasis on AA philosophy—the belief in the disease model of addiction instead of the moral shortcomings of addicts—and shorter durations of residency are two of the primary differences between MM and other therapeutic communities. Some clients of MM may participate in a therapeutic community, or extended care, after completing a program of inpatient care.

CRITICISMS AND SUCCESSES

Criticisms of MM often focus on aspects of the treatment philosophy instead of on the whole model itself. A common basis for criticism is found in the tenets of AA, such as the insistence on complete abstinence over controlled drinking; the emphasis on spirituality and a higher power, which may not resonate with all addicts; and the rigidness of the AA philosophy, resulting in an inflexible program. Addicts who do not wish to seek help from AA have few helpful exit strategies because of the intolerance of AA members to treatment alternatives.

Other criticisms are directed toward the disease concept of addiction, which some argue relieves the addict of too much responsibility for his or her addiction and which can reinforce self-indulgent behavior and undermine treatment. Despite criticisms, research suggests that the multiprofessional approach to treatment grounded in the principles of AA is a successful form of treatment for many addicts.

Although there are challenges in studying the success of treatment programs, and although many studies have methodological flaws, evidence shows that MM graduates do as well as, and possibly better than, graduates of other treatment programs. Completion of the program results in long-term abstinence for many addicts and shortens periods of repeated drug use for persons who may fail to maintain abstinence. There are documented improvements in the psychosocial well-being of graduates, improvements involving self-esteem, family relationships, and employment, and in overall physical health.

Michelle Petrie, PhD

FURTHER READING

Cook, Christopher. "The Minnesota Model in the Management of Drug and Alcohol Dependency: Miracle, Method, or Myth? Part I. The Philosophy and the Programme." *British Journal of Addiction* 83 (1988): 625–34. Print. An overview of the history, general treatment philosophy of the Minnesota model, and changes in treatment and daily residential life.

---. "The Minnesota Model in the Management of Drug and Alcohol Dependency: Miracle, Method, or Myth? Part II. Evidence and Conclusions." *British Journal of Addiction* 83 (1988): 735–48. Print. A review of empirical studies conducted on the effectiveness of the Minnesota model of treatment.

Spicer, Jerry. *The Minnesota Model: The Evolution of the Multidisciplinary Approach to Addiction Recovery.* Center City, MN: Hazelden, 1993. A comprehensive overview of the challenges, changes, history, and tenets of the Minnesota model.

WEBSITES OF INTEREST

Alcoholics Anonymous
http://www.aa.org

National Association of Addiction Treatment Providers
http:// www.naatp.org

National Institute on Alcohol Abuse and Alcoholism
http:// http://www.niaaa.nih.gov

See also: Alcohol abuse and alcoholism: Treatment; Alcoholics Anonymous; Betty Ford Center; Cognitive behavioral therapy; Hazelden Foundation; Residential treatment; Twelve-step programs for addicts

Models of addiction

CATEGORY: Diagnosis and prevention
DEFINITION: Addiction is a long-term relapsing disorder characterized by compulsive drug-taking behaviors.

ADDICTION MODELS

There are two predominant models to explain addiction: the disease model of addiction and the life-process model of addiction. The disease model considers addiction to be a life-long affliction arising from altered genetic and biological mechanisms. The life-process model considers addiction to be a learned behavior and source of gratification that can be explained through the context of social experiences and relationships.

Disease Model of Addiction

The disease model of addiction stresses the idea that addicts are born, not made. This model gained acceptance in scientific and government circles in the early 1960s when E. M. Jellinek discussed the model in his book *The Disease Concept of Alcoholism* (1960). Jellinek suggested that the disease model should be used because of the lack of clarity in the psychological pathologies that psychiatrists suggested were behind addiction. The model is now recognized by the World Health Organization and the American Medical Association and is utilized by both Alcoholics Anonymous (AA) and Narcotics Anonymous (NA) in their treatment and recovery plans.

Four stages of addiction comprise the disease model. In the presymptomatic stage, the use of the substance is not associated with any significant problems. In the prodromal stage, there is an increase of problems caused by the use of the substance, problems including psychological duress and increased consumption. In the crucial stage, the person attempts to control the substance abuse but fails; consequences increase with continued substance use. Finally, in the chronic stage, the addict consumes large amounts of the substance with great psychological and physiological repercussions.

The underlying neuronal mechanism implicated in the disease model of addiction is the dysregulation of the dopaminergic and glutamatergic pathways in the brain. These systems influence drug reward, dependence, and craving. In addition, long-term neuroadaptation to drug abuse can lead to drug tolerance. Withdrawal from drugs is characterized by depression, anxiety, irritability, and sleep disturbances, all of which lead to cycles of relapse. Withdrawal becomes a serious medical issue because of severe somatic symptoms associated with the withdrawal.

One of the fundamental aspects of the disease model of addiction is that a person cannot control his or her use of alcohol or drugs; furthermore, the person will feel compelled to confsume the substance. The duration of time in which the person becomes addicted is variable (days or months). As evidenced by the results of the AA and NA programs, treatment is specific and can be generalized to the whole population. However, the best recourse for the addicted person is abstinence.

Life-Process Model of Addiction

The life-process model of addiction directly opposes the disease model by stressing that the addiction can be controlled by the person addicted. Proponents of this model argue that specific biological mechanisms for addiction, as claimed by the disease model, have not been identified.

Addiction as explained through the life-process model is a way of coping with life experiences. Each person's addiction is singular to that individual and can be explained only through the context of each person's respective situation. In other words, a person becomes an addict for his or her own reasons, be it psychological or social. Reasons include stress, abuse, and an inability to cope. No specific or outlined progression of addiction exists. Consequently, the life-process model emphasizes treatments that are specific to the person and that stress changing the person's behavior and environment.

Individualized treatment employed in the life-process model varies greatly from those provided by group therapies like AA and NA. The individual, perhaps with the help of a therapist or mentor, discovers the source of the addiction and applies a specialized remedy. Unlike the disease model, the life-process model suggests that the individual does not need to indefinitely abstain from the addictive substance.

Elvin M. Jellinek: Alcoholism Is a Disease

Elvin M. Jellinek and his associates provided the basis for diagnosing the potential alcoholic in what became known as the Jellinek phases of alcoholism, or the Jellinek curve. Early warning signs of alcoholism include: sneaking and gulping drinks; worrying about consuming alcohol but not talking about drinking; and blacking out, forgetting what happened while consuming alcohol.

Jellinek was born in New York City on August 15, 1890. After his elementary and secondary education was completed, he became a student at three European universities: Berlin from 1908 to 1911, Grenoble in 1911, and Leipzig from 1911, until he received his master's of education degree there in 1914. Twenty-one years later, Jellinek earned a doctorate in science at Leipzig.

Following college, from 1914 until 1919, Jellinek was employed as a biometric consultant and as a library and field researcher. In the field of human physiology Jellinek was a biometrician at the Government School for Nervous Children in Budapest, Hungary, a post he held from 1915 until 1920.

Beginning in 1941, Jellinek taught at Yale University as an associate professor of applied physiology, and he directed the Yale School of Alcohol Studies at the university's Laboratory of Applied Physiology. At Yale, he subscribed to the principle that alcoholism is a disease and that the alcoholic is a sick person, that alcoholics can be helped and are worth helping, and that alcoholism is a public health problem and therefore a public responsibility.

Jellinek wrote two texts on alcohol and was generally considered an authority on that subject and on the science of biometrics, the statistical analysis of biological observation.

SUMMARY

As a chronic disease, addiction is the culmination of biological, psychological, and social maladjustments. It is a complex disorder shaped by substance exposure, genetic susceptibility, and environmental influences. Therefore, better understanding of the neurobiological factors and analysis of cognitive and social learning models would aid in the development of novel therapeutic interventions for drug-dependent persons.

Poonam Bhandari, PhD

FURTHER READING

Brandon, Thomas H., et al. "Cognitive and Social Learning Models of Drug Dependence: Implications for Assessment of Tobacco Dependence in Adolescents." *Addiction* 99, suppl. 1 (2004): 51–77. Print. Examines social and cognitive models of tobacco addiction in youth.

Erickson, Carlton. *The Science of Addiction: From Neurobiology to Treatment.* New York: W. W. Norton, 2006. A strong reference book for anyone in the field of addiction medicine. Provides a neurobiological perspective on addiction for general readers and specialists.

Everitt, Barry J., et al. "Neural Mechanisms Underlying the Vulnerability to Develop Compulsive Drug-Seeking Habits and Addiction." *Philosophical Transactions of the Royal Society* B 363 (2008): 3125–35. Print. Explains how initial voluntary drug-use transitions into compulsive drug-seeking habits.

Feltenstein, M. W., and R. E. See. "The Neurocircuitry of Addiction: An Overview." *British Journal of Pharmacology* 154 (2008) 261–74. Print. Summarizes the molecular mechanisms and pathways involved in addiction.

Koob, George F. "The Neurobiology of Addiction: A Neuroadaptational View Relevant for Diagnosis." *Addiction* 101, suppl. 1 (2006): 23–30. Print. Reviews the diagnosis of addiction.

Schaler, Jeffrey. *Addiction Is a Choice.* Peru, IL: Carus, 2000. Examines the life-process model of addiction. Describes addiction as a choice rather than a disease.

WEBSITES OF INTEREST

AddictionInfo.org
http://www.addictioninfo.org

ExploreAddiction.com
http://exploreaddiction.com/training/exploring-addiction

National Institute on Drug Abuse
http://drugabuse.gov

See also: Addiction; Genetics and substance abuse; Physiological dependence; Psychological dependence; Socioeconomic status and addiction

Monitoring the Future

CATEGORY: Diagnosis and prevention

DEFINITION: Monitoring the Future is an annual study that tracks the attitudes of secondary school students, college students, and young adults in the United States about drug and alcohol use and abuse.

BACKGROUND

Monitoring the Future (MTF) is conducted by researchers at the Institute for Social Research at the University of Michigan. Funded by competitive federal research grants from the National Institute on Drug Abuse since its beginnings in 1975, the study reports annual national data collected on eighth-, tenth-, and twelfth-grade students from across the United States. On average, the reports are based on responses from some fifty thousand students in four hundred twenty different schools.

Originally, only senior-level classes were surveyed, and in its early years MTF surveyed an average of sixteen thousand students annually in approximately 133 public and private high schools. Surveys started with randomly selected samples from each senior-level class, with participants resurveyed biannually. In 1991, similar survey samples of eighth and tenth graders were conducted, in efforts to catch potential dropouts while they were still in school.

On average, the eighth-grade samples contain about eighteen thousand students in about one hundred fifty schools annually, and the tenth grade samples contain about seventeen thousand students in about one hundred forty schools annually. Although the first surveys are given at schools, after graduation respondents receive a mail questionnaire at their place of residence.

Data from students is collected during the spring, with a multistage random-sampling procedure used to guarantee a representative sample for each of the three grade levels. Randomness is exercised at three levels: geographic area, schools in the areas chosen (with probability proportionate to size), and classes within each chosen school, with up to 350 students per school eligible for inclusion. The design allows for tracking four kinds of change: change reflected over time (period effects); change based on age (age effects); differences among peers through the life cycle (cohort effects); and differences based on environment, such as high school, college, workplace, or familial home, and on associated role transitions, such as marriage or parenthood (environmental effects). Students are surveyed on various attitudes, and resurveys follow some students into adulthood.

Among the phenomena tracked by MTF is substance abuse (of both licit and illicit drugs and alcohol). Surveys track initiation, habitual use, and cessation. Also surveyed are attitudes toward drugs in general, perceived availability, attitudes toward peer pressure, and perceived norms. By tracking cohort-sequential longitudinal data on drug abuse, MTF measures three figures: developmental (changes over the years), periodic (historical), and cohort (peer norms). Reports for each category are based on a diverse set of determinants. For example, the 2010 study of students in 396 public and private schools found that teenagers were more likely to use marijuana and ecstasy, and that the percentage of high school seniors, tenth graders, and eighth graders who reported daily marijuana use had risen from

2009. The report also noted that ecstasy use among eighth graders grew, although the 2010 MTF report found little change in the abuse of other illicit and prescription drugs.

Published as full text on the MTF website and in print through the National Institute on Drug Abuse, MTF reports have been used in many ways. For example, the reports helped to correlate data that tracks phenomena such as whether employment affects drug abuse and delinquency, helped to examine self-reported rationale for substance abuse among high school seniors from 1976 through 2005, and helped to examine the relationship between sports participation and steroid use among African American and Caucasian high school boys from 1991 through 2007 (to determine the effects of that time period's Major League Baseball steroid-use scandal). Reports also have been used to track differences in usage patterns based on student ethnicity and on the role of school sports.

MTF data has been used in articles in diverse scholarly journals, including the *American Journal of Public*

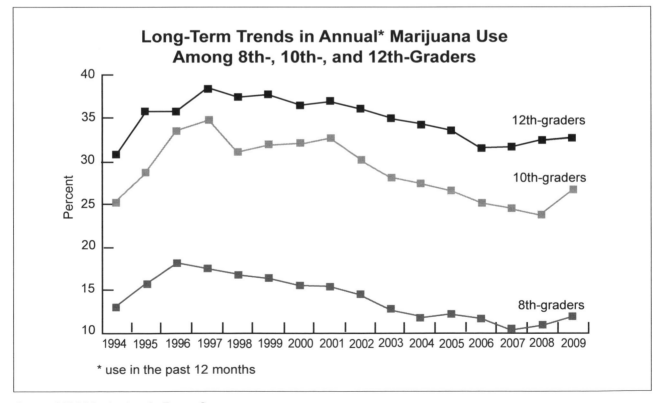

Source: 2009 Monitoring the Future Survey

Health, Education Week, the *Journal of the American Medical Association, Criminology,* the *Journal of Child and Adolescent Substance Abuse,* the *American Journal of Health Studies, Alcoholism and Drug Abuse Weekly, Substance Use and Misuse, Addiction,* the *Journal of Drug Issues,* and *Challenge: A Journal of Research on African American Men.*

Surveys similar to MTF include the Youth Risk Behavior Surveillance System, conducted by the Centers for Disease Control and Prevention, and the National Survey on Drug Use and Health (formerly the National Household Survey on Drug Abuse), conducted by the Substance Abuse and Mental Health Services Administration's Office of Applied Studies.

MISSION AND GOALS

The mission of the MTF project is to produce longitudinal data that allows for studying changes in the beliefs, attitudes, and behaviors of youth in the United States. Specifically, the goal of MTF is to track changes in public opinion toward government and politics, alcohol and other drug use, gender roles, and the environment by surveying youth over time. A major MTF objective is to make this data useful to policymakers at all levels of government and to scholars in various disciplines.

Anthony J. Fonseca, PhD

FURTHER READING

Bachman, J. G., et al. *The Education-Drug Use Connection: How Successes and Failures in School Relate to Adolescent Smoking, Drinking, Drug Use, and Delinquency.* New York: Erlbaum, 2008. The authors interpret MTF data to demonstrate that drug use affects the performance of youth in school.

---. "Racial/Ethnic Differences in the Relationship between Parental Education and Substance Use among US 8th, 10th, and 12th Grade Students: Findings from the Monitoring the Future Project." *Journal of Studies on Alcohol and Drugs* 72.2 (2011): 279–85. Print. The authors found a link between substance use among students and parental education level, with the greater problem existing among Caucasians than among African Americans or Hispanic Americans.

Johnston, Lloyd. "National Survey Results on Drug Use from the Monitoring the Future Study, 1975–1995." Washington, DC: GPO, 1997. Tallies results of the twenty-first national MTF survey, with an emphasis on secondary school samples.

WEBSITES OF INTEREST

Monitoring the Future
http://monitoringthefuture.org

National Survey on Drug Use and Health
https://nsduhweb.rti.org

Youth Risk Behavior Surveillance System. Centers for Disease Control and Prevention
http://www.cdc.gov/healthyyouth/yrbs

See also: Education about substance abuse; National Institute on Drug Abuse (NIDA); Prevention methods and research; Teens/young adults and alcohol abuse; Teens/young adults and drug abuse

Morphine

CATEGORY: Substances
DEFINITION: Morphine is a pure opioid agonist in the same class as oxycodone, hydromorphone, and fentanyl. The primary therapeutic action of morphine is analgesia. Like other pure opioid analgesics, the analgesic effects are limited only by adverse effects such as somnolence and depression and not by a ceiling of analgesic effect.
STATUS: Legal in the United States and worldwide
CLASSIFICATION: Schedule II controlled substance
SOURCE: First isolated from the opium poppy, *Papaver somniferum,* in 1803
TRANSMISSION ROUTE: Exists as a tablet, capsule, powder, rectal suppository, oral suspension and solution, and solution for injection; ingested orally, snorted, or injected intravenously

HISTORY OF USE

Morphine was first isolated in the early nineteenth century by Friedrich Sertürner in Germany. The word *morphine* is derived from the term *morphium,* for Morpheus, the Greek god of dreams. Within twenty years, morphine was available across Europe as an agent for treating pain and for many other uses, including treating alcohol abuse.

In the United States, morphine became a controlled substance in 1914 under the Harrison Narcotics Tax Act. Morphine is now the gold-standard by which other analgesics are measured. The drug is used for treating moderate and severe pain, both acute and chronic. Many available painkillers, such as codeine, are chemically related to morphine.

Illicit opioid use, including the use of morphine, is more common now than the use of cocaine, heroin, or methamphetamine (as reported by the 2008 National Survey of Drug Use and Health). Studies have shown that up to 40 percent of people who report abusing opioids have tried intravenous injection of opioids. Intravenous injection produces the fastest onset both of euphoric and of negative effects, including respiratory depression and central nervous system (CNS) effects. Oftentimes these prescription opiates are legally prescribed for a friend or family member and then obtained by the drug abuser. Because of the legitimate pain-relieving properties of morphine, the drug is highly prescribed and used. This high level of use increases opportunities for diversion and abuse.

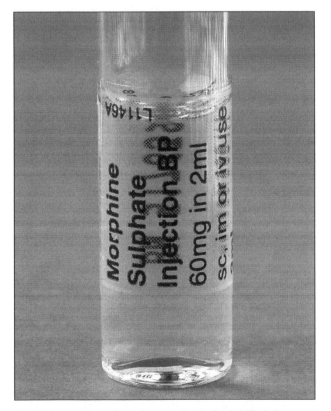

Morphine sulphate is used as analgesic (painkiller) for severe pain. It is a opioid or narcotic analgesic that mimicks the actions of natural pain-reducing chemicals. (Getty Images)

EFFECTS AND POTENTIAL RISKS

Decreased respiratory rate and sedation are two common adverse effects of morphine, effects experienced even in patients treated with normal doses and dosing regimens. However, these normal adverse effects can become extremely problematic and even fatal in acute morphine overdoses or with chronic administration. Respiratory depression occurs more commonly in elderly patients and in patients with underlying respiratory conditions, and it occurs to a higher extent with intravenous administration. Respiratory complications and sedative effects are also much more common in patients who are opioid naïve.

Like other mu (µ) opioid agonists (such as oxycodone and hydrocodone), morphine causes a feeling of euphoria, which can lead to psychological dependence. Following intravenous administration, euphoria can occur within five minutes, and although the physiological effects can last for greater than six hours, the feeling of euphoria generally dissipates sooner. This can lead an abuser to re-inject the medication at a time when his or her body is still reacting to the respiratory and CNS effects of the initial dose of morphine; this can lead to death. Intravenous injection also increases the risk of infection and vessel occlusion, both of which can have serious and fatal consequences.

Chronic morphine users who abruptly stop use can experience withdrawal. Signs and symptoms of withdrawal include nausea and diarrhea, profuse sweating, twitching muscles, and temperature disturbances, all of which can persist up to two weeks in some persons.

Allison C. Bennett, PharmD

FURTHER READING

Degenhardt, Louisa, et al. "Trends in Morphine Prescriptions, Illicit Morphine Use and Associated Harms among Regular Injecting Drug Users in Australia." *Drug and Alcohol Review* 25 (2006): 403–12. Print. A review of morphine prescriptions from 1995 to 2003 obtained from an Australian government agency. Just less than one-half of all injection drug users surveyed responded that they had used morphine illicitly.

Stoops, William W., et al. "Intravenous Oxycodone, Hydrocodone, and Morphine in Recreational Opioid Users: Abuse Potential and Relative Potencies." *Psychopharmacology* 212 (2010): 193–203. Print. A double-blind, placebo-controlled, randomized study designed to evaluate the relative abuse potential of three opioids: morphine, oxycodone, and hydrocodone. Study concluded that in the nine subjects completing the study, modest potency differences were seen among the three opioids, and that abuse potential was similar.

Tschacher, Wolfgang, Robert Hammig, and Nina Jacobsen. "Time Series Modeling of Heroin and Morphine Drug Action." *Psychopharmacology* 165 (2003): 188–93. Print. A study of morphine and heroin to determine the differences in perceived positive and negative effects by the drug user. Reports that adverse effects experienced in heroin use were linked to higher levels of euphoria, whereas with morphine users, adverse effects were linked to lower levels of euphoria.

WEBSITES OF INTEREST

Drug Information Portal: Morphine
http://druginfo.nlm.nih.gov/drugportal

National Institute on Drug Abuse
https://www.drugabuse.gov

Substance Abuse and Mental Health Services Administration
http://www.samhsa.gov

See also: Opioid abuse; Oxycodone; Painkiller abuse

Mothers Against Drunk Driving (MADD)

CATEGORY: Diagnosis and prevention
DEFINITION: Mothers Against Drunk Driving (MADD) is an activist organization whose mission is to assist persons affected by drunk driving, to advocate for stricter drunk driving laws and enforcement, and to promote public awareness and educational programs.
DATE: Established on September 5, 1980

BACKGROUND

Candace Lightner founded Mothers Against Drunk Drivers (MADD) after a drunk driver killed her thirteen-year-old daughter, Cari, on May 3, 1980, in Fair Oaks, California. Cari had been walking with a friend in a bicycle lane to a church carnival and was struck from behind. The forty-seven-year-old driver's blood alcohol content (BAC) was 0.20 percent, about twice the legal limit.

The driver, who fled the scene after hitting Cari, had five previous drunk driving convictions and had just been released from jail for another hit-and-run accident. The driver was sentenced to two years in prison for Cari's death, a sentence that her mother found too lenient. In response, Lightner formed MADD to help keep drunk drivers off the road and to help ensure that these drivers receive stricter penalties.

Shortly after starting the organization, Lightner met Cindi Lamb, whose daughter Laura had become the youngest quadriplegic in the United States, at the age of less than six months, after a drunk driving accident. Lamb had already been writing letters to law enforcement and other agencies when she met Lightner; soon, the two women joined forces. MADD was the subject of a television movie in 1983. The movie, *M.A.D.D.: Mothers Against Drunk Drivers*, starred Mariette Hartley as Candy Lightner and was produced and written by Michael Braverman.

In 1984, MADD changed its name to Mothers Against Drunk Driving to reflect its focus on the act of drunk driving. A board of directors, national president, and national board of advisors oversee MADD. The national office is in Irving, Texas. By the end of 1982, there were about one hundred local chapters. That number grew to 320 across the United States by 1985 and more than 600 chapters by 2001. International chapters are located in Canada, Great Britain, New Zealand, Australia, Guam, and Puerto Rico. Membership is not restricted to mothers of victims or to the victims themselves; all persons who are concerned about drunk driving can join.

MADD has more than twelve hundred victim advocates in most US states. In addition to trained staff, the organization also has volunteer counselors for its toll-free helpline. The nonprofit relies on membership dues and individual donations to fund its efforts. MADD also receives federal and state grants. It conducts a number of fundraising events, such as Walk Like MADD, which is sponsored in more than thirty locations; the event raised more than $3 million in 2009.

MISSION AND GOALS

MADD accomplishes its mission through public awareness and education, advocacy, and assistance. The initial mission was "To aid the victims of crimes performed by individuals driving under the influence of alcohol or drugs, to aid the families of such victims, and to increase public awareness of the problem of drinking and drugged driving." The original mission of MADD has evolved as the organization has grown.

The mission has been updated several times as MADD continues to broaden its work. In 1999, the mission was further updated, and simplified, to the following: "To stop drunk driving, support the victims of this violent crime, and prevent underage drinking."

In 2008, MADD served about 55,000 persons across the United States. Furthermore, MADD has helped save more than 300,000 lives. MADD's efforts to pass public health laws have saved an estimated 27,000 lives overall. Since the organization's founding, alcohol-related traffic fatalities have decreased by nearly 50 percent. MADD's goal is to reduce drunk driving fatalities to 10,000 or fewer people per year.

MADD has lobbied for many judicial changes with great success. In 1984, the US Congress passed a law requiring states to increase their minimum drinking age to twenty-one years or be penalized through lower federal funding. In 1984, only twelve states had a minimum drinking age of twenty-one years, but by the end of that year, another twelve had changed that minimum. By the early 1990s, nearly all US states had changed the minimum.

Other legislative actions inspired by MADD include early changes by states to toughen their drinking and driving laws, such as requiring mandatory jail sentences for first-time offenders. In 2000, US president Bill Clinton signed a law requiring states to set their maximum allowable BAC level to just under 0.08. Before this time, most states allowed drivers' BAC to be just under 0.10. Other laws inspired by MADD include requiring ignition interlock devices for all convicted drunk drivers and for those convicted of driving under the influence.

Patrice La Vigne

FURTHER READING

Blocker, Jack S. Jr., Ian R. Tyrrell, and David M. Fahey. *Alcohol and Temperance in Modern History: An International Encyclopedia.* Santa Barbara, CA: ABC/CLIO, 2003. A brief overview of MADD in historical context.

Korsmeyer, Pamela, and Henry R. Kranzler. *Encyclopedia of Drugs, Alcohol, and Addictive Behavior.* 3rd ed. Detroit: Macmillan, 2009. A good source of historical information about MADD.

Polacsek, Michele. "MADD Victim Impact Panels and Stages-of-Change in Drunk-Driving Prevention." *Journal of Studies on Alcohol* 62 (2001): 344–50. Print. A study that found no difference between the effects of MADD's victim impact panels and its driving-while-intoxicated school in preventing drunk drinking and drunk-driving recidivism.

WEBSITES OF INTEREST

Al-Anon/Alateen
http://www.al-anon.alateen.org

Mothers Against Drunk Driving
http://www.madd.org

National Highway Traffic Safety Administration
http://www.nhtsa.dot.gov

Students Against Destructive Decisions
http://www.sadd.org

Car Breathalyzer

A car breathalyzer is a device that is installed in a vehicle to prevent a person from driving while drunk. The driver breathes into the device, and if his or her blood alcohol level registers above the allowed limit, the car will not start. Car breathalyzers are most often installed in the vehicles of persons who have been convicted of driving under the influence of alcohol.

The purpose of the ignition interlock device is to save lives on the road. Another is to separate drinking from driving in the mind of the person who has consumed alcohol and who plans to drive. According to Mothers Against Drunk Driving, better known as MADD, three of four drivers who have had their license suspended because of driving drunk still drive without a license. Furthermore, the US Centers for Disease Control and Prevention reports that the use of car breathalyzers reduces the rearrest rates of convicted drunk drivers by a median of 67 percent.

See also: Designated drivers; Drugged driving; Drunk driving; Students Against Destructive Decisions (SADD)

Mushrooms/psilocybin

CATEGORY: Substances

ALSO KNOWN AS: Magic mushrooms; shrooms

DEFINITION: The drug substances in "magic" mushrooms, psilocybin (4-phosphoryloxy-N,N-dimethyltryptamine) and psilocin (4-hydroxy-N,N-dimethyltryptamine), are hallucinogenic. They have properties similar to LSD, or acid, and produce alterations of digestive and cardiac function, motor reflexes, behavior, and perception.

STATUS: Illegal in the United States and numerous countries worldwide

CLASSIFICATION: Schedule I controlled substance

SOURCE: Certain mushrooms native to tropical and subtropical regions of South America, Mexico, and the United States

TRANSMISSION ROUTE: Oral

HISTORY OF USE

Hallucinogenic mushrooms containing psilocybin are thought to have existed as long or longer than the human race. Historically, artwork such as pictures, statues, and carvings depicting the mushrooms have been seen near tribal settlements. In Central and South America, psilocybin-containing mushrooms were commonly used in religious ceremonies until Spanish settlers spread Catholicism and banned their use. Mushrooms are sacred to indigenous peoples and are considered entheogens, psychoactive substances that guide their religious path through the spirit world.

In the early twentieth century ethnobotanists Richard Evans Schultes and Blas Pablo Reko traveled to Mexico and sought out these mushrooms. Schultes published a report of his findings in 1939. After hearing of this work, ethnomycologists Roger Heim and R. Gordon Wasson and pediatrician Valentina Wasson traveled to Central America to investigate the use and effects of the mushrooms. In 1957 the Wassons published the article "Seeking the Magic Mushroom" in *Life* magazine.

Mushrooms symbolized hippie counterculture in the 1960s and 1970s and were commonly used in the

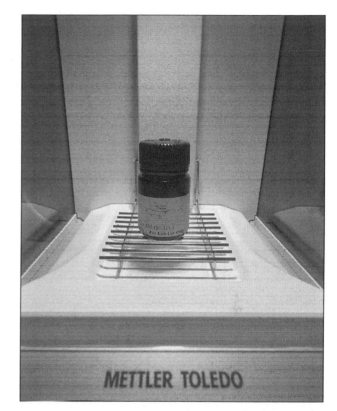

Synthetic psilocybin is displayed New research in psychedelics such as psilocybin, the main ingredient in "magic mushrooms," aims for therapeutic uses, such as treatments for anxiety, headaches or quitting smoking. (Bloomberg via Getty Images)

United States and Great Britain. The mushrooms led to the discovery of LSD, a synthetic hallucinogen.

It is difficult to determine the level of use of psilocybin-containing mushrooms because most studies of drug use neglect to include this drug. The Monitoring the Future survey published in 2008 reported that 7.8 percent of high school seniors had used hallucinogens other than LSD. This group of drugs includes peyote and psilocybin. Use in the previous year by participants was reported as 5 percent.

EFFECTS AND POTENTIAL RISKS

Psilocybin and its active form, psilocin, are not inactivated by heating or freezing. To mask its bitter flavor, the mushroom is brewed into tea or cooked with other foods. Digestion and absorption of the psilocybin take about twenty minutes, and the effects last from four to six hours.

Psilocybin can produce relaxation or weakness of the muscles, lack of coordination, excessive pupil dilation, nausea, vomiting, and drowsiness. Mushroom abusers are at risk of poisoning if poisonous mushrooms are accidentally ingested with psilocybin mushrooms.

The psychological effects of psilocybin use include hallucinations, an altered perception of the passage of time, and confusion between fantasy and reality. Panic and psychosis also may occur, especially with high doses. Persistent use comes with flashbacks, risk of psychiatric disease, memory impairment, and tolerance.

Kimberly A. Napoli, MS

FURTHER READING

Laing, Richard R., ed. *Hallucinogens: A Forensic Drug Handbook*. San Francisco: Elsevier, 2003.

National Institute on Drug Abuse. "Hallucinogens: LSD, Peyote, Psilocybin, and PCP." 2009. Web. 10 Mar. 2012. http://www.nida.nih.gov/infofacts/hallucinogens.html.

"Psilocybin Mushrooms." Web. 26 Mar. 2012. http://www.erowid.org/plants/mushrooms/mushrooms.shtml.

WEBSITES OF INTEREST

AbovetheInfluence.com
http://www.abovetheinfluence.com/facts/drugshallucinogens

National Drug Intelligence Center
http://www.justice.gov/ndic/pubs6/6038

National Institute on Drug Abuse
http://www.drugabuse.gov

See also: Hallucinogen abuse; Hallucinogens: Short- and long-term effects on the body; LSD; MDMA; Mescaline; PCP; Psychosis and substance abuse

N

Naloxone

CATEGORY: Treatment

ALSO KNOWN AS: Narcan

DEFINITION: Naloxone is a synthetic opioid antagonist used as an antidote for opioid overdose. Naloxone reverses the life-threatening respiratory depression caused by natural and synthetic opioids, including heroin, morphine, propoxyphene, and methadone. Naloxone is not a controlled substance, but it is available only by prescription.

USES

Naloxone is a pure opioid antagonist that completely displaces narcotics from the opioid receptor sites in the central nervous system. Naloxone is the treatment of choice for emergencies involving opioid overdose and intoxication. It is most often administered intravenously because of the need for a rapid onset of activity. Naloxone's effects are usually seen within two minutes of administration and last for thirty to forty-five minutes. Repeat doses of naloxone may be necessary if complete reversal of opioid intoxication is not achieved.

Naloxone is never used alone for long-term addiction treatment. The drug is available in combination with buprenorphine for long-term maintenance therapy of opioid addiction, usually in an outpatient, office-based setting. Naloxone is included in the formulation to prevent potential abuse of buprenorphine. In rare instances, naloxone may be used postoperatively to reverse the effects of anesthesia.

Naloxone distribution programs have been implemented in cities worldwide to provide naloxone to opioid abusers and their acquaintances to be used in the case of an overdose. The effectiveness of these programs in reducing morbidity and mortality associated with opioid abuse remains controversial.

PRECAUTIONS

Naloxone may cause increased heart rate, elevated blood pressure, and pulmonary edema, but these adverse effects do not usually warrant avoiding its use, given the life-threatening nature of opioid overdose. However, naloxone may precipitate withdrawal symptoms in opioid-dependent persons.

If doses of up to 10 milligrams fail to reverse overdose symptoms, the patient is likely to be suffering an acute intoxication of a substance other than an opioid.

Jennifer L. Gibson, PharmD

FURTHER READING

Bazazi, A. R., et al. "Preventing Opiate Overdose Deaths: Examining Objections To Take-Home Naloxone." *Journal of Health Care for the Poor and Underserved* 21.4 (2010): 1108–13. Print.

Dawson, Andrew H. "Naloxone, Naltrexone, and Nalmefene." *Medical Toxicology*. Ed. Richard C. Dart. 3rd ed. Philadelphia: Wolters, 2004.

Fukuda, Kasuhiko. "Opioids." *Miller's Anesthesia*. Eds. Ronald D. Miller et al. 7th ed. Orlando, FL: Churchill, 2009.

Mintzer, Ira L., et al. "Treating Opioid Addiction with Buprenorphine-Naloxone in Community-Based Primary Care Settings." *Annals of Family Medicine* 5 (2007): 146–50. Print.

Sporer, Karl A., and Alex H. Kral. "Prescription Naloxone: A Novel Approach to Heroin Overdose Prevention." *Annals of Emergency Medicine* 49.2 (2007): 17–77. Print.

WEBSITES OF INTEREST

DailyMed
http://dailymed.nlm.nih.gov

The Merck Manuals
http://www.merckmanuals.com/professional/sec15/ch198/ch198f.html?qt=naloxone&alt=sh

National Institute on Drug Abuse
http://www.drugabuse.gov/NIDA_notes/NNvol23N1/Young.html

See also: Addiction medications; Emergency treatment; Opioid abuse; Overdose

Naltrexone

CATEGORY: Treatment

ALSO KNOWN AS: Naltrexone hydrochloride; Revia; Vivitrol

DEFINITION: Naltrexone is a medication prescribed for the treatment of alcohol and opiate use disorders.

HOW DOES NALTREXONE WORK?

Naltrexone is an antagonist that binds to the mu (μ) opioid receptors in the brain but does not stimulate them. This is important because naltrexone is used to treat addictions, but like some addiction medications, it does not result in euphoria. When used with psychosocial therapy, naltrexone has been shown to be an effective adjunct for the treatment of addiction disorders.

Once naltrexone has reached a therapeutic level in the patient's system (in as little as a few hours) a couple of processes occur. First, there is typically a significant drop in cravings for the drug, and second, if opiates or alcohol are used, no euphoria is experienced. Naltrexone blocks the activation of the receptors of the dopamine that is typically released when opiates or alcohol are consumed: No dopamine, no euphoria.

Furthermore, because these receptors are accustomed to being stimulated, a lack of dopamine results in more cravings. With naltrexone occupying those receptors, cravings are decreased significantly. The decrease in cravings, coupled with the loss of the euphoria experienced when drinking or using opiates, may dramatically reduce the chances of relapse and provide the patient with the extra assistance needed to participate in psychosocial treatment. It must be noted that because naltrexone will remove any chemical currently occupying the receptor, withdrawal symptoms will follow. Because of this, the patient must be free of opiates (such as heroin, morphine, and buprenorphine) before being given naltrexone.

Side effects of naltrexone include nausea, headache, dizziness, anxiety, fatigue, and trouble sleeping. Hepatotoxicity, or chemical-induced liver damage, has been found when naltrexone is given in excessive doses. The specificity and intensity of the side effects may depend on the form in which the medication is taken.

DRUG FORMS

Naltrexone is prescribed in two different forms—oral (Revia) and in an intramuscular injection (Vivitrol). Revia is typically prescribed in a 50 milligram dose, once daily. Reactions to Revia vary. Some patients have reported side effects severe enough to discontinue use. However, frequency of side effects is greatly reduced with the once-monthly injectable form of naltrexone (Vivitrol).

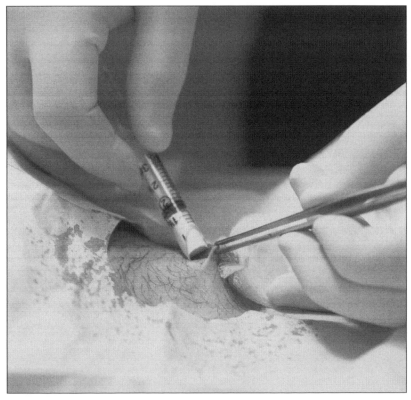

A doctor inserts a Naltrexone implant into a patient's lower abdomen. (AP Photo)

EFFICACY

Naltrexone has been shown to have positive, albeit varied results. Some research indicates that patients on naltrexone report significant reductions in their average drinking days and in heavy drinking days (more than four to five drinks per day). Other research indicates positive treatment outcomes in the areas of retention, compliance, and group therapy attendance. However, other studies report some problems with medication adherence.

CONTRAINDICATIONS

Naltrexone in either form (oral or injection) is contraindicated for anyone with active hepatitis, liver failure, or severe liver disease. In addition, anyone who is actively taking opiates (either illicitly or for pain) should not take naltrexone because it will negate any opiate-based effects (for example, pain reduction or management). Additional contraindications may depend on the form of the medication.

Desirée Akasha Crèvecoeur-MacPhail, PhD

FURTHER READING

AHFS Consumer Medication Information. "Naltrexone." February 2009. Web. http://www.ncbi. nlm.nih.gov/pubmedhealth/PMH0000853. Provides introductory information on the use of naltrexone and discusses special precautions associated with its use.

Gihyun Yoon, Suck Won Kim, Paul Thuras, and Joseph Westermeyer. "Safety, Tolerability, and Feasibility of High-Dose Naltrexone in Alcohol Dependence: An Open-Label Study." *Human Psychopharmacology: Clinical and Experimental* 26.2 (2011): 125–32. Print. Evaluates the safety and tolerability of high-dose naltrexone for treating alcoholism.

Lobmaier, Philipp P., Nikolaj Kunøe, Michael Gossop, and Helge Waal. "Naltrexone Depot Formulations for Opioid and Alcohol Dependence: A Systematic Review." *CNS Neuroscience and Therapeutics* 17.6 (2011): 629–36. Print. Discusses the effectiveness and side effects of naltrexone for opioid and alcohol dependence.

WEBSITES OF INTEREST

Medline Plus: Naltrexone
http://www.nlm.nih.gov/medlineplus/druginfo/ meds/a685041.html

SAMHSA: Naltrexone
http://dpt.samhsa.gov/medications/naltrexone. aspx

See also: Addiction medications; Alcohol abuse and alcoholism: Treatment; Opioid abuse

Narcotics abuse

CATEGORY: Substance abuse
ALSO KNOWN AS: Opioid abuse
DEFINITION: Narcotics include a variety of natural and synthetic substances, including opium, morphine, heroin, oxycodone, fentanyl, Demerol, and methadone, which are used to reduce pain. Some are used medicinally to suppress cough, treat diarrhea, ease pain, and induce sleep or stupor. Narcotics bind to opioid receptors in the central nervous system. When taken at prescribed levels, it is very unlikely that the user will become addicted. Narcotics can be abused at higher dosages in order to achieve intoxication.

CAUSES

Narcotics produce their effect by binding to opioid receptors in the central nervous system. The human body contains opioid receptors to respond to naturally occurring opioids in the body known as endorphins. Endorphins serve to block or suppress the feeling of pain, having an analgesic and sedative effect. Narcotics lead to euphoria and sedation, produced by stimulation of the opioid receptors.

RISK FACTORS

The type of narcotic abused can be a factor in addiction potential. Heroin, the most frequently abused narcotic, can cause addiction after one use; second in potency is morphine. Other risk factors for narcotics abuse include psychological mind-sets such as antisocial attitudes and sensation-seeking during adolescence. Environmental risk factors include dysfunction family relationships, poverty, gang membership, urban living, disposable income, family history of substance abuse, and low self-esteem.

SYMPTOMS

Narcotics intoxication may include sensations such as euphoria, a rush of pleasure, relaxation, and drowsiness, followed by sedation or sleep. Users report feeling free from cares and worries, a lessening of anxiety and tension, and a sense of escapism from life. The feeling is so pleasurable that the user often develops an irresistible urge to use again, an urge that may eventually develop into an addiction.

Some of the negative effects of narcotics abuse are sleep disturbances, sexual dysfunctions, anxiety, drowsiness, inability to concentrate, apathy, lethargy, flushing of the face and neck, constipation, nausea, and vomiting. A person prescribed a narcotic may develop some withdrawal symptoms over time if use is suddenly interrupted. Generally, if narcotics are prescribed for a longer time for pain relief, the dosage is progressively lowered through the weeks to prevent withdrawal symptoms.

Withdrawal symptoms for narcotics are some of the worst exhibited for any abused substance. Early symptoms of withdrawal may appear within a few hours, but typically appear within six to thirty-six hours of the last dose. Symptoms of withdrawal are typically the reverse of the pleasurable effects produced by the narcotic and include anxiety, irritability, loss of appetite, tremors, salivation, yawning, flu-like symptoms, and sweating. More serious withdrawal symptoms include abdominal cramping, fever, gooseflesh, gastrointestinal upset, confusion, and convulsions. Less acute withdrawal symptoms, which may persist for months after the last dose, include anhedonia, insomnia, and drug craving. The severity of symptoms is proportionate to dosage and duration of abuse.

SCREENING AND DIAGNOSIS

Persons suspected of narcotics overdose require immediate emergency medical attention. With an unconscious person suspected of narcotics overdose, doctors will look for physical signs of overdose, such as shallow breathing and small pupils. Patients are then administered naloxone, an opioid antagonist, to reverse the possibility of coma (which can occur in as quickly as one minute).

To diagnose abuse, a doctor will question a person about his or her history of drug use, including use under dangerous conditions, and will ask about failures to meet obligations, legal problems, and impairments of social or occupational functioning caused by narcotics use.

TREATMENT AND THERAPY

Treating people who are addicted to narcotics is difficult, mainly because of denial and the severity of withdrawal symptoms. Detoxification is the first step, and the most common long-term treatment is to substitute methadone (a synthetic narcotic with less addictive potential) for the abused drug, followed by weaning the abuser off the methadone. Buprenorphine is another medicine that can be used in the same manner for detoxification. The drug clonidine is also sometimes used to help alleviate some of the symptoms of withdrawal, particularly salivation, runny nose, sweating, abdominal cramping, and muscle aches. Also, recovery groups such as Narcotics Anonymous provide an important source of community support for persons who are overcoming narcotics addiction.

PREVENTION

To prevent possible addiction and dependence, it is important to use opioid medications only at the prescribed dosages, or to avoid narcotics altogether. A recovering addict must deal with the intense, long-term psychological dependence on narcotics. Counseling, self-help groups, halfway houses, and group therapy may help recovering addicts maintain abstinence.

Eugenia M. Valentine, PhD

FURTHER READING

Glass, George. *Narcotics: Dangerous Painkillers.* New York: Rosen, 2000. Written for young adult readers, this book gives a history of use of narcotics, warns of the dangers of abuse, and provides information on how to get help if using or addicted.

Narcotics Anonymous World Services. *Narcotics Anonymous: White Booklet.* New York: BN, 2007. The text is used at Narcotics Anonymous meetings. Written by former addicts, it lists the twelve steps to recovery and contains personal stories of recovery and inspiration.

Sanburg, Paul R., Michael D. Bunsey, and Solomon H. Snyder. *Prescription Narcotics: The Addictive Painkillers.* New York: Chelsea House, 1991. A comprehensive history of narcotic use throughout the world, illustrated with period photographs. Also covers modern synthetic narcotics and narcotics use, abuse, and treatment.

WEBSITES OF INTEREST
Narcotics Anonymous
http://www.na.org

National Institute on Drug Abuse
http://www.nida.nih.gov

"Painkillers, Narcotics Abuse, and Addiction."
  WebMD.com
http://www.webmd.com/pain-management/
  painkillers-and-addiction-narcotic-abuse

See also: Codeine; Fentanyl; Heroin; Hydrocodone; Methadone; Morphine; Narcotics: Short- and long-term effects on the body; Opioid abuse; Opium; Oxycodone; Painkiller abuse; Vicodin

Narcotics Anonymous

CATEGORY: Treatment
DEFINITION: Narcotics Anonymous is a nonprofit group-support organization of recovering drug addicts with a global network of approximately 58,000 weekly meetings in 131 countries.
DATE: Established in July 1953

BACKGROUND
Narcotics Anonymous (NA) grew from the organization Alcoholics Anonymous during the mid-twentieth century in Southern California. The twelve steps of NA are adaptations from those of its predecessor with only minor alterations, namely an expanded concept of addiction to include all substances of abuse. Many people were involved in the genesis of the society, including nonaddict participants in the medical, psychiatric, and religious communities. James P. Kinnon (Jimmy K.), who died in 1985, is usually regarded as having been most influential.

The organization of NA has changed significantly since 1953. Through 1966, only ten weekly meetings existed, and a basic text was not published until 1982. The 1970s saw the most rapid period of structural development, including the formation of a contemporary fellowship.

Tradition dictates that each NA group is officially autonomous, except when decisions bear on other groups or society as a whole. Participation is voluntary and groups are financially self-sufficient. Governance is based on a model of decentralized and democratic consensus. Local meetings often delegate members to serve as representatives in an area committee, which in turn delegates members to serve in a regional committee. An NA "world service" office, located in Van Nuys, California, ensures the common welfare of NA globally.

Although formats vary, a general outline can be found in the majority of meetings. A session might open with a call to order followed by a reading of some of the fellowship's core literature. If the literature is read, then it is generally divided among a number of participants rather than monopolized by a single person. A speaker, who is selected by a chairperson, who is in turn elected on a rotating basis to coordinate the meeting, then shares for a specified time. Sharing is usually biographical in scope and oriented around a particular topic (for example spirituality). The speaker then either calls on participants to share or opens the meeting for discussion of the topic at hand.

Meetings are generally sixty to ninety minutes in duration. The gathering is adjourned after either a prayer, more reading from the literature, or both. Each group is free to format its meeting however it collectively agrees.

MISSION AND GOALS
NA has one stated primary purpose: to develop a therapeutic environment in which former substance abusers can assist each other to abstain from using drugs and to recover. Part of this environment is the cultivation of sponsorship. Members who have "worked the steps" volunteer to help newcomers through the program. Sponsors provide mentorship and friendship and are regarded by the fellowship as indispensable to the recovery process.

Other instruments of the program include literature, social support networks, and service roles. These roles include chairing meetings and acting as treasurer for a group. Other functions are more simple and include brewing coffee and greeting members at the door.

Additional services are often delegated to service boards or committees at the intergroup level of the fellowship. Because NA is nonprofessional, groups often find it difficult to carry out certain types of service activities. Phone lines, public relations, and panels conducted at hospitals and institutions are examples. NA maintains a policy of neither affiliating with nor endorsing any cause or outside organization. Hence, although many treatment centers adopt a twelve-step orientation to their services, no institution is managed by nor bears the name of NA.

The best estimates of demographics are that, over time, membership approximates the ethnic, social class, and religious composition of the host country or region. The modal average length of abstinence is between one and five years. Evaluations of the program tend to support its effectiveness in treating substance use disorders across a broad range of populations. Recent years have witnessed a surge in the number of countries in which NA operates.

Tony N. Buell, MA

FURTHER READING

Anderson, Tammy L., and Lynn Bondi. "Exiting the Drug-Addict Role: Variations by Race and Gender." *Symbolic Interaction* 21.2 (1998): 155–74. Print. Explores variations in the process of creating a recovering-addict role within the constraints of twelve-step ideology.

Crape, Byron L., et al. "The Effects of Sponsorship in 12-Step Treatment of Injection Drug Users." *Drug and Alcohol Dependence* 65 (2002): 291–301. Print. Explains that among adult heroin and cocaine injectors, being a twelve-step sponsor predicts one's sustained abstinence whereas having a sponsor exerts no independent effect.

Frois, Catarina. *The Anonymous Society: Identity, Transformation, and Anonymity in 12 Step Associations.* Newcastle upon Tyne, Eng.: Cambridge Scholars, 2009. Ethnographic study of Narcotics Anonymous, Alcoholics Anonymous, and Families Anonymous in Portugal.

Krentzman, A., et al. "How Alcoholics Anonymous (AA) and Narcotics Anonymous (NA) Work: Cross-Disciplinary Perspectives." *Alcoholism Treatment Quarterly* 29 (2011): 75–84. Print. Presents findings of an academic conference on recovery from the fields of psychiatry, social psychology, and history.

Narcotics Anonymous. *Miracles Happen: The Birth of Narcotics Anonymous in Words and Pictures.* Chatsworth, CA: Author, 1998. Describes the first three decades of Narcotics Anonymous history, and includes facsimiles of historical interest.

Toumbourou, John W., et al. "Narcotics Anonymous Participation and Changes in Substance Use and Social Support." *Journal of Substance Abuse Treatment* 23 (2002): 61–66. Print. Employs quasi-experimental method to evaluate outcomes of Narcotics Anonymous participation.

WEBSITES OF INTEREST

Addiction Recovery Guide
http://www.addictionrecoveryguide.org/resources/recovery

Narcotics Anonymous
http://www.na.org

See also: Abstinence-based treatment; Group therapy for substance abuse; Outpatient treatment; Sponsors; Support groups; Twelve-step programs for addicts

Narcotics: Short- and long-term effects on the body

CATEGORY: Health issues and physiology

DEFINITION: *Narcotic* is another word for opioid drugs, or opiates, which have been used throughout human history to relieve pain. Historically, narcotics were naturally derived from the poppy plant. The narcotics prescribed today may be natural or synthetic. These drugs include morphine, heroin, codeine, opium, hydrocodone, oxycodone, meperidine, and methadone.

ADDICTION TO NARCOTICS

Substance use is a choice, but over time the use of substances can develop into dependency. The overuse, or abuse, of substances brings lasting physiological changes to the brain that lead to psychological and behavioral changes. With the abuse of narcotics, the damage to the brain is profound.

Addiction is a brain disorder. Narcotics disrupt the biochemical processes of the brain, eventually leading to addiction. To understand the damage of narcotics abuse requires an understanding of why narcotics are used and how they alter the brain.

Because narcotics (opioids) produce a euphoric state of relaxation, even sleep, they serve a medical purpose for controlling pain. Narcotics affect the mu (μ) opioid receptors in the brain, also known as the painkilling parts of the brain, or the reward pathway. When abused, narcotics block endorphins, the brain's natural pain-control chemical. A person with narcotics addiction experiences profound disruptions to normal brain activity and therefore feels a powerful need for the drug in order to maintain normal functioning and avoid withdrawal symptoms. Increasingly, the addict needs higher doses to feel the same effects.

In his book *Helping the Addict You Love*, Laurence W. Westreich warns the friends and relatives of addicts about the damage to the brain that substance abuse causes and how it leads to the impairment of judgment and common sense. Love and logic are not enough to convince an addict to stop using the substance. Much more occurs in the body physiologically with addiction that can hamper the addict's decision-making abilities and impulse control.

According to Westreich, several models explain why a person becomes addicted to a substance. Based in neuroscience, the learning theory model suggests that addiction evolves from the reward mechanism in the brain. The high is the reward, and the brain adjusts to receive more of the reward. The self-medication hypothesis suggests that people abuse substances as a way of coping with traumatic events and stress in life.

The biopsychosocial model assumes that addiction is driven by a combination of psychological and social factors and, therefore, must be treated at the same time other underlying factors are treated. The moral model assumes a fault in the addict's moral character as the fundamental cause for the development of the addiction. Conversely, the disease model considers addiction a disease or a medical condition that must be treated medically, and not as a defect in the addict's moral character.

In their book *Freedom from Addiction*, David Simon and Deepak Chopra summarize the impact of narcotic drugs on the body this way: "Opiate-derived chemicals directly activate the pleasure receptors of the brain, bypassing all usual methods to achieve comfort." They continue, "When the opiates are metabolized, the body is left without intrinsic or extrinsic pain relievers." Therefore, the short-term impact on the body is intense pleasure and pain relief, while the long-term impact is the inability of the brain to regulate pleasure and pain in the body normally.

NARCOTICS ABUSE VERSUS DEPENDENCY

In *Addiction: Why Can't They Just Stop?*, researchers John Hoffman and Susan Froemke define *substance abuse* and *substance dependence*. Accordingly, *abuse* is "a pattern of substance use that causes someone to experience harmful consequences," which includes failing to meet key responsibilities; engaging in reckless activity; and refusing to resist the substance despite recurrent interpersonal, occupational, and financial problems brought on by drug use. *Dependence* is a physical addiction to a substance resulting in physiological and behavioral changes to the user. Physiologically the dependent person needs increasingly higher doses of the substance to achieve a high. He or she then experiences intense withdrawal symptoms when deprived of the substance. Behaviorally the person is obsessed with acquiring the next dose, prioritizing the substance over all relationships and obligations, including care for his or her own health.

Some people can become addicted to narcotics without necessarily abusing narcotics. Rather, they may become dependent on narcotics from using them to manage chronic physical pain over an extended period of time. Even when narcotics are prescribed by a doctor, patients must be aware of the drugs' potential for dependency and addiction.

A continuum exists among opioid abuse, opioid dependence, and addiction. Signs of abuse include the user's inability to fulfill normal responsibilities and the prevalence of interpersonal problems. Dependence is characterized by the consumption of larger and more frequent doses of the narcotic over a span of time, an increased tolerance of the effects (the high) of the narcotic, and a clear demonstration that the user is obsessed with acquiring the narcotic regardless of cost to his or her own health and personal relationships. Addiction is the state in which the craving for the narcotic becomes so compulsive and overpowering that the addicted person's behavior becomes grossly self-destructive.

SHORT-TERM EFFECTS

Opiate narcotics like heroin, morphine, and prescription painkillers (such as oxycodone and Vicodin) will produce a surge of euphoria and drowsiness. The short-term effects of narcotics include relaxation, sleepiness, pain relief, an inability to concentrate, apathy, flushing of the face and neck, constipation, and nausea and vomiting.

Opiates also can slow systems in the body, such as the nervous, respiratory, and digestive systems. Physical dependence can become severe and can gravely affect the body's normal nervous, respiratory, and digestive functions. Heroin tricks the brain's neurotransmitters by activating abnormal messaging. In effect, the reward circuit of the brain is overstimulated.

LONG-TERM EFFECTS

Long-term abuse causes the brain to adapt to the drug-induced surges of dopamine, thereby producing less of its own dopamine naturally. The most significant long-term effect of narcotics abuse is this reduction of dopamine and dopamine receptors in the brain. The brain then cannot stimulate the reward circuit on its own. The neurotransmitter glutamate is permanently altered, and the brain develops a drive to achieve messaging to the reward center through narcotics. This desire trumps all other decisions and judgments.

Addiction is the underlying long-term effect on the body. The body craves the substance biologically just like it does food. "The addict's need for his or her substance of choice is like a starving person's primal need for food," Westreich explains. "Drugs and alcohol literally 'hijack' the brain, physically and emotionally driving the addict to find, use, and keep using whatever drug he or she has chosen." Once addicted, withdrawal is a necessary challenge to overcome when first embarking on the journey of recovery. In withdrawal from opiates, whether street heroin or prescription pain pills, the addict will experience extreme restlessness, severe pain in the muscles and bones, diarrhea, vomiting, and cold sweats. Heroin and morphine use can also cause permanent damage to the body through bacterial infections of the blood, heart valves, liver, or kidneys. Heroin, morphine, and prescription painkillers also can cause serious damage to the lungs if inhaled or snorted.

Melissa Walsh

FURTHER READING

Hoffman, John, and Susan Froemke, eds. *Addiction: Why Can't They Just Stop?* New York: HBO, 2007. The companion book to the HBO documentary of the same name, offering information and testimonies about addiction in the United States.

Lawford, Christopher Kennedy. *Moments of Clarity.* New York: Morrow, 2009. First-person accounts of addiction and the journey of recovery.

Simon, David, and Deepak Chopra. *Freedom from Addiction.* Deerfield Beach, FL: Health Communications, 2007.

Westreich, Laurence M. *Helping the Addict You Love.* New York: Simon & Schuster, 2007. A guide for families and friends of addicts in how to lead the addict into and through treatment and recovery.

WEBSITES OF INTEREST

American Council for Drug Education
http://www.acde.org

Center for Substance Abuse Treatment
http://csat.samhsa.gov

Narcotics Anonymous
http://www.na.org

WebMD: Narcotic Abuse
http://www.emedicinehealth.com/narcotic_abuse

See also: Codeine; Fentanyl; Heroin; Hydrocodone; Methadone; Morphine; Narcotics abuse; Opium; Oxycodone; Painkiller abuse; Vicodin

National Institute on Alcohol Abuse and Alcoholism (NIAAA)

CATEGORY: Diagnosis and prevention

DEFINITION: The National Institute on Alcohol Abuse and Alcoholism, part of the National Institutes of Health, develops and conducts comprehensive health education, training, research, and planning programs for the prevention and treatment of alcohol abuse and alcoholism.

DATE: Established on December 31, 1970

BACKGROUND

The National Institute on Alcohol Abuse and Alcoholism (NIAAA) was established on December 31, 1970, by the Comprehensive Alcohol Abuse and Alcoholism Prevention, Treatment, and Rehabilitation

Act (also known as the Hughes Act), as part of a new emphasis by the US government to solve the nation's alcohol abuse problems. Since its founding, the NIAAA has led increasingly effective efforts to define alcohol abuse as a medical problem and to address the problem by applying research-based findings. In 1971 it issued its first special report to the US Congress on alcohol and health.

In 1974 the NIAAA became an independent institute within the NIH's Alcohol, Drug Abuse, and Mental Health Administration. Its research responsibilities were expanded at this time and again in 1976. In 1977 the NIAAA organized the first international research conference on fetal alcohol spectrum disorders. Based on research from this conference, the first US Surgeon General's Advisory on Alcohol and Pregnancy was issued in 1981. The advisory was updated in 2005. In 1988, with NIAAA support, legislation was passed that required labels on alcoholic beverage containers that warned of the adverse effects of alcohol on the developing fetus.

Another major focus of the NIAAA is alcohol abuse among minors and young adults. NIAAA-sponsored research has shown that adolescents are more vulnerable to alcohol abuse and its negative consequences than are adults, and that the earlier in life a person begins abusing alcohol the more likely the user is to become an alcoholic.

The NIAAA was instrumental in establishing the minimum legal drinking law in 1988. In 1998 it created the Task Force on College Drinking, a three-year investigation that brought together educators, administrators, researchers, and students to address the problem. In 2002 the NIAAA published *A Call to Action: Changing the Culture of Drinking at US Colleges*. In 2004 it established the Underage Drinking Research Initiative. *The Surgeon General's Call to Action to Prevent and Reduce Underage Drinking*, released in 2007, was based primarily on NIAAA research.

The NIAAA has been instrumental in supporting studies of the genetic components of alcohol abuse, focusing on determining who is at greatest risk of developing an alcohol abuse disorder based on inborn characteristics. In 1989 the NIAAA initiated Collaborative Studies on Genetics of Alcoholism, a series of ongoing studies of twins, families, and adoptees to identify the genes underlying a person's vulnerability to alcoholism. To date, more than twenty genes associated with alcoholism have been identified.

NIAAA-supported epidemiologic studies help to define the scope and content of alcohol problems in the United States. In 1991 the NIAAA launched the National Epidemiologic Survey on Alcohol and Related Conditions (NESARC), which remains the largest survey ever conducted on alcoholism and associated medical and psychiatric conditions. Between 2001 and 2005 the National Longitudinal Alcohol Epidemiologic Survey, building on NESARC findings, focused on alcohol use disorders and comorbid psychiatric illnesses.

MISSION AND GOALS

The mission of the NIAAA, which believes that alcoholism is a curable public health problem, is to conduct, promote, and support research on alcohol abuse and its health and societal consequences. It promotes research in a wide range of scientific disciplines, including genetics, epidemiology, neuroscience, and the behavioral sciences to determine the most effective ways to prevent and treat alcoholism and to reduce the consequences of alcohol abuse.

A primary function of the NIAAA is to coordinate the research on alcohol abuse by different federal agencies and to collaborate with other US and international research centers. The agency disseminates research findings with a perspective and language level appropriate to the targeted audiences. These audiences include researchers, policymakers, health care providers, and segments of the general population, including adolescents, young adults, and pregnant women.

In 2006 the NIAAA released a five-year plan, the NIAAA Strategic Plan for Research. It employs a new framework, labeled a lifespan perspective, for organizing future research. The NIAAA funds approximately 90 percent of the ongoing research in the United States on the causes, consequences, treatment, and prevention of alcohol abuse and alcohol-related problems.

Since its founding in 1970, the NIAAA has built a solid base of biomedical and behavioral knowledge that has been applied to improved prevention and treatment of alcohol-related problems. Building on evidence-based findings, the NIAAA promotes government policies, medical practices, interventions, and outreach programs that effectively address alcohol abuse.

Ernest Kohlmetz, MA

FURTHER READING

Foroud, T., H. J. Edenberg, and J. C. Crabbe. "Genetic Research: Who Is at Risk for Alcoholism? *Alcohol Research and Health* 33.1–2 (2010): 64–75. Print. Reviews NIAAA and other research centers exploring the genetic components of alcoholism.

Thomas, J. D., K. R. Warren, and B. G. Hewitt. "Fetal Alcohol Spectrum Disorders: From Research to Policy." *Alcohol Research and Health* 33.1–2 (2010): 118–26. Print. Discusses the initial and ongoing work of the NIAAA in relation to fetal alcohol distress syndromes.

Warren, K. R., and B. G. Hewitt. "NIAAA: Advancing Alcohol Research for 40 years." *Alcohol Research and Health* 33.1–2 (2010): 5–17. Print. A detailed history of the NIAAA's efforts to advance alcohol research from its inception in 1970 through 2010.

Windle, M., and R. A. Zucker. "Reducing Underage and Young Adult Drinking: How to Address Critical Drinking Problems During this Developmental Period." *Alcohol Research and Health* 33.1–2 (2010): 29–44. Print. Shows how research on underage and young adult drinking can influence policy decisions.

WEBSITES OF INTEREST

TheCoolSpot.gov
http://thecoolspot.gov

Task Force on College Drinking
http://www.collegedrinkingprevention.gov

See also: Education about substance abuse; Genetics and substance abuse; National Institute on Drug Abuse (NIDA); Prevention methods and research

National Institute on Drug Abuse (NIDA)

CATEGORY: Diagnosis and prevention
DEFINITION: The National Institute on Drug Abuse is a US government organization focused on substance abuse and addiction research.
DATE: Established in September, 1973

BACKGROUND

The National Institute on Drug Abuse (NIDA) was established by the US Congress in late 1973 in an attempt to stem the tide of drug addiction in the United States. In its early days, NIDA, under its first medical director, Robert L. DuPont, focused on demand reduction (decreasing the desire for drugs) while law enforcement agencies focused on supply reduction (decreasing drug availability to potential addicts).

For eighteen years after its inception, NIDA was responsible both for overseeing research related to substance abuse and for delivery of service to patients. When NIDA became part of the National Institutes of Health (NIH) in 1992, its focus shifted entirely to research, with provision of services moving to the Center for Substance Abuse Treatment and the Center for Substance Abuse Prevention.

Since becoming an institute under the NIH, NIDA has been responsible for overseeing a huge number of research projects involving substance abuse and addiction. One of the best known of these studies is the NIDA Collaborative Cocaine Treatment Study, which was a multicenter trial studying nearly five hundred persons being treated for cocaine addiction. As a result of this study and thousands of others done under the purview of NIDA, addiction has come to be thought of as a chronic illness, rather than as the result of a lapse in moral judgment. This point of view is generally attributed to Nora Volkow, another NIDA director.

MISSION AND GOALS

Since 1992, the focus of NIDA has been predominantly drug abuse and addiction research and the dissemination of information to professionals in the field and to the public. In its 2010 strategic plan, major goals were identified in four areas: prevention, treatment, research on human immunodeficiency virus (HIV) and acquired immune deficiency syndrome (AIDS), and cross-cutting priorities (dealing with the impact of other fields of health on issues of addiction).

In prevention, NIDA's aim is to keep people from becoming involved with drugs and to stop addiction. For treatment, research is aimed at developing better treatment modalities for addiction. NIDA ensures that this research is translated into treatment and that this treatment will be more accessible to all persons in need. Through extensive research NIDA hopes to learn more about the transmission of HIV in the drug-addicted population, about decreasing the spread of HIV among drug users, and about improving the means of treatment for those drug abusers who are affected by HIV.

Research in the area of cross-cutting priorities is aimed at investigating the impact of other health issues on drug addiction. Other goals in this area include eliminating health disparities experienced by people who are known drug users, educating society about addiction, and encouraging people from many backgrounds to become involved in drug abuse research, prevention, and treatment. By fulfilling these strategic goals, NIDA will accomplish its basic mission of fostering research in the field of drug use, leading to a better understanding of addiction, translating research findings into practice in the prevention and treatment of addiction, and the transmission of this information to the public.

Robin Kamienny Montvilo, PhD

FURTHER READING

Condon, Timothy P. "Reflecting on Thirty Years of Research: A Look at How NIDA Has Advanced the Research, Prevention, and Treatment of Drug Abuse and Addiction." *Behavioral Healthcare* 26 (2006): 14–16. Print. A brief overview of the impact that NIDA has had on the field of drug addiction.

Courtwright, David T. "The NIDA Brain Disease Paradigm: History, Resistance, and Spinoffs." *BioSocieties* 5.1 (2010): 137–47. Print. Reviews the notion espoused by NIDA that addiction is a chronic illness, presenting evidence that favors this idea and evidence to the contrary. Examines the impact of this notion on the field of addiction.

Crits-Christoph, Paul, et al. "The National Institute on Drug Abuse Collaborative Cocaine Treatment Study: Rationale and Methods." *Archives of General Psychiatry* 54 (1997): 721–26. Print. Outlines the plans and goals for one of the best-known research projects done under the auspices of NIDA.

---. "Psychosocial Treatments for Cocaine Dependence: National Institute on Drug Abuse Collaborative Cocaine Treatment Study." *Archives of General Psychiatry* 56 (1999): 493–502. Print. This follow-up article reports the results of the five-hundred-patient multicenter trial dealing with treatment of cocaine addiction. One of the seminal studies overseen by NIDA.

DuPont, Robert L. "National Institute on Drug Abuse at Its First Thirty-Five Years." *Drug and Alcohol Dependence* 107.1 (2010): 80–81. Print. NIDA's first medical director looks briefly at the organization's history while also reflecting on its future.

Lamb, Sara, Merwyn R. Greenlick, and Dennis McCarty, eds. *Bridging the Gap between Practice and Research: Forging Partnerships with Community-Based Drug and Alcohol Treatment.* Washington, DC: National Academy, 1998. Outlines the steps taken by NIDA to keep addiction research from being isolated from the treatment providers whom it was intended to inform.

WEBSITES OF INTEREST

National Institute on Drug Abuse
http://drugabuse.gov

NIDA for Teens
http://teens.drugabuse.gov

See also: Drug abuse and addiction: Overview; Education about substance abuse; National Institute on Alcohol Abuse and Alcoholism (NIAAA); Prevention methods and research

Newborn addicts

CATEGORY: Health issues and physiology

DEFINITION: A newborn addict is an infant born exposed to a substance of abuse. Newborn addicts display physical symptoms typical of chronic drug users and psychological symptoms of withdrawal after birth, when the maternal drug source is removed. Newborn addicts often have deficits particular to damage during fetal development stages; they require specialized care not only for their addiction but also for behavioral and physical disabilities immediately after birth and throughout life.

CAUSES

Newborns are born with addictions to substances of abuse when their mothers choose to use drugs while pregnant—either as a conscious choice (such as to drink alcohol or smoke a cigarette) or as a result of chronic addiction. Abusive substances include prescription opioids, alcohol, tobacco, and illicit street drugs such as cocaine and heroin.

Maternal drug use affects the fetus during every stage of pregnancy. Infant liver function is underdeveloped in the womb, so substances are not removed from the fetus's body efficiently; thus, the fetus, more so than the pregnant woman, is exposed to even more prolonged, damaging drug amounts.

RISK FACTORS

Even limited maternal drug use can lead to addiction in the fetus, because drug effects are quite variable. However, the highest-risk infants are those with mothers who have an extended history of abuse or who have had children born with addiction.

SYMPTOMS

Symptoms common to newborn addicts include premature birth, low birth weight, and congenital defects, such as heart problems. Newborn addicts frequently experience trembling and excessive crying; they startle at touches, sounds, or lights and are easily unsettled. Often, these infants cannot be comforted and become withdrawn.

Some symptoms are drug specific, such as cocaine-induced jitters and irritation or marijuana- or alcohol-related growth delays after birth. Infants diagnosed with fetal alcohol syndrome display facial defects in the eyes and nasal groove, mental disabilities, and poor coordination and attention.

Long-term drug effects can be subtle, such as adulthood attention or sleep problems in newborns addicted to marijuana. Long-term effects also can be pronounced, such as neurologic deficits and hyperactivity in teenagers who were chronically exposed to alcohol before birth.

SCREENING AND DIAGNOSIS

Addiction in a newborn can be anticipated by maternal use patterns; conversely, diagnosis can be challenging if mothers are uncooperative or hide their addictions to avoid losing their newborns to social service programs. To complicate the diagnostic workup, symptoms associated with particular drugs of abuse are difficult to clarify because many newborns have been exposed to multiple substances.

Diagnosis of alcohol syndrome in a newborn addict is comparatively easy, because of the classic triad of symptoms. Suspected toxicities can be verified with blood tests that screen for positive drug concentrations. General indications that support a diagnosis of newborn addiction include premature birth, clinically low birth weight, and small head circumference. Although these symptoms occur frequently with abusive drugs, they are not specific to addiction problems.

Withdrawal symptoms definitively support an addiction diagnosis but develop after days without a drug source, not immediately after birth. A suspected newborn addict should therefore remain in the hospital for a minimum of four or five days under close observation for withdrawal onset.

TREATMENT AND THERAPY

Treatment of the newborn addict rarely begins before birth, even when the mother's substance abuse history is confirmed. Few health professionals are knowledgeable specialists in addiction care during pregnancy, and treatment entails risks of severe fetal consequences from withdrawal.

If a physician considers treatment, methadone administered to the mother can prevent extreme in utero complications and ease treatment of the newborn addict after birth. However, methadone use causes its own side effects after birth and requires careful weaning in newborns.

Treatment of the newborn focuses on acute and chronic needs. Immediate care includes support for vital functions to maintain adequate blood flow, respiration, and body temperature. Addicted babies often require isolated, reduced-stimuli settings to foster adjustment to life without drugs. Opioid addiction often requires slow weaning of dosages to minimize withdrawal. Pharmacologic care for the addicted newborn has little research or standards; treatment guidelines by the American Academy of Pediatrics focus on opioid withdrawal concerns specifically.

Withdrawal medications may be warranted, especially for infants addicted to opioids. Methadone is a traditional withdrawal treatment with mixed activity at opioid receptors. Clonazepam may be administered to slow the metabolism of methadone. Buprenorphine, a weak opioid agonist, has fewer supporting studies for use in newborn addicts but is associated with generally minimal withdrawal symptoms.

Many growing newborn addicts require treatment for lack of early pediatric care, for poor nutrition during neonatal development, and for exposure to sexually transmitted diseases. Stable environments are essential to minimize long-term addiction effects. The full effects of long-term consequences of newborn addiction are uncertain. Even infants who receive early detoxification can develop permanent disabilities from drug use. Cognitive learning disabilities, physical deformities, and emotional or behavioral disorders have all been connected with maternal substance abuse and newborn drug exposure.

PREVENTION

According to the Centers for Disease Control and Prevention, addiction in newborns is becoming epidemic in the United States. However, state tracking of diagnoses is sporadic, so the true number of affected children is unknown. The best prevention is maternal avoidance of abusive substances; often, no amount of a drug is safe for developing infants. Prevention of drug use during pregnancy hinges on public awareness, both universally through public service announcements and selectively for women who have histories conducive to drug abuse.

Nicole M. Van Hoey, PharmD

FURTHER READING

Guidelines for Identifying Substance-Exposed Newborns. Phoenix: Arizona Department of Economic Security, 2005. State-specific guidance on diagnosing newborn addicts and withdrawal symptoms to provide early care and follow-up.

Hankin, Janet R. *Fetal Alcohol Syndrome Prevention Research.* Bethesda, MD: National Institute on Alcohol Abuse and Alcoholism, 2002. Thorough documentation about the broad effects of any amount of alcohol on developing infants, with a focus on use prevention strategies.

Hudak, Mark L., et al. "Neonatal Drug Withdrawal." *Pediatrics* 129.2 (2012): 540–60. Print. Clinical guidelines covering the risks, symptoms, and evidence-based treatment methods for withdrawal.

Rayburn, William, F. "Maternal and Fetal Effects from Substance Use." *Clinical Perinatology* 34 (2007): 559–71. Print. Discusses the effects of drug use on pregnant women and their developing fetuses. Touches on biological and psychological needs of the patients and deals with the ethical and legal issues that result from drug use.

Wang, Marvin, et al. "Perinatal Drug Abuse and Neonatal Drug Withdrawal." 19 Jan. 2012. Web. 3 Apr. 2012. http://emedicine.medscape.com/article/978492-overview. Review of multiple studies on short- and long-term care of symptoms of illicit drug addiction in newborns.

WEBSITES OF INTEREST

Children's Hospital Boston: Neonatal Abstinence Syndrome
http://www.childrenshospital.org/az/Site1338/mainpageS1338P0.html

Fetal Alcohol Spectrum Disorders Center
http://www.fasdcenter.samhsa.gov

March of Dimes
http://www.marchofdimes.com/pregnancy/alcohol_illicitdrug.html

National Center on Birth Defects and Developmental Disabilities
http://www.cdc.gov/ncbddd

See also: Birth defects and alcohol; Birth defects and drug use; Fetal alcohol syndrome; Pregnancy and drug use

Nicotine addiction

CATEGORY: Substance abuse

DEFINITION: Unlike many damaging addictions (with the exception of alcohol abuse), the smoking or chewing of tobacco is legal in most countries. Cigars, cigarettes, and pipe and chewing tobacco contain many chemicals, but the addictive substance is nicotine, which creates a craving in many people that may be as difficult to break as addiction to heroin, cocaine, or other drugs.

STATUS: Legal in most of the world, but restricted by location of use and age of user worldwide

SOURCE: Tobacco plant *Nicotiana tabacum*

TRANSMISSION ROUTE: Inhalation, oral ingestion

HISTORY OF USE

Nicotine was named for the tobacco plant *Nicotiana tabacum*, which itself was named for Jean Nicot de Villemain, a French ambassador, who imported the

Nicotine

Nicotine is a highly toxic, colorless, oily liquid alkaloid best known as the addictive substance in tobacco. Cigarettes, cigars, and chewing tobacco are the principal ways in which nicotine is ingested. One of the world's most heavily-used drugs, nicotine has complex effects on the human body depending on dose size, period of use, health and genes of the user, and other factors.

As chemists were discovering the structure and dangerous properties of nicotine, other researchers were beginning to delineate some of the deleterious effects of nicotine in tobacco products. This led, in the twentieth century, to studies establishing nicotine's addictiveness, its link with heart disease, and its role in several other health problems. These studies led to US government warnings that smoking is dangerous to health and to advertising bans and bans on smoking in many public places.

plant to Portugal in 1560 as a medicine. The colony of Jamestown, Virginia, began to cultivate tobacco on a large scale around 1616. Starting in 1617, exports rose from 20,000 pounds to 1.5 million by 1629.

What had been characterized as a detestable weed soon began to be used by the English, who were told that the tobacco would improve their health. The colonists abandoned other ventures to cultivate tobacco, drawing about forty-six hundred new colonists from Europe in about fifteen years, flooding onto lands that the Powhatans had used to grow food and hunt game.

The smoking or chewing of tobacco became popular for centuries. Until the 1950s, many university lecture halls were built with ashtrays. Indoor smoking was widely accepted. The newsroom of the *New York Times*, for example, was used by so many chain smokers in the 1930s that by the end of each work day janitors swept away cigarette butts with pushbrooms.

The US surgeon general in 1963 issued a detailed report that associated the use of tobacco with many health problems, including heart disease, stroke, and cancer. Since then, even the inhalation of tobacco smoke from other people's lungs (secondhand or passive smoking) has been associated with health risks.

The nicotine itself usually does not cause health risks. Most of the physical damage is caused by other substances, including tar and various chemicals. In

2009, about 20 percent of adults in the United States still used tobacco.

EFFECTS AND POTENTIAL RISKS

The human body receives nicotine (and other addictive substances) through acetylcholine receptors in the brain, increasing the levels of neurotransmitters that regulate mood and behavior. The use of nicotine provides a shot of dopamine, a neurotransmitter that briefly produces a sense of euphoria and relaxation, rewarding continued use and thus reinforcing addiction. The use of nicotine also increases the flow of the stimulating hormone adrenaline (epinephrine). Nicotine also increases heart rate by about twenty beats per minute, elevating blood pressure and constricting arteries.

Burning tobacco contains a minimum of sixty cancer-causing chemicals. The smoking of tobacco plays a role in about 90 percent of lung-cancer cases and many cases of emphysema and chronic bronchitis; it also aggravates asthma. Inhalation of burning tobacco also provokes cancers of the esophagus, larynx, mouth, and throat (pharynx). It also negatively affects the stomach, pancreas, kidneys, bladder, cervix, stomach, and other parts of the body, and it can increase the risk of infertility and impotence.

The use of tobacco at a young age increases the likelihood of serious addiction. Dependence becomes slightly more intense each time the drug is used. Thus, while going without the drug is easier for younger people, the addiction becomes more trenchant with age. Going without nicotine causes withdrawal symptoms (such as irritability and anxiety) that vary in intensity and duration among different users.

Other symptoms of nicotine withdrawal include difficulty concentrating, restlessness, a depressed mood, frustration, anger, hunger, occasional insomnia, and constipation or diarrhea. The use of tobacco even after onset of serious health problems is a sign of serious addiction. Some people continue using tobacco even after lung-cancer surgery, and some people defend their "freedom" to be addicted.

Although nicotine addiction is physiological, it also involves psychological cues. The desire experienced by smokers to raise their nicotine levels is often associated with daily rituals, including a cup of morning coffee, free time between work tasks, or an evening over drinks at a familiar bar.

Meeting with friends (especially those who smoke) also can intensify the urge. Smoking also can be associated with specific sites, or a ride in a familiar automobile. Psychological stress can raise anxiety levels and increase the desire to smoke. Smelling burning tobacco also may increase a smoker's desire to use the substance.

People who experience schizophrenia, depression, or other mental illnesses are more likely to smoke tobacco than those without such illnesses. Abusers of alcohol and illegal drugs also use tobacco at higher rates. Nicotine has been studied as a treatment for attention deficit hyperactivity disorder, Parkinson's disease, and schizophrenia. Products meant to aid smokers in quitting have become a worldwide industry on which several billion dollars are spent each year.

Bruce E. Johansen, PhD

FURTHER READING

Benowitz, Neal L., ed. *Nicotine Safety and Toxicity.* New York: Oxford UP, 1998. A wide-ranging study of nicotine pathology.

Bock, Gregory, and Jamie Goode, eds. *Understanding Nicotine and Tobacco Addiction.* Hoboken, NJ: Wiley, 2006. An overview of nicotine's addictive properties and medical pathologies.

Kozlowski, Lynn T., Jack E. Henningfield, and Janet Brigham. *Cigarettes, Nicotine, and Health: A Biobehavioral Approach.* Thousand Oaks, CA: Sage, 2001. A guide to the many health risks of tobacco use and nicotine addiction.

Wagner, Eric F., ed. *Nicotine Addiction among Adolescents.* New York: Haworth, 2000. Discussion of young people's health risks, with chapters taken mainly from the *Journal of Child and Adolescent Substance Abuse.*

WEBSITES OF INTEREST

American Heart Association
http://www.americanheart.org

National Institute on Drug Abuse
http://www.nida.nih.gov/researchreports/nicotine/nicotine.html

See also: Cancer and substance abuse; Dopamine and addiction; Mental illness; Smoking; Smoking cessation; Smoking: Short- and long-term effects on the body; Tobacco use disorder

Nicotine replacement products

Category: Treatment
Definition: Nicotine replacement products are used to help people stop smoking. These products work best as part of a program that also includes education, counseling, and psychological support.

HOW NICOTINE REPLACEMENT PRODUCTS WORK

Nicotine replacement products provide nicotine, without delivering the other harmful carcinogens found in cigarettes, and help to wean a person's body off of nicotine. The typical effects of withdrawal are minimized as one's body adjusts to not smoking and progressively lower doses of nicotine, until the use of the nicotine replacement product is stopped completely.

Nicotine patches release nicotine through the skin and into the bloodstream. Nicotine gum is chewed slowly. It is then stored between the gum and cheek so that the nicotine can be absorbed through the mouth's lining and into the bloodstream. Nicotine lozenges dissolve slowly in the mouth to release nicotine at a slow, sustained rate. Nicotine nasal spray contains small doses of nicotine that are sprayed into the nasal passages and absorbed into the bloodstream. Nicotine inhalers contain nicotine that is inhaled through the mouth and absorbed in the mouth and throat.

Sometimes these products are used in combination, such as the patch with lozenges, which may help some people stay smoke-free.

Smoking Cessation Medications

Type of medication (brand name):

- Nicotine patch and transdermal nicotine (Habitrol, NicoDerm CQ, Nicotrol, ProStep)

- Nicotine gum and lozenges (Nicorette/ Commit)

- Nicotine nasal spray (Nicotrol NS)

- Nicotine inhaler (Nicotrol Inhaler)

Smoking cessation drug Chantix. (Bloomberg via Getty Images)

PRECAUTIONS

Smoking and using nicotine replacement products can be dangerous because nicotine can build up to toxic levels. Since the goal is to quit smoking entirely, one should not smoke while using a nicotine replacement product. One study has shown that the use of nicotine replacement products before the actual quit day could be beneficial. People who combine several quitting strategies often have the most success.

After quitting smoking, the goal is to end the use of the nicotine replacement products as well. It may be appropriate for some people to continue using nicotine replacement products longer than the recommended duration. Some people continue to use them for twelve months or longer. Weaning off the medicine is encouraged, but continuing it is preferable to smoking because cigarette smoke contains many harmful chemicals in addition to nicotine.

The presence of other conditions may affect the use of nicotine replacement products. These conditions include, but are not limited to allergies (nasal spray only); asthma or breathing problems (with inhaler and nasal spray); type 1 diabetes; heart or blood vessel disease; high blood pressure; liver disease; overactive thyroid; stomach ulcer; and recent stroke.

Karen Schroeder Kassel, MS, RD, Med

FURTHER READING

Fiore, Michael C., et al. *Treating Tobacco Use and Dependence: 2008 Update. Public Health Service Clinical Practice Guideline.* Rockville, MD: US DHHS, 2008. Identifies effective, experimentally validated tobacco dependence treatments and practices.

Piper, M. E., et al. "A Randomized Placebo-Controlled Clinical Trial of 5 Smoking Cessation Pharmacotherapies." *Archives of General Psychiatry* 66.11 (2009): 1253-1262. Reports results of a study that tested five methods for smoking cessation. Concludes that the nicotine patch plus lozenge had the most benefit.

Strandberg-Larsen, K., et al. "Use of Nicotine Replacement Therapy During Pregnancy and Stillbirth: A Cohort Study." *BJOG: International Journal of Obstetrics and Gynaecology* 115.11 (2008): 1405-1410. Results from a study which found that the use of nicotine replacement therapy (NRT) during pregnancy does not increase the risk of stillbirth.

WEBSITES OF INTEREST

American Cancer Society
http://www.cancer.org

Smokefree.gov
http://www.smokefree.gov

See also: Nicotine addiction; Smoking; Smoking cessation; Smoking cessation for older adults; Smoking: Short- and long-term effects on the body; Tobacco use disorder

---

Nitrazepam

CATEGORY: Substances

ALSO KNOWN AS: The don; Mogadon; moggies; moogles; nitros

DEFINITION: Nitrazepam is a central nervous system depressant and part of the benzodiazepine family of drugs. Nitrazepam is considered a tranquilizer with sedative and hypnotic properties similar to barbiturates.

STATUS: Legal by prescription in the United States and worldwide

CLASSIFICATION: Schedule IV controlled substance

SOURCE: A synthetic material with no natural source; obtained through prescription

TRANSMISSION ROUTE: Oral ingestion, inhalation, intravenous injection

HISTORY OF USE

Nitrazepam was first synthesized in Europe in 1962 by Hoffman-La Roche Pharmaceuticals following the synthesis of chlordiazepoxide, diazepam, and oxazepam. Nitrazepam became widely prescribed as a sleeping aide in the United Kingdom in the 1970s. Benzodiazepines were viewed as a safe and less habit-forming replacement for barbiturates. By the 1980s, these drugs had become the most commonly prescribed drugs in the world.

Nitrazepam is classified as a schedule IV controlled substance as a drug with lower abuse potential and a legitimate medical use. Marketed as Mogadon, nitrazepam was found to have an abuse profile similar to that of diazepam (Valium). It became popular as a recreational drug with polydrug users and alcoholics to enhance effects of the primary drug, alleviate withdrawal and hangover symptoms, and relieve anxiety related to alcohol use. Although nitrazepam is no longer marketed in some countries, its abuse still remains a concern.

EFFECTS AND POTENTIAL RISKS

Nitrazepam is a central nervous system depressant with sedative and motor-impairing properties. It acts by stimulating the release and binding of gamma-amino butyric acid, a natural nerve-calming agent, to receptors in the brain. This effect causes activity in the brain to slow, inducing sleep, reducing anxiety, and relaxing muscles.

Nitrazepam induces a mellow and peaceful feeling of relaxation and reduced anxiety. These short-term effects are attributed to its properties as a sedative and also include feeling euphoric, energetic, drunken, socially uninhibited, and talkative. Negative short-term effects include lightheadedness, vertigo, and drowsiness, and impaired judgment, speech, coordination, and balance.

Many polydrug users engage in nitrazepam abuse to enhance and prolong the high obtained from other drugs, including heroin. Users of stimulants such as cocaine, amphetamine, and ecstasy take nitrazepam as a "downer" to minimize withdrawal and hangover effects, including anxiety and insomnia.

Long-term nitrazepam use can lead to mental difficulties, depression, chronic fatigue, and aggressive behavior. Nitrazepam dependence often leads to addiction and benzodiazepine withdrawal syndrome, while large doses of benzodiazepine can cause respiratory depression.

Rose Ciulla-Bohling, PhD

FURTHER READING

Kuhn, Cynthia, Scott Swartzwelder, and Wilkie Wilson. *Buzzed: The Straight Facts about the Most Used and Abused Drugs From Alcohol to Ecstasy.* New York: W. W. Norton, 2003.

Longo, Lance P., and Brian Johnson. "Addiction Part I. Benzodiazepines: Side Effects, Abuse Risk, and Alternatives." *American Family Physician* 61.7 (2000): 2121–28. Print.

Vermeeren, Annemiek. "Residual Effects of Hypnotics: Epidemiology and Clinical Implications." *CNS Drugs* 18.5 (2004): 297–328. Print.

WEBSITES OF INTEREST
National Institute on Drug Abuse
http://www.drugabuse.gov/researchreports/Prescription/prescription3.html

US Drug Enforcement Administration
http://www.justice.gov/dea/concern/b.html

See also: Benzodiazepine abuse; Depressants abuse; Depression

Nitrous oxide

CATEGORY: Substances
ALSO KNOWN AS: Buzz bomb; laughing gas
DEFINITION: Nitrous oxide (N_2O) is an inorganic volatile gas that produces chemical vapors.
STATUS: Legal
CLASSIFICATION: Noncontrolled substance
SOURCE: Obtained illicitly from medical and dental practices or, more often, from household or commercial products
TRANSMISSION ROUTE: Inhalation

HISTORY OF USE

Nitrous oxide was first synthesized in the late eighteenth century. By the mid-nineteenth century, it was being used by dentists for pain relief and as an anesthetic. Because of the euphoria it induces, it came to be known as laughing gas. Today, it is used in medical settings for minor procedures that do not require loss of consciousness and to augment other anesthetics and sedatives.

Along with other inhalants, nitrous oxide is used as a recreational drug to induce a psychoactive (mind-altering) effect. Most first-time and frequent users are minors. The most common sources for nitrous oxide are whipped-cream aerosols, for which nitrous oxide is the propellant, and whippits, which are small and tapered cylinders containing nitrous oxide that are used to pressurize reusable, commercial or home-use, whipped-cream dispensers.

EFFECTS AND POTENTIAL RISKS

In clinical settings, nitrous oxide has few adverse effects. Recreational use can have serious consequences, however. Abusers inhale nitrous oxide to obtain a rapid high similar to that obtained when using alcohol. The initial euphoria, lightheadedness, and disinhibition are soon followed by agitation, then drowsiness.

Abusers must inhale frequently to maintain a high. With intense, repeated inhaling, the nitrous oxide replaces oxygen in the lungs. The result is hypoxia, which deprives the whole body, including the brain, of its needed supply of oxygen. An abuser can lose consciousness, stop breathing, and even die. Abusers may inhale the nitrous oxide through a plastic or paper bag or other such device, which can lead to suffocation. Nitrous oxide can damage the outer layer and deeper tissue of the nose, mouth, windpipe, and lungs.

Long-term use of nitrous oxide can break down myelin, a fatty tissue that surrounds and protects some nerve fibers. Loss of myelin can result in muscle spasms and tremors and permanent problems with coordination, walking, and talking. Inhaling nitrous oxide while under the influence of alcohol or ketamine can cause brain toxicity and death.

Ernest Kohlmetz, MA

FURTHER READING
Kuhn, Cynthia, Scott Swartwelder, and Wilkie Wilson. *Buzzed: The Straight Facts about the Most Used and Abused Drugs from Alcohol to Ecstasy*. 3rd ed. New York: W. W. Norton, 2008.
National Survey on Drug Use and Health. "Trends in Adolescent Inhalant Use: 2002 to 2007." *NSDUH Report*, 16 Mar. 2009, 136–38. Print.
Savelli, Lou. *Street Drugs: Pocketguide*. Flushing, NY: Looseleaf Law, 2008.

WEBSITES OF INTEREST
Alliance for Consumer Education, Inhalant Abuse Prevention Program
http://www.inhalant.org

National Institute on Drug Abuse
http://www.drugabuse.gov/publications/infofacts/inhalants

See also: Anesthesia abuse; Inhalants abuse; Recreational drugs

O

Obsessive-compulsive disorder (OCD)

CATEGORY: Psychological and behavioral issues

DEFINITION: Obsessive-compulsive disorder is an anxiety disorder marked by obsessions, or recurrent and persistent thoughts going beyond normal worries about everyday problems, and by compulsions, or those repetitive behaviors or mental acts that one feels they must perform to reduce anxiety and distress or to prevent some dreaded situation. The obsessions and compulsions cause significant distress, consume at minimum one hour each day, interfere with normal functioning, and are unrelated to another diagnosis, to medication, or to an abusive substance.

CHARACTERISTICS AND SUBTYPES

According to various community surveys, obsessive-compulsive disorder (OCD) is highly prevalent; estimates put the general population prevalence at 2 to 4 percent. A common disorder in children and adolescents, OCD has a prevalence rate in that age range of 1 to 2 percent. Males and females are equally affected, although onset is earlier in males and more likely to occur in childhood. Age at onset of OCD symptoms has been variously reported: from 80 percent by eighteen years of age to a mean age at twenty to twenty-five years.

Rather than constituting a single, unitary disorder, OCD may include a spectrum of behaviors and syndromes with overlapping features. To impose order on an unwieldy set of behaviors, a factor analysis based on thousands of participants with OCD identified four distinctive symptom clusters. These behaviors are placed in the following groups:

- washing, cleaning, fear of contamination
- repeated checking, religious obsessions, intrusive aggressive or sexual thoughts and images
- hoarding
- ordering, counting, arranging, and an intense need for symmetry

Persons with OCD generally have difficulties with tasks of executive functioning, or the ability to formulate goals or strategies and adapt to changing circumstances. In tests that measure executive functioning, responses of persons with OCD are delayed and repetitive compared with responses of control subjects.

Multiple subtypes characterize OCD, some of which are thought to be genetically determined. Familial OCD, for example, differs from sporadic OCD. Familial cases generally have an earlier onset and lesser response to treatment. Comorbid disorders—occurring simultaneously in the same person—are more likely in familial OCD. Comorbid Tourette's syndrome, or a chronic tic disorder, may accompany early-onset OCD. First-degree relatives of OCD probands, even without criteria for OCD, also have an increased risk for these disorders. Depression and other anxiety disorders also frequently co-occur.

One of the intriguing findings of family studies has been the connection between the onset of OCD, a tic disorder, or both, which closely follows Group A streptococcal infection in children. The sequential occurrence has been given the name PANDAS (pediatric autoimmune neuropsychiatric disorders associated with streptococcal infections). An abnormality in cell-mediated immunity has been proposed to explain the abrupt development of OCD.

Investigators have long noted clinical, familial, and other similarities between OCD and a group of disorders classified as impulse-control disorders. These include pathologic gambling and kleptomania. Proposals to incorporate impulse-control disorders within a newly categorized obsessive-compulsive spectrum have gained support.

THE NEUROBIOLOGICAL BASIS OF OCD

It is generally accepted that OCD can be traced to aberrant circuitry in the brain, but the clinical heterogeneity of OCD has hampered efforts to come up with a definitive hypothesis. Information in the form of nerve impulses normally passes in a loop from frontal lobes of the cerebral cortex to subcortical structures deep within the brain and back again. Functional neuroimaging studies have implicated circuits within this loop as dysfunctional.

Distinctive symptom complexes and subtypes may be mediated by different, albeit contiguous, circuitry. Because the circuits participate in a range of behavioral and cognitive functions, dysfunction can cause deficits in attention, learning, and executive function and changes in personality and mood. The circuits also are subject to excitatory and inhibitory neurotransmitters, any of which may contribute to the pathology of OCD.

In comparing gray-matter volumes between persons with OCD and healthy control subjects, findings have been largely inconsistent, perhaps because of heterogeneous recruited samples. Significant reductions and increases in gray matter have been found in areas of the cortex thought to be related to OCD. White-matter volume abnormalities in both directions have also been reported.

Although OCD is classified as an anxiety disorder, some of its features resemble addictive behaviors. Abnormally activated circuitry in the brain associated with OCD is also concerned with reward processing; compulsions in OCD may function as rewards by relieving anxiety, thereby fostering psychological dependence. Drawing a diagnostic line between OCD and substance addiction or such impulse-control disorders as pathologic gambling is difficult. They may share the same hyperactive brain circuits and share behavior characterized by disinhibition.

THE GENETIC BASIS OF OCD

As yet undefined, the genetic basis of OCD also mirrors its clinical heterogeneity. Little doubt exists that OCD has genetic determinants, but none has priority. Basic questions remain to be answered, including, is there a major gene responsible or do multiple genes interact to cause the disorder? Does each phenotype have its own distinctive genetic basis? How much influence does environmental stress exert?

That multiple cases of OCD commonly occur in families has been known since the 1930s; early studies, using the techniques then available, focused on family inheritance patterns and on twin pairs. In family history studies, parents of children with OCD often were found to meet OCD criteria, and first-degree relatives had an increased rate of obsessive traits.

Twin studies offer strong evidence that OCD is genetically based. Consistently higher concordance rates are observed in monozygotic (identical) twins than in dizygotic (fraternal) twins. In one such study, the concordance rate was 87 percent for monozygotic twins and 47 percent for dizygotic twins. The higher rate still leaves substantial room for environmental factors in the development of OCD. For example, susceptibility to OCD following streptococcal infection may combine a genetically determined vulnerability in immune response with the infection acting as an environmental trigger.

Candidate genes that have biologically plausible roles in OCD have been the subjects of intensive research. Candidate genes are genes that function primarily in neurotransmission of, for example, serotonin, dopamine, glutamate, and GABA, the major inhibitory neurotransmitter.

The efficacy of selective serotonin reuptake inhibitors (SSRIs), which have achieved some success in treating persons with OCD, accounts for the currency of a serotonin-related dysfunction as a cause of OCD; genes related to serotonergic neurotransmission have been widely researched. Glutamate, another neurotransmitter implicated in OCD, also is the subject of research scrutiny. (The neuronal glutamate transporter gene was found to be associated with OCD.) Altered glutamatergic transmission is implicated too, based on converging clinical, neuroimaging, and candidate gene studies. A major excitatory neurotransmitter, glutamate participates in such processes as learning and memory.

The genetic basis of OCD is likely to be as complex as the clinical spectrum and the neuropathologic underpinnings. Genetic heterogeneity might account for childhood versus adult onset, familial versus sporadic forms, and the increased rate of comorbid disorders in families.

TREATMENT AND THERAPY

Treatment delay is common in OCD. Patients may hide the condition or try to avoid the stigma attached to seeking treatment. Two treatments are considered first-line: SSRIs, which are antidepressants, and cognitive-behavioral therapy (CBT), which aims to prevent exposure and response to OCD triggers. Clomipramine, another antidepressant medication, also has been effective. Neuroimaging studies have shown that abnormally increased activity in brain structures related to OCD decreased after successful treatment with SSRIs and with behavioral therapy.

About 30 to 40 percent of persons with OCD do not respond to SSRIs, and atypical antipsychotics have been used as augmenting agents when response to SSRIs is deficient. In children and youths with OCD, the most likely initial treatment will be CBT. Other drug classes, such as opioid antagonists and anti-inflammatory agents, have been tried, but with limited success. Drug strategies under investigation are based on expanding knowledge of neurologic mechanisms underlying the development of OCD.

Judith Weinblatt

FURTHER READING

Baer, Lee. *The Imp of the Mind: Exploring the Silent Epidemic of Obsessive Bad Thoughts.* New York: Penguin, 2001. The author, who treats OCD, describes the differences between routine worries and OCD in an accessible, reader-friendly style.

Gilliam, Christina M., and David F. Tolin. "Compulsive Hoarding." *Bulletin of the Menninger Clinic* 74.2 (2010): 93–121. Part of a special issue on compulsive hoarding, this article describes the cognitive-behavioral therapy model and treatment of hoarding.

McGrath, Patrick B. *The OCD Answerbook.* Naperville, IL: Sourcebooks, 2007. Written by a cognitive-behavioral therapist, this book responds to common questions with straightforward, practical answers. Includes a bibliography and an index.

WEBSITES OF INTEREST

International OCD Foundation
http://www.ocfoundation.org

National Institute of Mental Health
http://www.nimh.nih.gov/health/topics/obsessive-compulsive-disorder-ocd

See also: Behavioral addictions: Overview; Cleanliness addiction; Compulsions; Hoarding; Sex addiction

Opioid abuse

Category: Substance abuse
Definition: Opioid abuse occurs when the compulsive use of opioids harms a person's health or social functioning. It also occurs when a person is addicted to or physically dependent on opioids. Opioids are a class of drugs made from opium, as well as synthetic or semi-synthetic drugs that resemble these opium-based drugs. Examples of these drugs are heroin, morphine, codeine, hydrocodone, oxycodone, and fentanyl. Opioids are also often referred to as narcotics.

CAUSES

Opioids produce a quick, intense feeling of pleasure (euphoria), followed by a sense of well-being and calm drowsiness. Opioid drugs produce their effects by binding to the opioid receptors of the central nervous system, which respond to the body's intrinsic opioids known as endorphins to naturally block or suppress the sensation of pain. When opioid drugs are used repeatedly, the level of natural endorphins in the body is diminished and the brain is likely to become dependent on the drug. Opioids are highly addictive.

RISK FACTORS

Risk factors that increase the chances of developing opioid abuse include a history of abuse of other types of drugs and the presence of a psychological disorder. Men between the ages of twenty and twenty-nine are also at a greater risk of developing opioid abuse.

SYMPTOMS

There are several symptoms of opioid abuse. One symptom is tolerance, or the need to increase the dose in order to achieve the same effect. Another symptom is increased amounts of time spent drug-seeking. Other symptoms include the interference of drug or drug-seeking behavior with social, occupational, or school functioning; the continued use of drugs despite social, legal, occupational, or interpersonal problems stemming from drug use; desire or efforts made to decrease or stop drug use without success; and withdrawal, the adverse symptoms that occur when the drug is not taken.

Symptoms of withdrawal are many, such as aching, fever, sweating, chills, and craving. Some other symptoms of withdrawal are diarrhea, nausea, and vomiting; sleeplessness; abdominal pain and muscle aches; restlessness; tearing eyes and runny nose; yawning; panic; and irritability.

SCREENING AND DIAGNOSIS

A diagnosis by a medical expert will include questions about the symptoms of opioid abuse as well as questions pertaining to a patient's medical history. A physical examination is also performed. Urine and blood tests may also be conducted.

TREATMENT AND THERAPY

The treatment options for opioid abuse consist of rehabilitation programs, support groups, behavioral therapy, and medications. In rehab programs, people with opioid abuse stay in a controlled environment for six to twelve months, during which they learn how to return to a drug-free lifestyle. It may be necessary to be in a detoxification center initially, where the side effects of drug withdrawal can be safely managed. One support group, Narcotics Anonymous, is a twelve-step program that has a good record for supporting people who are recovering from addiction to opioid drugs.

Behavioral therapy is another valuable treatment option. Behaviorual therapy is designed to modify people's attitudes and behaviors related to opioid abuse. In therapy, a person will learn how to avoid and cope with situations in which he or she is most likely to use drugs.

Medicines that have been shown to be effective in reducing withdrawal symptoms are methadone, buprenorphine (Subutex), and buprenorphine and naloxone (Suboxone). When combined with therapy, these medicines may help an individual adjust to not using drugs. They may also help an individual go through withdrawal at home, rather than at an inpatient facility.

PREVENTION

The best way to prevent this condition is to never use opioids. For persons taking prescription opioid medications for pain management, it is important to use the drug only at the prescribed dosages in order to prevent the development of drug dependence.

Krisha McCoy, MS

FURTHER READING

Edlund, M., et al. "Risk Factors for Clinically Recognized Opioid Abuse and Dependence Among Veterans Using Opioids for Chronic Non-Cancer Pain." *Pain* 129.3 (2007): 355-362. Results of a study conducted in light of the need to balance the risk of opioid abuse with the benefits of pain relief.

Hall, Wayne, Chris Doran, Louisa Degenhardt, and Donald Shepard. "Illicit Opiate Abuse." *Disease Control Priorities in Developing Countries.* 2nd ed. Ed. D. T. Jamison, et al. Washington, DC, DC: World Bank, 2006. Covers the nature, causes, and health consequences of opioid use; its contribution to the global burden of disease; interventions for opioid dependence; and its relevance to developing countries.

"Mind Over Matter: Opiates." *National Institute on Drug Abuse: NIDA for Teens.* National Institutes of Health. 2012. Web. 30 Mar. 2012. An overview of opiates for teenagers, including how the brain responds to opiates, how opiates work, how a person can become addicted, and other facts.

WEBSITES OF INTEREST

American Council for Drug Education
http://www.acde.org/

National Institute on Drug Abuse
http://www.drugabuse.gov/

See also: Codeine; Fentanyl; Heroin; Hydrocodone; Methadone; Morphine; Naltrexone; Narcotics abuse; Narcotics: Short- and long-term effects on the body; Opium; Oxycodone; Painkiller abuse; Vicodin

---

Opium

CATEGORY: Substances

DEFINITION: Opium is a narcotic drug produced from the poppy plant that binds to specific opioid receptors in the central nervous system to relieve pain.

STATUS: Legal with a prescription; illegal as the street drug heroin

CLASSIFICATION: Schedule I and II controlled substances

SOURCE: Dried latex of the outer skin of the poppy plant (*Papaver somniferum*)

TRANSMISSION ROUTE: Oral, intravenous, intramuscular, parenteral, transdermal, rectal, inhalant

HISTORY OF USE

Opium is processed in a manner that has changed little from fifth-century methods. Ancient peoples too used the plant to alleviate pain and anxiety and to perform minor surgeries. Early civilizations wrote about the healing powers of opium, as did such early physicians as Dioscorides, Galen, and Avicenna. Throughout these times, written records indicate that opium was considered primarily a healing tool and not a recreational drug.

China was the next great civilization to be introduced to the opium plant through trade with the Islamic world around the fifteenth century. The Chinese also used opium for medicinal purposes, but as opium use spread, people began to find a new use for the plant. The gummy rolled-up balls of the poppy plant, which resemble clay, were smoked in special pipes that circulated air under the opium balls. The result was a euphoric and hallucinogenic experience. While smoking opium was by no means epidemic, it was popular and highly addictive.

By 1900, Friedrich Sertürner had isolated morphine from opium, Pierre Jean Robiquet had discovered codeine, and opium and opium derivatives were becoming the most popular medicines in the United States. Produced by Bayer, Heroin (the brand name) was given to children as a cough syrup. Laudanum, a tincture of opium, was one of the most highly prescribed medicines, primarily to middle-class women for menstrual pains, creating countless addicts. Soon, the Harrison Act of 1914 was passed to regulate opiate use in the United States.

Opiates now are integrated into medicine as necessary tools for pain control. However, physicians are facing more and more regulation in prescribing these drugs. Strict regulation of opioid drugs has gained support due to the rising rates of abuse by a small group of physicians and by the alarming rates of prescription medication abuse. This regulation has affected patient care, as physicians, especially those who care for persons with chronic pain and those who provide end-of-life or palliative care, often fear prescribing opiates. However, studies have shown that the first group, people in chronic pain, has little to no risk of becoming addicted to pain medications. For the second group, those needing palliative care, physicians argue that denying dying patients pain medicine for fear they will get addicted goes against the Hippocratic oath. Even physicians who do not treat patients needing such care tend to underprescribe pain medications. Studies show that about 50 percent of patients report that they are not receiving adequate treatment for their pain.

Afghan poppy farmers extract raw opium from poppy heads in fields in Zhera district, and west of Kandahar city, Afghanistan. (Reuters/Landov)

EFFECTS AND POTENTIAL RISKS

Opiates work by disrupting the signals of pain sent to the brain from various channels. Some signals move through the nervous system. Other signaling systems are chemical and involve a biochemical cascade. One of the reasons why opiates are so effective is that they can block pain at many of these points.

Opiates are quick acting: A patient in severe pain will feel instant relief through the aid of intravenous morphine, for example. Oral medication takes about twenty to thirty minutes before acting but is extremely effective at controlling pain.

The most common side effects of opiates are constipation, sedation, nausea and vomiting, respiratory distress, tolerance, and addiction. For persons with cardiac or pulmonary disease, careful monitoring is necessary to check the patient's breathing. This is especially relevant in hospice care, where patients may be receiving high doses of morphine, which can severely impair breathing.

Detoxification from any opiate, whether a street drug like heroin or a legally prescribed medication, is extremely difficult and can, for some people, be life threatening if not performed under medical supervision. Any person taking large doses of an opiate who attempts to detox can suffer seizures, prolonged insomnia, severe depression, suicidal thoughts, anxiety, and panic attacks. Physical symptoms include vomiting, shaking, anorexia, fever, and chills. It is recommended that a person who needs help with any kind of opium addiction seek the help of a physician.

S. M. Willis, MS, MA

FURTHER READING

Booth, Martin. *Opium: A History.* New York: St. Martin's, 1999. A comprehensive history of the oldest known drug used by humankind.

Harris, Nancy, ed. *Opiates.* Farmington, MI: Greenhaven, 2005. Dozens of entries covering the history and abuse of opiates and the treatment of opiate addiction, among other topics.

Kenjhan, Refik. "Opioids and Pain." *Clinical and Experimental Pharmacology and Physiology* 22 (1995): 397–403. Print. A description of the physiological pathways of pain to the brain.

Nicholson, Bruce. "Responsible Prescribing of Opioids for the Management of Chronic Pain." *Drugs* 63 (2003): 17–30. Print. Assessing the challenge of finding appropriate pain relief for patients with chronic pain and patients who are terminal.

WEBSITES OF INTEREST

National Institute on Drug Abuse
http://www.drugabuse.gov

WebMD: Narcotic Abuse
http://www.emedicinehealth.com/narcotic_abuse

See also: Codeine; Fentanyl; Heroin; Hydrocodone; Methadone; Morphine; Naltrexone; Narcotics abuse; Narcotics: Short- and long-term effects on the body; Opium; Oxycodone; Painkiller abuse; Vicodin

Outpatient treatment

CATEGORY: Treatment
ALSO KNOWN AS: Ambulatory care
DEFINITION: Two treatment options are available to those in need of medical care: inpatient treatment and outpatient treatment. Outpatient treatment does not offer either twenty-four-hour care at a live-in facility or overnight hospitalization. Outpatient services include wellness and prevention treatments such as counseling services, diagnosis such as laboratory tests, treatments such as dialysis and chemotherapy, and rehabilitation services such as drug and alcohol addiction treatment.

WELLNESS AND PREVENTION SERVICES

Michael Mulvihill, a health care executive, defined health promotion as "A set of organized activities and systematic interventions, offered through corporations/worksites, managed care organizations, and governmental/community agencies, whose primary purposes are to provide health education, identify modifiable health risks, and influence health behavior changes."

Health promotion also involves outpatient preventive treatments and services. Children, for example, receive immunizations that prevent them from contracting illnesses such as polio, measles, and mumps. During annual doctor visits, physicians chart children's annual growth, make parents aware of age-specific milestones, and offer nutrition and fitness information as a way to prevent the rising rates of child diabetes and obesity.

As men and women age, more preventive outpatient screenings become necessary. For example, sexually active women should have an annual Pap test to screen for cervical cancer. An obstetrician or gynecologist usually performs this test. Once women reach age forty years, they should have an annual mammogram to screen for breast cancer. Some outpatient facilities specialize in this screening. However, some obstetricians and gynecologists also offer this service in their offices.

Women age fifty years and older also should be tested for colorectal cancer, and women age sixty-five years and older should receive bone density tests to screen for osteoporosis. Men's weight, cholesterol, and blood pressure should be tested annually. Once men reach age fifty years, they too should be screened for colorectal cancer and for prostate cancer.

Michael O'Donnell of the *American Journal of Health Promotion* defined wellness as "the science and art of helping people change their lifestyle to move toward a state of optimal health." Many counselors assist people with the different areas of wellness. Counselors offer their services in schools, hospitals, and rehabilitation facilities. They also work in private and group practices. Counselors often specialize in a certain area, such as marriage and family, guidance and career, rehabilitation, mental health, and substance abuse.

According to the National Institute of Mental Health, about 26 percent of adults in the United States have some type of mental illness. Mental illness includes anxiety disorder, attention deficit disorder, bipolarity, borderline personality disorder, depression, eating disorder, obsessive-compulsive disorder, panic disorder, post-traumatic stress disorder, schizophrenia, and social phobia. Counselors, psychotherapists, and psychiatrists often treat these mental illnesses using a combination of therapy, counseling, and medication. Most people with mental illness are treated on an outpatient basis.

DIAGNOSIS

To treat patients effectively, health care professionals need much information about those patients. One way to gather this information is through laboratory testing. Most diagnostic tests are done on an outpatient basis and include blood tests, prenatal tests, X-rays, magnetic resonance imaging, and sleep disorder testing. Conducting such outpatient tests allows physicians to determine the overall health of a patient; to examine bones, lungs, blood vessels, and other internal organs; and to diagnose diseases and illnesses such as multiple sclerosis, brain tumors, torn ligaments, tendonitis, and cancer. These tests are often conducted at hospitals or special testing centers. However, an overnight stay is unnecessary. Many blood collection centers do not even require an appointment.

TREATMENT TYPES

Outpatient treatment ranges from an orthopedist setting a broken bone and applying a cast to actual surgery. More than 60 percent of all surgeries are performed on an outpatient basis. Many experts predict that this number will rise to 75 percent by 2017. Much of this can be attributed to the development of better and more efficient medical tools and technologies.

Noninvasive surgery requires minimal postoperative care, allowing many patients to have surgery and return home the same day. For example, pacemaker implantations and tonsillectomies (tonsil removal) are now considered outpatient procedures. Other outpatient procedures are acupuncture or chiropractic treatment, cataract removal, hip replacement, and laser eye surgery and vision correction. Continual treatments such as dialysis for kidney function and chemotherapy, a treatment for cancer, are normally also performed on an outpatient basis. These treatments usually take several hours to complete but do not require an overnight stay in a hospital or medical facility.

Another reason outpatient care has become more common is the rising costs of medical care. Postoperative care is expensive, so many health insurance companies have categorized more and more surgeries as outpatient procedures. However, even when an insurance company deems a procedure to be outpatient in nature, other factors, such as the patient's personal medical history and the overall invasiveness of the surgery, should be considered.

REHABILITATION SERVICES

According to HealthSouth, a health care provider specializing in rehabilitation, rehabilitation is "specialized healthcare dedicated to improving, maintaining, or restoring physical strength, cognition, and mobility with maximized results. Typically, rehabilitation helps people gain greater independence after illness, injury, or surgery."

Rehabilitation services address a patient's physical and psychological needs. For example, there are many reasons why a person would need to restore the use of his or her muscles. Perhaps an arm has been in a cast for many weeks, or a person just had orthopedic surgery on a limb or joint and his or her mobility has been compromised. Maybe a person suffered a serious accident and his or her mobility has changed dramatically.

Outpatient physical therapy helps patients regain and improve movement and flexibility. Physical therapists often combine massage techniques with therapeutic exercises to improve movement of the foot and ankle, lower back, shoulders, neck, hips, and other areas of the body.

Occupational therapy is another area of rehabilitation and assists in improving a patient's daily living skills. Occupational therapists may assist children with disabilities so they can attend school and participate in social gatherings. Occupational therapists also assist people who are recovering from an injury or accident so they can regain their skills. They also assist adults with physical and cognitive changes. Occupational therapists often evaluate a person's environment and adapt it to fit that person's needs.

Speech and language therapy helps to improve a patient's speech, language, communication, and swallowing. Therapists in this area often work in outpatient facilities such as community health centers, hospitals, schools, children's day-care centers, jails and prisons, and in private practices. Speech and language pathologists work with babies, children, and adults.

Outpatient Treatment for Addictions and Substance Abuse

Persons suffering from an addiction, such as a drug or alcohol addiction, may require rehabilitation to overcome their dependencies and resume a normal life. Rehabilitation for addiction often involves a series of steps.

First, patients must go through detoxification. This is the process of removing toxic substances from the body. Even in an outpatient program, this first step is most often done on an inpatient basis because many addicts experience withdrawal symptoms, such as tremors, paranoia, and depression, and they require continuous medical attention.

Many addicts also have a mental illness. Therefore, many types of therapy are used to help the addicted individual deal with whatever situation has most likely contributed to the addiction. Cognitive therapy, family therapy, and group therapy are often used to help addicts understand their patterns of maladaptive behavior and to teach them better strategies for identifying and coping with the situations that trigger the addictive behavior. Medications such as Campral may be used to help people with alcohol addictions. Suboxone may be used to assist drug addicts by reducing withdrawal symptoms and cravings. Therapists also may introduce a twelve-step program, which involves group therapy and support to keep addicts clean and sober.

Outpatient treatment is most often used for persons who come from a somewhat stable environment. For example, someone who is married and has a steady job would benefit from outpatient treatment. However, a celebrity who travels from city to city or someone who lives in an extremely unstable, chaotic environment would most benefit from an inpatient program. Additionally, someone with a severe psychiatric illness would benefit from an inpatient program.

Challenges

In a study conducted by the *Journal of the American Medical Association* in 2011, the number one problem related to outpatient care facilities is diagnostic error. Additionally, physicians in outpatient facilities must rely on the patient to follow the directions they receive for care. Physicians who work in inpatient settings, such as hospitals, have more control over their patients' care because the care extends for a longer period. Furthermore, patients often see different providers in the outpatient setting, leading to misunderstandings about the patient's diagnoses and treatment.

Gina Kuchta

Further Reading

Gottheil, Edward, ed. *Intensive Outpatient Treatment for the Addictions.* New York: Haworth Medical, 1997. Provides descriptions, discussions, and outcomes of intensive outpatient treatment and compares traditional methods of treatment with intensive outpatient methods.

Jonas, Steven, et al. *Jonas and Kovner's Health Care Delivery in the United States.* 10th ed. New York:

Springer, 2011. A textbook for graduate and advanced graduate students presenting the critical issues and challenges surrounding health care in the United States.

Shi, Leiyu, and Douglas A. Singh. *Delivering Health Care in America: A Systems Approach*. Burlington, MA: Jones, 2012. Textbook discussing how the health care system in the United States is organized and structured.

WEBSITES OF INTEREST

American Rehabilitation Counseling Association
http://www.arcaweb.org

Betty Ford Center
http://www.bettyfordcenter.org

National Institute on Drug Abuse
http://www.drugabuse.gov

Substance Abuse and Mental Health Services Administration
http://www.samhsa.gov

Urgent Care Association of America
http://www.ucaoa.org

See also: Alcohol abuse and alcoholism: Overview; Drug abuse and addiction: Overview; Mental illness; Outpatient Treatment; Rehabilitation programs

Overdose

CATEGORY: Health issues and physiology
ALSO KNOWN AS: Toxicity
DEFINITION: An overdose involves an acute ingestion of an excessive amount of a drug beyond the recommended quantity. Overdoses may be intentional or accidental and are especially likely when the substance content of a drug is unknown or when multiple drugs are taken together. Overdoses are common with drugs of abuse, such as heroin, opioids, and barbiturates. Though overdoses can be fatal, they are also preventable.

CAUSES

Overdoses result from taking too much of a dangerous substance, whether an illicit substance of abuse or medications (such as prescriptions and over-the-counter drugs) approved by the US Food and Drug Administration. For example, accidental overdose can occur when a person mistakenly ingests a repeated, or double, dose of a prescription. Excessive drug ingestion can occur with a single drug or with a combination of drugs that have overlapping effects.

Fatal overdoses primarily involve dangerous drug mixtures, such as concomitant alcohol and benzodiazepine use, or a mixture of heroin and benzodiazepine. Combinations of alcohol with street drugs appear to be the most deadly.

The amount of a drug needed to cause an overdose varies by person, by type of drug, and by substance purity or potency. For example, increased potency of heroin products in the early twenty-first century compared with their historical content resulted in greater rates of heroin-associated fatal overdose.

Prescription-associated overdoses most often involve sedatives or painkillers, such as hydrocodone, methadone, oxycodone, and oxymorphone. In 2007, there were twenty-seven thousand accidental overdoses in the United States. Prescription drug abuse is a growing cause of fatal overdoses, particularly as a result of opioid misuse. According to the Centers for Disease Control and Prevention (CDC), overdose deaths increased from 1999 to 2004 because of painkillers, cocaine, and sedatives, and not because of heroin or methamphetamine.

RISK FACTORS

The populations at greatest risk for overdose are illicit drug users, youth, and elderly prescription-drug users. The risk of overdose increases when multiple drugs are prescribed or when illicit drugs are mixed with each other or with alcohol. In addition, risks increase in recovering drug users who experience relapse because they develop a lower tolerance to the drug before returning to the same level of substance abuse.

Long-term illicit drug users tend to overdose because they are overconfident; they often use drugs in solitary settings, which presents added danger and risk. Taking drugs by inhalation or injection is also more likely to result in toxicity because drug concentrations reach the brain more rapidly.

Painkiller overdose is associated with risk populations distinct from those of illicit drug use. Prescription misuse and overdose most commonly develop in middle-aged persons and with people living in poverty or in rural areas, such as the South or Midwest areas of the United States. White people overdose with prescription drugs more often than do black people, and Native Americans overdose more often than do whites. Long-term opioid users or people who receive painkiller prescriptions from multiple prescribers are more likely to receive unsafe drug quantities and to ingest toxic dosages. People with existing mental health problems, such as depression, also experience greater rates of overdose with prescription or illicit drugs.

Symptoms

Side effects of overdoses are often particular to the type of drug ingested, although some signs of overdose are consistent with general toxicity. Common symptoms of excessive substance use include nausea, vomiting, prolonged sleep, lack of consciousness, snoring and gurgling, blue lips, and blue nails. Additional symptoms relate to sedative or stimulatory effects on nervous system and organ functions. These symptoms include abnormal breathing, slurred speech, poor coordination, slow or fast pulse, high or low body temperature, large or small pupil size, flushing and perspiration, nonresponsive sleep, violent outbursts, and delusions or hallucinations.

Typically, overdose symptoms mimic and extend the clinical effect of the drug, whether the drug is sedating or stimulatory. For example, such stimulants as cocaine can cause seizures and heart arrhythmias, whereas sedating benzodiazepines can induce coma. However, paradoxical effects are possible, and toxic amounts of both sedatives and stimulants impair crucial breathing functions.

Screening and Diagnosis

Identification of people at risk for substance abuse or prescription misuse is critical to screening for potential overdose. These users have lower inhibitions about drug dosing, blunted emotional responses and impulse control to guide appropriate drug use, and lower likelihood of having social contacts that discourage inappropriate drug use. Although identification of a substance abuse problem does not guarantee an ingestion of toxic dosages, it does lead to active monitoring of a risk group.

Polydrug use is a large overdose risk factor that can be identified in a screening of patient-specific prescription habits or pharmacy refill rates. Alcohol is the most frequent substance identified in combination overdoses, so screening for levels of alcohol use before prescribing high-risk medications is another useful way to identify overdose likelihood.

Recognition and diagnosis of an overdose in the emergency room setting should be done quickly for appropriate care. Considerations include consciousness, shallow breathing, and slurred speech as traditional signs of substance abuse. Blood tests should be performed to screen for substances in the system so that the appropriate treatment can be employed to counteract damaging symptoms. Diagnosis of a drug overdose is particularly challenging when the patient is unconscious and the substances remain unknown.

In a community setting, early signs that can indicate an increased risk for potential drug overdoses include frequent morning hangovers from alcohol abuse, red streaks in the whites of the eyes, purchase of large drug quantities, appetite changes, and new sleep patterns. Extreme behavior changes, such as hostility, depression and mood swings, secretive actions, confusion, and social isolation, likewise represent uncontrolled drug use that can lead to overdose.

Treatment and Therapy

Effective treatment hinges on early recognition of the overdose. Treatment is often administered in an emergency room setting and can be complicated by the inability to identify the ingested drugs and by combative patients who intentionally ingested excessive quantities.

Care after an actual or suspected overdose begins with basic functions. Any airway barriers must be cleared and oxygen levels should be restored and maintained during treatment. Intravenous fluids may be necessary to assist with electrolyte balance; monitoring of vital organs, such as the cardiac and pulmonary systems, confirms stability and treatment response and can aid in diagnosing what drugs were involved.

As an overdosed patient achieves stable heart and lung function, considerations begin for substance removal. Gastric lavage and activated charcoal remove excessive medication from the stomach through the esophagus or through binding within the stomach, respectively. However, these methods are not recommended for every substance, and they do not fully remove drugs, which are already circulating in the blood. In some circumstances, hemodialysis can be used to filter substances from the blood and to prevent kidney damage. Infrequently, antidotes to specific substances cause rapid resolution of overdose symptoms. For example, the benzodiazepine antagonist flumazenil blocks toxic amounts of benzodiazepine at their receptors to counteract overdose symptoms. The drug naloxone is an opioid antagonist that displaces narcotics from the opioid receptor site, and is used as an antidote to opioid overdose.

To supplement emergency treatment, psychological needs might be evaluated, especially for cases of intentional overdose. Mental health counseling or behavioral care should be implemented when necessary to prevent future attempts at overdose.

PREVENTION

The CDC encourages state and federal tracking of overdose trends and increased education about these trends to improve substance abuse and overdose prevention efforts. Public health strategies emphasize avoidance of prescription drug sharing and awareness of available prescription-medication disposal programs. The Office of National Drug Control Policy enforces initiatives to restrict illicit drug use through education, drug tracking, and law enforcement options.

Known illicit drug users should be advised about the greater risks of overdose during withdrawal or relapse periods after tolerance diminishes. Prevention of accidental overdose in particular hinges on counseling and communication.

Overdose of prescription medications has the most potential for prevention success. Limiting access to the highest-risk drugs, providing proactive mental health care, reducing insurance coverage of multiple painkillers, and increasing health professional awareness and education all support lower rates of overdose in the general population. Trained health professionals can identify at-risk patients, such as those with multiple prescriptions, before an overdose occurs. With increased prescription drug monitoring and pain clinic oversight, professionals and patients can minimize the occurrences of prescription drug overdose.

Nicole M. Van Hoey, PharmD

FURTHER READING

Paulozzi, Leonard, et al. "CDC Grand Rounds: Prescription Drug Overdoses—A US Epidemic." *MMWR Weekly* 61.1 (2012): 10–13. Print. Reports on growing trends of prescription misuse and the safety effects of excessive use, particularly of opioid painkillers. Identifies target demographics and national and health professional initiatives to prevent overdose and death.

Shannon, Michael W., Stephen W. Borron, and Michael J. Burns, eds. *Haddad and Winchester's Clinical Management of Poisoning and Drug Overdose.* 4th ed. Philadelphia: Saunders, 2007. Professional reference guide on the thorough treatment of all types of toxic drug ingestion, often in an emergency setting. Identifies practical suggestions for care combined with expert background reasoning for the methods.

Substance Abuse and Mental Health Administration. "Drug Abuse Warning Network, 2006: National Estimates of Drug-Related Emergency Department Visits." Aug. 2008. Web. 3 Apr. 2012. http://www.samhsa.gov/data/DAWN/files/ED2006/DAWN2k6ED.htm. Analysis of emergency treatment of prescription misuse, combination substance overdoses, and intentional overdose treatment.

WEBSITES OF INTEREST

Centers for Disease Control and Prevention
http://www.cdc.gov/homeandrecreationalsafety/rxbrief

MedlinePlus: "Drug Abuse First Aid"
http://www.nlm.nih.gov/medlineplus/ency/article/000016.htm

See also: Alcohol poisoning; Emergency treatment; Naloxone

Overeaters Anonymous

CATEGORY: Treatment

DEFINITION: Overeaters Anonymous (OA) is a twelve-step recovery program based on the methods and philosophy of Alcoholics Anonymous. OA members profess that they are "powerless over food" and that their "lives have become unmanageable." The purpose of the group is not to promote weight loss and dieting but to support inner changes and daily actions that remove the feeling that one must consume excess and addictive foods.

DATE: 1960

BACKGROUND

Overeaters Anonymous (OA) was founded by Rozanne S., Jo S., and Bernice S. in 1960 after Rozanne had attended a Gamblers Anonymous (GA) meeting to support a friend. Rozanne discovered that the members' stories of compulsive gambling mirrored her own story of compulsive overeating. She recognized that the twelve steps and twelve traditions of recovery that were the foundation of Alcoholics Anonymous (AA) and adopted by GA could be applied to recovery from compulsive overeating.

The OA program is based on twelve steps, twelve traditions, and eight tools of recovery. The twelve steps are almost identical to those of AA. In AA literature, the word *alcohol* can be replaced with *trigger food* and the word *drinking* can be replaced with *compulsive overeating* to make the principles applicable to OA members. However, an important distinction between the two groups is that although AA members can abstain from all alcohol, OA members cannot abstain from all food.

Persons who wish to disengage from compulsive overeating must identify and refrain from ingesting specific food ingredients that trigger the compulsion. The most common trigger foods are wheat and sugar. In addition, compulsive overeating may be triggered by compulsive food behaviors, such as the need to empty a package of food or the need to finish food on a plate rather than leaving a portion or discarding food. In 2009, OA defined *abstinence* as "the action of refraining from compulsive eating and compulsive food behaviors."

The twelve traditions, nearly identical to those of AA, are guidelines for conducting meetings and sustaining the principles of the organization. Each of the twelve traditions has a related spiritual principle: unity, trust, identity, autonomy, purpose, solidarity, responsibility, fellowship, structure, neutrality, anonymity, and spirituality.

By using the eight tools of recovery, members are better able to achieve and maintain abstinence from compulsive overeating. The first tool is a plan of eating. (OA does not promote a specific dietary plan but encourages members to develop a personal eating plan after consulting a physician or dietitian and identifying trigger foods to avoid.) The second tool is sponsorship. A sponsor is an experienced OA member who helps a new member understand and work the twelve steps. The third tool is the OA meeting, which provides regular support from other OA members and helps members to overcome the isolation and shame that impede recovery.

The fourth tool of recovery is the telephone. Members are encouraged to ask for help from one another, especially when emotions are overwhelming. The fifth tool is writing as a way of examining one's reactions to difficult situations and discovering alternative coping mechanisms. The sixth tool is literature, particularly the publications of OA and the *Big Book* of AA. Such reading material provides insight into the nature and consequences of compulsive overeating and provides hope for recovery.

The seventh tool is anonymity, which protects members from gossip as they express their pain and struggles and also asserts equality among members. The eighth tool is service. Members are asked to sustain the organization with acts such as welcoming new members, setting up and cleaning up meeting rooms, and sharing news of upcoming OA events.

OA is a nonprofit organization. All funding comes from the sale of OA literature and voluntary contributions collected at meetings. The program has not changed over time. The demographics of its members have changed only as a reflection of trends in the general population. More participants today have college degrees, more work full-time, and more are divorced.

MISSION AND GOALS

The official literature of OA states that "Our primary purpose is to abstain from compulsive overeating and to carry this message of recovery to those who still suffer." OA has an estimated fifty-four thousand members in more than seventy-five countries, with sixty-five hundred groups meeting each week. Most members are white females who have been in the program an average of 5.7 years. They began the program with moderate obesity.

Although OA does not focus on diet and calorie counting, members of OA experience an average weight loss of 21.8 pounds as a result of working the program. Like other twelve-step programs, OA seeks to improve the physical, mental, and spiritual facets of the lives of its members. A 2002 survey found that 90 percent of OA members reported improvements in these areas.

Specific OA practices have a demonstrated significant relationship with the maintenance of abstinence from foods that trigger compulsive overeating: weighing and measuring foods on a deliberate food plan; regular communication with other OA members, specifically a sponsor; spending time in introspection; writing as a form of personal expression and investigation; attending OA meetings regularly; reading OA literature for inspiration; and working the steps, particularly the fourth and ninth steps. Abstinence and spirituality were strongly correlated with self-reported success.

Bethany Thivierge, MPH

FURTHER READING

Alcoholics Anonymous. *Alcoholics Anonymous Big Book.* 4th ed. New York: Author, 2007. The bible of twelve-step recovery programs, including Overeaters Anonymous.

Costin, Carolyn. *The Eating Disorder Sourcebook.* New York: McGraw-Hill, 2006.

Overeaters Anonymous. *For Today.* Torrance, CA: Author, 1982. Daily affirmations and readings to inspire compulsive overeaters and food addicts in recovery.

---. *Overeaters Anonymous.* 2nd ed. Torrance, CA: Author, 2001. A collection of short personal accounts of persons who have successfully worked the OA program.

WEBSITES OF INTEREST

HealthyPlace.com
http://www.healthyplace.com/eating-disorders

Overeaters Anonymous
http://www.oa.org

See also: Behavioral addictions: Treatment; Food addiction; Outpatient treatment; Sponsors; Support groups; Twelve-step programs for addicts

---

Over-the-counter drugs of abuse

CATEGORY: Substance abuse
ALSO KNOWN AS: Pharming
DEFINITION: Over-the-counter (OTC) drugs are medications that do not require a prescription and are sold at supermarkets, drug and convenience stores, pharmacies, and over the Internet. OTC abuse is the use of nonprescribed medications for reasons other than instructed by a health care provider or listed on the medication's label. OTC drugs are considered to be abused when taken more frequently, at a greater dose, or for a longer time than directed, in order to produce changes in mental or physical status.

CAUSES

OTC medications are readily obtainable, making them easy to abuse. Also, these substances are difficult to detect in urine drug tests, which allows for abuse without consequences at school or work. The most commonly abused OTC drugs include cough syrup, cold medications, and antihistamines. Other OTC medications of abuse include sleep aids, herbal supplements, steroids, and aspirin and other pain relievers.

The main ingredient of abuse in cough and cold medications is dextromethorphan hydrobromide (DXM), which causes hallucinations at high doses, but the other ingredients in cough medicines such as acetaminophen and pseudoephedrine can lead to fatal overdoses when taken at high levels. Additionally, five percent of persons of Caucasian ancestry are unable to metabolize DXM properly, which causes a buildup of toxic levels of the substance and causes more severe drug effects.

Diphenhydramine is a common antihistamine that is often abused for its sedative effects. Diphenhydramine can compound the sedative properties of anti-anxiety medications, particularly benzodiazepines, and abusers often take these drugs in combination to increase their high.

RISK FACTORS

Persons who abuse OTC medications are most often Caucasian females, although all ethnicities, ages, and genders abuse these drugs. Adolescents are at particularly high risk because the substances are easy to obtain. Substance abusers often seek OTC drugs when they are unable to acquire other illegal drugs or alcohol. Persons with a psychiatric diagnosis also are at greater risk, and those who are suicidal are more likely to use OTC medications with alcohol to attempt suicide. Medical personnel have an increased risk for antihistamine abuse because these medications are easily accessible at their place of employment.

SYMPTOMS

OTC medications cause different symptoms when they are used according to the drug's label than when they are abused, or used off-label. Also, each OTC medication has a different set of effects. For example, cold and cough medications are intended to act as decongestants and cough suppressants. When taken in high doses, the DXM in these medications acts like the illegal drugs phencyclidine (PCP) and ketamine. DXM, PCP, and ketamine cause euphoria, hallucinations, dissociation, and psychosis. The stimulants in many of these medications can lead to prolonged sexual performance and erection, but also to agitation, priapism, and dangerous elevations in heart rate.

Dietary supplements and herbal medications can cause psychosis when taken in large quantities. The misuse of sedatives may induce coma, and steroid abuse may cause aggressive behavior.

SCREENING AND DIAGNOSIS

Emergency physicians often do not inquire about what OTC medications a patient is taking or the reasons why he or she is using them. Therefore, OTC abuse is often identified only during a regular medical appointment or during a mental health screening. Many of the OTC medications will not appear on a routine

Over-the-counter drugs sit on shelves in front of the pharmacy at a Wal-Mart store. (Brian Kersey/UPI/Landov)

urine drug test, but abuse of DXM at high doses may cause a drug screen to be abnormal for PCP.

TREATMENT AND THERAPY

Withdrawal symptoms have been reported with OTC abuse and differ based on the specific medication used. As with many substances of abuse, a gradual tapering of the OTC medication may help with the detoxification process and may minimize withdrawal symptoms. Persons who have an addiction may be referred to Pills Anonymous to complete a twelve-step, group therapy program, which is similar to the programs of Alcoholics Anonymous or Narcotics Anonymous. Outpatient or inpatient therapy for substance abuse is also available although often underutilized for OTC abuse.

PREVENTION

Supermarkets and pharmacies have started to enforce stricter policies regarding the purchase of many OTC medications. While cold, cough, and allergy medications traditionally have been found in the aisles of stores, many are now located behind the counter of a store's pharmacy and require proof of legal age (eighteen years) to purchase. Also, there are limits to the number of packages of medications a customer can purchase per day. While these are not foolproof methods to reduce OTC medication abuse, they do make it more difficult for minors to abuse OTCs and for any person to obtain large quantities of the substances at one time. For adolescents, parental education and awareness about OTC medication abuse has been demonstrated to successfully reduce the problem of OTC abuse.

Janet Ober Berman, MS, CGC

FURTHER READING

Gracious, Barbara, Naomi Abe, and Jane Sundberg. "The Importance of Taking a History of Over-the-Counter Medication Use: A Brief Review and Case Illustration of 'PRN' Antihistamine Dependence in a Hospitalized Adolescent." *Journal of Child and Adolescent Psychopharmacology* 20.6 (2010): 521–24. Print. Case report of a teenager who abused antihistamines; presents an example of how OTC abuse is often undetected and undiagnosed.

Lessenger, James, and Steven Feinberg. "Abuse of Prescription and Over-the-Counter Medications." *Journal of the American Board of Family Medicine* 21 (2008): 45–54. Print. Provides a list of the most commonly abused OTC medications and their respective symptoms.

National Survey on Drug Use and Health. "Characteristics of Primary Prescription and OTC Treatment Admissions, 2002." Washington, DC: SAMHSA, 2004. One of the only reports that provides nationwide data on the understudied field of OTC medication abuse.

WEBSITES OF INTEREST

Over-the-Counter Products. FamilyDoctor.org
http://familydoctor.org/familydoctor/en/drugs-procedures-devices/over-the-counter.html

StopMedicineAbuse.org
http://www.stopmedicineabuse.org

Teen Drug Abuse of Cough and Cold Medicine. WebMD.com
http://www.webmd.com/parenting/teen-abuse-cough-medicine-9

See also: Cough and cold medications; Sleeping pills; Steroid abuse

Oxycodone

CATEGORY: Substances

ALSO KNOWN AS: Blue; hillbilly heroin; kicker; OC; OX; oxy; oxycotton

DEFINITION: Oxycodone is an opioid analgesic similar to morphine. It has strong pain-relieving, sleep-inducing, and anxiety-relieving properties. Oxycodone is the active component in Percocet, Percodan, Tylox, and OxyContin.

STATUS: Legal by prescription in the United States and worldwide

CLASSIFICATION: Schedule II controlled substance

SOURCE: Synthesized from thebaine, a constituent of the poppy plant

TRANSMISSION ROUTE: Ingested orally, snorted, or injected

HISTORY OF USE

Oxycodone was first synthesized in 1916 at the University of Frankfurt in Germany. It was developed as a nonaddictive substitute for opioids including morphine, heroin, and codeine.

Oxycodone initially became available in the United States in 1939 but its abuse potential was not recognized until the 1950s, when Percodan, an oxycodone and aspirin combination, was introduced. As a result, all oxycodone-containing products are classified as schedule II controlled substances, the strictest classification for legal medications. Schedule II drugs are those with a high abuse potential and a legitimate medical use.

The illicit abuse of oxycodone dramatically increased in 1996 in the United States after the marketing by Purdue Pharma of OxyContin, the controlled-release prescription form of oxycodone. OxyContin, consumed for its relaxing and euphoric effects, became the best-selling narcotic pain reliever on the market.

Although oxycodone is not as potent as heroin, it remains one of the most highly addictive and widely abused prescription drugs of all time. Despite numerous efforts to curb the illegal use of oxycodone-containing products, its abuse remains a major concern in the United States.

EFFECTS AND POTENTIAL RISKS

Oxycodone is structurally similar to codeine and hydrocodone but pharmacologically resembles morphine. It acts through opioid receptors to alter the brain's response to pain, lessening pain sensations. Like other opiates, oxycodone elevates dopamine levels, the neurotransmitter linked to pleasurable experiences.

Oxycodone's short-term effects include a rush of euphoria and joy leading to a dreamy relaxed state. Negative short-term effects include nausea, vomiting, constipation, dizziness, and sedation.

Many people use oxycodone to achieve an opiate-like high, while others use it to minimize withdrawal symptoms of morphine and heroin addiction. Oxycodone users achieve the greatest high by bypassing OxyContin's controlled-release mechanism, consuming the entire dose at once. Typically, pills are either chewed or crushed and snorted or mixed with a liquid and injected.

Oxycodone use can lead to dependency and addiction. Long-term abuse may affect brain functioning because of hypoxia (low blood-oxygen levels) in the brain that results from repeated respiratory depression.

Rose Ciulla-Bohling, PhD

FURTHER READING

Aquina, Christopher T., et al. "OxyContin Abuse and Overdose." *Postgraduate Medicine* 121.2 (2009): 163–67. Print.

Ginther, Catherine. *Drug Abuse Sourcebook.* Detroit: Omnigraphics, 2004.

Kuhn, Cynthia, Scott Swartzwelder, and Wilkie Wilson. *Buzzed: The Straight Facts about the Most Used and Abused Drugs from Alcohol to Ecstasy.* New York: W. W. Norton, 2003.

WEBSITES OF INTEREST

American Council for Drug Education
http://www.acde.org

Center for Substance Abuse Research
http://www.cesar.umd.edu

US Drug Enforcement Administration
http://www.deadiversion.usdoj.gov/drugs_concern/oxycodone/summary.htm

See also: Codeine; Fentanyl; Heroin; Hydrocodone; Methadone; Morphine; Naltrexone; Narcotics abuse; Narcotics: Short- and long-term effects on the body; Opioid abuse; Opium; Painkiller abuse; Vicodin

P

Pain addiction

CATEGORY: Psychological issues and behaviors

ALSO KNOWN AS: Algolagnia

DEFINITION: Pain addiction involves the infliction of pain or physical injury to the body in order to release pleasure-causing endorphins. The addiction is usually regarded as pathological only if it results in injury from illegal and unwanted aggression. Pain addiction exists at the nexus of pleasure and pain, most notably for sexual stimulation. Experts continue to debate whether the infliction of pain in search of pleasure is a true addiction.

BACKGROUND

From the days of René Descartes, philosophers including Baruch Spinoza and Jeremy Bentham have speculated that pain and pleasure are connected. The biological sciences provide strong evidence that the neurochemical pathways used for the sensation of pain and pleasure are related.

After an injury, the body releases endorphins to counteract pain. This connection has long been exploited for sexual stimulation that derives pleasure from the infliction of pain. These forms of stimulation include bondage, sadomasochism, "erotic spanking," and "love biting."

Sadomasochism (or S&M) as a concept originated with the French aristocrat Marquis de Sade in the late eighteenth century and with writer Leopold von Sacher-Masoch in the nineteenth century. Both had explored relations between people who enjoy giving pain (sadists) and those who enjoy receiving pain (masochists). A sadomasochist can fill both roles.

Sadomasochism may fall short of the clinical definition of paraphilias, but a medical diagnosis may follow the infliction of clinically significant distress or impairment. Usually sadomasochism involves mutual consent, in contrast with criminal acts involving sexual violence or other forms of illegal aggression.

The sexual tendency that derives sexual stimulation and pleasure from the infliction of physical pain is called algolagnia, so named in 1892 by psychiatrist Albert von Schrenck-Notzing. Algolagnia is regarded as a physical phenomenon in which a person's brain interprets pain signals as pleasurable. This tendency is at the root of sadomasochism, which has been refined since the early nineteenth century into several variants, including bondage and discipline (B&D).

POTENTIAL RISKS

No significant connection has been found between algolagnia or the related forms of sadomasochism and violent crime. However, pain addiction can be connected to accidents, sometimes fatal, and to depression and suicide. Some people with pain addiction may scar themselves or cut their wrists, legs, arms, or necks.

Algolagnia is not listed in the American Psychiatric Association's *Diagnostic and Statistical Manual of Mental Disorders* (DSM-IV-TR). The intentional infliction of pain is called "active algolagnia" in *Mosby's Medical Dictionary* and is considered a form of sadism. *Mosby's* also lists a form of masochism as "passive algolagnia." Neither is regarded as pathological unless it involves inflicting pain on nonconsenting persons or if it causes "marked distress or interpersonal difficulty."

Physically, a person does not become addicted to the pain itself, but to the hormone-like endorphins released by the body to control pain's effects. These affect the body much like opiates, such as morphine and heroin, producing an anesthetizing numbness. Vigorous exercise, emotional pain, and other forms of stress also release endorphins. Pain addiction is progressive, requiring increasing, sustained stimulus over time to maintain endorphin levels. Increasing intensity of pain (emotional, physical, or both) stimulates additional endorphin release. Pain also can force family and friends to focus attention on the addict.

Both emotional and physical pain may become addictive. Feelings of worry, anger, depression, grief, or fear may become so habitually familiar that an addict believes he or she cannot live without those emotions. There are physical and mental reasons for emotional pain addiction. Someone who is often stressed by emotional pain may develop dependence on stress-related biochemistry. Changing these habitual pain-related patterns may become as difficult as "kicking" an addiction to nicotine, alcohol, cocaine, or heroin. Much of this behavior becomes unconscious, a major reason many people maintain painful relationships or habits despite negative consequences.

An addict may seek to maintain pain more fiercely as the addiction intensifies, and may do so in many ways. A pain addict may even attribute pain to the will of a higher power or as punishment for past misbehavior. Pain even may be regarded as a refuge from a stressful family life.

Group support for recovering pain addicts is rare; there are no "pain addicts anonymous" groups. Anger, criticism, and the provocation of guilt usually do not aid in recovery for pain addicts; such strategies may even drive a person to seek more intense pain. Aid from a therapist familiar with addictive behavior and the chemistry of the brain may be necessary to break this cycle.

Bruce E. Johansen, PhD

FURTHER READING

Levinthal, Charles F. *Messengers of Paradise: Opiates and the Brain—The Struggle over Pain, Rage, Uncertainty, and Addiction.* New York: Anchor, 1988. Mental processes that associate pleasure and pain, as both relate to addiction.

White, J. M. "Pleasure into Pain: The Consequences of Long-Term Opioid Use." *Addiction and Behavior* 29.7 (2004): 1311–24. Print. Examines the role of opiates in the release of endorphins that provide a buffer for pain.

WEBSITES OF INTEREST

Pain and the Erotic
http://www.wellcome.ac.uk/en/pain/microsite/culture1.html

PhilPapers: Pain and Pleasure
http://philpapers.org/browse/pleasure-and-pain

See also: Body modification addiction; Cutting and self-mutilation; Paraphilias; Self-destructive behavior and addiction; Sex addiction

Painkiller abuse

CATEGORY: Substance abuse

ALSO KNOWN AS: Analgesic abuse

DEFINITION: A painkiller is an opioid medication used to reduce or alleviate pain. Painkiller abuse is the excessive use of painkilling drugs or use for nonmedical purposes. Painkiller addiction is the condition of physical or psychological dependence on a painkiller. The drugs are obtained legally through prescription or by purchasing as an over-the-counter medication, or they are bought illegally.

CAUSES

Opioids come in two forms: natural and synthetic. Natural opioids are derived from the opium plant; synthetic (artificial) and partially synthetic opioids are structurally similar to natural opioids. Morphine and codeine are purified from the crude opium latex. Partially synthetic drugs derived from morphine include heroin, oxycodone (OxyContin), hydromorphone (Dilaudid), and oxymorphone (Numorphan). Synthetic compounds that resemble morphine in their chemical structure include fentanyl (Duragesic), levorphanol (Levo-Dromoran), meperidine (Demerol), methadone, and dextropropoxyphene (Darvon).

All opioids exert their effect by modifying the transmission of the nerve impulse between neurons (nerve cells). Neurons are separated from each other through short spaces called synapses. When the nerve impulse reaches the terminal end of one neuron, neurotransmitters are released into the synapse. The neurotransmitter travels across the synapse and binds to receptors on the terminal of the next neuron to allow continuation of the nerve impulse. In the case of opioids, this neurotransmitter is dopamine.

Opioids act to increase and maintain the concentration of dopamine in the synapse by two methods. Some drugs prevent the reuptake of dopamine from the synapse by binding to proteins that normally transport dopamine. Other drugs act to increase the release of more dopamine from the presynaptic neuron terminal. The result is the maintenance and enhancement of the pleasurable effect promoted by dopamine.

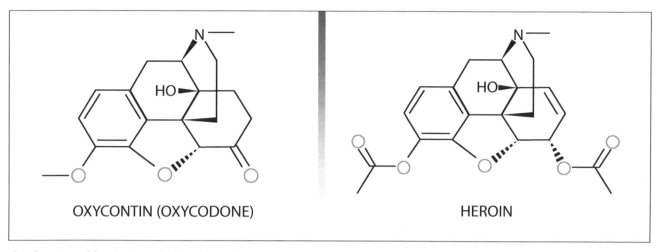

OXYCONTIN (OXYCODONE)

HEROIN

OxyContin and heroin have similar chemical structures and bind to the same receptors in the brain.

Opium and its synthetic counterparts have structural similarities to natural pain relievers in the body called endorphins. Endorphins are secreted by the pituitary gland in response to pain stimuli, resulting in the relief of pain by binding to pain receptors and preventing transmission of the pain impulse. Endorphins are also secreted in response to pleasurable activities, such as eating and sex, resulting in a high that is similar to that caused by morphine. Endorphins are more potent than morphine, but they do not lead to addiction because they are broken down by enzymes and do not accumulate.

Nonsteroidal anti-inflammatory drugs (NSAIDs) are painkillers that act in the body by a different mechanism. The most common NSAIDs are acetaminophen, acetylsalicylic acid (aspirin), and ibuprofen and are readily available over the counter. NSAIDs act by inhibiting the cyclooxygenase enzymes 1 and 2 that are involved in the synthesis of prostaglandins. Prostaglandins are involved in a variety of body processes, including sensitization of nerve endings.

NSAIDs are most commonly used for headache relief; however, they are often used to treat symptoms for which they are not recommended, such as anxiety, sleep problems, and stress. Authorities generally agree that the use of NSAIDs rarely leads to physical dependence.

RISK FACTORS

Painkiller abuse may include self-medication, or the use of the drugs without a prescription to relieve pain or other symptoms. Chronic pain is a common cause of painkiller abuse. A person with chronic pain may begin to take painkiller medication beyond the physician's prescription in larger doses or more frequently. People also use drugs for recreational purposes to produce euphoria, an emotional state of intensely pleasurable feelings.

More painkillers are available than ever before because of an increasing awareness and desire of physicians to reduce severe pain in their patients. In many cases, only opioid drugs can reduce severe pain. Physicians need to balance the need for relieving a patient's pain versus the chance that the patient's opiate use may lead to addiction. The ready availability of painkiller drugs can lead the patient to ignore alternative means of pain control. Additionally, many new pain medications first became available in the 1990s.

Social factors can be important in painkiller abuse. Exposing drugs to adolescents and young adults is a critical factor, as it can lead to a lifetime of drug abuse. A family structure lacking stability or that is disruptive and violent can result in a lack of good role models and a poor sense of direction for children. Pain medications may be readily available at home, leading teens to take them to relieve pain or stress without a doctor's prescription.

Peer pressure, the influence of friends and acquaintances in school and on the street, can be an important driving force, too. Adolescents often seek acceptance within particular groups, and adolescents may be prone to drug experimentation within these groups. Some persons of any age are more likely to become drug dependent, especially those who lack confidence or self-esteem, who may look to drugs to fill a void or to overcome loneliness or depression.

Genetic susceptibility can be a factor in painkiller abuse, although it is difficult to separate genetic from environmental influences. An estimated 40 to 60 percent of the variability of addiction is caused by genetic factors or by combined genetic and environmental interactions.

SYMPTOMS

Signs of painkiller abuse can be psychological or physical. Psychologically, the person abusing drugs is focused on obtaining more drugs. He or she may increase the dose over time and often continues to use drugs after his or her medical condition has improved. Physical appearance often declines, and the person may show shifts in energy, mood, and concentration. He or she may withdraw from family and friends and might neglect household and work responsibilities.

Typical symptoms of painkiller addiction are feelings of euphoria, lethargy, mental confusion, nausea, and poor judgment. Less specific symptoms include slurred speech, shallow breathing, bloodshot eyes, constipation, and unusual drowsiness. The addict eventually develops a tolerance for the drug, requiring higher doses to obtain the same effect. Withdrawal symptoms often occur if the addict abruptly stops using the drug. Withdrawal symptoms may include agitation, muscle aches, insomnia, anxiety, cramps, and nausea and vomiting.

SCREENING AND DIAGNOSIS

A physician will take a complete history of the patient, perform a physical examination, and send blood or urine samples to a laboratory to test for the presence of suspected drugs. Although blood tests are more likely than urine tests to detect drugs, urine tests are more common. Opiates are usually found in the urine within twelve to thirty-six hours of last use. A particular drug abuse screening test was developed in 1982, and it consists of questions to be answered by persons concerned about their involvement with drugs.

TREATMENT AND THERAPY

Treatment of painkiller addiction requires the person to stop using the drug. Abrupt discontinuation of drugs by long-term users, that is, going "cold turkey," results in severe withdrawal symptoms. A more practical treatment involves slowly decreasing the use of the drug (through a process known as detoxification); complete abstinence follows.

Newer drugs, such as buprenorphine and naltrexone, block the effect of opiates on the body, thereby reducing withdrawal symptoms and the length of withdrawal. Patients taking buprenorphine also can become mildly addicted to that drug. A newer version of the drug has been introduced; it is combined with another drug, naloxone. When this drug combination is injected, the person goes into withdrawal, thus preventing abuse in use.

Psychological addiction may continue long after physical withdrawal from the drug. The recovering addict can experience difficulties in coping with daily activities, and there is a great danger the user will return to drug use. Each patient needs to be treated on an individualized basis. The detrimental mental and emotional states that led to drug use need to be identified and addressed, and the patient needs to be taught how to avoid drugs and drug culture. These changes may include new activities and new social and relational contacts.

PREVENTION

Prevention is based on removing the risk factors. Education of children by family and teachers about the dangers of painkiller abuse is paramount. Parents need to keep prescription pain medications away from children, and sharing information about drug use can become part of a school's science curriculum. Additionally, for persons taking prescription painkillers to manage chronic pain, it is important to use the medication only at the prescribed dosages to avoid developing a dependency.

David A. Olle, MS

FURTHER READING

Abbott, Francis, and Mary Fraser. "Use and Abuse of Over-the-Counter Analgesic Drugs." *Journal of Psychiatry and Neuroscience* 23.1 (1998): 13–34. Print. Examines the widespread use and abuse of over-the-counter painkillers from the perspective of psychiatry.

Byrne, Marilyn, Laura Lander, and Martha Ferris. "The Changing Face of Opioid Addiction: Prescription Pain Pill Dependence and Treatment."

Health Social Work 34.1 (2009): 53–56. Print. A clinical-health perspective on changes in social work to address the abuse of painkillers and other opioids.

Twombly, Eric, and Kristen Holtz. "Teens and the Misuse of Prescription Drugs: Evidence-Based Recommendations to Curb a Growing Societal Problem." *Journal of Primary Prevention* 29.6 (2008): 503–16. Print. Discusses the abuse of prescription drugs, including painkillers, among youth.

WEBSITES OF INTEREST

Drug Dependence. PubMed Health
http://www.ncbi.nlm.nih.gov/pubmedhealth/PMH0002490

National Institute on Drug Abuse
http://www.drugabuse.gov

See also: Codeine; Hydrocodone; Morphine; Narcotics abuse; Narcotics: Short- and long-term effects on the body; Opioid abuse; Oxycodone; Prescription drug addiction: Overview; Soma; Tramadol; Vicodin

Panic disorders and addiction

CATEGORY: Psychological issues and behaviors
DEFINITION: Panic disorder is an anxiety disorder that is characterized by sudden episodes of intense fear that appear without warning. These episodes are known as panic attacks. People with panic disorder live in fear of having another attack. Panic attacks can feel like a heart attack, like one is "losing" his or her mind, or like one is on the verge of sudden death.

BACKGROUND

Panic attacks occur frequently and without warning. They even can begin during sleep. Over time, persons with panic disorder may begin to avoid situations they believe can trigger a panic attack or may, for example, stop leaving their homes because they fear that no place is safe.

SYMPTOMS

People with panic disorder are plagued by feelings of impending doom. The symptoms of panic disorder also include sweating, chest pain or pressure, irregular heartbeat, shortness of breath, a feeling of choking or being smothered, dizziness, a sense of unreality, a tingling sensation in the hands or feet, chills, flushing, nausea, a pressing desire to escape, and difficulty sleeping.

According to the Anxiety Disorders Association of America, approximately 6 million adults in the United States experience panic attacks each year. Women are twice as likely to be affected.

HOW PANIC DISORDER CAN LEAD TO ADDICTION

The symptoms of panic disorder can be extremely uncomfortable and overwhelming, so many people with the disorder turn to drugs and alcohol to relieve their symptoms. This action is known as self-medicating. Central nervous system depressants, such as alcohol, marijuana, and opiates, are commonly used to self-medicate. Long-term use of any of these substances can lead to addiction.

Over time, people who use drugs or alcohol to self-medicate will build up a tolerance to the drug, so that they will eventually need to increase the amount of the substance to get the same effect. For example, a person who may at first be having a drink or two to relax at the end of the day may find that, eventually, three, four, or more drinks are needed to feel relaxed. A person who began taking one pain pill a day to relieve symptoms of panic disorder may need to take two or three pills a day to get the same relief.

Self-medication also can lead to other problems. That is, the relief from self-medicating is temporary, the side effects of long-term drug or alcohol use can be severe, and the underlying cause of the panic disorder is ultimately not treated.

HOW ADDICTION CAN LEAD TO PANIC DISORDER

Panic disorder also can be caused by substance abuse. Certain substances, such as caffeine, tobacco, cocaine, and methamphetamine, can trigger panic attacks. Panic disorder symptoms caused by substance abuse may include irregular heart rate, flushing, dizziness, sweating, and difficulty sleeping. These symptoms can last long after the effects of the drug wear off, which often makes the person want to use the substance again.

Additionally, withdrawal from alcohol or opiates can cause symptoms of panic disorder. Panic disorder symptoms caused by alcohol or opiate withdrawal may include sweating, rapid heartbeat, dizziness, flushing, and difficulty sleeping. Therefore, a person who is self-medicating to avoid symptoms of panic disorder may be increasing his or her risk of a panic attack through substance abuse and subsequent withdrawal.

THE ANXIETY AND PANIC DISORDER CYCLE

Panic disorder and substance abuse often coexist in a vicious cycle. Although central nervous system depressants are often used to relieve panic disorder symptoms, the symptoms of panic disorder escalate when a person discontinues the depressant drugs and experiences withdrawal symptoms. This leads the person with the panic disorder to repeat the self-medicating behavior. When panic disorder is caused by addiction, the panic that is caused by the substance abuse is often further "treated" by using and abusing the substance.

Julie Henry

FURTHER READING

"Anxiety Disorders." Web. 21 Mar. 2012. http://www.webmd.com/anxiety-panic/guide/mental-health-anxiety-disorders. A detailed description of common types of anxiety disorders and their symptoms, causes, diagnoses, and treatment options.

Anxiety Disorders Association of America. "Panic Disorder and Agoraphobia." Web. 21 Mar. 2012. http://www.adaa.org/understanding-anxiety/panic-disorder-agoraphobia. An overview of panic disorder, including symptoms, treatment options, and links to additional research.

---. "Substance Abuse." Web. 21 Mar. 2012. http://www.adaa.org/understanding-anxiety/related-illnesses/substance-abuse. A discussion of the relationship between anxiety disorders and substance abuse.

Stewart, Sherry H., and Patricia J. Conrod, eds. *Anxiety and Substance Use Disorders: The Vicious Cycle of Comorbidity.* New York: Springer, 2008. Chapters cover findings, theories, and intervention strategies for panic and anxiety disorders, both across types of substance and across the range of such disorders.

WEBSITES OF INTEREST

Anxiety Disorders Association of America
http://www.adaa.org

National Institute of Mental Health
http://www.nimh.nih.gov

National Institute on Drug Abuse
http://www.drugabuse.gov

Substance Abuse and Mental Health Services Administration
http://www.samhsa.gov

See also: Anxiety; Anxiety medication abuse; Behavioral addictions: Overview; Caffeine addiction; Caffeine: Short- and long-term effects on the body; Mental illness; Withdrawal

Paraphilias

CATEGORY: Psychological issues and behaviors
ALSO KNOWN AS: Deviant sexual behaviors
DEFINITION: A paraphilia is a condition in which a person's sexual arousal depends on fantasizing about and engaging in sexual behavior that is considered atypical or abnormal.

BACKGROUND

A paraphilia can be centered on a particular object (animals, clothing, etc.) or on a particular act (inflicting pain, exhibitionism, etc.). A paraphilia is characterized by a preoccupation with the object or behavior to the point of dependence on that object or behavior for sexual gratification. Most paraphilias are much more common in men than in women.

Paraphilias are divided into three categories: sexual arousal and preference for nonhuman objects (as in fetishes and transvestism); sexual arousal and a preference for situations that involve suffering and humiliation (such as in sadism and masochism); and sexual arousal and preference for nonconsenting partners, behaviors that include exhibitionism, voyeurism, and child molestation.

SPECIFIC TYPES OF PARAPHILIA

Fetishism. Fetishism involves sexual urges associated with nonliving, or inanimate, objects, including clothing items.

Frotteurism. Frotteurism is characterized by a man rubbing his genitals against a nonconsenting, unfamiliar person.

Pedophilia. Pedophilia is characterized by fantasies or behaviors that involve sexual activity with a child.

Masochism. Sexual masochism is a paraphilia in which one incorporates his or her sexual urges into suffering to achieve sexual excitement and climax.

Sadism. Sexual sadism involves persistent fantasies in which sexual excitement results from inflicting suffering on a sexual partner. Extreme sadism involves illegal activities such as rape, torture, and murder.

Transvestism. Transvestism refers to the practice of dressing in clothes associated with the opposite sex to produce or enhance sexual arousal.

Voyeurism. Voyeurism involves achieving sexual arousal by observing an unsuspecting and nonconsenting person who is undressing or unclothed or engaged in sexual activity. The voyeur does not seek contact with the person that he or she is observing.

Other paraphilias. Some paraphilias are relatively rare, and include apotemnophilia (sexual attraction to amputations), coprophilia and urophilia (sexual excitement derived from contact with human waste), and necrophilia (sexual attraction to corpses).

SYMPTOMS

A paraphilic person is distinguished by the insistence and relative exclusivity with which his or her sexual gratification focuses on the acts or objects in question. For many paraphilic persons, orgasm is not possible without the paraphilic act or object. Paraphilic persons often have difficulty developing personal and sexual relationships with others, and frequently exhibit compulsive behavior. Although it is not known for certain what causes paraphilia, some experts have theorized that paraphilias may develop in response to childhood trauma, such as sexual abuse.

SCREENING AND DIAGNOSIS

The American Psychiatric Association's *Diagnostic and Statistical Manual of Mental Disorders* lists two basic criteria for diagnosing paraphilia: one, the unusual sexual behavior should occur over a period of six months and, two, the sexual behavior causes a clinically significant distress or impairment in social, occupational, or other important areas of functioning.

The second criterion differs for some disorders. For pedophilia, voyeurism, exhibitionism, and frotteurism, the diagnosis is formulated if acting out on these urges or if the urge itself causes a significant distress or interpersonal difficulty. For sadism, a diagnosis is made if these urges involve a nonconsenting person. For the other paraphilias, a diagnosis is made when the sexual behavior, urges, or fantasies cause substantial distress or disability in important areas of life.

TREATMENT AND THERAPY

Most cases of paraphilia are treated with counseling and therapy in an effort to help patients modify their behavior. Research suggests that cognitive-behavioral models are especially effective in treating persons with paraphilias. Group therapy involves breaking through the denial associated with paraphilias by surrounding the paraphilic person with other people who share their illness. Once they begin to admit that they have a sexual deviation, a therapist can address individual issues, such as past sexual abuse, that may have led to the disorder. Many physicians and therapists refer persons with paraphilias to twelve-step programs designed for sexual addicts. The programs incorporate cognitive restructuring with social support to increase awareness of the problem.

Also used in treatment are drugs called antiandrogens, which drastically lower testosterone levels in men temporarily. These medications help to decrease compulsiveness and reduce deviant sexual fantasies. In some cases, hormones such as medroxyprogesterone acetate (Depo-Provera) and cyproterone acetate (Androcur) are prescribed for persons who exhibit dangerous sexual behavior. These medications work by reducing one's sex drive. Antidepressants such as fluoxetine (Prozac) work in a similar manner but have not been shown to effectively target sexual fantasies.

Gerald W. Keister

FURTHER READING

American Psychiatric Association. *Diagnostic and Statistical Manual of Mental Disorders.* 4th ed. Washington, DC: Author, 2000. This standard reference on mental disorders discusses the various paraphilias in detail in a way that is understandable to general readers.

Bhugra, D. "Paraphilias across Cultures: Contexts and Controversies." *Journal of Sex Research* 47.2–3 (2010): 242–315. Print. Suggests that characteristics of cultures may influence the rate of reporting paraphilias and the rate of paraphilias themselves. Also explores whether paraphilias can be seen as culture-bound syndromes, and recommends consideration of a number of conceptual issues regarding the diagnosis and prevalence of paraphilias as future cross-cultural studies on this topic are developed.

Laws, R. D., and W. T. O'Donohue, eds. *Sexual Deviance: Theory, Assessment, and Treatment.* 2nd ed. New York: Guilford, 2008. Contains comprehensive presentations and discussions of all the paraphilias and sections on sexual deviance and the law, neurobiological processes and comorbidity in sexual deviance, and medical models and interventions in sexual deviance.

WEBSITES OF INTEREST

ForensicPsychiatry.ca
http://www.forensicpsychiatry.ca/paraphilia/overview.htm

Medscape: Paraphilias
http://emedicine.medscape.com/article/291419-overview

See also: Behavioral addictions: Overview; Pain addiction; Self-destructive behavior and addiction

Parenting and alcoholism

CATEGORY: Psychological issues and behaviors

DEFINITION: The connection between parenting and alcoholism is two-pronged. One facet is the effect upon the family system when one or both parents abuse alcohol. A specific category, identified as the children of alcoholics, incorporates both young children in the home and adults who grew up with alcoholic parents as children. The second facet represents parents who have one or more children who abuse alcohol. The largest group of children in the home who are alcohol abusers are teenagers, although college-age and young adult children for whom parents feel partially responsible also make up a large percentage of alcohol abusers.

ALCOHOLISM AND THE PARENTAL ROLE

Every alcoholic has a direct effect on several people, the majority of whom will be spouses, children, and parents. Although disagreement exists on a definition for *alcoholism*, there is general agreement that the term must be understood in context. As such, the most immediate and basic context is that of the family.

More than six million children under the age of eighteen years live in households with an alcoholic parent or parents. When a parent is an alcoholic, the result is often destructive, evidenced by higher rates of domestic violence, child neglect, health problems, and alcohol-related death. Families with an alcoholic parent are more likely to experience conflict and to face financial challenges.

Many persons, however, have coped effectively with the trauma of growing up with an alcoholic parent and have become competent adults. Longitudinal studies have noted that such persons relied on significantly more sources of support in their childhood and youth than was true of children of alcoholics who demonstrated coping problems. This notes the importance of environmental and individual resilience factors that can assist in both prevention and adaptation.

Many substance abuse therapists and organizations accept the premise that a biological vulnerability exists for alcoholism. Others disagree with the importance given to the genetic influence and prefer to focus on individual behaviors and environmental influences. Research has illustrated the importance of the home atmosphere; for example, families who ate dinner together (even families with one alcoholic parent) were less likely to pass alcoholism from parent to child. The sense of structure and of being cared for was assumed to be a contributing factor. In another longitudinal study, mothers who were warm and supportive were less likely to have children who grow up to become alcoholics.

PARENTS WHO ABUSE ALCOHOL

Nearly 18 percent of persons in the United States have an alcoholic parent. Over time, parental patterns of behavior and communication are affected as a result of alcohol abuse, and these patterns often keep families from dealing with general parental and child problems because alcoholic behavior becomes the primary focus. In the recovery process, a parent becoming sober is a necessary but insufficient goal. Also needing to be addressed are the distorted behavioral and communication patterns that have developed in the family. Treatment is essential if the abstinence is to be maintained.

Research shows a link between substance abuse and child maltreatment. In one large study, 40 percent of reported cases of child abuse involved the use of alcohol or other drugs, with an even higher percentage of cases of emotional abuse and neglect. In effect, children of alcoholics are more likely to have behavioral problems and conduct disorders, and to report higher levels of depression, anxiety, and stress.

Alcoholism in the family is not just about one person affecting others. All family members and persons in close relationship with the alcoholic are affected. Possibly the ones most vulnerable are younger children, because of their small physical size and their dependent status. How effectively a family with an alcoholic will function depends on the degree to which that family provides for the physical, social, emotional, and psychological well-being of family members.

When a parent is an alcoholic, the family system becomes organized around the alcohol abuse. Therefore, an effective recovery process requires change in the system itself, referred to as second-order change in family therapy, so that the family can develop patterns based on strengths, resiliency, and coping mechanisms.

INTERVENTION

Fifteen years after Bill Wilson founded Alcoholics Anonymous, his wife, Lois Wilson, founded Al-Anon to help family and friends recover from the effects of someone else's drinking. The preamble for Al-Anon Family Groups, as the organization is known officially, states that alcoholism is a family illness and that recovery is assisted by changed attitudes. Other organizations and approaches may state their purpose somewhat differently, but they all generally agree that the entire family benefits from inclusion in the recovery process.

The focus on adult children of alcoholics started as a grassroots movement, initiated primarily by those who had experienced living with one or more family members who abused alcohol. Their desire to receive assistance for themselves was often overlooked by helping professionals who concentrated on the alcoholic.

Although family therapy as a form of treatment has not been commonly utilized for families of alcoholics,

related intervention programs have shown effectiveness in the treatment of families affected by alcohol abuse. One approach in particular, multidimensional family therapy (MDFT), has combined resources to treat issues related both to substance abuse and to conduct disorders. The effectiveness of this therapeutic model lies in its careful design, which considers the chemical-dependent issue as being both family-based and multisystemic.

PARENTING CHILDREN WHO ABUSE ALCOHOL

Viewed from the parental role, concern over a child's alcohol abuse usually begins with adolescents and includes early adult years, especially the time when children are in college. In most family settings, the parental role will be more hands-on with adolescents and more distant with college students. The increasing number of young adults who return home after leaving the home for the first time also increases the likelihood that parents will extend their time of direct involvement. In such cases, the parent and the returning young adult may disagree over what constitutes alcohol abuse.

By the time young adults who drink alcohol reach their late twenties, many will have reduced their use of alcohol, often without clinical help or focused dialogue with their parents. These adult children often do not abstain from alcohol entirely but are not likely to abuse alcohol. Those who do not emerge from this phase of alcohol use are more likely to be at serious risk because they have family members who are or who have been addicted to some substance, including alcohol.

INTERVENTION STRATEGIES FOR PARENTS

Parents should learn how to detect a true alcohol abuse problem with their teens and young adult children. The American Psychiatric Association's *Diagnostic and Statistical Manual of Mental Disorders* distinguishes between alcoholic behaviors as abuse disorders and the more severe diagnosis, dependence disorders.

Research shows that some types of treatment for alcohol abuse by adolescents and young adults are more effective than others. Intervention strategies identified as more effective are those that provide motivation, tools, and support to produce change. Effective treatments draw upon strengths, motivation, and existing support networks. Young people possess many assets that assist them in making the necessary changes. By recognizing and using the resources available, changes are more likely. A parent is a primary resource.

Two treatment strategies that are effective with young people are MDFT and motivational interviewing (MI). The MDFT model considers multiple areas of an adolescent's life, including emotional and cognitive functioning and family and peer relationships. A carefully designed, family-based model will focus on the adolescent's particular developmental stages and his or her position within the family system.

MI is designed for therapy in general but has been especially effective for working with adolescents who abuse alcohol. MI is based on the premise that motivation to change should be elicited from the patient-client. Although MI does seek to "confront" clients with the reality of alcoholism, the technique differs substantially from more aggressive styles of confrontation over abusive behaviors.

Lillian J. Breckenridge

FURTHER READING

Brown, Stephanie, and Virginia Lewis. *The Alcoholic Family in Recovery: A Developmental Model*. New York: Guilford, 1999. The authors provide a developmental model of recovery with specific stages. The focus is the recovery process for the family system, rather than just recovery for the alcoholic.

Jay, Jeff, and Debra Jay. *Love First*. 2nd ed. Center City, MN: Hazelden, 2008. Shows how families, friends, and professionals can focus on love as an approach to intervention for alcoholism.

Miller, W. R., and S. Rollnick, eds. *Motivational Interviewing: Preparing People for Change*. 2nd ed. New York: Guilford, 2002. Proposes a treatment approach called motivational interviewing and advocates its use instead of twelve-step programs. The authors believe that young people who abuse alcohol respond best to therapy in which they are asked to examine their habits relative to their own values and goals.

Peele, Stanton. *Addiction-Proof Your Child*. New York: Three Rivers, 2007. Argues that parents will be able to protect their children from addiction with a focus on the right values. An innovative book that helps parents to determine their views on the more traditional perspectives of dealing with alcoholic behaviors.

WEBSITES OF INTEREST

Al-Anon and Alateen
http://www.al-anon.alateen.org

National Association for Children of Alcoholics
http://nacoa.org

National Families in Action
http://www.nationalfamilies.org

See also: Adult children of alcoholics; Families and substance abuse; Marriage/partnership and alcoholism; Parenting and behavioral addictions; Parenting and substance abuse

Parenting and behavioral addictions

CATEGORY: Psychological issues and behaviors

DEFINITION: Parents and primary caregivers of children and adolescents influence the development, identification, and treatment of addictions that do not involve substances but observable behaviors such as gambling, shopping, eating, and video gaming.

PARENTAL INFLUENCE ON BEHAVIORAL ADDICTION

Parents have three potential mechanisms by which they influence the development of behavioral addictions in their children. However, none of these mechanisms directly causes behavioral addictions.

The first and most fundamental parental mechanism is genetic inheritability. Addiction is promoted through a neuronal reward system in which the pleasure areas of the brain are stimulated and the behavior that brought the pleasurable experience is identified and repeated. A well-known example is the endorphin release or rush experienced by runners, cyclists, and other extreme athletes. At some point during the activity, the physical expenditure of energy triggers a release of brain chemicals (neurotransmitters), most notably endorphin, which the athlete experiences as pleasurable.

While this pleasurable response to vigorous exercise is almost universal and can be brought about by any number of strenuous physical activities, individual sensitivity is primarily genetically inherited. If it takes a lot of exercise before a parent experiences the pleasure of endorphin release, it is likely that his or her children will require much exercise before they experience the endorphin rush. What a parent contributes here is his or her child's sensitivity to having the pleasure centers of the brain stimulated.

In the example of the runners' high, just how much running has to occur before endorphins are released will vary among individuals, with most of the variation accounted for by how much exercise their parents would have had to do before their own endorphins were released. Largely determined by what was true for one's parents is how much activity one has to engage in to bring on the pleasurable experience, how intense (and thus addictive) is that experience, and how long that experience lasts.

Parents' genetic contributions influence their children's addictive sensitivity, pleasurable intensity (which corresponds to addictive potential with the more the intensity, the greater the potential), and duration. Duration involves the length of the experience and how much behavior was required to result in the reward. Parents pass down a tendency toward or a tendency away from pleasurable addiction; they do not pass down specific behavioral addictions like pornography or kleptomania. The more excitable the parents' brains, the more excitable the children's brains are likely to be.

The second mechanism through which parents influence the development of behavioral addiction is through imitative, behavioral, and social learning. Parents who are addicted to exercise, gambling, social networking, or shopping, for instance, show their children that these behaviors are within the range of what this family will accept. Most behavioral addictions are merely extreme examples of normally encountered and readily observed behaviors that all individuals exhibit. When parents are addicted to any of these behaviors, children are exposed to the idea that the behaviors are acceptable or normal to some degree; the parents legitimate the behaviors through their actions. For example, most children will not see a spotlessly clean home as normal unless they are raised in an environment in which compulsive cleaning is the norm.

The third and most common mechanism for parents to influence and sustain behavioral addictions

in their children is enabling. The cycle begins with children engaging in a commonly accepted behavior, such as video gaming. There also is a good chance that children have participated with their parents in that activity. It is common for parents, for example, to play video games with their children. However, because the threshold between normal, daily activity and driven addiction is more nuanced and not well defined, it usually takes a substantial period of time to go from family entertainment to individual addiction.

The behavior crosses the threshold into addiction when it directly or indirectly harms the child, interferes with other health- and growth-promoting activities (such as school work, socializing with friends, participating in family functions), and becomes the major focus or prime motivation for how the child allocates his or her time. Addicted children, like their adult counterparts, are on a quest to satiate urges and avoid the anxiety they will feel when those urges are not met. The addict's focus is on how soon he or she will be able to satisfy the next urge.

Even with the foregoing conditions as a guideline, it still can be difficult to distinguish passion and dedication from compulsion and absorption. For example, when does excessive football practice become exercise addiction? Addiction is usually difficult to determine until the addiction is well established; at this point parents are at risk of knowingly or unknowingly promoting the addiction by sustaining the addictive behavior of the child.

The behavior that is troubling to parents and harmful to their children is allowed to continue because of parents' uncertainty, unreliability, and hesitation about how they should respond to their child and his or her problem. Parents have ultimate authority and influence over their children's lives; they provide life's essentials—food, clothing, shelter, and security. They also provide life's social essentials—identity, belonging, and support for a life outside the home through financial and material means.

Helping children is generally natural for parents. This predisposition becomes problematic when children begin to manipulate parents and other family members to fulfill their addictive cravings. When parents minimize or deny that their child's behavior, such as excessive shopping or compulsive eating, is a problem, they enable the child to engage in these behaviors without having to identify that they have a problem.

Subconsciously, children study parental behavior and learn from it. This behavior cues children about what is allowable, what will be confronted, what will be ignored, and what will or will not be tolerated. By failing to identify the behavior and its impact on children and family as a problem, parents subconsciously influence how children see the addictive behavior. The addiction becomes something that is acceptable, "a phase," or something that the child will outgrow.

Placed between the emotionally difficult situation of loving and supporting their children without unnecessarily challenging them, parents often take responsibility for the actions and behaviors of their children. This allows the child to dismiss responsibility for the consequences of their behaviors. This feeds the addiction because the child is never forced to look at the harmful consequences of his or her behavior.

Children with behavioral addictions often display both an alarming lack of concern for those they affect and a disarming, narcissistic, self-concern. In the jargon of addiction treatment, this behavior becomes an example of "It's not the person but the addiction speaking." At this stage, children have learned to manipulate their parents' confusion and concern. Parents' attempts to control children's environments are vigorously opposed or cleverly bypassed. Children may lie, steal, and mislead to overcome the obstacles. The home environment becomes hostile, discordant, and conflict-ridden.

To establish stability, calm, and peace, parents begin to second guess how they should act around their addicted children, what they should or should not say, and what feelings they should share or keep to themselves. The relationship between parents and the addicted child may feel strained, forced, uncomfortable, and unfamiliar.

In an environment of indecision, addicted children will continue to accept that all is well; they will do this until parents express concern or confrontation. Children then often respond in the extreme. Pleading, promises, punishment, coercion, and reward have lost their effectiveness at this point. Even if both parents and child do not want a discordant climate, they lack the language and direction to make sustainable changes for the better. However, in any family that is understood to function as a system, it takes only one member to effect change in the rest of the family and to prompt the family toward a healthier direction.

Knowing what type of help to get, and where to get it, is critical to family recovery.

PARENTING AS A CURE

At the most basic level, parents must acknowledge how their responses may have made the addiction worse and treatment more difficult. Going against better judgment; not standing their ground; and punishing, bribing, and codependently watching and reacting to their troubled child have all made the family system less functional, trustworthy, and effective.

The first step in treating the addict and his or her family is for parents to accept how they may have helped sustain an addiction in their child. Parents can rarely control their children's harmful behaviors, but they can control their responses to those behaviors. They can begin to control their dysfunctional responses.

Parents must educate themselves about addiction in general and the specific behavioral addiction of their child. This will include demonstrating healthier behaviors for the child. Parents should understand that they may do whatever they can to help their child but do nothing that supports the addiction.

Parents did not create the addiction, and they cannot control or cure it. Parents who educate themselves about healthy actions, rather than reactions, can begin to support their addicted child.

Progress is likely to be uneven. Parents can make great strides in recovery while the child seems to regress, or the reverse can occur. Critical to this stage of recovery is accepting that recovery from addiction involves a long-term commitment to practicing healthy behaviors. As long as one side incorporates even some positive behavioral changes, the entire family system will improve and the relationship between child and parents will begin to mend.

While these behavioral modifications are critical first steps toward a healthier, addiction-free life, they are not usually enough to address all aspects of the addiction. Routinely, parents' and children's recoveries will involve multidimensional treatment, often with a specially trained clinician and with group support. Some addicts will need to enroll in a treatment facility to facilitate their recovery.

It is vital that parents and the child work separately at modifying their behaviors first. The best place to start is with a counselor who is trained to work with addicts and their parents. The counselor will be able to set up a proper treatment plan and refer the patients to the right resources.

Parents should seek professional help and support groups for themselves too. Self-help groups such as Al-Anon, Alateen, and Co-Dependents Anonymous also are available for parents and other family members to receive additional support.

Paul Moglia

FURTHER READING
American Academy of Child and Adolescent Psychiatry. "Facts for Families." Washington, DC: AACAP, 2011. An informational series for parents and families facing a variety of real-world issues, including behavioral addictions.
Sadock, B. J., and V. A. Sadock, eds. *Kaplan and Sadock's Comprehensive Textbook of Psychiatry.* Philadelphia: Lippincott, 2000. Contains detailed descriptions of various behavioral addictions, written for clinicians but comprehensible to general readers.

WEBSITES OF INTEREST
Al-Anon Family Groups
http://www.al-anon.alateen.org

Families Anonymous
http://www.familiesanonymous.org

See also: Behavioral addictions: Overview; Children and behavioral addictions; Families and behavioral addictions; Marriage/partnership and behavioral addictions; Parenting and alcoholism; Parenting and substance abuse

Parenting and substance abuse

CATEGORY: Psychological issues and behaviors
DEFINITION: More than eight million children in the United States live with a parent (or parents) who abuses or depends on alcohol or drugs. Children of substance abusers are more likely to be physically abused, neglected, and injured and are more likely to abuse drugs or alcohol as adults.

INTRODUCTION
In 2005 the American Psychiatric Association set forth four major criteria for drug and alcohol use to be classified as substance abuse. The criteria include repeated instances of drugs and alcohol preventing a parent from fulfilling crucial obligations at work or home, the continued placement of oneself or one's children in potentially physically hazardous situations, the recurrence of substance-related legal infractions, and the continued abuse of substances after the recurrence of one or all of these problems.

Alcohol and substance abuse during pregnancy has been definitively proven to be detrimental to the fetus. In addition to the well-documented damages caused by fetal alcohol syndrome, both alcohol and drug abuse place the fetus at risk for intrauterine growth retardation and higher susceptibility for infectious disease before birth.

Children who are reared by a parent or parents with substance abuse problems also have been shown to have impaired cognitive and social development skills, slowed learning skills, and a wide range of mental health problems, including depression and anxiety.

ALCOHOL ABUSE
Data from the National Survey on Drug Use and Health indicate that of the more than eight million children in the United States living with a substance abusing parent, the majority of those children (more than seven million) has a parent who abuses or is dependent on alcohol specifically. Young children of alcoholics are habitually given less attention than the alcohol itself by their parents. This leads to low self-esteem and decreased self-worth in the children, fostering fears of helplessness and abandonment.

The mood swings and erratic behavior of alcoholic parents also can lead to stress-induced nightmares, paranoia, and bedwetting in young children. Young children of alcoholics also are placed at a much higher risk of injuries, which result from inadequate supervision in the home or vehicular accidents caused by alcohol-impaired drivers.

Instances of incest and domestic violence also occur with considerably higher frequency in families in which alcoholism is prevalent. Because young children are poorly equipped to handle the emotional trauma that results from these incidents, they are at higher risk of lifelong psychological and mental disorders, including anxiety and depression.

The general alienation by and mistrust of adults also can lead young children into deviant behavior at school and in their community. This mistrust acts as a barrier for the children of alcoholic parents to seek solace or support from other adults, both outside the home and within their immediate families. The inability to relate and the lack of understanding in interactions with children from households unaffected by alcoholism also can lead to anger, hostility, and erratic behavior in peer interactions. This leads to further isolation and social abandonment.

DRUG ABUSE

While less prevalent nationwide than instances of parental alcohol abuse, parental drug abuse is equally hazardous to the health and proper development of children. As with abusive alcohol use, the number of potential prenatal dangers is lengthy and widely documented by medical research.

Pregnant women who use drugs, particularly those who ingest drugs intravenously, risk exposing the fetus to infectious disease. Severe brain damage, stroke, low birth weight, and organ failure are also common problems associated with prenatal use of illicit drugs.

Maltreatment such as sexual abuse and battery and habitual periods of neglect are of higher prevalence in families with one or more drug-using parent. The lack of structure and routine in the lives of children of substance abusers can also lead children to lash out at school and at day care.

While alcohol can be acquired legally and is readily available, controlled substances must be obtained through illicit transactions, often in environments that are unsuitable or unsafe for children. These environments include violent and crime-ridden neighborhoods.

Children of drug abusers are frequently exposed to these dangerous environments or experience lengthy periods of neglect in their own home while their parents seek the drugs. Lengthy neglect is particularly challenging for the older siblings of young children, who often have the responsibility of parenting their younger siblings when they are themselves lacking in the proper emotional, physical, and psychological abilities to navigate everyday life.

Similarly, children preoccupied with concern for their drug-abusing parents place education at a lower priority, resulting in less-than-adequate academic development and achievement. Shame, mistrust, and fear also hinder the children of drug-abusing parents. The children have trouble building trusting relationships both with their own peers and with adults, which further perpetuates feelings of isolation and helplessness.

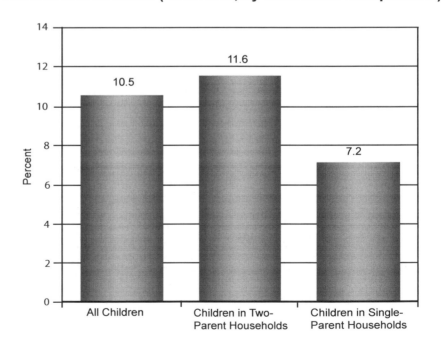

Percentage of Children Living with a Parent with a Past-Year Alcohol Use Disorder (2005-2010, by Household Composition)

Source: National Survey on Drug Use and Health (NSDUH), Substance Abuse and Mental Health Services Administration (SAMHSA)

TROUBLED ADULTHOODS

Children raised in drug-free homes or by parents with normative behaviors toward drugs and alcohol may experiment with such substances themselves. Children of substance-abusing parents, however, are raised in an environment that promotes alcohol and drug use as an acceptable and preferable way to combat the stresses, emotions, and responsibilities of life. Many children of addicts resort to the use of drugs and alcohol to ease the psychological and emotional pains of childhood, or they simply view such behavior as normal, leaving them vulnerable to abuse themselves.

Although there is little evidence to prove a genetic predisposition to illicit drug use, a large body of evidence exists to show a genetic connection between alcoholism in the children of alcoholic parents. According to the National Association of Children of Alcoholics (NACA), biological children of alcohol-dependent parents are four times as likely to become alcoholics themselves.

Children of substance abusers face difficult circumstances even if they manage to avoid the patterns of alcoholism and drug use demonstrated by their parents. Academic underachievement is common among children of substance abusers. These children repeatedly underperform on all standardized tests measuring academic skills, such as reading comprehension and mathematics. In one study reported by the NACA, 41 percent of children with drug- or alcohol-abusing parents repeat an academic grade because of poor performance or lagging academic comprehension. This lack of academic preparedness leaves children of substance abusers with fewer skills, interests, and motivations to apply toward careers and hobbies as adults.

The cyclical nature of damaging, abusive, and neglectful childhoods is perhaps the most severe consequence of substance abuse on parenting. Substance abuse can affect families for several generations. Early education on the dangers of alcohol abuse and illicit drug use has become a key tool in addressing the problem in the United States. Also critical is the establishment of effective outreach and social programs in which at-risk children can communicate about abusive behaviors and harmful home environments and can find support from their school or community.

John Pritchard

FURTHER READING

"Children Living with Substance-Dependent or Substance-Abusing Parents: 2002 to 2007." National Survey on Drug Use and Health. 16 Apr. 2009. Web. 20 Apr. 2012. http://www.samhsa.gov/data/2k9/SAparents/SAparents.htm.

Greenberg, Rivka, Annabelle Bonifacio, and Deborah Werner. *Children of Substance Abusers: COSA Resource List.* Substance Abuse and Mental Health Services Administration. 2008. Web. 20 Apr. 2012. http://womenandchildren.treatment.org/documents/cosa-resource-508v.pdf.

National Association for Children of Alcoholics. "Children of Addicted Parents: Important Facts." Web. 20 Apr. 2012. http://www.nacoa.net/pdfs/addicted.pdf.

Sims, Armethia L. "A Substance Abuse Prevention Guide for Parents." National Association of School Nurses. Web. 20 Apr. 2012. http://www.nasn.org/Portals/0/resources/pd_toolkit_parents_comp_booklet.pdf.

WEBSITES OF INTEREST

American Council for Drug Education
http://www.acde.org/health/riskfact.htm

Child Welfare Information Gateway: Parental Substance Abuse
http://www.childwelfare.gov/can/factors/parentcaregiver/substance.cfm

Hope Networks
http://www.hopenetworks.org/addiction/Children%20of%20Addicts.htm

National Center on Substance Abuse and Child Welfare
http://www.ncsacw.samhsa.gov

See also: Families and substance abuse; Marriage/partnership and substance abuse; Parenting and alcoholism; Parenting and behavioral addictions

PCP

CATEGORY: Substances

ALSO KNOWN AS: Angel dust; embalming fluid; phencyclidine; Sernyl; wet; whack

DEFINITION: PCP is a recreational drug with hallucinogenic and dissociative properties. It was first produced as a potential agent for anesthesia but was later recognized as a dangerous substance of abuse that can significantly alter mental status.

STATUS: Illegal in the United States and worldwide

CLASSIFICATION: Schedule II controlled substance

SOURCE: No natural source; illegally synthesized by combining several chemicals into a crystal or powder

TRANSMISSION ROUTE: Snorted in powder form or smoked when applied to other substances such as marijuana or an herb; injected intravenously, subcutaneously, or intramuscularly; orally ingested as a tablet or capsule

HISTORY OF USE

Phencyclidine (PCP) was originally synthesized in 1926 as 1-(1-phenylcyclohexyl)piperidine. It was intended for use as an intravenous surgical anesthetic during World War II because it caused decreased sensitivity to pain (analgesia) without decreasing heart and lung function or muscle tone. Its use was discontinued for this purpose after patients had adverse psychological side effects that included increased agitation and psychosis.

PCP was patented 1963 as the anesthetic Sernyl by Parke-Davis Pharmaceutical but was taken off the market two years later because of the drug's negative psychological effects and long half-life. PCP reappeared for veterinary use in 1967 as an animal tranquilizer.

PCP gained popularity as a recreational substance in the late 1960s because of the psychological effects. In 1969, however, PCP was made an illegal substance to possess, sell, or manufacture. In the early 1970s, the drug was categorized as a schedule III controlled substance. It was moved from schedule III to schedule II in 1978.

Since the 1970s, PCP's popularity has substantially decreased, but the drug remains readily available. Initial data from the peak of PCP use in 1979 revealed that 7 percent of high school students had used the drug. Data in 2009 from the National Survey on Drug Use and Health showed that only 122,000 Americans had used PCP within the previous calendar year; 1 percent of these persons were high school students.

Many persons are exposed to PCP without their knowledge. One study found that almost 25 percent of marijuana also contained trace levels of PCP. Additionally, PCP and other recreational drugs are gaining popularity as alternative drugs for treating chronic pain.

EFFECTS AND POTENTIAL RISKS

PCP acts as an N-methyl d-aspartate (NMDA) receptor antagonist by blocking NMDA receptor activity. It also inhibits the nicotinic acetylcholine receptor channels. By both of these mechanisms, PCP interferes with the brain's natural neurotransmitter responses. The actions of PCP on the brain are complex, causing both stimulation and depression of the central nervous system. This explains why some users may have a calming response to PCP exposure, while others may have an agitated or aggressive reaction.

The timing of drug effects depends on the mode of administration. Inhalation of PCP is the most common route because the drug works quite rapidly if inhaled; symptoms can be observed within about five minutes. With oral ingestion, symptoms can take up to one hour to be realized. The first effects of PCP last for approximately four to seven hours, but the long-lasting consequences continue for several days or even one week.

Initial effects of low doses (3 to 5 milligrams [mg]) resemble those of alcohol intoxication, including slurred speech and an unsteady gait (ataxia), and a numbing of the arms and legs. There is a significant increase in blood pressure (hypertension), pulse rate (tachycardia), and analgesia.

At increased doses (of more than 5 mg) PCP causes a decrease in respiratory rate, an irregular heart beat (arrhythmia), increased muscle tone (hypertonia), and seizures. In addition to the physiological effects, PCP also produces significant alterations in mental status at high doses. The psychological effects include hallucinations, delusions, an "out-of body" experience, amnesia, paranoia, a catatonic state, and disorganized thinking. Depression and psychosis may persist for an extended time after withdrawal.

The risk of permanent schizophrenic-like symptoms exists with PCP abuse rather than with occasional recreational use. PCP is unpredictable in how mood and mental status will be changed, and some users have negative experiences that lead to an increased tendency for suicidal thoughts or committing violent acts. Hospitalization may be required to closely monitor symptoms while recovering.

Coma and deaths have been reported from cardiac arrest, strokes from hypertension, increased body temperature (hyperthermia), breakdown of muscle (rhabdomyolysis), and increased potassium levels (hyperkalemia). Suicides and accidents secondary to violent behavior also are commonly reported. Deaths also occur because of the consumption of an unknown dosage, the presence of contaminated materials in substances that have been illegally manufactured and distributed, underlying medical issues, and the use of other drugs simultaneously.

Janet Ober Berman, MS, CGC

FURTHER READING

Bey, Tareg, and Anar Patel. "Phencyclidine Intoxication and Adverse Effects: A Clinical and Pharmacological Review of an Illicit Drug." *California Journal of Emergency Medicine* 8.1 (2007): 9–14. Print. Comprehensive review of the biochemistry, physiological and psychological effects, and medical management of PCP.

Deroux, Stephen, Anthony Sgarlato, and Elizabeth Marker. "Phencyclidine: A 5-Year Retrospective Review from the New York City Medical Examiner's Office." *Journal of Forensic Sciences* 56.3 (2011): 656–59. Print. Results of a study that found that lower doses of PCP can be fatal if a user has additional medical concerns.

Liu, F., et al. "Changes in Gene Expression after Phencyclidine Administration in Developing Rats: A Potential Animal Model for Schizophrenia." *International Journal of Developmental Neuroscience* 29.3 (2011): 351–58. Print. Results of a study of rats that found PCP alters gene expression and thus increases neuronal cell death, with discussion of the implications for potential treatment of schizophrenia symptoms in humans.

WEBSITES OF INTEREST

National Institute on Drug Abuse
http://www.drugabuse.gov/infofacts/hallucinogens.html

The Partnership at DrugFree.org
http://www.drugfree.org/drug-guide/pcp

See also: Hallucinogen abuse; Hallucinogens: Short- and long-term effects on the body; Recreational drugs

Peer pressure

CATEGORY: Psychological issues and behaviors
ALSO KNOWN AS: Peer influence
DEFINITION: A peer is any person who approximately shares one's age, social status, and interests. Peer pressure to experiment with alcohol or drugs is predictive of substance use, especially among youth.

CONCEPTUAL ISSUES

Biological development may vary among peers. Children and adolescents may or may not have a single best friend and may join different social groups with different norms; their relationships with parents may vary too. These differences must be considered when studying the influence of peers on one another's behaviors.

Often, this influence is tested by gathering a self-report of the target person's behavior (for example, substance use and sexual behavior) and also by measuring that target's report of a peer's behavior. These measurements are then correlated. The typical finding is that the target's behavior is related systematically to a peer's behavior, and this is taken as evidence of peer influence. Although there is abundant evidence of peer influence for substance use and abuse using this strategy, this effect may be inflated because of serious methodological artifacts.

SCIENCE OF PEER INFLUENCE

Peer influence indexed through self-reports ignores a number of alternative processes that could produce positive correlations between a target person's substance use and that of a peer.

One alternative process is called common developmental trajectory. Two peers of identical age may also be developing biologically in a similar way and can thus display and promote similar behaviors (such as substance use or sexual behavior) at the same time. What may appear as peer influence is actually a common developmental trajectory.

Group norms too can affect the behavior of peers similarly. A person may be a member of a group that values alcohol and drug consumption, and all members of the group share a similar attitude toward the behavior. This is a mutual influence effect.

Multiple groups can have different norms regarding substance use, and there can be more variability among groups than among individuals within groups. The ecological context can affect the behavior of group members; the substance use of adolescents in a peer group can be affected by the substance use of the adults in their community. This feature of social ecology causes members within the same environment to behave similarly.

If one were to consider communities in which adult substance use was low and other communities in which adult substance use was high, the ecological model would predict greater adolescent substance use in the latter than in the former. Peers may also selectively form relationships with peers similar to them; the similarity of their behavior is not necessarily the result of one peer's influence on another, but is, instead, a form of selective relationship formation. For example, female adolescents who have experienced parental abuse may form relationships and engage in risky behavior that are ultimately consequences of their shared developmental experiences and not necessarily peer influence effects.

EMPIRICAL FINDINGS

Only recently has peer influence research on substance use acknowledged and attempted to control for the different causal mechanisms that can produce artificial evidence of peer influence. The use of statistical methods to isolate the peer influence effect, after controlling for other effects, yields statistically significant, though modest, peer influence effects on substance use.

In 2010, researchers reported that "a 10 percent increase in close friend drinking will increase the likelihood of drinking by more than 2 percent" and that "a 10 percent increase in drinking among grade-level peers is associated with a 4 percent increase in individual drinking." Similarly, in 2005, researchers concluded that, after controlling for possible artifacts, the peer influence effect of a close friend on binge drinking was relatively weak. To the extent that there was a peer influence effect on adolescents' binge drinking, both peers had evidenced similar developmental histories and dissatisfaction with the parental relationship.

One possibility for this outcome is that when an adolescent's relationship with a parent is unsatisfactory, that adolescent's behavior may be more easily influenced by peers. In a 2002 study of young adults aged nineteen to twenty-five years, researchers found that a target person's same- and opposite-gender friends' binge-drinking and cigarette use was associated with their own use of these substances. Because alcohol and tobacco are legal substances, their use may be more acceptable in the peer group, especially when group members use these substances.

INTERVENTION

Developmental scientists recognize that behavior is a function of the individual; the social environment, including peers; and the ecological context. To understand peer influence on substance use and abuse, one must understand the determinants at multiple levels of analysis. The peer influence effect must be disentangled from other causal mechanisms that also have implications for substance use and abuse interventions.

If, for example, adolescent substance use is determined more strongly by group norms than by the influence of specific peers, then interventions should target these norms rather than emphasize resistance to persuasive messages by peers to use substances. In future work, it will be particularly important to understand the moderation of peer effects on substance use and also how the effect is mediated. It is important to recognize that peer influence on substance use is much more complicated than previously recognized, and may not be as strong as once thought.

Thomas E. Malloy, PhD

FURTHER READING

Ali, Mir M., and Deborah S. Swyer. "Social Network Effects in Alcohol Consumption among Adolescents." *Addictive Behaviors* 35 (2010): 337–42. Print. An analysis of peer influence that attempts to control for variables other than peer influence that affect alcohol use among adolescents.

Andrews, Judy A., and Hyman Hops. "The Influence of Peers on Substance Use." *Handbook of Drug Use Etiology: Theory, Methods, and Empirical Findings.*

Ed. L. Scheier. Washington, DC: American Psychological Association, 2010. A review of the peer influence literature that brings together scientific thinking and research.

Andrews, Judy A., et al. "The Influence of Peers on Young Adult Substance Use." *Health Psychology* 21 (2002): 349–57. Print. Provides a look at peer influence among young adults and its effect on substance use among young adults.

Dodge, Kenneth A., Thomas J. Dishion, and Jennifer E. Lansford. "Deviant Peer Influences in Intervention and Public Policy for Youth." *Social Policy Report* 20.1 (2006): 2–19. Web. http://www.srcd.org/documents/publications/SPR/spr20-1.pdf. 23 Apr. 2012. Reviews the evidence on group interventions for deviant adolescents and makes recommendations that address the public policy problem of placements for deviant youth.

Jaccard, James, Hart Blanton, and Tonya Dodge. "Peer Influence on Risky Behavior: An Analysis of the Effects of a Close Friend." *Developmental Psychology* 41 (2005): 135–47. Print. An analysis of peer influence that controls for variables other than peer influence that affect risky sexual behavior and substance use.

WEBSITES OF INTEREST

NIDA for Teens
http://www.teens.drugabuse.gov

TheCoolSpot.gov
http://www.thecoolspot.gov

See also: Gateway drugs; Teens/young adults and alcohol abuse; Teens/young adults and drug abuse; Teens/young adults and smoking

Phoenix House

CATEGORY: Treatment

DEFINITION: Phoenix House is a therapeutic community that treats a variety of substance addictions. Programs include assessment and evaluation, inpatient detoxification, residential and outpatient care, and programs for teenagers.

DATE: Established 1967

BACKGROUND

Phoenix House was established in Manhattan, New York, in 1967. The program developed out of a small group meeting of addicts that included psychiatrist Mitchell S. Rosenthal, who became a leader in implementing the residential treatment program. Phoenix House, modeled after the earliest forms of the therapeutic communities Daytop Village and Synanon, was led by graduates of these communities and by counselors from New York City's Addiction Services Agency.

Seven additional Phoenix House communities emerged within one year and, in 1972, Phoenix House became a nonprofit foundation. Phoenix House is now the largest nonprofit substance abuse treatment organization in the United States, with more than 120 programs around the country.

Phoenix House was the first treatment program to include prisoners when it started a program at Riker's Island, New York. Residents of Phoenix House have been diverse in terms of gender, age, race, and socioeconomic status, although some specialized programs treat specific addict populations, including adolescents, residents with co-occurring mental illnesses, men, and women. Phoenix House Academies, established in 1983, provide residential high schools for substance abusing youth with mental illnesses.

MISSION AND GOALS

The goals of Phoenix House focus not only on abstinence but also on inward growth and maturation. These goals are realized through a combination of self-help and mutual aid within a peer community. Underlying this treatment approach is the belief that addicts have a "defective" character disorder and that drug abuse is both an escape from and a symptom of this disorder. Within this view, sobriety is achieved by reshaping one's personality. The addict is considered immature, irresponsible, and selfish, and to have a flawed value system. Through treatment, the addict undergoes a resocialization process to establish new values through personal growth and through adopting a mature identity.

New residents start at the bottom of a hierarchy and work their way up to more desirable positions in the peer community. Jobs enhance work habits and self-reliance, assist residents in adapting to change, and allow residents to eventually assume positions of leadership by supervising others. Phoenix House works to be as economically independent as possible, with most routine services performed by house members. Residents are taught vocational skills and interpersonal skills that facilitate personality change and the acceptance of criticism, humiliation, and the following of orders.

The treatment model is organized around a confrontational style of group psychotherapy called the encounter. Limited to a small number of residents, the encounter encourages residents to express themselves honestly but nonviolently.

The model of substance abuse treatment provided by early programs, including Phoenix House, serves as the backbone of contemporary therapeutic communities. The mission of therapeutic communities remains much the same as in early years, although treatment innovations and programs recognizing the individual needs of clients have been adopted. Treatment of the whole person, including restructuring identity and enhancing self-esteem, continues to be of crucial importance. Although the general approaches of these types of therapeutic communities remain diverse, essential elements are the same: the promotion of community, honesty, and the reshaping of one's morals.

The encounter continues to be a primary form of group therapy. Program goals of communication, psychological growth, and vocational education are important objectives for successful recovery. Programs now include a variety of nonaddict professional and clinical staff in addition to former addicts. Preventive education programs also are offered in the community.

Through meetings, encounter groups, and jobs, resident involvement in the peer community reinforces life skills and morals that coincide with the expectations of society. Addressing how addicts think, behave, and communicate is fundamental to achieving personal growth and sobriety.

Residents progress through stages of treatment with typical program completion taking about two years, although residents live outside the residential community before graduation. During these stages residents increasingly earn more freedom as they prepare for their new lives outside the community. Many residents in later stages of treatment work fulltime, in or outside the residential community, or attend school. Aftercare is emphasized to maintain sobriety. Therapeutic communities continue to evolve but retain their emphasis on self-reliance, prosocial values, and behavior with the peer community as a facilitator of these changes.

Michelle Petrie, PhD

FURTHER READING

De Leon, George. *Phoenix House: Studies in a Therapeutic Community (1968–1973)*. New York: MSS, 1974. This edited book of essays provides a history of Phoenix House, a review of the main models of treatment, and a description of daily life. Includes a review of studies conducted on the first few years of Phoenix House that explore how neighborhoods have responded to having a therapeutic community on their block, the demographics of addicts, how length of stay affects treatment outcomes, and how dropping out affects future criminal activity.

---. *The Therapeutic Community.* New York: Springer, 2000. A general overview of the method, model, and theory underlying therapeutic communities. Emphasizes the common elements of therapeutic communities as they have evolved. Explores the philosophy behind treatment, the components of the peer community as a method of treatment, and the process of achieving sobriety through personal growth and lifestyle changes. Outlines daily residential life and stages of treatment.

National Institute on Drug Abuse. *Therapeutic Community: Advances in Research and Application.* Research Monograph 144. Rockville, MD: Author, 1994. This collection of essays reviews advances in therapeutic communities and includes an emphasis on specialized programs such as those for women, prisoners, and persons with co-occurring mental health issues.

WEBSITES OF INTEREST

National Institute on Drug Abuse
http://www.drugabuse.gov/podat/podatindex.html

Phoenix House
http://www.phoenixhouse.org

See also: Abstinence-based treatment; Group therapy for substance abuse; Prison and substance abuse; Rehabilitation programs; Residential treatment; Treatment methods and research

Physiological dependence

CATEGORY: Health issues and physiology
ALSO KNOWN AS: Physical dependence
DEFINITION: Physiological dependence refers to the adaptive changes made by the body to the continued presence of some drugs. These changes are observed when the dependent person experiences a drug-specific withdrawal syndrome, which is a set of unpleasant symptoms experienced when the drug is abruptly discontinued. Drugs of abuse can vary in the extent to which they produce physiological and psychological dependence.

BACKGROUND

Physiological dependence occurs when the body adapts to the continued presence of a drug. These adaptations lead to negative symptoms when the drug is removed or when the dose is dramatically reduced. As such, the presence of a drug-specific withdrawal syndrome, or a set of symptoms associated with drug removal, provides evidence for physiological dependence.

Many researchers use the term *physiological dependence* a bit more broadly, though, and would define it as including both tolerance and withdrawal. *Tolerance*, which typically develops before withdrawal, refers to the need to increase the dosage of a drug in order to achieve the same effect across time and with repeated dosing. In other words, with more experience taking the drug, more of the drug must be taken to maintain the drug's effectiveness.

Alcohol and opiate drugs, such as heroin, produce classic physiological dependence. For example, when a person takes an opiate drug, the initial effects include a significant reduction in pain, euphoria, and constipation. If the person takes the drug only occasionally, the body may not adapt to the presence of the drug in significant ways; therefore, the same dose may be sufficient to produce the initial effects. However, if the drug is taken repeatedly, tolerance may develop in a matter of weeks or even days. The initial dose will no longer be as effective in reducing pain or in increasing euphoria and constipation. If one wants to maintain the initial effects, the dose will need to be increased and will continue to need to be increased as more and more tolerance develops.

The drugged state is the body's "new normal." One can observe how much the body has adapted to operating in the presence of a drug by observing the drug-specific withdrawal symptoms after the drug is removed (or stopped). In cases of physiological dependence, withdrawal symptoms are basically the opposite of the effects produced by the drugs themselves. These often unpleasant symptoms can be easily eliminated, with another dose of the drug. Though alcohol also produces tolerance and withdrawal, the specific symptoms will be quite different, because the effects of the drug itself are different, requiring different adaptations.

IS PHYSIOLOGICAL DEPENDENCE ADDICTION?

Physiological dependence has sometimes been considered synonymous with the concept of addiction. This view, however, has changed as researchers and clinicians have recognized the importance of other factors, including psychological dependence, on addictive behavior.

Instead of producing physiological withdrawal symptoms, repeated abuse of a drug produces a preoccupation with the drug, a pattern of escalating and uncontrolled use, craving, and other maladaptive behavior changes. Physiological and psychological dependence do not necessarily go together. Some drugs of abuse have a high probability of producing psychological dependence but vary dramatically in the extent to which they produce clear drug-specific symptoms of withdrawal (if they produce any symptoms of withdrawal). However, in some cases drugs that were not thought to produce clear physiological dependence (such as cocaine and marijuana) have since been found to do so.

Finally, the opposite can be true as well. Some drugs may produce strong physiological dependence without producing strong psychological dependence. A good example of this is caffeine. The most noticeable withdrawal symptom of caffeine dependence is headache, which can easily be alleviated with another cup of coffee or a caffeinated beverage. Caffeine headaches are clear and consistent markers of physiological dependence, but having these headaches are not associated with addiction. That is, daily coffee drinkers with caffeine headaches are not considered addicts because they rarely exhibit the maladaptive behavioral changes associated with addiction.

The vast majority of caffeine drinkers, though they may be physiologically dependent upon caffeine, are not psychologically dependent in any clinically relevant way. Most habitual coffee drinkers do not become preoccupied with caffeine; they do not typically develop escalating and uncontrolled patterns of caffeine use or other maladaptive behavioral changes.

Furthermore, many drugs produce changes in the body that lead to tolerance and withdrawal that are not related to substance abuse in any way. For these reasons, physiological dependence is no longer used as a synonym for addiction. Though physiological dependence can occur with substances of abuse, it need not. The capacity to produce physiological dependence is neither necessary nor sufficient to describe a drug's addictive potential.

TREATMENT

Most acute withdrawal symptoms last for days, but in some cases they can be extraordinarily unpleasant (as is the case with opiates) if not medically dangerous (as is the case with alcohol). Therefore, the treatment of many addictions must begin with treating the withdrawal symptoms. This is particularly important in alcohol treatment, where withdrawal symptoms can include life-threatening seizures.

Substitute drugs that have some central nervous system effects in common with alcohol can be provided for a period of time, as the brain and body adjust to the removal of alcohol. Effective drugs for alleviating symptoms of alcohol include a class of tranquilizing drugs called the benzodiazepines. The benzodiazepines themselves, however, also can produce physiological dependence. This illustrates an important challenge for drug treatment.

Ideally, one would like to alleviate the symptoms of withdrawal without perpetuating or worsening physiological dependence. This may not always be easy to accomplish, as substitute drugs that are effective in treating withdrawal often produce physiological dependence themselves. Another example is methadone treatment of opiate withdrawal.

An additional challenge in treating physiological dependence is the possibility of negative symptoms that persist beyond the period of acute withdrawal. These symptoms are referred to as post-acute withdrawal symptoms (PAWS) and can include anhedonia (the inability to experience pleasure), drug craving, tendency to relapse to using the drug, and cognitive impairment.

These symptoms are far less drug-specific, may occur to some extent even with drugs that do not produce acute withdrawal effects, and can last for months, years, or even decades after the initial withdrawal from the drug of abuse. Though less understood, PAWS may indicate that the notion of physiological dependence may need to be expanded with improved understanding of these longer-lasting changes.

Linda R. Tennison, PhD

FURTHER READING

Julien, Robert M., Claire D. Advokat, and Joseph E. Comaty. *A Primer of Drug Action.* 12th ed. New York: Worth, 2011. An excellent, thorough text covering uses and effects of both psychiatric substances and drugs of abuse.

Ksir, Charles, Carl Hart, and Ray Oakley. *Drugs, Society, and Human Behavior.* 12th ed. Boston: McGraw-Hill, 2006. An entry-level textbook on substances of abuse.

WEBSITES OF INTEREST

MedlinePlus: Drug Dependence
http://www.nlm.nih.gov/medlineplus/ency/article/001522.htm

National Institute on Drug Abuse
http://www.drugabuse.gov

See also: Alcohol: Short- and long-term effects on the body; Caffeine: Short- and long-term effects on the body; Dependence; Narcotics: Short- and long-term effects on the body; Psychological dependence; Symptoms of substance abuse; Withdrawal

Pipes and hookahs

CATEGORY: Substance abuse
ALSO KNOWN AS: Bong; chillum; nargile; shisha; water pipe
DEFINITION: Pipes used to smoke marijuana consist of a bowl made of heat-resistant material such as stone, glass, ivory, metal, or clay. At the funnel-shaped base of the bowl, the smoker places marijuana, tobacco, or a mixture of the two, and then burns the mixture, drawing through the pipe to

inhale the smoke. Hookahs, traditionally used to smoke tobacco, include a heat-resistant bowl, a shaft that connects the bowl to a water vessel, and a hose through which the smoker draws the smoke.

MARIJUANA PIPES

Pipe smoking is a traditional method for smoking marijuana (dried leaves and flowers of the cannabis plant), ganja (sap-carrying tops of female cannabis), and hashish (dried resin from cannabis flowers). Using the traditional pipe, the chillum, four or five people gather around the pipe to smoke marijuana, tobacco, or a mixture of the two.

Another marijuana pipe is the one-hitter, a miniature smoking-pipe with a screened bowl designed for a single "hit" (inhalation) of marijuana. The screen catches the ash but allows the cannabinoids, which are an active component of marijuana, to pass through easily when burnt. So-called "stealth" pipes, which are designed to camouflage or hide the pipe, are designed to look like markers, fountain pens, flashlights, and bracelets, for example.

Marijuana also can be smoked through a water pipe. The water-pipe smoker burns marijuana in the head of the pipe. The base is partially filled with water. The smoker inhales through a hose and draws smoke down through the water. The smoke bubbles up out of the water and into the smoker's mouth. A bong is a small water pipe with a water filtration system. Hookahs are water pipes used to smoke tobacco.

HOOKAHS AND TOBACCO

Hookahs are ornately made pipes that come in many shapes and are made from various materials, such as brier (a thorny plant), stone, clay, wood, porcelain, meerschaum (a soft white mineral), metal, and glass. Hookahs are thought to have originated in Africa or Asia as early as the fourteenth century. People in the Middle East have been smoking hookah since the early seventeenth century.

Maassel is the most common type of tobacco smoked in a hookah. The sweet tobacco is fermented in molasses and fruit to produce many flavors, such as cherry, apple, blackberry, grape, orange, and mint. Groups of people meet at hookah bars, coffeehouses, and restaurants, which are often exempt from laws that prohibit smoking indoors. The water pipe can be

A hookah, or water pipe, is shown. People who smoke tobacco with a hookah believe it to be safer than smoking cigarettes. (Jim Middlekauff/Express-Times/Landov)

shared as it is passed from one person to another, or it can be used by an individual smoker.

People who smoke tobacco with a hookah believe it to be safer than smoking cigarettes. The smoke is indeed mild, but it is high in nicotine. Smoke from a single session of hookah (commonly thirty to sixty minutes) exceeds the nicotine content of a cigarette. Hookah smokers believe that the water in the pipe filters the nicotine, but the water in this type of pipe filters less than 5 percent of the nicotine from the smoke, leaving enough nicotine to make hookah smoking addictive.

Tobacco from a hookah is burned at a lower temperature than a cigarette, encouraging the smoker to inhale deeply and, thereby, pull more smoke into the lungs. The smoke contains twenty times more tar than the smoke of a cigarette, and the hookah produces as much smoke as more than one hundred cigarettes. The nicotine absorption is equivalent to smoking ten cigarettes per day.

Furthermore, the charcoal used to heat the tobacco in the hookah pipe produces toxic fumes. Hookah smokers are exposed to twice the level of carbon monoxide as cigarette smokers. Being exposed to secondhand smoke from a hookah may be just as dangerous as from a cigarette.

Smoking hookah may lead to health problems that include heart disease, lung cancer, respiratory diseases, and decreased fertility. Pregnant women are more likely to have babies with low birthweights. Viruses such as herpes simplex and Epstein-Barr are potentially spread by sharing hookah pipe mouthpieces.

In the United States hookah smoking is popular with college students, who consider the method safer and more acceptable than smoking cigarettes. The students perceive hookahs as novel, exotic, sensual, relaxing, and intimate. It is a social event promoting conversation among friends. Smoking hookah also is popular among teenagers.

Elizabeth Marie McGhee Nelson, PhD

FURTHER READING

Barnett, Tracey E., et al. "Water Pipe Tobacco Smoking among Middle and High School Students." *American Journal of Public Health* 99.11 (2009): 2014–19. Print. Examines water-pipe use among middle and high school students.

Beresteine, Leslie. "Healthy or Not, the Hookah Habit Is Hot." *Time* 161 (2003): 10. Print. Reports on hookah use among college students.

Kandela, Peter. "Nargile Smoking Keeps Arabs in Wonderland." *The Lancet* 356 (2000): 1175. Discusses the cultural importance of hookah smoking and the potential hazards.

Maziak, Wasim. "The Waterpipe: Time for Action." *Addiction* 103 (2008): 1763–67. Print. Discusses public health issues among hookah smokers.

Noonan, Devon. "Exemptions for Hookah Bars in Clean Indoor Air Legislation: A Public Health Concern." *Public Health Nursing* 27.1 (2010): 49–53. Print. Examines legal exemptions for smoking hookah pipes in indoor settings.

Noonan, Devon, and Pamela A. Kulbok. "New Tobacco Trends: Waterpipe (Hookah) Smoking and Implications for Healthcare Providers." *Journal of the American Academy of Nurse Practitioners* 21 (2009): 258–60. Print. Discusses hookah smoking from the clinical perspective.

Primack, Brian A., et al. "Prevalence of and Associations with Waterpipe Tobacco Smoking among US University Students." *Annals of Behavioral Medicine* 36 (2008): 81–86. Print. Results of a study that investigated the prevalence of hookah smokers among college students.

WEBSITES OF INTEREST

American Lung Association
http://www.lungusa2.org/embargo/slati/Trendalert_Waterpipes.pdf

Centers for Disease Control and Prevention
http://www.cdc.gov/tobacco/data_statistics/fact_sheets/tobacco_industry/hookahs

NIDA for Teens: Tobacco Addiction
http://teens.drugabuse.gov/facts/facts_nicotine1.php

See also: Drug paraphernalia; Hashish; Marijuana; Smoking

Poppers

CATEGORY: Substances

ALSO KNOWN AS: Alkyl nitrite; amyl nitrite; butyl nitrite; cyclohexyl nitrite; isobutyl nitrite; isopropyl nitrite

DEFINITION: Poppers are alkyl nitrites, a class of chemicals that are inhaled for recreational purposes, often to enhance sexual pleasure. The inhalation of popper vapors leads to a warm sensation, dizziness, and a sense of relaxation. Legal and easily available, the more popular brands include Hardware, Kix, Locker Room, Manscent, Pearls, Quicksilver, Ram, Rave, Rockhard, Rush, and Snappers.

STATUS: Legal in the United States and most countries worldwide

SOURCE: Alykl nitrites do not occur naturally, but are chemical compounds. Amyl nitrite, a form of alkyl nitrite, and its isomers feature an unreactive amyl group attached to a functional nitrito group, which generally functions as a source of nitric oxide. In mammals, including humans, nitric oxide causes relaxation of the involuntary muscles.

TRANSMISSION ROUTE: Poppers, in their amyl nitrite form, were originally sold in small, mesh covered glass ampoules that were crushed to release their vapors. These vapors are inhaled through the nose or mouth. In all forms, poppers are generally liquid nitrites (and generally volatile) that are inhaled.

HISTORY OF USE

Scottish physician Thomas Lauder Brunton pioneered the use of amyl nitrite in 1867 to treat angina (chest pain); the substance dilates the coronary arteries, making blood flow more freely to the heart. Now manufactured by Burroughs Wellcome (now GlaxoSmithKline) and Eli Lilly and Company, amyl nitrite was first sold in glass ampoules, or vials.

Light alkyl nitrites are effective antidotes to cyanide poisoning, and they are therefore carried by first responders. Light alkyl nitrites became available by prescription in 1937 and continued in that form through 1960, when they were made legal without a prescription. In 1969, they were available only with a prescription by the US Food and Drug Administration because of an increase in recreational use and abuse. Following the passage of the Anti-Drug Abuse Act of 1988, some alkyl nitrites were outlawed in the United States. The law, which also established the US Office of National Drug Control Policy, took effect in 1990, but it included exceptions for commercial purposes. Commercial manufacturers simply changed the chemical's formula and marketed alkyl nitrites as cleaners of carburetors and video player heads.

Amyl nitrite became known as poppers because of the popping sound made when the user crushes the ampoule containing the clear yellowish, unpleasant-smelling liquid to inhale its vapors. Butyl or cyclohexyl nitrite, sold as a video head cleaner (and referred to as rush, locker room, or climax), is often inhaled for a brief high. Isobutyl nitrite, a pungent colorless liquid that acts as a vasodilator, or a chemical that widens capillaries to increase blood flow, is used in the newest versions of poppers. These are sold under brand names such as Rush, Locker Room, Snappers, and Liquid Gold.

Used as a recreational drug for enhancing sexual pleasure, poppers create a sense of euphoria, relaxing smooth muscles like the sphincter muscles and the vagina, and are believed to cause more intense orgasms if inhaled immediately beforehand. Poppers also cause the smooth muscle surrounding blood vessels to relax, resulting in an immediate increase in heart rate and blood flow.

The legal status of poppers varies worldwide, and they are often sold as air fresheners and other common consumer products. Part of a multimillion-dollar industry since the 1970s, poppers are readily available online. In the United Kingdom, for example, poppers are sold in sex shops as room odorizers.

EFFECTS AND POTENTIAL RISKS

The effects of poppers on the human body are arguably less severe than those of many other recreational drugs. Although there are no withdrawal symptoms, and effects are instantaneous and short-lived (minutes), various studies have indicated the possible link between the drug and adverse effects. Accidental swallowing of the liquid can prove fatal (as cyanosis or methemoglobinemia), and if the liquid is spilled on the skin, it may cause serious burns.

The most common severe side effect has to do with vision. Recreational users of poppers can experience temporary vision problems, and heavy long-term use has been linked to worsening glaucoma by causing intraocular pressure. There is also potential for neurological damage. More common effects include headaches, and some men report short-term erectile dysfunction. Rare side effects include asphyxia, arrhythmias, carbon monoxide poisoning, and facial dermatitis. If used while taking prescription vasodilators (such as Viagra), poppers can cause a serious decrease in blood pressure, leading to fainting, stroke, or heart attack.

Although no definite proof exists, poppers have been associated with human immunodeficiency virus (HIV) infection and, more specifically, with Kaposi's sarcoma (a form of cancer and a complication of acquired immunodeficiency syndrome [AIDS], which is caused by HIV). More likely is the correlation between the use of poppers as a sexual enhancement drug and engaging in higher-risk sexual behavior. Finally, poppers may alter immune system function.

Anthony J. Fonseca, PhD

FURTHER READING

Joseph, Donald, ed. *Drugs of Abuse.* Washington, DC: GPO, 2005. The US Department of Justice's Drug Enforcement Administration offers concise, scientific information about drugs, including photographs and substance charts.

Shenton, Joan. *Positively False: Exposing the Myths around HIV and AIDS*. New York: Tauris, 1998. Challenges many common beliefs about acquired immunodeficiency syndrome (AIDS) by questioning many commonly argued hypotheses, including the role of poppers in the transmission of the virus that causes AIDS.

Stolberg, Victor B. "Amyl Nitrite." *Encyclopedia of Substance Abuse Prevention, Treatment, and Recovery*. Eds. Gary L. Fisher and Nancy A Roget. 2 vols. Thousand Oaks, CA: Sage, 2009. An encyclopedia entry detailing the history of poppers and their use.

Wills, Simon. *Drugs of Abuse*. 2nd ed. Chicago: Pharmaceutical, 2005. The author examines alkyl nitrites in chapter 18.

Wu, L. T., W. E. Schlenger, and C. L. Ringwalt. "Use of Nitrite Inhalants ('Poppers') among American Youth." *Journal of Adolescent Health* 37 (2005): 52–60. Print. Discusses the use of poppers by young people in the United States.

WEBSITES OF INTEREST

DanceSafe.org
http://dancesafe.org/drug-information/poppers

"Huffing, The Abuse of Inhalants." National Drug Intelligence Center
http://www.justice.gov/ndic/pubs07/708

"Inhalants." National Institute on Drug Abuse
http://www.drugabuse.gov/publications/infofacts/inhalants

See also: Club drugs; Inhalants abuse; Recreational drugs

Pornography addiction

CATEGORY: Psychological issues and behaviors
ALSO KNOWN AS: Cybersex addiction
DEFINITION: Pornography addiction is the excessive viewing of pornographic or sexually explicit material that results in negative consequences (relational, social, professional, financial) and that interferes with daily life and healthy psychological functioning. There is debate among researchers and clinical practitioners about whether or not porn addiction exists and if the language of drug addiction is appropriate in describing porn addiction.

BACKGROUND
There is no diagnosis of pornography (porn) addiction in the American Psychiatric Association's *Diagnostic and Statistical Manual of Mental Disorders* (DSM). However, porn addiction is under consideration as a particular variant of hypersexual disorder to be included in the revised DSM.

In many cases porn addiction may be better understood as overuse or problematic or compulsive use of sexually explicit materials without severe negative consequences, which often accompany other behavioral or drug addictions. Many psychologists who consider porn to be addictive also consider porn that is available online to be more problematic than traditional porn because of its ease of access. Also, online porn can be anonymously acquired, and it is affordable.

Advocates of the diagnosis of porn "addiction" argue that it is a behavioral addiction that activates the underlying neurological circuit involved in addictive drug use. Proponents also argue that the behavioral patterns of porn addiction are similar to those seen in drug addiction.

CAUSES
Given the nature of the human sex drive and the variety of psychological needs that sexual arousal and gratification serve, there is no one root cause for porn addition. Researcher Patrick Carnes has identified four core beliefs of persons struggling with sex or porn addictions: they are essentially bad, unworthy persons; they are unlovable as they currently are; their needs will never be met if they depend upon others to meet them; and satisfaction of their sexual needs is the most important thing in their life.

Several researchers and therapists have proposed stages of porn addiction, but these stages are not necessarily sequential. Also, there exists no general agreement on these stages. Reasons for excessive consumption of porn appear to be rooted in a desire for sexual pleasure or sexual variety, an escape from stress, and a way to cope with negative emotions.

RISK FACTORS

Research indicates that adolescent and young adult men are the primary consumers of sexually explicit materials and are most likely to develop maladaptive patterns of porn consumption. Other factors include early exposure to sexually explicit material, poor emotional attachment styles, and using porn as a masturbatory aid. Generally, the maladaptive pattern of use and sexually acting-out is developed between adolescence and early adulthood; however, it can begin later in adulthood.

SYMPTOMS

Symptoms of porn addiction are wide-ranging, but they generally follow those listed in the DSM for substance abuse (with appropriate modification). These symptoms include combinations of the following: recurrent viewing of pornographic material or images resulting in a failure to fulfill major role obligations at work, school, or home (such as repeated absences or poor work performance, suspensions or expulsion from school, or neglect of children or household); recurrent viewing of pornographic material or images that results in legal (criminal) problems; and continued viewing of pornographic material despite having persistent or recurrent social or interpersonal problems (for example, domestic and family) caused or exacerbated by their effects.

More specifically, the symptoms may include excessive personal (non-work-related) viewing of more than twenty hours per week, neglect or avoidance of previously rewarding personal relationships or interaction with peers, depression (either short- or long-term), underestimation of time spent viewing or searching for material, and pursuit of "highs" that have been experienced while online.

Generally, the porn addict is unable to choose whether or not to perform the behavior (and is addictive or compulsive) and continues to view porn in spite of clear, negative consequences (such as marital problems, financial problems, and sexual dysfunction). Also, the addict's thoughts center on the sexual content and the pornographic material (such as the next time it can be viewed, how to acquire it, anticipation of orgasm), which takes up a significant amount of the person's cognitive energy.

SCREENING AND DIAGNOSIS

Several screening tools have been developed to study porn addiction, none of which is considered a gold standard. Two screening tools of note are the pornography consumption inventory (a fifteen-item Likert-scale inventory with four subscales: sexual pleasure, emotional escape, sexual curiosity, and novelty) and the men's sexual addiction screening test (a twenty-five-item screening tool used in clinical settings that is simple, quick, and easy to score).

Given that porn addiction is not listed in the DSM, it is not considered a clinical diagnosis. Porn addiction, however, remains a popular diagnosis and may fit under the diagnosis of hypersexual disorder or sexual disorder with paraphilia. These paraphilic and hypersexual diagnoses may be the result of an underlying organic pathology relating to a brain lesion (trauma or tumor), the side effect of medication, or a symptom of endocrine abnormality, so these diagnoses should be investigated early in treatment.

Differential diagnosis can be indicated by atypical symptomology, such as onset in middle age or later, dramatic change from previously normal sexual habits or patterns, aggression, or seizure-like symptoms surrounding sexual arousal or behavior. Diagnosis of porn addiction as sexual paraphilia or hypersexuality should consider common addiction criteria such as tolerance, psychological or physiological withdrawal symptoms after extended periods of porn viewing abstinence, progressive viewing of more explicit content, and a cycle of abstinence followed by relapse. A diagnosis of pornography or masturbatory compulsivity or hypersexuality also should be considered.

TREATMENT AND THERAPY

Individual psychotherapy and psychoeducation about the effects of porn consumption are the most commonly used treatments. Interpersonal therapy and cognitive-behavior therapy are commonly employed to identify triggers and to treat comorbid psychological issues. In addition, support groups (such as Sexaholics Anonymous) and group therapy can be effective in treating porn addiction, provided these therapeutic approaches consider matters of access, coping skills, relapse prevention, and recovery.

Online communities for recovery also exist, although computer access, availability, and the anonymous nature of the Internet can be problematic for porn recovery. To address these issues, therapists can employ filtering software to monitor use and prevent access to sexually explicit material. Pharmacotherapy for pornography addiction or a related diagnosis (such as an anxiety, mood, or hypersexual disorder) should also be considered, especially in severe cases.

PREVENTION

Given that the development of porn addiction or compulsive viewing of porn is highly associated with sexually acting-out in response to the sexual arousal that viewing explicit material elicits, prevention is best achieved by avoiding the regular viewing of pornographic material. Refraining from viewing of sexually explicit materials as a regular part of sexual activity also is recommended.

William M. Struthers, PhD

FURTHER READING

Carnes, Patrick, David Delmonico, and Joseph Moriarity, eds. *In the Shadows of the Net: Breaking Free from Compulsive Online Sexual Behavior.* 2nd ed. Center City, MN: Hazelden, 2007. Edited volume that covers core issues and recovery for both general readers and professionals. Highlights the role of the Internet in the delivery of pornographic material and in fostering pornography addiction.

Cooper, Al, ed. *Sex and the Internet: A Guidebook for Clinicians.* New York: Brunner, 2002. A landmark text for clinicians who are working with porn and cybersex addicts.

Maltz, Wendy, and Larry Maltz. *The Porn Trap.* New York: Collins, 2008. A comprehensive text written from a clinical perspective on the development and treatment of pornography addiction.

Mouras, H., et al. "Brain Processing of Visual Sexual Stimuli in Healthy Men: A Functional Magnetic Resonance Imaging Study." *Neuroimage* 20 (2003): 855–69. Print. A brain-imaging study that reveals the neurological circuit activated when viewing pornography.

Reid, Rory C., et al. "Reliability, Validity, and Psychometric Development of the Pornography Consumption Inventory in a Sample of Hypersexual Men." *Journal of Sex and Marital Therapy* 37.5 (2011): 359–85. Print. Examines the development of the pornography consumption inventory and the implications for how pornography addiction might be better understood, classified, and diagnosed.

Štulhofer, Aleksandar, Vesna Buško, and Ivan Landripet. "Pornography, Sexual Socialization, and Satisfaction among Young Men." *Archives of Sexual Behavior* 39.1 (2010): 168–78. Print. An excellent article examining the effects of regular pornography viewing on the development of sexual attitudes.

WEBSITES OF INTEREST

Porn Addicts Anonymous
http://www.pornaddictsanonymous.org

Sexual Recovery Institute
http://www.sexualrecovery.com

See also: Behavioral addictions: Overview; Compulsions; Internet addiction; Sex addiction

Post-traumatic stress disorder and addiction

CATEGORY: Psychological issues and behaviors

DEFINITION: Classified as an anxiety disorder, post-traumatic stress disorder (PTSD) involves a constellation of symptoms resulting from exposure to an extreme traumatic stressor. A strong relationship exists between PTSD and the development of substance-related disorders. A prevailing hypothesis is that following the development of PTSD, a person often begins using alcohol or other substances to cope with symptoms associated with the traumatic exposure.

POST-TRAUMATIC STRESS DISORDER

The lifetime prevalence rate for exposure to a potentially traumatic event is approximately 70 percent, while the lifetime prevalence rate for post-traumatic stress disorder (PTSD) is approximately 8 to 12 percent. These statistics mean that not all people exposed to potentially traumatic events will develop subsequent PTSD.

A number of factors may mediate the relationship between the occurrence of a traumatic stressor and the development of PTSD symptoms, including the nature of the traumatic event, demographic characteristics of the person (for example, his or her age and gender), and the person's coping resources. For example, research indicates that women are twice as likely as men to develop PTSD. This statistic likely means that women are more likely than men to experience personally violent traumatic events (such as sexual assault). Research indicates that when men experience trauma such as sexual assault, their rates of PTSD can be as high as among women.

Events qualifying as potentially traumatic include natural disaster, motor vehicle accident, physical assault, sexual assault, childhood maltreatment, kidnapping or abduction, and combat or war zone exposure. While this list is not exhaustive, it captures the overall quality of extreme traumatic stressors. Additional qualifications include the criteria that the traumatic event was personal or direct and that the person's response to the event included intense fear, helplessness, or horror.

Concomitant symptoms of PTSD include nightmares related to the traumatic event, flashbacks ("daymares") or feeling as though one is reliving the event, intrusive thoughts or memories of the event, avoidance of traumatic reminders, decreased interest in previously enjoyable activities, feeling detached or estranged from people, difficulty sleeping, difficulty concentrating, irritability, hypervigilance (feeling "on guard"), and an exaggerated startle response (feeling excessively "jumpy"). This list of symptoms is not exhaustive and not all symptoms need be present to arrive at a diagnosis of PTSD. Of the seventeen PTSD symptoms, only six must be present for diagnosis.

DUAL DIAGNOSIS

An estimated 12 to 34 percent of people seeking treatment for substance-related problems also suffer from PTSD; the rate is much higher (33–59 percent) among women. One way a person might cope with the symptoms of PTSD is by abusing substances to self-medicate (that is, to decrease the presence or effect of unpleasant symptoms) or to punish oneself because of feelings of guilt, self-blame, and shame associated with the traumatic event.

A person might self-medicate to escape from the pain of post-traumatic symptoms and to enter into a state of oblivion. These coping responses, however, are generally unhelpful and counterproductive from the perspective of therapeutic recovery.

Alternatively, another mechanism of action between PTSD and substance abuse is the possibility that underlying substance-related problems may place a person at greater risk for developing PTSD. According to this model, recurrent substance abuse may increase the likelihood that a person is exposed to potentially traumatic situations and, therefore, to PTSD, as substance abuse reduces judgment and decision-making capabilities and increases risky behavior. It is likely that both of these models (that is, PTSD as a precursor to substance-related problems and substance-related problems as a precursor to PTSD) help to explain the relationship between PTSD and addiction.

Stefanie M. Keen, PhD

FURTHER READING

American Psychiatric Association. *Diagnostic and Statistical Manual of Mental Disorders*. 4th ed. Washington, DC: Author, 1994. Provides detailed information for the diagnosis of mental health disorders. In addition to providing the specific symptom criteria for each disorder, this manual includes prevalence estimates; information regarding course and prognosis; specific culture, gender, and age features; information regarding familial patterns; and considerations when making differential diagnoses.

Jacobsen, Leslie K., Steven M. Southwick, and Thomas R. Kosten. "Substance Use Disorders in Patients with Posttraumatic Stress Disorder." *American Journal of Psychiatry* 158.8 (2001): 1184–90. Print. A review of the scientific literature regarding the relationship between PTSD and substance use disorders that found high rates of comorbidity. Most reports supported a model in which the development of PTSD precedes substance-related problems.

Messman-Moore, Terri L., Rose Marie Ward, and Amy L. Brown. "Substance Use and PTSD Symptoms Impact the Likelihood of Rape and Revictimization in College Women." *Journal of Interpersonal Violence* 24.3 (2009): 499–521. Print. An empirical investigation of the relationship between prior trauma history, substance use, and sexual assault. Results of this study suggest that women with post-traumatic symptoms are at greater risk for sexual assault, especially if they self-medicate with alcohol or other drugs.

Najavits, Lisa M. "Helping 'Difficult' Patients." *Psychotherapy Research* 11.2 (2001): 131–52. Print. Outlines the background literature related to the dual diagnosis of PTSD and substance use disorders, specifically focusing on the treatment challenges faced by both patients and clinicians. Explains the rationale for the development of an integrated therapeutic program aimed at the concurrent treatment of both conditions.

WEBSITES OF INTEREST

National Center for PTSD
http://www.ptsd.va.gov

National Institute of Mental Health
http://www.nimh.nih.gov/health/topics/post-traumatic-stress-disorder-ptsd

See also: Anxiety; Mental illness; Military and substance abuse; Sexual assault and alcohol use; Sexual assault and drug use; Veterans and addiction

---

Poverty and substance abuse

CATEGORY: Social issues

DEFINITION: Substance abuse is thought to be closely related to living in poverty and that substance abuse may be caused by poverty. However, no evidence exists to show that poverty per se causes substance abuse.

POVERTY: DEFINITIONS AND DYNAMICS

Living in poverty is defined by the US federal government as living in a family unit with an income that is at or under a specified percentage of the US Census Bureau's poverty thresholds. With this formula, a family's income is divided by the appropriate threshold amount. This number is then indexed by the number of family members, so that the income is stated per person. In the United States, 15.1 percent of the population was living in poverty in 2010.

Many of the poor live their days trying to survive. The poor often use whatever resources they can muster to feed and clothe their family members. This may include borrowing money from their children or elderly parents and pawning anything of value. The poor tend to provide for their family one day at a time. They often do not have the money to purchase food in advance or to pay their bills. In some poor homes, there is no money to provide three meals a day, and poor children are often sent to school without breakfast and return home to no dinner.

Some poor people lack the skills to obtain a high-level job, or they are unemployed, underemployed, or inconsistently employed. Some poor parents, particularly single parents, may work more than one minimum-wage job. As a result, they may leave their children with inadequate caregivers, or with the oldest child in charge.

Children of the poor are forced to grow up early. Frequently, they are denied the childhood of their peers that extends into the teenage years. Children of the poor may not see much need for education, and they may drop out of high school or get a job after high school rather than going to college or a training school.

Emotional and physical abuse is thought to be common among the poor. Inadequate finances can lead a person to show his or her anger and frustration by harming family members. This type of abuse can lead to low self-esteem and depression for the abuser and the abused. Abuse behaviors are frequently passed from generation to generation, unless an adult gains insight and is able to break the pattern. Both adults and children are likely to feel hopeless in this type of situation.

The poor are represented in all groups of society. They may live in tenements in the city or in a run-down house in a rural area. Those living in poverty represent people from all racial and ethnic groups, although US poverty rates are lower among Caucasian and Asian people. Mental disorders are more common in the poor. Poverty may last for a short period of time, or it may continue for the long term. This depends on the reason for the poverty. For example, a student may be poor while attending school.

The homeless are a subgroup of the poor, and their incomes, financial reserves, and family members are often unknown. Accurate counts of the homeless are not available, as census workers may not be able to count them because they often tend to limit their social exposure.

SUBSTANCE ABUSE RISK FACTORS

Many factors can put a person at risk for substance abuse. It is thought that there may be an inherited genetic susceptibility for abusing drugs. In the absence of an inherited susceptibility, it is likely that substance abuse is passed from generation to generation as a learned behavior. Children tend to perceive their parents' behavior as the norm, and if a parent abuses a substance, his or her children are likely to abuse as well.

Substance abuse is more common in persons with certain mental illnesses, particularly personality disorders, schizophrenia, depression, and bipolar disorder. Certain personality traits also can lead to substance abuse. Some persons are said to have an addictive personality. These persons may be aggressive, thrill-seeking, and rebellious, or they may have low self-esteem. Other personality characteristics thought to lead to substance abuse are impulsiveness, poor ability to deal with stress, lacking goals, and having psychological problems.

Factors in the home also can lead to substance abuse. These factors include living in a home that is not cared for or maintained, having parents who are not nurturing, and having parents who distance themselves from their children. Children and adults who are physically, psychologically, or sexually abused in the home are also at an increased risk for substance abuse. These factors can lead to lack of confidence and low self-esteem, which put children and adults at risk for developing substance abuse problems. How a child is socialized to relate to other people also can put a child at risk for substance abuse. The behaviors most commonly associated with substance abuse are poor skills at relating to others, shyness, aggression, involvement with a negative peer group, poor achievement in school, and perceived approval for abusing substances.

Because of the nature of drugs of addiction, it is not possible to simply "try" a drug such as crack cocaine or heroin. These drugs make permanent changes in the brain. Some drugs act like neurotransmitters, which are chemicals in the brain that connect nerve cells and transmit nerve impulses, and they can disrupt the brain's normal communication patterns. Most drugs of addiction stimulate the production of large amounts of dopamine in the brain, leading to feelings of euphoria. Ongoing use of addicting drugs leads to decreased production of dopamine and a decreased number of dopamine receptors in the brain. As a result, the person needs to continue taking the drug to feel good and needs to take increasingly larger amounts of the drug. Consequently, taking a drug of addiction as an experiment can lead to addiction.

Substance abuse is most common in men between the ages of eighteen and forty-four years. Substance abusers are likely to be unmarried and in a lower socioeconomic group. People living in the western part of the United States are more likely to be substance abusers.

The homeless have the highest incidence of substance abuse. It is estimated that about 38 percent of the homeless are substance abusers. Mental health problems are extremely common in this group, and they often have little social support from family members or partners.

DOES POVERTY CAUSE SUBSTANCE ABUSE?

No clear evidence shows that poverty causes substance abuse. Most of the problems that are thought to characterize the poor and that might lead to substance abuse can also lead to substance abuse in persons with middle- and upper-class backgrounds. These problems include adult and child abuse, hopelessness, parents who abuse substances; low-level job skills, lack of community involvement, feelings of being alienated from the rest of society, mental health problems, lack of personal goals, and unemployment.

It does appear, however, that substance abuse can lead to poverty. A substance abuser is more likely to lose his or her job and to spend what money he or she has on drugs or alcohol.

Christine M. Carroll, RN, BSN, MBA

FURTHER READING

Gorski, Paul. "The Myth of the Culture of Poverty." *Poverty and Learning* 65.7 (2008). Web. http://www.ascd.org/publications/educational-leadership/apr08/vol65/num07/The-Myth-of-the-Culture-of-Poverty.aspx. The author attempts to dispel the belief that the poor are different than people in other social classes.

Kerr, Peter. "Rich vs. Poor: Drug Patterns Are Diverging." *New York Times* 30 Aug. 1987. Web. http://www.nytimes.com/1987/08/30/us/rich-vs-poor-patterns-are-diverging.html. Kerr discusses how substance abuse affects all parts of society.

National Coalition for the Homeless. "Substance Abuse and Homelessness." July 2009. Web. http://www.nationalhomeless.org/factsheets/addiction.html. This article discusses the causes of homelessness and its relationship to substance abuse.

Federal Poverty Guidelines. US Department of Health and Human Services
http://aspe.hhs.gov/poverty/11fedreg.shtml

National Coalition for the Homeless
http://www.nationalhomeless.org

See also: Economic impact of addiction; Health disparities and substance abuse; Homelessness; Socioeconomic status and addiction

Pregnancy and alcohol

CATEGORY: Health issues and physiology

DEFINITION: Alcohol use during pregnancy has been associated with fetal alcohol syndrome, fetal death, spontaneous abortion, and stillbirth. For the years 2008 and 2009, 10 percent of pregnant women age fifteen to forty-four years reported alcohol use, including 4.4 percent who were binge drinkers and 0.8 percent who were heavy drinkers. Although no limit on alcohol consumption has been established for pregnant women, major negative effects on the fetus have been observed with chronic alcohol use (six drinks per day), with binge drinking (five or more drinks in succession), or with drinking a total of forty-five alcoholic beverages per month.

FETAL ALCOHOL SYNDROME

Fetal alcohol syndrome (FAS) in children is the most widely recognized consequence of alcohol use during pregnancy. The syndrome was first recognized in the late 1960s as a pattern of physical abnormalities and mental impairment in children of alcoholic women.

Since the 1960s, other terms have been developed to encompass the broad spectrum of milder disorders associated with the effects of alcohol use on the fetus during pregnancy. These terms include fetal alcohol effects (FAE), fetal alcohol spectrum disorders (FASD), and alcohol-related neurological disorders.

FAS affects approximately 4 to 6 percent of infants of mothers who drink heavily while pregnant. The estimates of children with neurological impairment from prenatal alcohol exposure (not classified as FAS) are much higher. The statistics on the numbers of children with FAS may be underestimates, because the diagnosis of FASD is largely dependent on disclosure from the mother of her own alcohol abuse. Thus, the diagnosis of FAS is difficult to make and is determined primarily through reports of the mother's alcohol use during pregnancy in conjunction with a group of identifiable abnormalities in the child. The condition is characterized in a child by abnormal prenatal and postnatal growth, dysmorphic facial features, and central nervous system damage.

Alcohol use by pregnant women has been associated with growth deficiencies in both the fetus and the child after birth. Newborns have lower birth weights, and children with FAS demonstrate growth retardation even with sufficient nutrition. Weight and height remains in the lower one-tenth percentile for the child's age group. Additionally, the child may have a low weight-to-height ratio and a short stature.

There are characteristic abnormal facial features in children with FAS, most noticeably small head size. Also present is maxillary hypoplasia, the underdevelopment of the jawbones that, when combined with an underdeveloped midface, gives the illusion of a protruding lower jaw. This may also be accompanied by a small separation between the upper and lower eyelids (palpebral fissures); a small, flat, upturned nose; thin upper lip; and characteristically folded "railroad track" ears. These facial features may become less obvious as the child matures.

Neurological deficiencies are the most severe consequence of FAS. Fetuses of women who drink heavily have been found to have a lower prenatal cranial-to-body growth ratio, with brain abnormalities continuing throughout early childhood. It is believed that every episode of consumption of two or more alcoholic drinks by the pregnant woman leads to the death of a quantity of fetal brain cells. Children with FAS generally have IQs about ten points lower than average; those with the most extreme FAS symptomology can have IQs of 60 to 70. Delayed speech and speech and language difficulties may be present throughout childhood.

Maternal alcohol use during pregnancy has been associated with attention deficit hyperactivity disorder (ADHD) in children, with the degree of severity of the ADHD directly related to the amount of alcohol consumed by the mother while pregnant. Impaired or delayed development of fine motor skills has also

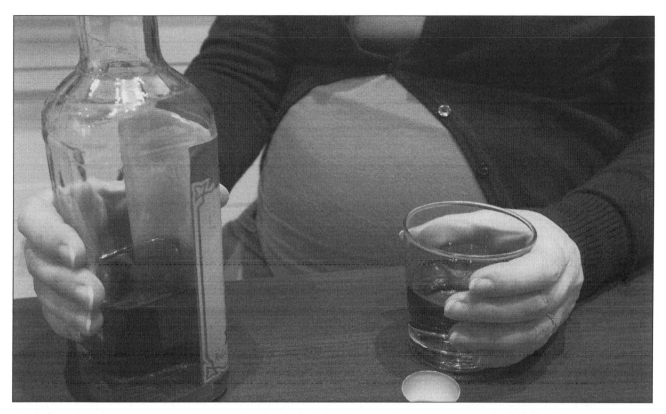

Alcohol use during pregnancy has been associated with fetal death, spontaneous abortion, and stillbirth. (Francois Destoc/ Maxppp/Landov)

been observed in toddlers with FAS. Psychiatric disorders such as substance abuse, paranoia, personality disorder, aggressiveness, and behavioral dysfunction occur at increased rates in children with FAS. Unlike the abnormal facial features that improve as the child matures, neurological deficiencies persist into adulthood and throughout life.

Less apparent effects of maternal alcohol abuse on the child after birth include abnormalities of the hand. The pinky finger is bent inward toward the other fingers, and the upper crease of the palm is prominent, ending between the index and ring fingers. Other possible symptoms of FAS are cardiac defects and excessive hair growth. Various types of hearing loss have also been attributed to FAS and may contribute to the developmental and social delays that children with FAS often experience.

The manifestations of FAS symptoms are highly variable among children and dependent upon the amount of alcohol consumed by the mother while pregnant. Relationships have been observed between the amount and frequency of alcohol consumed and the gestational age of the fetus. The first six weeks are critical to embryonic development, as are the last few months of pregnancy, when the fetus undergoes a period of extensive growth. Therefore, alcohol consumption during these periods of pregnancy poses a higher risk to the fetus.

Binge drinking appears to be particularly deleterious to the fetus, as it is exposed to a high level of alcohol. During binge drinking, the pregnant woman's liver takes longer to metabolize the large amount of alcohol, thereby also exposing the fetus to alcohol for an extended time.

Other factors may influence the severity of FAS symptoms exhibited by a child. It is theorized that the unique sensitivity of the pregnant woman to alcohol may moderate the effects of alcohol on the developing fetus. Variations in genes have been identified that influence the inclination to abuse alcohol, the rate of alcohol metabolism, and the tendency to develop FAS. Other factors present during pregnancy, such as maternal age, use of other drugs, nutrition, and even birth order, may influence the severity of FAS symptoms.

PREVENTION

Because no level of alcohol consumption by pregnant women has been determined to be safe for the developing fetus, the US surgeon general has recommended that women who are pregnant or intend to become pregnant in the near future, and those who are not using birth control, abstain from drinking alcohol entirely. This guidance is based on statistics showing that many pregnancies are unintentional, and women may drink alcohol before they realize they are pregnant.

The early weeks of pregnancy, including the time from conception to recognition of the first missed menstrual period, are critical to neurological development. Although alcohol use has been shown to decline after a woman realizes she is pregnant, the use of any alcohol during this time may be especially harmful to the embryo.

FAS is caused only by alcohol consumption by pregnant women and is a completely preventable cause of birth defects. Although FAS is not hereditary, the tendency to abuse alcohol may be. Health care providers can perform alcohol screening as part of routine prenatal care and can provide alcohol abuse information for their patients.

Alcohol use in the three months prior to pregnancy is also a good predictor of the pattern of alcohol use during the first three months of pregnancy. This information can be used to provide pregnant women with information on early intervention and abstinence programs. Women at high risk for alcohol abuse during pregnancy, however, frequently do not receive adequate prenatal care.

Deborah A. Appello, MS

FURTHER READING

Centers for Disease Control and Prevention. "A 2005 Message to Women from the US Surgeon General: Advisory on Alcohol Use in Pregnancy." 2005. Web. 22 Mar. 2012. http://www.cdc.gov/ncbddd/fasd/documents/SurgeonGenbookmark.pdf. Guidelines on the use of alcohol during pregnancy.

Ethen, Mary K., et al. "Alcohol Consumption by Women Before and During Pregnancy." *Maternal and Child Health Journal* 13 (2009): 274–85. Print. A study of the prevalence, patterns, and predictors of alcohol use before and during pregnancy in the United States.

Gray, Ron, Raja A. S. Mukjerjee, and Michaek Rutter. "Alcohol Consumption During Pregnancy and Its Known Effects on Neurodevelopment: What Is Known and What Remains Uncertain." *Addiction* 104 (2009): 1270–73. Print. A brief, high-level summary of potential risks to the fetus when exposed to alcohol in utero.

O'Leary, Colleen M. "Fetal Alcohol Syndrome: Diagnosis, Epidemiology, and Developmental Outcomes." *Journal of Paediatric and Child Health* 40 (2004): 2–7. Print. A review of the literature on FAS to increase awareness of the diagnostic features and epidemiology of FAS and the developmental deficiencies associated with this syndrome.

Ornoy, Asher, and Zivanit Ergaz. "Alcohol Abuse in Pregnant Women: Effects on the Fetus and Newborn, Mode of Action and Maternal Treatment." *International Journal of Environmental Research and Public Health* 7 (2010): 364–79. Print. Results of investigations of the effects of alcohol use on the developing embryo and fetus in both animal models and humans.

Wattendorf, Daniel J., and Maximillian Muenke. "Fetal Alcohol Spectrum Disorders." *American Family Physician* 72 (2005): 279–82. Print. A review of the epidemiology, clinical presentation, diagnosis, and management of fetal alcohol spectrum disorders.

WEBSITES OF INTEREST

Fetal Alcohol Spectrum Disorders, Center for Excellence
http://fascenter.samhsa.gov

National Organization on Fetal Alcohol Syndrome
http://www.nofas.org

See also: Alcohol: Short- and long-term effects on the body; Birth defects and alcohol; Fetal alcohol syndrome; Pregnancy and drug use; Pregnancy and smoking

Pregnancy and drug use

CATEGORY: Health issues and physiology

DEFINITION: Drug abuse during pregnancy frequently leads to spontaneous abortion, premature birth, stillbirth, low birth-weight infants, and an increased risk of sudden infant death syndrome. Birth defects caused by drug abuse during pregnancy are rare, however. Drugs considered to have abuse potential during pregnancy include marijuana, cocaine, heroin, hallucinogens, and prescription pain medications.

DRUG USE DURING PREGNANCY

For the years 2008 and 2009, 4.5 percent of pregnant girls and women age fifteen to forty-four years, including 7.1 percent of women age eighteen to twenty-five years, admitted to some kind of illicit drug use in the past month. Drug use was highest during the first trimester of pregnancy and decreased in the second and third trimesters. The most commonly reported illicit drugs used were heroin, cocaine, and benzodiazepines.

Certain factors in the life of a drug-abusing woman contribute to her reluctance to seek help, obtain prenatal care, or to stop using drugs during pregnancy. Many women who exhibit a pattern of drug use have mental, social, and financial problems. These situations contribute to an overall unhealthy routine that may include smoking, poor diet, stress, violence, and unpredictable living conditions, resulting in adverse pregnancy outcomes.

Drug-addicted women frequently are much more likely to smoke cigarettes and to use intravenous drugs during pregnancy, potentially exposing themselves to blood-borne infections. The high rates of mental illness in women who abuse drugs and illnesses that include anxiety, depression, and personality disorders contribute to a high rate of relapse among women who attempt to discontinue drug use while pregnant.

Women who abuse drugs may fail to obtain prenatal care for several reasons. For example, amenorrhea is a common side effect of drug abuse, so a woman may not realize she is pregnant. Drug use can be particularly risky to the fetus during the first eight weeks of pregnancy, a critical period of fetal development. Drug addiction also may lead to forgotten or missed appointments or to a lack of concern regarding the health of the fetus. Women who abuse drugs also endanger their own health through unhealthy lifestyles and relationships that may involve physical abuse, which also risks harm to the fetus.

COCAINE

The 1980s witnessed a significant increase in the use of cocaine and crack cocaine in the United States. Cocaine remains a serious public health issue in the United States, with the majority of cocaine-using women in their childbearing years.

It has been determined that when a pregnant woman uses cocaine, the drug crosses the blood-brain barrier and the placenta, becoming readily available to the developing fetus. Animal models have shown that cocaine interferes with fetal brain development because it interacts with neurotransmitters and affects gene expression, but the mechanisms for this are unknown. Children exposed to cocaine prenatally have demonstrated deficits in attention span and impulse control, which may be attributed to the effects of cocaine on areas of the brain regulating these functions.

Cocaine is known to be a vasoconstrictor and may contribute to spontaneous abortion and low birth weight from a lack of blood flow to the fetus. Cocaine use during pregnancy, especially crack cocaine, has been linked to deformed arms, legs, and internal organs because of this vasoconstriction effect during fetal development. Lack of blood flow across the placenta also prevents the transport of oxygen and nutrients to the fetus. Infants born to cocaine-addicted women also are more likely to be hospitalized in a neonatal intensive care unit.

Infants are also affected indirectly by their mother's cocaine use through the effects that use has on the area of the brain that controls maternal behavior. Cocaine disrupts the pathways in the brain that control maternal-infant bonding behavior and disrupts the production of oxytocin, a hormone that is key to triggering response behaviors in mothers.

OTHER SUBSTANCES

In addition to cocaine, other frequently misused substances, such as methamphetamine, marijuana, hallucinogens, and opiates, have demonstrated increased risk of premature labor and low birth-weight infants. Methamphetamine use has grown substantially in the United States, particularly in the western half of the country. Thus far, however, there have been few studies of the effect of methamphetamine use on the developing fetus.

It is known that methamphetamine interacts with biochemical transporters in the brain and is transported directly into cells. Once inside nerve cells, methamphetamine disrupts the release and metabolism of neurotransmitter molecules in the brain, impairing the development of the neurotransmitter system. Methamphetamine is a vasoconstrictor, similar to cocaine, and can have the same effect on the fetus through lack of blood flow.

Magnetic resonance imaging studies of children exposed to methamphetamine in utero have revealed abnormal brain structure in association with neurological developmental deficiencies. Newborn babies prenatally exposed to methamphetamine are usually underweight and have shown similar neurological effects as those exposed to cocaine. Animal models have demonstrated learning deficiencies, behavioral problems, and hyperactivity.

Heroin is a short-acting opiate that, with repeated use and withdrawal, can cause muscle contractions, leading to premature labor. However, no studies have shown that heroin use during pregnancy causes central nervous system damage in the developing fetus. Opiates cross the placenta, so opiate abusers may give birth to addicted newborns who must subsequently undergo withdrawal. These newborns experience irritability, central nervous system difficulties, gastrointestinal disorders, and respiratory symptoms for up to eight days after birth. As in the case of cocaine, it is difficult to determine if these symptoms are caused by the mother's heroin use or are consequences of other factors associated with the mother's lifestyle.

REMEDIAL ACTIONS

It is difficult to attribute specific fetal deficiencies to illicit drug use because of the many other confounding factors in the drug-addicted woman's life. These factors include smoking and poor nutrition, both of which may adversely affect the pregnancy too.

Residential treatment during pregnancy has demonstrated positive outcomes, but it is unclear if this outcome is from stabilization of the drug use or from an overall healthier lifestyle. Studies have shown that drug-addicted women who receive early intervention and extensive prenatal care and supervision can have pregnancy outcomes equivalent to women who do not use drugs. Comprehensive prenatal care can

substantially reduce the risk of premature labor and low birth-weight infants among drug abusers.

It is recommended that pregnant women stop using cocaine during pregnancy, but the cocaine must be reduced in a measured fashion to avoid side effects, such as maternal seizures. Methadone treatment has been found to stabilize opiate abusers during pregnancy by allowing the women to gradually diminish opiate abuse through the pregnancy without the repeated use and withdrawal of heroin. The effect of drug abuse on infant mortality remains to be studied and delineated.

Deborah A. Appello, MS

FURTHER READING

Burgdorf, Kenneth, et al. "Birth Outcomes for Pregnant Women in Residential Substance Abuse Treatment." *Evaluation and Program Planning* 27 (2004): 199–204. Print. An exploratory study investigating the effect of residential substance abuse treatment on pregnancy outcomes.

Hepburn, Mary. "Substance Abuse in Pregnancy." *Current Obstetrics and Gynaecology* 14 (2004): 419–25. Print. An overview of the management of high-risk pregnancies caused by drug or alcohol abuse.

Pinto, Shanthi M., et al. "Substance Abuse During Pregnancy: Effect on Pregnancy Outcomes." *European Journal of Obstetrics and Gynecology and Reproductive Biology* 150 (2010): 137–41. Print. A retrospective study of drug-abusing women in the United Kingdom in a four-year period to determine the effect of drug use on maternal and perinatal complications.

Prentice, Sheena. "Substance Misuse in Pregnancy." *Obstetrics, Gynaecology, and Reproductive Medicine* 20 (2010): 278–83. Print. A study of substance misuse during pregnancy and the role of the specialist midwife.

Roussotte, Florence, Lindsay Soderberg, and Elizabeth Sowell. "Structural, Metabolic, and Functional Brain Abnormalities as a Result of Prenatal Exposure to Drugs of Abuse: Evidence from Neuroimaging." *Neuropsychology Review* 20 (2010): 376–97. Print. A study of the effects on the fetal brains of humans and animals, using MRIs, of mothers who abused alcohol, cocaine, or methamphetamine during pregnancy.

Salisbury, Amy L., et al. "Fetal Effects of Psychoactive Drugs." *Clinical Perinatology* 36 (2009): 595–619.

Print. A study of the effects of cocaine, methamphetamine, and selective serotonin reuptake inhibitors on the developing brain and central nervous system of the fetus.

Strathearn, Lane, and Linda C. Mayes. "Cocaine Addiction in Mothers: Potential Effects on Maternal Care and Infant Development." *Annals of the New York Academy of Science* 1187 (2010): 172–83. Print. A study of how cocaine use affects maternal care and infant development in both humans and animal models.

WEBSITES OF INTEREST
Fetal Alcohol Spectrum Disorders, Center for Excellence
http://fascenter.samhsa.gov

National Institute on Drug Abuse
http://www.drugabuse.gov

See also: Birth defects and drug use; Hallucinogens: Short- and long-term effects on the body; Narcotics: Short- and long-term effects on the body; Newborn addicts; Pregnancy and alcohol; Pregnancy and smoking; Stimulants: Short- and long-term effects on the body

Pregnancy and smoking

Category: Health Issues and physiology

Definition: Through pregnancy, a few simple cells will grow to form the baby. Organs such as the heart, lungs, and brain go through intense periods of development, and it is important to have the right building blocks for all of this growth. Nutrients and oxygen that support a growing fetus are passed from mother to fetus through an organ called the placenta. Dangerous substances such as drugs, alcohol, and chemicals from recreational smoking, however, can also pass through the placenta to the baby. Chemicals from smoke are absorbed into the blood from the mother's lungs; many of the chemicals are not only toxic but also interfere with the delivery of oxygen and nutrients to the baby. These chemicals can cause serious and chronic illnesses in adults and children. In a developing baby, the chemicals can also impair development—some health issues may be seen at birth while others can develop later in a baby's life.

RISKS FOR MOTHER AND BABY

Researchers do not yet fully understand how every chemical in tobacco smoke affects a growing baby, but they do know that the health risks are high. If an expecting mother smokes, she is more likely to have pregnancy complications that put both herself and the baby at risk. Such complications may be pelvic pain; early rupture of the membranes; placental problems (detachment, tearing, or slipping); stillbirth; premature births; and miscarriages.

Smoking while pregnant also puts the baby at a higher risk for serious complications, such as being born underweight, which is a sign that the baby has not adequately developed. This puts the baby at high risk for serious health issues, including intellectual disability, cerebral palsy, and lung problems. Babies are also at a greater risk for sudden infant death

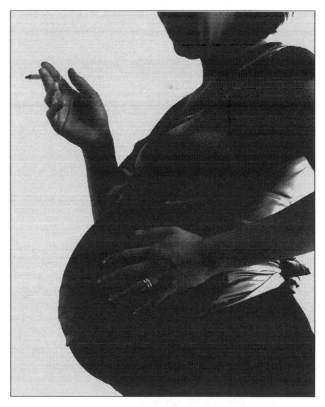

Research has shown that smoking during pregnancy damages a baby's airways before the child is born. (Getty Images)

syndrome (SIDS) and developing attention deficit and hyperactivity disorders.

It is also important to note that because the baby is exposed to nicotine through the placenta, smoking while pregnant can cause the baby to have nicotine withdrawal symptoms after birth. This can make the baby more jittery, nervous, and harder to soothe. The earlier an expectant mother stops smoking, the better it is for the baby and for the mother's own health. Even shortly after stopping, an expectant mother will begin to recover. For example, within minutes, heart rate and blood pressure will drop. Within twelve hours, carbon monoxide levels in the blood return to normal (carbon monoxide decreases the level of oxygen in the body). Within just a couple of weeks, circulation and lungs improve their function.

In addition, smokers that breastfeed continue to pass chemicals like nicotine on to the baby through breast milk. Babies are also very susceptible to second-hand smoke.

QUITTING SMOKING

After an individual quits smoking, the body goes through withdrawal. The individual may experience symptoms such as dizziness, depression, headaches, tiredness, irritability, and sleep problems. Withdrawal effects, however, are temporary, and cravings can be overcome by simple distraction techniques. Some distraction techniques are participation in such activities as walking; relaxation methods, such as deep breathing; drinking water; nibbling on healthy snacks, such as vegetables and fruits; sucking on a hard piece of candy; investing time into a hobby; and simply talking with others who have successfully quit smoking.

In addition, certain programs and smoking cessation tools can help to gradually decrease nicotine levels. However, certain smoking cessation products such as nicotine gum or patches may not be safe to use while pregnant.

Pamela Jones, MA

FURTHER READING

Anderson, Judith. *It's Your Health: Smoking.* North Mantko, MN: Smart Apple Media, 2005. Provides an introduction to smoking's negative effects on the body.

How Tobacco Smoke Causes Disease: The Biology and Behavioral Basis for Smoking-Attributable Disease: A Report of the Surgeon General. Rockville, MD: US DHSS, 2010. Contains information from thousands of studies proving that smoking has had ruinous consequences for the health of millions of Americans. List of tables and figures. Index.

Substance Abuse and Mental Health Services Administration. *Results from the 2009 National Survey on Drug Use and Health: Volume I. Summary of National Findings.* Rockville, MD: US DHSS Publication No. SMA 10-4856, 2010. Results from the 2009 survey, which is the primary source of information on the use of illicit drugs, alcohol, and tobacco in the United States.

WEBSITES OF INTEREST

The American Congress of Obstetricians and Gynecologists
http://www.acog.org/

American Lung Association
http://www.lung.org/

Nicotine Anonymous
http://www.nicotine-anonymous.org/

Smoke Free
http://www.smokefree.gov/

See also: Birth defects and smoking; Pregnancy and alcohol; Pregnancy and drug use; Smoking: Short- and long-term effects on the body

Prescription drug addiction: In depth

CATEGORY: Substance abuse

DEFINITION: Prescription drug addiction is a chronic, progressive disease characterized by the inability to abstain from prescription drug use, despite known harmful consequences. The prescription drugs that most often lead to addiction include opioid painkillers, central nervous system depressants, and stimulant medications.

CAUSES

When used as prescribed, prescription drugs can help to improve the quality of life for people with chronic pain or chronic health conditions, such as attention deficit hyperactivity disorder (ADHD), narcolepsy, anxiety, or sleep disorders. However, when used long term, some prescription drugs can lead to drug abuse and addiction.

Most people take prescription medications as they are prescribed, but according to the National Institute on Drug Abuse, a growing number of people are taking prescription medications for nonmedical reasons, and such abuse can lead to addiction. It is unclear why prescription drug abuse is on the rise. One theory is that prescription medications have become more accessible. More drugs are being prescribed than ever before, and pharmacies on the Internet have made it easy for people to obtain prescription drugs, even without a prescription. Some people also mistakenly believe that because prescription medications are prescribed for medical reasons, they are safer alternatives to street drugs.

Opioids. When used as prescribed, opioids are intended to treat pain in persons with chronic health conditions such as cancer, back pain, arthritis, muscle or bone pain, diabetic neuropathy, phantom limb pain, and pain caused by injuries that are slow to heal. Opioids also are used to treat severe short-term pain from surgical procedures, injuries, or painful medical conditions, such as shingles.

Opioids block the nerve receptors in the body that cause a person to perceive pain. They also affect the regions of the brain that perceive pleasure, which results in an initial feeling of euphoria followed by a calm, drowsy feeling. As a result, many people use them to feel good or to get high, to relieve stress, or to relax in social situations.

Central nervous system (CNS) depressants. CNS depressants, which are used to treat anxiety disorders, sleep disorders, muscle tension, and seizure disorders, slow brain function and produce a calm, drowsy effect. They are often used to get high, to relieve stress, to relax in social situations, or to counteract the effects of other drugs, such as stimulants.

Stimulants. Stimulant medications, which are used for the treatment of ADHD or narcolepsy, increase alertness, energy, and attention. When taken as prescribed, stimulant medications slowly increase the production of dopamine—a neurotransmitter that is responsible for feelings of pleasure—in the brain. However, when taken in higher than normal doses or by routes other than oral, they can cause a rapid increase in dopamine, which results in a feeling of euphoria. Stimulant medications are often used to get high or to decrease appetite.

RISK FACTORS

Risk factors for prescription drug addiction may include a genetic predisposition to addiction, but people who are not genetically predisposed to addiction can still become addicted. Other factors contribute to prescription drug addiction, including early onset of drug abuse (teenage years or early twenties); addictions to other substances, either past or present; peer pressure; and easy access to prescription drugs.

SYMPTOMS

Symptoms of prescription drug addiction will depend, somewhat, on the type of drug to which the person is addicted. However, symptoms that are common to all prescription drug addictions include taking a higher dose of the medication than what the doctor prescribed or taking the medication more frequently than called for by the prescription. People who are addicted to prescription drugs may find themselves calling the doctor's office more frequently for refills or asking the physician to prescribe higher doses.

Opioids. In addition to increasing the medication's dose and frequency without permission from the doctor, opioid addicts have the following symptoms from use: constipation, excessive sleeping, depression, confusion, slurred speech, poor coordination, itching, tiny pupils, paranoia, excessive sweating, poor judgment, low blood pressure, and shallow breathing.

CNS depressants. Symptoms of addiction to CNS depressants may include drowsiness or excessive sleeping, slurred speech, depression, confusion, unsteady gait, lack of coordination, impaired memory, poor judgment, slowed breathing, low blood pressure, and involuntary rapid eye movements.

Stimulants. A person who is addicted to stimulant medications may experience weight loss, staying awake for long periods of time, irritability, mood swings, excessive energy, poor judgment, bloodshot eyes, high blood pressure, rapid or irregular heartbeat, dangerously high body temperatures, anxiety, paranoia, and seizures.

Doctor Shopping

Doctor shopping, an illegal activity, is the intentional use of multiple doctors to secure prescription narcotics or other controlled substances while withholding that the drug in question has already been prescribed by another doctor. The patient may have real, chronic pain that is being undertreated, or may be faking or exaggerating illness or injury to satisfy an addiction or to obtain medication to sell illegally.

Patients seek prescription drugs from emergency rooms, walk-in clinics, physicians, specialists, and dentists. They also may buy them on the street; may steal prescription pads; may alter prescriptions to get additional refills; might steal drugs from a pharmacy, friends, and family members (especially the elderly); might obtain drugs from disreputable Web-based pharmacies; or might visit physicians in states that have weak doctor-shopping laws.

The controlled substances most often sought are narcotics such as Vicodin (hydrocodone), OxyContin (oxycodone), Darvocet, Demerol (meperidine), Percocet (oxycodone with acetaminophen), and morphine. Addicts also seek stimulants (amphetamines) and sleeping pills (benzodiazepines).

People who are addicted to prescription drugs may do things that they would not do otherwise. For example, to get more drugs or money to buy more drugs, people who are addicted to prescription medications might seek prescriptions from more than one doctor (a practice known as doctor shopping), steal money or items that they can sell for money, forge prescriptions, or engage in prostitution for money.

When people who are addicted to prescription drugs run out of drugs and are unable to get more, they may experience withdrawal symptoms. Symptoms of opioid withdrawal include fever, chills, shaking, stomach cramps, nausea or vomiting, diarrhea, muscle aches, increased sensitivity to pain, insomnia, watery eyes, runny nose, irritability, and panic. Symptoms of CNS depressant withdrawal include anxiety, insomnia, tremors, weakness, delirium, and seizures. Symptoms of stimulant withdrawal include intense cravings, irritability, headaches, nausea, vomiting, mood swings, anxiety, depression, increased appetite, fatigue, shaking, sweating, insomnia, and confusion.

Prescription drug addiction can lead to a number of complications, especially when the drugs are taken in large doses or combined with alcohol or other drugs. Opioids can increase a person's risk of choking. They also can slow breathing. If taken in large doses or used in combination with alcohol, antihistamines, barbiturates, or benzodiazepines, opioids can lead to respiratory depression, a life-threatening condition that can slow a person's breathing to a point where breathing may actually stop.

CNS depressants can cause memory problems and can also affect body temperature. If taken in large doses or used in combination with other substances that may cause drowsiness, such as alcohol, opioids, antihistamines, and some over-the-counter cold medications, CNS depressants can lead to respiratory depression, coma, and death.

Stimulant medications can cause increased blood pressure, irregular heart rate, increased body temperature, and a decrease in appetite, which can lead to malnutrition. In large doses, they can cause seizures, paranoia, or hallucinations, and stroke. If taken with certain over-the-counter cold medications, stimulant medications may raise blood pressure to a dangerously high level. They also may cause irregular heart rhythms.

Addiction to prescription medications may have other consequences, in addition to physical complications. For example, driving while under the influence can lead to a motor vehicle accident or arrest. Prescription drug addiction can also have an adverse effect on school or work performance.

SCREENING AND DIAGNOSIS

Physicians are in a unique position not only to screen patients for prescription drug abuse but also to help them recognize when they have a problem, to set recovery goals, and to seek treatment. Diagnosis of prescription drug addiction is usually based on the patient's symptoms and medical history.

Health care providers may screen patients by asking about past or present substance use or abuse, and by asking about current medication use, including the dosage, frequency, reason for use, and for what period of time the person has been taking the medication. Blood and urine tests also may be used to determine what prescription medications a patient has been taking and to track treatment progress.

Pharmacists can help screen patients for prescription drug addiction by checking prescriptions closely to see if they may have been forged or modified and by watching for multiple prescriptions from different doctors. Pharmacists also can alert nearby pharmacies when fraud or doctor shopping has been detected.

TREATMENT AND THERAPY

Prescription drug addiction is a treatable condition. The type of treatment will depend on the type of drug to which the person is addicted and on the needs of the individual. Successful treatment programs are usually a combination of detoxification, counseling, and, in some cases, medications. Many people go through more than one round of treatment before they are able to fully recover from their addiction.

Opioids. Initial treatment for opioid addiction may include medications to help alleviate the symptoms of withdrawal. Methadone and buprenorphine, both synthetic opioids, are the most commonly used drugs to treat symptoms of opioid withdrawal. Both are highly regulated drugs that are usually prescribed to people who are enrolled in a treatment program for opioid addiction.

Methadone and buprenorphine ease withdrawal symptoms and relieve cravings. Methadone has been used for decades to treat opioid addiction. Buprenorphine was approved by the US Food and Drug Administration for the treatment of opioid dependence in 2002. Patients will need medical supervision during treatment for opioid withdrawal.

Counseling following treatment for opioid withdrawal symptoms can help patients learn to function without drugs, handle drug cravings, and avoid people and situations that could lead to relapse. Support groups and twelve-step programs such as Narcotics Anonymous can help with the treatment of opioid addiction and with the adjustment to a new, drug-free lifestyle.

CNS depressants. People who are addicted to CNS depressants should not abruptly stop taking the medication because withdrawal from CNS depressants can be life-threatening. Instead, the medication dose must be gradually tapered until it is safe to stop taking the drug altogether. Patients will need medical supervision during treatment for withdrawal from CNS depressants. After the patient has been successfully weaned from the drug, cognitive-behavioral therapy can help the recovering addict to increase his or her coping skills, thereby eliminating the perceived need for the drug.

People who are addicted to CNS depressants often have co-addictions, such as alcoholism, so approaches to treatment must address all addictions. Support groups and twelve-step programs such as Narcotics Anonymous also can help with the treatment of addiction to CNS depressants.

Stimulants. There are no medications to help alleviate withdrawal symptoms in patients who are addicted to prescription stimulants. One approach is to slowly decrease the dosage until the patient has been weaned. Patients will need medical supervision during treatment for withdrawal from stimulant medications. Once the patient has stopped taking the medication, behavioral therapy is often used to help patients recognize risky situations, avoid drug use, and more effectively cope with problems.

Another treatment that has been proven effective for stimulant addiction is contingency management. During contingency management, patients are given vouchers for drug-free urine tests. The vouchers can be exchanged for rewards that promote healthy living. Support groups and twelve-step programs such as Narcotics Anonymous also can help with the treatment of prescription stimulant addiction.

PREVENTION

Most people who take prescription medications as prescribed do not become addicted. There are some steps that people can take to decrease their risk of addiction, including the following:

- Ask if the medication being prescribed is addictive and if there are any alternative medications.
- Follow the directions on the medication label without exception.
- Avoid increasing a medication dose without discussing it with the health care provider who prescribed the medication.
- Avoid taking medication that was prescribed for someone else.

Parents too can take steps to help ensure that their children do not become addicted to prescription drugs. Preventive steps include keeping prescription medications in a locked cabinet; discussing with children the dangers of prescription medications, including the dangers of sharing medications with others; and properly disposing of prescription medications.

Pharmacists can help prevent prescription drug addiction by giving patients clear information about how medications should be taken and by providing information about potential side effects or drug interactions. Prescribers can help to prevent prescription drug addiction by noting increases in the amount of drug a patient needs to get the same therapeutic effect and by tracking frequent requests for refills.

Julie Henry, RN, MPA

FURTHER READING

Fishbain, D. A., et al. "What Percentage of Chronic Nonmalignant Pain Patients Exposed to Chronic Opioid Analgesic Therapy Develop Abuse/Addiction and/or Aberrant Drug-Related Behaviors? A Structured Evidence-Based Review." *Pain Medicine* 9.4 (2008): 444–59. Print. A review of studies on the development of abuse and addiction and aberrant drug-related behaviors in chronic pain patients with nonmalignant pain on exposure to chronic opioid analgesic therapy.

Mayo Foundation for Medical Education and Research. "Prescription Drug Abuse." 25 Jun. 2010. Web. 10 Mar. 2012. http://www.mayoclinic.com/health/prescription-drug-abuse/DS01079. A detailed description of prescription drug abuse, including drugs most commonly abused, symptoms, causes, risk factors, complications, tests and diagnosis, prevention, and treatment options.

McCabe, S. E., C. J. Teter, and C. J. Boyd. "Medical Use, Illicit Use, and Diversion of Abusable Prescription Drugs." *Journal of American College Health* 54.5 (2006): 269–78. Print. A study of the medical use, illicit use, and diversion of four distinct classes of abusable prescription medications in a random sample of undergraduate students.

National Institute on Drug Abuse. "Prescription and Over-the-Counter Medications." Jun. 2009. Web. 10 Mar. 2012. http://www.nida.nih.gov/infofacts/PainMed.html. A detailed description of commonly abused prescription medications, including how they are abused, how they affect the brain, possible adverse effects, what happens when one stops taking the drugs, and treatment options.

---. "Prescription Drugs: Abuse and Addiction." Oct. 2011. Web. 10 Mar. 2012. http://www.nida.nih.gov/researchreports/prescription/prescription6.html. Examines the role of patients and pharmacists, physicians, and other health care providers in recognizing and preventing prescription drug abuse.

"Prescription Drug Abuse." 2010. Web. 10 Mar. 2012. http://www.webmd.com/mental-health/abuse-of-prescription-drugs. A detailed description of prescription drug abuse, including drugs most commonly abused, how those drugs work on the brain and body, why people become addicted, treatment options, and guidelines for using prescription drugs safely.

WEBSITES OF INTEREST

American Pharmacists Association
http://www.pharmacist.com

Centers for Disease Control and Prevention
http://www.cdc.gov

National Institute on Drug Abuse
http://www.drugabuse.gov

National Institutes of Health: MedlinePlus
http://www.nlm.nih.gov/medlineplus

See also: Amphetamine abuse; Anxiety medication abuse; Barbiturates; Benzodiazepine abuse; Codeine; Depressants abuse; Dextroamphetamine; Opioid abuse; Painkiller abuse; Sleeping pills

Prescription drug addiction: Overview

CATEGORY: Substance abuse

ALSO KNOWN AS: Prescription drug dependence

DEFINITION: Prescription drug addiction refers to dependence on scheduled prescription drugs obtained from a physician or through illicit means. The prescription drug addict has a psychological and physiological need for the drug. Prescription drug dependence often involves narcotic painkillers and psychiatric drugs such as amphetamines and benzodiazepines.

RISK FACTORS

According to the Substance Abuse and Mental Health Services Administration (SAMHSA), 1.9 million people in the United States age twelve years and older abused or were dependent on prescription pain relievers in 2009. An additional 481,000 persons abused or depended on tranquilizers, 371,000 persons abused or depended on stimulants, and 147,000 abused or depended on sedatives.

Anyone can become addicted to prescription scheduled drugs, but some persons have a greater risk. For example, alcoholics or persons who abuse illegal drugs have an elevated risk for dependence on prescribed drugs. Alcoholics may misuse drugs such as benzodiazepines to potentiate (increase) the effects of alcohol, while others addicted to stimulants such as methamphetamine or cocaine may use benzodiazepines as sedatives to fall asleep. Misuse can escalate into an addiction.

In general, women have a higher risk for prescription drug abuse and addiction than men. For example, about 55 percent of those who use prescription pain relievers for no medical reason are women, according to SAMHSA. In addition, incarcerated persons of both genders, particularly those in prison or on parole, have a higher risk for drug abuse and dependence than those not incarcerated or on parole.

According to an analysis by researcher Li-Tzy Wu and colleagues, adolescents aged twelve to seventeen years abuse prescription pain relievers, but only about 1 percent of this group is addicted. This research also indicates female adolescents have a higher risk for addiction to opiates than males. Other risk factors for addiction among adolescents include the abuse of multiple illicit drugs and the sale of illegal drugs to others. Adolescents who abuse or depend on prescription pain relievers are significantly more likely than others to have emotional or health problems and to have problems with family or friends.

An early nonmedical use of prescription drugs is predictive of adult prescription drug abuse and dependence, according to research by Sean E. McCabe and colleagues. The researchers found that nonmedical prescription drug abuse before age thirteen years was predictive for abuse and dependence of prescription drugs at age twenty-one years and older. Among early users, 25 percent became dependent on prescription drugs later in life, compared with 7 percent who initiated their prescription drug misuse at or older than age twenty-one years and then became abusers or addicts.

OBTAINING DRUGS OF DEPENDENCE

Some persons initially obtain dangerous prescription drugs from their physician because of a valid medical problem involving pain or a diagnosis of a psychiatric disorder. These persons may exceed the dosage recommended by the physician. To support this increased dosage, these users may seek a greater quantity of drugs from their doctors; if their doctor refuses, they often seek prescriptions through multiple physicians. This practice is referred to as doctor shopping.

In 2009 about one-half of persons who abused narcotics or psychiatric medications obtained these drugs from a friend or relative with that person's permission. Others obtain their drugs from the Internet or from drug dealers, or they steal drugs from friends and family members. Some addicts steal prescription pads from doctors and write their own prescriptions, while some with legitimate prescriptions are altered to obtain a greater quantity than ordered by the doctor. For this reason, doctors who prescribe pain medications often photocopy their original prescription.

Prescribed drugs are also stolen from pharmacies. For example, between January 2000 and June 2003, about 1.4 million OxyContin tablets were stolen from pharmacies. About two-thirds of these losses were attributed to break-ins or robberies, and 16.5 percent were attributed to employee theft.

Drug dealers also sell prescription drugs. A 2008 study of prescription opioid misuse among persons taking street drugs found that, based on a sample of 586 illicit heroin users in New York City, methadone was sold to them by 64.7 percent of drug dealers and OxyContin was sold by 41.4 percent. One-half of the drug dealers selling heroin and cocaine also sold prescription opioids and 25 percent of the drug dealers sold prescription opioids only.

Some people hire patients already legitimately receiving Medicare or Medicaid to complain to their doctors about pain to obtain drugs for diversion. Doctors who participate in this type of scam (and who receive illicit payments for their participation) give the patient a prescription for a large quantity of opiates. These prescriptions are then filled, given to the person who initially hired the patient, and then retrieved by drug dealers for illegal sale.

SYMPTOMS OF WITHDRAWAL

The problem of prescription drug dependence becomes evident when the person stops taking the addictive drug, whether voluntarily or because the person cannot obtain the drug. The addict will undergo withdrawal symptoms, which may be severe. Symptoms include such reactions as headache, tremors, vomiting, seizures, and even death.

Psychological symptoms too are common with a sudden withdrawal from prescription drugs of abuse; the person may experience severe anxiety, hallucinations, and delusions. To limit the withdrawal symptoms, persons who stop taking addictive prescription drugs should be under the care of a physician.

TREATMENT

According to SAMHSA, in 2009, 739,000 people received treatment for the misuse of prescription pain relievers and 421,000 received treatment for the misuse of tranquilizers. A treating physician may taper the person off the drug of abuse and substitute a safer drug in the same category, then taper the person off that drug. Such treatments can markedly reduce withdrawal symptoms.

Psychotherapy is a helpful adjunct to treatment with medications, and therapy is often ordered by courts when prescription drug dependence is related to the commission of a crime. There are many

---

Prescription Drug Addiction Prevention

The following steps will help a person reduce the chance of becoming addicted to a prescription drug:

- Carefully follow prescription directions.

- Be aware of potential interactions with other drugs.

- Talk with one's doctor before changing the dose.

- Avoid the use of another person's prescription.

- Tell one's doctor about all the medicines one is taking, including over-the-counter medicines and dietary and herbal supplements.

- Have a good relationship with one's children, which may reduce their risk of using drugs.

---

different types of therapies, but one popular form is cognitive-behavioral therapy, in which the person is trained to identify and challenge irrational or maladaptive thoughts in an active interaction with the therapist.

Group therapy is also commonly used so that the addict can relate to and learn from the problems of others. Pills Anonymous is a twelve-step support group for persons addicted to prescription drugs, but these groups are available only in a few US states. Some prescription drug addicts must enter residential treatment programs to detoxify from their addiction.

Christine Adamec, BA, MBA

FURTHER READING

Davis, W. Rees, and Bruce D. Johnson. "Prescription Opioid Use, Misuse, and Diversion among Street Drug Users in New York City." *Drug and Alcohol Dependence* 92 (2008): 267–76. Print. Discusses research on the diversion and misuse of prescription opiates among street-drug users in New York City.

Gwinnell, Esther, and Christine Adamec. *The Encyclopedia of Drug Abuse.* New York: Facts On File, 2008. This comprehensive source provides general information about the abuse of and dependence on illicit and prescribed drugs.

Inciardi, James A., et al. "Mechanisms of Prescription Drug Diversion among Drug-Involved Club- and Street-Based Populations." *Pain Medicine* 8.2 (2007): 171–83. Print. Results of a study on how people obtain prescription drugs of abuse, based on four populations: those who abused illicit drugs purchased on the street, those with human immunodeficiency virus infection, those on methadone maintenance treatment, and those in a club-type setting.

McCabe, Sean E., et al. "Does Early Onset of Non-Medical Use of Prescription Drugs Predict Subsequent Prescription Drug Abuse and Dependence?" *Addiction* 102.12 (2007): 1920–30. Print. This study compared prescription abuse and dependence among adults with the age at which they first began abusing prescription drugs. Those who began their abuse at age thirteen had a much higher risk than others for becoming dependent on prescription drugs as adults.

Substance Abuse and Mental Health Services Administration. *Results from the 2009 National Survey on Drug Use and Health: Volume 1: Summary of National*

Findings. Rockville, MD: Author, 2010. This annual publication provides basic and detailed statistical information on the abuse of illicit and prescribed drugs in the United States, based on an annual survey of nearly sixty-eight thousand people.

Wu, Li-Tzy, et al. "Prescription Pain Reliever Abuse and Dependence among Adolescents: A Nationally Representative Study." *Journal of the American Academy of Child and Adolescent Psychiatry* 47.9 (2008): 1020–29. Print. Provides analysis and data on prescription pain reliever abuse and dependence among adolescents, based on 18,678 adolescents who were interviewed in 2005 and 18,314 adolescents interviewed in 2006.

WEBSITES OF INTEREST

National Institute on Drug Abuse
http://www.drugabuse.gov

Pills Anonymous
http://www.pillsanonymous.org

See also: Amphetamine abuse; Anxiety medication abuse; Barbiturates; Benzodiazepine abuse; Codeine; Depressants abuse; Opioid abuse; Painkiller abuse

Prevention methods and research

CATEGORY: Diagnosis and prevention

DEFINITION: Prevention of substance abuse and addictive behavior disorders is concerned with stopping substance abuse before it starts (primary prevention), preventing the progression from infrequent use to addiction or encouraging current users to quit (secondary prevention), and preventing relapse among former addicts (tertiary prevention).

PREVENTION PROGRAM EFFICACY

Of the three levels of prevention, primary prevention receives most of the funding and attention, as it is often more effective and less costly than secondary or tertiary prevention. However, the effectiveness of a prevention program is difficult to determine without expensive, long-term studies. As a consequence, a large number of programs are in use in the United States that may not be effective. For example, an estimated 80 percent of youths age twelve to seventeen years were exposed to some form of education about drugs or alcohol in 2004, but only 20 percent were exposed to effective prevention programs.

Research on prevention methods may take the form of a randomized-controlled trial (RCT) or observational study or may use more informal evaluation methods. The most rigorous design tests the program's effects on a group that receives the intervention and compares results with a second group that did not receive the intervention (a control group).

One of the drawbacks of most of the studies conducted to evaluate prevention programs is that substance abuse is usually self-reported, and so studies may overestimate the benefits of the intervention because of underreporting by participants. In addition, short-term follow-up, lack of randomization, lack of blinding, and failure to control for confounders are all common in the research literature in this area and may cause results to appear more or less significant than if higher-quality research methods had been used.

Another method that is sometimes used to assess interventions is cost-effectiveness research, which includes an assessment of the cost of providing the program and the costs or losses prevented by the program. Taking both costs and benefits into account enables policymakers and communities to choose programs that not only are effective but also are efficient in the use of resources. However, cost-effectiveness is not often evaluated, and there are no requirements that a program be cost-effective for it to be used.

One notable feature of most of the research on substance abuse prevention is that the effect sizes are generally quite small. Therefore, to prevent substance abuse and its adverse consequences, a comprehensive program of intervention strategies is required. No single intervention can reduce the problem enough on its own.

ALCOHOL ABUSE

Prevention of alcohol abuse is a major public health goal, as alcohol abuse is the most costly substance abuse disorder and the consequences are severe. A number of laws and policies have proven effective in preventing alcohol-related problems.

Well supported in the research literature as both effective and cost-effective are alcohol excise taxes of up to 20 percent of the pretax selling price, a minimum legal drinking age of twenty-one years, and a curfew for novice drivers. Laws against serving patrons who are intoxicated and ensuring that servers are trained to recognize impairment are more costly to implement and enforce, and so may not be as cost-effective in the long run. Implementation of stringent drunk driving laws (such as lower blood-alcohol concentration laws, minimum legal drinking-age laws, and sobriety checkpoints) has been credited with reducing the number of alcohol-attributable traffic deaths in the United States since about 1970.

A number of programs aimed at young people have been identified as effective in reducing alcohol abuse in the long term. These programs include Botvin's LifeSkills Training (LST) and the family-based Strengthening Families Program (SFP). The LST program was designed to be delivered to students in seventh through ninth grades by trained teachers. It has two main goals: developing personal decision-making skills (competence-enhancement) and developing social skills to help students resist peer pressure to smoke, drink, and use drugs. In one RCT, students who attended more than 60 percent of the studied LST training sessions reported significantly lower prevalence rates for weekly drinking, heavy drinking, and problem drinking six years after the initial intervention.

Some LST programs have been specially designed for high-risk youth. In one such study, drinking frequency and drinking amount were significantly lower in students who received LST or a culturally focused intervention compared with students who received information only. In another study, students who received LST reported significantly fewer occasions of binge drinking compared with students who did not. Another variation of the LST program, which incorporated Native American values, legends, and stories and was delivered to Native American students in grades three through five, also reported positive long-term effects.

SFP, developed in the early 1980s, is a fourteen-session skills-training program aimed at preventing alcohol, tobacco, and drug abuse among high-risk families. More than fifteen independent studies have found similar positive results with families.

Secondary and tertiary alcohol-abuse prevention programs include screening and brief counseling interventions in primary care settings, employee assistance and skills-training programs in the workplace, and peer interventions and support groups. Brief interventions by clinicians have been shown to reduce alcohol consumption in men, but the evidence is less clear for women. However, heavy drinkers who received a brief (fifteen-to-twenty-minute) intervention have been shown to be twice as likely to decrease their alcohol consumption in the medium term (six to twelve months after an intervention) compared with drinkers receiving no intervention.

Minimal research exists on the effectiveness of workplace prevention programs. The effectiveness of skills training to reduce consumption among college students also has not been proven, although there is weak evidence of some effects. Also, peer-led programs may be more effective than teacher-led programs among young people.

TOBACCO USE

As with alcohol, a number of laws and policies have been used to prevent underage smoking and to encourage smokers to quit. Indoor and workplace smoking bans, enforcement of prohibitions on underage purchase, and increased taxes on tobacco products have all been shown to be effective in preventing smoking.

A strong relationship exists between increased taxes on tobacco products and rates of smoking among people of all ages. For example, after an increase of $1.25 in New York State's excise tax on cigarettes in 2008, the adult smoking rate dropped by 12 percent. Every 10 percent increase in the price of cigarettes reduces youth smoking by about 7 percent.

Going beyond smoke-free workplace policies, some employers have even instituted policies against hiring smokers, although the evidence base is limited in terms of the effectiveness of such policies in preventing smoking; about thirty states have passed laws protecting smokers who smoke on their own time.

The We Card Program, established by the Coalition for Responsible Retailing in 1995, "is a youth-smoking prevention" program in the United States. The program primarily involves tobacco sales training and education, which includes the display of graphical materials in retail locations that sell tobacco products. The program's effectiveness has been questioned in terms of preventing sales of tobacco products to minors. Some critics have argued that the program was intended to enhance positive perceptions of tobacco companies and to reduce law enforcement "stings" of retail establishments. The campaign may even be perceived by some high-risk youths as encouragement to smoke upon turning age eighteen years.

School-based programs for primary prevention of smoking include information campaigns, skills-training programs, and community interventions. School-based programs that simply provide information have not proven effective in preventing smoking. Although studies of programs that used a skills-training approach have found short-term effects in preventing youth smoking, the highest quality and longest trial (the Hutchinson Smoking Prevention Project, a fifteen-year randomized trial) found no long-term effects. Programs that teach social resistance skills (the ability to resist peer pressure) can

reduce the proportion of youth who initiate smoking by about one-third relative to controls, although the effects of the intervention dissipate by about three years after the program ends.

Groups that have been the targets of a number of secondary interventions aimed at preventing smoking in users include pregnant women, persons with heart disease, and persons who have had surgery. The most effective programs for these adults appear to be brief interventions delivered by clinicians. Brief smoking-cessation counseling offered at the first prenatal visit results in more women quitting than no intervention or in an education-only intervention. Full insurance coverage (removing copayments or coinsurance) for smoking cessation therapy, including nicotine replacement (such as nicotine gum or patches) or pharmaceutical products such as Zyban and Chantix, also is effective and cost-effective in reducing tobacco use in current smokers.

Public Service Announcements

A public service announcement (PSA) is any commercial-length television or radio broadcast or print or electronic advertising that promotes topics of social interest. Unlike commercial advertising, which tries to persuade persons to purchase a product or service, PSAs generally focus on building awareness for a specific issue.

The tone of the PSA usually is formulated to generate an emotional response, including empathy, fear, and anger. Examples of PSAs include those regarding drunk driving, seatbelt use, adoption, animal cruelty, cancer screening, tobacco use, and substance abuse.

Often, media outlets such as newspapers, television, radio, and websites donate advertising time or space. Sometimes, advertising and public relations agencies and production companies donate their services to produce the advertising. Although most media outlets will run PSAs free of charge, some organizations choose to purchase advertising space or broadcast time to launch their message to the public.

National PSA campaigns often feature celebrities, politicians, and athletes. Internet campaigns often use social networking sites such as *Facebook, Twitter,* and *MySpace,* or video sites such as *YouTube* and *Vimeo,* to direct consumers to specific websites for additional information.

ILLICIT AND NONMEDICAL PHARMACEUTICAL DRUGS
Laws and policies designed to prevent drug use are often more severe than those aimed at alcohol and tobacco. In an era of mandatory minimum sentencing and zero tolerance laws, one-half of all prisoners in US prisons are incarcerated for nonviolent drug offenses, and the United States has the highest per-capita prison population in the world. Although the Office of National Drug Control Policy (ONDCP) has asserted that prevention is the most cost-effective approach to the drug problem, funding for prevention programs makes up only a small portion of the ONDCP budget (7 percent); the majority of spending is on law enforcement and interdiction activities (63 percent).

Many employers require drug testing of employees, particularly those in transportation and security services. Research on the effectiveness of drug testing policies on preventing drug abuse is scarce, but some evidence suggests that productivity is actually lower in firms that have drug testing policies.

Another policy that has recently become more common is mandatory and random student drug testing (MRSDT), often required for student athletes and others who wish to participate in afterschool or other extracurricular activities. The effectiveness of such policies, in terms of their ability to prevent drug abuse, is not clear. A large study funded by the National Institute on Drug Abuse, called Monitoring the

Future, has found that schools with MRSDT had virtually identical drug use rates as schools without drug testing.

Many of the same approaches that are used in primary prevention programs for alcohol are also used in programs that aim to prevent drug use. Also, many programs aimed at youths are intended to prevent substance abuse of all types. However, since the 1980s, the emphasis of these programs, including the "Just Say No" national campaign, has typically been on illicit drugs such as marijuana, cocaine, and heroin. More recently, the nonmedical use of pharmaceutical drugs, such as painkillers and stimulants (such as Ritalin), has become a focus of concern.

One of the most commonly used educational programs has long been Drug Abuse Resistance Education (D.A.R.E.). In a comparison study in the mid-1990s and in a follow-up study about five years later, schools that used the D.A.R.E. program had no significant reductions in drug use relative to control schools. More broadly, much research has shown that education-only programs are not sufficient to change behavior, although they may be effective in changing knowledge or attitudes.

Programs that can be effective in changing behaviors are usually derived from psychosocial theories and focus on minimizing the risk factors for, and on enhancing the protective factors against, substance abuse initiation. Multiple evaluations since the early 1990s have found that a combination of social resistance skills-training and competence enhancement are among the most effective approaches. Programs that use these approaches and that have shown positive results in RCTs include LST and SFP and the programs Lions Quest Skills for Adolescence, Project ALERT, CASASTART, and Project STAR.

Mass media campaigns appear to have little effect on drug use rates. More than $1.7 billion has been appropriated by the US Congress since 1998 for the National Youth Anti-Drug Media Campaign, yet evaluations have found no evidence that the campaign had a positive effect on teen drug use and some indications of a negative effect. Although the program was retooled and refocused specifically to address marijuana use in the early 2000s, further evaluations found that the campaign has had no effect on youth marijuana-use rates.

Lisa M. Lines, MPH

FURTHER READING

McGrath, Yuko, et al. *Drug Use Prevention among Young People: A Review of Reviews.* London: National Institute for Health and Clinical Excellence, 2006. Web. 27 Mar. 2012. http://www.nice.org.uk/niceMedia/docs/drug_use_prev_update_v9.pdf. This report focuses on studies about what works to prevent and reduce illicit drug use among young people.

Miller, Ted R., and Delia Hendrie. *Substance Abuse Prevention Dollars and Cents: A Cost-Benefit Analysis.* Rockville, MD: Center for Substance Abuse Prevention, 2008. Web. 27 Mar. 2012. http://store.samhsa.gov/shin/content//SMA07-4298/SMA07-4298.pdf. This report provides estimates of the costs and benefits of programs designed to prevent abuse of alcohol, tobacco, and other drugs.

National Institute on Drug Abuse. *Preventing Drug Use among Children and Adolescents: A Research-Based Guide for Parents, Educators, and Community Leaders.* 2nd ed. Bethesda, MD: NIDA, 2003. Web. 27 Mar. 2012. http://www.drugabuse.gov/publications/preventing-drug-abuse-among-children-adolescents. This report details comprehensive strategies for implementing drug-use prevention programs in various communities.

O'Connell, Mary Ellen, Thomas Boat, and Kenneth E. Warner. *Preventing Mental, Emotional, and Behavioral Disorders among Young People: Progress and Possibilities.* Washington, DC: National Academies, 2009. Web. 27 Mar. 2012. http://www.nap.edu/catalog.php?record_id=12480. A holistic view of the prevention of substance abuse, placing it in context with the emotional and mental health issues that may underlie addictive behaviors.

Robinson, Matthew B., and Renee G. Scherlen. *Lies, Damned Lies, and Drug War Statistics: A Critical Analysis of Claims Made by the Office of National Drug Control Policy.* Albany: State U of New York P, 2007. Examines the drug war with a critical eye and includes a thorough policy analysis.

WEBSITES OF INTEREST

DrugWarFacts.org
http://www.drugwarfacts.org

National Institute on Drug Abuse
http://www.drugabuse.gov

*Substance Abuse and Mental Health Services
    Administration*
http://www.samhsa.gov/prevention

*US Food and Drug Administration: Break the Chain of
    Tobacco Addiction*
http://www.fda.gov/BreaktheChain

See also: Center for Substance Abuse Prevention
(CSAP); D.A.R.E. (Drug Abuse Resistance Education); Designated drivers; Drug testing; Education
about substance abuse; Government warnings; Just
Say No campaign; Monitoring the Future

Prison and substance abuse

CATEGORY: Social issues

DEFINITION: Substance abuse and addiction are major factors contributing to the growing US prison
population. A common outcome of substance use
disorder (SUD) is arrest and incarceration. SUD is
a primary disease that includes the progressive use
of alcohol or drugs that leads to severe psychosocial consequences.

DEMOGRAPHICS

The US criminal justice system is overburdened by
an epidemic of drug addiction and alcoholism. The
United States consumes two-thirds of the world's illegal drugs and incarcerates more than one-quarter
of the world's prisoners. According to a 2008 report
by the US Department of Justice, Bureau of Justice
Statistics (BJS), close to seven million people have
been identified within the criminal justice system as
incarcerated, on parole, or on probation.

In the second of a two-part landmark report, *Behind
Bars II: Substance Abuse and America's Prison Population*
(2010), published by the National Center on Addiction and Substance Abuse at Columbia University,
substance use disorders among inmates were found to
be at epidemic proportions. Prison inmates are seven
times more likely to have a substance use disorder
(SUD) than are persons in the general population.

The BJS noted in "Substance Dependence,
Abuse, and Treatment of Jail Inmates, 2002," a
survey of federal and state prisons, that 68 percent
of inmates, in the year before their imprisonment,
met the criteria of the American Psychiatric Association's *Diagnostic and Statistical Manual of Mental
Disorders* (DSM) for substance dependence or
abuse. An additional 16 percent acknowledged that
their convictions were directly related to obtaining
money for drugs, and more than one-half acknowledged the use of drugs or alcohol in the commission of a property crime or other violent crime. Of
inmates who did not meet the full DSM criteria for
SUD, an additional 20 percent acknowledged that
substance use was a factor in their crimes, that is,
the inmate had been under the influence at the
time of the offense or had directly violated alcohol
or drug laws.

The survey further showed that diagnoses of alcohol abuse and dependence (47 percent) and drug
abuse and dependence (53 percent) were fairly evenly
distributed within the prison population. Female prisoners (52 percent) were found to have higher rates
of substance dependence than males (44 percent),
although males had higher rates of substance abuse.
Race also varied among inmates. More white inmates
(78 percent) were diagnosed with SUD than were
black inmates (64 percent) or Hispanic inmates (59
percent). White women, although they represented
43 percent of all incarcerated women, had the highest
rates of SUD.

Age is also significantly related to SUD in the
prison population. The survey showed that younger
prisoners age twenty-five to forty-four years had
higher rates of SUD than prisoners age fifty-five
years or older, who had the lowest rates of SUD.
Younger inmates tended to abuse drugs, whereas
older inmates tended to abuse alcohol. Ten percent
of juvenile offenders were found to have been involved with drugs.

The family backgrounds of prisoners with SUD are
different from those inmates not diagnosed with addiction. Of those inmates who met criteria for SUD,
most had a previous criminal record and had a previous history of homelessness. Their family backgrounds showed that they were twice as likely to be the
child of a parent or guardian with a history of SUD as
an inmate who has no history of SUD. Almost twice
as many prisoners with SUD (21 percent) reported
being victims of physical or sexual abuse. More prisoners with a diagnosis of SUD had a parent who also
had been incarcerated.

BENEFITS OF TREATMENT

Since about 2000, substance abuse treatment has been offered to some people in the criminal justice system. Special attention has been focused on diversion programs and the use of drug courts to provide alternative paths to incarceration.

The National Institute on Drug Abuse issued several principles advocating treatment for the criminal offender. The principles acknowledge that drug abuse is a disease that requires proper assessment and treatment. Co-occurring mental and physical health issues, such as human immunodeficiency virus, acquired immunodeficiency syndrome, and hepatitis, should be addressed and treated. Drug treatment should be tailored to the criminal justice population. Special attention to treatment for the criminal offender must have strong drug-monitoring procedures and familiarity with correctional facility requirements. Treatment must target criminal behavior and thinking patterns and must help the inmate anticipate the consequences of his or her drug and alcohol use. Ideally, treatment should begin in prison and have aftercare programs in place within the community upon release.

In 2005, the US government spent $74 billion on incarceration, court proceedings, probation, and parole for offenders of substance-related crimes. However, the government committed less than 1 percent of that amount—$632 million—to prevention and treatment programs. In contrast, the National Drug Intelligence Center places the cost of effective prevention and treatment at $113 billion, which includes the cost of the criminal justice system itself and the cost of crime to its victims. An overwhelming body of evidence supports the inclusion of substance abuse treatment in the criminal justice system as a cost-effective and humanitarian way to reduce crime.

RECIDIVISM

Substance-involved offenders are more likely to recidivate (repeat crimes) than those who are not involved with substance use. More than one-half (52.2 percent) of substance-involved inmates have been previously incarcerated, compared with 31.2 percent of inmates who are not involved with substances.

SUD is preventable and treatable. Without treatment, however, the statistics suggest that substance-involved offenders will return to prison. Also, in spite of the recommendations for drug treatment, few inmates actually receive drug treatment that is adequate or tailored to their specific needs. Without treatment the rates of relapse will continue, driving up the rate of recidivism.

Amanda Leſkowitz, MA

FURTHER READING

Chandler, R. K., B. W. Fletcher, and N. D. Volkow. "Treating Drug Abuse and Addiction in the Criminal Justice System: Improving Public Health and Safety." *Journal of the American Medical Association* 301 (2009): 183–90. Print. Examines substance abuse among the prison population as a public health and safety issue.

Karberg, Jennifer C., and Doris J. James. "Substance Dependence, Abuse, and Treatment of Jail Inmates, 2002." Jul. 2005. Web. 3 Apr. 2012. http://bjs.ojp.usdoj.gov/content/pub/pdf/sdatji02.pdf. A twelve-page statistical report from the US Department of Justice, Bureau of Justice Statistics.

National Center on Addiction and Substance Abuse. *Behind Bars II: Substance Abuse and America's Prison Population.* Feb. 2010. Web. 3 Apr. 2012. http://www.casacolumbia.org/articlefiles/575-report-2010behindbars2.pdf. An extensive report, the second of two parts, on substance abuse among the incarcerated in the United States from the National Center on Addiction and Substance Abuse at Columbia University.

WEBSITES OF INTEREST

Bureau of Justice Statistics
http://bjs.ojp.usdoj.gov/content/dcf/contents.cfm

National Institute of Corrections
http://www.nicic.gov

National Institute on Drug Abuse
http://www.drugabuse.gov/publications/principles-drug-abuse-treatment-criminal-justice-populations

See also: Crime and substance abuse; Jail diversion programs; Phoenix House

Promises Treatment Center

CATEGORY: Treatment

DEFINITION: With locations in Malibu and West Los Angeles, California, Promises Treatment Center offers addiction recovery care for all clients, famous or not, through its specialized inpatient and outpatient treatment programs.

DATE: Established in 1998

BACKGROUND

Founded in 1998 by Richard Rogg, Promises Treatment Center offers treatment for a variety of addictions, including those to alcohol, prescription drugs, and cocaine and methamphetamine. The center also treats co-occurring psychological conditions, such as post-traumatic stress disorder, depression, attention deficit hyperactivity disorder, sleep disorders, and bipolar disorders. The center also offers programs to address marijuana abuse.

The center, which charges clients more than $35,000 per month, has treated a host of celebrities, including Lindsay Lohan, Brittany Spears, Ben Affleck, and Robert Downey Jr. It has a range of care specialties and a high staff-to-client ratio to ensure individualized and thorough care.

The center originated the Malibu model of substance addiction treatment, which is, essentially, individualized treatment for each client's unique experience and recovery needs. In the Malibu model, customized drug-addiction treatment integrates the detoxification (detox) process with specialized physical and psychological care, focusing on rehabilitating the mind, body, and spirit. The center features customized treatment for the addict, ensures confidentiality, and offers psychological care for the addict's family.

To ensure comprehensive, holistic care for each client, the center limits the number of clientele to twenty-four at each of its two locations. Recognizing the value a recovering addict's pet dog can offer to the treatment process, the center's Malibu location allows clients to lodge with their dog, if they have one, in residential treatment houses.

MISSION AND GOALS

Promises chief executive officer David Sack describes the center's mission as providing "a gateway to sobriety for you or a loved one and to aid in the achievement of lifetime dreams." Though the underlying foundation of treatment is the traditional twelve-step approach, each client's treatment team of specialists integrates adjunct methods and techniques to meet the needs of the client. These methods include medically monitored detox; psychiatric care; individual, family, and group psychotherapy; stress management education; art therapy; yoga and meditation; fitness and nutritional education; eye movement desensitization and reprocessing; dialectical behavioral therapy; and somatic therapy.

The main house of the the Promises Treatment Center in Malibu, California. (AP Photo)

The center offers brain imaging studies to discover whether and to what extent a client's brain has been affected by substance abuse. Through a technique known as digital electroencephalogram spectral analysis, specialists perform a computerized tomography scan to collect images of the brain regions affected by substance abuse. The imaging helps doctors analyze a client's central nervous system, input processes, and expression processes. Once specialists gather an analysis of how a client's substance abuse has physically affected his or her brain, they present the results to the client, thereby facilitating the client's understanding of how drugs and alcohol affect the brain and behavior.

The center's drug and alcohol addiction programs are designed to guide clients through recovery. Beginning with thirty days of residential treatment, clients stay in comfortable, home-like lodging, where physicians and specialists are always available. The next stage of the center's "continuum of care" features extended care treatment, which provides continued support as clients transition back into work and family life. Treatment covers relapse prevention and includes life coaching and individual and family therapy. Next, clients move on to day treatment, the stage in which they receive treatment five hours per day, five days per week. Clients have private meetings with a therapist, participate in group therapy and art therapy, and undergo random drug and alcohol testing.

Following day treatment, clients receive outpatient treatment, in which they fully reenter work and family life while regularly meeting with a local therapist or counselor. In lieu of outpatient care, a client may opt to, or be directed to, participate in sober living accommodations rather than return to his or her pretreatment living situation. Sober living homes require that residents attend twelve-step meetings, continue with therapy, and participate in random drug and alcohol testing. The homes also may impose additional house rules, such as an evening curfew.

Promises Treatment Center offers other addiction treatment programs, including those for sex addiction and video-game addiction. The center also offers care and counseling to the addicted patient's family, including intervention assistance, family therapy, and out-of-care transition support.

Melissa Walsh

FURTHER READING

"Gamers Anonymous: A Famed Rehab Takes on Joystick Addicts." *Los Angeles Magazine* 53.1 (2008): 34. Discusses the introduction of the gaming addiction program to the Promises Treatment Center in Malibu.

Ries, Richard K., et al., eds. *Principles of Addiction Medicine.* 4th ed. Philadelphia: Wolters, 2009.

Stillman-Corbitt, Shari. "How Promises Uses EEG Biofeedback to Improve Outcomes in Addiction treatment." 10 May 2010. Web. http://www.addiction-treatmentmagazine.com/addiction-treatment. Describes the therapeutic role of EEG biofeedback in addictions treatment at Promises Treatment Center.

WEBSITES OF INTEREST

The Addiction Recovery Guide
http://www.addictionrecoveryguide.org/resources/recovery

National Institute on Drug Abuse
http://drugabuse.gov

Promises Treatment Centers
http://www.promises.com

Substance Abuse and Mental Health Services Administration
http://www.samhsa.gov

See also: Alcohol abuse and alcoholism: Treatment; Behavioral addictions: Treatment; Celebrities and substance abuse; Outpatient treatment; Residential treatment; Twelve-step programs for addicts; Twelve-step programs for family and friends

Pseudoaddiction

CATEGORY: Psychological issues and behaviors

DEFINITION: A pseudoaddiction is drug-seeking behavior that mimics addiction. It occurs in persons who are not receiving adequate pain relief, and it indicates mismanagement of pain relief treatment.

INTRODUCTION

People experience pain in many ways and for many reasons, ranging from acute pain from injuries or surgery to chronic pain from long-term diseases such as arthritis. Health care practitioners provide pain-relieving medications, but these medications do not always work equally well for each person.

A dosage of a pain relief medication that may work for one person may be either inadequate or over-whelming for another person. In addition, certain types of pain relievers work better for some people than for others, even in persons with the same condition. For example, extra-strength acetaminophen may be sufficient for one person while for another, opioids may be needed to adequately relieve pain. Sometimes the level of pain relief can depend on the age of the person or on the amount of pain-relieving medication taken previously.

Pseudoaddiction was first described in 1989 in the case of a seventeen-year-old who had pain related to leukemia. Because the patient's pain was inadequately treated, the patient began exhibiting addictive behaviors. The patient's progression to pseudoaddiction was traced through phases, which are still used to describe pseudoaddiction. The phases are inadequate pain relief medications, demands by the patient for more painkillers and for more frequent doses of pain-killers (with accompanying behavior changes that attempt to convince caregivers that more pain relief is necessary), and mistrust between patient and his or her health care team about the severity of pain and the necessity of pain relief.

PSEUDOADDICTION VERSUS ADDICTION

Patients who are not receiving enough medication to alleviate their pain may begin to exhibit drug-seeking behaviors that mimic addiction. These behaviors include focusing on getting medication or watching the clock to monitor when the next dose of pain medication will be available. Patients also may moan or grimace in a way that seems excessive, may be deceptive about their use of painkillers, and might even seek illicit drugs for pain relief.

Pseudoaddicts are not addicted to the drug in the common sense; they are simply seeking adequate pain relief. Because their behavior may seem addictive to a person not familiar with the case, this condition is termed *pseudoaddiction*. One can determine if a patient is experiencing pseudoaddiction or is truly addicted by noticing if the drug-seeking behaviors cease once the patient receives adequate pain medication.

TREATING PSEUDOADDICTION

The first and most important activity in treating pseudoaddiction is to provide the patient with enough medication to adequately relieve pain. This may be difficult because by the time the patient is exhibiting drug-seeking behavior, health care providers may distrust the patient enough to refuse to provide any more pain medication. Providers may need to be convinced to attempt a trial of providing pain relief to the point that the patient actually feels relief and stops exhibiting this type of behavior, before a relationship of trust can once again be attempted.

Treatment of pseudoaddiction in the elderly can be particularly difficult. Though providers may believe that the dosage and frequency of pain-relieving medication is more than adequate, they should consider that aging organs might not be able to process medications to the point of providing relief. Thus, the patient will still experience pain even with frequent or high doses of medication. A movement has begun among health professionals treating pain in the elderly to ensure that doses of pain relief are adequate for the particular patient, and not based on suggested dosages only. The movement encourages a relationship of trust in which the provider believes the patient if the patient still complains of pain.

Marianne M. Madsen, MS

FURTHER READING

Sees, K. L., and H. W. Clark. "Opioid Use in the Treatment of Chronic Pain: Assessment of Addiction." *Journal of Pain and Symptom Management* 8 (1993): 257–64. Print.

Turk, D. C., H. D. Wilson, and A. Cahana. "Treatment of Chronic Non-Cancer Pain." *Lancet* 377 (2011): 2226–35. Print.

Weissman, D. E., and J. D. Haddox. "Opioid Pseudoaddiction: An Iatrogenic Syndrome." *Pain* 36 (1989): 363–66. Print.

WEBSITES OF INTEREST

American Academy of Pain Medicine
http://www.painmed.org

American Society of Addiction Medicine
http://www.asam.org/for-the-public/pain-and-
    addiction

*Beth Israel Hospital, Department of Pain Medicine and
    Palliative Care*
HealthCentral.com
http://www.healthcentral.com/chronic-pain/
    coping-279488-5.html

Pain Treatment Topics
http://www.pain-topics.org

See also: Opioid abuse; Painkiller abuse; Prescription
drug addiction: In depth; Science of addiction

Psychological dependence

CATEGORY: Health issues and physiology

DEFINITION: Psychological dependence is marked by
a strong desire for a substance (or activity) that
provides enjoyment or satisfaction. Psychological
dependence can occur with or without physiological dependence; the psychologically dependent
person's body may continue to function normally
without the substance, but he or she still feels a
strong urge for and preoccupation with that substance.

INTRODUCTION

Addiction is a complex issue, and persons who are
addicted may become physically dependent and
psychologically dependent on the substance they
abuse. People also can become addicted to behaviors,
which are generally only psychologically dependent
problems.

DEPENDENCE

A person can become physiologically and psychologically dependent on the same substance. Physiological
dependence occurs when the body becomes dependent on a substance, and physical withdrawal symptoms develop when the substance is no longer used.
These withdrawal symptoms may include accelerated
heartbeat, hypersensitivity, nausea and vomiting,
sweating, tremors, insomnia, and agitation. Some of

the substances most likely to cause physical dependence are alcohol, amphetamines, barbiturates, opiates, and nicotine.

Psychological dependence occurs when a person
derives reward or pleasure from a substance or an activity and when the desire to participate in that activity
is irresistible. Substances may be used to relieve anxiety, seek elation, avoid depression, and relieve pain
(physical or psychological). Behaviors involve activities of avoidance (such as playing computer games to
avoid work) and provide pleasure and reward (such as
sexual activity). Psychological withdrawal symptoms
occur when the activity (including substance use) is
discontinued. These symptoms may include craving,
depression, insomnia, and irritability.

TREATING PSYCHOLOGICAL DEPENDENCE

In treating any kind of addiction, it is important to
consider psychological dependence as integral to
the treatment program. Relapse rates in treating addiction are extremely high (80 percent for drug addiction and 86 percent for alcohol addiction), even
when the addicted person has gone through a physical detoxification process to ensure that the body
is no longer physically dependent on the substance.
This phenomenon adds weight to the argument that
a psychological dependence may be even stronger
than a physical dependence. Cognitive-behavioral
therapy or traditional psychotherapy may help to address underlying psychological reasons for addiction.

Another type of treatment that attempts to address the psychological underpinnings of addiction
is the popular twelve-step program, such as that of
Alcoholics Anonymous. These programs often focus
on behavior modification to address psychological
dependence, such as substituting a positive behavior
for an addictive behavior when craving strikes. Experimental treatments for psychological dependence
have involved surgeries to attempt to block those
areas in the brain, such as the nucleus accumbens,
that are thought to lead to psychological dependence.
Other treatments involve alternative therapies, such
as hypnotherapy or acupuncture, to try to overcome
psychological dependence. Still other treatment combinations addressing both physical and psychological
addiction boast relapse rates as low as 15 percent,
though these numbers have been disputed.

Some addictions have no real physical component,
leaving the psychological component as the only

element involved. Behaviors that may become addictive, such as gambling, shopping, and Internet use, should be treated psychologically. Even in these cases, however, a physical component exists. Addictive behaviors may allow the brain to release certain chemicals that enhance the pleasure-giving aspect of addiction. Amphetamine and cocaine use are strongly associated with the brain's dopaminergic, or reward, system.

Persons who become psychologically dependent may have certain personality or behavior characteristics that reinforce the tendency toward this type of addiction. Often, they have difficulty with consistency, commitment, impulse control, and project completion. They also may be confrontational and may lack communications skills. Genetic studies are looking at how gene mutations or certain genotype combinations may affect these tendencies.

Many clinicians make no distinction between psychological dependence and physical dependence in substance addiction because the problem remains the same: A person is addicted to a substance. Others believe that psychological dependence can be even stronger than physical dependence, and that even after physical dependence is overcome, a psychological dependence can linger, increasing the risk that a recovering addict may later relapse. However, most clinicians agree that whether physical or psychological, these dependencies are inseparably intertwined, thus making substance addiction a complicated and difficult condition to treat.

Marianne M. Madsen, MS

FURTHER READING

Blane, Howard T., and Kenneth E. Leonard, eds. *Psychological Theories of Drinking and Alcoholism.* New York: Guilford, 1999. Provides an overview of the psychology of alcoholism from leaders in the field, including thoughts on emotions, genetics, and neurobiology related to drinking.

Edwards, Griffith, and Christopher Dare, eds. *Psychotherapy, Psychological Treatments, and the Addictions.* New York: Cambridge UP, 1996. Classic discussions of psychological dependence and addiction, covering treatment strategies and approaches to therapy.

Gao, Guodong, et al. "Clinical Study for Alleviating Opiate Drug Psychological Dependence by a Method of Ablating the Nucleus Accumbens with

Stereotactic Surgery." *Stereotactic and Functional Neurosurgery* 81 (2003): 96–104. Print. Describes experimental surgery for persons with psychological addictions. Also discusses long-term results and patient outcomes.

Kuhn, Cynthia M., and George F. Koob, eds. *Advances in the Neuroscience of Addiction.* Boca Raton, FL: CRC, 2010. Discusses advancements in the psychological aspects of addiction at different levels, including genetics, behavioral, and psychological issues.

Orford, Jim. *Excessive Appetites: A Psychological View of Addictions.* 2nd ed. New York: Wiley, 2001. Covers a variety of addictions and includes information on psychological dependences. Discusses origins and processes of addiction and ways to treat addiction.

WEBSITES OF INTEREST

"Addiction." Treatment-Now.com
http://www.treatment-now.com/addiction

"Chronic Pain." HealthCentral.com
http://www.healthcentral.com/chronic-pain/
    coping-279488-5.html?ic=506011

"Psychological Addiction." Drug-Addiction-Support.org
http://www.drug-addiction-support.org/Psychological-Addiction.html

See also: Addiction; Dependence; Physiological dependence; Science of addiction

---

Psychosis and substance abuse

CATEGORY: Health issues and physiology

ALSO KNOWN AS: Psychosis and substance abuse comorbidity; psychosis and substance abuse dual diagnosis

DEFINITION: *Psychosis* is defined as an impaired ability to understand reality, think clearly, communicate adequately, and respond emotionally. Hallucinations and delusions (false beliefs) are often present. Psychotic symptoms occur in several mental disorders, such as schizophrenia, bipolar disorder, and depression. The pathway of association (comorbidity) of psychotic manifestations and substance abuse appears bidirectional, meaning that substance abuse can trigger or exacerbate psychosis, while psychosis may lead to substance abuse. A cycle is thus created, one that often renders diagnosis and treatment difficult.

SUBSTANCE ABUSE AND PSYCHOSIS

Clinical studies and community surveys document high rates of substance use disorders (SUD) in persons with psychotic symptoms. The lifetime prevalence of substance abuse among persons with psychotic illnesses such as schizophrenia and bipolar disorder can reach 60 percent, much higher than in the general population.

This comorbidity is most often associated with being male, single, young, and having a conduct or antisocial personality disorder. Persons with psychosis also tend to abuse multiple substances. The overlapping biological substrates responsible for this co-occurrence include structural brain abnormalities, genetic vulnerabilities, and early exposure to stress or trauma.

A high prevalence of substance abuse in persons with schizophrenia has been reported in numerous studies conducted in developed countries. According to the US National Institute of Mental Health, schizophrenia carries a 10.1 percent risk of drug abuse, and SUD may constitute the most common comorbidity of schizophrenia. Apart from tobacco and cannabis (the preferred substances), these persons also abuse alcohol, cocaine, and amphetamines.

When a person presents to mental health professionals with recent-onset psychosis associated with substance abuse, it becomes essential to establish whether the substance use caused the symptoms. Psychosis is considered to be independent of the SUD if the psychosis occurred before the substance use or if the psychosis persisted during long substance-free periods. An absence of disorientation (which occurs in substance-induced delirium) also may point to a distinct psychosis.

In practice, the aforementioned features can be difficult to ascertain. Persons with psychosis often do not

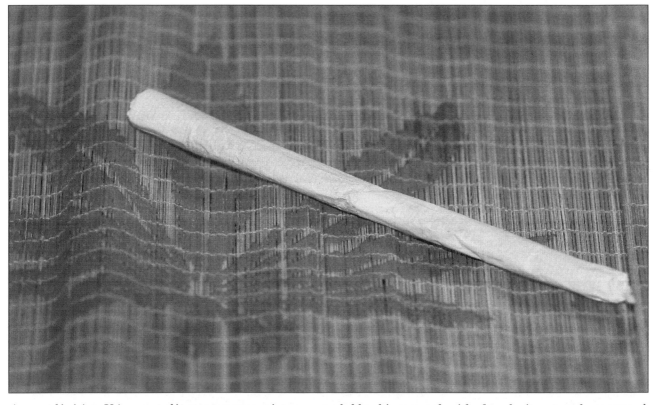

A cannabis joint. Using cannabis as a teenager or into young adulthood increases the risk of psychosis, experts have warned. (David Cheskin/PA Photos/Landov)

remember the exact sequence of events that contributed to the development of their disorder. Therefore, it becomes difficult to pinpoint the temporal relationship of psychotic symptoms and substance abuse. In addition, the patients may not experience significant substance-free periods. The diagnosis dilemma is further amplified by the similarity of symptoms, such as paranoia and auditory hallucinations, occurring both in independent psychosis and in psychosis induced by substances (especially stimulants). For this reason, persons with comorbid psychosis and SUD need to be thoroughly assessed at presentation, detoxified, treated immediately by interdisciplinary teams (using pharmacotherapy and cognitive behavioral-therapy among other approaches), and then monitored.

Overall, coexisting SUD imparts a more severe character and a poorer outcome to psychotic disorders, with frequent relapses and hospitalizations. Studies show, for example, that persons with defined comorbid SUD and first-episode psychosis are likely to have poorer treatment response than those with psychosis alone.

PSYCHOSIS TRIGGERS
Alcohol and illegal drugs (cannabis, amphetamines, cocaine, hallucinogens, and opiates) can cause psychosis, both during use and as a consequence of withdrawal. Severe psychiatric disorders appear to correlate with earlier and longer exposure to stimulants. This suggests the presence of a critical developmental stage, or a threshold effect, of the drug on psychosis development.

Up to 15 percent of cannabis users report psychotic symptoms immediately after use. The hypothesis that cannabis abuse also causes chronic schizophrenia-like psychosis has not been ruled out, although evidence remains insufficient. An increasing body of literature points to early exposure to cannabis as generating psychosis later in life. Cannabis use during adolescence is an independent risk factor for the onset of psychosis in adulthood (especially in at-risk subjects) and associates with an earlier onset of schizophrenia. Studies also suggest that heavy cannabis use precipitates psychotic relapses in person with schizophrenia who previously achieved remission.

Psychotic symptoms with paranoia and suspiciousness are reported during cocaine use and withdrawal. The propensity to experience cocaine-induced psychosis has been linked to mutations in genes coding for proteins involved in dopaminergic transmission.

Methamphetamine use is commonly associated with psychiatric conditions such as psychosis and depression. During both abstinent and intoxicated circumstances, persons who are methamphetamine-dependent are more likely to report psychotic symptoms than are cocaine addicts. Drug-induced psychotic syndromes are both positive (auditory hallucinations, persecutory delusions) and negative (poor speech, flattened affect). These psychotic states persist after the pharmacological effects of the methamphetamine have subsided, and they reappear upon reinjection. Furthermore, under stressful conditions, persons with a history of methamphetamine psychosis undergo spontaneous recurrence of their psychotic symptoms. Methamphetamine psychosis might therefore associate with persistent structural or functional brain damage caused by repeated drug administration.

PSYCHOSIS CAN LEAD TO SUBSTANCE ABUSE
It has been suggested that persons with schizophrenia may self-medicate with tobacco, alcohol, and drugs. The substances of abuse are often perceived as alleviating negative symptoms (such as depression and withdrawal), improving hallucinations and paranoid delusions, lessening adverse effects of medications (such as restlessness), and providing an avenue for social interaction. This causal relationship remains unclear, as some studies have contradicted the self-medication hypothesis for this comorbidity.

Mihaela Avramut, MD, PhD

FURTHER READING
Emmelkamp, Paul M. G., and Ellen Vedel. *Evidence-Based Treatment for Alcohol and Drug Abuse: A Practitioner's Guide to Theory, Methods, and Practice.* New York: Routledge, 2006. Excellent resource for professionals and caregivers interested in substance abuse disorders. Includes a detailed discussion of psychiatric comorbidities.

Tamminga, Carol A., et al., eds. *Deconstructing Psychosis: Refining the Research Agenda for DSM-V.* Arlington, VA: American Psychiatric Association, 2010. An updated, authoritative study of psychosis for advanced students. Includes an assessment of diagnosis difficulties in substance use disorder comorbidity.

Thakkar, Vatsal G. *Addiction*. New York: Chelsea House, 2006. Accessible overview of addiction topics, including the relationship with mental illness.

Volkow, Nora D. "Substance Use Disorders in Schizophrenia: Clinical Implications of Comorbidity." *Schizophrenia Bulletin* 35 (2009): 469–72. Print. Article written by an authority in the field of addiction research.

WEBSITES OF INTEREST

National Drug Intelligence Center
http://www.justice.gov/ndic/pubs7/7343/7343p.
pdf

National Institute on Drug Abuse
http://drugabuse.gov/researchreports/comorbidity/
whyoccur.html

See also: Cocaine use disorder; Depression; Marijuana; Mental illness; Methamphetamine; Schizophrenia and addiction

Pyromania

CATEGORY: Psychological issues and behaviors

DEFINITION: Pyromania is an impulse control disorder involving repeated failure to control an impulsive urge to set a fire that will not yield monetary or other gain. The reward is the fire itself, which relieves an inner tension and may confer pleasure or gratification. Consequences are disregarded by the pyromaniac.

PYROMANIA, FIRE SETTING, AND ARSON

The criteria set forth by the *Diagnostic and Statistical Manual of Mental Disorders* (DSM) for a diagnosis of pyromania are specific. To qualify for the diagnosis, those affected will have a fascination with fire and its aftermath. Motives other than the fire itself—for example, vengeance and political expression—exclude the diagnosis, as will such conditions as dementia or mental retardation.

Psychiatric disorders will also take precedence over the pyromania diagnosis. Importantly, pyromania is excluded if the fire setting is better explained by impaired judgment owing to alcohol intoxication or substance-abuse influence.

Restricted by the exclusions, pyromania is therefore a rare disorder, considerably less frequent than either arson or fire setting. *Pyromania, fire setting*, and *arson* are commonly confused terms, often used interchangeably. Arson is a criminal act, a felony, which assumes willful, deliberate destruction of property by fire—including one's own property. Fire setting, in contrast with both arson and pyromania, is a broad, inclusive term that implies no particular intent or pathology. Neither arson nor fire setting can assume pyromania is the cause.

Dubious understanding of the meaning of pyromania was demonstrated by a large group of professionals (police, firefighters, and fire investigators) attending an advanced training session. Despite the rarity of the psychiatric diagnosis, these personnel often used the term. Asked their definition of *pyromania*, the group demonstrated in open-ended responses that they were seriously misinformed about the term.

A much-quoted study analyzed the prison files and mental health records of 283 men and women convicted of arson. The pyromania diagnosis fit only 3 persons, or 1 percent of the group. Almost two-thirds (64 percent) had been abusing drugs or alcohol when they set their fires, and the overwhelming majority (90 percent) had histories of psychiatric disorders.

Spanning a twenty-one-year period, a Finnish study of 401 arsonists found twelve repeat offenders who fit the DSM pyromania definition; nine of the twelve, however, had been acutely intoxicated with alcohol at the time of the arson. The remaining three were volunteer firefighters. The authors of this study questioned whether substance intoxication should still exclude the pyromania diagnosis.

WHO SETS FIRES?

A series of 153 adults convicted of arson exemplified most of the criteria that would eliminate pyromania. Most were young men with a psychiatric disorder. One in four had educational deficiencies, either because of mental disability or because of a history of special schooling. Revenge was the motivation for one-third of the group. More than one-third were intoxicated when they set the fires.

Those who study the complex mix of behavioral factors that leads to fire setting generally consider children and adolescent fire setters as a distinct group. This population segment is responsible for a significant portion of the annual toll of property damage because of deliberate fire setting, but the path from normal to excessive interest in fires to pyromania is not well understood. Beginning as early as two to three years of age, children normally are interested in fire. By the time they reach six to ten years of age, the interest is a prevalent trait, particularly in boys.

Investigators have repeatedly tried to identify differences between children who set fires and their peers who do not. Young fire setters are a heterogeneous group, however, with varying motivations. Although consistent pictures have not yet emerged from multiple research approaches and disparate populations, some risk factors have become apparent.

Behavioral difficulties and conduct problems, such as disobedience and aggressive behavior, are frequently encountered in children and youths who set repeated fires. The family environments of many juvenile fire setters are marked by lax supervision and discipline, high levels of family conflict, and parental neglect and rejection. These factors have predicted repeated fire setting. Some young fire setters may have been subjected to severe emotional neglect and physical or sexual abuse. Ineffective monitoring leaves children with free access to incendiary materials, without consequences that would limit the behavior.

In a survey of almost four thousand community adolescents in grades seven through twelve, more than one-fourth—more than one thousand students—reported that they had set fires in the past year. The prevalence was higher among boys and among older students. Those who began setting fires before ten years of age were more likely to report frequent episodes in the past year. This early-onset group had a distinctive risk profile: psychological pathology and suicidal behavior, delinquency, and substance abuse. Another large national sample of children and adolescents yielded a composite picture of fire-setting juveniles with deficient social skills and difficult interactions with peers and teachers.

PREVENTION AND TREATMENT

Guidelines for the treatment of pyromania or fire setting have not been established. The mix of motivations, life situations, and legal standings of those who deliberately set fires can preclude a uniform treatment formulation. For children and adolescents, assessing family issues may be a first step, perhaps pointing to family therapy. Early intervention for abused and emotionally neglected children would aim at reducing destructive and aggressive behavior.

Complicating the choice of treatment is the high prevalence of psychiatric disorders in adult fire setters. Evaluating comorbid disorders might indicate the appropriate psychotherapeutic or pharmacologic treatment.

When specific treatments are suggested, cognitive-behavioral therapy, counseling, and pharmacologic treatment have been shown to be helpful. Research and prevention trials are needed. Given the substantial costs of arson and fire setting to lives and property, finding an effective treatment would pay large dividends.

Judith Weinblatt, MA, MS

FURTHER READING

Frierson, Cathy A. *All Russia Is Burning! A Cultural History of Fire and Arson in Late Imperial Russia.* Seattle: U of Washington, DC P, 2002. Illustrated and well written, this book explores the significance of fire from benevolent warmth to political statement.

Geller, J. L., M. McDermeit, and J. M. Brown. "Pyromania? What Does It Mean?" *Journal of Forensic Sciences* 42.6 (1997): 1052–57. Print. A study of more than three hundred police, firefighters, and fire investigators that concluded that pyromania remains an elusive concept.

Grant, Jon E., and S. W. Kim. *Stop Me Because I Can't Stop Myself: Taking Control of Impulsive Behavior.* New York: McGraw-Hill, 2003. Beginning with personal stories, experts offer understandable, comprehensive coverage of impulsive behavior.

Kolko, David J., ed. *Handbook on Firesetting in Children and Youth.* San Diego, CA: Academic, 2002. Contributions from multidisciplinary experts start with the preschool child.

Office of the Deputy Prime Minister (United Kingdom). *Evaluation of Interventions with Arsonists and Young Firesetters.* Web. 18 Apr. 2012. http://www.communities.gov.uk/documents/corporate/pdf/145135.pdf. This report investigates the range of fire-setting intervention schemes for children and young people undertaken by the UK Fire and Rescue Service, and also assesses the interventions of other stakeholders.

WEBSITES OF INTEREST

PubMed Health: "Conduct Disorder"
http://www.ncbi.nlm.nih.gov/pubmedhealth/
    PMH0001917

University of Minnesota, Impulse Control Disorders Clinic
http://www.impulsecontroldisorders.org

US Fire Administration
http://www.usfa.fema.gov

See also: Behavioral addictions: Overview; Conduct disorders; DSM-IV criteria for behavioral addictions; Impulse control disorders; Kleptomania

R

Recovery

CATEGORY: Treatment

ALSO KNOWN AS: Chronic sobriety; prolonged abstinence; sober living

DEFINITION: Recovery is a process of breaking one's addiction to an abusive substance, behavior, or other compulsion. Recovery involves maintaining abstinence from that addiction through behavior change and active effort. Recovery is not a single event but is a process of change and a new, sober way of living. Recovery takes practice, effort, and focus on daily living with support from health professionals, counselors, community members, and peer groups.

METHODS AND GOALS

The goal of sober living is not out of reach for any addict who can admit that his or her addiction has become a chronic illness. Recovery is intended to treat the illness of addiction and to break the habitual behaviors and viewpoints that fostered chronic abuse. Recovery is not a straightforward process for anyone; treatment plans differ for each addict, and the steps involved vary for each person.

Recovery typically involves long-term health care planning. Treatment might encompass substance detoxification and medication to reduce symptoms of drug withdrawal, integrated treatment of mental health issues by psychologists or addiction counselors, and development of a self-care routine with general practitioners to bolster physical health. New behavior skills and extended support systems that act as positive influences for a sober life also are frequently set in place during this treatment and recovery process.

Recovery often can involve a drastic change of life skills and beliefs from those expressed during addiction. For example, friendships, work settings, and homes that do not foster positive support of sobriety are not helpful and should be avoided during recovery. These components of the old lifestyle are best replaced with stable, sober living settings.

Recovery groups, such as twelve-step programs, help recovering addicts to identify a new set of colleagues and peers. Twelve-step and other recovery programs teach supportive behavior therapy, introduce new traditions for living, encourage reevaluation of ethics and fault, and identify risk behaviors or situations to avoid, all with a supportive sponsor and a community of peers with shared experiences.

Participation in social programs within the community boosts independence and expands sober relationships. Common populations that support societal involvement during recovery include neighborhood associations, lay counselors, clergy at religious institutions, physicians, and recovered peers within twelve-step programs or transitional living environments. Sober family members also provide crucial encouragement of sober living and recovery.

Temptations for substance use exist in society. Recovery depends upon minimizing and countering inevitable stressors, such as social events that involve alcohol or cigarettes. Balancing the temptation for substance abuse and triggers of cravings with sober alternatives, such as gum chewing, is a constant goal of recovery.

Psychological counseling can strengthen an addict's resolve to maintain abstinence during recovery, especially in early recovery periods in which withdrawal and cravings remain especially strong. Trust in the relationships and social system built during recovery care, rather than in those from addiction living, is essential to maintaining abstinence and fully experiencing sober society.

Developing new interests and hobbies not only expands recovery options by introducing new people into a support network; it also provides skills and commitments that can distract from inevitable temptations. For example, enrollment in a team sport or community center class provides a recovered addict a safe setting to mentally redirect anxiety, focus on positive skills, and interact with peers. Recovery is possible only with a commitment to some or all of these behavior-change and counseling methods.

By integrating positive habits and involvement with work, family, and neighborhood groups, a recovering addict develops coping skills and a solid network to minimize the inevitable stresses that increase the likelihood of relapse. The varied treatment and support programs offer different benefits to different people, but all options include goals of renewed commitment to physical and psychological health and to social and community participation. Long-term follow-through and continued development of reinforcements of sober living are crucial, ongoing goals of maintained recovery.

RECOVERY AS A PROCESS

A person begins to use a particular substance voluntarily, but the physical and psychological changes that result from substances of abuse formulate an addiction (which is nonvoluntary) that becomes a chronic disease. Like numerous other chronic diseases, addiction may never be fully cured. Instead, recovery is a prolonged arc that involves daily choices, decisions, and actions to minimize compulsions.

Successes alternate with challenges in an evolving process of growth. Multiple transitions are necessary to achieve sobriety. First, recovering addicts need to admit their problem and evaluate the choices that led to addiction; then, they need to address the problem with active medical treatment; finally, they need to learn to live without the substance or compulsive behavior to reenter society.

Recovered addicts must become focused and functional because they are constantly managing high levels of temptations, stress, and cravings. Repeated care during recovery is often required to prevent relapse and to sustain abstinence. Relapse is the recurrence of addiction symptoms (for example, drug use and compulsive behaviors) after recovery has been established—the slip in the climb toward unbroken periods of abstinence.

Typically, a recovered addict will experience multiple phases of relapse when his or her coping skills or other psychosocial supports falter. Thus, recovery is not a singular, one-time goal but instead comprises progressive struggles and achievements. By acknowledging recovery attempts and learning from past relapse experiences, future recovery goals are more likely to be achieved. Relapse is not failure or a sign of weakness. It is a common occurrence for many recovering addicts, and it frequently becomes a learning experience and an educational tool.

ADVOCACY AND SUPPORT

Because recovery is a way of life, not a static goal, and because recovered addicts are fully immersed in conventional society, support for sustained recovery is beneficial to public health and the wider community. Stigmas associated with substance abuse and addiction treatments can impede full involvement in work and community settings. Addiction and treatments are financial burdens to the recovered addict also.

Advocacy and support from government and private organizations improve public awareness of addiction as a disease and encourage public support for successful recovery and sobriety. The Substance Abuse and Mental Health Services Administration's Recovery Support Strategic Initiative, for example, educates recovered addicts and the public about four major dimensions of life in recovery: health, home, purpose, and community.

Recovered addicts not only overcome a disease; they also focus on living in a physically and emotionally healthy way. Their sobriety is best supported by a stable, safe living environment and by purposeful daily activities, such as work, school, family, and volunteer endeavors. Finally, through building new social networks and relationships in a positive community, a recovered addict experiences hope and support that foster daily recovery.

Nicole M. Van Hoey, PharmD

FURTHER READING

Coombs, Robert H., ed. *Addiction Recovery Tools: A Practical Handbook.* Thousand Oaks, CA: Sage, 2001. A text for addiction counselors and others who provide services for substance abuse recovery. Includes directions for multiple treatment methods and guidance principles that vary from traditional medical care to holistic support.

Kelly, John F., and William L. White, eds. *Addiction Recovery Management: Theory, Research, and Practice.* New York: Humana, 2011. Describes a health professional's direct approach to recovery, including evidence-based guidance about successful methods to support recovery at multiple stages of the process.

National Institute on Drug Abuse. *Drugs, Brains, and Behavior: The Science of Addiction.* Bethesda, MD: NIDA, 2010. A clinical review of how addictions develop and how to use that knowledge to break addictive behaviors, in part by combining medical treatment with behavior change and support systems for recovery.

WEBSITES OF INTEREST

HelpGuide.org
http://www.helpguide.org/mental/drug_abuse_
    addiction_rehab_treatment.htm

National Institute on Drug Abuse
http://www.drugabuse.gov/publications/infofacts/
    treatment-approaches-drug-addiction

Substance Abuse and Mental Health Services
    Administration
http://www.samhsa.gov/recovery

See also: Addiction medicine; Alternative therapies for addiction; Cognitive behavioral therapy; Group therapy for behavioral addictions; Group therapy for substance abuse; Outpatient treatment; Rehabilitation programs; Relapse; Residential treatment; Sober living environments; Sponsors; Support groups; Treatment methods and research

Recreational drugs

CATEGORY: Substance abuse
DEFINITION: Recreational drugs are drugs used casually for entertainment and other purposes, in contrast with medicinal, spiritual, and performance-enhancing uses.

HISTORY OF USE

The nontechnical term *recreational drug* identifies the casual use of drugs. The term, which became common in the 1990s, is now frequently employed in the mass media and in popular discourse. The concept of using drugs for "recreational" purposes differentiates such use from the four other established uses and effects: medicinal, spiritual, addictive, and performance-enhancing.

While such distinctions can usefully serve to denote the type of use, they do not neatly classify the types of drugs used, because the same drug can be used for more than one such purpose. For example, most of the legal drugs that are used recreationally, especially nicotine, alcohol, and caffeine, are often also addictive. Also, many of the prescription drugs used for medicinal purposes can also be used recreationally and can be addictive. Likewise, many illegal drugs, such as cocaine and heroin, are used recreationally and are addictive. Drugs such as LSD, mescaline, ecstasy, peyote, and marijuana are used for spiritual and recreational purposes, and the latter is now also commonly used for medicinal reasons.

Several of the drugs now used recreationally have been used throughout the history of civilization. Alcohol was first fermented in west Asia about 8000 BCE, marijuana was used in Asia as early as about three thousand years ago, and mushrooms containing the psychedelic chemical psilocybin have been available to humans for thousands of years. Initially, these drugs were used for medicinal and religious purposes, and recreational use emerged as a deviation.

Recreational drug use is endemic throughout all historical eras and geographic regions, but the particular drugs used vary widely across different cultures, places, and times. Alcohol and marijuana have been the two most prevalent across time and culture. Both have been the target of many unsuccessful attempts at prohibition. Among other drugs that have been in widespread recreational use for several centuries are coffee, tobacco, and opiates.

In the United States during the 1950s, two groups of prescription drugs were commonly used beyond their medicinal purposes: barbiturates, which were used as tranquilizers, and amphetamines, which were used as stimulants. Amphetamine came to be known casually as speed and was increasingly used recreationally through the 1960s and later. Also, LSD, which had been synthesized in 1943, was studied for its medicinal and therapeutic uses in the 1950s and early 1960s. Successful outcomes were indicated in the treatment of felons and alcoholics. Some performance-enhancement uses also were studied, mostly for artistic creativity. During the 1960s, the spiritual use of LSD became more common. With this widening pattern of use, LSD also came to be used recreationally, especially among college students, and it was made illegal in 1966.

Psychedelics derived from plants, especially mescaline and psilocybin, also became popular around the mid-1960s. Again, these substances were used first for spiritual purposes, which had been their long-standing function among the indigenous peoples in the United States and Mexico; a wider use by youth included recreational pursuits. Marijuana use also increased dramatically in the 1960s and early 1970s.

During the late 1970s, especially among the disco and punk music subcultures, the use of amyl nitrates (poppers) as inhalants became common. The 1980s saw the spread of ecstasy, especially among clubgoers. Though research showed that ecstasy may have medicinal value as an aid to marital or relationship therapy, it was made illegal in 1985. Later research indicated that ecstasy may also have medicinal value in treating post-traumatic stress disorder and cluster headaches.

In the first decade of the twenty-first century, methamphetamine has become a common drug of choice. Since the mid-twentieth century, the two most commonly used recreational drugs have been alcohol and marijuana, especially by youth, with the popularity of other drugs rising and falling.

The recent history of recreational drug use shows that the particular drugs used recreationally have tended to rise and fall according to their fashion for specific times and subcultures. Current trends in the United States likewise vary by age, race, and social class. Among poor children and adolescents, solvent inhalants, especially glues and aerosols, are commonly used recreational drugs. Among poor and working-class urban adolescents and young adults, heroin and crack cocaine are major drugs of choice. Among the rural poor and working class, methamphetamine is common.

For middle-class youth, alcohol, tobacco, and marijuana are the most prevalent. For the professional class, a wide range of so-called designer drugs are used, especially barbiturates, amphetamines, LSD, ecstasy, and ketamine. Most recently, synthetic chemicals that mimic the effects of marijuana have been produced. For each new synthetic drug, there is a lack of an official classification, which keeps the drug legal for a time. However, soon thereafter, government experts declare the substance illegal.

EFFECTS AND POTENTIAL RISKS

Given the extremely wide range of drugs that are used recreationally, the number of effects and potential risks is similarly large. It is possible to classify recreational drugs in terms of their effects on cognition, affect, or sensation. Furthermore, it is possible to specify whether they enhance or diminish such capacities.

LSD, for example, is used to enhance cognition, ecstasy to enhance affect, and marijuana to enhance sensation; cocaine and methamphetamine provide both a euphoric affect and a stimulation of cognition, whereas heroin provides a euphoric mood while leading to a drowsy cognitive state; alcohol typically enhances affect while decreasing cognition and sensation, and so forth. Such attempts at classifying the effects of drugs, however, falter upon the dilemma that, for most drugs with psychoactive effects, the exact effects are not universal, but rather vary considerably based upon two factors not tied to the drug itself: the mental state of the user and the setting in which the drug is used.

Just as the effects of so wide a range of drugs cannot be univocally specified, neither can their potential risks. For most drugs, one potential risk is the danger of dependence. Such addictive potential varies considerably across the spectrum of drugs used recreationally. Those that are legal—alcohol, nicotine, and caffeine—have the most widespread patterns of addiction. Among the illegal drugs with the greatest potential for addiction are heroin, cocaine, and methamphetamine. The drug whose use is most commonly prosecuted, marijuana, has been shown to have no addictive potential, though the possibility of a nonphysical, or psychological, dependency among some users remains disputed.

Beyond their addictive potential, many of the drugs used recreationally also pose a range of health risks, especially in the context of long-term heavy use. Alcohol in particular has been linked to organ damage, especially of the liver. Nicotine, when smoked, has been linked to lung cancer. Among illegal drugs, methamphetamine use can lead to brain damage and dental problems; cocaine to cardiovascular problems; and heroin to heart, lung, and liver damage.

Additional risks arise because of the illegal status of many recreational drugs. For example, additional unknown, harmful effects can arise. Blood-borne diseases are often caused by using needles for intravenous drugs. Also, adulterated or impure substances purchased on the black market can cause serious harm. The risk of arrest and the consequences of a conviction also must be counted among the harms in this category.

Christopher M. Aanstoos, PhD

FURTHER READING

Fadiman, James. *The Psychedelic Explorer's Guide*. Rochester, VT: Inner Traditions, 2011. Drawing on research in psychedelic science, this book offers a guide to the responsible and effective use of psychedelic drugs for personal growth.

Holland, Julie, ed. *The Pot Book: A Complete Guide to Cannabis*. Rochester, VT: Park Street, 2010. Using a broad spectrum of knowledge from science to culture, the authors explore the role of marijuana in society, medicine, history, and politics.

Nichter, Mark. "Generation RX: Anthropological Research on Pharmaceutical Enhancement, Lifestyle Regulation, Self-Medication, and Recreational Drug Use." *A Companion to Medical Anthropology*. Eds. Merrill Singer and Pamela I. Erickson. Malden, MA: Wiley, 2011. Chapter examines, from the perspective of anthropology, the use of recreational drugs, defining an entire age population.

Shapiro, Harry. *Recreational Drugs: A Directory*. London: Collins, 2004. A compendium of major recreational drugs that covers facts about use, effects, risks, and legal status.

WEBSITES OF INTEREST

Drugs Forum
http://www.drugs-forum.com

Multidisciplinary Association for Psychedelic Studies
http://www.maps.org

National Institute on Drug Abuse
http://www.drugabuse.gov

See also: Barbiturates; Coffee; Designer drugs; LSD; Marijuana; MDMA; Methamphetamine; Opium

---

Rehabilitation programs

CATEGORY: Treatment

DEFINITION: Treatment for substance abuse first involves an evaluation of the nature of the drug or drugs used. Also essential is knowing the extent of addiction because early identification usually lessens the difficulty of overcoming the physiological and psychological effects of drug abuse. Equally important is determining the degree to which the person is committed to his or her rehabilitation. Thus, rehabilitation programs should attempt to adjust their mission and goals, as well as their therapeutic methods, to meet a wide range of patient needs and capacities.

BACKGROUND

Since the mid-twentieth century, enormous amounts of money have been spent by individuals, families, governments, and private foundations to establish short- to long-term rehabilitation programs for addicts and substance abusers. Proponents of reducing the problems of drug addiction and substance abuse have long debated just how to accomplish this goal.

Some have favored strict enforcement of drug and drug-trade laws (thus identifying with the criminal justice system). Statistics suggest that this path demands higher levels of public funding than do programs aimed at the prevention of addiction and the rehabilitation of addicts. Supporters of early prevention emphasize the importance of educational programs, both in local communities and at all levels of the public education system. Thus, rehabilitation programs have never been excluded, but have been ranked variously in public opinion and among possible funding agencies, both public and private.

One of the earliest and most widely used methods for treating drug addiction (treatment that has gradually been replaced by more personal therapeutic approaches) involves the use of the drug methadone. Methadone (not to be confused with the highly addictive drug meth, or methamphetamine) is a synthetic opioid, a chemical that, like several highly addictive drugs, interacts with opioid receptors located mainly in the central and peripheral nervous system. Opium, as its name suggests, is the best-known drug containing natural opiates (alkaloids contained in the resin of the opium poppy), but other drugs, including heroin and morphine, have similar effects on the nervous system. The physiological effects of other well-known drugs, including cocaine, crack cocaine, and methamphetamine, are different, so addicts dependent on these narcotics do not respond to rehabilitation methods involving opioid substitutes like methadone.

Beginning in the late 1930s (when it was first produced by German chemists) methadone was used by

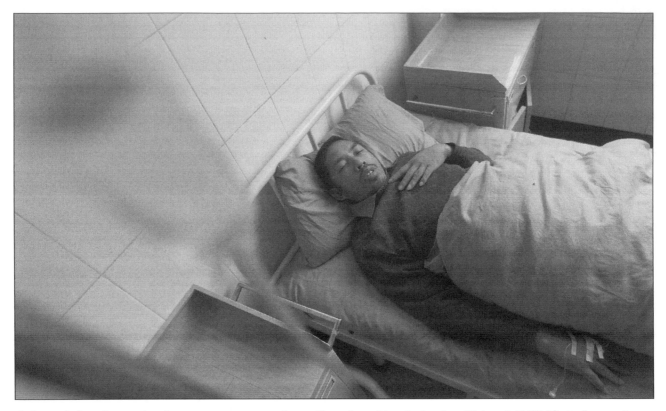

A drug rehab patient receives intravenous treatment for an illness brought on by heroin withdrawl. (AFP/Getty Images)

European doctors as an analgesic, or painkiller. After its introduction in the United States in 1947, physicians and hospitals working with patients who were addicted to opium, heroin, or morphine pioneered its use to counter (or to replace) the euphoric effects experienced by opioid-dependent patients. This method of rehabilitation came to be known as methadone maintenance treatment.

By administering controlled doses of methadone, usually through the agency of outpatient methadone clinics, physicians can essentially control patients' cravings for addictive drugs, and do so while avoiding the most dangerous chemical effects of true narcotic drugs. In later years a number of different products have joined and sometimes replaced methadone in cases where drugs are used in rehabilitation programs. One of these drugs, buprenorphine (sold by pharmacists as Subutex or Suboxone), is a high-strength compound extracted from thebaine, an alkaloid in opium poppies.

All opioids, whether illicit or substitutes used in medicinal rehabilitation, combine sedative effects with euphoric reactions. Additional, sometimes negative, effects include constipation and a tightening of the respiratory tract, which makes some opioids useful in cough depressant formulas. Proponents of medicinal rehabilitation programs generally argue that such side effects are clearly less harmful than allowing (still actively drug-dependent) patients to follow much longer rehabilitation programs based on individual or group counseling.

Whatever the specific addictive drug may be (and whatever therapeutic procedure is followed), chances for full rehabilitation are usually higher when the problem of addiction is identified in its early stages. This scenario is more likely to occur when the affected person becomes aware of the need to stop a drug habit before it becomes serious. Rehabilitation therapists also emphasize the importance of the family as a first-stage support group in such cases. Contrary conditions are often (but not always) associated with addicted persons who are somehow forced into a detoxification (or detox) program because they have reached physically dangerous levels of addiction, have exhibited recurring suicidal tendencies, or have been ordered to begin rehabilitation following arrest and prosecution by court authorities.

Among the first steps taken in the rehabilitation process is the attempt to evaluate the actual degree of motivation impelling addicts to seek help. If the process is essentially ordered by a court, levels of motivation tend to be lower.

Governmental agencies beyond the criminal and juvenile court systems are engaged in the task not only of evaluating statistics relating to drug addiction but also of providing informational support and funding for rehabilitation programs. It was not until 1992 that the US Congress mandated the creation of the Substance Abuse and Mental Health Services Administration (SAMHSA), an agency within the US Department of Health and Human Services. This move stemmed from a rising awareness that millions of substance abuse and mental health cases were being disregarded by the health care system, sometimes because of a person's inability to pay for assistance and sometimes because of inadequate awareness of what services exist, both in the private and public sectors.

A specific branch of SAMHSA, the Center for Substance Abuse Treatment (CSAT), manages a portion of SAMHSA's legislatively allotted budget and reviews applications for grants to fund state, local, and private clinics involved in rehabilitation programs. CSAT also provides the general public, professional service providers, and rehabilitation counselors with updated information on substance abuse trends and methods of prevention and treatment.

National statistics (much of its gathered by CSAT) make it possible to compare the availability, staff qualification standards, and application procedures for public and private rehabilitation programs and state-by-state levels of admission to rehabilitation facilities. Among the most developed examples of state-run programs are, as might be expected, states with large urban areas: California (with slightly more than 170,000 admissions in 2005) was closely followed in numbers of persons undergoing rehabilitation by New York State. Statistics for privately funded rehabilitation programs, which vary considerably both in the number of client-patients admitted and in the nature of therapeutic methods practiced, are less widely circulated.

MISSIONS AND GOALS

Continuous operation makes it possible to trace short-, medium-, and long-term missions and goals and accomplishments of two major (and internationally recognized) rehabilitation programs: the Odyssey House and Phoenix House.

The Odyssey House, founded in 1967 by psychiatrist Judianne Gerber of New York's Metropolitan Hospital, pioneered a new approach to rehabilitation, one that hoped to do away with, or reduce, reliance on drug replacement medications (primarily methadone) in treating patients. Gerber's (at that time innovative) approach involved founding the first Odyssey House Therapeutic Community (a direction that would be followed, almost simultaneously, by the Phoenix House movement) in a private building in East Harlem, New York. The first such therapeutic community began with seventeen addicts seeking to break their drug habit.

In the early 1970s, Odyssey House began to lay plans for two different complementary rehabilitation programs within its overall structure. One involved the establishment, with partial support from public revenue sources, of what was called the Teen Leadership Center. The center combined preventive programs (mainly by offering vocational training and placement services for teens) with special therapy sessions bringing individual drug users (or high-risk youth) together with their families. This latter aspect of the Odyssey House's approach to rehabilitation has been adopted, depending on available funding and the nature of training undergone by counselors, by many different programs in the United States.

Odyssey House also has gained national recognition for its efforts to structure rehabilitation programs to fit the needs of different age groups and persons with specific family needs. The first of these, a residential center called Mothers and Babies Off Narcotics (MABON) on Ward's Island, New York, and a second residence in East Harlem were designed to help addicted young parents who were trying to raise their children in a drug-free environment. Since about 1980, the original MABON program has increased its capacity so that it could assist more than two hundred mothers and their families. Again, depending on funding, this model has become part of rehabilitation clinics, sometimes as an outpatient procedure, in different states and localities.

Finally, during the 1990s, Odyssey House (by then beginning to expand operations to other regions of the United States) made other changes to meet the needs of specific groups experiencing substance-use dependence. It introduced in situ health-care clinics staffed by certified health practitioners and, in 1997, pioneered the first Odyssey Elder Care rehabilitation program specifically designed to assist drug dependent adults age fifty-five years and older.

Another outstanding and nationally recognized example of a rehabilitation program, Phoenix House, began in a local setting and gradually expanded operations to a number of branch locations nationwide. The initial stimulus came in 1967 from six heroin addicts, all of them participants in a New York City hospital detoxification program, who decided to form their own small community in which they would live together and dedicate themselves to mutual support in their desire to recover from addiction.

The original Phoenix group chose its name to symbolize their faith in the image of the Phoenix (a mythological bird that, in several ancient traditions, is reborn from the ashes after experiencing a long lifecycle and perishing in its own flaming nest). The group received vital support from psychiatrist Mitchell Rosenthal, then deputy commissioner for New York's Addiction Service Agency.

While programs such as these involve the need to provide permanent or semipermanent institutional settings for rehabilitation programs, Odyssey House (and many different publicly and privately sponsored programs that are less well known to the general public) believes that one-time-only events focusing on different preventive or "passive therapeutic" paths should be part of the overall effort to raise public consciousness of substance abuse. Such events vary from year to year and can include (as in the summer of 2011) special community art exhibits and Run for Life sporting events meant to engage young participants. The indicators of success associated with the Odyssey House and Phoenix House programs would lead to the establishment of similar therapeutic communities around the United States (notably in Utah, Louisiana, Michigan, and Texas) and other countries (the first being founded in Australia and New Zealand).

The high degree of moral commitment instilled in both counselors and addicts seeking rehabilitation through programs such as these was expressed eloquently by the president and chief executive of Odyssey House, Peter Provet, in a letter to the *New York Times* on July 12, 2011. Provet wrote that "Treatment, whether residential or outpatient, is a discrete, time-limited experience. Recovery must be a life-long process whereby individuals establish themselves within a community of their peers and together live out the principles learned in treatment."

Despite the wide range of institutional structures, sources of funding, and therapeutic methods used in rehabilitation programs, certain basic features appear to be fundamental to all. One source for understanding developments in the field of drug rehabilitation is the National Association of Alcohol and Drug Abuse Counselors, (NAADAC) founded in 1972. This professional organization exists in addition to a number of state-level associations. The NAADAC's magazine *Counselor*, is an excellent reference available not only to association members but also to the public at large to keep informed of issues and therapeutic methods relevant to rehabilitation. For example, news concerning evolving approaches to group (in comparison with individual) therapy and reviews of recently published professional articles appear in the magazine regularly.

Another of NAADAC's goals is to establish consensus on an unwritten code of ethics applying to relations between rehabilitation professionals and their clients. This can involve, among many other issues, recognizing and knowing how to deal with degrees of empathy or appropriate personal closeness, confidentiality, and avoidance of any form of discrimination, whether ethnic or gender related.

Finally, a primary responsibility for all rehabilitation service providers is to be prepared to refer clients to a different subfield of specialists or medical professionals or to appropriate support systems or community resources that may serve their needs more effectively. Because many such alternative paths are subject to unpredictable changes (owing to dependence on public tax-based funding or renewable grants), those involved in rehabilitation programs must remain closely informed at local, state, and national levels.

Byron D. Cannon, PhD

FURTHER READING

Falco, Mathea. *The Making of a Drug-Free America: Programs that Work.* New York: Times Books, 1994. This book deals with a wide range of topics, including ways to influence public conceptions (especially among youths) of drug addiction, stopping drug supplies at their source, and modes of treatment and rehabilitation.

Fisher, Gary L., and Thomas C. Harrison. *Substance Abuse: Information for School Counselors, Social Workers, Therapists, and Counselors.* Boston: Allyn & Bacon, 2000. A textbook that is representative of methods used for training professionals whose work relates either to drug-use prevention or to different public and private rehabilitation programs.

Lawson, Gary W., Ann W. Lawson, and P. Clayton Rivers. *Essentials of Chemical Dependency Counseling.* Gaithersburg, MD: Aspen, 2001. An informative handbook describing various methods used in rehabilitation both in institutional and community level programs.

US Department of Health and Human Services, Center for Substance Abuse Treatment. *Medication-Assisted Treatment for Opioid Addiction in Opioid Treatment Programs.* Washington, DC: SAMHSA, 2005. A publication for use by clinicians that covers methods of diagnosis and includes a comparison of the pharmacology of five different medications.

---. "What Is Substance Abuse Treatment? A Booklet for Families." Washington, DC: SAMHSA, 2008. A basic guide to help families identify both signs of substance abuse and appropriate steps to be taken to receive rehabilitation treatment.

WEBSITES OF INTEREST

Odyssey House
http://www.odysseyhouseinc.org

Phoenix House
http://www.phoenixhouse.org

See also: Abstinence-based treatment; Alcoholics Anonymous; Betty Ford Center; Cirque Lodge; Cocaine Anonymous; Debtors Anonymous; Hazelden Foundation; Narcotics Anonymous; Overeaters Anonymous; Phoenix House; Promises Treatment Centers; Twelve-step programs for addicts; Twelve-step programs for family and friends;

Relapse

CATEGORY: Treatment

DEFINITION: Since the 1980s, relapse has been conceptualized as a dynamic process through which an abstinent person gives in to the urge to resume substance use (such as drinking, smoking, or self-administering drugs). Relapse is distinguished from slips or lapses that are one-time (slip) or brief occurrences (lapses) during the recovery process. Relapse is not generally considered a failure of treatment but rather a common consequence of an attempt to change any chronic behavior, not just addictive behaviors.

WHAT IS RELAPSE?

There has been a major shift in how relapse is conceptualized by addiction researchers. Before the 1980s, the term *relapse* was used to signify any return to substance use following a period of abstinence, much as a disease state recurs following a period of remission. However, largely as a result of work by G. Alan Marlatt and colleagues, relapse is now viewed as a dynamic process through which a person gives in to the urge to resume drinking, smoking, or taking drugs following a period of sobriety or abstinence. An important feature of the dynamic process approach is that relapse is distinguished from slips or lapses that are one-time (slip) or brief occurrences (lapses) of substance use during the recovery process.

Despite wide variations in relapse criteria (from a single drink, cigarette, or drug use episode to a return to pretreatment substance use levels), studies have shown that recovery from substance abuse is typically characterized by repeated episodes of relapse, with the first episode most often occurring within one year of treatment. For alcohol-dependent persons who have undergone treatment, relapse is the most common outcome, with less than 25 percent remaining abstinent after one year. Approximately one-half of recovering cocaine addicts are reported to relapse within one year of detoxification. However, relapse rates for addictive behaviors are not significantly different from those of other chronic conditions such as asthma, diabetes, and hypertension.

RISK FACTORS

The use of electronic devices, such as ecological momentary assessment (EMA), for real-time monitoring has provided valuable information about external events, thoughts, and mood states that precede a slip, lapse, or relapse. Among the most common triggers reported for abstinence cessation are exposure to substance-related cues, negative mood states or stress, social interactions, and substance use even in small quantities.

In a 1996 analysis, negative mood states and interpersonal conflict were identified as triggers for more than 50 percent of all relapse episodes involving alcohol and smoking and for more than 40 percent for those involving heroin. However, these triggers do not inevitably precipitate a relapse. Researchers are paying more attention to individual differences in relapse risk and in the potential for predisposing factors, such as severity of dependence, genetics, and beliefs about drug effects and coping skills to moderate or interact with precipitating factors that increase the risk for relapse.

In studies of alcohol dependency, Marlatt and his colleagues described an emotional reaction to a lapse that can influence progression to a relapse. Persons who blame themselves for lapsing subsequently experience guilt and negative emotions and are then more likely to continue drinking than persons who perceive the lapse as an occasion to improve their coping skills. Studies using retrospective reports of the lapse suggest that the magnitude of this reaction is related to relapse; however, EMA studies have not observed this relationship.

Brain imaging studies have shown that specific regions of the corticostriatal limbic circuitry involved in stress-induced and drug-cue-induced craving states are associated with drug relapse outcomes. Moreover, some persons have less effective orbitofrontal cortex circuitry, making it more challenging to manage their urge to seek drugs and more difficult to make good decisions. These studies are important for developing new medications for use in relapse prevention.

Genetic differences have been shown to influence susceptibility to relapse through their interaction with medications. In a 2003 study using naltrexone to reduce craving in alcohol-dependent patients, the relapse rate was significantly higher (47.9 percent) in patients with the Asn40 variant in an opioid receptor gene compared with patients with the Asp40 variant (26.1 percent).

THEORIES OF RELAPSE

A number of models have been constructed to explain the phenomenon of relapse. One of the most influential models is Marlatt's cognitive-behavioral approach to relapse prevention. This model bases relapse risk on self-efficacy, outcome expectancies, attributions of causality, and decision-making processes. An abstinent person who encounters a high-risk situation (trigger) and engages in a successful coping response will heighten self-efficacy (confidence in ability to remain abstinent).

In contrast, an abstinent person with poor coping skills will be unable to manage the craving elicited by the trigger, leading to a reduction in self-efficacy, an increase in the expectation of a positive outcome, and an increased risk of lapsing. Lapses that are attributed to personal failure generate guilt and negative emotions and a further reduction in self-efficacy, thereby heightening the risk of relapse.

Conditioning models also have contributed prominently to the understanding of relapse. Cues associated with substance use are thought to be Pavlovian conditioned stimuli that come to elicit various conditioned responses, including drug craving. Human cue-reactivity studies have confirmed this account of craving. Several studies also have tested the prediction that exposure to such cues in the absence of substance use (cue exposure therapy, or CET) should be an effective extinction procedure for eliminating craving and guarding against relapse. Results have been mixed.

Researchers Peter Monti, Damaris Rohsenow, and colleagues showed that cue exposure combined with coping-skills training may result in increased use of skills, increases in days abstinent, and decreases in drinking. Other studies of alcohol dependency, however, have found little impact of CET in eliminating craving and reducing relapse.

Laboratory studies of extinction in animals may provide some insight in clinical studies about the apparent fragility of CET for relapse prevention. The phenomena of reinstatement, renewal, retraining, and spontaneous recovery collectively illustrate that extinction does not remove original learning. In a 2002 review paper, researcher Mark Bouton discussed how each of these phenomena may underlie relapse. For example, his research on renewal has shown that extinction is context specific, such that when an extinguished CS is presented in its original conditioning context, responses to the CS are renewed.

FUTURE DIRECTIONS

Addiction researchers are in general agreement that a multivariate, biopsychosocial approach to relapse is essential. In a 2006 commentary on relapse in the addictive behaviors, researchers Stephen Maisto and Gerard Connors recommended that more attention be paid to the operational definition of relapse, theory development and its systematic testing, modeling of the relapse process, and the role of moderating variables on relapse outcome.

Ruth M. Colwill, PhD

FURTHER READING

Bouton, Mark E. "Context, Ambiguity, and Unlearning: Sources of Relapse after Behavioral Extinction." *Biological Psychiatry* 52 (2002): 976–86. Print. Reviews the role of context in extinction and discusses its implications for relapse and relapse prevention.

Brandon, Thomas H., Jennifer Irvin Vidrine, and Erika B. Litvin. "Relapse and Relapse Prevention." *Annual Review of Clinical Psychology* 3 (2007): 257–84. Print. Comprehensive review of theories of relapse of addictive behaviors and strategies for relapse prevention.

Conklin, C. A., and S. T. Tiffany. "Applying Extinction Research and Theory to Cue-Exposure Addiction Treatments." *Addiction* 97 (2002): 155–67. Print. Finds little evidence for the efficacy of cue exposure treatments for addictions but also identifies several methodological weaknesses that undermine any conclusive assessment.

Maisto, Stephen A., and Gerard J. Connors. "Relapse in the Addictive Behaviors: Integration and Future Directions." *Clinical Psychology Review* 26 (2006): 229–31. Print. Identifies consistencies and future needs in relapse research in a special issue on relapse in the addictive behaviors.

Marlatt, G. Alan, and Dennis M. Donovan. *Relapse Prevention: Maintenance Strategies in the Treatment of Addictive Behaviors.* New York: Guilford, 2005. Chapters cover factors that may trigger relapse at different stages of recovery and describe procedures for teaching effective cognitive and behavioral coping strategies.

Shiffman, Saul. "Ecological Momentary Assessment (EMA) in Studies of Substance Use." *Psychological Assessment* 21.4 (2009): 486–97. Print. Review of EMA methods in substance use research. Focus is on tobacco and alcohol use and relapse.

Siegel, Shepard. "Drug Tolerance, Drug Addiction, and Drug Anticipation." *Current Directions in Psychological Science* 14 (2005): 296–300. Print. Discusses the contribution of drug-related stimuli to tolerance and withdrawal from a Pavlovian-conditioning perspective and the implications for cue-exposure therapies.

Sinha, Rajita, and Chiang-Shan R. Li. "Imaging Stress- and Cue-Induced Drug and Alcohol Craving: Association with Relapse and Clinical Implications." *Drug and Alcohol Review* 26 (2007): 25–31. Print. Reviews brain imaging studies, suggesting that specific regions of the corticostriatal limbic circuitry involved in stress-induced and drug cue-induced craving states are associated with drug relapse outcomes.

WEBSITES OF INTEREST

National Institute on Alcohol Abuse and Alcoholism
http://pubs.niaaa.nih.gov/publications/aa06.htm

National Institute on Drug Abuse
http://www.drugabuse.gov/publications/scienceaddiction

See also: Abstinence-based treatment; Recovery; Science of addiction

Residential treatment

CATEGORY: Treatment

ALSO KNOWN AS: Inpatient treatment; therapeutic community care

DEFINITION: Residential treatment is nonhospital care provided in centers that rely on a resident's full-time participation in a structured community as a key component of addiction care and recovery. Residential treatment centers house recovering addicts and support staff to interact as an enclosed society. A primary focus is the preparation of recovered addicts to return to an independent and drug-free life.

BACKGROUND

Centers for residential treatment, and the umbrella organizations that sponsor them, vary in structure and program depth, so no single date marks the beginning of their formation or popularity. However, one program for residential treatment, known as the therapeutic community or TC, has become more commonplace since the 1970s and into the twenty-first century.

TC efficacy is backed by decades of supporting research by the National Institute on Drug Abuse. Positive results attributed to treatment at these residential centers include reduction of depression, drug use, and criminal activity in recovered addicts. Similarly, residential treatment is provided through intensive and planned communities because the treatment facility is also the addict's home. Forty to eighty addicts often live in one treatment center with staff members.

Residential centers are more community-oriented than a hospital but are more constant in treatment than an outpatient drop-in program. Treatment encompasses not only medical detoxification or withdrawal care but also psychological counseling, training programs, and recovery support groups. The centers emphasize concentrated efforts toward personal responsibility and behavior change.

Residential treatment programs support the needs of any addict, but particularly persons with severe addiction problems, including those with criminal backgrounds; with impaired social functioning as a result of mental health disorders; and with special needs, such as pregnant women, persons infected with the human immunodeficiency virus, and persons with acquired immune deficiency syndrome.

Treatment at residential centers can be provided anywhere, from a prison setting to a shelter, camp, or suburban or rural housing site. The TC is only one example of a residential treatment center model.

Community-based residential centers are frequently removed from drug-heavy environments and are instead incorporated into neighborhoods that provide drug-free stability. Prison-based residential substance-abuse treatment programs are examples of intensive treatment centers within the justice system that are isolated from the general prison population; these programs offer continuous involvement with

The Center For Drug-Free Living in Orlando, Florida. (Getty Images)

counselors and support from family and friends to habituate the incarcerated addict to a stable environment after release and to reduce the likelihood of relapse and re-arrest.

Residential treatment programs typically require a long-term commitment from the patient to stay in group housing and to fully participate for well-rounded care; six to twelve months is considered an appropriate baseline duration. Although no time limit or requirement is identified for each patient, the outcomes are generally more positive when participatory care lasts eighteen to twenty-four months. Poor funding frequently results in shorter stays; conversely, well-funded programs can offer long-term, population-specific programming, such as diploma classes, work training, or child care instruction, which promotes successful and sober integration into society.

Regardless of the length of time, all residents progress through stages of care and are expected to be active and responsible through treatment. Each center functions as a private, structured society; thus, treatment incorporates counseling, prevention programs, socialization programs, and work habituation. Assigned responsibilities and community work by residents within the group are crucial to encourage actual living experiences and accountability on a small but increasing scale.

MISSION AND GOALS

Residential treatment is based upon two keystone principles: community as the primary agent of behavior change and self-help, as the addicted residents become the main contributors to the process of recovery and social independence for themselves and for all other residents. Although counselors are available in the living environment, the residents enter the treatment facility with baseline expectations of support from their peers as well. The residents and staff work together to encourage orderly living, moral and ethical functioning, and group influences on individual recovery.

Supportive psychosocial-care concerns that are addressed include self-esteem, coping strategies and skills, interpersonal skills, impulse control, and maturity. Treatment progresses in stages, which slowly introduces chores and household responsibilities within the living group. Concurrently, socialization begins through required in-house programs and support meetings on site. This around-the-clock, integrated

care ultimately emphasizes functional living that is based on the sober social skills developed within the community.

As treatment continues, addicts are slowly guided toward new values about drug use and prior behaviors while simultaneously receiving additional responsibilities in their new living arrangement. These immersive programs reinforce behaviors and skill sets necessary for reentry into a solid work and social experience. The addict makes decisions in a protective environment that expands to independence without reliance on substances of abuse or on compulsive behaviors.

The final goal of residential treatment is to transition the recovered addict into society with adequate coping mechanisms and behavior skills to flourish in a stable home and job situation. Treatment center completion, then, might be accompanied by outpatient counseling or a recovery support group such as Alcoholics Anonymous or Narcotics Anonymous to reinforce the changes learned from residential treatment.

Nicole M. Van Hoey, PharmD

FURTHER READING

Harrison, Lana D. *Residential Substance Abuse Treatment (RAST) for State Prisoners Implementation Lessons Learned.* May 2003. Web. 3 Apr. 2012. http://www.nij.gov/pubs-sum/195738.htm. Reviews the methods, successes, and overall results of prison-based addiction treatment programming through the RAST grant initiative.

National Institute on Drug Abuse. "Research Reports: Therapeutic Community." Aug. 2002. Web. 3 Apr. 2012. http://www.drugabuse.gov/publications/research-reports/therapeutic-community. Describes stage-based models of treatment in residential centers and identifies the importance of well-rounded and stratified responsibilities to the success of addiction care.

"What Is Substance Abuse Treatment? A Booklet for Families." 2004. Web. 3 Apr. 2012. http://kap.samhsa.gov/products/brochures/pdfs/WhatIsTx.pdf. Consumer-based guide to options for treatment settings for substance abuse care. Focuses on therapeutic communities and other residential treatment options as alternatives to hospitalization programs or outpatient clinics that do not involve the full spectrum of physical, psychological, and social addiction care.

See also: Abstinence-based treatment; Betty Ford Center; Cirque Lodge; Halfway houses; Hazelden Foundation; Phoenix House; Promises Treatment Centers; Sober living environments

Respiratory diseases and smoking

CATEGORY: Health issues and physiology

DEFINITION: Chronic bronchitis, emphysema, chronic obstructive pulmonary disease, and lung cancer are caused by smoking tobacco in a majority of cases. The first three affect lung functioning to varying degrees, depending on how far the condition has progressed; lung cancer is one of the fastest-spreading and most deadly forms of cancer.

CAUSES

Smoking tobacco is the primary cause of a number of respiratory diseases, the most serious being chronic bronchitis, emphysema, chronic obstructive pulmonary disease (COPD), and lung cancer. Most long-term smokers started as preteens or teenagers, became addicted to nicotine, and then subjected their respiratory systems to the toxins and carcinogens contained in the tobacco.

Tobacco smoke contains thousands of chemical compounds and more than four hundred toxic and carcinogenic substances. As a result, smoking-related respiratory diseases kill more than 440,000 people each year in the United States alone, including about 90 percent of deaths caused by lung cancer and more than 80 percent of those caused by COPD, the second and fourth leading causes of death, respectively.

Chronic bronchitis occurs when there is an increase in the size and number of mucous glands in the large airways of the lungs. The increased amount of mucus inflames and scars the airways, constricting air flow, which becomes more pronounced with continued scarring and thickening of the airway walls.

Emphysema results from damage to the lungs' alveoli, or air sacs, which facilitate the exchange of carbon dioxide and oxygen. This condition further compromises breathing because of the constriction of airways from the loss of lung elasticity.

COPD is a condition that usually includes a combination of chronic bronchitis and emphysema, resulting in forced and inefficient breathing. The degree of the contribution of each component condition to COPD varies from case to case. Lung cancer occurs when carcinogens, most often from cigarette smoke, cause damage to lung cells, leading to abnormal cellular replication that creates tumors in the larger airways or other parts of the lung.

RISK FACTORS

Although people who have never smoked can potentially develop respiratory ailments from factors such as genetics or exposure to job-related or general air pollution, the cause of 80 to 90 percent of all serious respiratory diseases is long-term tobacco smoking. Researchers estimate that approximately fifteen hundred preteens and teenagers each day become addicted to nicotine, and many of them will become life-long smokers.

There is a positive linear correlation between the risk of major respiratory disease and the duration of exposure, which is measured in "package-years," determined by years of smoking multiplied by the number of packs of cigarettes per day. This measurement places older chronic smokers at highest risk. Research shows that nonsmokers who are exposed to secondhand or passive smoke, because they live, work, or recreate in smoke-filled environments, are at a significantly increased risk of developing serious respiratory diseases.

SYMPTOMS

Chronic bronchitis, often called smoker's cough, is evidenced by the coughing up of sputum, or phlegm, for a minimum of three months during two or more consecutive years. Emphysema is characterized by severe shortness of breath that makes physical activity increasingly difficult as the disease progresses to the point of total disability. Common symptoms include exhaustion, coughing, heart problems, and enlarged chest because of labored breathing.

Indicators of COPD include all of the symptoms of chronic bronchitis and emphysema. As COPD progresses, respiratory inefficiency further increases carbon dioxide levels and reduces oxygen levels in the blood, which is evidenced by drowsiness, twitching, headaches, lips assuming a bluish pallor, severe shortness of breath, and swollen ankles from heart strain. Some symptoms associated with lung cancer are labored breathing, chest pain, hoarseness, phlegm containing blood, lack of strength in the hands or arms, and swollen face and neck.

SCREENING AND DIAGNOSIS

Because chronic bronchitis and emphysema are both obstructive pulmonary diseases that are typically combined in COPD (to some degree), the diagnostic tests for all three conditions are the same. In all three cases, patients are asked if they smoke or have ever smoked, or if they work with lung-damaging chemicals. A number of tests are then performed.

A spirometry test that shows that less than 70 percent of the air is expelled from the lungs during exhaling indicates COPD. X-rays and computed tomography (CT) scans can detect damage to lung tissue and increased air in the chest. Excessive air in the lungs can be determined with a lung volume test, which indicates COPD. Diffusing capacity and arterial blood gas tests measure how efficient the lungs are in eliminating carbon dioxide and supplying oxygen to the blood. A body plethysmography shows whether asthma is present in conjunction with emphysema, and an alpha-1 antitrypsin deficiency test can detect a relatively rare form of genetically inherited emphysema.

Lung cancer is diagnosed with X-rays or a CT scan to reveal the presence of tumors. If tumors are present, lung mucus or fluid is often examined for the presence of cancer cells. The definitive diagnosis usually involves the removal of a small sample of tissue from tumors with an instrument that is inserted through the air passage, on which a biopsy is performed to determine if the growths are cancerous.

TREATMENT AND THERAPY

Because chronic bronchitis, emphysema, and COPD are caused by smoking in a majority of cases, the first treatment strategy for patients who are active smokers is to quit. The body can repair lung damage in short-term smokers, and although the effects of advanced COPD are irreversible and progressive, smoking cessation can slow the rate of progression. While COPD is progressive and potentially fatal, management strategies can improve the patient's quality of life and extend longevity.

Patients with low oxygen levels can take supplemental oxygen from an oxygen cylinder or concentrator through nasal tubes or an oxygen mask, which allows them to lead more active lives. Oxygen dosages must be carefully monitored to avoid a number of serious side effects. Being overweight or underweight can affect the progression and severity of symptoms of COPD, so adjustments in diet in combination with counseling and an exercise program can reduce the degree of infirmity.

A number of medications can help to control COPD symptoms. Nebulizers are used to administer anticholinerics or B2 agonists. Both are bronchodilators that act quickly to improve air flow by relaxing muscles around airways. In advanced COPD cases, corticosteroids are administered to reduce airway inflammation, but the side effects include a higher probability of pneumonia. In some of the most advanced COPD cases, the patient may need surgery to remove the most severely damaged parts of the lungs, or a lung transplant may need to be performed.

The treatment for lung cancer varies depending on the type of cancer and how far the disease has progressed. Non-small-cell lung cancer develops relatively slowly and, if diagnosed early, is treated with surgery that may involve removing the tumor, a portion of the lung, or the entire lung. Often, radiation therapy, which kills cancer cells with X-rays, follows the surgery. Chemotherapy, which kills cancer cells with powerful medications, is sometimes used in conjunction with surgery and radiation therapy.

Small-cell lung cancer progresses and spreads to other organs relatively quickly and is usually treated with radiation therapy or chemotherapy.

All persons with cancer who also are smokers are strongly advised to quit smoking. Nicotine and the chemicals in cigarette smoke retard the healing process after surgery and appear to promote cancer cell growth while insulating cancer cells from the destructive effects of both radiation therapy and chemotherapy. After the initial treatment, cancer patients have ongoing follow-up care that includes X-rays and CT scans, blood work, and physical examinations to check for a possible recurrence of the disease.

PREVENTION

Because 80 to 90 percent of all cases of chronic bronchitis, emphysema, COPD, and lung cancer are caused by smoking, the most important preventive measures are to not start smoking, to quit if one already smokes, and to avoid secondhand smoke. Management and workers in industries in which the work environment exposes personnel to dust and harmful chemicals should be aware of the importance of adequate ventilation; of using respirators; and of monitoring and controlling dust, toxin, and carcinogen levels.

Jack Carter, PhD

FURTHER READING

Owing, J. H., ed. *Smoking and Health: New Research.* Hauppauge, NY: Nova Science, 2005. Posits that smoking is a global epidemic responsible for numerous pathological conditions that are leading causes of death and disability, based on the analysis of global research.

Slovic, Paul, ed. *Smoking: Risk, Perception, and Policy.* Thousand Oaks, CA: Sage, 2001. Presents the results of research showing that young people, a majority of new smokers, do not understand the health-related consequences of nicotine addiction, and calls for more preventive measures including education and access restriction.

Ward, Jeremy P. T., Jane Ward, and Richard M. Leach. *The Respiratory System at a Glance.* Hoboken, NJ: Wiley, 2010. Includes concise discussions of the effects, methods of diagnosis, and treatment of respiratory diseases related to smoking.

WEBSITES OF INTEREST

American Lung Association
http://www.lung.org

Centers for Disease Control and Prevention
http://www.cdc.gov/tobacco/basic_information

National Heart, Lung, and Blood Institute
http://www.nhlbi.nih.gov/health/public/lung/copd

See also: Cancer and substance abuse; Chronic bronchitis; Chronic obstructive pulmonary disease (COPD); Emphysema; Lung cancer; Smoking; Smoking: Short- and long-term effects on the body

Risk factors for addiction

CATEGORY: Diagnosis and prevention

DEFINITION: The underlying risks for drug abuse and addiction involve a complex mix of biological, psychological, and environmental factors. Medically, addiction is recognized as a chronic, recurrent brain disease expressed in the form of compulsive behaviors. Addiction is characterized by loss of control, craving or preoccupation with the addictive substance or activity, and continued use despite consequences. It is also a developmental disease that usually begins in adolescence.

THE ADDICTIVE PERSONALITY?

Solving the addiction problem is much more complex than "just saying no," as the antidrug campaign popularized by former US first lady Nancy Reagan encouraged. A major misconception about addiction is that certain substances, by themselves, can turn the unwary into "dope fiends." Because substance abuse involves problems with impulse control, many researchers believed that dependence is mostly a matter of personality, speculating that there may be a certain addictive personality profile that puts people at risk for addiction.

The National Survey of American Attitudes on Substance Abuse, an annual survey conducted by the National Center on Addiction and Substance Abuse at Columbia University, states that "Every child in America is at risk of using drugs, regardless of race, ethnicity, or economic status." People of all racial and ethnic groups can develop addictions, and most Americans have tried marijuana but do not become addicts. Only 10 percent of all people who experiment with drugs become addicted.

Why does addiction affect only some people and not others? The answer appears to lie not so much in a person's personality but more in a person's vulnerability to drug abuse and addiction. Vulnerability is a product of the interaction of a person's environment, age, and biology. The common denominator is body chemistry and how the brain reacts to addictive substances. The addictive process shares common elements and influences, although the pathways will differ from person to person.

A National Academy of Sciences study in the 1980s concluded that there is no single set of psychological characteristics that fit all addictions, but the study did report common elements in people from addiction to addiction. Personality characteristics that were studied include depression, anxiety, dependent or antisocial behavior, and difficulty formulating long-term personal goals.

There appear to be commonalities and valid risk factors but no true way to characterize an addictive personality. While certain personality traits play a role in addictive behavior, most behavioral experts concur that the triad of social factors, psychological factors, and physiological components is at the core of the addiction process, but the exact nature of their interplay remains unknown.

PSYCHOLOGICAL RISK FACTORS

Addiction comprises psychological conditions involving biological processes and genetics that have physical, environmental, and neurochemical aspects. Impulsivity and sensation-seeking are the psychological characteristics that have been commonly reported as factors associated with higher risk for addiction. Also considered is how a person perceives risk. Persons who have a low-risk perception tend to focus on potential benefits and cannot or do not see the adverse consequences in situations of uncertain outcome.

The prevalence of addiction to illicit drugs and to nicotine is higher in persons who also have a comorbid mental illness. More than 50 percent of persons with substance-related disorders have comorbid psychiatric disorders, namely, major depression, personality disorders, anxiety disorders, and schizophrenia. Nearly all personality disorders are marked by impairments in impulse control. Consequently,

people with such a diagnosis are at a higher risk for addiction. This is especially true for antisocial and borderline personality disorders. Antisocial personality disorder is a pervasive pattern of disregard for and violation of the rights of others and an inability or unwillingness to conform to social norms. Such persons are impulse-dysfunctional, have deficits in attention, lack the ability to reflect, and lack sensitivity. Borderline personality disorder is a pervasive pattern of instability in interpersonal relationships, self-image, affect regulation, and impulse control.

People with anxiety disorders are at increased risk for developing addictions because they may use substances to reduce their anxiety and control their symptoms. A National Epidemiologic Survey on Alcohol and Related Conditions found that any anxiety disorder of the *Diagnostic and Statistical Manual of Mental Disorders*, diagnosed in the year of the survey, was associated with a 13.02 percent prevalence of alcohol use disorder, which increased with a diagnosis of two coexisting disorders.

A later study of patients from three urban, university-affiliated outpatient clinics investigated the association of individual anxiety and mood disorders and drinking patterns, defined as three drinks, two or more times a week for heavy drinking and four or more times a week for frequent drinking. Overall percentages were 6.19 percent for heavy drinking and 8.31 percent for frequent drinking. Post-traumatic stress disorder was associated more with heavy drinking and panic disorder more with frequent drinking (but with less heavy drinking). No significant relationship was found between alcohol use and two or more coexisting disorders.

Persons with attention deficit hyperactivity disorder (ADHD) in general are at higher risk for addictions because one of the primary features of ADHD is impulsivity, which involves premature, risky behavior and poorly conceived actions. Aside from their impulsivity, people with the disorder have difficulty recognizing risks and do not associate them with negative consequences; people with ADHD lack sound judgment and become frustrated easily, all of which makes them highly susceptible to addictive behavior.

Approximately one-half million teenagers struggle with eating disorders. While not strictly an adolescent disorder, the median age of onset for an eating disorder is between twelve and thirteen years old for the three major disorders (anorexia nervosa, bulimia nervosa, and binge eating), according to a 2010 study released by the National Eating Disorders Association. These addictions manifest as intense preoccupations with food, weight, and body image but are complex conditions involving physical, psychological, interpersonal, and social issues. Like other addictions, eating disorders have patterns, although no one factor causes an eating disorder.

Risk factors for anorexia include fear of growing up, inability to separate from the family, need to please or be liked, perfectionism, need to control, need for attention, lack of self-esteem, high family expectations, parental dieting, and family discord. Risk factors for bulimia include difficulty regulating mood, impulsive acts (such as shoplifting and substance abuse), sexual abuse, and family dysfunction.

BIOLOGICAL FACTORS

Since the early 1990s, scientists have amassed a wealth of data about the neurophysiologic processes and biologic mechanisms that underlie the triggering of pleasure, reward, and addiction, resulting in the classification of addiction as a biological brain disease. These neurochemical changes and genetic influences, which account for up to 40 to 60 percent of the predisposition to addiction, along with family history of addiction, age, and gender, are all biologically based risk factors that affect a person's vulnerability to addiction.

The prefrontal cortex (the gray matter of the anterior part of the frontal lobe) is part of the cerebral cortex, the convoluted outer layer of gray matter of the cerebrum that coordinates sensory and motor information. The prefrontal cortex is involved in behavior control through executive functioning (EF)—abstract thinking, motivation, planning, and inhibition of impulsive responses. The prefrontal cortex is highly developed in humans but is not fully developed until adulthood. Thus, certain groups, such as people with ADHD and antisocial personality disorder, and adolescents, who have deficient, dysfunctional, or immature EFs, will be predisposed to impulse control problems and have a higher risk for substance abuse and addiction.

With chronic substance abuse, the brain's ability to control impulses becomes further compromised because addicting substances reduce functioning specifically in that area. Simply put, this initiates a vicious cycle of impulse control problems leading to

dangerous behavior that perpetuates the impulsivity.

The limbic system controls basic emotions, drives, and behaviors and affects motivational and mood states. Because it links certain brain structures that regulate people's ability to feel pleasure, the limbic system is essential to the brain's reward circuitry.

The neurotransmitter dopamine has long been known to become activated and to regulate feelings of pleasure, and it now appears to also be key in determining the motivational state. With chronic drug use, the persistent release of dopamine programs the limbic brain regions and the prefrontal cortex to embed drug cues into the amygdala (one of the limbic system structures), a process that floods the brain's reward system, enhances the motivational state, and creates the obsessive craving for drugs. Hence, there is an inherent risk cycle of reinforced drug taking that leads to addiction. This compulsive drive toward drug use is exacerbated by deficits in impulse control and decision making.

Personal relevance, the state of being able to relate internal and external stimuli to establish a sense of belonging, is important in personality development. The bilateral caudate nucleus (BCN) and pregenual anterior cingulate cortex (PACC) are both known to be active in this process. BCN is a medial basal ganglia involved in motor control. PACC is found in the frontal part of the cingulate cortex surrounding the corpus callosum; it is involved in emotional aspects of brain function and linked to anhedonia.

Another brain region, the bilateral anterior insula (BAI), not previously reported to be active in personal relevance, was investigated specifically during personal relevance in an experiment into neural responses evoked by reward and the attribution of personal relevance. BAI is normally involved in empathy, compassion, and interpersonal phenomena, and in decision-making under complex and uncertain situations. Based on analyses, the response to personally relevant stimuli is dependent on the novelty seeking personality trait, and the neuronal responses of BAI, BCN, and PACC may be predictors of addiction risk.

Other studies have found evidence of additional biological risk factors. Deficient cortisol reactivity to a variety of stressors has been implicated as a risk factor for alcohol and nicotine dependence. In addition, persons with alcohol and drug-abusing parents who show preexisting alterations in frontal-limbic interactions with the hypothalamic-pituitary-adrenocortical axis may be more vulnerable to addiction. Task-based activation in the inferior frontal gyrus and right insula has been associated with risk aversion, and activation in the nucleus accumbens and parietal cortex has been associated with both risk seeking and risk aversion. According to the investigators, these findings indicate that individual differences in attitudes toward risk taking are reflected in the brain's functional architecture and may have implications for engaging in real-world risky behaviors.

Children and adolescents who exhibit aggressive behaviors, who demonstrate a lack of self-control, and who have a difficult temperament may be at risk for drug addiction, especially if they have been physically abused or have parents who are dependent on drugs or alcohol. These children and adolescents usually view authority with disrespect and feel out of control. Those who have been abused may be consumed by feelings of violence and may turn to drugs to suppress the anger, anxiety, and aggression caused by earlier trauma.

RISK FACTORS RELATED TO AGE AND GENDER

Because the prefrontal cortex is the last part of the brain to develop, thirteen to nineteen year olds tend to use other parts of the brain (for example, emotional areas) when making decisions and are at high risk for substance abuse and addiction. Adolescent characteristics are predictors of adult alcohol use and abuse, and their effect varies as a function of age and type of alcohol outcome.

According to the Substance Abuse and Mental Health Services Administration, twelve to seventeen year olds who smoke, compared with nonsmoking youth, are more than eight times more likely to use illegal drugs and more than seventeen times more likely to drink heavily. In the same age group, weekly marijuana users are nine times more likely than nonusers to experiment with illegal drugs or alcohol.

There is a robust association between age at first drink and risk of alcohol use disorder, reflecting willful rather than uncontrolled heavy drinking. Heavy episodic drinking is a measure of higher-risk drinking. Substance abuse prevalence is greatest among eighteen to twenty-five year olds and more common in men than in women, but the relative risk of marijuana use is approximately equal for men and women.

Males and females experience adolescence differently because of various social, cultural, physiological, and psychological differences. In males, puberty tends to increase aggressive behavior and causes them to crave being an adult; males at this age also experiment with sexual behavior and with alcohol, tobacco, or illegal drugs. In females, puberty tends to increase the incidence of depression, lessen self-confidence and self-worth, and reduce physical activity, school performance, and aspirations; females at this age become more vulnerable to negative outside influences and mixed messages about risky behaviors. They are also at higher risk for sexual abuse, which has been associated with substance abuse.

In aging adults, fewer women than men consume alcohol, women who do drink consume less alcohol than men, and total alcohol intake decreases after retirement. Despite the latter, alcohol abuse and alcoholism may be under-recognized and, in terms of absolute numbers, may be becoming a silent epidemic, despite the overall decrease in alcohol consumption with increasing age.

ENVIRONMENTAL FACTORS

Environmental risk factors are those characteristics in a person's surroundings and everyday life that increase his or her likelihood of becoming addicted to drugs. These characteristics include one's family dynamics, social and cultural surroundings, housing, school, employment status, economic status, education level, and peer group.

Risk of drug abuse increases substantially during times of transition—changing schools, moving, divorce, and puberty. One of the biggest factors contributing to drug abuse risk is having friends who engage in addictive behavior. Teens are six times more likely to use marijuana when they believe that all or most of the students in their grade use drugs.

Lackadaisical family attitudes about drugs and alcohol, family substance use, dysfunctional parenting, and parental abuse (physical, emotional, or sexual) are contributing risk factors to substance abuse and addiction. If parents use alcohol, tobacco products, or other substances, their children are more likely to use them too.

Excessive deprivation or overindulgence in early life and inconsistencies in parental behavior, such as too much or too little love or discipline, or frequent instances of sudden switching from unrealistic praise to destructive criticism, can make a child more likely to use drugs or alcohol. Studies have found that latchkey children who are left home alone two or more days per week were four times more likely to have gotten drunk than those who had parental supervision five or more times per week; children who have the least adult monitoring start using drugs at earlier ages; and the earlier a child starts using drugs, the greater the likelihood a serious problem will develop.

Cultural beliefs, availability of drugs in the community, and acceptability of use within a person's social environment and peer group contribute to drug use. People living in urban communities are more at risk for drug and alcohol abuse than those living in rural communities.

Academic failure, particularly in later elementary years, is a risk factor for addictions because it begets low self-esteem. According to a 2003 National Household Survey on Drug Use, children age twelve to seventeen years who enjoyed going to school, felt that their assigned schoolwork was meaningful, or believed that what they learn in school would be important later in life, were less likely to have used illicit drugs or alcohol compared with those who did not have the same positive attitudes toward school. Female students were more likely than male students to have positive attitudes toward school, and Asian, black, and Hispanic youths were more likely than white youths to have these positive attitudes.

Teens are more likely to smoke, drink, or use illegal drugs if they have a negative attitude, difficulty adapting to change, and an inability to "go with the flow." Teens at risk are those with changing family structures; easy access to alcohol, tobacco, or illegal drugs; adverse peer pressure; little adult supervision; unsafe places to learn, play, and socialize; and no good role models.

PERSPECTIVES

Resolving the monumental problem of substance abuse and addictive disorders will require education about addictive substances, recognition of susceptible personality traits and risk factors associated with addiction, and better understandings of the complex interactions of psychological, environmental, and biological factors that contribute to the development of addiction.

Barbara Woldin, BS

FURTHER READING

Barnes, Gordon, Robert Murray, and David Patton. *The Addiction-Prone Personality.* New York: Springer, 2007. Describes the addiction-prone personality, linking personality traits to the development of alcohol abuse.

Courtwright, David. *Forces of Habit: Drugs and the Making of the Modern World.* Cambridge, MA: Harvard UP, 2001. Compelling commentary on the drug problem, described in terms of big business.

Nakken, Craig M. *The Addictive Personality: Understanding the Addictive Process and Compulsive Behavior.* 2nd ed. Center City, MN: Hazelden, 1996. Discusses how a person becomes an addict and explains the addiction process. Covers genetic factors and cultural influences.

Thombs, Dennis. *Introduction to Addictive Behaviors.* 3rd ed. New York: Guilford, 2006. Covers theories of addiction, prevention, comorbidity, motivation enhancement and harm reduction, and psychoanalytic, cognitive, family, and sociocultural issues.

WEBSITES OF INTEREST

American Society of Addiction Medicine
http://www.asam.org

National Institute on Drug Abuse
http://www.drugabuse.gov

Substance Abuse Mental Health Services Administration
http://www.samhsa.gov

See also: Addictive personality; Anxiety; Cross-addiction; Depression; Dopamine and addiction; Genetics and substance abuse; Mental illness; Models of addiction; Science of addiction; Socioeconomic status and addiction

Ritalin

CATEGORY: Substances
ALSO KNOWN AS: Methylphenidate
DEFINITION: Ritalin is a central nervous system stimulant that shares many characteristics with amphetamines. It is a controlled substance that is most often prescribed for attention-deficit hyperactivity disorder.

STATUS: Legal in the United States and worldwide
CLASSIFICATION: Schedule II controlled substance
SOURCE: Synthetic substance with no natural sources
TRANSMISSION ROUTE: Oral, inhalation, intravenous

HISTORY OF USE

Although originally synthesized in 1944, Ritalin was not studied for its therapeutic effects in humans until the mid-1950s. Early on, Ritalin was used to treat narcolepsy (a sleep disorder), depression, and chronic fatigue. By the 1960s it was discovered to produce a calming effect in children who had been diagnosed with symptoms of attention-deficit hyperactivity disorder (ADHD).

When Ritalin is administered orally, its effects are slowed by the gastrointestinal tract, which effectively prevents the user from experiencing a euphoric high. However, when the drug is crushed and snorted or used intravenously, it can lead to intense feelings of pleasure that some have equated with cocaine usage.

Ritalin abuse has been on the rise. This increase has been driven by two primary factors.

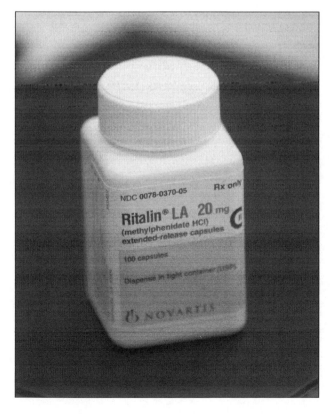

A bottle of Ritalin. (Getty Images)

First, there has been an increase in the number of people diagnosed with ADHD. Second, persons without ADHD have learned that Ritalin can be used as a cognitive enhancer for improving academic performance on tasks that require sustained, focused attention.

Estimates indicate that between 3 and 10 percent of school-aged children in the United States meet the diagnostic criteria for ADHD. This trend has increased the overall availability of the drug. Adolescents and young adults more often abuse Ritalin by snorting it or by ingesting larger quantities to experience exhilaration. In 2010, researcher Eric Racine and his colleague and co-author Cynthia Forlini looked into rates of lifetime nonmedical stimulant use and found that the prevalence for using stimulants, including Ritalin, to augment cognition ranged from 3 to 11 percent of college students.

EFFECTS AND POTENTIAL RISKS

Ritalin increases the presence of the neurotransmitter dopamine in the brain by blocking its reuptake by the cells that release it. Short-term adverse effects include headache, nausea, irregular heartbeat, wakefulness, agitation, anxiety, increased blood pressure, and, in rare instances, seizures. Long-term adverse effects include anxiety and sleeplessness. Initial reports of suppression of growth have been placed in doubt by later studies. Physical and psychological dependence can occur with chronic abuse.

Bryan C. Auday, PhD

FURTHER READING

Iversen, Leslie. *Speed, Ecstasy, Ritalin: The Science of Amphetamines.* New York: Oxford UP, 2008. Provides information on the medical and nonmedical history of amphetamine use, including Ritalin.

Levinthall, Charles F. *Drugs, Behavior, and Modern Society.* 7th ed. Boston: Pearson, 2012. An informative text describing the effects and history of a wide range of substances of abuse.

Racine, Eric, and C. Forlini. "Cognitive Enhancement, Lifestyle Choice, or Misuse of Prescription Drugs?" *Neuroethics* 3 (2010): 1–4. Discusses the medical and nonmedical use of stimulant drugs and explores ethical issues involving the use and prescription of cognition-enhancing products.

See also: Dopamine and addiction; Prescription drug addiction: Overview; Stimulant abuse; Stimulants: Short- and long-term effects on the body

Rohypnol

CATEGORY: Substances

ALSO KNOWN AS: Circles; date rape drug; flunitrazepam; forget-me pill; La rocha; lunch money drug; Mexican Valium; R-2; Reynolds; roachies; roofies; rophies; Row-shay; wolfies

DEFINITION: Rohypnol is the brand name for flunitrazepam, a potent benzodiazepine with strong sedative-hypnotic properties similar to Valium. It is considered a central nervous system depressant that slows brain activity to induce sedation.

STATUS: Illegal in the United States but legal in many countries worldwide

CLASSIFICATION: Schedule IV controlled substance; numerous US states consider it a schedule I controlled substance

SOURCE: Synthetic compound with no natural sources and smuggled into the United States

TRANSMISSION ROUTE: Oral ingestion (as tablet and liquid); also snorted in its crushed form

HISTORY OF USE

Flunitrazepam (Rohypnol) was first synthesized in Europe in 1972 by Hoffman-La Roche Pharmaceuticals as a sleeping aid and an anesthetic. Its illicit use began in 1975, once it was marketed as Rohypnol. Rohypnol became a popular recreational drug because of its intoxicating effects. By the 1990s, Rohypnol gained recognition in the United States as a club drug among young adults in bars and nightclubs and at raves and concerts. Rohypnol quickly achieved a reputation as a "date rape" drug for use in sexual assaults because it readily disappears in drinks and then sedates, incapacitates, and erases the memory of persons who consume it. Rohypnol became one of the most dangerous benzodiazepines available.

Rohypnol is not approved for any use, even medical, in the United States but is legal in numerous countries worldwide. It is classified with other benzodiazepines as a schedule IV controlled substance under the Controlled Substances Act (1970) as a drug with potential dependence. Once Rohypnol's dangers were recognized, numerous US states reclassified it as a schedule I controlled substance with no

The hands of a young female drug addict disolve a dose of the barbiturate Rohypnol on a spoon at an aid center for drug addicts. (Boris Roessler/dpa/Landov)

legitimate medical use. This prompted the US Congress to pass the Drug-Induced Rape Prevention and Punishment Act of 1996 to increase penalties for distributing a controlled substance to unknowing persons. Despite reformulation efforts to increase the visibility of Rohypnol tablets in drinks, its misuse remains a concern.

EFFECTS AND POTENTIAL RISKS

Like other benzodiazepines, Rohypnol acts by stimulating the release and binding of gamma-amino butyric acid, a natural nerve-calming agent, to receptors in the brain. This effect causes brain activity to slow and then to induce sleep, reduce anxiety, and relax muscles.

Rohypnol's short-term effects are attributed to its sedative properties. It induces feelings of euphoria, relaxation, and intoxication. Negative short-term effects include amnesia, blackouts, drowsiness, confusion, nausea, and impaired coordination.

Rohypnol is a dangerous and potent substance. It is often used with other drugs, such as heroin or cocaine, to enhance a high or to alleviate withdrawal symptoms. When combined with alcohol, Rohypnol can cause serious disorientation and memory loss. Furthermore, it is a tasteless and odorless drug that is easily, and often unknowingly, consumed.

Similar to other benzodiazepines, long-term Rohypnol use can lead to mental difficulties, aggression, dependence, and addiction. High doses of Rohypnol can cause respiratory depression.

Rose Ciulla-Bohling, PhD

FURTHER READING

Adams, Colleen. *Rohypnol: Roofies—"The Date Rape Drug."* New York: Rosen, 2007. An informative resource on the physical and psychological effects of Rohypnol and its use as a date rape drug.

Doweiko, Harold. *Concepts of Chemical Dependency.* Belmont, CA: Brooks, 2009. A valuable text describing the science of chemical dependency and addiction. Chapter 10 discusses the use and abuse of benzodiazepines, including Rohypnol.

Ginther, Catherine. *Drug Abuse Sourcebook.* Detroit: Omnigraphics, 2004. Provides foundational information on the risks, effects, and patterns of use of illicit, prescription, and over-the-counter drugs.

WEBSITES OF INTEREST

Center for Substance Abuse Research
http://www.cesar.umd.edu/cesar/drugs/rohypnol.asp

National Institute on Drug Abuse
http://www.drugabuse.gov/infofacts/clubdrugs.html

US Drug Enforcement Administration
http://www.justice.gov/dea/concern/flunitrazepam.html

See also: Benzodiazepine abuse; Club drugs; Date rape drugs

Routes of administration

CATEGORY: Substance abuse
ALSO KNOWN AS: Modes of administration
DEFINITION: The manner in which a drug is introduced into the body can affect how rapidly it is absorbed and delivered to the brain, which may alter the drug's effects and its addictive potential. Common routes of administration of addictive substances include oral, injection, inhalation, and administration through the skin and mucous membranes.

BACKGROUND

For drugs to affect a person's psychological experience, they must reach the brain. This statement is rather obvious, but what may be less obvious is how the path a drug takes to the brain can affect the experience and consequences associated with taking the drug. All things being equal, the faster an addictive substance is delivered to the brain, the more that drug tends to be abused and addictive. One variable that plays a large role in determining how quickly a drug is delivered to the brain is the route of administration, or the method used to get the drug into the body.

ORAL ROUTE

Perhaps the most common route of administration is the mouth. The introduction of drugs into the body by swallowing them is referred to as oral administration. Pills are administered this way, as are liquids such as alcohol.

In addition, drugs that are consumed in whole-foods forms, for example, marijuana baked into brownies or hallucinogenic mushrooms brewed into tea, also are administered orally. When orally administered, drugs will be partially absorbed in the stomach and intestine, where the active ingredients are absorbed into the bloodstream and then carried to the brain.

The oral route of administration is a relatively slow way to deliver drugs to the brain. Because the active ingredients are absorbed through digestive processes, the speed of onset can be influenced by a variety of stomach and intestinal variables. A prominent example of this process is alcohol consumption, in which approximately 20 percent of the alcohol is absorbed in the stomach and the rest in the upper intestine. The speed with which this occurs is affected by how fast the stomach empties; this, in turn, is related to how much food is already in the stomach. This factor explains why people are more rapidly influenced by the effects of alcohol when they drink on an empty stomach.

In addition, men have more of a particular gastric enzyme that metabolizes a portion of the consumed alcohol before it is absorbed into the bloodstream. This partly explains why men will be somewhat less influenced by the effects of alcohol than will women, even when the number of drinks and body size are held constant.

INJECTION

A second route of administration is intravenous (IV), intramuscular, and subcutaneous. In an IV administration, the drug is injected with a syringe and needle, often directly into the bloodstream through a vein. Drugs also can be injected directly into muscle (an intramuscular injection) or just under the skin (a subcutaneous injection). However, most drugs of abuse that are taken through self-injection are delivered intravenously.

IV injection is relatively dangerous because it is fast and irreversible. Once the drug has been injected, it cannot be retrieved; the injection cannot be reversed. In addition, IV injection bypasses virtually all barriers to absorption. The drug that is injected will be completely and rapidly available. In some cases the rapid

availability of the drug can itself become a problem. The dose of a drug that is administered orally will gradually become available to the brain as the dose dissolves and is absorbed. The same dose delivered intravenously will be available to the brain all at once. Serious problems can occur if the user has an allergic reaction, miscalculates the dosage, or has an unanticipated side effect.

Finally, it can be difficult for IV drug users to obtain safe and clean needles. Shared or reused needles can spread infection and blood-borne diseases, including hepatitis virus infection and infection with the human immunodeficiency virus.

INHALATION

Another common route of administration among drug users is the lungs, in which the substance of abuse is inhaled. The inhalation route includes smoking, in which the drug of abuse is heated or burned to suspend its particles in smoke or vapor.

Inhalation is a popular way to administer tobacco, marijuana, and smoked versions of cocaine, methamphetamine, and heroin. Also, chemicals that are found in many household products, including some paints, cleaners, and glues, also can be administered as substances of abuse if their fumes are inhaled. The lungs absorb the inhaled chemicals rapidly and efficiently and send them directly to the heart and brain. As a consequence, drugs that are inhaled will have an extremely fast onset, sometimes even faster than IV injection.

Inhalation has the potential to damage the lungs themselves. In many cases the lung damage is not directly caused by the drug itself, but by other drugs and toxins that are delivered to the lungs at the same time. An additional problem associated with inhalation is that the amount of oxygen absorbed and made available to cells of the body is often reduced. Reducing the amount of oxygen available to the brain leads to a dangerous condition called anoxia.

Anoxia is a common and especially devastating problem with the abuse of chemicals in household cleaners, glues, and paints. In this case, the anoxic effects produced by the chemicals themselves are compounded by efforts that inhalant abusers often take to concentrate the gasses they are inhaling, such as covering the mouth with chemical-soaked rags or plastic bags.

OTHER MODES OF ADMINISTRATION

Drugs also can be absorbed through nasal or oral mucous membranes (mucous administration). This route of administration is common with tobacco chew and snuff, in which the nicotine is absorbed through tissue in the mouth and nose, respectively. Mucous administration also is the method used to absorb cocaine or powdered forms of other drugs, which are snorted (sniffed into the nose).

Drugs also can be absorbed directly through the skin (transdermal administration). The most familiar example of transdermal administration of drugs is the nicotine patch, but this strategy is gaining popularity for the delivery of other drugs, including pain medications.

Linda R. Tennison, PhD

FURTHER READING

Julien, Robert M., Claire D. Advokat, and Joseph E. Comaty. *A Primer of Drug Action.* 12th ed. New York: Worth, 2011. An excellent, thorough text covering uses and effects of both psychiatric substances and drugs of abuse.

McCabe, Sean E., Carol J. Boyd, and Christian J. Teter. "Motives, Diversion, and Routes Of Administration Associated with Nonmedical Use of Prescription Opioids." *Addictive Behaviors* 32 (2007): 562–75. Print. Reports the results of a large web-based survey of undergraduate students investigating the ways that students abuse opioid medications for nonmedical purposes and their motivations for doing so.

Samaha, Anne-Noel, and Terry E. Robinson. "Why Does the Rapid Delivery of Drugs to the Brain Promote Addiction?" *Trends in Pharmacological Sciences* 26 (2005): 82–87. Print. Proposes a theory of brain function and summarizes alternative theories for why increasing the speed of delivery of drugs to the brain increases their addictive potential.

WEBSITES OF INTEREST

Drug and Alcohol Services Information System
http://oas.samhsa.gov/2k7/crackTX/crackTX.htm

The Merck Manual Home Health Handbook
http://www.merckmanuals.com/home/sec02/ch011/ch011a.html

National Institute on Drug Abuse
http://www.drugabuse.gov

See also: Inhalants abuse; Intravenous drug use and blood-borne diseases; Physiological dependence; Science of addiction

S

Safe and drug-free schools

CATEGORY: Diagnosis and prevention

DEFINITION: Safe and Drug-Free Schools is a program funded by the US government to prevent school violence; to prevent illegal use of alcohol, tobacco, and drugs; to improve community environments; and to support student academic achievement.

DATE: Created July 1, 2002

BACKGROUND

The US Safe and Drug-Free Schools and Communities Act was included as part of the No Child Left Behind Act of 2001, a reauthorization of the Elementary and Secondary Education Act of 1965. George W. Bush, US president at the time, believed that school improvement could not happen without the establishment of safe, drug-free schools and local communities.

The Goals 2000 Educate America Act, which was passed in 1994, included a similar goal statement: "Every school in the United States will be free of drugs, violence, and the unauthorized presence of firearms and alcohol and will offer a disciplined environment conducive to learning." This goal was not achieved by 2000, ensuring the enactment of the Safe and Drug-Free Schools and Communities Act in 2001. In 2011, the Office of Safe and Drug-Free Schools (OSDFS) and its programs were incorporated into the Office of Safe and Healthy Students (OSHS), within the Office of Elementary and Secondary Education. The OSHS will continue the mission of the OSDFS in coordinating policy efforts aimed at drug and violence prevention.

MISSION AND GOALS

The purpose of the Office of Safe and Healthy Students is to support programs that prevent violence near schools; that prevent the illegal use of alcohol, tobacco, and drugs; and that involve parents and communities in efforts to reduce and eliminate drug use. Another goal is to bring together federal, state, school, and community efforts and resources to foster a safe and drug-free learning environment to enhance student academic achievement.

To achieve these goals, the Office of Safe and Healthy Students performs the following functions:

- Provides funding through grants to support drug- and violence-prevention programs aimed at students in elementary schools, secondary schools, and colleges. Recipients of grants could be state and local educational agencies and public and private nonprofit groups.
- Participates in the development of federal-level education policy related to drug and violence prevention.
- Participates in committees, partnerships, and interagency groups related to drug and violence prevention; coordinates with other federal agencies on issues of school health, and advises the secretary of education on related issues.
- Participates with other federal agencies in developing a national research strategy for drug and violence prevention.
- Administers programs related to character and civics education.

ORGANIZATION

The Office of Safe and Healthy Students has a number of initiatives. Each of them is administered by a program or subgroup.

The Health, Mental Health, Environmental Health, and Physical Education group administers programs that promote the health and well-being of students and families. Basically, this group oversees the provision of discretionary grants to states to support program goals.

The Drug-Violence Prevention (DVP) program provides financial assistance for state and local drug- and violence-prevention activities in elementary and secondary schools and in institutions of higher education. A separate branch of the DVP handles federal programs of a larger scope.

The Character and Civic Education (CCE) subgroup provides financial assistance for character and citizenship education activities in elementary and secondary schools and in institutions of higher education. CCE also reports on issues and programs, disseminates information, and provides technical assistance to state agencies and state and local correctional institutions.

A final subset works across group boundaries to emphasize coordinated, collaborative responses to developing and maintaining safe and drug-free learning environments. This subset office supplies discretionary grants to states for such programs as Readiness and Emergency Management, Safe Schools/Healthy Schools, and School's Emergency Response to Violence programs.

Mary C. Ware, PhD

FURTHER READING

Barton, Elizabeth A. *Leadership Strategies for Safe Schools.* Thousand Oaks, CA: Corwin, 2009. Focuses more on school safety than on drug-free schools, but offers valuable tips and suggestions for principals and school leaders.

King, Keith A., Donald I. Wagner, and Bonnie Hedrick. "Safe and Drug-Free School Coordinators' Perceived Needs to Improve Violence and Drug Prevention Programs." *Journal of School Health* 71 (2001): 236–41. Print. Reports on a study in which coordinators of safe and drug-free schools were polled to determine obstacles to their work and what they would need to be more successful.

Knowles, Cynthia R. *Prevention That Works! A Guide for Developing School-Based Drug and Violence Prevention Programs.* Thousand Oaks, CA: Corwin, 2001. Considered an invaluable guidebook; includes suggestions for creating school-based drug and violence prevention programs.

Wilson, Richard, and Cheryl Kolander. *Drug Abuse Prevention: A School and Community Partnership.* 3rd ed. Boston: Jones, 2010. A thorough study of drug prevention programs in schools and communities, updated to include information about the success of safe and drug-free schools programs.

WEBSITES OF INTEREST

Office of Safe and Drug-Free Schools
http://www2.ed.gov/about/offices/list/osdfs

Office of Safe and Healthy Students
http://www2.ed.gov/about/offices/list/om/fs_po/oese/safehealth.html

Safe and Supportive Schools
http://safesupportiveschools.ed.gov

See also: Education about substance abuse; Legislation and substance abuse; Prevention methods and research; Schools and substance abuse

Salvia divinorum

CATEGORY: Substances

ALSO KNOWN AS: Diviner's sage; magic mint; mystic sage; sadi; Sally-D; ska Maria Pastora

DEFINITION: The herb *Salvia divinorum* stimulates kappa-opioid receptors in the brain, causing hallucinogenic effects such as dissociation and synesthesia. The leaves of the plant are available fresh, dried, and in aerosol preparations.

STATUS: Illegal in several countries and banned in many parts of the United States, although unregulated nationally

CLASSIFICATION: Drug or chemical of concern

SOURCE: Few restrictions on its sale in US states where the plant is not banned; also available for purchase on the Internet

TRANSMISSION ROUTE: Chewed, snorted, and smoked

HISTORY OF USE

Salvia divinorum was first used by indigenous peoples in the mountains of southern Mexico for religious purposes. To the Mazatec people, its use allowed transcendence and communion with higher powers. In the 2000s, *Salvia* became the most commonly used hallucinogen in the United States, although not for spiritual reasons. Its increased use has been linked to the availability of information about it on the Internet, to the belief that it is fairly safe, to its legality in many parts of the world, to its potent and short-lived hallucinogenic effects, and to its being undetectable in routine drug tests.

EFFECTS AND POTENTIAL RISKS

Salvia's psychoactive component, salvinorin A, selectively activates a specific type of opioid receptor, the kappa-opioid receptors (KOR). These are found in several areas of the central nervous system, including the hypothalamus, the claustrum, the central gray

Bags of confiscated Salvia, *an addictive herb, are shown.* (Jon Fabrigar/Xinhua/Landov)

matter of the midbrain, and the spinal cord. A few minutes after stimulation, KORs cause vivid dissociative effects, including depersonalization and sensory confusion. Additionally, KOR stimulation decreases one's sensation of pain and increases urination and perspiration. The effects of smoked *Salvia* typically last fewer than thirty minutes. If chewed, the effects can persist for about one hour.

There does not appear to be significant risk of addiction with *Salvia*. Salvinorin A has no affinity for the mu (μ) opioid receptors, which are stimulated by substances such as heroin and morphine and have been implicated in the reward system that drives addiction.

Although nonaddictive, *Salvia* is not harmless. Its vivid hallucinogenic effects can be unpleasant and can produce heightened anxiety or panic. Other negative symptoms include paranoia, thought blocking, and mental slowing. Moreover, because it is a non-water-soluble compound, the long-term effects of salvinorin A are unpredictable.

Michael R. Meyers, PhD

FURTHER READING

Babu, Kavita, Christopher R. McCurdy, and Edward Boyer. "Opioid Receptors and Legal Highs: *Salvia divinorum* and Kratom." *Clinical Toxicology* 46 (2008): 146–52. Print. Describes the psychoactive effects of *Salvia* and its increasing popularity as a recreational drug.

Brown, David Jay. "Salvia on Schedule." *Scientific American* 301.2 (2009): 20–21. Print. Reviews the debate surrounding the regulation of saliva and discusses the potential effects of criminalizing the drug on research efforts studying the drug's medicinal properties.

Mysels, David. "The Kappa-Opiate Receptor Impacts the Pathophysiology and Behavior of Substance Use." *American Journal on Addictions* 18 (2009): 272-76. Print. Reviews research on the kappa-opiate receptor and its role in substance abuse and addiction.

Sanders, Laura. "Lab Study Probes Psychoactive Drug." *Science News* 179.2 (2011): 15. Print. Describes the psychopharmacological effects of *Salvia*.

See also: Hallucinogen abuse; Hallucinogens: Short- and long-term effects on the body; Psychosis and substance abuse

Schizophrenia and addiction

CATEGORY: Psychological issues and behaviors

DEFINITION: Schizophrenia is a severe mental disorder characterized by impaired functioning in cognition, perception, emotions, and behavior. In its acute stage, it manifests as psychosis. Schizophrenia is highly associated with substance abuse, and the link between the two is thought to be disturbances in signaling pathways involved in the brain's rewards system.

BACKGROUND

Schizophrenia is a chronic and often severe mental disorder. Affecting approximately 1 percent of the population, schizophrenia usually develops during adolescence or early adulthood. Patients are diagnosed as having paranoid, catatonic, disorganized, undifferentiated, or residual schizophrenia, according to their positive symptoms (exaggerations of normal functioning) and negative symptoms (deficiencies in normal functioning). The hallmark of the disease is psychosis, wherein the person with schizophrenia loses touch with reality (and experiences delusions and hallucinations).

The complexities of schizophrenia are yet to be fully unraveled, and the psychiatric community still grapples with what constitutes psychosis. There is mounting evidence that malfunctioning dopamine and glutamate systems in the brain play a major role in the development of schizophrenia.

BIOLOGICAL AND GENETIC FACTORS IN SCHIZOPHRENIA

Unlike many other psychiatric disorders, schizophrenia impairs multiple areas of brain functioning.

Since the mid-twentieth century, technological advances have enabled neuroscientists to study the brain more fully, shedding light on the structural and genetic variants seen in schizophrenia.

Through a variety of dynamic imaging and brain mapping techniques, researchers have found that persons with schizophrenia have various anomalies in brain structure and morphology, displaying abnormalities such as loss of gray and white matter, enlargement of the ventricles, and displacement of other structures. Persons with schizophrenia also show disturbances in neurotransmission, particularly in the glutamate and dopamine signaling pathways.

The availability of genome-wide association studies has made the search for genetic markers of complex diseases a reality. The most likely candidate genes associated with schizophrenia have been located on chromosomes 1 (DISC1 and RG542), 6 (DTNBP1), 7 (GRM3), 8 (NRG1), 13 (DAOA), 17 (PPP1R1B), and 22 (COMT). Most of these genes make proteins involved in dopamine or glutamate signaling; others are growth factors involved in nerve development.

The bulk of these structural and genetic aberrations correlate with known functional impairment in persons with schizophrenia—namely, deficits in cognitive and executive functioning, information processing, verbal memory, planning, and self-awareness.

THE SCHIZOPHRENIA AND ADDICTION CONNECTION

Researchers have been investigating the relationship between substance use disorder (SUD) and schizophrenia since about 1980. Studies have shown that 40 to 60 percent of people with a diagnosis of a schizophrenia spectrum disorder also have a diagnosis of SUD. Aside from nicotine, the most frequently used substances are alcohol, cannabis (marijuana,) and cocaine. Despite the health hazards, 50 to 90 percent of people with schizophrenia also smoke cigarettes.

In persons with schizophrenia, risk factors for developing SUD are younger age, male gender, earlier onset of the disease, and lower level of negative symptoms. Persons with comorbid schizophrenia and SUD have worsening signs of illness, including deteriorating function over time, reduced memory and attention, decreased adherence to medications, higher rates of relapse, increased frequency of hospitalizations, decreased employment opportunities, and increased rates of homelessness.

Integrated treatment in which the substance abuse and schizophrenia are treated simultaneously is recommended for persons with a dual diagnosis. Of the atypical antipsychotic agents, clozapine has been the drug more thoroughly studied for use in dual diagnosis. The drug has been shown to reduce psychotic symptoms seen in both schizophrenia and substance abuse and to reduce rates of substance abuse.

The reasons for the comorbidity between schizophrenia and substance abuse are not entirely understood, but there is growing evidence that this comorbidity is caused by disturbances in signaling pathways involved in the brain's rewards system. The dopamine system is involved in several brain functions, including attention, executive function, working memory, and reward mechanisms, and it has been studied extensively for its role in schizophrenia, psychosis, and substance abuse.

The basis for the dopamine theory in schizophrenia is that the manifestation of psychosis arises from imbalances in dopaminergic neuronal pathways, evidenced by increased dopamine production and release observed in the brains of unmedicated patients during a psychotic episode. Dysfunction in the regulation of dopamine levels and signal transduction of dopamine receptors causes excess release of dopamine, which is thought to be the primary trigger of schizophrenic psychosis.

The role of the dopamine system in addiction has been clearly demonstrated. One function of the dopaminergic neuronal pathway is to connect the nucleus accumbens (NAC), a collection of neurons in the basal forebrain, with the ventral tegmental area (VTA), a brain structure involved in reward mechanisms and motivation. Most psychotropic drugs increase dopamine levels in the NAC and appear to transmit the rewarding effects of the drug by activating dopamine cells in the VTA, especially on initial use. This intensifies the motivation for repeated use and fosters addiction.

Another connection between schizophrenia and SUD is incentive salience, a concept initially used in the context of drug addiction and later applied to schizophrenic psychosis to describe a person's motivational state in regard to a particular experience. Medical experts hypothesized that dopamine mediates the attribution of incentive salience to conditioned cues that predict reward, and that dopamine activation appears to be sufficient to enhance cue-triggered incentive salience. In schizophrenia, dopaminergic neurons attribute incentive salience to irrelevant stimuli, indicating that the attribution of salience to reward-predicting stimuli is impaired and that this dysfunction contributes to delusion formation.

However, it is now known that, although dopamine is necessary for normal wanting, dopamine release is not directly rewarding but reflects more of an error in reward prediction. In other words, when the actual reward exceeds predicted reward, the positive difference between the two is reflected in increased dopamine firing. Conversely, dopamine firing is reduced when expectations are higher than outcomes. When the difference is zero (actual and expected reward are the same), no dopamine is released, indicating that it is independent of "consuming" the reward.

Schizophrenia is a life-long disorder with a high burden of illness, compounded by the great emotional toll it has on patients, families, and communities. Schizophrenia accounts for more than 2.5 percent of all medical expenditures (about $50 billion per year) and about 50 percent of all occupied beds in mental hospitals. Added to these burdens is the tendency for patients with schizophrenia to use and become addicted to substances of abuse.

Barbara Woldin, BS

FURTHER READING

Brunette, Mary F., Douglas L. Noordsy, and Alan I. Green. "Co-Occurring Substance Use and Other Psychiatric Disorders." *Essentials of Schizophrenia.* Eds. Jeffrey A. Lieberman, T. Scott Stroup, and Diana O. Perkins. Washington, DC: American Psychiatric Association, 2012. This chapter examines substance use by persons with schizophrenia. Part of an academic resource for advanced students and clinicians.

Katz, Brooke. *I Think I Scared Her: Growing Up with Psychosis.* Bloomington, IN: Xlibris, 2004. Author describes her experiences with psychosis and how she finds treatment; insightful for parents struggling with a child diagnosed with schizophrenia.

Miller, Rachel, and Susan Elizabeth Mason, eds. *Diagnosis: Schizophrenia.* New York: Columbia UP, 2002. Recounts personal stories of thirty-five persons with schizophrenia who describe how it feels to have the disease. Book was reviewed by a panel of experts.

Mueser, Kim T., and Susan Gingerich. *The Complete Family Guide to Schizophrenia: Helping Your Loved One Get the Most Out of Life.* New York: Guilford, 2006. Guides readers through treatment and support options and provides guidance on family issues, substance abuse, psychosis, and more.

Wagner, Pamela Spiro, and Carolyn Spiro. *Divided Minds: Twin Sisters and Their Journey through Schizophrenia.* New York: St. Martin's, 2005. Memoir written in alternating voices by identical, middle-aged twins, about their lives, mental breakdowns, and hospitalizations in the face of schizophrenia.

WEBSITES OF INTEREST

CNS Spectrums
http://www.cnsspectrums.com/aspx/diseasestates.aspx

National Institute of Mental Heath
http://www.nimh.nih.gov/health/topics/schizophrenia

PsychCentral.com
http://psychcentral.com/disorders/schizophrenia

Schizophrenia.com
http://www.schizophrenia.com

See also: Anhedonia; Mental illness; Psychosis and substance abuse

---

Schools and substance abuse

CATEGORY: Social issues

DEFINITION: The prevalence of drug abuse among middle and high school students in the United States is rooted in societal, behavioral, and psychological causes. Because data about drug and alcohol abuse vary so disparately across generations, particular substances, and communities, the problem continues to defy simple explanation.

SUBSTANCE ABUSE PREVALENCE

According to findings made by the American Academy of Child and Adolescent Psychiatry in 2008, children in the United States begin to experiment with drugs and alcohol as early as age twelve. Marijuana, cocaine, and opiates are among the most commonly used drugs by middle and high school students.

Experimental or recreational drug and alcohol use has long been considered a cultural rite of passage or inevitable societal precursor to adulthood in the United States. The continued prevalence of drug and alcohol abuse among young children and teenagers, however, has long been considered developmentally problematic and wrought with potential negative long-term consequences.

The National Institute on Drug Abuse (NIDA) reports that as of 2009 more than 20 percent of American high school students had used marijuana and more than one-half had used alcohol on a recreational basis. Use of the psychoactive drug ecstasy rose 3 percent among eighth grade students between 2009 and 2010. Nonmedical use of prescription drugs such as OxyContin, Vicodin, and Adderall and of over-the-counter cough and cold medicines also has risen significantly since about the year 2000, according to NIDA studies.

CAUSES

Schools and their surrounding communities are often criticized when the potential causes of teenage substance abuse are examined by parents, medical professionals, and sociologists. This is to be expected because of the long tradition of collecting drug use data through in-school surveys, coupled with positive and negative peer influences.

Despite the long association between drug use and educational institutions, contemporary data on the influences that lead to substance abuse among school children illustrate that the reasons may be far more personal and individualized. Researchers have also begun to deconstruct many long-held truisms surrounding the connection between substance abuse and educational performance to unveil a more complex relationship.

According to a leading drug-abuse prevention resource, The Partnership at Drugfree.org, the outside influences affecting teenage drug and alcohol abuse are many, and they do not stop at peer pressure. Popular media and adult influences are two major factors in a teen's decision to experiment with drugs and alcohol. Drug and alcohol abuse has proven to be higher among groups of students who have more exposure to the widespread use of drugs and alcohol in R-rated films, according to DrugFree.org research.

The notion that drug and alcohol use is an expected, temporary, and easily escapable episode in the lives of American teenagers has been trumpeted in American film, music, and literature for decades. A landmark 1999 study by the Office of National Drug Control Policy (ONDCP) showed that of two hundred contemporary films surveyed, 93 percent depicted alcohol use and 51 percent depicted marijuana use.

Frequent exposure to drugs and alcohol and lax attitudes on the use of such substances by parental figures, older siblings, and other family members also influence teenagers' decisions to abuse substances. Familial influence runs parallel to the misinformation perpetuated through society about the dangers of drug and alcohol abuse. Despite decades of scientific evidence to the contrary, many American teenagers simply do not regard short-term or occasional substance abuse as dangerous or wrought with negative long-term consequences.

While researchers have often noted the use of illicit substances as an act of teenage rebellion, new findings also attribute boredom and a search for instant gratification as potential influences. Similarly, many children revert to the use and abuse of illicit substances simply to find common ground with their peers outside institutionalized or supervised environments.

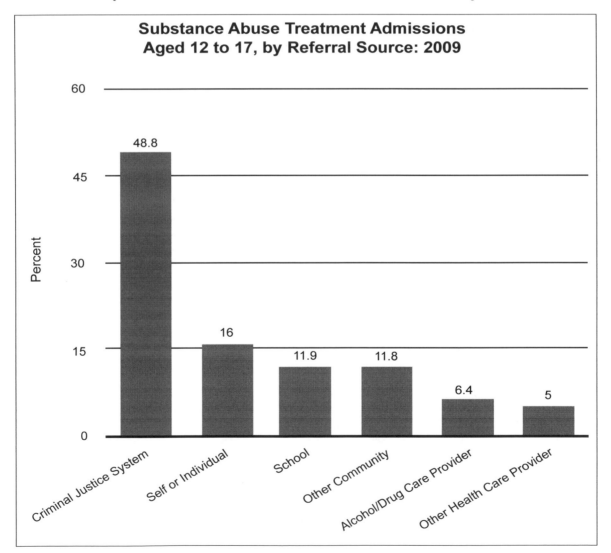

Source: Substance Abuse & Mental Health Services Administration

LONG-TERM EFFECTS

Teenage substance abuse has both short- and long-term negative consequences. The physiological and mental health consequences of substance abuse are particularly harmful to young people, negatively affecting concentration, learning, and social development. Studies have long shown that substance abuse can lead to truancy and legal problems, which hamper educational progress.

Data from the Office of Juvenile Justice and Delinquency Prevention, however, indicate that not all young people who partake in substance abuse have extended absences from school or serious legal consequences. While many students prone to substance abuse remain physically present in the classroom, their valuation of and commitment to education can often wane. Such students simply go through the motions of participation, which results in underachievement and underappreciation of academic development.

Depression, apathy, and psychosocial dysfunctions are the most common problems associated with alcohol abuse among young people and adolescents. The US Department of Health and Human Services reports that alcohol is a major contributor to fatal injury, which is the leading cause of death for Americans younger than age twenty-one years. Adulthood alcohol dependence is five times more likely in persons who report that their first use of alcohol was before the age of fifteen years.

Similarly, teenage abuse of illicit drugs causes considerable damage to a person's ability to successfully transition to adulthood. Symptoms include psychosomatic impairment such as stress disorders, impaired romantic attachments, and improper or unbalanced emotional functioning. Such impairments can lead to difficulty in building interpersonal and professional relationships.

Significant teenage drug abuse, namely the type that occurs with a frequency beyond the norms of occasional experimentation, can set the stage for difficulties in social-psychological functioning in adulthood. These malfunctions include poor impulse control; defiance toward social, personal, and professional expectations; and introversion and depression.

METHODS OF PREVENTION

Since the mid-twentieth century, a number of programs have attempted to educate youth about the dangers of drug and alcohol abuse. Such programs have been designed at the local, state, and federal level and have had varying degrees of success.

Former US first lady Nancy Reagan's Just Say No campaign was one of the first antidrug campaigns in the United States at the nationwide level. The program led to the founding of more than ten thousand Just Say No clubs nationwide. Cocaine use by high school seniors dropped to decade-low rates during the campaign's height in the mid-1980s. The effectiveness of the campaign, however, dwindled in the years after the Reagan Administration.

Los Angeles Police Department chief Daryl F. Gates initiated the Drug Abuse Resistance Education (D.A.R.E.) program in California schools in 1983. The program grew throughout the 1980s and early 1990s to become the most widely implemented youth substance-abuse prevention program in US history. However, D.A.R.E.'s enormous popularity ultimately proved overblown. By 2001 the program's ineffectiveness in preventing teenage substance abuse led US surgeon general David Satcher to deem the program a failure, and all federal support for the program was ended.

The failure of school-based campaigns has given rise to new strategies to combat school-age substance abuse among American youth. Organizations such as The Partnership at Drugfree.org and the National Youth Anti-Drug Media Campaign have designed programs aimed at altering individual decision-making at the home level.

The ONDCP's Above the Influence campaign has begun to show success, according to sociological studies. A 2011 study in the journal *Prevention Science* showed that students exposed to the advertising-style Above the Influence campaign were less likely to begin recreational marijuana use than those who had not seen the campaign's message.

It remains the hope of substance-abuse professionals and contemporary antidrug programs that parents who have experienced the internal and external pressures to experiment with drugs and alcohol during adolescence will act as a trusted resource to their own children. Parents can do this by presenting to their teen children the alternatives and by discussing the numerous potential long-term consequences of substance use and abuse.

John Pritchard

FURTHER READING

Bachman, Jerald, et al. *The Education-Drug Use Connection: How Successes and Failures in School Relate to Adolescent Smoking, Drinking, Drug Use, and Delinquency.* New York: Erlbaum, 2008.

Bonnie, E. D. *Reducing Underage Drinking: A Collective Responsibility.* Washington, DC: National Academies, 2004.

Cohen, Donald. *Developmental Psychopathology, Risk, Disorder, and Adaptation.* Indianapolis: Wiley, 2006.

Franklin, Cynthia, Mary Beth Harris, and Paula Allen-Meares, eds. *The School Services Sourcebook : A Guide for School-Based Professionals.* New York: Oxford UP, 2006.

Hanson, Glen R., Peter J. Venturelli, and Annette E. Fleckenstein. *Drugs and Society.* 11th ed. Sudbury, MA: Jones, 2012.

WEBSITES OF INTEREST

Above the Influence
http://www.abovetheinfluence.com

American Academy of Child and Adolescent Psychiatry
http://aacap.org/cs/root/facts_for_families/facts_for_families

Partnership at DrugFree.org
http://parent.drugfree.org/UnderstandingTeens/Articles/Why_Teens_Try_Alcohol_and_Drugs.aspx

National Institute on Drug Abuse
http://www.drugabuse.gov/publications/infofacts/high-school-youth-trends

Office of Juvenile Justice and Delinquency Prevention
http://www.ojjdp.gov/pubs/drugid/ration-03.html

TeenDrugAbuse.us
http://www.teendrugabuse.us/overindulgent_parents.html

See also: College and substance abuse; Education about substance abuse; Safe and drug-free schools; Teens/young adults and alcohol abuse; Teens/young adults and drug abuse; Teens/young adults and smoking

Science of addiction

Category: Health issues and physiology

Definition: Neuroscientists define addiction as a chronic, relapsing brain disease. Addiction is considered a brain disease because it alters the brain's structure and chemistry in fundamental, long-lasting ways.

STAGES OF ADDICTION

There are three related stages in addiction: acute drug effect, transition to addiction, and end stage addiction. In the early stage, the individual experiences the rewarding effects of the addictive drug. Dopamine is the key brain chemical involved at this stage. At the second stage, the individual transitions from recreational use to addiction. Glutamine is the key brain chemical involved at this stage. At the third and final stage, the individual experiences a strong urge to obtain the addictive drug, loses control of the drug-seeking desire, and experiences a diminished pleasure after using the addictive drug, requiring larger and more frequent dosing to achieve the same initial effects.

Scientists have worked out the two major pathways in the brain responsible for addiction. First, there is the mesolimbic pathway mediated by dopamine. Second, the prefrontal cortex, the decision-making center, is responsible for controlling any inappropriate reward responses. Drug addiction can lead to physical changes in these pathways.

Neuro-imaging techniques, such as PET scans and MRIs, have documented changes in the size and shape of nerve cells in the brains of addicts. Networks of nerve cells determine a person's feelings and behavior. Drugs influence behavior by transforming the way these networks function.

THE DOPAMINE CONNECTION

The biological link among all addictions is dopamine. This brain chemical is released during pleasurable activities, ranging from sex to eating, to more detrimental behaviors such as drinking and taking drugs. A powerful drug like crack cocaine elevates dopamine levels much faster than normal pleasurable activities. It creates the classic drug-induced feelings of exhilaration and power. In a landmark 1950s experiment, scientists stimulated rodent brains and found that the animals kept returning to the place where they received the stimulation.

Coming down from a drug high is caused by a decrease in dopamine levels. If a person's brain cells produce excessive dopamine on a regular basis, such as through repeated exposure to an addictive substance, the cells adjust to the unnaturally elevated levels of dopamine in the brain and begin to produce less dopamine. Over time, addicts need drugs just to stimulate dopamine to normal levels. They become trapped in a cycle of cravings and addiction to avoid withdrawal symptoms and depression. It is believed that once a person crosses the line from user to addict, the brain is so changed that he or she can no longer control his or her behavior.

This transformation helps to explain why it is so difficult to break an addiction. Cravings are more significant than physical withdrawal in keeping an addict hooked. Drugs like cocaine and methamphetamine, unlike heroin and alcohol, do not produce intense physical withdrawal symptoms, but they do produce powerful

psychological symptoms, including overwhelming cravings. These cravings can be aroused by external or internal stimuli that are as innocuous as walking by a pub or feeling sad.

AN ADDICTIVE PERSONALITY?

Many addiction professionals believe that addiction stems from a combination of biological, psychological, and environmental factors. Many support groups for addictions recovery also follow this belief. For example, Alcoholics Anonymous describes alcoholism as a physical, emotional, and spiritual disease.

The progression to addiction can develop in this way: A person may have a genetic or biological predisposition to an addiction. If he or she grows up in a family and environment without addiction or stress, he or she may never begin casual use. However, if the person grows up in a stressful environment where substance abuse is common and encounters more stressors over time, he or she may begin casual use and, because of the permanent changes in the brain caused by repeated drug use, become a full-blown addict.

Children of alcoholics are at a higher risk of becoming alcoholics themselves than the children of nonalcoholics. Scientists are also studying whether addicts are born with inadequate endorphins, the brain chemicals that regulate stress.

NEW TREATMENTS

For years, heroin and narcotics addictions have been treated successfully with methadone, which eases withdrawal and blocks the effect of drugs. Naltrexone is another drug commonly used for alcohol and narcotics addiction. Another drug, buprenorphine, has shown promising results in treating narcotics addicts. Useful for detoxification, buprenorphine (usually combined with naltrexone) can also be used for maintenance therapy. Buprenorphine can be prescribed by psychiatrists and other doctors who have received special training. Methadone, in contrast, can only be dispensed from a specially-licensed clinic.

It is unlikely that a magic pill will be found that "cures" addiction. On the other hand, aerobic exercise offers a simple and natural way to help combat addiction. During aerobic exercise, dopamine levels increase in the areas of the brain involved with addiction, and feelings of depression and anxiety decrease.

Elaine Gottlieb

Diagnosing Addiction

You may have a problem with drugs or alcohol if you:

- cannot predict whether or not you will use drugs or get drunk

- believe that you need to drink or use drugs to have fun

- turn to alcohol or drugs after a confrontation or argument or to relieve uncomfortable feelings

- need to drink more or use more drugs to get the same effect that you used to get

- drink or use drugs by yourself

- have periods of memory loss

- have trouble at work, in school, or in your personal relationships because of drinking or using drugs

- make promises to yourself or others that you will stop getting drunk or using drugs but are unable to keep those promises

- feel alone, scared, miserable, and depressed

Adapted from "Just the Facts," from the US Substance Abuse and Mental Health Services Administration.

FURTHER READING

DiClemente, Carlo C. *Addiction and Change: How Addictions Develop and Addicted People Recover*. New York: Guilford Press, 2003. Describes the common features of addictive behavior, broadly defined, and discusses the development of and recovery from addictions as a stage theory.

Erickson, Carlton. *The Science of Addiction: From Neurobiology to Treatment*. New York: W. W. Norton, 2006. A reference for anyone in the field of addiction medicine. Provides a neurobiological perspective on addiction that can be understood by lay people.

Hart, Carl L., Charles Ksir, and Oakley Ray. *Drugs, Society and Human Behavior*. 12th ed. Boston: McGraw-Hill-Hill, 2006. An easy to read, entry-level textbook on substances of abuse.

Schaler, Jeffrey. *Addiction Is a Choice*. Peru, Il: Carus Publishing Company, 2000. This book provides a life-process model of addiction point of view. The author describes addiction as a choice rather than a disease.

WEBSITES OF INTEREST

National Institute on Drug Abuse
http://www.nida.nih.gov/

The Substance Abuse and Mental Health Services Administration
http:// samhsa.gov/

See also: Addiction; Addictive personality; Brain changes with addiction; Dopamine and addiction; Drug interactions; Genetics and substance abuse; Models of addiction; Psychological dependence; Psychosis and substance abuse

Screening for behavioral addiction

CATEGORY: Diagnosis and prevention

DEFINITION: Screening for behavioral addiction is a process in which mental health professionals determine whether a person is likely to engage in or does engage in problem behaviors to the point of addiction. Screening shows if a person may need further help for addictive behavior problems.

INTRODUCTION

Behavioral addictions are patterns of behavior that follow a cycle similar to that of chemical addiction. Persons addicted to certain behaviors, such as gambling, exercising, computer gaming, Internet use, shopping, eating, or sexual activity, crave the activity and engage in that activity at the risk of causing problems in important life areas.

Behavioral addicts often recognize that their actions are causing a problem, but as with any addiction, they find the behavior impossible to control. Behavior addiction can be socially and psychologically damaging, rivaling substance addiction in the ability to cause havoc in family structure. However, behavioral addictions are often overlooked, even though its markers are similar to those of substance addiction.

Many health care professionals believe that addiction in one area is indicative of addictive tendencies in general, and persons who have these tendencies are likely to exhibit addictive behavior in many areas of life. Thus, substance abuse and behavioral abuse often go hand-in-hand, and screening for one type of addiction should include screening for all types.

RISK ASSESSMENT SCREEN

A diagnosis of substance addiction is often fairly clear. However, behavioral addiction is a much harder diagnosis for a professional to make. Often, this type of addiction is overlooked even though it coexists with substance addiction.

Clinical psychologist James Slobodzien introduced a tool called behavior risk assessment screen (BRAS) for professionals to use when they suspect addictive behavior. This tool screens for addictive behavior in seven areas: substance intake (nicotine, alcohol, illicit drugs, caffeine), eating attitude, exercise patterns, sleep patterns, sexual practice, gambling practices, and risky behaviors (impulsive behaviors with negative consequences such as reckless driving and starting fires).

Each of the seven areas includes two or three statements read by the tested subject. The subject then decides which of the statements best describes his or her behavior. Each statement is then given a standardized weighted classification, and the number of points is totaled for a cumulative score called a prognostic assessment gauge score, which ranges from 0 to 100.

This score is further broken into twenty-point categories ranging from excellent (80–100), good (60–80), fair (40–60), poor (20–40), and guarded (0–20). These point categories characterize how well the subject is coping with addictive behavior. The final score represents a person's overall psychological, social, and occupational function and is comparable to a global assessment of functioning score (part of the *Diagnostic and Statistical Manual of Mental Disorders*).

CAGE ASSESSMENT TOOL

The CAGE assessment tool screens for alcohol abuse. However, because it attempts to identify addictive behaviors, this simple tool is used by many providers as a basis for any type of addiction, including behavioral addictions, by substituting the type of addictive behavior for the term *drinking* in the questions.

The screen consists of four questions: Have you felt the need to cut down on your drinking? Do you feel annoyed or angered by others' criticism of your drinking? Have you ever felt guilty about your drinking? And do you need to drink soon after waking as an eye-opener?

In using this tool to screen for behavioral addiction, two additional questions have been suggested to form the acronym "CAGED": Do you feel empty when you're not (for example) eating or gambling? Does (for example) eating or gambling disrupt your life or are you neglecting parts of your life because of it? These two additional questions may help pinpoint and further define behavioral addiction. Addictive tendencies may be a concern if the person being screened answers "yes" to two or more of the questions.

SCREENING FOR SPECIFIC BEHAVIOR ADDICTIONS

The BRAS and CAGE or CAGED assessments can give an idea of whether a person has addictive tendencies, including both behavioral and substance addictive tendencies. However, each type of addictive behavior has specific, though similar, screening instruments to determine whether the screening subject has that specific behavior addiction. Some examples follow.

Gambling. The LIE/BET screening for gambling consists of two questions: Have you ever had to lie to people important to you about how much you gambled? Have you ever felt a need to bet more money? A "yes" answer to either question would indicate that a person should be evaluated further. The South Oaks gambling screen is more complex, with sixteen questions (and several subquestions) rating the behavior of the person being screened. The questions are answered with the terms *not at all, less than once a week,* or *once a week or more.* This screening tool asks questions about the amounts of money used in gambling, family or friends who gamble, and several more related to gambling behavior. Answers to these questions are then weighted and scored, with a score of 5 or more indicating problem behavior. Gamblers Anonymous also has a twenty-question screening tool; seven or more yes answers means the person is likely to be a compulsive gambler.

Sexual activity. The WASTE Time tool is a quick screening for sex addiction. This tool assesses functional indicators such as withdrawal, adverse consequences, inability to stop, tolerance or intensity, and escape, with time spent on sexual activity being the final element of the screen. Answering "yes" to even one of the screening questions indicates a possible problem; answering "yes" to two or more questions indicates a high probability of sex addiction. Another screening for sexual addiction is the sexual addiction screening test, which consists of forty-five questions. Answering "yes" to more than seven of the first twenty questions indicates a sexual addiction, while the rest of the questions are intended to help pinpoint the problem's manifestations.

Eating disorders. EAT-26 is a common screening tool to assess eating behavior addictions such as overeating, anorexia nervosa, or bulimia nervosa. The tool consists of personal-information questions that assess attitudes about ideal weight, with twenty-six yes/no questions, and six behavioral questions. Items are scored on a scale of 1 to 3; if the total score is above 20, further help may be needed. However, even a score of less than 19 may refer a person for further help if binging or purging behavior is indicated by the screening.

Internet use. The Internet addiction test may be used as a screening tool for Internet addiction. The test screens with twenty questions that are rated on a scale using the terms *does not apply* or *rarely to always.* Each question is scored, and a total score is assigned (between 0 and 100). These scores are broken into ranges of 0–19 (below average), 20–49 (average), 50–79 (above average), and 80–100 (significantly above average). A score of 80 or above is cause for referral for further help.

Work. The work addiction risk test consists of twenty-five questions pertaining to attitudes toward work and to related behaviors in particular and life in general. The person being screened answers each question on a scale of 1 to 4, with 1 representing "never true" and 4 representing "always true." The numbers are then added into a total score, in which 25–54 represents "not work addicted," 55–69 represents "mildly work addicted," and 70–100 represents "highly work addicted."

Marianne M. Madsen, MS

FURTHER READING

Crozier, Mary K., and Steven R. Sligar. "Behavioral Addiction Screening during the Vocational Evaluation Process." *Vocational Evaluation and Work Adjustment Association Journal* 37 (2010): 45–57. Print. Provides basic information about screening for behavioral addiction, particularly as it relates to job performance. Defines and identifies behavioral addiction indicators.

Freimuth, Marilyn. "The 'New Look' in Addiction Assessment: Implications for Medical Education." *Annals of Behavioral Science and Medical Education* 16.1 (2010): 30–34. Print. Argues that to provide a well-rounded assessment of addictive behavior, medical health professionals need to screen for behavioral addiction and substance addiction.

Whitlock, Evelyn, et al. "Evaluating Primary Care Behavioral Counseling Interventions: An Evidence-Based Approach." *American Journal of Preventive Medicine* 22.4 (2002): 267–84. Print. Discusses studies showing that screening for behavioral addictions results in better health care outcomes for subjects engaging in such behaviors or in other types of addictive behaviors.

WEBSITES OF INTEREST

American Psychological Association
http://www.apa.org

Center for Internet Addiction Recovery
http://www.netaddiction.com

Gamblers Anonymous
http://www.gamblersanonymous.org

International Institute of Trauma and Addiction Professionals
http://www.sexhelp.com/sast.cfm

See also: Behavioral addictions: Treatment; Diagnosis methods; Gambling addiction; Gaming addiction; Internet addiction; Prevention methods and research; Risk factors for addiction; Sex addiction; Work addiction

Secondhand smoke

CATEGORY: Health issues and physiology
ALSO KNOWN AS: Environmental tobacco smoke; involuntary smoke; passive smoke; tobacco smoke pollution
DEFINITION: Secondhand smoke is a combination of two types of exposure to tobacco smoke in the environment: mainstream and sidestream. Mainstream smoke involves exposure to smoke that has been exhaled by a smoker. Sidestream smoke is that smoke emitted from a lit tobacco product, such as a cigarette, cigar, or pipe. Sidestream smoke is the more dangerous of the two because it contains a much larger concentration of cancer-causing (carcinogenic) and toxic agents, which are small enough to easily enter the body and damage a variety of cells.

HEALTH EFFECTS

The effects of secondhand smoke on persons who share an environment with smokers are similar to the effects on smokers themselves. In 2006, US Surgeon General Richard Carmona issued a statement on secondhand smoke that concluded that both children and adults who have never smoked can get sick and die as a result of exposure to secondhand smoke.

Secondhand smoke is categorized as a type A carcinogen, meaning there is strong evidence of its cancer-causing effects in human beings. Cancer is only one of the effects that secondhand smoke can have on the body. Secondhand smoke also has been found to increase the incidence of heart disease, respiratory infections (such as bronchitis, pneumonitis, and pneumonia), asthma, middle ear infections, and sudden infant death syndrome, among other disorders. Even brief exposure to secondhand smoke can damage the lining of blood vessels and cause clumping of platelets, both of which can result in heart disease.

Secondhand Smoke

Even for persons who do not smoke, exposure to tobacco smoke is dangerous. Consider the following:

- Secondhand smoke causes disease and premature death in children and adults who do not smoke.

- Children exposed to secondhand smoke are at risk for sudden infant death syndrome, lung infections, ear problems, and severe asthma.

- Being exposed to secondhand smoke while pregnant can increase the risk of stillbirth and birth disorders and defects.

- Parents who smoke can cause breathing problems and slow lung-growth in their children.

- Secondhand smoke affects the heart and causes coronary heart disease and lung cancer in adults.

TOXINS

Smoke (whether primary or secondhand) consists of several thousand different chemicals, hundreds of which are toxic and more than fifty of which are known to be carcinogenic. Toxins that are found in secondhand smoke include formaldehyde, benzene, vinyl chloride, carbon monoxide, hydrogen cyanide, butane, ammonia, arsenic, and lead. These toxins can directly and indirectly affect almost any organ in the body. According to most research, any exposure to secondhand smoke can be harmful, even minimum exposure.

Studies indicate that the greatest amount of secondhand smoke exposure takes place in enclosed spaces, such as in the home or in vehicles. The US Environmental Protection Agency has urged people who smoke to refrain from doing so in their homes or automobiles.

Robin Kamienny Montvilo, PhD

FURTHER READING

Barnoya, Joaquin, and Stanton A. Glantz. "Cardiovascular Effects of Secondhand Smoke: Nearly as Large as Smoking." *Circulation* 111 (2005): 2684–98. Print. Describes the dangers of secondhand smoke exposure to cardiovascular health.

Glantz, Stanton A., and William W. Parmley. "Even a Little Secondhand Smoke Is Dangerous." *Journal of the American Medical Association* 286 (2001): 462–63. Print. Provides information regarding the damage to the body caused by secondhand smoke.

Parker, Philip M., and James N. Parker, eds. *Second-Hand Smoke: A Medical Dictionary, Bibliography, and Annotated Research Guide to Internet References.* San Diego, CA: Icon Health, 2004. An informative medical dictionary providing detailed information on the properties and effects of secondhand smoke.

WEBSITES OF INTEREST

Mayo Clinic
http://www.mayoclinic.com/health/secondhand-smoke/CC00023

Medline Plus: Secondhand Smoke
http://www.nlm.nih.gov/medlineplus/second-handsmoke.html

National Cancer Institute
http://www.cancer.gov/cancertopics/factsheet/Tobacco/ETS

US Environmental Protection Agency
http://www.epa.gov/smokefree/healtheffects.html

See also: Cancer and substance abuse; Respiratory diseases and smoking; Smoking; Smoking: Short- and long-term effects on the body; Tobacco use disorder

Sedative-hypnotic abuse

CATEGORY: Substance abuse

ALSO KNOWN AS: Barbiturates (barbs, block busters, Christmas trees, goof balls, Mexican yellows, pinks, purple hearts, red devils, yellow jackets); BDZs (benzodiazepine, benzos, downers, Mexican Valium, rope, wolfies); NB-NBDZs (methaqualone, ludes, sopors)

DEFINITION: Barbiturates, BDZs, and NB-NBDZs are groups of drugs within the class known as sedative-hypnotics or central nervous system depressants. This class has sleep-inducing and anxiety-decreasing (sedative, tranquillizing) effects because of its capacity to enhance the effects of gamma-amino-butyric acid, the most prominent inhibitory neurotransmitter in the central nervous system.

STATUS: Prescription-only drugs accepted for medical use worldwide

CLASSIFICATION: Barbiturates are schedule II to IV controlled substances; BDZs and some NB-NBDZs (such as zolpidem, zopiclone, chloral hydrate, paraldehyde, meprobamate) are controlled in schedule IV; glutethimide (originally a schedule III drug) was upgraded to schedule II; methaqualone and gamma-hydroxybutyric acid are schedule I controlled substances in the United States

SOURCE: Legally available through prescription; illegally purchased without a prescription

TRANSMISSION ROUTE: Ingestion; intravenous and intramuscular administration; suppository

HISTORY OF USE

Bromide, the first sedative-hypnotic, originated in 1838 and was followed by chloral hydrate, paraldehyde, and barbiturates. Bromide compounds were frequently used as sedatives and anticonvulsants in the nineteenth and early twentieth century.

Barbiturates were first introduced for medical use in the early twentieth century. Since then, approximately fifty barbiturates were marketed but less than fifteen remain in medical use. Barbiturates became popular in the 1960s as treatment for anxiety, insomnia, and seizure disorders, but the dependence-producing potential and the dangers of overdose restricted their use significantly. Since the 1970s, barbiturates were largely replaced by the safer BDZ group.

The first BDZs, chlordiazepoxide and diazepam, were introduced in clinical practice in the early 1960s. Although more than two thousand different BDZs have been synthesized, less than twenty are currently approved in the United States. BDZ usage increased dramatically in the 1970s, with total sales accounting for about 10 percent of all prescriptions in many Western countries. The perceived desirable properties of anxiety alleviation, euphoria, disinhibition, and sleep promotion have led to the compulsive misuse of virtually all of the drugs classed as sedative-hypnotics.

EFFECTS AND POTENTIAL RISKS

Graded, dose-dependent depression of the central nervous system (CNS) function is characteristic of sedative-hypnotics. At low doses, they produce sedation (relieving anxiety and promoting relaxation), whereas at higher doses they have a hypnotic effect.

Barbiturates

Barbiturates are classified three ways. Those three ways, and the associated barbiturate, are ultrashort-acting methohexital (Brevital), thiamyl (Surital), and thiopental (Pentothal); short- and intermediate-acting amobarbital (Amytal), pentobarbital (Nembutal), secobarbital (Seconal), butalbital (Fiorinal), butabarbital (Butisol), talbutal (Lotusate), and aprobarbital (Alurate); and long-acting phenobarbital (Luminal) and mephobarbital (Mebaral).

Barbiturates produce a wide spectrum of CNS depression, from mild sedation to coma, and are used as sedatives, hypnotics, anesthetics, and anticonvulsants. The ultrashort-acting barbiturates produce anesthesia within one minute of intravenous administration and are used for minor surgery or as preoperative anesthetics for major surgery. The long-acting barbiturates are used in some forms of epilepsy or to treat convulsions caused by cocaine and other stimulant drugs. Barbiturates have a narrow therapeutic index and can cause coma or death if taken inappropriately, especially in children and elderly persons.

The toxicity of barbiturates is likely when the dose exceeds five to ten times the hypnotic dose. The potentially fatal dose for phenobarbital is 6 to 10 grams, but only 2 to 3 grams for pentobarbital or secobarbital. Barbiturates also are addictive if taken daily for longer than about one month and can cause a life-threatening withdrawal syndrome upon discontinuation.

Symptoms of withdrawal include tremors, difficulty sleeping, agitation, hallucinations, high temperature, and seizures. In pregnant women barbiturates can cause dependence and newborn withdrawal syndrome. Barbiturates are commonly used in suicide attempts. Although the medical use and street abuse of barbiturates has declined since the 1970s, surveys suggest that abuse has been rising since about 2000. Barbiturates are commonly abused to counteract the symptoms of such stimulating drugs as cocaine and methamphetamine.

BDZs

BDZs (also known as minor tranquilizers) are effective in a wide range of medical and psychiatric conditions, such as anxiety and sleep disorders, panic attacks, agoraphobia, acute stress reactions, convulsive and spastic disorders, presurgical sedation, and detoxification from alcohol. They are usually classified by their duration of action, which ranges from less than six hours to more than twenty-four hours as ultra-short acting midazolam (Versed) and triazolam (Halcion); as short-acting alprazolam (Xanax), lorazepam (Ativan), estazolam (ProSom), temazepam (Restoril), and oxazepam (Serax); and as long-acting chlordiazepoxide (Librium), diazepam (Valium), clonazepam (Klonopin), flurazepam (Dalmane), and clorazepate (Tranxene).

BDZs are widely prescribed, and four of them—alprazolam, clonazepam, diazepam, and lorazepam—are among the top forty prescription medications sold. Alprazolam and diazepam are the two most frequently encountered BDZs on the illicit market.

Signs and symptoms of acute toxicity or overdose may include drowsiness, confusion, dizziness, blurred vision, weakness, slurred speech, lack of coordination, difficulty breathing, and coma. Fatal overdoses usually involve the combination of BDZ and alcohol. When used chronically, for longer than four to eight weeks, BDZ can be addicting. BDZ, particularly those having a rapid onset—the highly lipophilic (such as diazepam) and the short-acting/high-potency BDZ (such as alprazolam or lorazepam)—are the most reinforcing and, therefore, most likely to be associated with abuse. They are used recreationally to induce relaxation and are abused to produce a euphoric effect.

BDZ also are used to augment alcohol's effects and to manage withdrawal states. BDZ have a relatively low potential for abuse in persons without a history of substance use disorders but moderate-to-high potential for people with a history of substance abuse or dependence.

NB-NBDZs

NB-NBDZs include chemically heterogeneous compounds that do not fall into either the barbiturate or the BDZ group. Chloral hydrate (Somnote, Aquachloral) is a fast-acting sedative-hypnotic with long-lasting effects. It had widespread use (including recreationally) in the late nineteenth century. A solution of chloral hydrate in alcohol was known as knock-out drops or Mickey Finn (a drink designed to incapacitate the person who drinks it).

Methaqualone (Quaalude) possesses sedative-hypnotic, anticonvulsant, antispasmodic, local anesthetic, antitussive, and weak antihistaminic properties. It produces a dissociative high that resembles those of opiates (heightened sensitivity and euphoria) without the drowsiness caused by barbiturates. Methaqualone became a popular recreational drug in the 1960s and 1970s. Because of its high abuse potential, methaqualone has been removed from the market in many countries. In the United States, the marketing of methaqualone stopped in 1984.

OTHER USES OF SEDATIVE-HYPNOTICS

Some of the sedative-hypnotics are used to commit sexual assaults. Because these drugs are sedating and induce a temporary amnesia, they are sometimes added to alcoholic beverages and soft drinks to incapacitate the intended victim of a rape. Flunitrazepam (Rohypnol), also known with the street names rophies, roofies, and roach, is a long-acting BDZ used as a favored sedative of abuse among adolescents and adults, and it is typically used in combination with alcohol as a party and a date rape drug.

Flunitrazepam has never been approved for medical use in the United States. Gamma-hydroxy butyrate (GHB), a natural CNS depressant resulting from the metabolism of the inhibitory neurotransmitter GABA, has emerged as a significant drug of abuse. It gained popularity for recreational use because of its pleasant, alcohol-like, hangover-free high with aphrodisiac properties.

Body-builders abuse GHB for its alleged utility as an anabolic agent. GHB is often taken by young polydrug abusers (who are called clubbers and ravers) in combination with amphetamines to produce euphoria and a hallucinatory state. Because of concerns about GHB abuse and date rape usage, in 2000 this drug was made a schedule I controlled substance. Because flunitrazepam and GHB are illegal in the United States, they are available only through the underground market.

Those who chronically abuse sedative-hypnotics prefer the short-acting barbiturates, the barbiturate-like depressants glutethimide and methaqualone, and the faster-acting BDZs diazepam, alprazolam, and lorazepam. Persons who abuse sedative-hypnotics are most likely to be those who use drugs to relieve stress; who use drugs to counteract unpleasant effects of other drugs of abuse; and who combine CNS depressants with alcohol or opiates to potentiate their effects.

Significant safety concerns with sedative-hypnotics include important drug interactions (for example, the inhibitors of drug metabolism such as antifungals, erythromycin, clarithromycin, or cimetidine significantly prolong their effect and increase their toxicity) and their appropriate use in special populations (elderly people, pregnant women, and persons with a history of substance abuse). Overdosing on sedative-hypnotics is among the most common methods for attempting suicide.

Katia Marazova, MD, PhD

FURTHER READING

Hanson, Glen R., Peter J. Venturelli, and Annette E. Fleckenstein. *Drugs and Society*. 11th ed. Sudbury, MA: Jones, 2012. Written by prominent experts in the field of pharmacology, toxicology, neuroscience, and neurochemistry of drug abuse. Provides updated information on a broad range of topics related to drug use, dependence, and abuse.

Lader, Malcolm. "History of Benzodiazepine Dependence." *Journal of Substance Abuse Treatment* 8.1–2 (1991): 53–59. Print. Review article on the history of sedative-hypnotics written by an expert in the field of psychopharmacology. Examines benzodiazepine dependence.

O'Brien, Charles P. "Benzodiazepine Use, Abuse, and Dependence." *Journal of Clinical Psychiatry* 66, suppl. 2 (2005): 28–33. Print. Provides an overview of the abuse potential of benzodiazepines. Discusses withdrawal syndrome and clinical options for discontinuing benzodiazepine treatment.

Posternak, M. A., and T. I. Mueller. "Assessing the Risks and Benefits of Benzodiazepines for Anxiety Disorders in Patients with a History of Substance Abuse or Dependence." *American Journal on Addictions* 10.1 (2001): 48–68. Print. This review article is based on a MEDLINE search to examine the English-language literature on benzodiazepines and substance abuse published between 1966 and 2001. Focuses on the efficacy of benzodiazepines in anxiety disorders and their side effects and toxicity.

WEBSITES OF INTEREST

National Institute on Drug Abuse
http://www.drugabuse.gov

US Drug Enforcement Administration
http://www.justice.gov/dea

See also: Anxiety medication abuse; Barbiturates; Benzodiazepine abuse; Date rape drugs; Depressants abuse; Sleeping pills; Soma; Temazepam

---

Self-destructive behavior and addiction

CATEGORY: Psychological issues and behaviors
DEFINITION: Self-destructive behaviors are unhealthy responses to feelings of shame and powerlessness. Substance abuse is a self-destructive behavior caused by chemical changes in the brain from drug use. Self-destructive behaviors can arise from psychological trauma that can range from birth complications to child sexual abuse to loss of self-esteem from factors such as parental unemployment or addiction, being bullied, or experiencing violence in the home.

PROGRAMMED BEHAVIOR?

The tendency toward negative thinking and self-destructive behavior might be psychologically programmed at birth. Researchers in Stockholm studied the records of 412 alcoholics, drug addicts, and persons who committed suicide to see if obstetric procedures were linked to harmful events later in life, as data from the United States seemed to indicate.

The results of the study also showed that people who committed suicide by asphyxiation had close association with asphyxia at birth; those who died by violent mechanical means had experienced a mechanical birth trauma; and people who became addicts were born to women who had been given opiates or barbiturates during labor. The research team concluded that obstetric procedures should be reexamined in light of a possible imprint for self-destructive behavior that manifests later in a person's life.

SELF-ESTEEM

Birth is only the first opportunity for the kind of psychic trauma that can put a person on a self-destructive spiral toward substance abuse or suicide. Early exposure to sexual abuse has been found to cause profound dissociation and lead to alcohol and drug abuse.

Other notable factors, such as parental unemployment, exposure to violence in the home, or being bullied at school, all can drain self-esteem, according to researchers. Being separated from parents, either physically by protective services or emotionally because of parental substance abuse, significantly increases the risk of self-destructive behavior.

SUICIDAL IDEATION

Self-destructive thoughts can lead to dangerous actions. Suicidal thoughts build along a continuum from mild self-criticism to angry self-attacks and thoughts of suicide. Self-destructive behaviors exist in parallel, on a continuum that ranges from accident proneness to drug abuse, alcoholism and other compulsions to premature death.

Substance abuse is considered the third major risk factor for suicide, behind previous suicide attempts and depression. Substance abuse is a slow form of suicide. Research has shown that people who drink heavily and use drugs die thirty years earlier, on average, than the general population.

HUMAN DRIVES

Research suggests that visceral influences—drive states such as hunger, thirst, sexual desire, emotions, physical pain, and addictive cravings—can "crowd out" a person's better intentions with the sole mission of mitigating the visceral urge. All focus turns to the moment and the drive. During binges, the thoughts of cocaine addicts, for example, are focused solely on the drug; sleep, money, survival, loved ones, and other responsibilities lose significance.

This change in focus also is evident in binge eating. Binge eaters have high standards and expectations of themselves and are acutely sensitive to the demands of others. When they feel they have fallen short of expectations, they become negatively self-conscious, resulting in emotional distress, anxiety, and depression. To escape from this painful state of being, binge eaters narrow their attention to immediate stimuli and avoid thinking on a broader level, researchers say.

GENETIC FACTORS AND ENVIRONMENTAL TRAUMA

People who suffer the sorts of trauma mentioned above and who are genetically predisposed to addiction are at the highest risk for substance abuse. Some people are more prone to substance abuse through inheritance of gene mutations such as D2A1, the dopamine receptor found in 69 percent of severe alcoholics, 40 to 55 percent of persons with post-traumatic stress disorder, and 20 percent of nonalcoholics.

Dopamine works with serotonin in areas of the brain responsible for emotion and attention. Abnormal serotonin levels in substance abusers' brains are linked to a mutation of the enzyme tryptophan oxygenase, which breaks down tryptophan.

Teenagers who receive important social supports such as family counseling after traumatic events fare better than those who are left to cope alone, whether they have the gene mutations or not. Recovery from substance abuse requires finding new pleasure-inducing activities, coping mechanisms, relaxation methods, and relapse prevention.

Laura B. Smith

FURTHER READING

Baumeister, Roy F., and Steven J. Scher. "Self-Defeating Behavior Patterns among Normal Individuals: Review and Analysis of Common Self-Destructive Tendencies." *Psychological Bulletin* 104.1 (1988): 3–22. Print. Evaluates three levels of self-destruction by reviewing twelve categories of self-defeating behavior patterns from research literature in social psychology.

Christoffersen, Mogens Nygaard. "Child Maltreatment, Bullying in School, and Social Support." 9 Apr. 2010. Web. 20 Apr. 2012. http://www.sfi. dk/publications-2773.aspx. Examines how child maltreatment influences both low self-esteem and suicidal ideation directly, but also indirectly through decreased social support and increased risk of being bullied in school.

Firestone, Robert W., and Richard H. Seiden. "Suicide and the Continuum of Self-Destructive

Behavior." *Journal of American College Health* 38.5 (1990): 207–13. Print. Provides a chart depicting increasing suicidal intent along a continuum. Understanding where a person can be placed on the continuum can assist clinicians in diagnoses and can pinpoint students at risk for suicide.

Frederick, Calvin J., Harvey L. P. Resnik, and Byron J. Wittlin. "Self-Destructive Aspects of Hard Core Addiction." *Archives of General Psychiatry* 28.4 (1973): 579–85. Print. Found that overall, heroin addicts are more depressed than the study's control group. Methadone proved helpful except when addicts abstained from taking it.

Heatherton, Todd F., and Roy Baumeister. "Binge Eating as Escape from Self-Awareness." *Psychological Bulletin* 110.1 (1991): 86–108. Print. Proposes that binge eating is motivated by a desire to escape from self-awareness.

Jacobson, Bertil, et al. "Perinatal Origin of Adult Self-Destructive Behavior." *Acta Psychiatrica Scandinavica* 76.4 (1987): 364–71. Print. Suggests that trauma at birth imprints in the brain and predicts violent outcomes in adulthood.

Rodriguez-Srednicki, Ofelia. "Childhood Sexual Abuse, Dissociation, and Adult Self-Destructive Behavior." *Journal of Child Sexual Abuse* 10.3 (2002): 75–89. Print. Associates sexual abuse in childhood with self-destructive behaviors later in life.

WEBSITES OF INTEREST

American Psychological Association
http://www.apa.org

National Child Traumatic Stress Network
http://www.nctsnet.org

National Institute of Mental Health
http://www.nimh.nih.gov

See also: Behavioral addictions: Overview; Body modification addiction; Cutting and self-mutilation; Pain addiction; Paraphilias

Self-medication

CATEGORY: Psychological issues and behaviors
DEFINITION: Self-medication involves the use of drugs to treat a health problem without the guidance of a health professional.

BACKGROUND

Humans have always treated themselves with medicines. Modern medicines include herbals, vitamins, supplements, and over-the-counter drugs. These medicines are legal, but not always controlled, substances. Self-medication also occurs with prescribed medicines, as when a person takes more or less of his or her doctor's recommended dose.

People with mental illness, such as depression or bipolar disorder, may use legal or illegal drugs as a way to relieve symptoms. Alcohol, tobacco, prescription opioids (painkillers), sedatives (sleeping pills), stimulants (energy boosters), cannabis, cocaine, and heroine are common drugs of self-medication. Although these drugs might provide temporary relief, they can increase symptoms or trigger latent problems. They also can lead to dependence or addiction.

THE SELF-MEDICATION HYPOTHESIS

In 1974, two researchers independently published reports of clinical studies suggesting that drug abusers use their drug of choice specifically to relieve the symptoms of an underlying mental condition. This theory is known as the self-medication hypothesis.

Psychiatrist Edward Khantzian and colleagues developed one model of the self-medication hypothesis. This model takes a psychoanalytic approach. In treating heroin addicts, Khantzian observed that many had histories of depression, often accompanied by anger and rage, long before they began using illegal drugs. Many reported that heroin relieved their feelings of anger. Khantzian concluded that his patients' tendency to abuse heroin stemmed from these problems with anger. In additional studies, Khantzian expanded the hypothesis to include cocaine addiction and alcohol addiction as outcomes of underlying mental problems.

Psychologist David Duncan proposed the other model of the self-medication hypothesis. Duncan took a behavioristic approach. He argued that dependence and addiction are forms of escape or avoidance behavior, known as negatively reinforced behaviors. The theory, according to behavioral psychology, is that elements of addiction, such as the continued use of a substance even with the user's awareness of negative consequences and the likelihood of relapse, are common characteristics of all negatively reinforced behaviors. Negative reinforcement, according to behavioral psychology, reinforces a behavior because a negative condition such as mental distress is halted or avoided because of the behavior.

Although medical professionals use both models of the self-medication hypothesis to treat drug addiction, the theory has its detractors. Some researchers have claimed that it ignores research on the biological mechanisms of motivation and reward and the effects on mood brought about by drug use. Other researchers have asserted that the addiction itself is the cause of mental distress rather than a response to it, and that it remains unclear what comes first: the addiction or the underlying disorder that leads to addiction.

Wendell Anderson, BA

FURTHER READING

Harris, Katherine, and Mark Edlund. "Self-Medication of Mental Health Problems: New Evidence from a National Survey." *Health Services Research* 40.1 (2005): 117–34. Print. Presents a study involving persons with mental disorder symptoms and analyzes their patterns of drug use against the quality and availability of mental health care.

Khantzian, Edward, and Mark Albanese. *Understanding Addiction as Self Medication: Finding Hope Behind the Pain.* Lanham, MD: Rowman, 2008. An analysis of the core reasons behind a number of addictions through the lens of the self-medication hypothesis.

Robinson, Jennifer, et al. "The Role of Self-Medication in the Development of Comorbid Anxiety and Substance Use Disorders." *Archives of General Psychiatry* 68.8 (2011): 800–07. Print. Assesses self-medication behaviors in the development of comorbid anxiety and substance use disorders.

WEBSITES OF INTEREST

Comprehensive Drug Self-Administration and Discrimination Bibliographic Databases
http://www.drugrefs.org

National Institute on Drug Abuse
http://www.drugabuse.gov

See also: Addiction; Mental illness; Opioid abuse; Painkiller abuse; Sleeping pills; Stimulant abuse

Sex addiction

CATEGORY: Psychological issues and behaviors

DEFINITION: Sex addiction is not recognized as a diagnosis in the current edition of the American Psychiatric Association's *Diagnostic and Statistical Manual of Mental Disorders.* In clinical settings and popular psychology circles, the label is often applied when a person engages in sexual behavior that is excessive in frequency, intensity, or duration and that leads to adverse consequences, such as subjective distress or impairment in social or occupational roles. Common manifestations include excessive use of pornography, compulsive masturbation, intercourse with many casual partners or with prostitutes, and cybersex, including "sexting" (exchanging text messages and photographs for the purpose of sexual arousal).

CAUSES

The causes of sex addiction are not known. Nevertheless, as with substance addictions, most research focuses on the structures of the brain's mesolimbic reward system and the neurotransmitter (chemical messenger) dopamine. Most researchers believe that the mesolimbic reward system evolved to sustain behaviors that are necessary for survival and reproduction, namely the pursuit of food, water, and sex.

Normal sexual arousal and orgasm involve excitation in the mesolimbic reward system. In sex addiction, repeated sexual behavior is hypothesized to result in excessive stimulation of dopamine pathways in structures of the mesolimbic reward system (for example, the striatum), thereby causing changes at the cellular level (fewer dopamine receptors) that lead to even greater desire and cravings to engage in the behavior.

As in substance addictions, classical conditioning appears to play a role in the development and maintenance of many sexually addictive behaviors.

Stimuli that are present when an addict engages in the problem behavior, such as a computer that the person uses to view pornography or a street where the person has often visited a strip club, can become powerful triggers for the desire to engage in the addictive behavior.

RISK FACTORS

Men are at higher risk than women for sex addiction. Although high-quality epidemiological data are lacking, the substantial majority (80 percent or more) of sex addicts addressed in published work are male. Access to numerous sexual partners also may be a risk factor. Thus, men who are famous or socially powerful may be at especially heightened risk for sex addiction.

In 2010, tremendous media attention focused on the alleged sex addiction of golf superstar Tiger Woods, who was reportedly treated for the condition. In 2011, Anthony Weiner resigned from the US House of Representatives because of his alleged involvement in a sexting scandal. Although both Woods and Weiner and numerous other high profile persons with "excessive" sexual activity were labeled as sex addicts by much of the popular media, it is not known whether either men met any formal or informal criteria for sex addiction.

Some experts have suggested that childhood sexual abuse may play an important role in the development of sex addiction. Nevertheless, available research suggests that childhood sexual abuse is a nonspecific risk factor for a broad range of mental health difficulties during adulthood rather than a specific risk factor for sex addiction.

Although pornography viewing and masturbation are common manifestations of sex addiction, these behaviors are common among adult men, and the vast majority of these men will never develop behaviors that are compulsive or otherwise problematic. Thus, masturbation and pornography are not considered risk factors for sex addiction.

Some clinicians believe rates of sex addiction have increased in recent years because of the Internet. They argue that the Internet has made pornography, and connection with casual sex partners and prostitutes, far more accessible, anonymous, and affordable than ever before. This claim is plausible, but there is no firm data to support or refute it.

Cybersex Addiction

Cybersex addition is the compulsive use of the Internet to achieve sexual arousal or gratification. A cybersex addict will spend hours online seeking out sexual partners, participating in online adult fantasy roleplay, frequenting adult chat rooms, and viewing pornography. As with other addictions, these activities are done without regard to potential negative consequences in the addict's life, including the loss of one's job, health, and personal relationships.

Sexual addicts may turn to cybersex because of the anonymity of the Internet and the convenience with which it can provide an escape from reality. Cybersex also allows for sexual gratification without the risk of disease. Resources available for cybersex addicts seeking help include therapy, screening tests, online support groups, and twelve-step programs.

SYMPTOMS

The manifestations of sex addiction are diverse. Nevertheless, all manifestations involve a preoccupation with sexual thoughts, fantasies, or urges and sexual activity that is excessive in frequency or duration. The behavior is pursued despite obvious costs and consequences, such as loss of a job or relationship or getting a sexually transmitted disease. Many sex addicts have repeatedly attempted to discontinue or curb their behavior unsuccessfully.

There is controversy concerning whether sex addicts exhibit tolerance and withdrawal. In support of the view that tolerance develops, some have observed that many sex addicts take greater risks over time and engage in increasingly extreme or unusual sex acts. Similarly, some argue that withdrawal is evident in the frustration and anger sex addicts experience when they cannot engage in the desired sexual behaviors.

Many clinicians have reported that sex addicts use sexual behavior as a way to cope with unpleasant emotions; this possibility needs to be examined in systematic research. Data are limited, but preliminary information suggests that sex addiction is highly comorbid (overlapping), not only with substance addictions but also with anxiety and mood disorders.

Sex addiction may manifest differently in women than in men. Rather than focusing on fantasies and behaviors associated with sexual gratification, as do most men with sex addiction, some women who self-identify as sex addicts appear to experience an ongoing series of intense romantic attachments toward new partners. The romantic attachments may develop toward inappropriate persons (such as a coworker or boss) and despite possible negative consequences (such as the loss of one's marriage). Although no systematic data are available, there have been occasional reports of men who experience such a series of attachments to many partners over time. Some authors refer to this ongoing pattern of new romantic attachments as love addiction.

SCREENING AND DIAGNOSIS

As noted, sex addiction is not recognized as a formal mental health diagnosis. However, because of the need for a diagnosis for sexual behavior (intercourse or masturbation) that is excessive in frequency or duration and causes subjective distress or impairment in social or occupational functioning, a related diagnosis of hypersexual disorder is being considered for inclusion in the fifth edition of the *Diagnostic and Statistical Manual of Mental Disorders* (DSM-V).

Hypersexual disorder has a narrower focus than does sex addiction. Whereas the former refers only to "normal" sexual behaviors that are habitual and cause distress or impairment, sex addiction refers either to such normal sexual behaviors or to unusual sexual behaviors (such as exhibitionism and fetishes) that are habitual and cause distress or impairment.

A clinician who suspects sex addiction should conduct a thorough interview, inquiring about the person's sexual behaviors, urges, and fantasies and their frequency, duration, and consequences. Clinicians also may screen for sex addiction using various checklists and questionnaires.

TREATMENT AND THERAPY

Little research has been conducted on the efficacy of treatments for sex addiction. However, most treatment approaches for sex addiction parallel effective treatments for substance addictions. These approaches include behavioral therapy and cognitive-behavioral therapy. Such treatments teach addicts how to recognize and avoid stimuli that increase the risk of engaging in sexually inappropriate behavior. Such stimuli generally include people, places, and Internet sites associated with the addict's previous maladaptive sexual behavior.

Because many sex addicts engage in sexually inappropriate behaviors in response to negative emotions, sex addicts may be taught skills that enable them to cope with negative feelings more adaptively and to identify situations that may trigger unpleasant emotions, such as anger or feelings of loneliness. Cognitive-behavioral therapy interventions also seek to identify and correct erroneous beliefs (for example, "I will be miserable if I cannot have sex when I have the urge to do so") that the addict maintains about sex or romantic relationships.

In addition to embracing traditional psychotherapy, many clinicians and recovering sex addicts believe twelve-step programs (support groups modeled after Alcoholics Anonymous, or AA) are helpful to recovering sex addicts. Note, however, that whereas AA promotes complete abstinence from alcohol, twelve-step groups for sex addicts promote responsible sexual behavior rather than abstinence. Inpatient treatment programs for sex addiction exist and are typically used when outpatient treatments fail to curb life-threatening behaviors, such as frequent unprotected sex with strangers.

In extreme cases in which a sex addict's behavior is illegal or harmful to others (such as with exhibitionism), anti-androgen medications (including Depo-Provera, or depot medroxyprogesterone acetate) are sometimes prescribed to reduce the person's sex drive. Nevertheless, controlled studies to ascertain whether these medications are effective for sex addiction are lacking.

PREVENTION

No research has been conducted on the prevention of sex addiction.

Glenn Hutchinson, PhD
Scott O. Lilienfeld, PhD

FURTHER READING

Carnes, Patrick J. *Don't Call It Love: Recovery from Sexual Addiction.* New York: Bantam, 1991. Provides an excellent description of the clinical features of sex addiction. However, Carnes based many of his claims on a survey that had low participation rates.

Cooper, Alvin. "Sexuality and the Internet: Surfing into the New Millennium." *Cyberpsychology and Behavior* 1.2 (1998): 187–93. Print. Argues that Internet accessibility, anonymity, and affordability create new risks for sex addiction.

Kafka, Martin P. "Hypersexual Disorder: A Proposed Diagnosis for DSM-V." *Archives of Sexual Behavior* 39.2 (2010): 377–400. Print. Provides rationale for including hypersexual disorder in the next version of the DSM, although the author does not argue that hypersexual disorder should be considered an addiction.

WEBSITES OF INTEREST

American Psychiatric Association, DSM-5 Development
http://www.dsm5.org

Sex Addicts Anonymous
http://www.sexaa.org

See also: Behavioral addictions: Overview; Internet addiction; Men and behavioral addictions; Pornography addiction; Sexual stimulant abuse

---

Sexual assault and alcohol use

CATEGORY: Social issues

DEFINITION: Sexual assault is physical attack by means of forced, or nonconsensual, sex. Alcohol consumption does not cause sexual assault, but they are highly correlated. Alcohol-induced cognitive impairment disinhibits inappropriate behavior by making it more difficult to process inhibitory cues.

PREVALENCE

The prevalence of sexual assault, involving or not involving alcohol intoxication, cannot be accurately determined because it is often unreported. Estimates are based on reports from law enforcement and on random samples of crime victims, interviews with incarcerated rapists and others imprisoned for assault, interviews with victims who seek hospital treatment, general population surveys of women, and surveys of male and female college students.

This research suggests that approximately one-half of all sexual assaults involve alcohol consumption by the perpetrator, the victim, or both; 34 to 74 percent occur when the perpetrator is under the influence of alcohol; and 30 to 79 percent are associated with the victim's alcohol consumption.

Findings suggest two distinct subtypes of sexual assault involving substance abuse: those involving mutual substance use and those in which only the perpetrator abused a substance. Assaults involving mutual substance abuse tend to occur between acquaintances rather than intimates, to originate outside the home, and to result in rape or attempted rape rather than sexual coercion. Women who were assaulted by a substance-using perpetrator but who did not use a substance themselves reported lower income, lower rates of employment, and the highest rates of partner physical aggression and injury. When assault occurs in close relationships, women whose partners abuse alcohol are 3.6 times more likely than other women to be assaulted by their partners.

Sexual assaults involving alcohol are more likely than other sexual assaults to occur between men and women who know each other but not well (for example, dates, acquaintances, and friends). These assaults also tend to occur at parties or in bars. The typical scenario involves a woman who is assaulted by a single man who uses verbal and physical pressure, which the woman attempts to resist.

PSYCHOLOGICAL CORRELATIONS

Men who report that they drink heavily are more likely than other men to report having committed sexual assault. A man's behavior can be influenced by certain situations, such as when consensual sex is a possible outcome. Research demonstrates that when people have an expectation about a situation, they tend to more heavily observe cues that fit that expectation. Studies confirm that a man's misperception of a woman's degree of sexual interest is a significant predictor of sexual assault.

Many men expect to feel more powerful, disinhibited, and aggressive after drinking alcohol. Men with these expectations may feel more comfortable forcing sex when they are drinking because they can later justify that the alcohol made them act accordingly. Heavy drinkers may routinely use intoxication as an excuse for engaging in socially unacceptable behavior, including sexual assault. Alcohol also is used by a perpetrator to incapacitate the person assaulted. Furthermore, certain personality characteristics (such as impulsivity and antisocial behavior) may increase a man's propensity both to drink heavily and to commit sexual assault.

Women who drink alcohol are often perceived as being more sexually available and promiscuous, compared with women who do not drink, which may put them at an increased risk for being targeted for assault. Although a woman's alcohol consumption may increase her risk of sexual assault, she is in no way responsible for the assault.

PHARMACOLOGIC CORRELATIONS

Laboratory studies that examine alcohol's effects on responses to sexual and aggressive stimuli have shown that alcohol consumption disrupts higher-order cognitive processes, including abstraction, conceptualization, planning, and problem-solving. As a result, alcohol consumption may lessen a perpetrator's ability to generate nonaggressive solutions to sexual satisfaction.

Intoxication narrows the perceptual field of drinkers so that they focus on what is most important to them in a given situation. Hence, a perpetrator will focus only on social cues that indicate interest in sexual activity. Cognitive deficits lead to a focus on gratification, sense of entitlement, and anger, rather than on empathy and consequences. Once aggression is begun, it is difficult to stop. Alcohol's effects on motor skills may limit the victim's ability to resist effectively, thus heightening the likelihood of a completed assault.

MITIGATION

Sexual assault and heavy drinking are separate issues. A perpetrator must recognize that sexual contact without consent is sexual violence, whether alcohol is involved or not. However, it is useful to focus on the use of alcohol in dating and sexual situations in models of alcohol's role in sexual assault, rather than on general drinking patterns, because the level of alcohol consumption does not differ between perpetrators and nonperpetrators.

Effective sex offender programs teach four principles of sexual consent: privilege, permission, justification/intent, and responsibility.

1. Privilege: Sex is never a right; it is always a privilege.
2. Permission: A person needs to be sober enough to know whether or not they have

been given permission; and the other person must be capable, at the time, of giving permission. If someone is passed out, unconscious, or asleep, they are legally incapable of giving consent.
3. Justification/Intent: No minimization of the use of aggression as a result of alcohol or drug use, stress, deviant arousal patterns, loss of control or misunderstandings.
4. Responsibility: The only person who ever is responsible for a sexual assault is the perpetrator.

Stephanie Eckenrode, BA, LLB

FURTHER READING

Abbey, Antonia, et al. "Alcohol and Sexual Assault." *Alcohol Health and Research World* 25.1 (2001). Web. 28 Mar. 2012. https://www1.columbia.edu/sec/cu/health/pdfs/alcohol_sexual_assault.pdf. An overview of the evidence correlating alcohol consumption and sexual assault.

Dawgert, Sarah. *Substance Use and Sexual Violence: Building Prevention and Intervention Responses, A Guide for Counselors and Advocates.* Enola: Pennsylvania Coalition Against Rape, 2009. Examines drug and alcohol use, abuse, and addiction as it relates to sexual violence.

LeBeau, Marc A., and Ashraf Mozayani, eds. *Drug-Facilitated Sexual Assault: A Forensic Handbook.* San Diego, CA: Academic, 2001. A handbook for investigators of sexual crimes that covers how drugs are used to facilitate sexual assaults.

WEBSITES OF INTEREST

Centers for Disease Control and Prevention
http://www.cdc.gov/ViolencePrevention/sexualviolence

Men Can Stop Rape
http://www.mencanstoprape.org

Sexual Assault Awareness Month
http://www.nsvrc.org/saam

See also: Crime and substance abuse; Domestic violence and addiction; Sexual assault and drug use; Substance abuse

Sexual assault and drug use

CATEGORY: Social issues

ALSO KNOWN AS: Date rape; drug-facilitated sexual assault

DEFINITION: Sexual assault is any form of sexual activity, including rape and sexual harassment, where consent is not freely given. Drug use is defined as the use or misuse of any legal or illicit psychoactive, mood-altering chemical, including alcohol, marijuana, stimulants, hallucinogens, benzodiazepines, sedatives, and opiates.

DRUG-FACILITATED SEXUAL ASSAULT

According to the US Department of Health and Human Services, sexual assault includes the non-consensual acts of inappropriate touching; vaginal, anal, or oral penetration (rape); attempted rape; and child molestation. Sexual assault can be verbal, visual, or involve coercive physical attempts to engage another person in unwanted sexual contact or attention.

Sexual assault often involves the use of psychoactive mood-altering drugs and alcohol. According to the US Department of Justice, close to 40 percent of all rapes and other forms of sexual assault in a given year in the United States involve alcohol use by the offender. Drug use in addition to the alcohol use accounted for 18 percent of sexual assaults.

Drug-facilitated sexual assault involves the administration of drugs that usually induce amnesia in the victim. This type of assault often occurs in bars or nightclubs. The drug is usually slipped into an alcoholic beverage without the victim's knowledge. These drugs are often referred to as date rape drugs, the most common of which are sedative hypnotics such as gamma hydroxybutyrate, Rohypnol, ketamine, and Soma.

Date rape is common during college years. Drugs and alcohol play significant roles in date rape, with as much as 75 percent of men and 50 percent of women in college involved in a sexual assault reporting having been under the influence at the time of the assault. In eighty percent of sexual assaults the victim and perpetrator are known to each other, and more than 50 percent of sexual assaults occur close to the victim's home. The most common profile of the sex offender is white, male, and age thirty-one years.

Neither drugs nor alcohol excuses a perpetrator seeking sexual relations without consent. Programs to rehabilitate sex offenders attempt to help the offenders make the distinction that drugs and alcohol do not give license for sexual abuse. Drug and alcohol problems are considered separate from deviant sexual behavior.

VICTIMS OF SEXUAL ASSAULT

The profile of an assault victim is generally female, age twelve to thirty-four years. Girls and women age sixteen to nineteen are at highest risk. Boys also can be victims of sexual assault. By the age of eight years, one in four girls and one in six boys has been sexually assaulted.

Crime rates are often misleading when it comes to the statistical reportage of sexual assault and drug use. These crimes are vastly underreported because of a deep sense of shame, embarrassment, and guilt induced in the victim. Another factor leading to underreporting of sexual assault occurs because of the effect of drugs or alcohol on memory. Often the drugs interfere with the recall of the assault, leaving victims unable to remember if they consented to engage in sex.

POST-TRAUMATIC STRESS AND SELF-MEDICATION

Sexual assault, including rape, is a leading cause of post-traumatic stress disorder (PTSD). In general, women are two to three times more likely than men to develop PTSD. One of the leading risk factors of PTSD is sexual assault that causes the victim to feel powerless.

Studies consistently demonstrate high rates of co-morbidity between PTSD and substance abuse disorder. Specifically, there exists a strong relationship between drug use and victimization through sexual assault. Often, the victim of a sexual assault will use drugs and alcohol to self-medicate the symptoms of the trauma. Rates of substance abuse disorder are as high as 30 to 50 percent of the population of women diagnosed with PTSD, according to the National Comorbidity Study. An Office of Justice Programs report on substance abuse and victimization notes that victims of sexual assault are 5.3 percent more likely than nonvictims to use prescription drugs, 3.4 times more likely to use marijuana, and 10 times more likely to use hard drugs to cope with their assault.

However, there is a tendency to blame the victim because drugs are often involved at the time of sexual assault for both the perpetrator

and the victim. This also is true when victimization leads to substance abuse, and the victim is further stigmatized. Research shows that being sexually assaulted puts one at higher risk for a repeated assault. For these reasons, research points to the need for gender-sensitive treatment to address sexual assault, PTSD, victimization, and empowerment.

Amanda Lefkowitz, MA

FURTHER READING

Breslau, N., et al. "Vulnerability to Assaultive Violence: Further Specification for the Sex Difference in Post-Traumatic Stress Disorder." *Psychological Medicine* 29 (1999): 813–21.

Jackson-Cherry, Lisa R., and Bradley T. Erford. *Crisis Intervention and Prevention.* Upper Saddle River, NJ: Pearson, 2010.

Koss, M. P. "Hidden Rape: Incident, Prevalence, and Descriptive Characteristics of Sexual Aggression and Victimization in a National Sample of College Students." *Rape and Sexual Assault II.* Ed. Ann W. Burgess. New York: Garland, 1988.

"Sexual Assault and Substance Abuse." *Research and Advocacy Digest* 8.1 (2005): 1–15. Web. 6 Apr. 2012. http://www.mecasa.org/joomla/images/pdfs/substance_use/sexual_assault_and_sub_abuse.pdf.

US Bureau of Justice Statistics. *Sexual Assault of Young Children as Reported to Law Enforcement.* Washington, DC: DOJ, 2000.

WEBSITES OF INTEREST

National Center for PTSD
http://www.ptsd.va.gov

National Violence Against Women Prevention Research Center
http://www.musc.edu/vawprevention

Rape, Abuse, and Incest National Network
http://www.rainn.org

See also: Crime and substance abuse; Domestic violence and addiction; Narcotics abuse; Sexual assault and alcohol use; Substance abuse

Sexual stimulant abuse

CATEGORY: Substance abuse

DEFINITION: Sexual stimulants are prescription medications designed to produce, enhance, or prolong sexual arousal. The US Food and Drug Administration has approved prescription sexual stimulants only for the treatment of erectile dysfunction in men.

HISTORY OF USE

The active ingredients in sexual stimulants include sildenafil citrate, vardenafil, and tadalafil, all of which are synthetic compounds. Sexual stimulants are produced in tablet and capsule form and are intended to be ingested orally.

The brand-named sexual stimulant Viagra (sildenafil citrate) was approved by the US Food and Drug Administration as a prescription erectile dysfunction (ED) medication in 1998. By the time brand competitors Levitra (vardenafil) and Cialis (tadalafil) arrived on the market in late 2003, studies had already begun to indicate incidences of abuse among men across all sexual orientations.

A 2000 study from Cedars-Sinai Medical Center in Los Angeles, California, analyzed more than fourteen hundred medical emergencies involving Viagra. The study found that more than five hundred of the cases led to death, the majority of which occurred in men younger than age sixty-five years who had no previous heart conditions.

Despite widespread clinical evidence indicating that men without erectile problems receive no benefit from the drugs, it was not long before ED drugs gained a false reputation as an aphrodisiac among both gay and heterosexual men. While ED drugs pose little negative effect to users when taken on their own, the combination of their active ingredients with other illicit drugs poses tremendous health risks.

EFFECTS AND POTENTIAL RISKS

ED medications stimulate erectile capability in men by dilating blood vessels. As a result, the combination of these medications with other stimulant drugs like cocaine, ecstasy (methylenedioxymethamphetamine), and poppers (amyl nitrate) can result in fatal blood pressure loss, heart attack, and stroke.

These are some of the sexual stimulants sold on open display at convenience stores. (Jason Arthurs/MCT/Landov)

While ED medications are not physiologically addictive, abusive users may develop psychological dependency on the drug. Both dealers and ED drug abusers have been known to lie to medical professionals and to exaggerate symptoms of ED to obtain the drug. As with any illegal drug, there is no way to ensure the authenticity, ingredients, or potential dangers in illegal ED medication.

Research also has revealed widespread use of ED drugs by young men attempting to combat the erectile impairment caused after heavy alcohol consumption. Researchers believe that the impression of false sexual prowess combined with impaired cognitive decision-making can lead men who combine ED medications and alcohol into higher-risk sexual behavior, which can lead to unwanted pregnancies and sexually transmitted diseases.

John Pritchard

FURTHER READING

Morgentaler, Abraham. *The Viagra Myth: The Surprising Impact on Love and Relationships.* Hoboken, NJ: Jossey, 2003.

"The New Young Face of Viagra Abuse." Chicago Tribune, 27 Dec. 2003. Web. 21 Apr. 2012. http://www.azcentral.com/health/men/articles/1226viagra-abuse-ON.html.

Peterson, Karen. "Young Men Add Viagra to Their Drug Arsenal." USA Today, 21 Mar. 2001. Print.

Salyer, David. "The Dangers of Using and Abusing Viagra." The Body, Nov./Dec. 2004. Web. 21 Apr. 2012. http://www.thebody.com/content/art32246.html.

WEBSITES OF INTEREST

Viagra.com
http://www.viagra.com/questions.aspx

Viagraholics Anonymous
http://www.viagraholics.com

See also: Pornography addiction; Prescription drug addiction: In depth; Sex addiction; Stimulant abuse; Stimulants: Short- and long-term effects on the body

Shopping/spending addiction

CATEGORY: Psychological issues and behaviors

ALSO KNOWN AS: Compulsive buying disorder; oniomania; shopaholism

DEFINITION: Shopping or spending addiction is a behavioral addiction in which a person is excessively preoccupied with shopping or spending money. The behavior interferes with the person's social, academic, family, or workplace functioning, whether or not the person is spending beyond his or her means. It is possible to have a compulsive buying disorder without making many purchases; some persons with the disorder simply spend large amounts of time window-shopping, including shopping online.

CAUSES

The causes of shopping and spending addiction are debated. German psychiatrist Emil Kraepelin was the first medical expert to describe the condition in 1915; he called it oniomania (from two Greek words meaning "to sell" and "insanity"). Eugen Bleuler, a Swiss expert on schizophrenia, defined shopping addiction in 1924 as an impulse-control disorder in the same category as kleptomania and pyromania.

More than 90 percent of persons with the disorder also meet the *Diagnostic and Statistical Manual of Mental Disorders* (DSM) criteria for anxiety or mood disorders, eating disorders, substance abuse disorders, and axis II disorders (personality disorders). Obsessive-compulsive, borderline, and narcissistic personality disorders in particular have been associated with compulsive buying disorder (CBD). Because of this extensive overlap, some observers question whether compulsive spending is a separate mental disorder or simply a secondary feature of other disorders. Furthermore, there is no evidence of a genetic factor in shopping or spending addiction.

Some experts regard CBD's underlying cause as poor ability to tolerate anger, sadness, boredom, or other negative feelings. Others believe that a search for personal identity through purchasing prestigious brand-name products is the underlying cause. Other causes that have been suggested include early childhood deprivation, leading to compensating in adult life by purchasing special items; a need for excitement and stimulation; seeking approval by purchasing clothing or other items owned by one's peers; social isolation and loneliness; perfectionism (needing to dress or look perfect); and a feeling of inner emptiness.

RISK FACTORS

Risk factors for CBD include being female; being in one's late teenage years through early twenties; living in a developed country with a market-based economy; and a family history of substance abuse or mood disorders. It is estimated that about 8 percent of the general North American population are compulsive shoppers.

The disorder also has been reported and studied by psychiatrists in France, Canada, the United Kingdom, Germany, and Brazil. The rate is expected to increase worldwide because of widespread access to the Internet and online shopping, the easy availability of credit cards, and advertising that encourages the purchase of consumer goods as a way to increase self-esteem and social acceptance.

SYMPTOMS

The symptoms of CBD include excessive time spent shopping and excessive spending, in most cases leading to impaired cognitive, social, and occupational functioning. Spending beyond the person's means (beyond available income) usually creates tension in interpersonal relationships and financial and legal difficulties; these difficulties may include bankruptcy, ruined credit, or prosecution for shoplifting, check forgery, or embezzlement.

The person typically displays anxiety or emotional distress regarding the shopping and spending behavior. Denial is relatively uncommon; most affected persons (more than 85 percent) acknowledge that their shopping behavior is problematic.

Some psychiatrists identify four distinct phases or stages in an episode of compulsive shopping: anticipation, in which the person develops an urge to buy a specific item or to go on a shopping trip; preparation, in which the person decides which stores to go to, how to get there, what to wear, and even which credit cards to use; the actual shopping, which some persons describe as exciting or even sexually arousing; and the act of purchase, which is often followed by feelings of disappointment or anxiety over one's loss of self-control. Compulsive shopping is a solitary behavior in most cases, although some persons with CBD report that they go shopping with a friend or partner who shares the addiction.

The most common items purchased by both men and women are clothing, shoes, compact discs (CDs), and household items. Women with CBD often purchase jewelry and cosmetics, while men typically splurge on hardware, electronic gadgets, or automotive equipment. In most cases the individual items purchased are not expensive; however, persons with CBD often buy in quantity, such as eight or ten CDs instead of one. Researchers report that the average cost of a compulsive buying spree is between $100 and $150 (in US dollars).

SCREENING AND DIAGNOSIS

There are no standardized diagnostic criteria for shopping and spending addiction. An earlier edition of the DSM (DSM-III-R) classified CBD as an impulse-control disorder not otherwise specified, while the current DSM (IV) does not mention it at all. Proposed diagnostic criteria for the disorder in revised versions include intense preoccupation with shopping or spending, significant impairment in functioning, and shopping or spending that does not occur as part of a manic episode.

Several questionnaires and "screeners" for shopping addiction have been developed since the late 1980s. The oldest English-language instrument is the compulsive buying measurement scale (1988), or CBMS, which measures four dimensions of compulsive buying: the urge to spend, guilt after making the purchase, a general tendency to spend money freely, and a troubled family environment. In 1990, a German version of the CBMS, known as the Hohenheimer Kaufsuchttest or Hohenheim shopping addiction test, was published and used in several European studies.

The Minnesota impulsive disorder interview, or MIDI (1994), includes a subsection intended to diagnose compulsive buying, although no data have been published regarding its reliability or validity. The Yale-Brown obsessive-compulsive scale (Y-BOCS) was modified in 1996 to develop a ten-item scale called the Y-BOCS shopping version, or Y-BOCS-SV. In 2005 an English-language screener called the compulsive buying scale was introduced and rated for validity and reliability.

In some cases affected persons will screen themselves for the disorder through an online shopaholics self-test, by reading a book on the disorder, or by completing the fifteen-questions assessment tool of Debtors Anonymous (DA), and will then seek professional help after admitting to themselves that they have a problem.

TREATMENT AND THERAPY

A number of different treatments for CBD have been tried. Antidepressant medications, particularly the selective serotonin reuptake inhibitors, have been used but appear to be relatively ineffective, as does psychodynamic psychotherapy. Group therapy and a twelve-step program such as DA are helpful to some persons with CBD, as are simplicity study circles—small groups that meet to redefine the good life, to encourage self-reflection, and to help people make such changes as turning away from shopping or other forms of social competition.

Some compulsive shoppers also benefit from bibliotherapy (reading self-help books) or from bibliotherapy combined with cognitive-behavioral therapy (CBT). In some cases financial counseling is a useful adjunct to CBT. One expert in CBD offers patients five points of advice: they should not rely on antidepressants or other medications to treat CBD, they should acknowledge that they have the disorder, they should destroy all credit cards and checkbooks, they should go shopping only with friends or companions who do not have CBD, and they should find activities other than shopping to fill leisure time.

PREVENTION

Prevention of CBD is difficult because shopping and spending addiction is often rooted in the affected person's family of origin—which means that the behavior typically develops before the person recognizes that he or she is at risk for a behavioral addiction and may already suffer from an eating disorder or other impulse control disorder. Adolescents are particularly susceptible; however, there is no single family structure or characteristic that is useful in predicting the likelihood that a specific family member will develop CBD. Possible preventive strategies include parental oversight of teenagers' spending habits and early training in the responsible use of income, whether the money comes from allowances or part-time employment.

Rebecca J. Frey, PhD

FURTHER READING

Albrecht, Ulrike, et al. "Diagnostic Instruments for Behavioural Addictions: An Overview." *GMS Psycho-Social Medicine* 4 (2007): 1–11. Print. A review article of diagnostic instruments for several behavioral addictions; the second section deals with instruments for compulsive buying.

Benson, April L. *To Buy or Not to Buy: Why We Overshop and How to Stop.* Boston: Trumpeter, 2008. Interactive self-help book about compulsive buying disorder written for the general public.

Black, Donald W. "Compulsive Buying Disorder: A Review of the Evidence." *CNS Spectrums* 12.2 (2007): 124–32. Print. A comprehensive overview of the characteristics of CBD, its risk factors, and treatment options, written by an expert on the disorder.

Coombs, Robert H., ed. *Handbook of Addictive Disorders: A Practical Guide to Diagnosis and Treatment.* Hoboken, NJ: Wiley, 2004. A standard reference work on substance and behavioral addictions. Chapter 13 deals with understanding and diagnosing compulsive buying and chapter 14 discusses its treatment.

Mueller, Astrid, et al. "Latent Profile Analysis and Comorbidity in a Sample of Individuals with Compulsive Buying Disorder." *Psychiatry Research* 178.2 (2010): 348–53. Print. Suggests classifying compulsive shopping and spending as an associated feature of other psychiatric disorders rather than as a stand-alone condition.

WEBSITES OF INTEREST

Debtors Anonymous
http://www.debtorsanonymous.org

Illinois Institute for Addiction Recovery
http://www.addictionrecov.org/Addictions/index.aspx?AID=34

Shopaholics Anonymous
http://www.shopaholicsanonymous.org

See also: Behavioral addictions: Overview; Compulsions; Impulse control disorders

Slang

CATEGORY: Social issues

ALSO KNOWN AS: Street terms

DEFINITION: Slang is informal communication within a particular group. In reference to illicit drugs, slang involves the use of nonstandard words or invented phrases in place of the actual drug names and descriptions. Using slang allows dealers, addicts, and casual users to discuss drug abuse without being obvious to others about their intentions. Slang develops informally and typically addresses the drugs, users, dealers, equipment, methods, and effects of use to convey meaning within the group. Drug slang is not a simple dialect or a unique language; instead, it is an evolving method of street communication among dealers and substance abusers.

WHO USES SLANG AND WHY

As with slang (or street terms) for any niche, slang for drugs is used to build community or group inclusion. Using slang as a way to communicate includes and associates a person in a group or community and excludes others. Users and dealers use slang to distinguish themselves as a group. Youth are particularly susceptible to slang use because of their desire for inclusion. Street terms are often distinct enough from chemical or trade names to allow users to communicate in public safely without drawing attention to their substance use.

People use slang to more easily describe a drug or method of abuse and to identify combinations of drugs used together for different effects. For example, cocaine plus the hallucinogenic substances LSD (lysergic acid) and MDMA (ecstasy) is known as candy flipped on a string. Slang terminology provides easily remembered, unassuming names for unique multiple-drug combinations: A chocolate chip cookie refers to a wafer of MDMA and heroin or methamphetamine.

Using a single phrase for drugs in combination simplifies communication between substance abusers and dealers. Similarly, informal words or phrases are frequently applied to drugs approved by the US Food and Drug Administration that are commonly abused. Certain benzodiazepines, as commonly abused prescription sedatives, are referred to as roofies or goofballs, for example.

Slang describes not only single or combined substances but also particular forms of the same drug and the associated methods of ingesting the drug. Cocaine ingested as coke may be called blast, whereas cocaine inhaled in powder form is better known as snort. Tools and quantities associated with drug use also receive informal names; crack pipes may be called uzis and an eight ball refers to one-eighth ounce of a drug for purchase. The effects or emotions experienced during substance trips can direct the popular street terms too. Liquid incense refers to inhaled amyl nitrate as a mellowing depressant; rush refers to the same drug but describes more excitatory sensations of use.

Finally, street terms convey details about the drug users in a group or a shared event as a whole. Raves are hallucinogenic dance parties; mules are drug carriers. Individual drug users receive slang names too. For example, a person who uses heroin may be called a channel swimmer by other users. The groups of people who communicate using street terminology are as numerous and varied as the types of slang descriptions available.

How and Where Slang Develops

Slang names may develop regionally as jargon (for example, Spanish-language terms common near the Texas border with Mexico), they may develop from brand names (for example, robotripping from Robitussin medicine as a source of dextromethorphan), they can develop from the drug's organic sources (for example, poppy seed), or can develop from a drug's effects (for example, ecstasy). Slang often spreads according to drug popularity and by its increased use within and across addict groups. Slang, with the drug of abuse itself, can move rapidly across regions or particular populations, such as school campuses.

Some slang terms wane in popularity as a reflection of the dialect of a small group; these terms can be limited and local. Slang is more likely to spread when it is used more frequently and by more people within a group or across different substance abuser groups. When slang overlaps in populations, the same term can be used to refer to different but related drugs (for example, sniffing in reference to any type of inhalant) and can evolve according to the established drug of choice for an area or time period.

Slang may develop from the abbreviation of chemical or brand names (triple C in reference to the brand Coricidin Cough and Cold), by describing the drug's appearance (cheese as slang for black tar heroin combined with acetaminophen and diphenhydramine), and by nearly any method of invented phrasing used frequently in a community. The street terms in the drug world evolve with usage trends and even on the basis of packaging changes or new methods of use.

Slang is not static, and it changes with trends or drug popularity. As new substances, such as *Salvia*, become more common, different drug combinations and new terminology result. Often, related drugs are connected by alternatives of the same slang name, so that the terminology grows as informal terms overlap. Metaphors or similes also become used as slang to describe drug effects. Terms constantly evolve, as drug users switch street terms to avoid detection associated with commonly known names. However, some slang is universal and established across the globe.

Slang's Importance to Health Professionals and Caregivers

Communication between recovering addicts and their health care providers is traditionally a struggle. Vernacular references to drug trips and drugs of choice make identification of an actual substance and an accurate patient history quite difficult. Patients are often unaware of the chemical or trade names of many substances; by becoming familiar with street slang, health care professionals and caregivers can bridge the communication gap.

Addressing patients within their communicative ability can build trust so that practitioners can provide better quality care. At minimum, health care providers can use slang terms to learn what drugs and what methods their patients use. Greater familiarity with slang can provide insight into the patients' experiences, drug combinations tried, and the duration of abuse. Knowing the prevailing language increases outreach, especially to reticent patients; increases compassion during treatment; eases recognition of problems; and improves the likelihood of treatment success.

The National Institute on Drug Abuse supports the expansion of health professionals' knowledge by acknowledging the importance of using slang dictionaries from private, nonprofit sources and by increasing awareness of common slang terms. These lexical guides are tools to help gather accurate information about a substance abuser and to expand understanding about the ways drugs are abused. In addition to health providers, others with a vested interest in learning drug slang are caregivers, law enforcement, parents, family, and friends. These populations should stay abreast of word changes to maintain open communication with an addict.

Nicole M. Van Hoey, PharmD

FURTHER READING

Hamid, H., R. S. el-Mallakh, and K. Vandeveir. "Substance Abuse: Medical and Slang Terminology." *Southern Medical Journal* 98.3 (2005): 350–62. Print. A literature report that sets a call to action for health professionals. Goals include better communication with substance abuse patients by incorporating their unique lexicon of slang terms.

Johnson, Jay, Jane Carlisle Maxwell, and Marian Leitnerschmidt. *A Dictionary of Slang Drug Terms, Trade Names, and Pharmacological Effects and Uses.* Austin: Texas Commission on Alcohol and Drug Abuse, 1997. A collection of terminology specifically related to informal use by substance abusers rather than health professionals, developed as a guide for professionals and caregivers to foster communication.

Johnson, N. P., P. J. Michels, and C. W. Davis. "The Importance of Street Drug Terms as Diagnostic Clues." *Journal of Health and Social Policy* 3.1 (1991): 45–53. Print. An early review of slang as a lexical tool for the provider during diagnosis and treatment periods.

World Health Organization. *Lexicon of Alcohol and Drug Terms.* Geneva: WHO, 1994. Glossary-style collection of vocabulary related to substance abuse, geared toward professional readers. Slang terminology is included but is not specifically featured.

WEBSITES OF INTEREST

Addictions.org
http://www.addictions.org/slang.htm

Drug Slang Dictionary
http://www.noslang.com/drugs/dictionary.php

National Institute on Drug Abuse
http://www.drugabuse.gov/publications/
     media-guide/z-listing

See also: Age and addiction; Peer pressure; Socioeconomic status and addiction; Stigma of addiction

Sleeping pills

CATEGORY: Substances

DEFINITION: Nonbenzodiazepine sleeping pills include both prescription and over-the-counter (OTC) medications. Prescription medications, especially those that act on the GABA-A receptor of the central nervous system, are more likely to be abused than are melatonin-like or OTC sleeping pills.

STATUS: Legal in the United States and worldwide

CLASSIFICATION: Various scheduled classifications

SOURCE: Natural and chemically synthesized

TRANSMISSION ROUTE: Oral ingestion of tablets and capsules

HISTORY OF USE

Zolpidem (Ambien), a nonbenzodiazepine sleeping aid, was approved as a prescription by the US Food and Drug Administration in 1992. Zapelon (Sonata) was approved in 1999 and eszopiclone (Lunesta) was

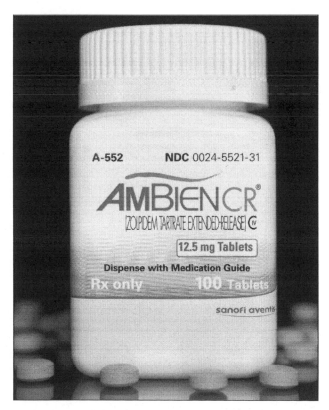

Ambien is used for the short-term treatment of insomnia. (Bloomberg via Getty Images)

approved in 2004. Since the introduction of zolpidem, there have been reports of diversion and abuse because of the addictive nature of these medications. When abused, these medications are often combined with alcohol or other sedating drugs, which heightens adverse reactions.

EFFECTS AND POTENTIAL RISKS

Zolpidem, zapelon, and eszopiclone all have mechanisms of action involving the GABA-A receptor within the central nervous system, whereas ramelteon (Rozerem) is a selective agonist of melatonin. Chemically, zolpidem and zapelon bind specifically to 1 subunits on GABA-A receptors.

Generally, these medications are indicated only for short-term management of insomnia and should be ingested only when the patient will get at least seven to eight hours of uninterrupted sleep. However, because of their addictive properties, these medications are often used for extended periods of time. Of the three sleeping medications, the only one that does not include a labeling restriction for short-term use only is eszopiclone. Overall, this medication has less potential for abuse or dependence in most patients.

Common adverse effects of this class of medications include daytime sedation, drowsiness, cognitive impairment, problems with motor coordination, and dependence. Although reported less frequently, more serious complications include sleep-related behaviors such as sleep-walking, sleep-eating, sleep-driving, and temporary amnesia. There also have been reports of worsening depression and suicidal thoughts, so a complete psychological history is an important factor in the decision of what sleeping medication, if any, to prescribe.

Allison C. Bennett, PharmD

FURTHER READING

Dolder, Christian, Michael Nelson, and Jonathan McKinsey. "Use of Non-Benzodiazepine Hypnotics in the Elderly: Are All Agents the Same?" *CNS Drugs* 21.5 (2007): 389–405. Print.

Rosenberg, R. P. "Sleep Maintenance Insomnia: Strengths and Weaknesses of Current Pharmacologic Therapies." *Annals of Clinical Psychiatry* 18.1 (2006): 49–56. Print.

Wagner, Judy, Mary L. Wagner, and Wayne A. Hening. "Beyond Benzodiazepines: Alternative Pharmacologic Agents for the Treatment of Insomnia." *Annals of Pharmacotherapy* 32.6 (1998): 680–91. Print.

WEBSITES OF INTEREST

National Institute on Drug Abuse
http://www.drugabuse.gov

Substance Abuse and Mental Health Statistics
http://www.drugabusestatistics.samhsa.gov

Substance Abuse Treatment Facility Locator
http://dasis3.samhsa.gov

See also: Over-the-counter drugs of abuse; Prescription drug addiction: Overview; Sedative-Hypnotic abuse; Self-medication

Smoking

CATEGORY: Substance abuse

DEFINITION: Smoking is the act of inhaling through the mouth the vapors emitted from any burning substance, particularly tobacco. The most popular means of ingesting smoke is the cigarette, made up of dried tobacco rolled in a thin paper with or without a fibrous filter tip. Alternate forms for inhalation include pipes and cigars. Other substances that are smoked are dried marijuana leaves, crack cocaine, opium, and methylamphetamine, or crystal meth.

HISTORY

Smoking in some form or another has been documented throughout human history in many indigenous cultures around the world. Ancient indigenous cultures usually did not partake in smoking as a recreational or leisure activity, however. Smoking of tobacco, opium, or other substances usually was performed as a ritualistic practice in religious ceremonies. In addition, smoking was believed to have therapeutic properties and was used in the treatment of disease.

The commercialization of smoking began when explorer Christopher Columbus's crew brought tobacco back to Europe from the New World. Smoking then proliferated throughout the world, and tobacco growing and production became a major industry and staple cash crop. The cigarette was created from the cigar when people who could not afford tobacco would collect discarded cigar stubs, remove the unburned tobacco, and roll it in paper to smoke. This "pauper's" cigar evolved into the modern cigarette, which features, usually, a fibrous filtered tip and special paper that burns only when the smoker is inhaling. This paper was developed to prevent smoking-related fires and burns.

Smoking peaked in the United States in the 1950s; however, the true dangers of the habit were documented about twenty years earlier. Before this, smoking was considered a harmless habit or recreation. Antismoking movements in the United States began around the turn of the twentieth century. However, the focus of these movements was centered on morality rather than health, as smoking and alcohol use were deemed by some religious groups as sinful vices. Antismoking movements later struggled against popular culture and advertising that portrayed smoking as pleasurable and fashionable.

Although smoking is legal, it is restricted in the United States and in Canada. The sale of tobacco products to children is illegal in most states. Alabama, Alaska, New Jersey, Utah, and three counties in New York have increased the legal age for tobacco purchase to nineteen years. Canada's federal law sets the sale-to-minors age at eighteen years too, but the legal age is nineteen years in six provinces (British Columbia, Newfoundland, New Brunswick, Ontario, Prince Edward Island, and Nova Scotia).

Advertising for smoking products also is restricted both in the United States and in Canada, and some local ordinances in both countries ban smoking in public places. Despite the decline in the number of smokers, the tobacco-product manufacturing industry made more than $46 billion (US) in revenue in 2010.

ADDICTION

A smoking addiction has two components: the chemical dependence and a behavioral habit. Chemical dependence involves tobacco's active ingredient, nicotine, which is a stimulant that causes increased heart rate and physical dependence. As a user smokes, his or her body craves more nicotine, which prompts the user to want more. This effect causes smokers to gradually increase the total number of cigarettes or other tobacco products smoked each day.

The behavioral component involves the act of smoking itself. The hand-to-mouth action of smoking

is so ritualistic that smokers find it comforting. Furthermore, the smoking ritual often coincides with normal activities during the day, such as finishing a meal or taking a break at work. These scenarios will often trigger the desire to smoke.

Although nicotine is a stimulant, people with a smoking addiction often crave tobacco products during times of stress and partake in the habit as a means to relax. This could be the case because the withdrawal symptoms cause more anxiousness than the nicotine itself, and the ritualized nature of smoking is thought to be soothing and relaxing.

RISK FACTORS

By far, age is the largest risk factor in developing a smoking habit or addiction. About 90 percent of adult smokers started smoking before they were age nineteen years. Close to one-fifth of high school students are smokers. Men are more likely than women to smoke.

Education level too plays a key role in developing a smoking habit. Adults without a high school diploma and persons who earned a general equivalency degree as their highest level of education are far more likely to smoke than are persons who have earned bachelor's and master's degrees. In addition, children with parents who smoke are more likely to pick up the habit than children who live in smoke-free households.

Smoking is often described as a social problem. People begin to smoke because others do it. Peer pressure, wanting to fit into a certain social group, and mimicking the habits of role models are reasons some people smoke. Others smoke because they want to rebel against their parents or against social rules.

Restrictions on smoking in media, such as on television, and strict advertising rules are in place because smoking is often portrayed as glamorous, fashionable, or otherwise "cool." Advocates of these restrictions argue that these messages prompt young people to start smoking because they are not yet capable of making informed decisions or able to understand the consequences of starting the habit.

SYMPTOMS

The first obvious symptom of a person with a smoking addiction is a distinct odor of residual smoke that lingers on hair, clothes, hands, and in living spaces where the person smokes, such as in the home or in an automobile. Habitual tobacco smoking will result in yellow stains on the teeth and bad breath. Because nicotine is addictive, smokers who do not regularly smoke will experience withdrawal symptoms of nervousness and irritability.

In addition to stained teeth, other changes occur from prolonged smoking, including wrinkling of the skin, particularly around the mouth and lips. Prolonged exposure to smoke causes changes in voice quality. A person who has smoked for several years will have a damaged larynx (voice box). His or her voice will begin to sound deeper and will have a raspy quality.

Because smoke is ingested through the upper respiratory system through the mouth, smokers often have chronic respiratory irritation, which results in nasal sinus infections and inflammation, cough, and lung infections such as bronchitis and pneumonia. The toxins in smoke leave deposits in the lungs and cause damage that reduces lung capacity and the ability of the lungs to work properly. In time, smokers will experience increasing shortness of breath during exertion, such as climbing a flight of stairs. Changes in the cells of the lungs from smoke exposure in time can lead to cancerous tumors.

SCREENING AND DIAGNOSIS

Every teenager and adult should be screened for a smoking habit at every wellness visit with a physician. Tobacco use is a basic question that is included in health histories in a patient's file, not only for primary care but also for visits to specialists and dentists. Because of the risk of many cancers (especially lung cancer), heart disease, and lung disease, as well as damage to nearly every system in the body, persons who reveal to their doctor that they use tobacco products are strongly advised to stop, even if they are addicted to smoking or only partake in the habit socially or occasionally.

TREATMENT AND THERAPY

Treatment of a smoking addiction (known as smoking cessation) can be self-guided or occur under the care of a physician or mental health professional who is an addiction specialist. One approach to smoking cessation is "cold turkey," in which the smoker abruptly and

---

Assessing Your Smoking Habit

Smoking is not only a physical addiction but also a psychological addiction (used as a coping mechanism) and a habit (reinforcement through repetition). Many people who have successfully quit smoking say that they found it helpful to understand their individual smoking-related habits.

Using a rating scale of 1 to 5 (1 = never, 2 = sometimes, 3 = often, 4 = very frequently, and 5 = always), rate the following statements. Your highest scores will show you which aspects of smoking are the most problematic for you so that you can develop alternatives.

- Smoking gives me an energy boost.
- I find smoking pleasurable and relaxing.
- I like holding a cigarette in my hand.
- Smoking is something I seem to do automatically.
- I smoke when I feel upset.
- I smoke when I feel that I'm starting to slow down.

- I enjoy the process of lighting up a cigarette.
- I smoke when I'm stressed out.
- It almost feels like torture when I can't smoke.
- I find cigarettes enjoyable.
- Sometimes I light up a new cigarette before I even finish the one that's in the ashtray.
- I'm very aware of when I need a cigarette.
- Smoking perks up my mood.
- I enjoy exhaling smoke.
- I tend to smoke more when I'm relaxed.
- Sometimes I'm not even aware that I have a cigarette in my mouth.
- I seem to crave a cigarette when I haven't had one for a while.
- I smoke when I feel sad or when I want to forget something painful.

entirely stops using tobacco products. The smoker experiences the acute withdrawal symptoms of nicotine until the chemical leaves the body, usually within forty-eight to seventy-two hours. The remaining desire to smoke is behavioral and is based on the hand-to-mouth habit and the soothing effect some smokers experience.

The desire to smoke after cessation is triggered by situations in which the smoker typically would partake of the habit, such as after a meal, while drinking alcohol, or during stressful situations. Former smokers redirect these urges by avoiding certain situations (going to a smoky bar, for example) or substituting the cigarette with something else, such as chewing gum, mints, toothpicks, or drinking straws to satisfy the oral fixation in a nontoxic, more socially acceptable manner. Exercise is also often suggested to promote the release of "feel-good" chemicals in the brain called endorphins, which mimic the soothing effects of nicotine.

Another approach is the step-down program, in which the smoker gradually weans him or herself from the habit by incrementally reducing the total number of cigarettes smoked each day. Although this approach takes longer than the cold turkey method, it often is more successful because the withdrawal symptoms are less severe, which helps to prevent relapse.

Pharmaceuticals are available to help the smoking cessation process. These are usually used with the step-down program. Pharmaceuticals include nicotine replacement products and medicines that help with the anxiety and other mood-related symptoms of withdrawal. Nicotine replacement products are available in several forms, including patches, gums, lozenges, and inhalers. The patches release nicotine into the bloodstream slowly to maintain a consistent level of nicotine in the body. The other forms of nicotine replacement provide a more immediate release of nicotine into the bloodstream and satisfy the oral habit associated with smoking.

Because nicotine is a stimulant that raises blood pressure and makes the heart work harder, nicotine replacement products need to be used as directed by the manufacturer and the smoker's physician. Some nicotine replacement products are available over the counter and others require a doctor's prescription.

Varenicline, marketed as Chantix, and bupropion, marketed as Zyban, are antidepressants that provide relief from the mood-related symptoms of withdrawal.

Unlike some nicotine replacement products that are available over the counter, a doctor's prescription is required to purchase these types of medications because they have been known to worsen depression in some people.

The best smoking cessation programs involve a multidisciplinary combination of antidepressant and anti-anxiety pharmaceuticals, behavior modification therapy by a trained addiction specialist, and nicotine replacement products. Support of family and friends also aids in successful cessation. Coverage for smoking cessation treatments varies by health insurance plan. Often, health insurance companies require a doctor's order before they will pay for treatments. Sometimes, insurance coverage will cover part of the treatment only.

Alternative therapies include acupuncture (a traditional Chinese medicine that involves hypnosis and therapeutic placement of needles under the skin at specific points on the body). Some persons report success using these modalities, but only conflicting scientific evidence is available to support their use, and most insurance companies do not cover alternative therapies.

PREVENTION

As with other addictive substances, avoiding the first smoking experience is the best prevention. Because most smokers begin at a young age, prevention consists of early education about the negative health effects of smoking. Education programs are available for children as young as five years old for use in the public school system. Also, parental reinforcement and example are key to preventing children from smoking tobacco and developing a smoking addiction.

In addition to covering the dangers of smoking, education programs usually include a self-esteem component that encourages young people to resist peer pressure. These programs take many forms, including patient and parent education by pediatric professionals, in-school programs, and public health campaigns directed to the general community. For adults, education includes patient education and information about how second-hand smoke harms not only smokers but also those around them.

Information is lacking regarding alternative forms of smoking that may falsely appear to be safe. The herbal cigarette, a tobacco alternative, is gaining popularity. Although these products contain no nicotine (usually they are a formulation of corn silk, banana peels, and other organic products), the smoke inhaled from these products still injures the lungs and leaves tar deposits. Clove cigarettes, sometimes called kreteks, are actually 60 to 80 percent tobacco; therefore, they provide no safety benefit. The flavor of these tobacco alternatives makes them attractive to new smokers, which can lead to smoking addiction.

Prevention also is critical to avoid many serious illnesses associated with smoking. Chronic lung conditions such as emphysema and chronic obstructive pulmonary disease are associated with smoking. Lung cancer, the leading cause of cancer deaths in the United States, can be largely prevented by avoiding or quitting smoking. Smoking and secondhand smoke exposure significantly increase the risk for developing cancer in other parts of the body too; for example smoke affects the mouth, throat, digestive system, and breasts. Smoking also increases the risk for heart disease and stroke.

Laura J. Pinchot, BA

FURTHER READING

Anderson, Judith. *It's Your Health: Smoking.* North Mankato, MN: Smart Apple, 2006. Provides an introduction to smoking's negative effects on the body. Written for juvenile readers.

Bingham, Jane. *Smoking.* Chicago: Heinemann Library, 2006. Examines why people smoke and the dangers of smoking.

Gilman, Sander L., and Zhou Xun, eds. *Smoke: A Global History of Smoking.* London: Reaktion, 2004. Provides an account of smoking among different cultures throughout human history.

Sanders, Bruce. *Let's Talk about Smoking.* North Mankato, MN: Stargazer, 2006. Provides a question-and-answer format on common social topics related to smoking. A brief book for juvenile readers.

US Department of Health and Human Services. "How Tobacco Smoke Causes Disease: The Biology and Behavioral Basis for Smoking-Attributable Disease—A Report of the Surgeon General." Atlanta: DHHS, 2010. Excellent review of literature related to the risks of smoking, including nicotine addiction.

WEBSITES OF INTEREST

American Cancer Society
http://www.cancer.org

Campaign for Tobacco-Free Kids
http://www.tobaccofreekids.org

Centers for Disease Control and Prevention
http://www.cdc.gov/tobacco

See also: Birth defects and smoking; Media and smoking; Men and smoking; Nicotine addiction; Nicotine replacement products; Pregnancy and smoking; Respiratory diseases and smoking; Smoking; Smoking cessation; Smoking: Short- and long-term effects on the body; Stress and smoking; Tobacco use disorder; Women and smoking

Smoking cessation

Category: Treatment

Definition: Quitting smoking is a daunting challenge. It is an addiction that is both physical and psychological, but quitting smoking can be done. In fact, nearly fifty million Americans are former smokers. There are plenty of reasons to quit when one considers smoking's fatal link with lung cancer, emphysema, and heart disease, as well as the harmful effects of secondhand smoke on immediate family.

THE MIND AND BODY CONNECTION

Smoking is addictive—both physically and psychologically. The physical addiction can be traced to the nicotine in each cigarette. It hooks an individual just as completely as heroin and cocaine, and the withdrawal symptoms—cravings, anxiety, agitation, nausea, cramps, depression, and dizziness—are similar.

Like these other drugs, nicotine surges through the bloodstream and gives smokers a high—a quick jolt that makes them think they feel better. In the meantime, what really happens is that smokers develop a tolerance for nicotine, which is why they go from a couple of cigarettes a day as a teenager to two and a half packs a day as an adult. The psychological addiction is, in its own way, just as bad. Smoking becomes second nature, like blinking or breathing. If one considers that a single pack of cigarettes per day can turn into two hundred puffs a day, seven days a week, fifty-two weeks a year, it is easy to see how hard it is to quit.

THE KEY TO QUITTING

The key to quitting is patience, perseverance, and having a plan. For many people, it is simply picking a reason that they believe in to quit smoking, whether for their family or for their own personal health. Changing one's environment is also useful, as it removes an individual from smoking triggers and can help that person avoid secondhand smoke. Tapering off is also a successful technique, though some studies show that a majority of permanent quitters achieved their goal by quitting "cold turkey." The key to tapering off is to cut down the number of cigarettes smoked each day. Techniques for this approach involve delaying the first cigarette of the day. Whether an individual decides to taper off or quit completely, the goal must be the same: abstinence.

Practicing the "Three D's"—delay, deep breathing, drink water—is also helpful for smoking cessation. This involves delaying smoking a cigarette when the need or craving arises, breathing deeply (while often counting to ten), and drinking a target of eight eight-ounce glasses of water each day. Water helps to flush nicotine out of the body. Keeping a diary is also an effective technique. A person can simply write down the time of day that they feel like having a cigarette, using a scale of one to three, with one representing the worst craving.

Medication has also proved to be successful for smoking cessation for some people. A medication called varenicline (Chantix) is a novel type of treatment that works by stimulating the release of low levels of dopamine in the brain. Nicotine in the cigarettes causes dopamine to be released, resulting in the positive feelings associated with smoking. At the time of smoking cessation, a drop in dopamine levels is related to the many withdrawals symptoms. By stimulating the release of this chemical in the brain, varenicline helps to reduce the signs and symptoms of withdrawal.

Varenicline also blocks nicotine receptors in the brain, so it helps the individual stay away from cigarettes. If a person resumes smoking while taking the medication, nicotine will not be able

---

Smoking Cessation: Exercise

Many people are concerned that they will gain weight if they quit smoking. However, with a healthy diet and regular exercise, this weight gain can be prevented. One also can lose weight with exercise. The longer a person is smoke-free, the easier it will be to breathe when he or she exercises. Also, regular exercise makes it less likely to start smoking again.

Exercise should be started slowly, but the key is to get into a routine of regular exercise. One should begin with three or four days of exercise per week, even if this involves only ten to twenty minutes of exercise each day. The time spent exercising each day should increase gradually. Persons who have been inactive or underactive physically should speak with their doctor before starting any exercise program.

---

to stimulate the brain's receptors the way it did in the past, making the habit much less pleasurable. Based on the research available thus far, it appears that varenicline works better than placebo and bupropion, another antidepressant used for quitting smoking. Taking varenicline has been associated, however, with some side effects. The most frequently reported include: nausea, headache, insomnia, bad dreams, and changes in the way food tastes. Varenicline and bupropion also may increase the risk of serious mood and behavior changes.

Other options to help a person quit smoking are: over-the-counter nicotine patches, gum, and lozenges, which may be used alone or in combination; prescription nicotine inhalers or nasal sprays; the prescription antidepressant bupropion; alternative therapies, such as hypnosis and acupuncture; and smoking cessation classes. Self-help programs such as Internet and computer-based programs are another option. There are also telephone quit lines, cell phone programs, and text messaging programs. For some, group behavior therapy may be more helpful than self-help programs. Trying a combination of these options may work best. For example, using a nicotine patch and going to group therapy may be the best option for some individuals.

Jeff Siegel

FURTHER READING

Potts, Lisa A., and Candice L. Garwood. "Varenicline: The Newest Agent for Smoking Cessation." *American Journal of Health-System Pharmacy* 64.13 (2007): 1381–1384. Reviews varenicline as an alternative to nicotine-replacement therapy and bupropion. Covers topics such as the pharmacology of varenicline, its clinical efficacy, its safety, and dosage administration.

White, Adrian R., Russell C. Moody, and John L. Campbell. "Acupressure for Smoking Cessation—A Pilot Study." *BMC Complementary & Alternative Medicine* 7.8 (2007): 14. Reviews a study that tested acupressure as a possible adjunct to nicotine-replacement therapy (NRT) and behavioral intervention.

Williams, Katherine E., et al. "A Double-Blind Study Evaluating the Long-Term Safety of Varenicline for Smoking Cessation." *Current Medical Research and Opinion* 23.4 (2007): 793–801. Covers a study that assessed the safety of long-term varenicline administration for smoking cessation.

WEBSITES OF INTEREST

American Lung Association
http://www.lung.org

Tobacco Information and Prevention Source (TIPS)
http://www.cdc.gov/tobacco/

See also: Bupropion; Nicotine addiction; Nicotine replacement products; Smoking; Smoking cessation for older adults; Tobacco use disorder

Smoking cessation for older adults

Category: Treatment

Definition: Many people do not realize that smoking cessation has immediate as well as long-term benefits. Seniors who quit smoking tend to enjoy better health and quality of life than their peers who continue to smoke.

GAINING HEALTH BENEFITS

For many long-term or older smokers, the drive to quit smoking is often comprised or derailed by the feeling that the "damage is already done." However, smoking cessation has numerous immediate health benefits, whether the smoker is young or old. They include, in just one day: an increase of blood circulation; a decrease in carbon monoxide levels in the blood; decreases in heart rate and blood pressure; and a decrease in the risk of having a heart attack. In several days to several weeks, smoking cessation can improve the sense of smell and taste, increase lung capacity, and ease breathing. In several weeks to nine months, ex-smokers should see energy levels increase and should have cleaner and more functional lungs.

Quitting smoking has additional health benefits as well. Colds and other respiratory tract infections become less common, and both sinus congestion and shortness of breath decrease. The risk of heart disease and lung cancer also decreases, and risk can eventually be similar to that of a lifelong nonsmoker. Additionally, smoking cessation decreases the risk of peripheral vascular disease, stroke, and chronic lung disease (bronchitis, emphysema, and asthma). Giving up cigarettes may also reduce the risk of cataracts, macular degeneration, thyroid conditions, hearing loss, erectile dysfunction, dementia, and osteoporosis.

Older smokers are usually more successful at quitting smoking than younger smokers. This is especially true if they already have health problems, particularly those associated with smoking. Studies suggest that elderly persons who ask their doctors about help for smoking cessation are more likely to receive that help and are more likely to be successful quitters. While quitting all at once tends to be most effective, selecting an appropriate method of quitting and learning how to handle stress are important for those considering smoking cessation. The following are imperative for successful smoking cessation: understanding cravings and how to handle them through distraction; understanding the importance of familial and other support; and avoiding weight gain by eating healthy and exercising. It should also be noted that most ex-smokers make several attempts to quit before they are successful.

Amy Scholten, MPH

FURTHER READING

Appel, D. W., and T. K. Aldrich. "Smoking Cessation in the Elderly." *Clinics in Geriatric Medicine* 19.1 (2003): 77–100. Discusses methods to help elderly smokers quit, even those with fatalism. Highlights the success of programs that stress the health benefits of cessation.

Elhassen, Amir, and R. Dobbin Chow. "Smoking Cessation in the Elderly." *Clinical Geriatrics* 15.2 (2007): 38–45. Discusses the trends in tobacco use over the past fifty years, demonstrates the benefits of smoking cessation in the elderly, and recommends treatment for people wishing to quit smoking.

Whitson, H. E., M. T. Helfin, and B. M. Burchett. "Patterns and Predictors of Smoking Cessation in an Elderly Cohort." *Journal of the American Geriatrics Society* 54.3 (2006): 466–471. Identifies patterns of cessation in elderly smokers and subject characteristics that predict cessation and relapse.

WEBSITES OF INTEREST
American Lung Association
http://www.lung.org

Tobacco Information and Prevention Source (TIPS)
http://www.cdc.gov/tobacco/

See also: Bupropion; Elderly and addictions; Nicotine addiction; Nicotine replacement products; Smoking; Smoking cessation; Tobacco use disorder

Smoking: Short- and long-term effects on the body

CATEGORY: Health issues and physiology

DEFINITION: Tobacco smoking leads to bodily changes such as increased blood pressure and heart rate within minutes or hours of inhalation. Habitual smoking has long-term consequences such as chronic lung and coronary heart disease and numerous cancers.

SHORT-TERM EFFECTS

A major reason for the spread and popularity of tobacco since the sixteenth century is connected to one of its short-term effects on the human body. An important active ingredient in tobacco smoke is nicotine, which is rapidly delivered into the bloodstream through the lungs. Nicotine is then transported to receptors in the central nervous system, increasing heart rate and the release of dopamine, a pleasure-inducing chemical. Tobacco smoke also contains chemical substances that increase heart rate and elevate blood pressure, sometimes causing dizziness and tremors because of a reduced flow of oxygenated blood to the brain and extremities.

Smoking also has short-term effects on the respiratory and digestive systems. Research on animals and humans has demonstrated that inhaling smoke from cigarettes impairs pulmonary clearance, which can lead to coughing and increased susceptibility to colds and allergens. Smoking attenuates the functioning of the lung's cilia and alveoli, reducing the lung's ability to oxygenate blood.

With regard to the digestive system, studies indicate that components of cigarette smoke foster increased acidity in the stomach, while other studies show that smoking may exacerbate gastric and duodenal ulcers. Deceptive advertisers have at times created the impression that one of the beneficial aspects of smoking is appetite reduction, instilling the fear that cessation of smoking will lead to weight gain. Many researchers, however, insist that this fear must be directly opposed because documented weight gain after cessation has complex causes.

The body's nervous, muscular, and reproductive systems are quickly affected by certain components in tobacco smoke. Because nicotine readily passes through the blood-brain barrier, it stimulates certain receptors that in novice smokers may induce nausea. In experienced smokers, however, this fact may explain why, with various physiological changes, some of them pleasurable, smoking becomes a deeply entrenched habit. Much research indicates that nicotine plays a significant role in establishing the smoking habit, though some smokers become dependent on nicotine-free cigarettes.

Because of smoking's negative effects on the muscular system, athletes have been perennially warned about smoking's ability to impair performance. Also, extensive research has been done on the immediate effects of the multiple harmful chemicals in cigarette smoke on the fetuses of animals and humans. These chemicals cause such effects as changes in fetal heart rate and placental circulation and metabolism; a rise in carboxyhemoglobin concentrations; and a host of other problems, which have led to a series of warnings that pregnant women should not smoke.

LONG-TERM EFFECTS

Scientific research has revealed that smokers are exchanging short-term pleasures for a devastating array of extremely negative long-term health consequences, including chronic problems for the circulatory, respiratory, and other bodily systems. Extensive research has shown that habitual smoking dramatically increases the risk for arteriosclerosis and coronary heart disease. General agreement exists that acute and chronic cardiovascular effects of smoking can be largely attributed to nicotine. Smoking also has been associated with narrowing of the blood vessels in the heart, brain, and other organs, significantly increasing the chances of stroke.

According to some analysts, the body's respiratory system experiences the most devastating damage from long-term smoking. Evidence shows a causal relationship between smoking and lung cancer, and that smokers are ten times as likely as nonsmokers to have lung cancer. These studies also indicate that more than 90 percent of all lung-cancer cases in men, and 80 percent in women, are caused by smoking. Furthermore, habitual smoking has been associated with increased susceptibility to such chronic obstructive lung diseases as emphysema and bronchitis.

Because smoking reduces the effectiveness of the body's immune system, habitual smokers readily have a variety of respiratory infections, including pneumonia. Other research has established a causal relationship between smoking and cancers of the digestive and urinary systems. For example, smokers are much more likely to develop and to die from cancers of the mouth, throat, esophagus, stomach, colon, pancreas, bladder, and kidneys. Indeed, several analysts believe that more than 30 percent of all cancer deaths in the United States can be directly attributed to smoking.

Much research has been devoted to studying the long-term health effects of smoking on the reproductive system. These studies have revealed negative effects from fertilization to birth. Smoking causes lowered fertility, stunted fetal growth, increased likelihood of miscarriages and premature births, and complications for normal-term births. Women who are habitual smokers also give birth to babies with weights much less than normal, and the harmful chemicals in the bodies of breastfeeding mothers who are smoking can be passed to their babies, causing immediate and long-term damage. The reproductive systems of men

Tobacco

Tobacco, used as a stimulant, is made up of the dried leaves of the plants *Nicotiana tabacum, N. rustica,* or other related *Nicotiana* species. Tobacco contains a number of alkaloids and other chemicals that give it its stimulant properties.

The primary component is the alkaloid nicotine. Most cured tobacco leaves contain 1 to 3 percent nicotine, but those derived from *N. rustica* and its hybrids can have as much as 9 percent nicotine. Nicotine binds to various nerve receptors, causing the stimulation and euphoria seen with tobacco use. In addition, nicotine paralyzes cilia in the respiratory and reproductive tracts, leading to increased infections and ectopic pregnancies. It also is an extremely addictive chemical.

Several of the other chemicals that are found in cured tobacco are carcinogens, and even more carcinogens are formed when cured tobacco is smoked. (Smoke from burning tobacco contains an estimated forty different carcinogens.) In addition to causing cancer, many of the components of tobacco smoke can damage lung tissue, leading to chronic bronchitis, chronic obstructive pulmonary disease, and emphysema.

also are affected by smoking, with reduced sperm count and increased impotency the most commonly reported problems.

Although the negative cosmetic effects of smoking are not as serious as the effects on the major systems of the body, they have, nevertheless, been studied. For example, smoking leads to premature aging of the skin, chiefly by interfering with the collagen production involved in renewing skin. Habitual smoking often results in bad breath, stained teeth, discolored fingers, and an unhealthy complexion.

Because of all the short- and long-term effects of smoking on the body, various institutions, including the World Health Organization, the US Office of the Surgeon General, and the American Heart Association, have persistently urged smokers to quit so that they might enjoy longer, healthier lives.

Robert J. Paradowski, PhD

FURTHER READING

Brandt, Allan M. *The Cigarette Century: The Rise, Fall, and Deadly Persistence of the Product That Defined*

America. New York: Basic, 2007. This historical account of how smoking became deeply ingrained in American culture contains a wealth of information about how researchers gradually discovered the deleterious effects of smoking and how the tobacco industry resisted these truths. Includes extensive references and an index.

Glantz, Stanton A., et al. *The Cigarette Papers.* Berkeley: U of California P, 1996. Based on four thousand pages of internal secret documents, this study reveals how the tobacco industry hampered the public's learning of the negative short- and long-term effects of their money-making products. Includes a document list, document index, and subject index.

How Tobacco Smoke Causes Disease: The Biology and Behavioral Basis for Smoking-Attributable Disease: A Report of the Surgeon General. Rockville, MD: DHHS, 2010. This report on the health effects of smoking contains information from thousands of studies proving that smoking has affected the health of millions of Americans. Includes a list of tables and figures and an index.

Lock, Stephen, Lois Reynolds, and E. M. Tansey. *Ashes to Ashes: The History of Smoking and Health.* Atlanta: Rodopi, 1998. This book, part of the Wellcome Institute series in the History of Medicine, contains chapters on such topics as the first reports on smoking and lung cancer. Also includes an introduction and concluding remarks that help to unify chapter themes. Includes an index.

WEBSITES OF INTEREST

American Cancer Society
http://www.cancer.org

American Lung Association
http://www.lung.org

Centers for Disease Control and Prevention
http://www.cdc.gov/tobacco

MedlinePlus: Smoking
http://www.nlm.nih.gov/medlineplus/smoking.
html

SmokeFree.gov
http://www.smokefree.gov

US Surgeon General
http://www.surgeongeneral.gov/tobacco

See also: Cancer and substance abuse; Chronic bronchitis; Chronic obstructive pulmonary disease (COPD); Emphysema; Lung cancer; Nicotine addiction; Respiratory diseases and smoking; Smoking; Tobacco use disorder

Sober living environments

CATEGORY: Treatment

ALSO KNOWN AS: Halfway houses; recovery residences; sober housing; supportive living; transitional living

DEFINITION: Sober living environments are group housing communities that are intended solely for recovering and recovered addicts. These are not permanent residences or treatment centers; instead, they are interim homes for sober residents who may have no stable place to live after completing an inpatient or outpatient treatment or rehabilitation program. Sober housing includes any living arrangement that temporarily provides structure and safety to a recovering addict without medical care; halfway houses and other transitional residences are specific examples of sober living arrangements in which residents benefit from the structure of a contained society as a bridge between fully supervised treatment programs and complete independence as a functioning member of society.

BACKGROUND

The sober living environment, because of its variety of development sources (for example, nonprofit, private ownership, and peer group initiatives), is a relatively new and little-studied development in standard addiction care. These environments are available across the United States. Some are faith-based and nonprofit, whereas others are privately funded; some are based in single-family group homes, and others are in apartment-style dwellings.

Sober living environments are homes that have little counselor supervision, unlike residential treatment centers, which are staffed with multiple social workers and counselors as community residents. Sober housing encourages sustained abstinence by providing a recovered addict a place to learn and practice independent coping skills away from drugs or behaviors related to addiction and abuse.

These homes promote sobriety in multiple ways. For example, they allow for a recovered addict to avoid frequenting old temptations and habits (such as particular places, hobbies, and people) by acting as a safe and stable environment. Also, they introduce recovered addicts to other people with similar concerns and histories to encourage socialization that supports continued recovery and promotes shared knowledge of relapse and recovery. The basic structure involves residency of 90 to 365 days, with rents charged to support the facility. Programs within the residence may be additionally supported by donations, nonprofit foundations, or grant awards.

Halfway houses and other sober living environments are particularly useful for people whose home or work environments before receiving addiction treatment were unstable or were not drug free. Recovery residences introduce experiences that model new, drug-free living for many struggling addicts.

At a minimum, each sober living environment has guidelines that the residents must follow to remain in the home. Most sober living environments assign housekeeping duties and curfews to residents; these responsibilities and expectations boost self-esteem and establish time for group participation. Thus, residents work and live together for the benefit of everyone in the home. Common transitional living rules include bans on overnight guests, prohibition of any substance of abuse, and required involvement in a peer group at the home.

Unlike patients of residential treatment or inpatient programs, the residents of sober housing are expected to hold a functional place in society outside the home, such as a work position, school enrollment, or other form of community involvement. Some halfway houses exist for adolescents only, while others exist for women or men only. Housing options involve wide ranges of supervision, and many employ random drug-testing to ensure abstinence.

MISSION AND GOALS
Sober living environments are common extenders of care in the twenty-first century, often because funding

for many treatment programs remains insufficient. Longer durations of structured programming, whether in hospitalized settings, prison settings, or full-time residential treatment centers, help prevent relapse.

Sober living facilities do not provide medical care or the same level of structure as treatment centers. However, they do embody abstinence-based living without the costs of specialized professional care, with a minimal cost burden. Sober living environments prolong the community and psychosocial support begun during detoxification or rehabilitation, after that stage of care is considered successful and complete.

A sober living environment aims to prevent recovered addicts from falling into old lifestyles that facilitate drug abuse after achieving treatment successes. Through group involvement, residents are guided toward goals of community development, in daily duties such as chores and in sharing of past treatment experiences. Sober housing frequently requires membership in a twelve-step model such as Alcoholics Anonymous or Narcotics Anonymous to foster recovery; thus, sponsors and meetings are incorporated into the sober living home to encourage trust and sobriety.

Often, members of a sober living arrangement have opportunities to participate in additional counseling or life training sessions at the residence. Freedom to leave the residence helps achieve the goal of independent, abstinent living in the larger society outside the home. The goal of any type of sober living environment is to provide safety, support, and accountability in the early period of this abstinent living.

Sober living environments provide a routine and a schedule that are likely new and beneficial to residents, who learn to manage time and share recovery goals with the other residents. Participants in sober living environments become a network of like-minded individuals, a network that can be extended even beyond the move to independent living circumstances.

Nicole M. Van Hoey, PharmD

FURTHER READING

Heslin, K. C., et al. "Alternative Families in Recovery: Fictive Kin Relationships among Residents of Sober Living Homes." *Qualitative Health Research* 21.4 (2011): 477–88. Print. Discusses the relationships that develop during a recovered addict's stay at a sober living home, which support the goal of abstinence even beyond the time of residence.

Polcin, D. C. "A Model for Sober Housing during Out-patient Treatment." *Journal of Psychoactive Drugs* 41.2 (2009): 153–61. Print. Reviews one example of a sober living environment and details the beneficial results of even short-term residence on a path to recovery.

Rasmussen, Sandra. *Addiction Treatment: Theory and Practice.* Thousand Oaks, CA: Sage, 2000. Distinguishes halfway houses, sober housing, and therapeutic communities as different types of residences that extend the accountability period for people recovering from substance abuse.

Youngs, Bettie B., Jennifer Leigh Youngs, and Tina Moreno. *A Teen's Guide to Living Drug-Free.* Deerfield Beach, FL: Health Communications, 2003. An informal guide to sober living for teenagers, who comprise a primary population that struggles with avoiding the temptations of drug and alcohol abuse.

WEBSITES OF INTEREST

Addiction Recovery Guide
http://www.addictionrecoveryguide.org/treatment/sober_housing

RecoveryCorps.org
http://www.recoverycorps.org

SoberLivingHouses.net
http://soberlivinghouses.net

Substance Abuse and Mental Health Services Administration
http://www.samhsa.gov

See also: Abstinence-based treatment; Alcohol abuse and alcoholism: Treatment; Halfway houses; Recovery; Residential treatment; Treatment methods and research

Social media addiction

CATEGORY: Psychological issues and behaviors
DEFINITION: Social media addiction represents a constellation of uncontrollable, impulsive, and damaging behaviors caused by persistent social media usage that continues despite repeated negative consequences.

BACKGROUND

The rise in popularity of social media websites, such as Facebook and Twitter, has spawned an age of social media consumption that is difficult to quantify. Rather than point to specific numbers or trends in everyday use, perhaps a better way of considering the effect of social media on society is to consider that two professional journals now chronicle the ongoing relationship with social media. The new journals are the *Journal of Social Media* and the *Journal of Cyberpsychology and Behavior*, both of which are relevant to studies of the effects of social media on human behavior.

Facebook, for example, has changed the way that people communicate and maintain social relationships, both in productive and nonproductive ways. Twitter has become a global vehicle through which people collect, report, and share the news of the moment. Communicating with other people has become easier and more immediate, while the boundaries, rules, and language that govern this communication have become more convoluted. As a result, research aimed at how and why people find themselves using social media (and technology in general) is on the rise.

Furthermore, features of one's personality that predict heavy (or limited) social media use are under investigation. So too are the merits of what widely interconnected, online relationships mean for face-to-face communication, intimacy, and privacy.

THE HUMAN RELATIONSHIP WITH TECHNOLOGY

Social media researcher Sherry Turkle has been exploring the interaction of human relationships and technology for decades. Her work has developed a collective understanding of how human beings interface with a technological society. Her seminal works applying self and interpersonal theories to social media relationships were predictive and formative. Turkle has shown that technological advances have made it virtually impossible to isolate oneself from complex interpersonal relationships. Additionally, technology has done as much to challenge self-representation as it has challenged interpersonal relationships. In so doing, the ways in which one's real life aligns with one's virtual life are telling and have become useful fodder for ongoing research.

Psychological Addiction? Loneliness, Anxiety, Shyness
Because of the long-held assumption that social media helps to foster meaningful, online relationships, and

because of the ease through which one can build a relationship with someone previously unknown to them, three psychological concerns in particular are now being studied: loneliness, anxiety, and shyness. No consensus exists on how these factors intersect with one's proclivity for social media (or for social media addiction), though there are a few interesting points to highlight.

First, research has shown a clear line of preference between people who self-identify as "lonely" and people who self-identify as "anxious"; specifically, lonely people prefer face-to-face communication (they find that social media lacks intimacy), whereas anxious people prefer electronic modes of communication. As such, loneliness has come to be better understood as something self-representational (with concerns hovering around issues of the self rather than of a specific fear of others or of socializing with others). Anxious people prefer social media because of the anonymity involved, making it easier to rationalize possible disapproval while having more control over how the other person experiences them. Lonely people seek levels of intimacy that, while possible through social media, are not easily attainable.

Second, shyness is not something that inhibits social media usage despite the likelihood that shy people will experience the same minimal amount of social contact online as they would otherwise. Despite reported difficulty maintaining online relationships, shy people report heightened satisfaction in their virtual worlds. This is likely because they are spending a greater amount of time seeking, surveying, and considering positive social encounters while online. Additionally, social media provide a rather safe and secure outlet for heightened social interaction.

Third, the issue of locus of control has come under scrutiny as it relates to potential social media addiction. Specifically, research has examined closely the types of reinforcements experienced by heavy social media users. People are less likely to become addicted to social media if they feel that they have control over their own lives (both online and off), whereas people are more likely to be addicted to social media if they feel as if others have greater control over them (both online and off).

Turkle's analysis of the Internet (and social media) as seductive is especially relevant here, particularly when one considers the fluid nature of a person's experience of social media. That is, a person can update, alter, change, or redefine his or her online identity in the click of a button.

Joseph C. Viola, PhD

FURTHER READING

Beard, Keith W. "Internet Addiction: A Review of Current Assessment Techniques and Potential Assessment Questions." *Cyberpsychology and Behavior* 8.1 (2007): 7–14. Print. A useful article for those looking to initiate research in this particular area. Examines the relevant methodological issues important to research into social media (as well as some of the common challenges).

Chak, Katherine M., and Lous Leung. "Shyness and Locus of Control as Predictors of Internet Addiction and Internet Use." *Cyberpsychology and Behavior* 7.5 (2004): 559–70. Print. Examines at internal versus external reinforcement factors and how they affect one's proclivity for social media usage. Relates well to Turkle's work on self and interpersonal theory, challenges several notions about shyness and social media, and captures ongoing dilemmas in research methodology.

Chia-Yi, Mba, and Feng-Yang Kuo. "A Study of Internet Addiction through the Lens of the Interpersonal Theory." *Cyberpsychology and Behavior* 10.6 (2007): 799–804. Print. Of particular interest in this article is the exploration of the negative correlation found between addiction and interpersonal relationships. Also explores reasons underlying addictive behaviors.

Lam, Lawrence T., et al. "Factors Associated with Internet Addiction among Adolescents." *Cyberpsychology and Behavior* 12.5 (2009): 551–55. Print. Attempts to identify relevant risk factors for addiction in a younger population. Of particular concern are adolescents who are male, dissatisfied with their family, and have recently experienced a stressful event.

Muise, Amy M., Emily Christofides, and Serge Desmarais. "More Information Than You Ever Wanted: Does Facebook Bring out the Green-Eyed Monster of Jealousy?" *Cyberpsychology and Behavior* 12.4 (2009): 441–44. Print. Counterbalances research suggesting long-term positive benefits of social media usage. Concerned with how social media can potentially introduce one to more jealousy-provoking information than would ordinarily be available.

Orr, Emily S., et al. "The Influence of Shyness on the Use of Facebook in an Undergraduate Sample." *Cyberpsychology and Behavior* 12.3 (2009): 337–40. Print. A good example of the type of research being conducted to better understand how increasing social media usage intersects with shyness.

Rosen, Larry D. *iDisorder: Understanding Our Dependency on Technology and Overcoming Our Addiction.* New York: Palgrave, 2012. Based on decades of research and expertise in the psychology of technology. Offers clear explanations for why many people are addicted to technology, including social media.

Stevens, Sarah, and Tracy Morris. "College Dating and Social Anxiety: Using the Internet as a Means of Connecting to Others." *Cyberpsychology and Behavior* 10.5 (2007): 680–88. Print. This article examines whether or not high levels of social anxiety (specifically, dating anxiety) are related to heightened social media usage.

Turkle, Sherry. "Whither Psychoanalysis in Computer Culture." *Psychoanalytic Psychology* 21.1 (2004): 16–30. Print. This article explores three competing (though related) theoretical orientations that help explain the human relationship with technology.

WEBSITES OF INTEREST

Center for Internet Addiction
http://www.netaddiction.com

Internet Addiction Guide
http://psychcentral.com/netaddiction

See also: Behavioral addictions: Overview; Computer addiction; Gaming addiction; Internet addiction

Socioeconomic status and addiction

CATEGORY: Social issues

DEFINITION: Socioeconomic status is the social classification of an individual by such measures as income, education level, occupation, and community of residence. Socioeconomic status is often subdivided into high, middle, and low categories. Addiction and substance abuse affect persons of all socioeconomic stratifications.

LOW SOCIOECONOMIC STATUS

When compared with persons of middle or high socioeconomic class, persons with a low socioeconomic status have lower salaries and accumulated wealth, may be unemployed, may have lower levels of education (often because of dropping out of school), and may face homelessness or the prospect losing their current place of residence. These stressors may lead to depression and anxiety.

In general, a depressed person is more likely to abuse substances to ease these feelings. Addiction, however, often perpetuates one's lower socioeconomic status because smoking, alcohol, and drug use all cost money; furthermore, abusing substances takes time from potential employment or from seeking employment. To maintain the addiction or substance abuse the person may undertake illegal activities, such as dealing drugs, prostitution, or stealing to pay for or obtain a substance.

A person with low socioeconomic status often resides in a neighborhood that may have higher risk factors for substance abuse and addiction. These risk factors include the ready availability of drugs, the prominence of successful drug dealers as role models or leaders in the neighborhood, and a lack of educational opportunities in areas without adequate funding resources. Homelessness also is included in this category. However, a common misconception is that addiction causes homelessness, but more often the reverse is true: Addiction is often a result of homelessness, which increases feelings of hopelessness and depression.

It is well documented that an addiction to smoking, alcohol, or drugs can lead to significant health concerns. Persons of lower socioeconomic status have limited and unequal access to health care. Untreated medical problems also contribute to feelings of stress and depression and can, therefore, perpetuate addiction. Some studies have found the lower one's socioeconomic status, the greater that person's risk of dying from complications of alcohol or drug abuse.

Lower educational levels also are associated with substance abuse. Some studies have found that the lower the person's educational level, the more likely that person will drink more alcohol per occasion. Other studies have found that whereas cocaine use is on the decline in persons of higher socioeconomic status, use in persons of lower socioeconomic status remains constant. This difference has been attributed to successful education programs in schools and communities regarding the health hazards of cocaine use.

Addiction also may create feelings of stigmatization and discrimination. For example, poor persons or those who are unemployed are stigmatized by society; addiction might stem from this stigma or enable it.

It is important to remember that while the variables mentioned here are risk factors for substance abuse, not all studies have documented that persons from low socioeconomic status groups have different addiction rates from persons of middle or high socioeconomic status groups. Some studies show that parenting skills and parental psychopathology play more of a role in the development of addiction than does socioeconomic status. There are many factors that

lead to drug and alcohol abuse, and continuing research is necessary to understand the contributions of these risk factors in addiction.

MIDDLE AND HIGH SOCIOECONOMIC STATUS

Early research on risk factors for substance abuse focused solely on persons from low socioeconomic backgrounds because of stereotypes and misconceptions. However, later research indicates that substance abuse occurs among persons of all socioeconomic statuses. Although depression and anxiety within the low socioeconomic status group may stem directly from financial and educational stressors, no person is immune to these psychological diagnoses.

Persons of middle and high socioeconomic status experience social and emotional stresses too, but

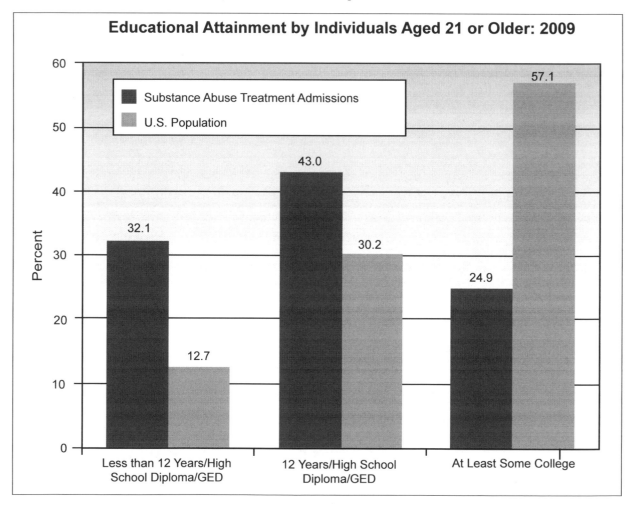

Source: Substance Abuse and Mental Health Services Administration (SAMHSA) Treatment Episode Data Set (TEDS), 2009

perhaps for different reasons. These stresses include the demands of a job, family, and school. Often a person's addiction is concealed at the place of employment or at home, leading to feelings of guilt and shame. Among persons in the middle and high socioeconomic status groups, teenagers are at greatest risk for substance abuse and addiction.

Typically, persons of middle and high socioeconomic status do not initially have the same financial pressures of addiction because, by definition, they begin with a greater individual or household income. Thus, money is available to support not only an addiction but also a more expensive addiction. Though research has demonstrated a higher rate of nicotine addiction in lower socioeconomic status groups, it has found an increased risk for alcohol, marijuana, and cocaine abuse in middle and high socioeconomic status groups. Teenagers who are experimenting with drugs have a greater ability to buy more expensive substances and in greater quantities.

Persons of middle and high socioeconomic status have more access to educational resources. As parents have typically obtained a college or higher degree, they encourage children to do the same. A teenage child who lives independently from his or her family at college has a greater risk for substance abuse because of this freedom from parental oversight. However, the younger the addiction begins, the more likely a person will not complete his or her education and obtain a job. This person also is more likely to be prosecuted for using illegal substances.

When an addiction becomes apparent within the wealthier family, more resources are often available for disease intervention and management. These families tend to have greater access to expensive inpatient treatment facilities, or they are more likely to be able to financially support the addict while in treatment or when facing criminal charges.

Family mobility, defined as families moving into and out of a community, also may play a role in addiction. Increased family mobility decreases the sense of community and social interaction within a neighborhood. Persons who cannot rely on established bonds within their community are at a greater risk for substance abuse and addiction.

PREVENTION AND TREATMENT

The challenge with treating and preventing addiction in all socioeconomic classes stems from the need to address a multitude of variables, including all of the aforementioned components of socioeconomic status and the family system. The process must start with treating any underlying psychological diagnoses such as depression or anxiety, with specific attention to the reason for these feelings. This treatment may involve psychotherapy alone, but it also may be combined with pharmacotherapy, if needed.

For persons of low socioeconomic status, vital to goal achievement are programs that help them obtain better jobs or receive higher education. The necessary tools or knowledge to help realize these goals may not be available, however.

It is extremely important for governmental programs to target not just one person with an addiction but the larger community too. Children and young adults often will succumb to peer pressure, and only when the entire community, including the family unit, helps to reduce the risk factors for addiction will neighborhood programs truly succeed. This approach also benefits societal goals for greater overall productivity and less energy use for prosecuting addicts and treating substance abuse.

Teenagers are considered to be at highest risk within the middle and high socioeconomic status groups, so interventions should target this population. Adolescents are at risk for continuing the addiction into adulthood. School and governmental programs can educate not only the teenager but also the parents, other family members, and educators. Also, parents should closely monitor and regulate their child's monetary allowances, which can be used to buy substances of abuse.

Janet Ober Berman, MS, CGC

FURTHER READING

Casswell, Sally, Megan Pledger, and Rhonda Hooper. "Socioeconomic Status and Drinking Patterns in Young Adults." *Addiction* 98.5 (2003): 601–10. Print. Research study that found that low socioeconomic status places a person at an increased risk for alcohol-related death; contradicts earlier research that found no differences among socioeconomic status groups.

Gallea, Sandro, and David Vlahov. "Social Determinants and the Health of Drug Users: Socioeconomic Status, Homelessness, and Incarceration." *Public Health Reports* 117, suppl. 1 (2002): S135–45. Print. Provides recommendations for public health policies to reduce addiction among persons of low socioeconomic status.

Humensky, Jennifer. "Are Adolescents with High Economic Status More Likely to Engage in Alcohol and Illicit Drug Use in Early Childhood?" *Substance Abuse Treatment, Prevention, and Policy* 5.19 (2010): 1–10. Print. Study demonstrates that high socioeconomic status is associated with an increased accessibility to drugs.

Wiles, Nicola, et al. "Socio-Economic Status in Childhood and Later Alcohol Use: A Systematic Review." *Addiction* 102 (2007): 1546–63. Print. Literature review that found no increased risk for alcohol addiction based on low socioeconomic status.

WEBSITES OF INTEREST

American Psychological Association, Socioeconomic Status Office
http://www.apa.org/pi/ses

National Institute on Drug Abuse
http://www.drugabuse.gov

US Census Bureau
http://www.census.gov

See also: Age and addiction; Crime and behavioral addictions; Crime and substance abuse; Economic impact of addiction; Elderly and addictions; Gender and addiction; Health disparities and substance abuse; Homelessness; Insurance for addiction treatment; Models of addiction; Poverty and substance abuse; Slang

Solvents

CATEGORY: Substances

ALSO KNOWN AS: Inhalants; volatile organic compounds

DEFINITION: Solvents are volatile organic liquids that readily dissolve other substances. When inhaled, solvents can act as central nervous system depressants similar to alcohol and anesthetics. Solvents are typically the first psychoactive substances misused by young people for mind-altering and rec-reational purposes because they are easily obtainable and relatively inexpensive.

STATUS: Legal in the United States and worldwide; restrictions on the sale of solvents to minors

CLASSIFICATION: Nonscheduled status

SOURCE: Household and commercial chemicals such as toluene, benzene, chloroform, coolants, paints, glues, gases, petroleum products, cleaning fluids and sprays

TRANSMISSION ROUTE: Inhaled through the nose and mouth from the container (sniffing or snorting), sniffed from inside a plastic or paper bag (bagging), put on a rag before sniffing (huffing), or sprayed directly into the mouth (spraying)

HISTORY OF USE

Experimentation with solvent inhalation originated hundreds of years ago for medicinal and recreational purposes. During the nineteenth century, anesthetics such as chloroform, nitrous oxide (laughing gas), and ether were commonly inhaled at "sniffing parties" to achieve intoxication.

Solvents encompass a broad range of poisonous chemicals that were never meant for human consumption. Solvent inhalation is a dangerous and highly toxic method of intoxication. For many users, solvents are considered a gateway drug that leads to illicit drug and alcohol abuse.

Modern-day solvent misuse began among young Americans in the mid-twentieth century with the sniffing of gasoline fumes and glue containing toluene. By the 1970s, inhalant abusers began using more dangerous products, such as aerosols, propellants, and coolants. During this time, the euphoric effects of solvent intoxication were fully recognized. Solvent abuse became a social activity among young people at "sniffing dens." By the 1980s the incidence of volatile solvent misuse increased substantially.

The widespread misuse of solvents prompted the English government to pass the Intoxicating Substances (Supply) Act in 1985. This law restricted the sale of solvents for inhalation to minors under the age of eighteen years. Some US states have enacted similar laws restricting the sale of solvents to minors. Most solvents are not considered controlled substances because of their legitimate everyday uses.

Solvent inhalation still remains a serious issue among young people; it is the third most abused substance worldwide after alcohol and tobacco. It is especially prevalent among "street children" and by peoples in developing countries. In South America solvents are considered the drugs of poor people, used by a significant number of young children to dull pain and hunger.

EFFECTS AND POTENTIAL RISKS

Solvent vapors are inhaled and quickly absorbed into the bloodstream and passed to the brain. The effects of solvent inhalation are rapid and short-lived. Solvent inhalation produces effects similar to those of alcohol and anesthetics by depressing the central nervous system. These chemicals act by stimulating the release and binding of gamma-amino butyric acid, a natural nerve-calming agent, to receptors in the brain. This effect causes activity in the brain to slow, inducing sleep, reducing anxiety, and relaxing muscles.

The short-term effects of solvent inhalation resemble alcohol intoxication. Solvent inhalation rapidly produces a surge of euphoria, exhilaration,

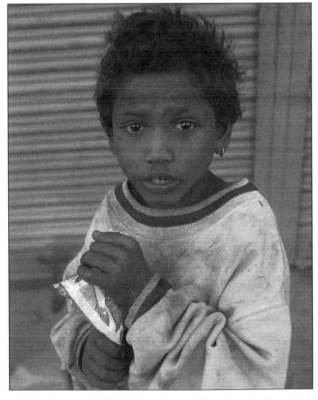

A Nepali street child holds a glue-sniffing bag in the capital Kathmandu. (Gopal Chitrakar/Reuters/Landov)

power, and loss of inhibition. Once the brief high subsides, the chemicals act like depressants, slowing bodily functions. This causes the user to feel depressed, tired, and physically ill, symptoms similar to those of a hangover. Users frequently mix solvents with other psychoactive substances or repeatedly inhale solvents to extend the intoxication.

Negative short-term effects of solvent use include nausea, vomiting, headache, dizziness, flushing, abdominal cramps, tinnitus, coughing, sneezing, increased salivation, slurred speech, blurred vision, loss of coordination, forgetfulness, confusion, fatigue, muscle weakness, chest pain, impaired judgment, agitation, delusions, lightheadedness, and hallucinations. Long-term solvent abuse can be associated with oral ulcerations, muscle spasms, numbness, memory loss, irritability, hostility, lethargy, severe depression, paranoia, anorexia, and depressed respiration.

Serious medical complications associated with solvent use include fatal overdose, accidental injury, hearing and vision loss, temporary unconsciousness, coma, brain damage, kidney and liver complications, neurological impairment, cardiac arrhythmia, and heart failure. Excessive solvent exposure may result in an increased risk of cancer and embryonic birth defects from carcinogenic and teratogenic properties. Sniffing high-solvent concentrations may be life threatening and result in unconsciousness and instant death, known as sudden sniffing death.

Some users may become psychologically dependent on solvents to compensate for personal problems. Suddenly stopping solvent use may induce symptoms similar to those of alcohol withdrawal. These symptoms include headaches, chills, shaking, muscle spasms, abdominal pain, and hallucinations.

Rose Ciulla-Bohling, PhD

FURTHER READING

Balster, Robert L., et al. "Classification of Abused Inhalants." *Addiction* 104.6 (2009): 878–82. Print. Examines inhalant abuse and the usefulness of classifying inhalants based on chemical and pharmacological qualities.

Fields, Richard. *Drugs in Perspective: Causes, Assessment, Family Prevention, Intervention, and Treatment.* 8th ed. New York: McGraw-Hill, 2012. Designed for drug- and substance-abuse counseling programs.

Discusses the consequences of drug addiction and dependency as well as treatment options.

Ginther, Catherine. *Drug Abuse Sourcebook*. 2nd ed. Detroit: Omnigraphics, 2004. Provides basic information about illegal drugs, health and treatment issues, and drug prevention programs.

Hanson, Glen R., Peter J. Venturelli, and Annette E. Fleckenstein. *Drugs and Society*. 10th ed. Sudbury, MA: Jones, 2009. Examines the impact of drug use and abuse on individuals and society. Provides detailed information on drug laws, commonly abused drugs, and substance abuse treatment and prevention options.

Koellhoffer, Tara, and Ronald J. Brogan. *Junior Drug Awareness: Inhalants and Solvents*. Philadelphia: Chelsea House, 2008. A basic overview of the household products abused as inhalants and solvents and their damaging effects on the body.

Kuhn, Cynthia, Scott Swartzwelder, and Wilkie Wilson. *Buzzed: The Straight Facts about the Most Used and Abused Drugs from Alcohol to Ecstasy*. 3rd ed. New York: W. W. Norton, 2008. A clear and comprehensive drug handbook describing how different drugs function in the body and affect behavior.

Williams, Janet F., and Michael Storck. "Inhalant Abuse." *Pediatrics* 119.5 (2007): 1009–17. Print. Reviews aspects of inhalant abuse in children and the pediatrician's role in managing and preventing it.

WEBSITES OF INTEREST

Inhalant.org
http://inhalant.org

National Inhalant Prevention Coalition
http://www.inhalants.org/guidelines.htm

National Institute on Drug Abuse
http://www.drugabuse.gov/publications/infofacts/inhalants

World Health Organization
http://www.who.int/substance_abuse/activities/volatilesolvent

See also: Ethanol; Gasoline; Household chemicals of abuse; Inhalants abuse

Soma

CATEGORY: Substances

ALSO KNOWN AS: Carisoma; carisoprodol; sanoma; sopradol; vanadom

DEFINITION: Soma (carisoprodol) is a skeletal-muscle relaxant that acts on the central nervous system to promote sedation and pain relief.

STATUS: Legal by prescription in the United States and banned in many countries around the world

CLASSIFICATION: Unclassified

SOURCE: Synthetic

TRANSMISSION ROUTE: Oral

HISTORY OF USE

Since the mid-1950s, the North American market for tranquilizing medications has been enormous. Most tranquilizers developed at this time were designed to overcome specific problems that had become apparent in earlier medications. For example, carisoprodol (brand name Soma) was developed because of problems with meprobamate, an older anxiolytic medication that had both high potential for dependence and difficult withdrawals.

The brand name "Soma" refers both to the drink of the gods in Hindu religious literature and to a fictional medication in the dystopic novel *Brave New World* (1932) by Aldous Huxley. Since the late 1950s, the medical and scientific communities have come to recognize that although Soma is an effective skeletal-muscle relaxant, it also has a high potential for abuse, dependence, and illegal purchase.

EFFECTS AND POTENTIAL RISKS

How Soma works in the brain is not well understood, although studies have suggested that it stimulates the receptors for gamma-aminobutyric acid, which in turn prompts overall relaxation of skeletal muscles and then sedation. Because of these two effects, Soma has been frequently prescribed along with anti-inflammatory medications as an aid for muscle sprains.

However effective in the short-term, Soma has significant potential risks. Some users have experienced anterograde amnesia after taking large doses, during which they have driven vehicles or engaged in other dangerous behaviors. Like other tranquilizing medications, Soma can cause dependence; predictably, those who become dependent tend to take larger doses to achieve desired effects, which in turn substantially increases the subsequent risk of cardiac problems, coma, and death. Withdrawal from Soma also is difficult, as its symptoms include increased sensitivity to pain and anxiety, jitteriness, hallucinations, and bizarre behavior.

Michael R. Meyers, PhD

FURTHER READING

Bramness, Jørgen G., Svetlana Skurtveit, and Jørg Mørland. "Impairment Due to Intake of Carisoprodol." *Drug and Alcohol Dependence* 74.3 (2004): 311–18. Print.

Gonzalez, Lorie A., et al. "Carisoprodol-Mediated Modulation of GABAA Receptors: In Vitro and In Vivo Studies." *Journal of Pharmacology and Experimental Therapeutics* 329.2 (2009): 827–37. Print.

Reeves, Roy, et al. "Carisoprodol (Soma): Abuse Potential and Physician Unawareness." *Journal of Addictive Diseases* 18.2 (1999): 51–56. Print.

Tone, Andrea. *The Age of Anxiety: A History of America's Turbulent Love Affair with Tranquilizers.* New York: Basic, 2008.

WEBSITES OF INTEREST

National Institute on Drug Abuse
http://www.drugabuse.gov

PubMed Health: Carisoprodol
http://www.ncbi.nlm.nih.gov/pubmedhealth/
PMH0000717

See also: Painkiller abuse; Prescription drug addiction: In depth; Sedative-Hypnotic abuse

---

Sponsors

CATEGORY: Treatment

DEFINITION: Sponsors are recovered addicts who have completed a twelve-step program and have remained with the program for social support of their abstinence. Sponsors encourage and guide new program participants, working as long-term role models of recovery for themselves and for the persons sponsored. Participating in a twelve-step program does not require being a sponsor, but the role is considered vital for the recovery of new addicts and is beneficial for the sponsor, as it helps to maintain his or her sobriety and sense of worth.

BECOMING A SPONSOR

Three well-known and successful treatment recovery programs center on the twelve-step model of addiction recovery and abstinence. These programs are Alcoholics Anonymous (AA), Narcotics Anonymous (NA), and Cocaine Anonymous (CA). Each program provides group recovery meetings for discussion and encouragement.

Although the entire service group of each twelve-step program is considered a sponsorship in itself for people who desire addiction recovery, single sponsors commonly help new addicts. The step recovery model is supported by the group but is encouraged more closely by an individual sponsor, who has lived through and sustained the recovery experience.

No strict guidelines exist to define or restrict the position of a sponsor; instead, the post has developed naturally as a result of treatment program fellowships. Empathy from a fellow recovered addict can help another in recovery. Thus, anyone sober who has completed the twelve steps and who continues to participate in the fellowship can be a sponsor.

The AA, NA, and CA programs all suggest that anyone considering a sponsorship role be addiction free for a minimum of one year to provide the best counsel; however, a baseline time limit is not enforced, and the person's strength of character during sobriety is often more relevant than the length of sobriety itself.

A sponsor's level of patience and willingness also are key factors in appropriate selection. In addition, AA suggests that sponsors ideally be the same gender as the new addict, to encourage focus on the recovery process and not on a potential personal relationship. In addition, a single sponsor is considered sufficient for ultimate bonding, focus, and discussion about the addiction recovery process. Selecting a sponsor early in the program, but doing so with care and consideration, is highly recommended for the best chance at recovery.

Becoming a sponsor is as simple as connecting with a new member in a mentorship position; a new member simply asks an existing recovered addict to sponsor his or her twelve-step recovery, often after forming a bond with the sponsor at an early meeting.

By participating in group meetings, a new addict can identify with a recovered addict he or she desires to emulate or with whom he or she has shared experiences of abuse and recovery. An addict-sponsor relationship relies upon compatibility and the assurance of sobriety in the sponsor. The sponsor should continue to live according to the twelve steps and traditions of the program.

ROLES AND RESPONSIBILITIES

Upon voluntarily sponsoring a recovering addict, a sponsor's role varies. Sponsors provide informal, individualized support; at minimum, the sponsor attends meetings with the recovering addict and assists the addict through the twelve-step path. In addition, sponsors encourage the new lifestyle promoted by recovery programs—one that is moral and often faith-based.

A sponsor should be available to the recovering addict between meetings to answer questions about the recovery process and to provide deeper and more personal discussions of relevant issues than are possible during group settings. Sponsors provide individual care and attention, and they ultimately guide an addict to recovery and abstinence by developing a close, confidential relationship built on mutual trust and respect.

Although a sponsor can encourage a recovering addict by sharing his or her past experiences, the sponsor cannot be available at all times, cannot provide medical advice, and is not expected to provide financial or other social support and guidance. The burden is on the recovering addict to maintain open communication with his or her sponsor, to progress along his or her own twelve-step path, and to be responsible for his or her own personal recovery. Sponsors introduce the new addict to other members, provide opportunities for sober interactions, and offer literature to support the addict.

Sponsors also experience benefits from their roles and responsibilities. The twelfth step of recovery typically involves helping another addict by introducing him or her into a recovery program. Sponsorship itself is not a step, but it is a continuous relationship that supports lasting twelfth step work.

Being a sponsor is an important responsibility that can strengthen personal sobriety, provide a continued role for the recovering addict in the program, and provide an active mentorship connection without temptation of abuse. Sponsor roles are privileged and must be well-balanced among the members of a service group; a one-on-one relationship serves both the addict and the sponsor by providing opportunities to a variety of group members.

Nicole M. Van Hoey, PharmD

FURTHER READING

Alcoholics Anonymous. "Questions and Answers on Sponsorship." 2010. Web. 8 Apr. 2012. http://aa.org/pdf/products/p-15_Q&AonSpon.pdf. Details the selection of a sponsor, expectations for the person sponsored, and guidance for potential sponsors within a twelve-step program.

Hamilton, B. *Twelve Step Sponsorship: How It Works.* Center City, MN: Hazelden, 1996. Describes the role and importance of sponsorship in addiction recovery.

Moos, R., and C. Timko. "Outcome Research on Twelve-Step and Other Self-help Programs." *Textbook of Substance Abuse Treatment.* Eds. M. Galanter and H. O. Kleber. 4th ed. Washington, DC: American Psychiatric, 2008. Reviews positive results associated with recovery programs that supplement or extend behavioral change after treatment programs.

Narcotics Anonymous. "For Those in Treatment." 1991. Web. 8 Apr. 2012. http://www.na.org/admin/include/spaw2/uploads/pdf/litfiles/us_english/IP/EN3117.pdf. Addresses questions frequently posed by new or potential members, including "What is a sponsor?" and "How do you get a sponsor?"

WEB SITES OF INTEREST

Alcoholics Anonymous
http://www.aa.org

Cocaine Anonymous
http://www.ca.org/literature/choosesponsor.htm

HelpGuide.org
http://www.helpguide.org/mental/drug_abuse_addiction_rehab_treatment.htm

Narcotics Anonymous
http://www.na.org

See also: Abstinence-based treatment; Alcohol abuse and alcoholism: Treatment; Alcoholics Anonymous; Cocaine Anonymous; Narcotics Anonymous;

Overeaters Anonymous; Support groups; Treatment methods and research; Twelve-step programs for addicts; Twelve-step programs for family and friends

Steroid abuse

CATEGORY: Substance abuse
ALSO KNOWN AS: Doping
DEFINITION: Steroid abuse is the misuse of anabolic-androgenic steroids to enhance one's physique and athletic performance. Such misuse is considered abuse when it harms a user's health or social functioning or when a user becomes psychologically dependent on steroids.

CAUSES

Unlike most other abused drugs, anabolic steroids do not cause euphoria or other immediate pleasurable reactions. Rather, the steroid abuser is seeking a change in body configuration—a build-up in muscle mass—and to improve athletic performance. Abusers do not become physically addicted to steroids, but they can develop a compulsive reliance on them.

The frequency and amount of dosing increase through continued use. Abusers may start taking several different formulations simultaneously; such formulations may include pills, intramuscular injections, and topical creams, gels, or transdermal patches. Down time or withdrawal from the drugs becomes increasingly uncomfortable.

RISK FACTORS

Adolescents, especially boys involved in such competitive sports as weightlifting, football, and wrestling, and professional athletes are the most likely to use anabolic-adrenergic steroids. Most do so to boost athletic performance and increase muscle mass. A wide range of steroids are readily available at gyms and through websites.

SYMPTOMS

Steroid abusers may develop severe acne on the face, shoulders, and back; excessive facial or body hair; pigmented lines (striae) on the skin; and voice changes. In men, the testicles may shrink and the breasts may show evidence of development. In women, the clitoris may become enlarged and breast development may be delayed. Behavioral consequences of steroid abuse may include "roid rage," which consists of mood swings, anxiety, irritability, and aggressiveness.

Withdrawal from steroids can cause depression, headaches, fatigue, loss of appetite, and insomnia. Depression can lead to suicidal thoughts and actions. Other controlled substances may be used to ease the adverse effects of steroid abuse. The suppliers of steroids often deal in other illegal drugs.

SCREENING AND DIAGNOSIS

Treatment providers should screen for steroid abuse in young patients with low body fat, extreme muscularity, and a disproportionately large upper torso. In addition to the symptoms outlined above, needle marks may be detected in large muscles (gluteals, thighs, deltoids). The history of athletic or fitness activity may reveal an obsession with weight training and body conditioning, often coupled with dissatisfaction with appearance, despite what others perceive. This is defined as body dysmorphic disorder.

Standard urine tests do not screen for steroids. Urinalysis must be done at a specialized laboratory equipped to test for steroids. Even then, abusers may be taking newer formulations not as yet included in the screening choices. Abusers also employ "stacking," in which they combine relatively small quantities of several steroids administered by different routes, in part to keep individual steroid types below detection levels. Abusers also will temporally suspend usage if they suspect or know that testing will occur.

TREATMENT AND THERAPY

If a person admits to steroid abuse, the physician or drug counselor needs to query that person regarding his or her perception of the benefits and understanding of the consequences of using steroids. The health professional needs to establish when steroids were first and most recently used and to determine the pattern of use (for example, on-and-off periods); what steroids were used, how they were administered, and at what dosage; how the steroids were obtained; and whether the patient is using other drugs to augment the steroids effects, to reduce side effects, or to cope with depression or other adverse effects during off periods. In all this, the health provider should convey a supportive rather than judgmental attitude.

All substances being used need to be addressed. The abuser should be told about the risks involved in abusing steroids. Patients who injected steroids should be tested for blood-borne diseases, including human immunodeficiency virus infection and hepatitis B and C virus infection.

Not all changes caused by the abuse of steroids can be reversed. Adverse sexual side effects may require hormonal therapy under the direction of an endocrinologist. Depression related to withdrawal of steroids may need to be addressed by a mental health professional. Severe or persistent depression may respond to selective serotonin reuptake inhibitors, such as fluoxetine (Prozac). Headaches and muscle and joint pain related to withdrawal are responsive to analgesics. Lifestyle changes may be required to maintain abstinence. The abuser may need to switch gyms, workout friends, competitive events, and sport types to avoid the risk of relapse.

PREVENTION

Most prevention efforts focus on athletes involved in professional and Olympic sports. The primary approach to prevention is to expose steroid abuse through testing and banning of abusers from competition and to strip athletes of records and rewards that were attained while using banned steroids. It is hoped that the consequences of these actions will deter current and potential users.

Most first-time users of banned steroids are high school students. However, few schools at this level have offered steroid abuse programs. Even if testing were more widely utilized at this level, it is not clear how great an effect it would have on preventing use. Providers of steroids offer new formulations that they claim cannot be detected by current tests and abusers stack several different steroids or temporally stop using them.

Simply warning students about the adverse effects of steroid abuse does not convince them that they will be adversely affected. They often believe that they can beat the odds. It may even pique their interest in the drugs, pushing them to try them. Steroid drug-testing among adolescents has not gained wide acceptance. Legal and cost concerns are raised by parents and school districts.

What appears necessary is an approach that, in addition to explaining the risks involved in using steroids, offers effective and healthy alternatives. Such an approach would allow students to make decisions based on informed knowledge and experience. To this end, for example, the Oregon Health and Science

Steroid Abuse: Steroid Use in Teenagers

Illegal steroid use by Olympic, college, and professional athletes often makes the news, but the abuse of these drugs by teenagers has not received as much attention. What is most troubling is that the health dangers can be especially devastating for teenagers.

Taken as a pill or as an injection, anabolic steroids are derived from and mimic the effects of the male sex hormone testosterone. In males, testosterone's role in the body is twofold. First, it maintains the reproductive system, including production and maintenance of the male sexual characteristics (such as deeper voice, greater amounts of body hair, larger body size, and greater muscle mass). Second, for a short time at the onset of puberty, testosterone production rises dramatically to stimulate the bulk of the physical maturation process. This involves full bone growth, deepening voice, and growth of facial hair.

It is this ability to promote muscle growth, increase lean body mass, and decrease body fat that entices teenagers to take anabolic steroids. Those striving to improve their strength, speed, and stamina often consider steroid use a quick way to push heavier weights and to look better.

The high doses that are necessary to affect these body changes come with health dangers. Teens are at risk for accelerated puberty and skeletal development that leads to irreversible stunted growth.

University, with sponsorship from the US government, developed the Athletes Training and Learning to Avoid Steroids (ATLAS) program. ATLAS was initially developed for use with high school football players. It is now more widely applied. Athletes Targeting Healthy Exercise and Nutrition Alternatives (ATHENA), a similar program, was developed for high school girls on sports teams.

With these programs, coaches and team leaders are trained to present information to small groups of students engaged in a shared experience as an integral part of athletic training. Students learn through an interactive approach that they can build strong bodies and improve athletic ability without the use of steroids. Strength-training and nutritional habits that promote healthy muscular conditioning without the use of drugs are put into practice as part of the programs.

A research study on ATLAS has shown that one year after completing the program, study participants versus a control group of similar student athletes who did not participate had one-half the incidence of new steroid abuse and less intention to abuse in the future. Noncontrol group participants also showed less abuse of other athletic-enhancing supplements and of alcohol, marijuana, amphetamines, and narcotics.

Ernest Kohlmetz, MA

FURTHER READING

Goldberg, Linn, et al. "The Adolescents Training and Learning to Avoid Steroids Program: Preventing Drug Use and Promoting Health Behaviors." *Archives of Pediatrics and Adolescent Medicine* 154.4 (2000): 332–38. Print. Results of a study of high school athletes.

Rosen, Daniel M. *Dope: A History of Performance Enhancement in Sports from the Nineteenth Century to Today.* Westport, CT: Praeger, 2008. A thorough presentation of the history of the use of anabolic steroids and other performance-enhancement drugs.

Yasalis, Charles E., ed. *Anabolic Steroids in Sport and Exercise.* Champaign, IL: Human Kinetics, 2000. Each chapter is written by an expert in the field. Chapter 4 is on prevention, chapters 6 through 8 on causes, chapter 10 on treatment, and chapters 12 and 13 on testing.

WEBSITES OF INTEREST

The Hastings Center: Sports Enhancement
http://www.thehastingscenter.org/Publications/ BriefingBook/Detail.aspx?id=2206

National Institute on Drug Abuse
http://www.drugabuse.gov/drugs-abuse/steroids-anabolic

Oregon Health and Science University, Health Promotion and Sports Medicine
http://www.ohsu.edu/xd/education/schools/ school-of-medicine

See also: Anabolic steroids; Men and substance abuse; Over-the-counter drugs of abuse

Stigma of addiction

CATEGORY: Psychological issues and behaviors
DEFINITION: Stigma is the exclusion of a person from social acceptance because of some characteristic, including being addicted to a substance of abuse or having a behavioral addiction.'

THEORIES OF STIGMA AND ADDICTION

No single theoretical model of stigma guides empirical work on this phenomenon, even though there exists a substantial body of theoretical and empirical work on stigma in general and on the stigma of addiction in particular. Canadian sociologist Erving Goffman's (1963) original analysis emphasized the effect of the stigmata (the devalued marker) on one's sense of social identity and the negative effect of stigma on social interaction with others. The stigmatized person may not feel fully human, and the responses of avoidance and disdain by others serve to confirm this compromised humanity.

Psychologist Edward Jones and colleagues (1984) considered the social-cognitive response of others to a person marked by stigmata. The researchers' basic claim was that the stigma engenders consensual social attributions about the person's dispositions. An addicted person, for example, may be consensually judged as weak, out of control, and possibly immoral. Research in 1982 proposed that social stigma legitimizes the social exclusion of a person and that social norms governing everyday social interaction do not apply to the stigmatized person. In the workplace, for example, a person with hypertension may be encouraged by coworkers and supervisors to use stress reduction strategies, exercise, and avoid salt. An addicted person may not be afforded such normative support, and plans may be laid to exclude the employee from the workplace.

Social psychologist Jennifer Crocker and colleagues (1998) took a social psychological perspective on stigma and focused on group membership that may be a basis of stigma. From the perspective of nonaddicted people, those with an addiction are devalued, likely to be judged negatively, and likely to be seen as interchangeable entities. That is, the addicted person will be judged as inferior and will be undifferentiated; people will use the "they're all the same" bias when evaluating addicts.

Another theoretical approach to stigma, by researchers Robert Kurzban and Mark R. Leary (2001), conceptualizes this phenomenon from the perspective of evolutionary theory. Their theory assumes an evolved brain mechanism that functions to avoid exposure to those who may carry pathogens that can compromise one's adaptive potential. This mechanism may have a propensity for false positives such that those who are different on a broad array of dimensions (for example, addicted people, the mentally ill, the obese, gay and lesbian individuals, persons with cancer, and persons from different racial and ethnic backgrounds) are evaluated negatively and avoided. For example, this avoidance might occur when one discovers that a potentially attractive romantic partner is in the process of addiction recovery, leading the discoverer to change his or her mind about pursuing the relationship further. While distinct, all theories of stigma acknowledge the negative effects on the self-assessment of the person with the stigmata and the social avoidance it promotes in others.

ADVERSE CONSEQUENCES

Stigma can adversely affect entry into treatment for substance abuse. More recent research (Keyes et al., 2010) documented that persons with an alcohol disorder who believe that alcoholism is a stigmatizing condition are less likely to seek clinical treatment. In a large national sample of 34,653 people with an alcohol use disorder, those who judged their disorder as stigmatizing were 37 percent less likely to seek treatment. Social interventions are needed to reduce the stigma associated with addiction because of the barriers posed for those who need clinical intervention to recover from a substance use disorder.

Thomas E. Malloy, PhD

FURTHER READING

Crocker, Jennifer, Brenda Major, and Claude Steele. "Social Stigma." *The Handbook of Social Psychology.* Eds. Daniel. T. Gilbert, Susan T. Fiske, and Gradner Lindzey. Vol. 2. 4th ed. Boston: McGraw-Hill, 1998. A review of the social psychological literature on social stigma and the effects in social interaction.

Goffman, Erving. *Stigma: Notes on the Management of Spoiled Identity.* Englewood Cliffs, NJ: Prentice Hall, 1963. A seminal work on the analysis of stigma written by a noted sociologist. Also discusses the history of stigmatization and the social consequences for an individual.

Jones, Edward E., et al. *Social Stigma: The Psychology of Marked Relationships.* New York: Freeman, 1984. A collaborative project by scientists who were fellows at the Center for Advanced Studies in the Behavioral Sciences. A central focus is on the social-cognitive processes in stigmatization.

Keyes, Kathleen, et al. "Stigma and Treatment of Alcohol Disorders in the United States." *American Journal of Epidemiology* 172 (2010): 1364–72. Print. Documents the adverse effects of perceived stigma on alcoholism treatment among those with an alcohol use disorder.

Kurzban, Robert, and Mark R. Leary. "Evolutionary Origins of Stigmatization: The Functions of Social Exclusion." *Psychological Bulletin* 127 (2001): 187–208. Print. A newer theoretical analysis of stigma that considers the evolutionary origin of social exclusion.

Room, Robin. "Stigma, Social Inequality, and Alcohol and Drug Use." *Drug and Alcohol Review* 24 (2005): 143–55. Print. A review of the literature on the role of stigma in psychoactive substance use.

Smith, Sharon M., et al. "Examining Perceived Alcoholism Stigma Effect on Racial-Ethnic Disparities in Treatment and Quality of Life among Alcoholics." *Journal of Studies on Alcohol and Drugs* (2010): 231–36. Print. Considers the effects of stigma on the quality of life of alcoholics but fails to confirm that stigma is a differential effect on racial and ethnic minorities.

WEBSITES OF INTEREST

ScienceDaily.com
http://www.sciencedaily.com/releases/2010/12/101202171057.htm

Stigma and Global Health Conference
http://www.stigmaconference.nih.gov

See also: Marriage/partnership and alcoholism; Marriage/partnership and behavioral addictions; Marriage/partnership and substance abuse; Mental illness; Socioeconomic status and addiction

Stimulant abuse

CATEGORY: Substance abuse

DEFINITION: Stimulant abuse is diagnosed when the recreational use of stimulants negatively affects health, interferes with daily functioning, and results in physical dependency. Stimulants, substances that excite the central nervous system, include herbal mixtures, beverages, cigarettes, diet pills, legal prescriptions, and illicit drugs such as cocaine, ecstasy, and methamphetamine. Stimulant abuse is treatable but difficult to overcome.

CAUSES

Stimulants have been prescribed to treat a variety of medical conditions, including narcolepsy, attention deficit hyperactivity disorder, Parkinson's disease, asthma, and obesity. Stimulants interfere with nerve cell communication by causing dopamine, a neurotransmitter responsible for the sensation of pleasure, to accumulate in the brain.

Stimulant use rapidly elevates dopamine levels, causing a surge of euphoria and energy that users desire. The continued use of stimulants can quickly lead to drug tolerance, physical and psychological dependency, and addiction.

Stimulant abuse is habit forming, risky, and dangerous. Stimulants can be abused orally, crushed and snorted, heated and smoked, or dissolved and injected. Suddenly stopping stimulant use can lead to withdrawal symptoms, intense drug cravings, and possible relapse. Withdrawal symptoms may include fatigue, headaches, nausea, vomiting, intense hunger, mood swings, fear, shaking, irritability, anxiety, depression, aggression, violence, mental confusion, paranoia, psychosis, suicidal thoughts, and possible anhedonia, the inability to experience pleasure.

RISK FACTORS

The majority of stimulant users are adolescents and young adults between the age of twelve and twenty-five years. Other risk factors may include a history of drug abuse, family conflicts, mental illness, post-traumatic stress disorder, attention deficit disorder, impulsive and aggressive behavior, mental illness, depression, and childhood sexual abuse.

SYMPTOMS

Stimulant side effects vary in severity depending on the drug. The short-term effects associated with stimulant use may include euphoria, hyperactivity, alertness, abdominal cramps, nausea, vomiting, headache, decreased appetite, insomnia, dilated pupils, mood swings, dizziness, irritability, anxiety, depression, sweating, dry mouth, muscle spasms, irregular heartbeat, shortness of breath, increased heart and respiration rates, elevated blood pressure, and sudden death.

Long-term use of stimulants can be associated with compromised health, poor hygiene, dental problems, dermatitis, memory loss, anorexia, violent behavior, aggressiveness, hostility, depression, psychosis, delusions, paranoia, hallucinations, and suicidal thoughts. The most detrimental long-term effect of stimulant abuse is physical and psychological tolerance and addiction, which can occur quickly; users require increasingly large doses of the drug to achieve the original high. Serious medical complications associated with stimulant abuse can include stroke, heart failure, respiratory depression, organ toxicity, cerebral hemorrhaging, dangerously high body temperature (hyperthermia), seizures, convulsions, brain damage, coma, and death.

SCREENING AND DIAGNOSIS

A physician suspecting stimulant abuse should perform a physical examination and obtain a thorough medical history of illicit drug use, prescribed medications, and symptoms to determine the type of drug abused and any associated psychological complications. Diagnostic screenings may include urine, blood and hair analysis, and an electrocardiogram to detect heart damage.

TREATMENT AND THERAPY

Stimulants can be highly addictive and difficult to overcome; treatment depends on the drug, length of use, and the severity of the symptoms. Physician-supervised stimulant-abuse treatment programs may be inpatient, outpatient, or residential. Treatment programs typically begin with medically assisted drug detoxification, slow tapering of drug use, and treatment of withdrawal symptoms.

No medications are available for the effective treatment of stimulant abuse, but some antidepressant medications can help with minimizing withdrawal symptoms and treating underlying issues, such as depression and anxiety. Behavioral therapies that encourage patients to modify thinking, expectations, and behaviors are effective treatment options for stimulant abuse.

Contingency management therapy enables patients to earn vouchers and rewards for drug-free behaviors and healthy living. Cognitive-behavioral therapies teach patients the skills to resist cravings, identify triggers and risky situations, effectively cope with stress, and avoid relapse. Other beneficial treatment options include mental health and substance abuse counseling, recovery support groups, and social services.

PREVENTION

The best preventive measure is to avoid stimulant use and better manage any underlying conditions associated with its use. Patients should be informed about the health hazards associated with stimulant abuse because many of the substances are highly addictive and habit forming.

Rose Ciulla-Bohling, PhD

FURTHER READING

Fields, Richard. *Drugs in Perspective: Causes, Assessment, Family Prevention, Intervention, and Treatment.* 8th ed. New York: McGraw-Hill, 2012. Designed for drug and substance abuse counseling programs. Describes the consequences of drug addiction and dependency and treatment options.

Ginther, Catherine. *Drug Abuse Sourcebook.* 2nd ed. Detroit: Omnigraphics, 2004. Provides basic information about illegal drugs, health and treatment issues, and drug prevention programs.

Hanson, Glen R., Peter J. Venturelli, and Annette E. Fleckenstein. *Drugs and Society.* 10th ed. Sudbury, MA: Jones, 2009. Examines the impact of drug use and abuse on individuals and society. Provides detailed information on drug laws, commonly abused drugs, and substance abuse treatment and prevention options.

Kuhn, Cynthia, Scott Swartzwelder, and Wilkie Wilson. *Buzzed: The Straight Facts about the Most Used and Abused Drugs from Alcohol to Ecstasy.* 3rd ed. New York: W. W. Norton, 2008. A clear and comprehensive drug handbook describing how different drugs function in the body and affect behavior.

Walker, Pam, and Elaine Wood. *Stimulants.* San Diego, CA: Lucent, 2004. Discusses the history, health effects, and dangers associated with legal and illegal stimulant use. Also discusses treatment and prevention strategies.

Warburton, Lianne, Diana Callfas, and Ronald J. Brogan. *Junior Drug Awareness: Amphetamines and Other Stimulants.* New York: Chelsea House, 2008. A basic overview of the science and history of stimulants and of treatment and addiction options. Written for juvenile readers.

WEBSITES OF INTEREST

National Institute on Drug Abuse
http://www.drugabuse.gov

National Institutes of Health: "Treatment for Stimulant Use Disorders"
http://www.ncbi.nlm.nih.gov/books/NBK64333

NIDA for Teens
http://teens.drugabuse.gov

YouthOnDrugs.com
http://youthondrugs.com/drugs/stimulants

See also: Amphetamine abuse; Caffeine addiction; Coffee; College and substance abuse; Dextroamphetamine; Ephedrine; Methamphetamine; Ritalin; Sexual stimulant abuse

Stimulants: Short- and long-term effects on the body

CATEGORY: Substance abuse

DEFINITION: Stimulants are drugs such as caffeine, cocaine, and amphetamine that alter physiological responses by increasing blood pressure, heart rate, and motor activity. Changes in psychological states include euphoria, increased focus, alertness, and energy. Using higher quantities for a long time can lead to both physical and psychological dependence.

CAUSES

The most frequently ingested stimulant is caffeine, which is used by 80 percent of the adult population of the United States. Caffeine, a member of a class of chemicals known as xanthines, is found not only in coffee, tea, and soda beverages but also in a number of foods. Caffeine affects the nervous system by inhibiting the neurotransmitter substance adenosine.

Adenosine is an inhibitory brain chemical that brings on sleepiness, slows the heart rate, and lowers blood pressure and body temperature. Because caffeine interferes with the inhibitory action of adenosine, the resulting effect is an increase in brain activity, which leads to heightened alertness and a lack of fatigue. Consuming too much caffeine can lead to caffeinism, which is a temporary condition characterized by insomnia, restlessness, nervousness, and anxiety.

Two other stimulants, cocaine and amphetamine, exert their effects by increasing the availability of three primary neurotransmitter substances: dopamine, norepinephrine, and serotonin. Although the mechanisms through which each drug alters the presence of these brain chemicals differ, the end product—having an abundance of a particular neurotransmitter in the synapse—is responsible for the behavioral and physiological changes that occur. Although the connection between cocaine and excessive amounts of dopamine is believed to be responsible for the rapid and strong dependency that can form, the latest research reveals a more complex picture that implicates interactions among several additional neurotransmitters.

RISK FACTORS

Stimulant overuse and abuse is more likely to occur in adults younger than age forty years, with the majority being males. Most persons who experiment with cocaine do so to experience a euphoric high; however, competitive athletes and college students are more likely to use stimulants to enhance physical or cognitive performance. Of all the stimulants, cocaine and methamphetamine pose the greatest risk of dependency.

SYMPTOMS

Physiological and psychological symptoms associated with the ingestion of stimulants are determined by several factors. These factors include the method of drug delivery (snorting, taking a pill), the specific dosage, and the length of time that the drug has been used.

Low-dosage, short-term side effects associated with stimulant usage include such changes as appetite suppression; increased alertness, particularly for persons diagnosed with attention deficit disorder; euphoria; an increased confidence in task performance; hypertension; pupil dilation; and delayed onset of sleep. With acute use of cocaine and methamphetamine, even at low dosages, initial feelings of euphoria and elation will dissipate and frequently result in depression, anxiety, and a desire or craving to ingest more of the drug.

Higher dosages of stimulants used for a long time can lead to drug tolerance. Essentially, increased amounts of the drug are needed to produce the same psychoactive effects. This condition sets the stage for chronic abuse. Long-term effects of stimulants can result in anxiety, depression, paranoia, seizure, pulmonary edema, stroke, gastrointestinal complications, and sudden death from cardiac complications.

Cocaine and methamphetamine abuse can lead to a drug-induced psychosis, which is characterized by visual and auditory hallucinations, incoherent speech, paranoia, and abnormal sleeping patterns. In addition, chronic usage of stimulants can lead to dependence, which results in drug craving. This intense craving can lead to behavioral changes, in which a drug user may forego social, family, and work responsibilities to acquire the drug.

SCREENING AND DIAGNOSIS

A licensed clinical psychologist or medical doctor will ask a battery of questions that assess previous drug history, family history, and the degree to which current use of stimulants is affecting the person's physical, social, and psychological health.

TREATMENT AND THERAPY

For stimulants that produce dependency, no pharmacological treatment exists that directly targets the mechanisms that brought on the addiction. Antidepressant drugs are used in persons who experience depression during detoxification. Cognitive-behavioral therapies are used to help persons acquire new coping strategies to refrain from going back to using a stimulant.

PREVENTION

In terms of caffeinism, adverse symptoms can be resolved by simply reducing the amount of caffeine one normally consumes. For prescribed medications such as amphetamines, it is important to monitor any potential adverse side effects. If these emerge, one should contact the medical doctor who authorized the prescription. Cocaine use should be avoided because of its potential for harmful side effects.

Bryan C. Auday, PhD

FURTHER READING

Iversen, Leslie. *Speed, Ecstasy, Ritalin: The Science of Amphetamines.* New York: Oxford UP, 2008. This book is devoted to discussing what is understood about amphetamines and nonamphetamine drugs, such as Ritalin.

Levinthall, Charles F. *Drugs, Behavior, and Modern Society.* 7th ed. Boston: Pearson, 2012. A highly readable account of the major categories of psychoactive drugs, such as the stimulants, to better understand how these substances travel within the body, affect the central nervous system, and exert their behavioral effects.

Maisto, Stephen A., Mark Galizio, and Gerard J. Connors. *Drug Use and Abuse.* 6th ed. Florence, KY: Cengage, 2010. Introduces the reader to the central substance abuse and treatment issues. Includes good information on cognitive and behavioral treatment approaches that are used to treat drug abuse.

Meyer, Jerrold S., and Linda F. Quenzer. *Psychopharmacology: Drugs, the Brain, and Behavior.* Sunderland, MA: Sinauer, 2005. The chapters on stimulants are well documented with examples from research that address results from brain imaging studies and clinical trials for therapeutic applications.

Rasmussen, Nicolas. *On Speed: The Many Lives of Amphetamine.* New York: New York UP, 2008. Features one of the best historical introductions to the use of amphetamines as a behavioral and cognitive enhancer primarily by military personnel in the United States and Great Britain.

WEBSITES OF INTEREST

Behavioral Biology Research Center, Johns Hopkins University
http://www.caffeinedependence.org/caffeine_dependence.html

Center for Substance Abuse Research
http://www.cesar.umd.edu/cesar/drugs/ritalin.asp

Cocaine Anonymous
http://www.ca.org

NIDA for Teens: Stimulants
http://www.teens.drugabuse.gov/facts/facts_stim1.php

See also: Amphetamine abuse; Birth defects and drug use; Caffeine: Short- and long-term effects on the body; Dextroamphetamine; Methamphetamine; Pregnancy and drug use; Sexual stimulant abuse

---

Stress and alcohol

Category: Substance abuse
Also known as: Anxiety and substance abuse; addiction and anxiety
Definition: Stress is a physiological response to certain negative stimuli, including illness, injury, extreme temperatures, and fear. It is commonly associated with the fight-or-flight response and can be associated with alcohol use. Though not everyone drinks in response to stress, a number of factors can help to determine whether a person will drink during a stressful situation. Some of these factors are genetics, usual drinking behavior, former experiences with alcohol or other drugs, and the availability of social support.

BACKGROUND

When the body experiences stress, it responds by secreting hormones into the blood in an attempt to cope with the stressor. This stress response affects the way the body functions and alters body temperature, appetite, and mood. This is one reason some people turn to alcohol after a stressful event. In many cases, people will turn to alcohol when a stressful situation feels out of their control. For example, many war veterans treated for post-traumatic stress disorder (PTSD) have alcohol-use disorders. Many studies have also shown that stressful situations can lead to relapse among recovering alcoholics. People who do not have the resources—such as a social support network—to cope with stress are more likely to drink in response to a stressful situation. They use alcohol to help buffer the effects of stress.

Alcohol is not a healthy way of dealing with stress. Drinking to deal with stress can interfere with work, relationships, finances, and lead to more problems, such as alcoholism and health complications. Symptoms of stress include headaches, stomach aches, feeling tired or overwhelmed, and having difficulty sleeping.

CONTROLLING STRESS

There are numerous strategies to reduce or control stress. Some of these are: learning to say no and to set boundaries, which means not taking on more than one can handle; taking on one thing at a time—if the workload seems unbearable, an individual should pick one urgent task to focus on; meditating, which often takes only ten to twenty minutes each day; eating healthy and exercising, including at least thirty minutes of physical activity on most days of the week; limiting the intake of caffeine and alcohol, both of which interfere with sleep; learning to breathe properly (breathing techniques are a useful tool in combating stress); and sharing one's feelings. This latter strategy is important; a friend or family member's love, support, and guidance can help those suffering from stress through a particular situation. Professionals are trained to assess levels of stress and recommend coping and relaxation strategies. In addition, a supplement with vitamin B complex and magnesium may help to offset the effects of chronic stress.

Krisha McCoy, MS

FURTHER READING

Barnes, Gordon, Robert Murray, and David Patton. *The Addiction-Prone Personality.* New York: Springer, 2007. Describes Addiction-Prone Personality, linking personality traits to the development of alcohol abuse.

Slone, Laurie B., and Matthew J. Friedman. "Recognizing Other Mental Health Issues." *After the War Zone.* Boston: Da Capo Press, 2008. Experts from the VA National Center for PTSD offer guidance to service members and their families for dealing with deployment- and combat-related stress issues.

Stewart, Sherry H., and Patricia Conrod, eds. *Anxiety and Substance Use Disorders.* New York: Springer, 2008. Examines how substance use disorders are associated with anxiety and vice versa.

WEBSITES OF INTEREST

Mental Health America
http://www.nmha.org/

Mental Health Canada
http://www.mentalhealthcanada.com/

National Institute on Alcohol Abuse and Alcoholism
http://www.niaaa.nih.gov/

See also: Anxiety; Economic impact of addiction; Military and substance abuse; Post-traumatic stress disorder and addiction; Stress and drug abuse; Stress and smoking

Stress and drug abuse

CATEGORY: Substance abuse

DEFINITION: Stress, a physiological reaction of the body to tension, is commonly associated with the body's fight-or-flight response. Stress can be associated with drug use, which is the maladaptive pattern of use of a substance.

BACKGROUND

Stress has long been associated with drug abuse. The connection has been especially strong with drug relapse, and it also has been linked with the initiation of drug use. Correlations have been found between stressful life events and the use of substances. The higher rates of substance use by vulnerable populations have been attributed to the higher rates of stress from discrimination and socioeconomic disadvantage that group members often experience. Additional stressors that group members are disproportionately exposed to are violent and criminal environments.

Research has found that most people are affected by stressful events of great intensity. What is not well understood is why people react to stress differently. Also unclear are the determining factors for these differences. An additional area in need of investigation is why some persons react to stress by using drugs specifically.

Ethnographic researchers found that after life-threatening, stressful, catastrophic events, such as Hurricane Katrina (2005) and the acts of terrorism of

September 11, 2001, street addicts show a greater demand for drugs. Similarly, stress under conditions of war combat has led to elevated levels of substance use and subsequent addiction among soldiers and other military personnel. The implication is that some persons cope with stressful events by self-medicating with drugs.

Stress has been associated with the use of several different types of drugs. Studies have demonstrated, for example, that under laboratory-induced stress, animals were prone to relapse and to self-administer amphetamines, heroin, cocaine, alcohol, and nicotine. Also, cocaine abusers reported more cravings for cocaine and alcohol when cued with imagery that was considered stressful versus imagery that was considered neutral.

BRAIN SCIENCE RESEARCH

While many studies have demonstrated a correlation between stress and drug use, the science has not been able to explain the mechanism by which the two are intertwined. Research on humans and nonhuman animals has shed new light on how this mechanism might work. New discoveries in brain science have been especially exciting.

Persons under chronic stress have been found to have problems with the regulation of stress-induced corticotropin releasing factor (CRF), which stimulates hormonal responses that are a part of the fight-or-flight (stress) response. In such a case, the hormones and thus the person's biophysiological responses are not returning to normal (to homeostasis) once the stress is over. This process is thought to enhance a person's susceptibility to stress-related illnesses and drug use. An impaired hormonal regulatory system that renders a person chronically hypersensitive may lead that person to cope with that impairment by self-medicating with drugs. The body's naturally occurring opioid peptides function to inhibit the release of the CRF and, thus, to suppress the fight-or-flight response under normal circumstances when no threat is present or when the cause for alarm has ended.

Opioids, such as heroin, morphine, and methadone, act similarly to the opioid peptides and may thus explain their self-medicating properties, which dull stressful emotions for some persons. However, during periods of absence from the drugs (withdrawal), hypersensitivity to stress returns at even greater levels, as does the need to self-medicate with the opiates. Cocaine is thought to operate similarly. Methadone maintenance is theorized to be effective for heroin addiction by helping to stabilize the self-regulatory system.

Persons with post-traumatic stress disorder also appear to have a propensity for drug abuse, possibly because of a problem with their own hormonal system not properly self-regulating. Challenges for researchers and clinicians working in psychology and addiction include developing better treatment and prevention programs that teach healthier stress-management strategies to those persons vulnerable to stress-induced drug use.

Debra L. Murphy, PhD, MPH

FURTHER READING

Al'Absi, Mustafa. *Stress and Addiction: Biological and Psychological Mechanisms.* San Diego: Academic, 2007. Outlines the mechanism between stress and drug use based on state-of-the-art biological and psychological research.

Bride, Brian E., and Samuel A. MacMaster. *Stress, Trauma, and Substance Use.* New York: Routledge, 2009. Examines the interrelationships among stress, trauma, and substances of abuse.

Stewart, Sherry H., and Patricia Conrod. *Anxiety and Substance Use Disorders.* New York: Springer, 2008. Examines how substance use disorders are associated with anxiety, and vice versa.

WEBSITES OF INTEREST

National Center for PTSD (Post-Traumatic Stress Disorder)
http://www.ptsd.va.gov

National Institute on Drug Abuse
http://www.drugabuse.gov

Substance Abuse and Mental Health Services Administration
http://www.samhsa.gov

See also: Anxiety; Anxiety medication abuse; Economic impact of addiction; Military and substance abuse; Post-traumatic stress disorder and addiction; Stress and alcohol; Stress and smoking

Stress and smoking

CATEGORY: Psychological issues and behaviors

DEFINITION: Stress is tenuously associated with smoking addiction and relapse, but the complex connections between smoking and stress remain unresolved. Nicotine, the primary addictive substance in cigarettes and other inhaled tobacco products, appears to both ease and instigate stress in a conflicting manner.

STRESS RESPONSES

Stress is a natural, reactive response involving physical and psychological changes that helps the body adapt to a variety of events and exposures. Stress responses trigger the hypothalamic-pituitary axis (HPA), which regulates multiple hormones simultaneously and connects their actions to chemicals in the nervous system.

During an acute stress event, hormonal and chemical fluctuations facilitate tension in the body; epinephrine, also known as adrenaline, and cortisol peak and cause increased heart rate and blood pressure, sweating, muscle tension, headache, and rapid respiration. Cortisol guides an inflammatory response and can counteract immune system functions.

Acute stress is useful when these processes activate the body's defenses or increase the adrenaline necessary to overcome a challenge. However, neurochemical responses can result in psychological changes that can lead to short- and long-term emotional instability and anxiety. With chronic stress exposure, deeper problems develop: Excessive stimulation of cortisol release causes obesity, heart disease, depression, and other chronic diseases. Chronic stress increases the likelihood that a person will turn to substance abuse in an attempt to counteract the body's hyper-reactive state; drug and food abuse can relieve immediate psychological anxiety through dopamine release but cannot stop the long-term physical or psychological damages of stress.

NICOTINE AND STRESS

Smoking physically stresses the body immediately and in the long term, worsening other conditions and increasing anxiety. When inhaled nicotine enters the bloodstream, the HPA is triggered to release epinephrine and cortisol—the same physical response to everyday stressors. Thus, heart rate, respiratory rate, and blood pressure all increase after nicotine use.

Tolerance to the nicotine effect on the HPA builds as smoking continues; although the physical effects wane, the levels of cortisol and epinephrine in the body remain high with chronic HPA activation. The result is a blunted natural stress reaction that prevents the body from responding appropriately to other stressors.

Nicotine also increases glucose secretion and prevents insulin release, causing chronically high blood sugar concentrations that stress organ functions. Oxidative stress reactions to nicotine throughout the body cause damage to cells and change cellular DNA (deoxyribonucleic acid), which impairs the immune response, worsens existing diseases, and increases inflammation.

In the central nervous system, nicotine use is rewarded by an apparent and immediate relief of anxiety through neurochemical changes. When tobacco is inhaled, nicotine enters the brain within ten seconds to stimulate dopamine, acetylcholine, and norepinephrine. Through these actions, nicotine quickly induces pleasure, improves mood, and enhances concentration and focus. Each cigarette provides hundreds of rapidly fleeting nicotine hits that in turn cause short bursts of euphoria. The subjective psychological boost hides the physical impairment and is short lived as the body develops tolerance to the fleeting neurologic highs.

Although smokers generally believe that nicotine reduces their stress, the repeated dopamine stimulation provides negative reinforcement of cigarette use. Chronic smoking leads to the compulsion of greater use to try to minimize the anxiety that results from lower dopamine levels when the nicotine effect wears off between cigarettes.

STRESS FUELS NICOTINE ADDICTION

Smoking and nicotine addiction are aggravated by additional, outside sources of stress, as smokers report higher cigarette use during times of known external stressors. In addition, the body of a smoker develops chronic physical health problems from nicotine damage that facilitate stress responses.

Smokers claim to have more psychological stress than nonsmokers, and stress is provided as a reason for smoking because of its apparent relaxing effects. However, no empiric evidence supports a consistent difference in stress between smokers and nonsmokers until after smoking begins. Nicotine heightens baseline stress between cigarette use, and smokers only attain normal, lower stress signals when cigarettes are used.

Stress is a vital body mechanism for protection, but it contributes to smoking addiction and the frequency of relapse, as smokers use nicotine to relieve immediate sensations of anxiety. When nicotine is chronically present, the nervous system and HPA adapt to it as a stressor; even more nicotine is needed to respond to daily stress.

Stress itself increases the craving for nicotine as tolerance builds, and anxiety encourages drug-seeking behavior. As the central nervous system adapts to frequent and repeated norepinephrine and dopamine stimulation, more nicotine is necessary to obtain the same pleasure, focus, and stress-relief responses. Relief of stress is harder to achieve as smoking continues. Thus, stress increases the amount, frequency, duration, and intensity of cravings for nicotine.

Withdrawal from nicotine is probably the best example of the connection between stress and smoking habits. Although physical withdrawal from nicotine can cause increased appetite and headaches, the psychological reactions of withdrawal are the key causes of stress and ultimate nicotine dependence. Irritability, attention problems, sleep disturbances, and tobacco cravings are common and are a sign of the damaging changes from smoking, not proof of nicotine's stress-relieving effects.

Without the rapid and repeated bursts of nicotine, anxiety and physical stress become evident. Nicotine abstinence breaks the cycle of stress-induced smoking and smoking-induced stress, but it ultimately requires learning new coping skills to manage stress.

Nicole M. Van Hoey, PharmD

FURTHER READING

Cougle, J. R., et al. "The Role of Comorbidity in Explaining the Associations between Anxiety Disorders and Smoking." *Nicotine and Tobacco Research* 12 (2010): 355–64. Print. Relates research to connect and explain the greater rates of smoking in people who have clinically diagnosed anxiety, depression, or other mental health disorders.

Mendelsohn, C. "Women Who Smoke: A Review of the Evidence." *Australian Family Physician* 40 (2011): 403–7. Print. Highlights the connection between stress, particularly in women, and nicotine use, especially rates of use and means of counteracting nicotine use in women with apparently high stress levels.

"Psychological Stress and Cancer: Questions and Answers." 29 Apr. 2008. Web. 8 Apr. 2012. http://www.cancer.gov/cancertopics/factsheet/risk/stress. A brief overview of the connections between psychological stress and the development of cancer, including cancer from smoking.

Richards, J. M., et al. "Biological Mechanisms Underlying the Relationship between Stress and Smoking: State of the Science and Directions for Future Work." *Biological Psychology* 88.1 (2011): 1–12. Print. Discusses outstanding questions about the connection between smoking and physical stress responses through the hypothalamic-pituitary axis, and examines the intricacies of physical and psychological changes that take place during and between nicotine use.

WEBSITES OF INTEREST

Cancer.gov
http://www.cancer.gov/cancertopics/tobacco/
    smoking

SmokeFree.gov
http://www.smokefree.gov

Substance Abuse and Mental Health Services Administration
http://www.samhsa.gov

See also: Anxiety; Economic impact of addiction; Military and substance abuse; Post-traumatic stress disorder and addiction; Smoking; Smoking: Short- and long-term effects on the body; Stress and alcohol; Stress and drug abuse

Students Against Destructive Decisions (SADD)

CATEGORY: Diagnosis and prevention
ALSO KNOWN AS: Students Against Driving Drunk
DEFINITION: Students Against Destructive Decisions is a peer-to-peer education and prevention organization that provides children and young adults with resources and activities that encourage them to reject illegal substances, including alcohol and

drugs, and detrimental behaviors, such as drunk driving, binge drinking, bullying, and violence.

Date: Established 1981

Background

Robert Anastas, a health educator and counselor at Wayland High School in Massachusetts, had the idea to create an organization called Students Against Driving Drunk (SADD) in 1981 after the deaths of two athletes he had coached. Both boys had been inebriated when they were in separate fatal automobile accidents. Anastas soon developed and taught a class focusing on the ramifications of driving drunk.

Anastas and fifteen of his students then established SADD. The students served as peer leaders and role models who created and presented projects that focused on changing teenagers' attitudes about driving and intoxication. The peer leaders stressed that drinking is not essential for students to attain popularity and acceptance by classmates. In 1997, as the organization's goals and missions expanded beyond a sole focus on drunk-driving prevention, the group changed its name to Students Against Destructive Decisions, reflecting its commitment to reducing other dangerous behaviors, including binge drinking, drug use, and violence.

SADD, now based in Marlborough, Massachusetts, expanded nationally, as students formed chapters throughout the United States. Soon after the organization's creation, SADD leaders introduced the Contract for Life, which involves both youths and their parents. Advice columnists Dear Abby and Ann Landers republished SADD's Contract for Life in their columns. CBS television followed by broadcasting the film *Contract for Life: The SADD Story* (1983). By this time SADD chapters also were being established internationally, and the organization extended its membership to include college and middle school students and youth at summer camps, churches, and community clubs.

Since 1991, SADD has designated a student of the year. Many members attend SADD's annual national conference. Government, business, and nonprofit organizations help to fund SADD programs. SADD provides helpful information on its website and on social networks such as Facebook and Twitter and it publishes the electronic newsletter *SADDvocate*. SADD's public service messages are televised nationally.

The US Department of Health and Human Services (HHS) presented Anastas with an appreciation award for his service to SADD and selected Carl Olsen, who was the first SADD president while at Wayland High School, to serve on a government panel studying alcoholism. SADD members have represented the organization at international meetings focused on driving safety, hosted by the World Health Organization and the United Nations.

Mission and Goals

SADD's mission is exemplified by its Contract for Life. Signers of the contract state they are aware of risks associated with driving drunk and agree not to drink, use drugs, drive impaired, or ride in vehicles operated by substance-impaired drivers. They promise to wear seatbelts and contact parents when exposed to alcohol or drug hazards.

Illegal alcohol consumption is consistently the greatest problem affecting adolescents, so the organization's primary goal has been to prevent fatalities associated with drunk drivers. SADD chapters present programs covering accident simulations that show emergency responders removing bodies from vehicles and law enforcement personnel arresting inebriated drivers.

SADD supplements its general programs with discussion of the dangers of cell-phone use while driving. The organization also supports mental health programs for students in kindergarten through high school that focus on preventing stress, depression, and suicide. SADD programs also address obesity, eating disorders, bullying, hazing, and youth violence.

Youth are discouraged from using tobacco products, steroids, and prescription drugs not prescribed to them. Organization materials address teenage sexuality, pregnancy, and sexually transmitted diseases. Leaders urge students to remain in school and graduate.

Partnering with other organizations, including the National Highway Traffic Safety Administration, SADD assists in devising programs to address issues of drinking and substance use at graduations and proms. Liberty Mutual Insurance helps SADD by acquiring information from teenagers about their experiences with illegal substances and their attitudes toward risky behaviors.

SADD supports legislation that enforces and maintains the nationwide drinking age of twenty-one years. The organization also endorses legislation requiring seatbelt use and the implementation of graduated driver's licenses, which are obtained by youth who undergo several stages with varying restrictions as they gain driving experience and awareness of driving-associated responsibilities. SADD also promotes the proposed Students Taking Action for Road Safety Act.

By the early twenty-first century, SADD has guided approximately seven million youth. Researchers estimate that SADD has helped to reduce teenage drunk-driving fatalities as much as 60 percent since the organization's founding in 1981.

Elizabeth D. Schafer, PhD

FURTHER READING

Anastas, Robert, and Kalia Lulow. *The Contract for Life.* New York: Pocket, 1986. SADD's founder discusses why he created the organization and looks at its accomplishments in the group's first five years.

"Prom, Graduation Season, and the SADD Pledge." *Alcoholism and Drug Abuse Weekly* 18.16 (2006): 5. Print. Present methods that SADD chapters can implement to present information to students and seek assistance from adults, including teachers, to combat drunk driving, especially in relation to traditional student celebrations.

Rosenberg, Merri. "Kids as Messengers on Teenage Drinking." *New York Times*, 20 Apr. 2003, p. 2. Discusses SADD activities at several high schools and includes quotations from students and school counselors concerning their experiences. Explains how SADD differs from other antidrinking strategies.

Wallace, Stephen. *Reality Gap: Alcohol, Drugs, and Sex—What Parents Don't Know and Teens Aren't Telling.* New York: Union Square, 2008. A SADD official and counselor analyzes youths' and adults' attitudes, behaviors, and misperceptions about alcohol, drugs, and other social issues.

WEBSITES OF INTEREST

National Organizations for Youth Safety
http://www.noys.org

National Student Safety Program
http://www.adtsea.org/nssp

Students Against Destructive Decisions
http://www.sadd.org

See also: Designated drivers; Drugged driving; Drunk driving; Mothers Against Drunk Driving (MADD)

Suboxone

CATEGORY: Treatment
ALSO KNOWN AS: Box; bupe; buprenorphine with naloxone; saboxin; sobos; stop signs; stops; sub; subs
DEFINITION: Suboxone is a sublingual tablet or film consisting of buprenorphine and naloxone, used for the treatment of opioid addiction.
STATUS: Legal in the United States and worldwide
CLASSIFICATION: Schedule III controlled substance
SOURCE: Synthetic compounds derived from the thebaine alkaloid of the opium poppy
TRANSMISSION ROUTE: Sublingual

HISTORY OF USE

Buprenorphine has been available since the 1980s in injectable and sublingual dosage forms prescribed for pain management. Since 2002, sublingual formulations with and without naloxone have been used primarily as safer alternates to methadone in opioid detoxification and dependence programs. Subutex, a formulation containing only buprenorphine, is sometimes ground up and injected or inhaled by patients to maximize the euphoric effects of the drug. Including naloxone in a one-to-four-part ratio with buprenorphine limits the abuse potential of the drug; naloxone blocks the effects of opiates such as heroin and leads to immediate withdrawal symptoms.

Use in the United States is limited by the Drug Addiction Treatment Act of 2000. A Risk Evaluation and Mitigation Strategy, approved by the US Food and Drug Administration, is available for the drug to ensure proper medication use and to limit abuse and diversion; this program allows primary care physicians to prescribe the medication, improving access to treatment. A transdermal patch containing buprenorphine (Butrans) is available for pain management only.

EFFECTS AND POTENTIAL RISKS

Buprenorphine is a potent partial agonist at the mu (µ) opioid receptor. Because buprenorphine binds more strongly than other opioids to receptors in the brain, it limits the effect of opioids in patients taking buprenorphine and can effectively block the effect of high-dose heroin, making it ideal for opioid treatment programs.

The side-effect profile is similar to that of other opioids, including nausea, vomiting, constipation, sweating, headache, drowsiness, and dizziness; side effects are less frequent than with morphine. Respiratory depression is not likely to occur unless buprenorphine is taken with central nervous system depressants, such as alcohol or benzodiazepine; deaths have been reported in persons taking benzodiazepine who also inject buprenorphine products.

Naloxone is a mu (μ) antagonist used in opioid overdose, primarily in cases involving heroin or morphine. It is not an effective antagonist to buprenorphine because of the high binding affinity of buprenorphine to the opioid receptors. The drug combination is preferred in cases where unsupervised administration of the drug is occurring, as both buprenorphine and naloxone can block or reverse opiate effects from other opioids such as heroin, morphine, and methadone; intravenous abuse of Suboxone leads to immediate withdrawal symptoms in persons continuing to abuse other opioids.

Karen Nagel Edwards, PhD

FURTHER READING

Collins, Gregory B., and Mark S. McAllister. "Buprenorphine Maintenance: A New Treatment for Opioid Dependence." *Cleveland Clinic Journal of Medicine* 74 (2010): 514–20. Print.

Kahan, Meldon, et al. "Buprenorphine: New Treatment of Opioid Addiction in Primary Care." *Canadian Family Physician* 57 (2011): 281–89. Print.

Lang Walter, et al. "From Research to the Real World: Buprenorphine in the Decade of the Clinical Trials Network." *Journal of Substance Abuse and Treatment* 38, suppl. 1 (2010): S53–60. Print.

WEBSITES OF INTEREST

National Institute on Drug Abuse
http://archives.drugabuse.gov/drugpages/buprenorphine.html

Suboxone.com
http://www.suboxone.com/pdfs/Medication_Guide.pdf

See also: Addiction medications; Narcotics abuse; Opioid abuse; Overdose

---

Substance abuse

CATEGORY: Substance abuse
ALSO KNOWN AS: Drug abuse
DEFINITION: Substance abuse is the ingestion, inhalation, or injection of a product that is harmful to one's health, usually for psychoactive (mood-altering) purposes. Legal substances that are commonly abused include alcohol, tobacco, prescription drugs, and over-the-counter medications. Illegal substances of abuse include cocaine, marijuana, methamphetamine, and heroin. Other substances of abuse include hallucinogens, inhalants, solvents, and anabolic steroids.

OVERVIEW

According to the National Survey on Drug Use and Health, an estimated 21.8 million Americans age twelve years and older (8.7 percent of the population) used illicit drugs within one month of the survey. This total includes psychoactive prescription drugs used for nonmedical reasons.

Marijuana is the most commonly used illegal drug, followed by cocaine, methamphetamine, and hallucinogens. Drug abusers comprise all ages. Many abused substances have addictive properties; the user becomes dependent on the regular use of the substance and experiences withdrawal symptoms when use is discontinued. Withdrawal symptoms range from depression and anxiety to seizures.

Society has determined that the use of illegal substances is harmful; thus, laws are applied to protect both the individual and society from the harmful consequences of their use.

ABUSE OF LEGAL SUBSTANCES

Tobacco
Tobacco can be smoked or chewed. Nicotine, contained in tobacco, is highly addictive; it is a psychoactive substance that produces temporary physical and mood-altering effects in the brain. Nicotine also is a vasoconstrictor (blood vessel constrictor); thus, it increases the risk of cardiovascular disease.

Tobacco also is a well-known carcinogen, and tobacco's use is the leading cause of preventable illness and death in the United States. In addition to lung, throat, and mouth cancer, tobacco has been associated with cancers of the nasal cavity, esophagus, stomach, pancreas, breast, kidney, bladder, and cervix. The smoking of tobacco results in lost time at work either because of smoking breaks or because of respiratory illnesses, which are more common in smokers.

According to the National Cancer Institute:

- Cigarette smoking causes an estimated 443,000 deaths each year, including approximately 49,400 deaths from exposure to secondhand smoke.
- Lung cancer is the leading cause of cancer death among both men and women in the United States; 90 percent of lung cancer deaths among men and approximately 80 percent of lung cancer deaths among women are caused by smoking.
- Persons who smoke are up to six times more likely than nonsmokers to have a heart attack, and the risk increases with the number of cigarettes smoked. Smoking also causes most cases of chronic lung disease.
- In 2009, approximately 20.6 percent of adults in the United States were cigarette smokers.
- Nearly 20 percent of high school students smoke cigarettes.

Alcohol
Alcohol consumption involves the ingestion of ethanol (C_2H_5OH), which is a component of alcoholic beverages (beer, wine, and hard liquor). Alcoholism is a chronic condition in which a person is dependent upon regular ingestion of alcoholic beverages. Alcoholics are unable to control their drinking and continue to drink even though doing so interferes with their health, interpersonal relationships, or work.

Alcohol abuse refers to excessive drinking—enough to cause problems in daily life—without complete dependence upon the substance. The combination of alcohol abuse and tobacco use markedly increases the risk of cancers of the oral cavity. Approximately 50 percent of cancers of the mouth, pharynx (throat), and larynx (voice box) are associated with heavy drinking. Even in nonsmokers, a strong association exists between alcohol abuse and cancers of the

upper digestive tract, including the esophagus, the mouth, the pharynx, and the larynx.

Prescription Medication
Prescription drug abuse involves the ingestion of medication that has been obtained without a prescription or that is used inappropriately (that is, not according to prescription instructions). According to the National Institutes of Health, in 2009, 16 million Americans age twelve and older had taken a prescription pain reliever, tranquilizer, stimulant, or sedative for nonmedical purposes one or more times in the year before being surveyed.

Not infrequently, prescription drug abusers take medication with alcohol or combine stimulants and depressants. These combinations increase the risk of permanent damage to the user's health or death. Commonly abused types of prescription medications include narcotics such as hydrocodone (Vicodin), meperidine (Demerol), and oxycodone (OxyContin); central nervous system depressants such as alprazolam (Xanax), diazepam (Valium), and pentobarbital (Nembutal); and stimulants such as dextroamphetamine (Dexedrine) and methylphenidate (Ritalin). Narcotics and central nervous system depressants cause drowsiness and respiratory depression; stimulants can cause seizures, irregular heartbeat, paranoia, and dangerously elevated body temperatures.

In some cases, a prescription may be obtained from a health care professional by feigning symptoms such as pain; however, most health care professionals are adept at spotting a drug abuser. Most abused prescription medication is purchased from a drug trafficker or stolen by the user.

ABUSE OF ILLEGAL SUBSTANCES
Illegal substances have the added risk of containing contaminants, which can increase the health risk. For example, marijuana may be mixed with phencyclidine (PCP). PCP was developed as an anesthetic, but its medical use was discontinued a few years after its introduction because of its harmful effects on the brain. It is not uncommon for an abuser of illegal substances to combine a drug with other illegal substances, prescription drugs, or alcohol.

Marijuana
Smoked marijuana and smoked tobacco are chemically similar; thus, like cigarettes, the greatest health

hazard of marijuana is from smoking the substance. The psychoactive component of marijuana leaves is delta-9-tetrahydrocannabinol (THC), which is a relatively safe drug. However, smoked marijuana is a health risk. Scientific analyses have identified a minimum of six thousand of the same chemicals in marijuana smoke that are present in tobacco. The chief difference between the two plants is that marijuana contains THC and tobacco contains nicotine. Moreover, one of the most potent carcinogens in tobacco smoke, Benzo[a]pyrene, is present in larger quantities in marijuana smoke.

Another factor increasing the carcinogenic risk is in the way it is inhaled. Marijuana smokers frequently inhale and hold the smoke in their lungs for an extended time to increase the drug's effects; this practice increases the amount of tar deposited in the respiratory tract by about a factor of four.

Cocaine and Crack Cocaine

Cocaine is the most abused central nervous system stimulant in the United States and is a frequent cause of emergency room visits. Ingestion of cocaine can produce seizures, strokes, or heart attacks. Some users claim that it is not addictive because it does not produce physical withdrawal symptoms, which do occur with alcohol or heroin addiction. However, cocaine has powerful psychological addictive properties. Users will often go to extraordinary lengths to obtain the drug.

Methamphetamine

Methamphetamine is a highly addictive street drug that can be readily and inexpensively manufactured from the ingredients of common household products. Use of the highly addictive substance has reached epidemic proportions in the United States. Psychological effects of the substance include agitation, depression, euphoria, mood disturbances, psychosis, and violent behavior. In addition to being less expensive than cocaine, its effects are longer lasting.

The use of methamphetamine can result in permanent injury to the brain, heart, and lungs. Furthermore, the volatile substances used in its manufacture can lead to fires and explosions.

Heroin

Heroin (diacetylmorphine) is a potent analgesic (painkiller). It is abused for the intense euphoria it produces. It is highly addictive, as tolerance to the drug develops quickly. As a result, users need more of the drug to achieve the same effects. When injected intravenously, heroin produces a greater degree of euphoria than other opiates, such as morphine.

TREATMENT

Many substance abusers either deny that they have a problem or simply state that the pleasure derived from the substance outweighs the negative impact on their life, family members, and friends; thus, treatment is often initiated by a triggering event or by the urging of another person.

A triggering event may be conviction for driving under the influence, a health condition (such as pancreatitis or cirrhosis of the liver), a threat of divorce, a threat of a job loss, or a threat of loss of child custody. A spouse, relative, coworker, or boss may be influential in initiating treatment. However, some substance abusers ignore a triggering event or advice from others and continue to abuse substances.

A number of treatment options are available to substance abusers. These vary markedly by the type of substances and by individual circumstances. In some cases, a brief intervention by a health care professional may be sufficient. Other cases require enrollment in an outpatient program, which includes counseling. More severe cases require an inpatient program.

The following steps are involved in treatment for persons requiring inpatient or intensive outpatient treatment:

Detoxification. For most drug addictions, detoxification (also called detox) is necessary. Sedatives are often necessary to reduce withdrawal symptoms, which may include shaking, confusion, or hallucinations. Withdrawal may last one or two weeks and usually requires inpatient care at a hospital or a treatment center.

Reprogramming. A recovering substance abuser, with the help of professionals skilled in substance abuse treatment, learns new skills and formulates a treatment plan. The plan should include behavior-modification techniques, counseling, goal setting, and use of self-help manuals or Internet resources.

Psychological counseling. Counseling on an individual or a group basis is an essential treatment component. Group therapy is particularly valuable because it allows interaction with other substance abusers. It promotes the idea that one's problems are not unique. Therapy may include the presence of a spouse or other family members. Family support is a significant component of the recovery process.

Medication. Following medication for detox, long-term pharmaceutical treatment may be used in some cases. Oral medications such as disulfiram, acamprosate, and naltrexone are used for alcoholism. These medications produce unpleasant physical reactions such as flushing, headaches, nausea, and vomiting. Methadone is commonly used in the treatment of heroin addiction; however, its use is controversial. Critics claim that treating recovering addicts with methadone is simply substituting one addictive drug for another. Despite this opinion, many addicts claim that they never could have ended their heroin habit without help from methadone.

Follow-up support. Aftercare programs and support groups are essential for the recovering substance abuser. These programs help the abuser to avoid (or manage) relapses and deal with the necessary lifestyle changes to maintain a drug-free existence. For alcoholics, regular attendance at a support group such as Alcoholics Anonymous (AA) is often an important component of follow-up care. Follow-up often includes psychological and medical care.

Substance abuse commonly is a component of other mental health disorders. For persons with mental health issues, psychological counseling or psychotherapy may be recommended. Substance abusers also can have medical conditions that require treatment. These conditions include hypertension (high blood pressure), diabetes, heart disease, and liver disease (such as cirrhosis of the liver). If a substance abuser remains drug-free, some medical conditions may decrease in severity or may resolve. Treatment for depression or anxiety also may be a part of follow-up.

Beyond counseling and medication, other modalities may be helpful. For example, in September 2010, researchers at the University of California, Los Angeles released the results of a clinical trial involving a unique new therapy that applies electrical stimulation to a major nerve emanating from the brain. The technique, trigeminal nerve stimulation, achieved an average of a 70 percent reduction in depression in the eight-week study period.

Inpatient treatment. For persons with a serious substance abuse problem, inpatient care is often necessary. These programs include detox followed by counseling, group therapy, and medical treatment. A benefit of an inpatient program is that it greatly reduces the risk of a patient gaining access to harmful substances. Regular outpatient follow-up also is essential.

Rural Areas and Substance Abuse

People living in rural areas are vulnerable to becoming addicted to various illegal and legal substances because of distinctive socioeconomic, demographic, and cultural factors associated with those communities. The US Substance Abuse and Mental Health Services Administration periodically issues statistics from its National Survey on Drug Use and Health, revealing greater percentages of rural substance abusers. Of these abusers, youths routinely represent the greatest rates, compared with urban populations.

The physical isolation of rural locations appeals to illegal substance manufacturers, traffickers and dealers, and users who recognize the minimal chance that their activities will be detected by law enforcement. Furthermore, the erratic aspects of agricultural production, a traditional income source of rural areas, frequently leads to substance use and abuse. Rural residents, like people in all areas in general, tend to use substances to numb their reactions to negative events in everyday life. Common negative effects of rural life that can lead to substance use and abuse are employment and income loss, crop failures, and natural disasters.

Drug abuse researchers identify excessive alcohol consumption as the most dangerous addiction among rural youths. In 2011, University of Kentucky researchers estimated that 13 percent of rural youths abused prescription drugs, particularly painkillers and tranquilizers, and that those teenagers had a 26 percent greater risk than adolescents outside rural areas to become addicted.

Methamphetamine (meth) has also grown in popularity in rural areas. The availability of agricultural chemicals, such as anhydrous ammonia in fertilizer and iodine, aids the rural production of meth. In the early twenty-first century, law enforcement authorities reported that the state of Missouri had the highest number of meth laboratories in the United States, mostly in the rural communities of the Ozarks. Experts estimate that the rate of rural youths using meth is almost double that of youth meth users in urban areas.

Many medical centers include treatment for substance abuse. Stand-alone facilities also are present throughout the United States and other developed nations. Some provide care in a basic, clinical setting while others function in a resort-like setting. One well-known facility is the Betty Ford Center in Rancho Mirage, California, which was founded by former US first lady Betty Ford. The one-hundred-bed nonprofit residential facility offers inpatient, outpatient, and day treatment for recovering substance abusers and addicts. It also provides prevention and education programs for family members (including children) of substance abusers and addicts.

Support groups. A variety of support groups are available to a substance abuser who admits he or she has a problem. Treatment centers may have their own support groups or may refer patients to outside programs they deem suitable. A recovering alcoholic may have to try a variety of resources before finding the best fit.

Religious support. Churches and synagogues often sponsor support for recovering alcoholics. Members can use available services, which are often integrated with other organizations and social services in the community. Sometimes, an alcoholic who has no religious faith will start recovery by accepting a religious faith. Although nonsectarian and nondenominational, AA is a faith-based organization as exemplified by its twelve-steps program. The twelve steps include the acknowledgement of the existence of a supreme being.

GENETIC FACTORS

Significant evidence exists that genetic factors are involved in the development of substance abuse and addiction, particularly alcoholism. The interaction of genes and environmental factors that influence substance dependence is a complex scientific topic.

Since 1989, the US-government-funded Collaborative Study on the Genetics of Alcoholism (COGA) has been tracking alcoholism in families. COGA researchers have interviewed more than 14,000 people and sampled the DNA of 262 families. They have found evidence for the existence of several alcohol-related genes. COGA researchers are increasingly convinced that different types of alcoholics are representative of a number of genetic variations.

SOCIAL IMPLICATIONS

Substance abuse has a tremendous impact on society. For example, many people are injured or killed by substance abusers who drive under the influence of one or more psychoactive substances (for example, alcohol or marijuana). Family members of substance abusers suffer from the emotional and financial burden placed on them by a substance abuser. Furthermore, substance abusers accrue countless hours of lost and unproductive work.

All developed nations have extensive legislation regarding substance abuse and age limits for legal substances. For example, in the United States the legal drinking age is twenty-one years and the legal smoking age is eighteen years. However, some nations have more lenient restrictions. Some substances deemed illegal by one government are considered legal by another.

An example of a substance with varying degrees of legality is marijuana. The substance is deemed illegal by the US government; however, it is available in the Netherlands, with some restrictions. In the United States, the use of medical marijuana remains a contentious topic. Medical marijuana has been legalized in some US states to allow usage for legitimate medical reasons, such as for glaucoma or for pain relief from cancer. However, there is a concern that the substance will be dispensed for frivolous, nonmedical reasons or diverted for illegal use.

Robin L. Wulffson, MD

FURTHER READING

Fisher, Gary, and Thomas Harrison. *Substance Abuse: Information for School Counselors, Social Workers, Therapists, and Counselors.* 4th ed. Boston: Allyn & Bacon, 2008. Incorporating actual clinical examples with solid research, this text provides counselors and social workers with a detailed overview of drug addictions.

Ketcham, Katherine, et al. *Beyond the Influence: Understanding and Defeating Alcoholism.* New York: Bantam, 2000. The authors define *alcoholism* as "a genetically transmitted neurological disease" and not the result of a character defect or moral weakness. They explain the effects of "the drug alcohol" on the human body and brain in both alcoholics and nonalcoholics.

Liptak, John, and Ester A. Leutenberg. *The Substance Abuse and Recovery Workbook.* Duluth, MN: Whole Persons, 2008. Contains self-assessments, exploratory activities, reflective journaling exercises, and educational handouts to help participants discover habitual and ineffective methods of managing substance abuse and to explore new ways of healing.

Miller, William. *Rethinking Substance Abuse: What the Science Shows, and What We Should Do about It.* New York: Guilford, 2010. Reviews what is known about substance abuse and offers overviews of biological, psychological, and social factors involved in the treatment of substance abuse. Also anticipates future developments and evaluates them for their potential effects on prevention and treatment.

Seixas, Judith. *Children of Alcoholism: A Survivor's Manual.* New York: Harper & Row, 1986. Focuses on children of alcoholics and the specific problems they face.

WEBSITES OF INTEREST

Al-Anon and Alateen
http://www.al-anon.alateen.org

Alcoholics Anonymous
http://www.aa.org

National Institute on Alcohol Abuse and Alcoholism
http://www.niaaa.nih.gov

National Institute on Drug Abuse
http://www.nida.nih.gov

Substance Abuse and Mental Health Services Administration
http://www.samhsa.gov/

See also: Alcohol abuse and alcoholism: Overview; Alcoholics Anonymous; Cocaine Anonymous; Cocaine use disorder; Heroin; Marijuana; Methamphetamine; Narcotics abuse; Narcotics Anonymous; National Institute on Alcohol Abuse and Alcoholism (NIAAA); National Institute on Drug Abuse (NIDA); Opioid abuse; Painkiller abuse; Substance Abuse and Mental Health Services Administration (SAMHSA)

Substance Abuse and Mental Health Services Administration (SAMHSA)

CATEGORY: Diagnosis and prevention

DEFINITION: The Substance Abuse and Mental Health Services Administration, a branch of the US Department of Health and Human Services, provides services that address addiction, substance abuse prevention, and mental health. The agency is guided by a series of eight strategic initiatives.

DATE: Established in 1992

BACKGROUND

Established by the US Congress, the Substance Abuse and Mental Health Services Administration (SAMHSA) consists of four centers tasked with helping to guide health care practitioners on issues of substance abuse, addiction, and mental illness. SAMHSA comprises the Center for Mental Health Services (CMHS), the Center for Substance Abuse Prevention (CSAP), the Center for Substance Abuse Treatment (CSAT), and Center for Behavioral Health Statistics and Quality (CBHSQ).

CMHS is charged with promoting mental health and preventing mental illness; CSAP is charged with the prevention of addiction problems related to alcohol, drugs, and smoking; and CSAT provides for substance abuse treatment services through community-based services and nationwide referrals.

The fourth center, CBHSQ, handles all issues dealing with research, including disseminating information on evidenced-based practices in the field of behavioral health. This center was formerly known as the Office of Applied Studies.

MISSION AND GOALS

SAMHSA's primary mission is to reduce the harm of substance abuse, especially as it intersects with mental illness. As part of this mission, SAMHSA works to facilitate recovery and build recovery capital for people who are at risk for addiction or mental illness. To fulfill this mission, SAMHSA, as outlined in its 2011–2014 Strategic Plan, developed a number of strategic initiatives to guide the agency's work. The eight strategic initiatives also provide a mechanism that determines how resources should be used to best deal with the issues of addiction and mental illness. The eight strategic initiatives are delineated and discussed here.

1. Prevention of substance abuse and mental illness. This initiative, which reiterates the primary mission of SAMHSA, helps to focus the utilization of resources in this key area.

2. Trauma and justice. This initiative deals with the effects of trauma on the victim, as trauma can contribute to mental illness and substance abuse issues. By utilizing better screening and treatment techniques with trauma victims, this initiative could significantly decrease the incidence of these co-occurring disorders. Additionally, this initiative involves meeting the mental health and treatment needs of people who are involved with the criminal justice system.

3. Military families. This initiative focuses on members of the military and their families. SAMHSA partners with the US Department of Defense and the Department of Veterans Affairs to improve access to and types of behavioral health care.

4. Recovery support. This initiative acknowledges that while screening, prevention, and treatment for mental health and addiction problems have improved, recovery support services are lacking. It indicates that health, home (permanent housing), purpose (employment or education), and community (peer support) are essential to support recovery.

5. Health reform. Based on the Patient Protection and Affordable Care Act of 2010, this initiative calls for an improvement in the nation's behavioral health care and access to that care. As part of this initiative, SAMHSA works to improve treatment for persons who, for example, are infected with the human immunodeficiency virus or who have acquired immune deficiency syndrome.

6. Health information technology. This initiative focuses on the use of electronic health records and health information technology to improve the behavioral health care of those in need. The hope is that technology will allow better interaction between primary care practitioners and behavioral-health-care practitioners.

7. Data, outcomes, and quality. This initiative calls for improved tracking of data and better use of outcomes to improve the quality of behavioral health care.

8. Public awareness and support. This initiative mandates the provision of information on mental health and substance abuse disorders with the intention of preventing discrimination and improving attitudes toward those with behavioral health issues.

These eight initiatives provide the framework for SAMHSA to ensure that its mission is fulfilled and that its resources are expended in the areas of greatest need.

Robin Kamienny Montvilo, PhD

FURTHER READING

Brounstein, P. J., S. E. Gardner, and T. Backer. "Research to Practice: Efforts to Bring Effective Prevention to Every Community." *Journal of Primary Prevention* 27.1 (2006): 91–109. Print. A review of SAMHSA work to inventory and evaluate evidenced-based practices in addiction prevention, thus allowing wider dissemination of this research to those working in the field.

Drake, R. E., and G. R. Bond. "Implementing Integrated Mental Health and Substance Abuse Services." *Journal of Dual Diagnosis* 6 (2010): 251–62. Print. Demonstrates the use of SAMHSA's model for dealing with co-occurring disorders. This model makes use of the SAMHSA toolkit Integrated Treatment for Co-Occurring Disorders.

Herr, E. C. M., M. J. English, and N. B. Brown. "Translating Mental Health Services Research into Practice: A Perspective from Staff at the US Substance Abuse and Mental Health Services Administration." *Alzheimer's Care Quarterly* 4.3 (2003): 241–53. Print. Reviews the history of SAMHSA and traces its functioning from its inception to the present. Describes how research is relayed to professionals in the field and how this shapes practice, focusing on older adults as clients.

Power, A. K. "Transforming the Nation's Health: Next Steps in Mental Health Promotion." *American Journal of Health* 100 (2010): 2343–46. Print. Describes the role that SAMHSA plays in promoting mental health. Emphasizes the important role of this agency in promoting the general health of the individual and society.

WEBSITES OF INTEREST
National Institutes of Health
http://www.nih.gov

Substance Abuse and Mental Health Services Administration
http://www.samhsa.gov

See also: Education about substance abuse; Monitoring the Future; National Institute on Alcohol Abuse and Alcoholism (NIAAA); National Institute on Drug Abuse (NIDA); Substance abuse

Sugar addiction

CATEGORY: Psychological issues and behaviors
ALSO KNOWN AS: Sugar dependence
DEFINITION: Sugar addiction is the compulsive physiological need for sugar. This compulsive need constitutes a behavioral addiction, an interpretation that is reinforced when sugar addicts, long habituated to large amounts of sugar, experience classic withdrawal symptoms when their sugar intake is reduced.

CAUSES

Just as the search for explanations of addiction to alcohol and other drugs has been complicated by the nature-nurture debate, so too have been the controversies over sugar addiction. Some medical researchers and physicians believe that sugar addiction might be genetic, that is, that the biological nature of certain humans or, more specifically, the information programmed into their deoxyribonucleic acid (DNA), can explain why some people become addicted to sugar (in a way similar to how others become addicted to, for example, alcohol, nicotine, or heroin).

Other researchers have traced the pleasurable physiological state (popularly known as a sugar high) induced by an intake of sugar to the activation of certain receptors in the brain. Sugar is said to affect the same neurotransmitters in the brain associated with the pleasure produced by such substances as nicotine in cigarette smoke.

Those who emphasize the cultural rather than the genetic causes of physiological addiction to sugar point out that refined sugar (or sucrose, largely derived from sugar cane and sugar beets) has been a relatively recent addition to the human diet. Throughout most of the evolution of *Homo sapiens* and the early history of civilized humans, the dietary need for glucose was satisfied by the ingestion of fruits, vegetables, and fats, which could, as needed, be metabolized into glucose.

Even after techniques were discovered allowing sugar to be extracted from plants, most humans were unable to use this sugar because of its expense. Sugar did not become an inexpensive commodity until the eighteenth century, when doctors began to discover some of its negative effects on the human body. For some historians, the origin of sugar addiction can be traced to this period, when laborers could be inexpensively fed with sweetened foods and drinks rather than with costly meats, fruits, and vegetables.

Contemporary analysts now believe that sugar addiction has both genetic and cultural causes. However, because of the uniqueness of every person's biochemistry, it is difficult if not impossible to precisely divide causality for this relatively recent medical phenomenon into its biological and environmental sources.

RISK FACTORS

Scientists have discovered a number of medical conditions that predispose a person to sugar addiction. For example, a weak adrenal gland results in an insufficient quantity of glucocorticoid hormones to properly regulate glucose levels in the blood, leading to an intense craving for sugar. Furthermore, persons with a penchant for overeating are often susceptible to sugar addiction.

Cultural factors also can pose risks. For instance, in many advanced societies the processed food industries add massive amounts of refined sugar to numerous products, thus allowing for large numbers of suitably predisposed persons to become sugar addicts.

SYMPTOMS

A common symptom of sugar addiction is the overpowering urge, several times a day, to consume something sweet. If afflicted persons are unable to satisfy these urges, they often feel weak, apathetic, and dizzy. These symptoms may be relieved by the ingestion of sugar-containing foods and sweetened beverages, but continued dependence on sugar results in tolerance with increased consumption needed to relieve symptoms and re-experience the pleasurable feelings that sugar consumption initially created.

With the removal of sugar from the addict's diet, withdrawal symptoms often occur, such as tremors of the extremities, painful headaches, and digestive difficulties, including nausea. Psychological symptoms include irritability, depression, and drastic mood changes.

Researchers have noted numerous long-term health problems associated with sugar addiction, including such well-known consequences as obesity and dental decay. The American Diabetes Association regards the overconsumption of sugar as a major cause of degenerative diseases in the United States, including diabetes, heart disease, and cancer. Sugar also has a negative effect on the body's immune system by depleting white blood cells, thus reducing this system's ability to fight infectious agents.

SCREENING AND DIAGNOSIS

Screening for sugar addiction has not been a part of most routine physical examinations, with the exception of physical exams of the obese and of persons showing clear symptoms. For those who believe that sugar addiction is endemic to Western society, this neglect to screen for the addiction imperils the health of many people.

This lack of monitoring for sugar addiction has led to numerous books on this disorder, many of which contain guidelines for self-diagnosis. However, self-diagnoses can be inaccurate, even dangerous. Blood tests exist to monitor symptoms before and after the ingestion of sugar, and these tests can provide reliable evidence leading to a diagnosis of sugar addiction.

TREATMENT AND THERAPY

According to some advocates, the world is facing a crisis centered on the treatment of sugar addiction that faces several cultural barriers. Sugar has become "a legalized recreational drug" that is "socially acceptable to consume." Sugar addiction is considered an acceptable addiction, one wholly separate from other addictions; this is an alarming perspective to those calling for prevention and treatment of sugar addiction.

The treatment of sugar addicts is also hindered by the denial of their dependence in a manner reminiscent of classic drug addicts. Also, similar to another addictive product—tobacco—countries frequently subsidize sugar production because of its importance to their economies. Furthermore, it is common for

sugar and its presence in numerous foods and drinks to receive much more legal immunity than tobacco.

Therapy for sugar addiction can be a long and difficult process. Sugar addicts should not expect their sugar cravings to vanish in a few weeks or months. Most physicians and nutritionists begin treatment with diet modification. After tests, doctors generally attempt to stabilize blood sugar levels by getting their sugar-addicted patients to eat modest meals rich in protein. A nutritious breakfast is especially important, as is the elimination of sugar and artificial sweeteners from all meals and snacks.

Some doctors insist on treating sugar addiction the way they treat alcohol and other drug addictions, that is, by insisting their patients avoid all refined sugars and sugar-containing foods and drinks from their diet. This can be daunting because so many processed foods contain fructose, dextrose, maltose, and other sugary additives such as corn syrup. Some nutritionists even suggest a drastic reduction in the consumption of fresh fruits and fruit juices, which contain sugar. Others, though, allow some fruit in the diet during the transition to a totally sugar-free diet.

Doctors also can prescribe medicines that may help reduce the craving for sugar, and nutritionists may advise recovering sugar addicts to take amino acids, such as glutamine and tyrosine, to help reduce cravings. Others have found that chromium supplements help to balance blood sugar.

Orthomolecular physicians believe that good health can be achieved by balancing substances normally present in the body or by adding essential vitamins and minerals to the diet. These practitioners tend to agree with believers in sugar addiction that this sweet substance is alien to the body and poses a danger to health. For orthomolecular physicians, megavitamin therapy, along with the elimination of sugars and other processed foods that are incompatible with the body's normal and natural array of molecules, is optimum for health.

Other therapies add behavioral modifications for the treatment of sugar addiction. These therapies include exercise, especially relaxed walking, and eight hours of sleep every night. For serious cases, some professionals recommend psychotherapy, because certain patients become addicted to sugar to assuage feelings of loneliness or self-hatred. Therapists often try to discover why patients crave sugar; oftentimes, this craving is caused by past trauma.

With increasing awareness of sugar addiction, many treatment options have become available. Professionals now promote their services in treating this disorder. Treatment centers that include group therapy for sugar addiction also are available.

PREVENTION

Curbing sugar addiction involves both the individual and society. Even those skeptical of this addiction agree that most persons consume far too much sugar and that this overconsumption contributes to many health problems. Evolution has not prepared the human body to handle an average intake of 150 to 300 pounds of sugar each year. Several states in the United States have failed in their attempts to put a tax on sugary soft drinks. In concept, the prevention of sugar addiction is simple: Drastically reduce sugar consumption. In reality, though, individuals and societies rarely are willing to accomplish this.

Robert J. Paradowski, PhD

FURTHER READING

Appleton, Nancy, and G. N. Jacobs. *Suicide by Sugar: A Startling Look at Our #1 National Addiction.* Garden City, NY: Square One, 2009. Written by a long-time believer in the dangerous reality of sugar addiction, Appleton and her coauthor have collected data linking sugar consumption to a range of disorders, from dementia to cancer.

Avena, Nicole M., Pedro Rada, and Bartley G. Hoebel. "Evidence for Sugar Addiction: Behavioral and Neurochemical Effects of Intermittent, Excessive Sugar Intake." *Neuroscience and Biobehavioral Reviews* 32.1 (2008): 20–39. Print. Results of a study using rats to determine whether or not sugar can be a substance of abuse and lead to a natural form of addiction. Concludes that the evidence supports the hypothesis that under certain circumstances rats can become sugar dependent.

Bennett, Connie, and Stephen T. Sinatra. *Sugar Shock! How Sweets and Simple Carbs Can Derail Your Life— and How You Can Get Back on Track.* New York: Berkley, 2006. This popular paperback, intended for a wide readership, marshals much evidence for how eating massive amounts of sugar has harmed the health of millions of people. Offers advice on ending one's sugar habit. Index.

Macinnis, Peter. *Bittersweet: The Story of Sugar.* Boston: Allyn & Bacon, 2002. This narrative of how sugar processing became big business contains "very few heroes and many villains." Some who made sugar hoped to save lives, others to make money, but they all ended up harming the common good, the health of sugar consumers. Glossary, references, and index.

Minitz, Sidney W. *Sweetness and Power: The Place of Sugar in Modern History.* New York: Viking, 1985. An anthropologist explains how politics and slavery transformed sugar from "a rare foreign luxury" to a necessary commodity in industrialized societies. Bibliography, notes, and index.

Yudkin, John. *Sweet and Dangerous.* New York: Bantam, 1974. A pioneer in analyzing the connections between sugar and many health problems summarizes research on sugar. An account that many have found "prophetic" and as relevant today as it was when first published. Yudkin's research had a strong influence on Linus Pauling and the other founders of orthomolecular medicine.

WEBSITES OF INTEREST

Academy of Nutrition and Dietetics
http://www.eatright.org

American Diabetes Association
http://www.diabetes.org

Food Addicts Anonymous
http://www.foodaddictsanonymous.org

See also: Addiction; Compulsions; Food addiction

Suicide and addiction

CATEGORY: Psychological issues and behaviors

DEFINITION: Addiction is associated with suicidal behavior more frequently than mood disorders and schizophrenia. Addiction also increases social problems and mental health issues associated with suicide attempts and completed suicides. The complex relationship between addiction and suicide must be better understood to improve treatment outcomes for substance use disorders and suicide prevention programs.

SUICIDALITY

Suicide is a serious public health problem and a leading cause of death among substance abusers and among persons who are chemically dependent. Heavy substance users are more likely than the general population to die by suicide. The risk of suicide increases as substance use progresses into abuse and addiction.

Addiction is a primary contributor to suicide risk. The risk of suicide attempts is highest among people who abuse amphetamine, methamphetamine, and cocaine; however, more suicide attempts are associated with alcohol abuse because more people consume alcohol. Determining a primary substance can be difficult because substance abusers often use multiple substances in combination. Multi-substance abusers are more likely than single-substance abusers to engage in suicidal ideation, or thoughts about taking one's own life.

Suicidal ideation is a predictor of suicide among substance abusers. People with substance use disorders who have thoughts about attempting suicide are more often depressed, take more health-related risks, and show more aggression than substance abusers who have not thought about suicide. Suicidal ideation often occurs during the "crash" or withdrawal phase, in which the pleasurable effects of a drug give way to agitation and depression, increasing the risk of suicide.

The relationship between suicide and substance abuse is complex. Suicide and substance abuse are not consequences of one single cause. They are behavioral outcomes that result from a combination of interacting stressors. The risk factors that contribute to suicide also can contribute to substance abuse.

RISK FACTORS

Factors associated with increased risk for suicide and addiction often overlap and include childhood abuse or trauma, sexual abuse, poor family relationships, poor communication and interpersonal conflict, family psychiatric history, unemployment and financial stress, biological correlates, impulsivity, hopelessness, previous suicide attempt, history of violence, and mental health problems including depression, bipolar disorder, and generalized anxiety disorder.

Substance abuse increases the risk of suicide by affecting cognition, mood, and impulsiveness. Substance abuse impairs judgment, increases affective instability, and reduces inhibition. This makes self-directed aggression more likely, particularly for people who have access to firearms or other means of suicide. Substance-related suicide attempts are more likely to have an impulsive component and to occur during a short-term crisis, during stress, or following a loss.

Gender also may have a part in mortality rates from suicide. Female suicide mortality rates are strongly related to alcohol consumption. The social stigma and inaccurate stereotypes attached to women with drinking problems can contribute to guilt and shame and can serve to increase a woman's sense of isolation and loneliness. The exacerbation of these feelings by alcohol use adds to the likelihood of suicidal ideation and suicide attempts, creating a history of suicidal behavior that, in turn, has been linked to later alcohol problems among women.

Among men, serious substance abuse and addiction are correlated with higher rates of completed suicides.

The majority of persons who attempt suicide suffer from comorbidity, or the presence of more than one disorder that coexists with a primary disorder but may be unrelated. Depression or other mental health problems, such as bipolar disorder, along with a substance use disorder may overlap and contribute to suicidal behavior.

It is not uncommon for persons with a psychiatric illness to self-medicate with drugs or alcohol. If the person enters a treatment program or abstains from substance use, then the effects of the illness can escalate, creating stress in the user and contributing to suicide risk. Effective prevention and treatment programs need to focus on psychiatric disorders and addiction, especially among multi-substance abusers who are more likely to die by suicide than are single-substance abusers.

TREATMENT

Treatment of addiction is an important part of a comprehensive approach to suicide prevention. Addiction counselors need to know how to screen for suicide risk and assess the risk of suicidal danger. Examples of screening and assessment tools include the modified mini screen, which is used to identify people who need a mental health assessment, and the addiction severity index, which is designed to assess factors contributing to substance abuse problems.

Evaluating the risk for suicide in a patient who has a substance abuse disorder is not easy. The patient may not be able to remember the details of a suicide attempt. It also may be difficult to establish that the patient intended to attempt suicide, as in the case of an overdose, which may appear to have been accidental. The difficulty in assessing and evaluating risk for suicide in addiction treatment programs and a lack of knowledge about the correlation between addiction and suicide has resulted in moving patients out of addiction treatment programs and into the mental health system. This places suicidal patients at greater risk for self-harm because the addiction, which is a primary contributor to suicide risk, is no longer being treated. To improve outcomes for persons with substance use disorders, suicide prevention programs need to include addiction treatment programs.

Patients in treatment for substance use disorders, and who have attempted suicide, report more psychiatric illnesses and more problematic substance abuse. These patients benefit from inpatient treatment and increased intensity of care during the early phases of treatment. Motivational interviewing, which helps the patient understand the problems and consequences of substance abuse; continuing care; and psychosocial therapy, which focuses on improving communication skills and interactions a patient has with family and friends, also have contributed to improved treatment outcomes for persons with substance use disorders and a history of suicide attempts. Effective strategies for suicide prevention include restricting access to firearms and other means of suicide, gatekeeper training to enhance communication and intervention skills, public education campaigns, crisis hotlines, physician training, addiction treatment programs, and controlling the availability of drugs and alcohol.

Anne M. W. Kelly, PhD

FURTHER READING

Glass, Joseph E., et al. "Inpatient Hospitalization in Addiction Treatment for Patients with a History of Suicide Attempt: A Case of Support for Treatment Performance Measure." *Journal of Psychoactive Drugs* 42.3 (2010): 315–25. Print. Recommendations for improved substance use disorder treatment for persons with a history of suicide attempt.

Kaminer, Yifrah, and Oscar G. Bukstein, eds. *Adolescent Substance Abuse: Psychiatric Comorbidity and High-Risk Behaviors.* New York: Routledge, 2008. Reviews mental health problems, treatments, and interventions associated with adolescent substance use disorders.

Landheim, A. S., K. Bakken, and P. Vaglum. "What Characterizes Substance Abusers Who Commit Suicide Attempts? Factors Related to Axis I Disorders and Patterns of Substance Use Disorders." *European Addiction Research* 12 (2006): 102–8. Print. Underlines the need for a comprehensive approach to suicide prevention and substance use disorder treatment programs.

Mann, Robert E., et al. "Alcohol Factors in Suicide Mortality Rates in Manitoba." *Canadian Journal of Psychiatry* 53.4 (2008): 243–51. Print. Identifies alcohol-related factors that contribute to suicide mortality rates.

Mino, Annie, Arnaud Bousquet, and Barbara Broers. "Substance Abuse and Drug-Related Death, Suicidal Ideation, and Suicide: A Review." *Crisis: The Journal of Crisis Intervention and Suicide Prevention* 20.1 (1999): 28–35. Print. Reviews the literature on substance abuse and suicidal ideation and suicide attempts, risk factors for suicide, and protective effects of treating substance abuse on suicidal behavior.

Nunes, Edward V., et al., eds. *Substance Dependence and Co-Occurring Psychiatric Disorders: Best Practices for Diagnosis and Clinical Treatment.* Kingston, NJ: Civic Research Institute, 2010. Includes an overview of suicide and substance abuse, suicide risk factors, and screening patients for suicide risk.

WEBSITES OF INTEREST

American Association of Suicidology
http://www.suicidology.org

Substance Abuse and Mental Health Services Administration
http://www.samhsa.gov

Suicide Awareness Voices of Education
http://www.save.org

Suicide Prevention Resource Center
http://www.sprc.org

See also: Addiction; Dependence; Gender and addiction; Genetics and substance abuse; Risk factors for addiction; Substance abuse

Support groups

Category: Treatment

Definition: Support groups are generally composed of small numbers of people who are facing similar challenges in their lives. They meet, with or without a trained facilitator, to explore their reactions, problems, solutions, feelings, frustrations, successes, and needs in relation to those challenges. They build bonds of trust, and members show compassion for one another. Groups may provide material support or simply assure the individual member that he or she is not alone. They help to minimize stress and maximize coping. They model strategies for dealing with the given challenge, provide information, nurture their members, and encourage the application of new learning. Through this sharing, each member grows, and through individual growth, the group matures.

History and Ideology of Support Groups

The history of support groups in modern times begins with the formation of the Oxford Group in 1908 and the subsequent development of Alcoholics Anonymous. For the participants, support groups reduce feelings of isolation, offer information, instill hope, provide feedback and social support, and teach new social skills. At the beginning of the twenty-first century, support groups exist for persons suffering from all kinds of medical and psychological conditions and for the victims of violent crime.

Humans are social animals in that they live in groups. These networks among people are powerful in shaping behavior, feelings, and judgments. Groups can lead to destructive behavior, such as mob violence and aggression, but they can also encourage loyalty, nurturing of others, and achievement, as is found in cancer-support groups. A group may be permanent or temporary, formal or informal, and structured or unstructured. Support groups may share any of these characteristics. Scientific investigation of how groups affect human behavior began as early as 1898, but the main body of research on group functioning began only in the 1940s and 1950s. The study of groups is still a major topic of scientific inquiry.

Why do human beings seek out groups? Social learning theorists believe that humans learn to depend on other people because most are raised within families, where they learn to look to other people for support, validation, amusement, and advice. Exchange theorists, on the other hand, reason that groups provide both rewards (such as love and approval) and costs (such as time and effort). Membership in a group will benefit the individual if the rewards are greater than the costs. Yet another set of theorists, the sociobiologists, believe that humans form groups because this has a survival benefit for the species. They hypothesize a genetic predisposition toward affiliation with others. From an evolutionary standpoint, it is within groups that people have the greatest chance of survival.

Whatever the reason for forming groups, all groups have important characteristics that must be addressed in understanding why support groups work. First of all, group size is important. Larger groups allow more anonymity, while smaller groups facilitate communication, for example. Group structure includes such elements as status differences, norms of conduct, leaders and followers, and subgroups. Individuals in groups develop social roles—those expected behaviors associated with the individual's position within the group. Roles are powerful in influencing behavior and can even cause individuals to act contrary to their private feelings or their own interests. These roles carry varying degrees of status within the group—who is influential and respected and who is less so. Groups may have subgroups based on age, residence, roles, interests, or other factors. These subgroups may contribute to the success of the whole group or may become cliquish and undermine the main group's effectiveness.

Groups also have varying degrees of cohesion. Cohesion reflects the strength of attachments within the group. Sometimes cohesion is a factor of how well group members like one another, while other times it is a factor of the need to achieve an important goal. Cohesion can also be a factor of the rewards that group membership confers. All groups have communication networks, or patterns of openness and restrictions on communication among members.

Group norms are the attitudes and behaviors that are expected of members. These norms are helpful to the group's success because they make life more predictable and efficient for the members. Leadership may be formal or informal, may be task-oriented or people-oriented, and may change over time. Finally, all groups go through fairly predictable stages as they form, do their work, and conclude. The comprehensive term for the way a group functions is "group dynamics."

How Groups Influence Individuals

Researchers have found that for all animals, including human beings, the mere presence of other members of the same species may enhance performance on individual tasks. This phenomenon is known as social facilitation. However, with more complex tasks, the presence of others may decrease performance. This is known as social inhibition or impairment. It is not clear whether this occurs because the presence of others arouses the individual, leads individuals to expect rewards or punishments based on past experience, makes people self-conscious, creates challenges to self-image, or affects the individual's ability to process information. Most theorists agree that the nature of the task is important to the success of the group. For example, a group is more likely to succeed if the welfare of individual members is closely tied to the task of the group.

Groups model behavior deemed appropriate in a given situation. The more similar the individual doing the modeling is to the individual who wants to learn a behavior, the more powerful the model is. Groups reward members for behavior that conforms to group norms or standards, and they punish behaviors that do not conform. Groups provide a means of social comparison—how one's own behavior compares to others' in a similar situation. Groups are valuable sources of support during times of stress. Some specific factors that enhance the ability of groups to help individuals reduce stress are attachment, guidance, tangible assistance, and embeddedness. Attachment has to do with caring and attention among group members. Guidance may be the provision of information or it may be advice and feedback provided by the group to its members. Tangible assistance may take the form of money or of other kinds of service. Embeddedness refers to the sense of belonging that the individual has within the group. Some researchers have shown that a strong support system actually increases the body's immune functioning.

Alcoholics Anonymous and Other Groups

The most well-known support group is Alcoholics Anonymous (AA), formed in Akron, Ohio, in the late 1930s. AA groups now number in the tens of thousands and are found across the globe. What is less well known is that AA is an outgrowth of the Oxford Group, an evangelical Christian student and athlete group formed at Oxford University in England in 1908. The Oxford Group's ideals—self-examination, acknowledgment of character defects, restitution for harm done, and working with others—directly influenced the steps to recovery practiced by members of AA and other twelve-step groups, including Al-Anon, Narcotics Anonymous, and Smokers Anonymous.

For addicts, support groups are important for a number of reasons. They provide peer support for the effort to become "clean and sober." They provide peer pressure against relapsing into substance use. They assure addicts that they are not alone—that others have suffered the hardships brought about by drinking or drug use. Addicts in twelve-step groups learn to interact with others on an emotional level. Importantly, members of AA and other support groups for addicts are able to confront the individual's maladaptive behaviors and provide models for more functional behavior. The norm for AA is sobriety, and sobriety is reinforced by clear directions on how to live as a sober person. Another important aspect of AA is the hope that it is able to inspire in persons who, while using, saw no hope for recovery. This hope comes not only from seeing individuals who have successfully learned to live as sober persons but also from the group's emphasis on dependence on a higher power and the importance of a spiritual life.

Support Groups and the Internet

Support groups have traditionally met in person, but the Internet has altered this expectation. Many support groups now meet online. These may take the form of synchronous or asynchronous chat groups; bulletin boards; and websites with links to information sources, referrals, and collaboration with professionals. These groups, while not well-studied, seem to serve the same purposes as in-person groups. In addition, they provide a possible advantage: The anonymity of the Internet makes it possible to observe and to learn from observing without actually participating until one is comfortable doing so.

Rebecca Lovell Scott

Further Reading

Carlson, Hannah. *The Courage to Lead: Start Your Own Mutual Help Support Group—Mental Illnesses & Addictions.* Madison, CT: Bick, 2001. A complete how-to manual for creating small groups for persons striving against addiction or to overcome mental illnesses.

Klein, Linda L. *The Support Group Sourcebook: What They Are, How You Can Find One, and How They Can Help You.* New York: Wiley, 2000. A comprehensive guide on how groups work, develop, and assist people. Advice on how to start or find a group.

Mowat, Joan. *Using Support Groups to Improve Behaviour.* Thousand Oaks, CA: PCP/Sage, 2007. Describes how to change undesirable behaviors through support groups.

Nichols, Keith, and John Jenkinson. *Leading a Support Group: A Practical Guide.* New York: Open University Press, 2006. Explains the benefits of support groups and describes a step-by-step guide to forming and running one.

O'Halloran, Sean. *Talking Oneself Sober: The Discourse of Alcoholics Anonymous.* Amherst, NY: Cambria Press, 2008. Discusses the techniques followed by one of the best-known support groups.

WEBSITES OF INTEREST

Alcoholics Anonymous
http://www.aa.org

Gamblers Anonymous
http://www.gamblersanonymous.org

Narcotics Anonymous
http://www.na.org

Nicotine Anonymous
http://nicotine-anonymous.org/

Overeaters Anonymous
http://www.oa.org/

See also: Alcohol abuse and alcoholism: Treatment; Alcoholics Anonymous; Behavioral addictions: Treatment; Cocaine Anonymous; Debtors Anonymous; Drug abuse and addiction: Overview; Gamblers Anonymous; Group therapy for behavioral addictions; Group therapy for substance abuse; Narcotics Anonymous; Overeaters Anonymous; Sponsors; Twelve-step programs for addicts; Twelve-step programs for family and friends

Symptoms of substance abuse

CATEGORY: Health issues and physiology

DEFINITION: Substance abuse is characterized by the overuse of alcohol or drugs that leads to compulsive urges to consume the substance of choice. Substance abuse affects the user's quality of life and the ability to make good decisions. In addition to negative behavioral symptoms, substance abuse generates harmful physical symptoms—unseen physiological damage to internal organs and visible deterioration in the user's appearance.

RISK FACTORS

Experimentation with alcohol and drugs is the most prominent risk to becoming a substance abuser. Whether the reward of the high is physical pleasure, the temporary removal of a traumatic memory from the mind, or simply acceptance by a peer group, experimenting with substances is always risky. Symptoms of the substance use and its effects begin to appear immediately.

Many neuroscientists and mental health professionals assert that some persons are more susceptible than others to becoming addicted to alcohol or drugs because of genetic, biological, or environmental tendencies or exposure. Risk factors include a family history of substance abuse, mental disorders, childhood trauma, and early experimentation with substances. For persons with or without these risk factors, experimentation with certain substances could lead to addiction.

The earlier a substance abuser recognizes the symptoms of substance abuse and acknowledges the dangers of continued use, the earlier he or she can advance toward treatment and recovery. At any point between a substance abuser's experimentation and addiction, signs of dependency increasingly become apparent. Friends and family members may recognize the symptoms and then intervene to break a substance abuser's destructive patterns. By not confronting a person suspected of substance abuse, the problem will likely worsen.

Though a substance abuser is likely to admit to using a substance, he or she is less likely to admit to abusing that substance, which makes the process of intervention difficult. Still, the more proficient a loved one or friend is in recognizing the symptoms of substance abuse, the more confident he or she can be in intervening.

PHYSICAL SYMPTOMS

The most profound physiological symptoms of substance abuse stem from how substances radically alter the biochemical processes of the brain. Alcohol and drugs affect how the brain's nerve receptors receive, process, and send information by overtaking the brain's neurotransmitters and by overstimulating the brain's pleasure center.

This effect on the brain is manifested in a substance abuser's mood. He or she will seem cheerful or "normal" when feeling the initial effects, or the high, of the substance. Once the high wears off, he or she will be noticeably agitated or depressed. A substance abuser also requires increasingly higher and more frequent dosing of the substance of choice to achieve the same effects after physical dependence develops.

Without increasing dosage and frequency, the abuser will experience disruptive withdrawal symptoms. Other common physical warning signs of substance abuse include bloodshot and glassy eyes, sudden weight loss or weight gain, change in appetite, deteriorating personal appearance and hygiene, odor of alcohol or smoke emanating from the person's breath or clothing, tremors, lack of coordination, and changes in speech patterns like slurring.

Though all substances can generate short-term or long-term effects on the body, different substances affect the body differently and manifest different symptoms. Alcohol, for example, increases dopamine in the brain, and when abused it impedes the natural production and transmission of dopamine. As the brain's organic ability to generate pleasure chemicals is impeded by chronic alcohol consumption, the alcoholic develops a tolerance for alcohol and has difficulty functioning in daily life without it. Physical signs of alcoholism are the odor of alcohol on the breath and skin, bloodshot eyes, redness in the face, a bloated stomach, slurred speech, and a lack of coordination and focus.

Marijuana's main active chemical, delta-9-tetrahydrocannabinol (THC), impacts sites in the brain known as cannabinoid receptors. A marijuana user will have bloodshot and glassy eyes, impaired

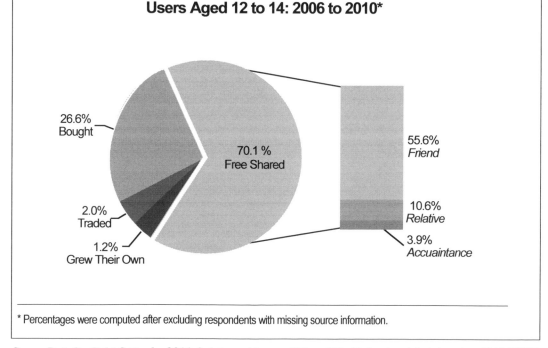

Source of Most Recently Used Marijuana among Past Year Marijuana Users Aged 12 to 14: 2006 to 2010*

26.6% Bought

70.1 % Free Shared

2.0% Traded

1.2% Grew Their Own

55.6% *Friend*

10.6% *Relative*

3.9% *Accuaintance*

* Percentages were computed after excluding respondents with missing source information.

Source: Data Spotlight, September 2011, Substance Abuse and Mental Health Services Administration. (SAMHSA)

coordination, difficulty with thinking, and memory loss. Because THC weakens the immune system, a chronic marijuana smoker frequently contracts respiratory infections.

Cocaine stimulates the nervous system by increasing the level of dopamine in the brain, and it adversely affects the ability of the brain to transmit dopamine organically. A cocaine user is hyperactive and talkative when high and appears fatigued and melancholy later, when the high has worn off. Chronic cocaine snorting causes a chronic cough, frequent nose bleeds, and even permanent damage to the nasal cavity, including a loss of the sense of smell and loss of appetite. Those who smoke crack cocaine or methamphetamine (meth) experience blemishes on the skin, weight loss from decreased appetite, and rotting teeth. Stimulants, such as cocaine, crack cocaine, and meth, also will manifest physical signs of dilated pupils, dry mouth, unusual sleeping and eating patterns, and increased heart rate and blood pressure.

Nonstimulant drugs generate different symptoms. Abusers of heroin, for example, exhibit weight loss; tremors and twitching; track marks on the arms, legs, or feet; paleness; sweating; and reduced heart rate and respiration. Abusers of narcotic depressants, including prescription painkillers, appear drunk and exhibit poor judgment, clumsiness, sleepiness, and an inability to concentrate.

BEHAVIORAL SYMPTOMS

Substance abuse inflicts long-term changes to the brain; the neuroadaptations the brain produces to control the release of dopamine and regulate emotions remain with the addict even after treatment and abstinence. Substance addiction also alters the prefrontal cortex of the user, causing the reduction in neuron activity in this part of the brain.

These changes to the brain also lead to the release of the neurotransmitter glutamate, which impairs the addict's decision-making ability. Glutamate facilitates impulsiveness and intense focus on achieving the immediate reward of pleasure. Consequently, addicts often engage in reckless behavior, and rehabilitated addicts are prone to relapse when faced with substance-related stimuli. In the amygdala, the part of the brain involved in memory formation, emotional memories associated with being high are enhanced, thereby making it difficult for the addict to resist stimuli that trigger these memories.

Because substance abuse radically affects the physiology of the brain, abuse also profoundly affects behavior. The need to consume the substance of choice increasingly dominates a substance abuser's sense of judgment and daily actions.

Substance abuse may be attributed to several disruptive and harmful behavioral patterns, such as family disintegration, loss of employment, domestic violence, and child abuse. Common behavioral symptoms include the inability to refrain from consuming the substance, an obsession with achieving the next high, an abandonment of important responsibilities and interpersonal relationships, and a disregard for the obvious harm the substance is causing to the body.

Consistent with the effect that substance abuse has on the brain, a substance abuser is more likely to drop out of school or quit a job, may change peer groups often, may experience conflicts with the law, and may experience mood swings, recklessness, laziness, and paranoia.

The classic behavioral symptom of persons with a substance abuse problem is that they sever important relationships by betraying those closest to them. Because the quest for the next high is so prominent in their mind, substance abusers will lie, cheat, and steal from strangers and loved ones alike to get the next fix.

Melissa Walsh

FURTHER READING

Fisher, Gary, and Nancy Roget. *Encyclopedia of Substance Abuse Prevention, Treatment, and Recovery.* Thousand Oaks, CA: Sage, 2009. An encyclopedia of key concepts and approaches used in the field of substance abuse.

Hoffman, John, and Susan Froemke, eds. *Addiction: Why Can't They Just Stop?* New York: HBO, 2007. The companion book to the HBO documentary of the same name, presenting information and testimonies about addiction in the United States.

Lawford, Christopher Kennedy. *Moments of Clarity.* New York: Morrow, 2009. First-person accounts of addiction and recovery.

"The Science of Drug Abuse and Addiction." Dec. 2011. Web. 9 Apr. 2012. http://www.drugabuse. gov/publications/media-guide/science-drug-abuse-addiction. An easy-to-read overview of substance abuse, including its symptoms.

WEBSITES OF INTEREST

American Council for Drug Education
http://www.acde.org

American Society of Addiction Medicine
http://www.asam.org

National Institute on Drug Abuse
http://drugabuse.gov

See also: Brain changes with addiction; Cancer and substance abuse; Cross-addiction; Flashbacks; Hallucinogens: Short- and long-term effects on the body; Heart attacks and substance abuse; Liver disease and alcohol use; Narcotics: Short- and long-term effects on the body; Overdose; Physiological dependence; Psychosis and substance abuse; Respiratory diseases and smoking; Smoking: Short- and long-term effects on the body; Tolerance; Withdrawal

T

Teens/young adults and alcohol abuse

CATEGORY: Social issues

DEFINITION: Alcohol abuse is a pattern of heavy drinking that significantly compromises a person's physical health and social functioning. In the United States, six percent of fourteen-year-old children, about one-third of eighteen year olds, and one-half of college students age eighteen to twenty-four years are binge or heavy drinkers. Despite intensive government efforts to curb the problem, the prevalence of underage alcohol abuse has remained constant since about 1990.

SCOPE OF THE PROBLEM

Alcohol use and abuse among young people in the United States is pervasive and destructive. Despite minimum legal drinking ages of between eighteen and twenty-one years since World War II, and despite a nationwide minimum legal age of twenty-one years since about 2000, 80 percent of Americans began drinking alcohol by age eighteen years; the peak age for binge drinking is eighteen to twenty-one years. A 2008 National Institutes of Health survey estimated that 1.4 million youth age twelve to seventeen years experienced alcohol abuse or dependence in the past year and that 2.3 million twelve to twenty year olds drank five or more drinks on an occasion, five or more times per month.

At age twelve, 11 percent of boys and 9 percent of girls have commenced drinking, and 1 percent of them are classified as binge and heavy users. By age fourteen years, the numbers are 31 and 33 percent for use, respectively, and 6 percent of them are binge or heavy users. At age eighteen years, 73 percent have commenced drinking, 42 percent have used alcohol in the past month, and 39 percent are heavy users. Girls age fourteen to eighteen years are somewhat more likely than boys to use alcohol regularly, probably because they are more mature physically and because they often associate with older boys. After age eighteen years, levels of problem drinking are higher among young men, although the gender differential has been steadily narrowing since the 1970s.

Alcohol dependence, characterized by maintenance drinking and an inability to regulate intake, affects 2 percent of twelve to seventeen year olds who drink, 12.2 percent of eighteen to twenty year olds, and 11 percent of young adults age twenty-one to twenty-four years. In contrast, only 3.8 percent of forty to forty-four year olds and less than 2 percent of persons older than age fifty years are dependent on alcohol.

People who commence heavy or episodic binge drinking before age sixteen years are more than twice as likely as people who start drinking after age eighteen years to develop alcohol dependence. This statistic is often cited as justification for higher drinking ages and for more diligent enforcement of laws against underage drinking. There is some controversy whether this is a matter of cause and effect. Early heavy drinkers usually have alcoholic parents or siblings and are probably genetically susceptible to alcoholism; as well, they probably are subject to environmental influences favoring alcohol abuse.

Rates of both alcohol abuse and alcohol dependence decline steadily after age twenty-five years, a pattern that has been consistent for many decades despite changing social attitudes. Among drinkers with a normal trajectory, work and family responsibilities reduce the opportunities for, and acceptability of, frequent intoxication. For those who develop alcohol dependence, a point is eventually reached in which the person either receives treatment and abstains, or dies of the disease.

Rates of teen and young-adult alcohol abuse in northern Europe are similar to those in the United States, except that the average age of onset of heavy drinking is lower; this is in part due to lower minimum legal drinking ages. A survey of fifteen to sixteen year olds in thirty-four European countries in 2007 showed more than 80 percent had drunk alcohol in the past year and 43 percent had been intoxicated or consumed more than five drinks on one occasion in the past thirty days. There is considerable variation from country to country, with abuse being less frequent in southern Europe.

In Great Britain, drinking among schoolchildren is a serious national problem of recent origin. Up until 1960, persons age sixteen to twenty-four years had the lowest per capita alcohol consumption of any adult group; since 1990, the situation has reversed. Some of this pattern (which is seen to a lesser extent in the United States) may be attributed to the rising age of workforce participation. Few sixteen to eighteen year olds are employed full time, and an increasing proportion of eighteen to twenty-four year olds are students with more leisure time and fewer responsibilities than working counterparts. In general, high rates of unemployment that are not accompanied by extreme economic privation produce high levels of alcohol abuse.

EFFECTS OF EARLY ALCOHOL USE AND ABUSE

Alcohol abuse exacts a heavy toll among young people. In 2007, 1,825 college students in the United States died in alcohol-related accidents, 599,000 were injured, 696,000 were involved in nonsexual assaults, 97,000 were sexually assaulted, 400,000 had unsafe sex while intoxicated, 3,360,000 reported driving drunk, about 5 percent were arrested for alcohol-related offenses, and 25 percent reported adverse academic consequences because of drinking. Twenty-five percent of "low-alcohol use" campuses and 50 percent of "high use" campuses reported property damage.

The negative effects on a person's life range from short-lived and inconsequential to profound. Drinking leads to a massive loss of productivity, both in poor academic performance and in the resources that college administrators divert from academics toward combating alcohol problems on campuses.

Statistics on alcohol use for persons eighteen to twenty-five years of age who are not enrolled in a college or university are not as comprehensive; in general, rates of binge drinking are lower but still significant. For both college

and university students and people in the workforce, an early and persistent pattern of alcohol abuse tends to translate into poorer career prospects and family instability, even if the drinker never becomes alcohol dependent or if the drinker later successfully enters a recovery program.

Alcohol can serve as a gateway drug. A high proportion of younger heavy drinkers also use marijuana, and the culture surrounding binge drinking among

---

Beer: A History of Its Consumption and Effects

Beer is one of the world's oldest beverages, dating to 3500 BCE or earlier for common usage. It is produced in varying levels of alcohol concentration during the fermentation process.

Today, beer as a product and its advertising are highly visible to persons of all ages. Being readily available and inexpensive, beer is a frequent beverage in initial alcohol consumption. Its abuse derives from overconsumption or a habitual pattern of use. Some studies have found that as many as one-half of thirteen-year-olds in the United States have consumed alcohol. Early consumption increases risk of alcohol dependence in adulthood. Adolescent risks include damage to the developing brain, physical or sexual assault, and reduced academic performance.

The alcohol in beer is rapidly absorbed into the bloodstream; short-term effects are proportional to consumption. Beer is a central nervous system depressant, and every organ is affected; reaction time, judgment, speech, and movement abilities may be compromised, contributing to the frequency of motor vehicle accidents.

Gender, age, weight, food consumption, and tolerance levels affect blood alcohol content (BAC), generally the best measure of short-term use and effects. Though initial feelings of euphoria, decreased inhibition, and extroversion may be present in moderate use, significant impairment, coma, or death may result when the BAC exceeds .30. No safe level of consumption has been established for girls and women who are pregnant or nursing.

Alcohol-related disorders may result from long-term use of beer, as with other alcoholic beverages. Chronic usage can damage the liver, heart, gastrointestinal tract, nervous system, bone marrow, and endocrine system, and it is associated with an increased cancer risk. In addition, vitamin deficiencies, alterations in blood sugar and fat levels, hepatitis, fatty liver, cirrhosis, esophagitis, gastritis, and dementia may develop. The physical and emotional effects of addiction can result in behavioral disorders, including violence and mood and anxiety disorders.

young people for whom it is illegal provides opportunities for experimenting with more dangerous street drugs. Many methamphetamine addicts report that they began using the drug to counteract the effects of alcohol on the job.

REDUCING UNDERAGE DRINKING

Federal, state, and local governments devote a great deal of energy to combat underage drinking through education and increased enforcement. Federal law in the United States now mandates a minimum state drinking age of twenty-one years as a condition of receiving federal highway funds. This law has reduced the availability of alcohol to middle and high school students but has had little effect on levels of consumption among eighteen to twenty-one year olds.

A comparison of the United States with European countries, where a drinking age of sixteen or eighteen years is typical, calls into question whether the approach in the United States is effective. In no European country is the level of problem drinking among eighteen to twenty-one year olds higher than in the United States. It can be argued that turning any alcohol consumption into a criminal activity increases the chances of excessive use and alcohol-associated risky behaviors, such as unsafe sex, without reducing the proportion of young adults whose use adversely affects their lives and the lives of those around them.

Revenue considerations often complicate efforts to curtail alcohol abuse among young people. Underage drinkers comprise a major market sector. Advertising campaigns continue to target this demographic despite government regulation. Flavored alcoholic beverages are of particular concern to regulators and to opponents of alcohol use among youth. Also, in college and university towns, the revenue stream generated by sporadic enforcement of liquor laws tends to undermine efforts at truly effective enforcement.

If statistics on traffic accidents are any indication, efforts made toward curbing underage drinking and reducing alcohol abuse among high school and college students do seem to have had a significant effect on driving behavior, but not on consumption. Effects of heightened education and enforcement on the population as a whole and on older age groups are not dramatic and can be partially explained by other factors, including an aging population and a persistent recession that tends to depress luxury consumption among people who are not alcohol dependent.

Also unknown, but probably significant, is the degree to which marginalized youth, who a generation ago would have abused alcohol, are turning to street drugs instead.

Martha A. Sherwood, PhD

FURTHER READING

Bellenir, Karen, and Amy Sutton. *Alcoholism Sourcebook.* Detroit: Omnigraphics, 2007. Consumer information about alcohol use, abuse, and dependence. Includes statistics on physical and social pathology.

A Developmental Perspective on Underage Alcohol Use. Spec. issue of *Alcohol Research and Health* 33.1 (2009): 1–76. Print. Seven research papers focusing on alcohol use in physical and social contexts.

Grant, Bridget, et al. "The 12-Month Prevalence and Trends in DSM-IV Alcohol Abuse and Dependence, United States, 1991–1992 and 2001–2002." *Drug and Alcohol Dependence* 74.3 (2004): 223–34. Print. A detailed statistical report and analysis.

Hingson, Ralph W., Wenxing Zha, and Elissa R. Weitzman. "Magnitude and Trends in Alcohol-Related Mortality and Morbidity among U.S. College Students Ages 18–24, 1998–2005." *Journal of Studies on Alcohol and Drugs* 16 (2009): 12–20. Print. A statistical paper, underscoring the need for intervention and counseling.

Monti, Peter M., Suzanne M. Colby, and Tracy O'Leary, eds. *Adolescents, Alcohol, and Substance Abuse: Reaching Teens through Brief Interventions.* New York: Guilford, 2001. A multiauthored volume with emphasis on clinical practice.

WEBSITES OF INTEREST

College Drinking: Changing the Culture
http://www.collegedrinkingprevention.gov

Institute of Alcohol Studies
http://www.ias.org.uk/resources/factsheets/adolescents.pdf

Mothers Against Drunk Driving
http://www.madd.org/underage-drinking

National Institute on Alcohol Abuse and Alcoholism
http://www.niaaa.nih.gov

National Institutes of Health Fact Sheets
http://report.nih.gov/NIHfactsheets

See also: College and substance abuse; Families and substance abuse; Parenting and alcoholism; Peer pressure; Schools and substance abuse; Teens/young adults and drug abuse; Teens/young adults and smoking

Teens/young adults and drug abuse

CATEGORY: Social issues

DEFINITION: Drug abuse is a complex disease that leads to changes in the structure and function of the brain in teenagers and young adults.

DRUG ABUSE

Teenagers and young adults who abuse drugs often display problem behaviors such as poor academic performance and dropping out of school. They also are at an increased risk of unplanned pregnancies, violence, and infectious diseases.

For most young people, the initial decision to take drugs is voluntary. However, the repeated use of substances such as drugs, alcohol, and tobacco causes changes in the brain that affect one's self-control and ability to make sound decisions. Drugs also cause the brain to send intense impulses that compel the user to take more drugs. Because of this, drug abuse can result in addiction.

The teen brain is still developing, making the effects of drug abuse even more complex for this population. One area of the brain still maturing during adolescence is the prefrontal cortex, which enables a person to consider situations fully, make solid decisions, and keep emotions and desires under control. Because this critical part of an adolescent's brain is still a work in progress, adolescents are at greater risk for poor decision-making (such as trying drugs or continued use). Also, using drugs while the brain is still developing may lead to profound and long-lasting consequences.

No single factor determines whether a person will become addicted to drugs. The overall risk for addiction is affected by the person's biological makeup and his or her environment. It can even be influenced by gender or ethnicity, a person's developmental stage, and the surrounding social environment (such as conditions at home, at school, and in the neighborhood). Scientists estimate that genetic factors account for 40 to 60 percent of a person's vulnerability to addiction, including the effects of environment on gene expression and function.

Adolescents and persons with mental disorders are at greater risk of drug abuse and addiction than the general population, making drug abuse prevention programs for teens critically important. Alcohol, tobacco, and illicit drug abuse are reduced when science-validated drug-abuse prevention programs are properly implemented by schools and communities. Such programs help teachers, parents, and health care professionals shape teens' perceptions about the dangers of drug abuse. While many events and cultural factors affect drug abuse trends, levels of abuse are reduced when teens and young adults learn that such abuse is harmful.

COMMONLY ABUSED DRUGS

Drug use in teenagers and young adults varies between ages thirteen and nineteen years. Younger teens are less likely to use most drugs than older teens. An exception is the use of inhalants, which is seen more in younger teens and less in older ones, in part because inhalants are readily accessible to teens. An average home has between thirty and fifty products with abuse potential. Also, inhalants are inexpensive and are legal to buy and possess. Additionally, the perceived risk of use is low.

More and more teens are abusing prescription drugs. Use of marijuana has remained stable but is more common. About 15 percent of high school seniors report having abused prescription drugs and about 32 percent report having used marijuana in the last year. According to the 2010 Monitoring the Future survey, prescription and over-the-counter drugs are among the most commonly abused drugs by twelfth graders; only alcohol, marijuana, and tobacco are used more often. Youth who abuse prescription medications also are more likely to report using other drugs.

Other drugs that are abused by teens and young adults include opioids (heroin, opium), stimulants (cocaine, amphetamine, methamphetamine), club drugs (methylenedioxy-methamphetamine, flunitrazepam, gamma-hydroxybutyrate), dissociative drugs (ketamine, PCP and analogs, *Salvia divinorum*, dextromethorphan), hallucinogens (lysergic acid diethylamide, mescaline, psilocybin), and anabolic steroids.

DRUG ABUSE AND ITS EFFECTS ON THE BRAIN

Drugs contain chemicals that interfere with the brain's communication system and change the way nerve cells normally send, receive, and process information. Drugs cause this interruption by imitating the brain's natural chemical messengers and by overstimulating the reward circuit of the brain.

Some drugs (such as marijuana and heroin) have a structure that is similar to chemical messengers called neurotransmitters, which are naturally produced by the brain. This similarity allows the drugs to fool the brain's receptors and activate nerve cells to send abnormal messages.

Other drugs, such as cocaine or methamphetamine, can cause the nerve cells to release large amounts of natural neurotransmitters (mainly dopamine) or to prevent the normal recycling of these brain chemicals, which is needed to shut off the signaling between neurons. The result is a brain full of dopamine, a neurotransmitter present in brain regions that controls movement, emotion, motivation, and feelings of pleasure. The overstimulation of this reward system, which normally responds to natural behaviors linked to survival (for example, eating and spending time with loved ones), produces euphoric effects in response to psychoactive drugs. This reaction sets in motion a reinforcing pattern that "teaches" a person to repeat the rewarding behavior of abusing drugs.

As a person continues to abuse drugs, the brain adapts to the overwhelming surges in dopamine by producing less dopamine or by reducing the number of dopamine receptors in the reward circuit. The result is a lessening of dopamine's effect on the reward circuit, which reduces the abuser's ability to enjoy the drugs, as well as the events in life that previously brought pleasure. This decrease compels the addict to keep abusing drugs to bring the dopamine function back to normal; however, larger amounts of the drug will be required to achieve the same dopamine high—an effect known as tolerance.

Long-term abuse also causes changes in other brain-chemical systems and circuits. Glutamate is a neurotransmitter that influences the reward circuit and the ability to learn. When the optimal concentration of glutamate is altered by drug abuse, the brain attempts to compensate, which can impair cognitive function.

Tough Love

Organizations that prescribe a tough-love perspective hold teenagers responsible for their behavior by helping them become aware of the consequences of their actions. Strategies often focus on confrontation and ultimatums and are considered a last response to behaviors that are self-destructive or dangerous to others.

In the 1960s, the tough-love approach was prescribed to parents who felt powerless because of their unruly, out-of-control children, many of whom were using drugs. Some persons credit David and Phyllis York as popularizers of this parenting approach in the 1980s. Many residential rehabilitation programs that provide addiction treatment represent this approach, some in the form of behavior modification centers or wilderness programs. The assumption is that certain rules and strategies will produce well-behaved, well-ordered teens.

The tough-love perspective has its critics, however. Opponents believe that parents can prevent children from "bottoming out" through a relationship that communicates understanding and support, rather than confrontation and ultimatums.

Brain imaging studies of drug addicts show changes in areas of the brain that are critical to judgment, decision making, learning and memory, and behavior control. Together, these changes can drive an abuser to seek and take drugs compulsively despite adverse, even devastating consequences; this is the nature of addiction.

TREATMENT

Drug abuse is a treatable disease with many effective treatments available. Some important points about drug abuse treatment include the following: Medical and behavioral therapy, alone or together, are used to treat drug abuse. Treatment can sometimes be done on an outpatient basis, but severe drug abuse usually requires residential treatment, in which the patient sleeps at the treatment center.

Treatment can take place within the criminal justice system, which can help to prevent a convicted person from returning to criminal behavior. Furthermore, studies show that treatment does not need to be voluntary to work.

Addiction is a difficult disorder to treat, especially if diagnosed late into the condition, although remissions can be achieved in up to 60 percent of patients. Whether or not treatment works depends on the patient's level of functioning at entry into treatment, premorbid functioning, comorbid conditions, and the support systems and resources available to the patient. Treating a substance abuser is not a hopeless process, but it can be a long and difficult one, similar to the treatment of any chronic disorder.

Claudia Daileader Ruland, MA

FURTHER READING

Gogtay, N., et al. "Dynamic Mapping of Human Cortical Development during Childhood through Early Adulthood." *Proceedings of the National Academy of Sciences* 101 (2004): 8174–79. Print.

Graham, A. W., and T. K. Shultz, eds. *Principles of Addiction Medicine*. 3rd ed. Chevy Chase, MD: American Society of Addiction Medicine, 2003.

National Institute on Drug Abuse. *Drugs, Brains, and Behavior: The Science of Addiction*. Bethesda, MD: NIDA, 2010.

---. *Preventing Drug Use among Children and Adolescents: A Research-Based Guide for Parents, Educators, and Community Leaders*. Bethesda, MD: NIDA, 2003.

Rehm, J., et al. "Global Burden of Disease and Injury and Economic Cost Attributable to Alcohol Use and Alcohol-Use Disorders." *Lancet* 373 (2009): 2223–33. Print.

WEBSITES OF INTEREST

GirlsHealth.gov
http://www.girlshealth.gov/substance

National Institute on Drug Abuse
http://www.drugabuse.gov

National Institute on Drug Abuse for Teens
http://teens.drugabuse.gov

See also: College and substance abuse; Families and substance abuse; Parenting and substance abuse; Peer pressure; Schools and substance abuse; Teens/young adults and alcohol abuse; Teens/young adults and smoking

Teens/young adults and smoking

CATEGORY: Social issues

DEFINITION: Tobacco smoking typically begins early in the teenage years—usually around age eleven to thirteen years—although many youths start earlier. Tobacco smoking includes the use of cigarettes (the primary form of smoked tobacco), cigars, pipes, and water pipes, also known as hookahs.

PREVALENCE OF SMOKING

In 2009, 36 percent of young adults ages eighteen to twenty-five years were cigarette smokers. Among teens, smoking had increased with age; only 1.4 percent of teens between age twelve and thirteen years smoked, compared with 7.5 percent of those between age fourteen and fifteen years and 17 percent of those between age sixteen and seventeen years. While this represents a significant decline from earlier in the decade, it still involves a large number of young people.

In addition, several studies conducted since 2006 in the United States and in Canada found that between 10 and 24 percent of young adults had smoked tobacco in a water pipe in the past month. Many had switched from cigarettes, believing that water pipes were safer. This represents a significant risk to smokers' health because the amount of nicotine absorbed by smoking a water pipe is comparable to that absorbed from cigarettes.

INITIATION AND CONTINUATION

Tobacco smoking typically begins around age eleven to thirteen years, although many youths start earlier. An increasing number of young adults are starting to smoke when they enter college.

Many factors influence whether a nonsmoking teen will experiment with cigarettes, including one's genetic makeup and whether parents or other adults in the household smoke; whether friends or acquaintances smoke; exposure to tobacco marketing or to tobacco use in films or video games; psychological factors such as anxiety, depression, poor coping skills, attention deficit disorder, and low self-esteem; and beliefs about tobacco use (for example, that smoking helps kids fit in or smoking makes a person look "cool").

One factor that has received considerable attention in recent years is the effect of exposure to tobacco marketing or to portrayals of tobacco use in entertainment media, both of which have been found to be at least as influential in getting teens or young adults to smoke as are family, friends, or psychological factors. These factors are particularly important, because avoiding such exposure is difficult but possible.

Simply puffing on a cigarette does not mean that a person will continue to smoke or become addicted to tobacco. Research indicates that the strongest predictors of a person's continuing to smoke and eventually becoming addicted are a relaxed, dizzy, or light-headed sensation after the first puff or two on a cigarette; being impulsive and seeking novelty; feeling depressed; smoking being permitted in the home; familiarity with tobacco marketing (for example, having a favorite cigarette advertisement); and believing that smoking helps a person "fit in."

BECOMING ADDICTED

It was once thought that a person had to smoke daily to become addicted, but research has shown this assumption to be false. Smokers can be said to be autonomous over their tobacco use if they can quit without experiencing discomfort or without expending effort.

Analogously, most people could give up eating broccoli or liver without difficulty or without suffering any ill effects, but the majority of people who smoke more than a few cigarettes in their lifetime go on to develop symptoms of diminished autonomy (that is, they become "hooked"). They find it difficult to quit or to cut down their smoking because they experience unpleasant symptoms. Often this occurs within only weeks of first inhaling cigarette smoke. A sizeable percentage of teens experience one or more symptoms of diminished autonomy after smoking fewer than five cigarettes in their lives, and more than 75 percent of teens experienced symptoms while smoking only a cigarette or two each week. Girls tend to become hooked faster than boys, although the reasons for this are unknown.

Nicotine (the major ingredient in tobacco smoke), even in low doses, causes the brain to remodel itself. In response to nicotine, neurons (the basic building blocks in the nervous system) literally change their physical characteristics and the ways in which they communicate with each other through neurotransmitters (the chemicals that carry signals from one neuron to another). While this happens throughout the nervous system, the effects are particularly marked in the reward system, the part of the brain that is responsible for the experience of good feelings and pleasure.

The first few doses of nicotine (the first few cigarettes) sensitize the brain so that it becomes more susceptible to later doses. Thus, the effects of nicotine make it easier for the brain to become accustomed to nicotine, which makes it more difficult for a person to remove nicotine from the body by cutting down or quitting smoking.

Becoming hooked is one step on the path to becoming dependent on, or addicted to, tobacco. A medical diagnosis of tobacco dependence can be made when the number of symptoms reaches a threshold specified by either the *Diagnostic and Statistical Manual of Mental Disorders* or the *International Classification of Diseases* (ICD). Factors that predict a teen smoker's developing a sufficient number of symptoms to meet the ICD-10 threshold include a relaxed, dizzy, or light-headed sensation after the first puff or two on a cigarette, and feeling depressed. The earlier a person begins to smoke, the greater the likelihood of that person becoming dependent and the worse the addiction (that is, the harder it becomes to quit).

E-cigarettes

E-cigarettes, or electronic cigarettes, are battery-powered devices available in a range of sizes and shapes. For example, some look like real cigarettes, cigars, or pipes, while others are designed to look more like pens.

In general, the devices are made up of a mouthpiece; a replaceable (or refillable) cartridge—the cartridge contains a liquid solution of nicotine, available in different strengths, as well as flavoring, water, and chemicals; an atomizer, which transforms the liquid solution into a vapor; and a rechargeable battery. Depending on the style, the battery end of the cigarette may have an LED light on the tip to look like the burning ember of a real cigarette. However, the LED light does not get hot, so it does not pose a fire hazard.

When the user inhales from the mouthpiece, the liquid is heated and the atomizer turns the liquid into a vapor. The vapor feels like smoke when inhaled by the user. When the user exhales, the vapor quickly disappears.

RISKS OF SMOKING

The US surgeon general has repeatedly warned of serious risks incurred by people who smoke tobacco. In a 2004 report, smoking was identified as a cause of twenty-nine diseases or serious medical conditions, including various cancers, cardiovascular and respiratory diseases, and reproductive or fertility related effects.

Cigarette smoking is considered the primary preventable cause of death, with approximately one in every five deaths in the United States (about 443,000 per year, or more than 1,000 per day) attributable to smoking. The diseases caused by smoking produce chronic disability in many people and are estimated to cost almost $200 billion per year in health care expenses and lost productivity in the United States alone.

It takes years of continued smoking to be affected by many of these diseases, but even teens and young adults suffer some serious consequences. For example, young women who smoke are more likely than their nonsmoking peers to experience infertility or delays in trying to become pregnant. If they become pregnant, their babies are at increased risk of low birth weight or sudden infant death syndrome. Young adults who smoke incur the risk of early onset reductions in lung function, which would make it difficult, for example, to exercise, dance, or sing. Smoking also increases asthma-related symptoms, and children and young adults are particularly susceptible to asthma and other respiratory diseases.

All available evidence suggests that avoiding smoking is one of the best steps a person can take to remain healthy, and that quitting smoking if one has started is also beneficial. The US surgeon general has concluded that there is no safe level of exposure to tobacco smoke; secondhand smoke (that is, smoke in one's immediate environment) is almost as dangerous as smoking itself.

CESSATION

There are many effective ways to stop smoking. Every US state and every Canadian province has a free telephone "quitline," and many offer help online. Hospitals and other health care facilities offer support groups and one-on-one help, and school and college health services usually provide information and support. For persons who need additional help, various over-the-counter nicotine-replacement products (such as patches, gum, and lozenges) are available, as are prescription medications.

Robert J. Wellman, PhD

FURTHER READING

DiFranza, Joseph R., et al. "Susceptibility to Nicotine Dependence: The Development and Assessment of Nicotine Dependence in Youth-2 Study." *Pediatrics* 120.4 (2007): 974–83. Print.

---. "Symptoms of Tobacco Dependence after Brief Intermittent Use: The Development and Assessment of Nicotine Dependence in Youth-2 Study. *Archives of Pediatrics and Adolescent Medicine* 161.7 (2007): 704–10. Print. These two articles present the results of a longitudinal study of teens and smoking and review related studies.

Dugas, Erika, et al. "Water Pipe Smoking among North American Youths." *Pediatrics* 125.6 (2010): 1184–89. Print. Discusses the results of a longitudinal study in Canada. Includes good references to similar studies.

US Department of Health and Human Services. "How Tobacco Smoke Causes Disease: The Biology and Behavioral Basis for Smoking-Attributable Disease—A Report of the Surgeon General." Atlanta: DHHS, 2010. Excellent review of literature related to the risks of smoking, including nicotine addiction.

Wellman, Robert J., et al. "The Extent to Which Tobacco Marketing and Tobacco Use in Films Contribute to Children's Use of Tobacco: A Meta-Analysis." *Archives of Pediatrics and Adolescent Medicine* 160 (2006): 1285–96. Print. Analysis of fifty-one studies with 142,000 participants.

WEBSITES OF INTEREST

Campaign for Tobacco-Free Kids
http://www.tobaccofreekids.org

Cancer.gov
http://www.cancer.gov/cancertopics/tobacco/smoking

Centers for Disease Control and Prevention
http://www.cdc.gov/tobacco/youth

SmokeFree.gov
http://www.smokefree.gov

See also: College and substance abuse; Families and substance abuse; Media and smoking; Parenting and substance abuse; Peer pressure; Smoking; Teens/young adults and alcohol abuse; Teens/young adults and drug abuse

Television addiction

CATEGORY: Psychological issues and behaviors

DEFINITION: No agreed upon definition exists for television addiction because there are no clear criteria on what constitutes normal versus problematic television watching. Experts have relied on self-reports from television viewers who typically report that they watch television to help them cope with negative and dysphoric mood states, loneliness, extreme anger, and social anxiety. Self-identified addicts look forward to television viewing because it imposes stability on an otherwise imbalanced mental state.

BACKGROUND

Television addiction is not listed in the *Diagnostic and Statistical Manual of Mental Disorders* (DSM) because of the range of factors that complicate a definition. A significant effort was made in the early 1990s not only to solidify a meaningful definition but also to better identify health and safety concerns associated with excessive television viewing.

Surveying the available literature on this topic reveals a fascinating archive of how modern society has changed through the years. For instance, the most relevant books and journal articles on the topic of television addiction were published between 1986 and 1991; the research emphasis then shifted to issues of definition and the development of empirical methods that would better identify how, why, and when television viewing becomes an addiction.

The twenty-first century has seen television addiction research neglected for research on Internet, video gaming, and social media addictions and for psychological and sociological inquiry into how attitudes about addiction are shaped by television. Also, later research has focused on comorbid factors related to the health and safety of children (for example, obesity, smoking, alcohol use, underlying depression, and social anxiety) who watch excessive amounts of television. All of these factors have led to a neglect of the question of whether television addiction is real.

Excessive television viewing can have deleterious effects on one's psychological and physical health, but it need not, and there is a growing body of research that suggests that television can be instructive, can provide needed escape, and can help children reach certain developmental milestones. Taken together though, several decades of research has not moved experts much closer to better understanding the dynamics of television addiction. Still, few people question that excessive television viewing can be problematic, particularly if persons find themselves unable to control or simply reduce their viewing habits.

No great concern has accompanied the inability to define television addiction. Rather than debate what number of hours and functional limitations define television addiction, research has taken up the task of exploring related pathogenic effects (physical and psychopathological) and of more methodically investigating the underlying psychological dynamics common to excessive television viewership.

SELF-IDENTIFICATION

Research into television addiction is plagued by the ubiquity of the self-report. The more serious attempts to create structured assessment protocol that differentiate normal versus problematic viewing have relied solely on persons self-referring and self-identifying as television addicts. This challenges both the validity and the reliability of television addiction research.

Still, much has been learned from researchers who have tried to create these assessment tools. Specifically, participant pools that self-identify as television addicts have opened the door to understanding many other psychological factors that contribute to excessive viewing.

It is not uncommon for people to report immediate relief in much the same way that substance abusers experience instant gratification after use, though a similar parallel emerges. The longer someone watches television the less likely it is that he or she continues to derive enjoyment from it. Whereas self-described television addicts report feeling immediately more relaxed after immersing themselves in television viewing, they also report feeling less stimulated over time (and oftentimes report feeling more emotionally and cognitively depleted).

People who experience social anxiety (or related loneliness) also may find themselves with decreasing levels of frustration tolerance over time, specifically with their own self-representations. Put another way, without the stimulation that television offers, addicts will experience increased frustration trying to cope with their own interpersonal and intrapersonal conflicts. As such, it becomes increasingly more difficult to understand and work through existing patterns of negative thoughts.

CONCLUSIONS

Behavioral addictions such as television addiction likely will receive more discussion in revised editions of the DSM. Still, other prevalent behavioral addictions, such as Internet, texting, and video gaming addictions, likely will not be considered at all. Given the already strong foundation of research into many of these areas since about 2005, it is likely that revisions of the DSM will more carefully consider the range of issues common to these behavioral addictions.

Television addiction specifically has been neglected alongside issues related to Internet and social media addictions. A cursory literature review indicates as much. Instead, focus has shifted toward the various health, safety, and psychological factors (such as underlying depression and anxiety) that conjoin with excessive television viewing. Furthermore, ongoing research is examining the role that substance-based addictions can have in perpetuating behavioral addictions, while related sociological research is examining the culture of reality television and how television, in general, shapes attitudes about addiction.

Efforts to define and discern television addiction from comorbid issues have largely abated. As a result, research paradigms have shifted toward the meaningful inclusion of television viewing into the analysis of other public health concerns and substance-based addictions.

Joseph C. Viola, PhD

FURTHER READING

Bryant, J., and D. Zillmann, eds. *Perspectives on Media Effects*. Hillsdale, NJ: Erlbaum, 1986. Explores television addiction research and the nascent stages of the movement and examines the various struggles of the time (trying to fit television addiction into an existing body of addiction literature dominated by substance use).

Condry, J. *The Psychology of Television*. Hillsdale, NJ: Erlbaum, 1989. An excellent book that covers the origins of research on television addiction and the struggles with a definition. Discusses the question of whether or not television addiction exists.

Hollen, Kathryn H. "Television Addiction." *Encyclopedia of Addictions*. Westport, CT: Greenwood, 2009. A brief but informative article on television addiction.

Horvath, Cary W. "Measuring Television Addiction." *Journal of Broadcasting and Electronic Media* 48 (2004): 378–98. Print. Examines the ways in which researchers have tried to develop assessment tools to better differentiate normal from problematic television viewing; two studies in particular are explored.

Kubey, R. W. "Television Dependence, Diagnosis, and Prevention." *Tuning In to Young Viewers: Social Science Perspectives on Television*. Ed. Tannis M. MacBeth. Thousand Oaks, CA: Sage, 1999. A careful look at how issues of television addiction align with existing frameworks of substance-based dependence. Also explores several related factors of television addiction, such as specific effects for children and adolescents and pornography and treatment considerations.

McIlwraith, R. D. "'I'm Addicted to Television': The Personality, Imagination, and TV Watching Patterns of Self-Identified TV Addicts." *Journal of Broadcasting and Electronic Media* 42 (1998): 371–86. Print. Examines issues of self-identification, what emerges when this is the primary vehicle of data collection, and how to best consider the many layers of excessive television viewing.

McIlwraith, R. D., et al. "Television Addiction: Theories and Data behind the Ubiquitous Metaphor." *American Behavioral Scientist* 35 (1991): 104–21. Print. An early work from a collection of research that explains the zeitgeist related to behavioral addictions, the relevance of television addiction in society, and related comorbid issues that complicate definition, diagnosis, and treatment.

WEBSITES OF INTEREST

American Psychiatric Association
http://www.psych.org

TurnOffYourTV.com
http://www.turnoffyourtv.com

See also: Behavioral addictions: Overview; Gambling addiction; Gaming addiction; Sex addiction; Work addiction

Temazepam

CATEGORY: Substances

ALSO KNOWN AS: Eggs; jellies; norries; Restoril; rugby balls; ruggers; tems

DEFINITION: Temazepam is a hypnotic benzodiazepine that slows brain activity to induce sedation. It is considered a tranquilizer that dulls and slows the central nervous system.

STATUS: Legal by prescription in the United States and worldwide; certain US states require specially coded prescriptions

CLASSIFICATION: Schedule IV controlled substance

SOURCE: Synthetic compound with no natural sources; obtained through prescription or manufactured in illicit, clandestine labs

TRANSMISSION ROUTE: Ingested orally, inhaled, or injected intravenously or intramuscularly

HISTORY OF USE

Temazepam was first synthesized in Europe in 1964 and marketed as a treatment for insomnia in 1969. During the Cold War in the 1970s, temazepam found a purpose in mind-control and brainwashing methods but proved unsuccessful as a "truth" serum because of its potent sedative effects.

Temazepam was marketed in the United States in 1981 as a sedative-hypnotic drug under the name Restoril. It became an effective sleep aide known as no-go pills for US Air Force pilots following missions. It is classified as a schedule IV controlled substance, which includes drugs with a low abuse potential and a legitimate medical use.

By the late 1980s, temazepam was one of the most widely abused prescription tranquilizers in Europe, especially in the United Kingdom, because of its sedative effects. It became the benzodiazepine of choice for intravenous drug use because of its easily injectable capsule contents. It is often used as an inexpensive alternative to heroin. Even though temazepam has been placed under stricter regulations, it remains a highly sought-after and abused benzodiazepine worldwide.

EFFECTS AND POTENTIAL RISKS

Temazepam functions as a tranquilizer and central nervous system depressant. It works by stimulating the release and binding of gamma-amino butyric acid, a natural nerve-calming agent, to receptors in the brain. This effect causes activity in the brain to slow, inducing sleep, reducing anxiety, and relaxing muscles.

Temazepam is a fast acting and rapidly absorbed benzodiazepine. Negative short-term effects include drowsiness, confusion, and dizziness, and impaired judgment, coordination, and balance.

Many temazepam users engage in injecting hard and soft gel-filled capsule contents to achieve a greater high. However, injecting capsule contents intended for oral use can cause serious circulation problems (such as vein blockage, gangrene, and limb amputations) and blood-borne infections (such as human immunodeficiency virus and hepatitis).

Long-term temazepam use can lead to mental difficulties, depression, chronic fatigue, and erratic behavior. Temazepam dependence can lead to addiction and benzodiazepine withdrawal syndrome.

Rose Ciulla-Bohling, PhD

FURTHER READING

Dobbin, Malcolm, et al. "Association of Benzodiazepine Injection with the Prescription of Temazepam Capsules." *Drug and Alcohol Review* 22.2 (2003): 153–57. Print.

Eddey, David P., and Mark J. Westcott. "The Needle and the Damage Done: Intra-Arterial Temazepam." *Emergency Medicine* 12.3 (2000): 248–52. Print.

Vermeeren, Annemiek. "Residual Effects of Hypnotics: Epidemiology and Clinical Implications." *CNS Drugs* 18.5 (2004): 297–98. Print.

WEBSITES OF INTEREST

PubMed Health: "Temazepam"
http://www.ncbi.nlm.nih.gov/pubmedhealth/PMH0000808

US Drug Enforcement Administration
http://www.deadiversion.usdoj.gov/drugs_concern/benzo_1.htm

See also: Benzodiazepine abuse; Depressants abuse; Prescription drug addiction: Overview; Sedative-Hypnotic abuse

Tobacco use disorder

CATEGORY: Substance abuse

ALSO KNOWN AS: Nicotine addiction

DEFINITION: Tobacco use disorder occurs when the use of tobacco harms a person's health or social functioning, or when a person becomes dependent on the nicotine in tobacco. Tobacco may be consumed in the form of cigarettes, smokeless tobacco products (including snuff and chewing tobacco), cigars, or pipes. This condition can be treated.

CAUSES

Tobacco products contain nicotine, which is transported to the brain and causes pleasurable sensations. The effects of nicotine dissipate within a few minutes, however. This causes tobacco users to continue using tobacco to maintain the pleasurable effects and prevent withdrawal. Other chemicals in tobacco products may also contribute to tobacco use disorder.

RISK FACTORS

There are many risk factors that increase the chance of developing tobacco use disorder, or nicotine addiction. Some risk factors are schizophrenia, posttraumatic stress disorder, bipolar disorder, major depression, and other mental illnesses.

SYMPTOMS

Symptoms related to tobacco use disorder include nicotine "highs," which are caused by an increase in blood pressure, blood sugar level, breathing rate, and heart rate. Symptoms of nicotine withdrawal include irritability, cravings, sleeplessness, increased appetite, nervousness, and headaches. Tobacco-related health problems may include smoker's cough and hot flashes in women. Throat cancer is also strongly associated with tobacco use disorder. There are other consequences of tobacco use disorder as well, such as cancers of the larynx (voice box), oral cavity, throat, esophagus, lung, and colon; chronic bronchitis; emphysema; chronic obstructive pulmonary disease; heart disease; stroke; dementia; and miscarriage or premature delivery.

SCREENING AND DIAGNOSIS

A diagnosis of tobacco use disorder will involve a doctor inquiring about symptoms and medical history, as well as a physical examination and lung function tests. Doctors will typically ask questions pertaining to the duration and the frequency of tobacco use.

TREATMENT AND THERAPY

Treatment may consist of nicotine replacement therapy (NRT) and behavioral therapy. Nicotine replacement therapy (NRT) is used to relieve nicotine

Chewing Tobacco

Chewing tobacco is made of whole or shredded leaves of the plant *Nicotiana tabacum* and is sold in three forms: loose leaf tobacco, plug tobacco, and twist tobacco. Plug tobacco is sold as sheets of sugar-cured leaves pressed into a brick, from which pieces are bitten off. Twist tobacco is a rope of braided leaves, from which pieces are cut off.

Chewing tobacco is legal in the United States for persons eighteen years of age and older, legal in Canada for persons age nineteen years and older, but illegal in the United Kingdom. The United States grows about 10 percent of the worldwide tobacco crop.

Chewing tobacco is placed in the mouth between the cheek and gum. The nicotine in the tobacco is absorbed through the mucosal membranes and goes straight into the bloodstream. Saliva mixed with tobacco components is usually spit out, but it may be swallowed. Chewing tobacco irritates the mouth, causing bleeding of the lips and gums. It also causes gum recession and bone loss around the roots of teeth, which cause teeth to loosen and fall out. Chewing tobacco also stains teeth and causes bad breath, and it kills taste buds on the tongue, resulting in loss of the ability to taste. The nicotine in the tobacco increases heart rate, blood pressure, and the risk of heart attacks and strokes, while the salts in chewing tobacco can cause kidney disease.

Chewing tobacco contains twenty-eight carcinogens (cancer-causing agents), including formaldehyde, cadmium, cyanide, arsenic, benzene, and lead. Oral cancer can occur in the lips, tongue, cheeks, and gums. Cancer-causing agents also can be passed along in the tobacco juice to the esophagus, stomach lining, and bladder. Chewing tobacco also has been associated with pancreatic cancer.

withdrawal symptoms. Examples of NRT products are nicotine gum, lozenges, nasal sprays, patches, and inhalers. Sometimes these products are used in combination, which may help some people stay smoke-free. Since NRT does not produce the pleasurable effects of tobacco, there is little chance that these products will be abused. According to various studies, NRT may help reduce the amount of tobacco consumed and help to control withdrawal symptoms after a person has quit smoking. NRT will also help smokers abstain from smoking.

Combining behavioral therapy with NRT may be even more helpful. Behavioral therapies are comprised of counseling, group behavior therapy, self-help classes and manuals, and text messaging programs. There is also cognitive-behavioral therapy, which teaches people to recognize high-risk tobacco situations, develop coping strategies, manage stress, improve problem-solving skills, and increase social support.

Certain medicines, such as some antidepressants, may help individuals quit smoking. Some medicines may help ease withdrawal symptoms and block nicotine effects if the person were to start smoking again. One side effect, however, is that these medicines may increase the risk of serious behavior changes.

PREVENTION

The best prevention is to never use tobacco products, as they are very addictive. One should also stay away from places where people are smoking to avoid harmful exposure to secondhand smoke.

Krisha McCoy, MS

FURTHER READING

Anderson, Judith. *It's Your Health: Smoking.* North Mantko, MN: Smart Apple Media, 2005. Provides an introduction to smoking's negative effects on the body.

Erickson, Carlton. *The Science of Addiction: From Neurobiology to Treatment.* New York: W. W. Norton , 2006. A reference for anyone in the field of addiction medicine. Provides a neurobiological perspective on addiction that can be understood by lay people.

How Tobacco Smoke Causes Disease: The Biology and Behavioral Basis for Smoking-Attributable Disease: A Report of the Surgeon General. Rockville, MD: US DHHS, 2010. Contains information from thousands of studies proving that smoking has had
ruinous consequences for the health of millions of Americans. List of tables and figures. Index.

WEBSITES OF INTEREST

American Cancer Society
http://www.cancer.org

American Lung Association
http://www.lung.org

Freedom From Smoking
http://www.ffsonline.org/

Smokefree.gov
http://www.smokefree.gov

See also: Media and smoking; Men and smoking; Nicotine addiction; Nicotine replacement products; Smoking cessation; Smoking; Smoking cessation for older adults; Women and smoking

Tolerance

CATEGORY: Substance abuse
ALSO KNOWN AS: Mithridatism
DEFINITION: Tolerance to a drug occurs when a drug progressively decreases in effectiveness, even with repeated administration. To maintain a drug's primary effect, the drug dosage must be increased.

BACKGROUND AND BASIC PRINCIPLES

For millennia, humans have sought to counteract the effects of harmful substances by taking small amounts of the substance and then gradually increasing its levels. This practice is called mithridatism, named for Mithridates VI, the former ruler of Pontus who, after his defeat by the Romans in 63 BCE, tried to commit suicide by taking poison. However, because he had built up immunity to diverse poisons by years of incremental exposure to them, the poisons did not end his life and he had to resort to demanding he be killed with a sword. Mithridatism can be effective if the substance does not pass through the body too quickly or accumulate to dangerous levels; it works because tolerance to the drug has been established.

Tolerance is influenced by diverse variables, including type of drug, dosage level, frequency of administration, environmental circumstances, psychological factors, and the drug user's physiology. Tolerance may develop to some effects of a drug; however, little or no tolerance may occur to other effects. Although tolerance normally develops slowly, it sometimes occurs after only one or a few administrations, a phenomenon called tachyphylaxis. The effects of tolerance may accrue to other, usually closely related, drugs, through cross-tolerance.

Drug tolerance typically dissipates when exposure to a drug is limited or stopped. Conversely, with reverse-tolerance, or sensitization, in which a drug's effectiveness progressively increases with repeated administration, the effect often persists long after a drug is discontinued.

TOLERANCE MECHANISMS

The complexity and diversity of tolerance phenomena indicate that multiple factors underlie its occurrence. Three main mechanisms of tolerance have been identified, two are physiological and one is more psychological. Metabolic tolerance (also known as dispositional tolerance) involves increased levels of enzymes in the body to metabolize a drug; subsequently, the level of the drug in the body decreases. Metabolic tolerance will diminish all effects of a drug because the amount of the drug throughout the body is lowered.

Cellular-adaptive tolerance (also known as pharmacodynamic or physiological tolerance) is the second main physiological mechanism of tolerance. Cellular-adaptive tolerance involves diverse adjustments by the body to restore its predrug functioning; this results in decreased drug effects. Essentially, cellular-adaptive tolerance is marked by the body's compensatory actions to reestablish the homeostasis (the normal physiological stability) disrupted by the introduction of a drug.

The compensatory processes can work at multiple levels. For example, an appetite-suppressing drug may lose its effectiveness at the cellular level because its blocking action at neuronal receptors is diminished. This diminishment occurs because, postsynaptically, more receptors are being produced and, presynaptically, more neurotransmitter is being produced. Conversely, for an appetite-suppressing drug that works by increasing neurotransmitter levels at neuronal receptors, the number of receptors and the amount of neurotransmitter produced may be decreased (a process

called down-regulation). The body may also compensate for the drug in other ways, such as by producing more ghrelin, a hormone that stimulates appetite, or by increasing activity in regions of the hypothalamus that stimulates appetite.

Environmental and psychological factors almost always alter the effectiveness of a drug through a third tolerance mechanism known as behavioral tolerance. Behavioral tolerance works through a variety of conditioning (learning) and psychological processes. Respondent (also called classical) conditioning, in which two stimuli are paired repeatedly and in which the response to one stimulus is eventually elicited by the other stimulus, was demonstrated by Ivan Pavlov (in the early twentieth century). The environment in which the drug is administered is a stimulus that is usually conditioned to the effects of the drug. What typically is conditioned is the body's attempt to resist the drug. Thus, the environment elicits compensatory actions that cause a drug to be less effective; tolerance, controlled by environment, develops. This can have dangerous consequences for a drug addict who has developed tolerance to lethal doses of a drug consistently taken in a particular setting. If the person takes the drug in a novel setting, the conditioned tolerance is absent; the loss of this tolerance may result in a fatal overdose.

Operant conditioning, in which the frequency of a behavior is determined by its consequences, also plays a role in tolerance development. Research by Muriel Vogel-Sprott and colleagues in the 1990s demonstrated that when people are rewarded for resisting the effects of a drug, they develop tolerance more rapidly than those who are not rewarded. Conversely, withholding a reward may prevent tolerance from developing. For example, amphetamine causes loss of appetite in diverse species; however, if the drug is administered to a hungry animal that is not given the opportunity to eat after being given the drug, tolerance to the appetite-suppressive effects of the drug will not evolve. Thus, whether or not tolerance develops depends on the conditions in which a drug is administered.

Paul J. Chara, PhD
Kathleen A. Chara, PhD

FURTHER READING

Hart, Carl L., Charles Ksir, and Ray Oakley. *Drugs, Society, and Human Behavior.* 14th ed. New York: McGraw-Hill, 2011. This popular textbook provides a comprehensive overview of drug principles, drug use, and its effects on the individual and society.

Julien, Robert M., Claire D. Advokat, and Joseph E. Comaty. *A Primer of Drug Action: A Comprehensive Guide to the Actions, Uses, and Side Effects of Psychoactive Drugs.* 12th ed. New York: Worth, 2011. Presents a thorough treatment of psychoactive drugs. The first three chapters provide a good introduction to psychopharmacology.

McKim, William A. *Drugs and Behavior: An Introduction to Behavioral Pharmacology.* 6th ed. Upper Saddle River, NJ: Pearson, 2007. Chapter 3 of this excellent book presents detailed coverage of drug tolerance.

Siegel, Shepard. "Drug Tolerance, Drug Addiction, and Drug Anticipation." *Current Directions in Psychological Science* 14.6 (2005): 296–300. Print. A leading expert in the study of drug tolerance describes how conditioning affects the expression of drug tolerance.

WEBSITES OF INTEREST

Drugs.com
http://www.drugs.com

National Institute on Drug Abuse
http://www.drugabuse.gov

See also: Alcohol: Short- and long-term effects on the body; Hallucinogens: Short- and long-term effects on the body; Narcotics: Short- and long-term effects on the body; Physiological dependence; Symptoms of substance abuse

Tramadol

CATEGORY: Substances

ALSO KNOWN AS: Ultram

DEFINITION: Tramadol is an opioid analgesic with morphine-like properties. It works as a central nervous system depressant and as an analgesic.

STATUS: Legal in the United States and worldwide

CLASSIFICATION: Nonscheduled status, but US state laws vary

SOURCE: Synthetic analog of codeine with no natural sources

TRANSMISSION ROUTE: Ingested orally, inhaled, or injected

HISTORY OF USE

Tramadol was first synthesized in 1962 by the German pharmaceutical company Grünenthal. Tramadol has been in clinical use in Germany since 1977. Originally marketed as a safe painkiller with a low risk of abuse, tramadol became the most prescribed opioid on the European market. It was introduced to the prescription drug market in the United States in 1995 as Ultram, a nontraditional, centrally acting analgesic. Tramadol has a nonscheduled status, meaning it has a low potential for abuse.

Tramadol produces pleasurable sensations and relaxation without increased drowsiness, enabling people to remain productive while managing pain. It is an easily available opiate and can be habit forming because of its morphine-like properties. Because of reports of increased tramadol misuse, it has been labeled a drug of concern by the US Food and Drug Administration and thus requires additional label warnings. Some US states have classified tramadol as a controlled substance.

EFFECTS AND POTENTIAL RISKS

Tramadol is a nontraditional, centrally acting opioid analgesic with morphine-like pain-relieving activity. It has a dual mechanism of pain relief because it includes a mixture of enantiomers.

Studies suggest that tramadol activity is mediated through both opioid and nonopioid or monoaminergic mechanisms. It exhibits opioid activity by binding to specific opioid receptors in the brain that decrease pain perception. Monoaminergic activity is displayed by inhibiting the reuptake of norepinephrine and serotonin, neurotransmitters responsible for altering pain response in the brain.

The short-term effects of tramadol include feelings of euphoria, mood elevation, and relaxation. Tramadol is usually well tolerated but can be associated with negative short-term effects, including nausea, vomiting, constipation, drowsiness, dizziness, vertigo, weakness, and headache.

Long-term use of tramadol can be associated with drug dependence and possible addiction. Abruptly stopping tramadol may generate opiate-like withdrawal symptoms such as anxiety, agitation, sweating, abdominal upset, and hallucinations.

Rose Ciulla-Bohling, PhD

FURTHER READING

Grond, Stefan, and Armin Sablotzki. "Clinical Pharmacology of Tramadol." *Clinical Pharmacokinet* 43.13 (2004): 879. Print.

Raffa, Robert B. "Basic Pharmacology Relevant to Drug Abuse Assessment: Tramadol as Example." *Journal of Clinical Pharmacy and Therapeutics* 33.2 (2008): 101–8. Print.

Senay, Edward C., et al. "Physical Dependence on Ultram (Tramadol Hydrochloride): Both Opioid-Like and Atypical Withdrawal Symptoms Occur." *Drug and Alcohol Dependence* 69.3 (2003): 233–41. Print.

WEBSITES OF INTEREST

eMedExpert: "Tramadol (Ultram)"
http://www.emedexpert.com/facts/tramadol-facts.shtml

PubMed Health: "Tramadol"
http://www.ncbi.nlm.nih.gov/pubmedhealth/PMH0000960

US Drug Enforcement Administration
http://www.deadiversion.usdoj.gov/drugs_concern/tramadol.pdf

See also: Depressants abuse; Morphine; Narcotics abuse; Opioid abuse; Painkiller abuse; Prescription drug addiction: Overview

Treatment methods and research

CATEGORY: Treatment

DEFINITION: Among medical and science professionals, drug and alcohol addiction is considered a disease. Addiction is treatable, but not curable, and no one treatment works for all addicts. Some addicts are prescribed medications to help control cravings and others have great success with individual, group, and behavioral therapies in outpatient or residential treatment programs. Some addicts receive both medication and therapy and still others seek alternative treatments.

ABSTINENCE-BASED TREATMENT

Medical professionals and other experts have been studying the effectiveness of abstinence-based treatment programs for decades. These treatment programs require patients who are addicted to or are abusing drugs and alcohol to stop using them entirely.

In programs in which abstinence is not the focus, counselors can teach patients how to drink alcohol or smoke cigarettes, for example, in moderation. Counselors and doctors in abstinence-based programs are not looking to help patients cut back on their drug or alcohol use. The goal of these programs is to help patients develop the strength to avoid drugs and alcohol for the rest of their lives. According to the World Health Organization, drop-out rates for abstinence-based treatment programs are quite high in the first three months of treatment. Once patients have cleared that hurdle, however, most complete the programs.

Addicts will have the most difficult time at the beginning stage of abstinence-based treatment: detoxification, which often involves withdrawal symptoms of nausea, headaches, muscle aches, and excessive sweating. Depending on the patients' health, addicts at this stage also may experience life-threatening symptoms such as heart attacks, strokes, or organ failure. Because of the risks associated with withdrawal, this stage of the treatment program is often completed under the supervision of medical professionals in a medical facility. Doctors will sometimes administer prescription medications, such as methadone, clonidine, subutex, and suboxone, to ease withdrawal symptoms.

Once patients have successfully completed detoxification, they can begin their treatment programs. Programs are outpatient and residential; residential programs are highly recommended for abstinence-based treatment, as they eliminate the risk of patients relapsing. Although the urge to use drugs remains, the chance is small that a patient in a rehabilitation facility will find and use the drugs he or she desires. In residential programs, patients meet in groups and with individual counselors to talk about their cravings, their experiences while using substances, and their goals for the future. Participants commit to the idea of abstaining from drugs and alcohol, and they learn life skills to keep them from relapsing upon release from treatment.

Outpatient abstinence-based programs are not as successful as residential programs because patients are permitted to come and go. The risk of patients being in areas where drugs are present is high. To encourage patients to abstain from drug and alcohol use, many programs offer abstinence-based vouchers as incentives. Patients can earn vouchers after undergoing a round of tests (often blood or urine) that reveal whether they have remained clean (drug and alcohol free). Patients collect vouchers and then trade them for particular items.

Researcher Alan J. Budney and colleagues at the University of Vermont spoke of the success of abstinence-based vouchers in their 2006 article "Clinical Trial of Abstinence-Based Vouchers and Cognitive-Behavioral Therapy for Cannabis Dependence" (*Journal of Consulting and Clinical Psychology*). They found that distributing vouchers alone produced the same success rate as behavioral therapy alone. Combining the vouchers with behavioral therapy produced even better outcomes than either individual approach.

GROUP THERAPY AND SUPPORT GROUPS

One of the most common approaches to recovering from a drug or alcohol addiction is group therapy. Highly recommended by drug and alcohol counselors, group therapy is helpful both in residential and in outpatient treatment programs. Group therapy brings like-minded people together under the supervision of a trained counselor or medical professional. Group therapy is often required by physicians or psychologists overseeing the treatment of their patients. Some insurance companies cover the cost of this treatment.

People who cannot afford to go to group therapy or who do not wish to participate in such a formal type of treatment may choose to attend support group meetings. Support group meetings are similar to group therapy in their setup: A group of persons struggling to overcome drug abuse or addiction meet to share their stories and to encourage others to quit using. Unlike group therapy, however, attendance is not required and is free of charge. Also unlike group therapy, support groups are typically sponsored by drug-free organizations and can be led by former drug addicts, by representatives of the sponsoring organizations, or by the family members of an addict. Sometimes support group leaders invite doctors, psychologists, or drug and alcohol counselors to their

meetings to speak about formal treatment options and new research about treatments and addiction. Support group meetings may also be held on the phone or online.

Regardless of whether the group is led by a medical professional or a former addict, the goals of group therapy sessions and support group meetings are similar. Including people who can relate to each other's circumstances is a way to offer comfort to newcomers. People struggling to overcome drug abuse and addiction should not feel as though they are alone; group therapy and support groups offer addicts a chance to tell their stories, to confess their fears and trepidations, and to receive practical advice and information about challenges they will eventually face. During these meetings, members should not feel as though they are being judged or isolated. Instead, their relation to and encouragement from other members in the group should make them feel empowered and in control of their lives.

A successful meeting is marked by a reduction in stress or depression and anxiety and by an increase in confidence and self-knowledge. These methods of treatment should provide members with the skills and information they need to cope with their cravings and to adjust to their new drug-free lives.

Traditionally in the United States, people seeking help for more than one condition would attend more than one meeting for treatment. For example, a person with a drinking problem who also is a domestic violence offender would need to attend one session with a drug and alcohol counselor and another with a domestic violence counselor. The same is true for people living with comorbidity, or the presence of a mental illness with a drug addiction. A cocaine addict who also has bipolar disorder would need to be treated for the two conditions separately. Medical professionals are now trying to develop more efficient treatment programs that do not require patients to compartmentalize their struggles.

In 2008, psychiatrist Alan S. Bellack and colleagues at the University of Maryland School of Medicine designed a program named Behavioral Treatment for Substance Abuse in Severe and Persistent Mental Illness (BTSAS) to bring treatments together. This group treatment program included motivational interviews, goal setting, social skills training, and informational meetings on drug abuse and addiction. It also featured an incentive program that involved urine tests. Every clean urine test led to a monetary award that could later be exchanged for desirable products.

In the study, after two months of treatment, BTSAS was producing impressive results compared with traditional group therapy (known in this study as STAR, or Supportive Treatment for Addiction Recovery). About 59 percent of participants in the BTSAS study produced drug-free urine tests on a regular basis, while only 25 percent of participants in STAR did the same. About 33 percent of participants in BTSAS maintained their abstinence past the eighth week of treatment; only 8 percent of STAR patients did the same. Bellack's research may lead medical professionals to combine treatment for drug abuse and treatment for mental illnesses into a single group effort.

BEHAVIORAL THERAPIES

Many types of behavioral therapies exist. Some occur in a group setting similar to group therapy, others work best using a one-on-one approach. Some psychologists or counselors find it best to invite spouses to behavioral therapy sessions; others ask the entire family and those closest to the patient to come to meetings.

The point of behavioral therapies, regardless of the location and participants, is to teach the patient new methods of dealing with his or her addiction. Although addiction can be treated, it cannot be cured, and the risk of relapse is always present. In behavioral therapy, patients learn new skills that will help them to beat the cravings when they reappear.

One of the most common types of behavioral therapy is cognitive-behavioral counseling. This type of treatment follows the theory that all behavior, whether healthy or destructive, is learned behavior. In therapy, patients learn skills that will help them take care of themselves in drug-free environments. The main focus of cognitive-behavioral therapy (CBT) is to teach patients how to conduct themselves in situations in which drugs may be present or at times when the craving for a drug becomes overwhelming. Much of this training is done through role playing; the counselor takes on the role of a friend offering drugs and the patient must decline the offer. According to the National Institute on Drug Abuse, many studies have shown that the behavior and lessons learned in CBT remain with patients long after therapy has ended.

Another effective type of behavioral therapy is motivational enhancement therapy (MET). Patients in MET are those who have yet to be convinced that they have a problem; many do not wish to alter the way they live their lives.

MET has two parts: an initial assessment and motivational interviews. During the initial assessment, counselors gather information about the patient's physical health and history of drug use. They then use this information in motivational interviews that occur in two or three counseling sessions with the patient. The information is used to try to persuade, or motivate, the patient to take control of his or her life and to commit to a treatment program. The counselors help the patient realize that he or she wants to get better and that life could be better without drugs or alcohol. In subsequent sessions, counselors monitor their patient's drug use and encourage the patient to keep working toward positive change. This type of therapy works well for alcoholics, people who are marijuana dependent, and adolescents who use a variety

Cold Turkey

Cold turkey is a method of addiction suppression. It consists of a process of immediate cessation of the substance or behavior with no gradual reduction or substitute substance or behavior.

In concept, quitting cold turkey is a simple process. One immediately stops consuming the substance or engaging in the behavior. Cold turkey can involve self-regulated restriction or can be monitored and supported by others. If successful, the person will refrain from further usage or action that was detrimental.

Cold turkey may be accompanied by a feeling of accomplishment, a reduction in risk and financial expense, and an opportunity to "start over" by adopting healthy behaviors and practices. More likely, though, is the occurrence of withdrawal symptoms, which can be particularly severe and even fatal, and that can challenge the person's ability to maintain a freedom from the addicting substance or behavior.

Research has shown that cold turkey is not a feasible method for many smokers, unless they have exceptional willpower, are light smokers, or are heavy smokers with discouraging health news. For an alcoholic, quitting cold turkey should not be attempted without medical supervision.

of drugs. Research has shown inconsistent results for people addicted to cocaine, heroin, and prescription drugs.

Abstinence-based incentives work well when combined with behavioral therapy. These incentives are sometimes called motivational incentives and can be used both in rehabilitation facilities and in outpatient therapies. These incentives can be cash-based or can be in the form of printed coupons.

MEDICATIONS

Medical professionals have been using medicines to treat addiction since the late nineteenth century. At this time, Sigmund Freud suggested alcoholics could be treated through the distribution of cocaine. By the early twentieth century, home remedies to treat alcohol addiction included combinations of alcohol, morphine, opium, cocaine, and cannabis. Doctors even used heroin as a treatment for alcoholism. Soon, people were addicted to more than just alcohol.

Opioid addiction became a serious concern in the mid-twentieth century. Scientists worked to develop medications that would counteract the effects of drugs such as opioids and alcohol. These medications would ideally help addicts avoid drugs of abuse and addiction as they started drug-free lives. In the mid-1950s, methadone became the first drug to show promise in helping a person overcome opioid addiction.

Scientists have since developed a handful of drugs approved by the US Food and Drug Administration for treating various addictions, including addictions to alcohol, opioids, and nicotine. Although many medications are effective, they are often only a part of the treatment programs patients must complete. Addiction medicines were designed to help dull the cravings, to balance chemicals in the brain, and to make certain substances less desirable to the user. Addiction medicines do not contain any elements that can help a patient relearn how to behave in social situations or to develop impulse control. This explains why medication is typically paired with group therapy, behavioral therapy, or individual counseling.

The most common medications administered for alcohol addiction today are naltrexone, acamprosate, and disulfiram. Naltrexone is a favorite among patients because it facilitates quitting alcohol. If a patient drinks while taking naltrexone,

he or she cannot feel the effects of the alcohol. The drug blocks the brain receptors that react to alcohol and therefore the patient cannot get drunk. This decreases alcohol's desirability.

Acamprosate, which is recommended for patients with severe alcohol dependency, calms the side effects that may accompany withdrawal, such as irritability, depression, and anxiety. Disulfiram also is effective in treating alcoholism, but only if the patient regularly uses the drug. Most patients request alternative medications after they have started taking disulfiram, as disulfiram causes patients to become nauseous if they consume alcohol with the medication in their systems. Patients who remain on disulfiram throughout treatment are more likely to be successful in staying alcohol-free.

Naltrexone is also used to treat persons with opioid addictions. Also effective are methadone and buprenorphine, but these drugs must be administered at different times. Methadone treatment can start before the patient begins withdrawal. This medication helps with withdrawal symptoms and helps the patient feel normal. The patient does not feel euphoric or depressed while using methadone. Medical professionals with a license to distribute buprenorphine are the only doctors allowed to do so. Taken at the incorrect time during the withdrawal process, buprenorphine can be deadly. Once the medication is safely in the patient's system, it reacts similarly to methadone.

Medications designed to help treat nicotine addictions are divided into two groups: first-line therapies and second-line therapies. Bupropion and varenicline are grouped among the patches, nasal sprays, lozenges, and chewing gums recommended for nicotine addiction. These first-line therapies are not as strong as second-line therapies and simply work to soothe withdrawal symptoms and calm cravings. Second-line therapies include nortriptyline and clonidine.

ALTERNATIVE THERAPIES

Many people do not believe in traditional approaches to addiction treatment; they do not wish to speak to a counselor, they do not want to be part of a support group, and they may not want to take any medications. Instead, they may try alternative therapies such as herbal therapy, hypnosis, acupuncture therapy, chiropractic therapy, or prayer.

Patients in withdrawal may not request the supervision of a medical professional and may not check themselves into a rehabilitation center. Instead, they may prefer to make home remedies containing vitamins and herbs, for example. To make up for the nutrients the body has lost because of the addiction, people may prepare foods and drinks packed with beta-carotene; zinc; vitamins A, B, C, and E; and selenium. They may begin diets that are low in sugars and refined carbohydrates, but high in complex carbohydrates. They also may cleanse their bodies with burdock root and echinacea.

Another alternative approach to traditional addiction therapy is avoiding a life of abstinence. Some programs exist in which the addict attempts to learn how to drink alcohol or smoke cigarettes in moderation. They learn how to avoid drinking to become drunk. They may learn to cut back to two cigarettes a day rather than two packs a day. These programs are typically disregarded by those in the medical community, but many psychologists and counselors in the field offer these opportunities to those patients not seeking abstinence.

Nicole Frail

FURTHER READING

Ghodse, Hamid. *Ghodse's Drugs and Addictive Behaviour: A Guide to Treatment.* New York: Cambridge UP, 2010. Examines various types of drug addictions and behavioral addictions, presents treatment options, and suggests methods of preventing substance misuse and addiction.

Gwinnell, Esther, and Christine A. Adamec, eds. *The Encyclopedia of Addictions and Addictive Behaviors.* New York: Infobase, 2005. Provides information about more than three hundred types of addictions. Discusses the historical and modern-day treatments of each addiction.

Hoffman, John, and Susan Froemke, eds. *Why Can't They Just Stop?* New York: Rodale, 2007. Written to supplement an HBO television documentary of the same name, this book offers insight into how a chemical dependency affects the lives of all involved. Includes personal narratives and success stories.

Ries, Richard K., ed. *Principles of Addiction Medicine.* Philadelphia: Lippincott, 2009. Textbook that pro-

vides information on how to diagnose, manage, and treat patients experiencing various types of addictions.

WEBSITES OF INTEREST

American Society of Addiction Medicine
http://www.asam.org

Betty Ford Center
http://www.bettyfordcenter.org

National Institute on Drug Abuse
http://www.drugabuse.gov

Substance Abuse and Mental Health Services Administration
http://www.samhsa.gov

See also: Alcohol abuse and alcoholism: Treatment; Alternative therapies for addiction; Behavioral addictions: Treatment; Behavioral therapies for addiction; Cognitive behavioral therapy; Detoxification; Group therapy for behavioral addictions; Group therapy for substance abuse; Halfway houses; Harm reduction; Intervention; Jail diversion programs; Outpatient treatment; Rehabilitation programs; Screening for behavioral addictions; Sober living environments; Sponsors; Support groups; Twelve-step programs for addicts; Twelve-step programs for family and friends

---

Trends and statistics: Alcohol abuse

CATEGORY: Social issues

DEFINITION: Alcohol abuse is a pattern of heavy drinking that significantly compromises a person's physical health and social functioning; alcohol dependence is physical addiction to alcohol. These two disorders affect about 8.5 percent of Americans age fourteen years and older, exacting a tremendous social and monetary toll.

ALCOHOL ABUSE BEFORE 1950

Alcohol abuse and dependence are mainly modern problems concentrated in areas with a predominantly

European culture and ancestry. Around much of the world, alcohol consumption is not part of the cultural tradition or is contrary to religious belief.

Several genetic factors have been identified that predispose people to alcohol abuse, and the frequency of these factors varies considerably among ethnic groups. A rough correlation exists between origin in high latitude regions and high alcohol abuse susceptibility that persists when groups immigrate to lower latitude regions.

Ancient and medieval references to alcohol abuse, including references in the Bible, stress bad behavior brought on by excessive alcohol consumption rather than a pattern of alcohol dependence, which was a luxury available only to the wealthy until the late seventeenth century. Distilled liquor, in the form of brandy, made its appearance in the fourteenth century but remained a scarce commodity until the advent of sugar cane growing in the West Indies. Before this time common people mainly drank beer (in northern Europe) and wine (in southern Europe) and could "afford" intoxication on special occasions only. Frequent drunkenness became a possibility for the masses, and persons with any genetic susceptibility to alcoholism began to show that they were much more vulnerable to developing the disease.

High levels of alcohol consumption characterized colonial America and the period immediately after the American Revolution. Taxes on hard liquor were significant sources of revenue for the young republic, encouraging growth of the liquor industry. Per capita consumption of distilled spirits in the United States peaked in 1820. Beer and wine consumption is harder to trace because taxation was not uniform and because many people made these beverages themselves. It is probable that there was a shift toward the consumption of beer and wine in the nineteenth century, along with an influx of immigrants from Germany and southern Europe.

Problems associated with alcohol abuse spawned numerous temperance movements that increasingly stressed total abstinence rather than simply abstaining from hard liquor and drunkenness. The temperance movement also drew support from anti-immigrant nativists and religious fundamentalists.

By the beginning of World War I, several US states had banned alcohol altogether. Support for a national ban gained impetus during the war and was tied to anti-German sentiment. In January 1919, the US Congress ratified the Eighteenth Amendment, prohibiting the sale of all alcoholic beverages. The degree to which the fourteen-year experiment in Prohibition curbed alcohol abuse is unknown. Total consumption declined, but turning drinking into a crime actually encouraged irresponsible use and favored hard liquor over beer and wine.

Statistics on alcohol consumption in the United States, compiled from state and federal tax records, show a per capita consumption of 1.2 gallons of pure ethanol (roughly 10 gallons of wine) in 1935, as opposed to 2.3 gallons in 1947. This increase reflects a readjustment in response to repeal but could also be a result of increasing prosperity.

CONSUMPTION PATTERNS, 1950 TO 2010

The National Institute on Alcohol Abuse and Alcoholism (NIAAA) estimates that rates of alcohol abuse rose from 3.03 percent in 1991–1992 to 4.65 percent in 2001–2002, while rates of alcohol dependence declined from 4.38 to 3.81 percent. The overall rate increased from 7.41 to 8.46 percent. The 2001–2002 figures translate into 9.7 million adult Americans who have experienced significant drinking related problems in a twelve-month period, and 7.9 million Americans who are chemically addicted.

Native American men age eighteen to thirty years have the highest rates of alcohol abuse and dependence (15.25 and 13.34 percent, respectively), while the rates for older Asian and Hispanic women are negligible. Young white men, who have both high rates and a large demographic share, dominate the raw numbers.

Rates of alcohol abuse among men and women have been converging. The male/female ratio was 3.09 in 1991–1992 and 2.72 in 2001–2002, with most of the difference concentrated in the younger age groups. While rates among younger white men remained steady, increases were noted among black, Hispanic, and Asian persons.

On a per capita basis, Americans age fourteen years and older consumed the equivalent of 2.04 gallons of pure grain alcohol in 1950. Consumption rose to 2.75 gallons from 1975 to 1980, declined to 2.15 gallons in 1996, and had risen to 2.3 gallons in 2008. There has been a steady shift from distilled spirits since 1950. (Figures are based on tax receipts; surveys of alcohol use are unreliable because heavy drinkers consistently underreport their consumption.) It has been estimated that 10 percent of drinkers account for one-half of the alcohol consumption in the United States.

Alcohol education and the expansion of treatment options account for some of the modest decline in consumption since the mid-1970s, but part of that peak can be attributed to baby boomers, who were, in the 1970s, mostly in their twenties, an age marked by high alcohol consumption.

MORTALITY, CRIME, AND ECONOMIC LOSS

Alcohol abuse exacts a huge social toll in the form of premature death, crime and other antisocial behavior, and lost productivity. A conservative estimate considers alcohol abuse to be responsible for 5 percent of deaths annually in the United States, mainly from cirrhosis of the liver and motor vehicle accidents. The impact is disproportionate because many of the victims are relatively young.

Trends in alcohol-related vehicle crashes are improving. In the mid 1970s, alcohol was a factor in more than 60 percent of traffic fatalities and accounted for two-thirds of traffic fatalities among those age sixteen to twenty years. In 1982 there were 43,945 traffic deaths, 59.6 percent of them alcohol related. In 2004 there were 42,836 deaths, 39.5 percent alcohol related, and the proportion among youth had fallen to 37 percent. Tougher laws against drunk driving, education campaigns in schools, and raising the legal drinking age are credited with much of the decline.

Alcohol-related cirrhosis of the liver was the twelfth leading cause of death in the United States in 2000, accounting for 1.1 percent of all deaths. This represented a decline from a high of 2.3 percent in 1910. Historically, rates of liver disease have tracked rates of alcohol consumption with a four to five year lag time. Rates

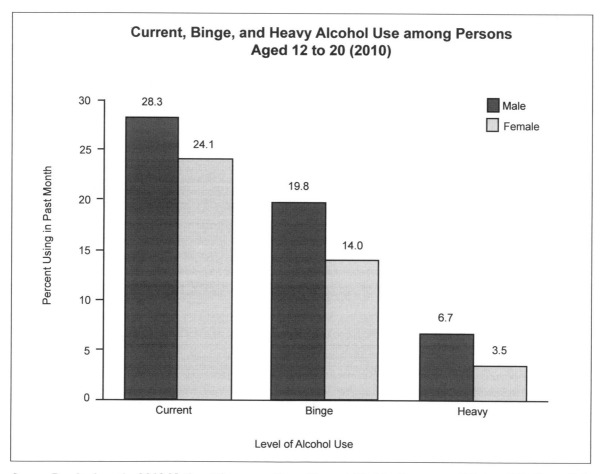

Source: Results from the 2010 National Survey on Drug Use and Health: Summary of National Findings, Substance Abuse and Mental Health Services Administration. (SAMHSA)

were low during Prohibition, rose to 2.1 percent in the mid 1970s, and then declined. Some rise is anticipated because of increasing rates of hepatitis C infection, which exacerbates the effects of alcohol. In addition to decreased consumption and more aggressive treatment for alcoholism, a switch from hard liquor to wine and beer may have aided the decline because these beverages have less effect on the liver even when the same amount of ethanol is consumed.

Alcohol consumption by perpetrator or victim, or both, is a factor in approximately one-half of all violent crimes and one-half of sexual assaults. These figures are based on surveys of fifty thousand households in the US Bureau of Justice Crime Victimization Survey. For reasons not entirely understood, this survey showed a 23 percent drop in reported victimizations and a 34 percent drop in alcohol-related victimizations between 1993 and 1998. The role of alcohol in property crimes is generally unknown.

A 1998 NIAAA estimate of the economic costs of alcohol abuse, taking into account alcoholism treatment and medical treatment of alcohol-related disorders, lost productivity, motor vehicle crashes, crime, and social welfare administration, showed a cost of $148 billion in 1992 and of $184.6 billion in 1998. The largest component was lost productivity from death, disability, and absenteeism.

Impact of Treatment and Other Interventions

Since about 1980 there has been a marked increase in efforts devoted to curbing alcohol abuse through education, medical treatment of alcoholism as a disease, and stricter laws against underage drinking and against driving under the influence of alcohol. Acceptance of alcoholism as a disease and successful efforts to force medical insurers to cover alcoholism treatment led to explosive growth in residential substance abuse treatment centers and college programs to train and certify counselors. This wave appears to be ebbing as the ranks of uninsured grow and as reimbursement rates drop. There also is growing skepticism about the effectiveness of intensive residential treatment programs in comparison with less costly outpatient programs or Alcoholics Anonymous.

If statistics on traffic accidents are any indication, efforts made toward curbing underage drinking and reducing alcohol abuse on college campuses do seem to be working. Effects on the population as a whole and on older age groups are not dramatic and can be explained, in part, by other factors, including an aging population and a persistent recession that tends to depress luxury consumption among people who are not alcohol dependent. Also unknown, but probably significant, is the degree to which marginalized youth, who a generation ago would have abused alcohol, are turning to street drugs instead.

Martha A. Sherwood, PhD

Further Reading

Barrows, Susanna, and Robin Room. *Drinking: Behavior and Belief in Modern History.* Berkeley: U of California P, 1991. Scholarly papers on the history of drinking and of temperance movements in colonial and nineteenth-century America.

Bellenir, Karen, and Amy Sutton. *Alcoholism Sourcebook.* Detroit: Omnigraphics, 2007. Basic consumer information about alcohol use, abuse, and dependence; statistics on physical and social pathology.

Grant, Bridget, et al. "The 12-Month Prevalence and Trends in DSM-IV Alcohol Abuse and Dependence, United States, 1991–1992 and 2001–2002." *Drug and Alcohol Dependence* 74.3 (2004): 223–34. Print. A detailed statistical report and analysis.

Mann, Robert E., et al. "Epidemiology of Alcoholic Liver Disease." *Alcohol Research and Health* 27.3 (2003): 209–19. Print. Statistics on mortality and morbidity from liver disease and their correlation with alcohol consumption.

Websites of Interest

National Council on Drug and Alcohol Dependence
http://www.ncadd.org

National Institute on Alcohol Abuse and Alcoholism
http://www.niaaa.nih.gov

National Institutes of Health Fact Sheets
http://report.nih.gov/NIHfactsheets

See also: Alcohol abuse and alcoholism: In depth; Trends and statistics: Behavioral addictions; Trends and statistics: Illegal drug use; Trends and statistics: Prescription drug abuse; Trends and statistics: Smoking

Trends and statistics: Behavioral addictions

CATEGORY: Social issues

DEFINITION: Behavioral addiction is the continuation of a certain behavior that has many costs and few gains. A person who cannot control or stop a behavior, even after experiencing negative consequences from engaging in that activity, may be considered a behavioral addict. These types of addictions can involve any type of behavior. However, some of the more recognized behavioral addictions involve sex, shopping, gambling, Internet use, video games, overeating, and pornography.

SEX ADDICTION

The National Council on Sexual Addiction and Compulsivity defines sex addiction as "engaging in persistent and escalating patterns of sexual behavior acted out despite increasing negative consequences to self and others." The first major study on sex addiction was published in 1991. Participants in the survey included 752 men and 180 women; all were diagnosed as sex addicts.

The results of the survey showed that 97 percent felt a loss of self-esteem following sexual relations, 96 percent felt lonely and isolated, 94 percent felt hopeless, 91 percent were acting against their own personal morals and beliefs, 88 percent felt as if they were living a double life, and 78 percent labeled themselves as emotionally unstable. The survey also found that 42 percent of those who participated in the survey also had substance addictions to drugs or alcohol.

The survey's findings are consistent with general overviews of those diagnosed with sex addiction. Sex addicts are generally preoccupied with thoughts and fantasies about sex, are often more interested in following sexual routines rather than climaxing, and often do not feel sexually satisfied after having sex. On the contrary, the sex addict feels depressed, remorseful, and powerless.

Fifty-eight percent of sex addicts have legal troubles and 60 percent have financial difficulties because of their addiction. Various methods of therapy and medications, usually antidepressants, are helpful in treating sex addiction, as it has been linked with other disorders.

SHOPPING ADDICTION

Shopping addiction, or oniomania, involves the purchase of unnecessary items, leading to excessive spending, usually outside a person's budget. Affecting about 6 percent of the population, mostly women, shopping addiction involves the need for instant gratification, which releases endorphins and dopamine in the brain to provide a feeling of euphoria and relaxation.

Research has shown that men with shopping addiction often buy electronics, tools, books, and music. Women with shopping addiction tend to buy clothes, makeup, and housewares. Many shoppers return what they purchase to alleviate the feelings of guilt and depression they feel after the high of shopping has subsided. However, some people buy more items to alleviate the feelings of guilt, leading to a vicious circle of consumption.

Lorrin M. Koran and colleagues, in a 2006 study of compulsive buying behavior in the United States, noted:

> Compulsive shoppers are actively acquiring the items, but they don't care about them after they have them. Women will hang new clothes in the closet, yet never take them out of the bag and never take off the tags. Men will leave the CDs wrapped in plastic and never listen to them.

A European Union report revealed that up to one-half of girls age fourteen to eighteen years in Scotland, Italy, and Spain showed symptoms of shopping addiction. Research done in the United States yielded similar results. However, the problem may be even greater because many people do not view their shopping habits as problematic and thus fail to report them.

As with many addictions, the behavior masks deeper issues such as low self-esteem, anxiety, and depression. Drugs such as antidepressants may help to improve a shopper's self-esteem, but the drug alone cannot treat the problem of shopping addiction. To be treated the shopper also must participate in therapy to understand the root cause of the addiction and to address the damage that has been done to the shopper's finances and personal relationships.

GAMBLING ADDICTION

Gambling addiction, also known as pathological gambling, is classified in the *Diagnostic and Statistical Manual of Mental Disorders* (DSM) as an impulse-control disorder not elsewhere classified. According to the Impulse-Control Disorders Clinic at the University of California, Los Angeles, "The essential feature of Impulse-Control Disorders is the failure to resist an impulse, drive, or temptation to perform an act that is harmful to the person or to others."

Studies using neuroimaging (brain images) show that the same regions of the brain involved in substance addiction also are involved in gambling addiction. The most notable regions of the brain affected in both instances are involved in executive functioning, planning, and memory. What this information proves is that gambling addiction is like substance addiction in that it is a brain disease.

Approximately 3 million Americans have a problem with gambling. The DSM lists ten criteria for diagnosing gambling addiction. If a person exhibits five or more of these behaviors, they are considered to have a gambling problem. The criteria include a preoccupation with gambling, the inability to stop gambling, reduced gambling leading to increased irritability, wagering higher sums, the use of gambling to reduce stress or escape problems, attempts to recover gambling losses by gambling, hiding the problem from others, carrying gambling debts, putting stress on personal and professional relationships because of gambling, and breaking the law to gamble.

A 2005 study showed that approximately 4 percent of Californians met the criteria for problem gambling. The study also showed that the most vulnerable populations are African Americans, the disabled, and the unemployed.

Many gambling addicts also have a mental illness, such as depression or anxiety. Medication may help alleviate these illnesses, which may be contributing to the addiction, but medication is not a substitution for therapy. Support groups such as Gamblers Anonymous offer twelve-step programs to assist gambling addicts and to teach coping mechanisms for dealing with the addiction.

INTERNET AND VIDEO GAME ADDICTION

Although little information exists about Internet addiction, which is not medically classified as an addiction, it is believed that between 5 and 10 percent of computer users have a form of Internet addiction. Internet addiction and video game addiction have both been compared with gambling addiction. Internet addiction comes in many forms.

Some people may be addicted to cybersex, pornography, online love affairs, multi-user role-playing games, online shopping, online gambling, or just extensive Internet browsing. It is believed that Internet addiction is really a mask for another disorder, such as depression, attention deficit disorder, anxiety, or impulsivity. As with any addiction, the signs and symptoms of Internet addiction include altered lifestyle and unhealthy interference of daily activities because of extensive Internet usage.

It remains disputable whether video game addiction is actually an addiction. The American Psychiatric Association does not list video game addiction in the DSM as a mental disorder, but it is being considered for inclusion in DSM revisions if adequate scientific evidence supports its categorization as an addiction.

More than 8 percent of American youths between the ages of eight and eighteen use video games enough to affect daily functioning. For example, engaging in video games extensively can result in physical and social harm.

In 2007, Iowa State University conducted a study on video game addiction. According to researchers, a child is addicted to video games if he or she displays six of the following eleven qualities: increased time thinking about video games, learning about video games, or planning the next playing opportunity; a need to spend more time and money on video games to feel the same excitement; inability to reduce the amount of time spent playing video games; becoming irritable when time is reduced or when it is time to stop playing; playing video games to escape problems or bad feelings; lying to friends or family about time spent playing video games; stealing a game or money to purchase a game; skipping household chores to play video games; skipping homework to play video games; receiving a poor grade on an assignment because time was spent playing video games; and borrowing money from friends or family because one's own money was spent on video games, software, or Internet fees.

THE DSM REVISION

The DSM is set for revision. Much debate has focused on whether or not behavioral addictions should be included in their own section or if these behaviors are the result of other classified disorders such as depression or anxiety. Addiction specialist Reef Karim posed a controversial and thoughtful question in the fall 2010 issue of *CSAM News*:

> Is it time that we open up this definition [of addiction] to include abnormal repetitive behavioral patterns as "non substance" forms of addiction? The inclusion of behavioral addictions may "medicalize" bad behaviors or bad habits, and where do we draw the line between an excessive bad behavior and a true addiction?

What is known about behavioral disorders and addictions is that defining conditions need to be outlined and valid screening measures must be put into place. Additionally, more research is necessary to determine whether addiction is a matter of a person's "addictiveness," a matter of the substance, or a matter of the behavior, or a combination of the three.

Gina Kutcha

FURTHER READING

Albanese, Mark J., and Edward J. Khantzian. *Understanding Addiction as Self Medication*. Lanham, MD: Rowman, 2008. Examines the emotional and mental issues behind addictions and examines whether addictions are a moral weakness or purely a brain disease.

American Psychiatric Association. *Diagnostic and Statistical Manual of Mental Disorders*. 4th ed. Washington, DC: APA, 1994. A professional manual outlining all topics relevant to psychiatric conditions and diagnoses.

WEBSITES OF INTEREST

American Psychological Association
http://www.apadivisions.org

American Society of Addiction Medicine
http://www.asam.org

National Center on Addiction and Substance Abuse at Columbia University
http://www.casacolumbia.org

See also: Behavioral addictions: Overview; Trends and statistics: Alcohol abuse; Trends and statistics: Illegal drug use; Trends and statistics: Prescription drug abuse; Trends and statistics: Smoking

Trends and statistics: Illegal drug use

CATEGORY: Social issues
ALSO KNOWN AS: Drug use evaluation
DEFINITION: Illegal drug use is tracked by a growing number of federal and private organizations in the United States and worldwide. Substance abuse statistics are measured against historical rates, and trends are evaluated to determine not only the effect of previous treatment campaigns and programs but also to identify new problems faced by regulatory bodies, public health programs, and health care providers into the future.

MEASURING ILLEGAL DRUG USE

Tracking drug use identifies connections with economic, cultural, educational, and age-related factors. The Centers for Disease Control and Prevention (CDC) and the National Institute on Drug Abuse (NIDA), for example, report on annual trends and statistics of drug use with age-specific population surveys. Youth are particularly targeted, because illegal drugs, especially marijuana, remain available to youth, and a person's first drug use usually occurs before the age of eighteen years.

The CDC Youth Risk Behavior Survey (YRBS) and the NIDA Monitoring the Future (MTF) survey provide data on usage rates by age groups of preteens, teenagers, and college-aged adults. The YRBS is released each summer and reports on six risk-behavior categories for students of grades nine through twelve. The MTF survey seeks to identify drug use in more than forty-five thousand children in grades eight, ten, and twelve; this survey has been released annually each fall since 1975.

These two well-known reporting tools are supplemented by trend evaluations, such as those by the Office on Drugs and Crime (ODC) and by the National Survey on Drug Use and Health (NSDUH). In the ODC report, drug use is measured according to timing:

across a lifetime, annually, or during the past thirty days (the latter to reflect current users). The results then provide a comparison across generations and between men and women. The NSDUH report includes more than sixty-five thousand people twelve years of age and older. Results are released one year after the MTF data. NSDUH data similarly measure periods of drug use by lifetime, past year, and past month.

Government monitoring agencies such as the Drug Abuse Warning Network (DAWN) track the rates of hospital admissions or adverse events related to drug use. Combining statistics of numerous organizations provides a more thorough picture of drug use; trends by age often distinguish differences between high school and college usage and identify broader trends in drug popularity. Most evaluations compare numerical data on illicit drug use according to the frequency of use as new, one-time, or chronic users.

FACTORS AFFECTING CHANGING TRENDS

Substance abuse affects all levels of society, but focal groups and drug preferences vary with time. Identifying factors that determine past trends can help to determine new trends and risk groups. Trends in illegal drug use reflect specific changes of the era, as the drug choices and rates fluctuate over time. Drug preferences vary according to what is available on the street or in schools and according to the cost of drugs and level of economic stability.

Trends also directly relate to mental health disorders. Chronic mental health problems are associated with a risk of dependence that is three times greater than the norm. Similarly, drug use problems increase in persons (such as preteens) who experience social exclusion on the basis of age or social status (for example, poverty level). Finally, public opinion actively affects drug use; resignation about a drug's presence in society encourages complacency about widespread use, especially in teen and preteen populations.

EFFECTS OF PUBLIC HEALTH CAMPAIGNS

Public opinion shapes the perception of the dangers of drug use, and the trends of drug preference can change in response to the prevailing public opinion of a drug's relative safety or danger. Thus, the acceptance of different drugs, or the complacency of adults about certain illegal drug use in teens, can directly increase the amount of users.

For example, although cigarette use is now actively discouraged in youth because of the known cancer risks, marijuana is now seen by teens and adults as a safer substance of abuse. In an MTF survey, children in all three grade levels expressed belief in the lesser harm of marijuana, a belief reflected by greater rates of use.

Contrasted with the complacency of marijuana use in the United States is the extended public campaign effort to reduce cigarette smoking, particularly in underage groups. US surgeon general warnings are required for all tobacco products sold in the United States, and newly updated warnings in 2012 will include graphic images of the harmful effects tobacco has on the body. Text, graphic, and point-of-purchase warnings make up public health efforts that have greatly reduced illegal tobacco use in youths.

CURRENT TRENDS AND STATISTICS

Youth-based surveys like MTF document changing trends by substance: Drugs of choice include alcohol, tobacco, and marijuana. Also included are illicit street drugs such as cocaine and heroin and stimulants such as methamphetamine. Surveys change to reflect popularity trends too, so club drugs and prescription drugs are being evaluated more frequently in the twenty-first century.

Although fewer people are using drugs regularly from a high of 25 million persons in 1979, drug use is still widespread. More than one-third of people age twelve years and older have tried an illicit substance at least once, and 60 million adults report a history of drug use before adulthood. In 1993, approximately 13 million people (or 6 percent of the population) age twelve years and older were current illicit drug users, according to the National Criminal Justice Reference Service.

Alcohol. Alcohol is still the most used drug by youth, but both alcohol and tobacco use have declined since the 1990s, according to 2009 NSDUH surveys. Similarly, trends in alcohol use across five years on the 2011 MTF survey identified lower rates of alcohol use in each grade level for binge use, past year rates, and daily use rates.

Despite these advances in reducing underage drinking, alcohol continues to cause 2.5 million deaths each year, 320,000 of them in people age nineteen to twenty-nine years. Nearly one-quarter of college students age eighteen to twenty-four years abuse alcohol each year, and approximately 375,000 of them report treatment admissions for abuse in 2009.

Tobacco. Tobacco trends have paralleled those of alcohol in youth surveys. Cigarette use is still prevalent, with three thousand new youth cigarette smokers each day in the United States. These numbers, however, are lower than twentieth century figures. The NSDUH reported a decrease in current cigarette users from 13 percent in 2002 to 9 percent in 2009 in children, and the MTF survey reported slow but decreasing trends of daily cigarette use in all grade levels in 2011. However, the 2010 MTF reported a new choice for tobacco use: Small cigars were smoked by 23 percent of high school students polled that year.

Marijuana. Contrasting with the downward trends of cigarette and alcohol use are data about marijuana use. The increase in overall drug use measured from 2000 to 2008 parallels marijuana use specifically on CDC and National Institutes of Health reports. Nearly 3 million more youth age twelve years and older reported illicit substance abuse in 2010 than in 2008 because of increased marijuana use. Marijuana use appears equal in college-educated and non–college-educated adults, and its use exceeded that of cigarettes in high school seniors in 2011.

Daily marijuana use increased in grades eight, ten, and twelve on the 2010 NSDUH survey. Five-year trends on the 2011 MTF survey reported that nearly 40 percent of twelfth-graders used marijuana one or more times in the past year.

Illicit Drugs. Although the number of one-time cocaine users is lower than its 1985 peak, 600,000 people remain addicted to heroin in the United States, and more youth continue to try it than were reported in 1970 and 1980. Use of stimulants like methamphetamine also was on the rise into the 1990s, but rates have dropped from 731,000 in 2006 to 353,000 in 2010.

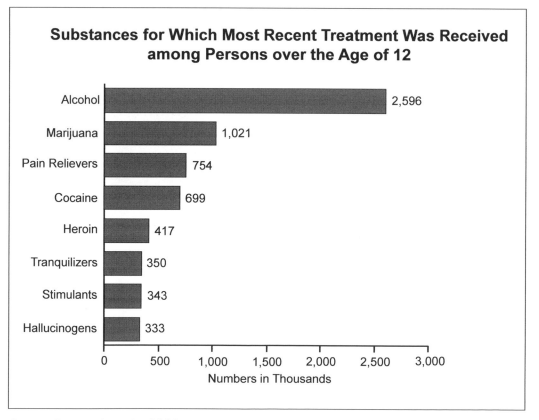

Source: Results from the 2010 National Survey on Drug Use and Health: Summary of National Findings, Substance Abuse and Mental Health Services Administration (SAMHSA)

The most recent changes in illicit drug use trends involve club drugs and prescription drugs. For example, ecstasy use increased 1 percent in eighth graders in 2009 and 2010 despite years of decline. The most commonly abused prescription drugs among high school students include methylphenidate and related stimulants, painkillers such as hydrocodone or oxycodone, and sedatives such as diazepam. According to DAWN, misuse of prescription drugs approved by the US Food and Drug Administration resulting in emergency room visits increased in 2005 to 1.4 million visits. The continued increase in abuse of these drugs likely results from the low cost and widespread availability of medications.

Nicole M. Van Hoey, PharmD

FURTHER READING

Degenhardt, L., and W. Hall. "Extent of Illicit Drug Use and Dependence and Their Contribution to the Global Burden of Disease." *Lancet* 379 (2012): 55–70. Print. A discussion of the harmful short- and long-term effects of illicit drugs, including prescription drugs of abuse, compared across countries of varied economies.

Henkel, D. "Unemployment and Substance Use: A Review of the Literature (1990–2010)." *Current Drug Abuse Review* 4.1 (2011): 4–27. Print. Thorough analysis of available reports on patterns of employment associated with drug misuse.

Substance Abuse and Mental Health Services Administration. *Drug Abuse Warning Network, 2009: Methodology Report.* Rockville, MD: SAMHSA, 2011. Detailed description of the Drug Abuse Warning Network function, process, and purpose; the specific data reported; and the agencies involved in data collection and evaluation.

US Department of Justice. "Bureau of Justice Assistance Fact Sheet: Combating Methamphetamine Abuse." Publication No. 000318. Washington, DC: DOJ, 2009. A law enforcement perspective on methods to counter rising stimulant abuse in the twenty-first century.

WEBSITES OF INTEREST

Centers for Disease Control and Prevention: Youth Risk Behavior Surveillance System
http://www.cdc.gov/healthyyouth/yrbs

National Institute on Drug Abuse
http://www.drugabuse.gov/publications/infofacts/
nationwide-trends

National Survey on Drug Use and Health
http://nsduhweb.rti.org

See also: Narcotics abuse; Recreational drugs; Trends and statistics: Alcohol abuse; Trends and statistics: Behavioral addictions; Trends and statistics: Prescription drug abuse; Trends and statistics: Smoking

Trends and statistics: Prescription drug abuse

CATEGORY: Social issues

DEFINITION: Prescription drug abuse is the use of prescribed medications for reasons other than intended by a medical professional. Prescription drugs are taken in excess quantity, more frequently, or for a longer time than prescribed in order to produce changes in mental or physical status. The abuse of prescription drugs is now considered an epidemic in both the United States and in Canada.

DATA COLLECTION

The collection of accurate data on prescription drug abuse is of paramount importance, as prescription drugs constitute the second most abused class of substances behind marijuana. The National Survey on Drug Use and Health (1992) reported that 4 million people in the United States abused or misused prescription pain relievers; this figure rose to 5 million in 1998, 6.5 million in 1999, and 8.4 million in 2001. Furthermore, there was an overall increase in the prevalence of prescription drug abuse (0.17 percent in 1991–1992 to 0.28 percent in 2001–2002).

The abuse of prescription drugs causes a great burden on individuals and on the health care system. The Drug Abuse Warning Network found a significant increase of 98.4 percent in emergency room visits related to prescription medication abuse from 2004 to 2009, from approximately 627,000 cases in 2004 to more than 1.2 million. A rise in deaths secondary to this abuse, specifically with opioids, also was observed. The amount of opioid-related deaths increased by 68 percent from 1999 to 2004. The economic impact is significant, with 2001 estimates for abuse of opioid medications revealing a $2.6 billion cost to the health care system for treatment, $1.4 billion cost to the criminal justice system, and $4.6 billion cost in the workplace of affected persons. Therefore, the collection of statistics on other prescription drugs of abuse and research on prevention and treatment are becoming public health priorities.

Statistics reveal that the majority of persons who abuse prescription drugs still do not receive proper medical or mental health treatment for the problem. While one study in the United States found that treatment admissions rose by one-third from 2001 to 2003, another study found that fewer persons enrolled in treatment in 2001–2002 than in 1991–1992 (by 36.4 percent); this translates into 86 percent of prescription drug abusers not receiving proper care in 2001–2002.

In Canada, the Centre for Addiction and Mental Health similarly found that only 11 percent of admissions to treatment programs for substance abuse were for prescription drug abuse. When persons sought treatment, they most commonly attended twelve-step programs such as Narcotics Anonymous. Some also attended drug rehabilitation programs or were aided by a psychologist, physician, or social worker. The underutilization of treatment demonstrates how greater effort is needed to understand why this population does not receive the same detoxification and psychological treatment as illicit substance and alcohol abusers.

DATA COLLECTION CHALLENGES

Until recently, there has been a paucity of reliable and valid medical literature on prescription drug abuse because the problem went either unrecognized or under-recognized by physicians and researchers. Health care providers and researchers often inquire only about illicit substances and neglect to ask patients about abusing prescription medications. Several national and international agencies and networks have since been established to obtain statistics and track trends of prescription drug abuse.

Additionally, there is no agreed-upon, standardized definition of what constitutes prescription drug abuse, and the medical literature does not agree on whether to classify the problem as abuse or misuse. This poses a challenge when attempting to collect and analyze data. It remains difficult to determine from an examination of medical records if a person took medication secondary to self-treating an actual medical diagnosis, such as chronic pain, anxiety, or sleep disorders, or if that person abused the drug to get high.

RISK FACTORS FOR PRESCRIPTION DRUG ABUSE

Teenagers and young adults age eighteen to twenty-five are typically considered the highest risk population for prescription drug abuse for two reasons: the ease of access to medications from family or friends and the general social acceptability of using prescription medications, instead of illicit drugs, to get high. One study of college students estimated that 20 percent of this population had misused prescription drugs; this figure has risen since about 1995. While men, overall, are more likely than women to abuse prescription drugs, women often misuse prescriptions to self-medicate rather than to get high.

Prescription drug abuse is more common among non-Hispanic Caucasians than among persons of other ethnic backgrounds. Data from 1999 hospital records revealed that 87 percent of persons admitted for prescription drug abuse were of Caucasian ancestry; later studies have confirmed this population as the greatest risk.

Furthermore, persons who abuse prescription drugs are more likely to consume alcohol and be diagnosed with other illicit substance disorders. The data have not found a change in this statistic over time, with most persons in this population being young and unmarried men. However, the population characteristics have been further elucidated. Persons of African American ancestry and those age forty-five years and older showed a significant increase in being diagnosed with both a prescription drug abuse and substance abuse or alcohol disorder. The reasons for the rise of concurrent disorders in other demographics need to be determined through further study.

TRENDS AND STATISTICS BY DRUG CATEGORY

Prescription drugs are divided into four categories for purposes of studying their abuse patterns: opioids; sedatives, hypnotics, and tranquilizers; stimulants; and anesthetics. However, the categories are not always mutually exclusive, as many persons abuse medications in multiple classes. One study found that 19.3 percent of persons abused medications from two classes, 11.1 percent from three classes, and 5 percent from all four classes.

Opioids. Opioids, such as oxycodone, methadone, hydrocodone, and codeine, constitute the most commonly abused class of prescription drugs and are intended to act as pain relievers. Data between 1991–1992 and 2001–2002 shows that the prevalence of opioid abuse increased significantly. This risc is attributable, in part, to opioids being the most frequently prescribed class of medications. Physicians prescribed hydrocodone-acetaminophen for pain management more than any other pain medication in 2008, a 6.9 percent increase from 2006. The use of fentanyl, which is an opioid patch, showed a similar increase in prescriptions and accounted for approximately six thousand more emergency room visits secondary to abuse in 2008 when compared with 2006.

Sedatives, hypnotics, and tranquilizers. Another popular class of prescription drugs includes sedatives, hypnotics, and tranquilizers. Commonly abused medications in this category include phenobarbital, methaqualone, clonazepam, and alprazolam. Physicians are more frequently prescribing these medications to reduce symptoms of insomnia, anxiety, and panic disorders. Women are more likely to be admitted for treatment with this category. Data from a ten-year span (1991–1992 to 2001–2002) shows an increase in the prevalence of sedative abuse. While tranquilizer abuse accounted for more emergency room visits in 2006 than in 2004 (36 percent), another large study did not find any significant increases in the prevalence of tranquilizer abuse in that same ten-year period.

Stimulants. Common stimulants include amphetamine, dextroamphetamine, and methamphetamine. The abuse of stimulants is on the rise because of the increasing amount of prescriptions written to treat attention deficit hyperactivity disorder (ADHD). The US Drug Enforcement Administration found a 600 percent increase in ADHD prescriptions between 1990 and 1995, many of which were then sold to others for nonmedical purposes. Not all studies, however, have found an increase in stimulant abuse. Because more prescriptions are given to younger school-age persons to treat ADHD, the age of hospital admission for this category is younger than for other classes of prescription drug abuse.

Anesthetics. The least commonly abused class of prescription drugs is anesthetics, as most of these require administration by a physician and are not generally prescribed. However, health care professionals who

have access to these medications, especially anesthesiologists, are at risk.

Janet Ober Berman, MS, CGC

FURTHER READING

Birnbaum, Howard, et al. "Estimated Costs of Prescription Opioid Analgesic Abuse in the United States in 2001." *Clinical Journal of Pain* 22.8 (2006): 667–76. Print. Study provides figures on the increasing costs of prescription drug abuse to both the medical and criminal justice fields.

Hernandez, S., and L. Nelson. "Prescription Drug Abuse: Insight into the Epidemic." *Clinical Pharmacology and Therapeutics* 88.3 (2010): 307–17. Print. Article lists a summary of current networks and studies that collect data on prescription drug abuse as well as some of the commonly misused substances.

McCabe, Sean, Carol Boyd, and Christian Teter. "Subtypes of Nonmedical Prescription Drug Misuse." *Drug and Alcohol Dependence* 102 (2009): 63–70. Print. Research data on prevalence of prescription drug abuse by type of drug and race and gender demographics.

McCabe, Sean, James Cranford, and Brady West. "Trends in Prescription Drug Abuse and Dependence, Co-Occurrence with Other Substance Use Disorders, and Treatment Utilization: Results from Two National Surveys." *Addictive Behaviors* 33 (2008): 1297–1305. Print. Study reports trends in prescription drug abuse and treatment from 1991–1992 and 2001–2002.

WEBSITES OF INTEREST

Canadian Centre on Substance Abuse
http://ccsa.ca

Center for Behavioral Health Statistics and Quality
http://www.samhsa.gov/about/cbhsq.aspx

National Institute on Drug Abuse
http://drugabuse.gov

See also: Narcotics abuse; Prescription drug addiction: In Depth; Trends and statistics: Alcohol abuse; Trends and statistics: Behavioral addictions; Trends and statistics: Illegal drug use; Trends and statistics: Smoking

Trends and statistics: Smoking

CATEGORY: Social issues

DEFINITION: Trends and statistics include numeric data regarding cigarette smoking prevalence. According to the US Centers for Disease Control and Prevention, in 2009, 20.6 percent (or about 46 million) people age eighteen years and older in the United States smoked. Historically, cigarette consumption peaked in the 1960s.

US TRENDS AND STATISTICS

With the discovery of the detrimental health effects of tobacco use and with subsequent public health education and legislation to reduce consumption, the number of smokers in the United States has steadily declined through the first part of the twenty-first century. The number of regular smokers stalled in 2005 and has remained stable since 2007.

The Centers for Disease Control and Prevention (CDC) defines current regular smokers as people who have smoked at least one hundred cigarettes in their lifetime and smoke every day or most days. More men (23.5 percent) than women (17.9 percent) smoke in the United States. The following statistics focus on cigarette consumption, as this is by far the most predominant form of tobacco smoking, compared with cigars and loose tobacco (pipes and self-rolling) usage.

Education and income play a key role in the prevalence of smoking. The CDC reports that nearly one-half (49 percent) of adults with a general equivalency diploma as their highest level of education attainment and more than one-third of those who never graduated high school are smokers, whereas only 5.6 percent of people with a master's degree are smokers. In regard to income, 31 percent of adults who live below the poverty line are smokers, whereas approximately 19 percent who live at or above the poverty line are smokers.

Persons who identified as being multiracial had the highest rate of smoking at 29 percent. Asian Americans reported the lowest smoking rates at 12 percent, followed by Hispanics (14 percent), non-Hispanic African Americans (21 percent), non-Hispanic Caucasians (22 percent), and Native Americans and Alaska Natives (23 percent). By state, Utah reports the lowest smoking rate at 9.8 percent, whereas Kentucky and West Virginia report the highest prevalence

of smokers at more than one-quarter of the adult population.

The 2004 Pregnancy Risk Assessment and Monitoring System compiled data from twenty-six states and determined that 13 percent of women smoke during the last three months of pregnancy. The prevalence of smoking during pregnancy reflects the general trends. Smoking is highest among women from lower socioeconomic backgrounds. Young, less educated women are more likely to smoke while pregnant than other pregnant women.

Children are a particularly vulnerable population regarding tobacco use in the United States. According to the nonprofit Campaign for Tobacco-Free Kids, approximately 400,000 children either try their first cigarette or become regular smokers each year. About 90 percent of adult smokers say that they started in their teens, and two-thirds are regular smokers by the time they are nineteen years old. About 19 percent of all teenagers who are in grades nine through twelve are regular smokers.

Teenage smokers are divided evenly among girls and boys, with statistics for both genders also at about 19 percent. In regard to ethnicity, smoking is most prevalent among white children at 22 percent. Hispanic children fall in the middle at 18 percent and African American children have the lowest smoking rates at 9.5 percent.

Despite laws in the United States to deter children from obtaining tobacco products, cigarettes are relatively easy for a minor to obtain. According to the National Survey on Drug Use and Health (2003), 77 percent of smokers age twelve to seventeen years purchased their cigarettes directly from a retailer or vending machine. Other methods include stealing, shoplifting, or obtaining from friends or family.

CANADIAN TRENDS AND STATISTICS

According to the Canadian Tobacco Use Monitoring Survey, an ongoing study about tobacco usage, 32 percent of young adults age fifteen to twenty-four years and 24 percent of adults age twenty-five years and older were regular smokers in 1999. The number of regular smokers decreased significantly to 18 percent for young adults and 17 percent for adults older than age twenty-five years in 2009.

Canada has almost 5 million smokers who are fifteen years of age or older. Overall, the provinces of British Columbia and Ontario report the lowest number of smokers fifteen years of age and older (15 percent), and the province of Saskatchewan reports the highest smoking rate at 22 percent.

The Canadian survey began in 1999 and records characteristics about who was most likely to smoke. Trends were comparable with those in the United States, in that men were more likely than women to smoke (27 versus 22 percent) and people who did not complete high school were more likely to smoke than their peers with college and university degrees.

Despite the publicized risks of smoking during pregnancy, the practice is prevalent among Canadian women. An average of 17 percent of pregnant women smoked up to the third trimester. Certain regions of Canada have higher incidences of smoking during pregnancy. For example, a survey reported that more than 26 percent of non-aboriginal women in Winnipeg and more than 25 percent of pregnant women in Nova Scotia smoked up to delivery. Statistical information for aboriginal women of Winnipeg recorded more than twice (61.2 percent) the incidence of smoking up to delivery than in other areas.

Like children in the United States, children in Canada obtain cigarettes either socially or by purchasing or stealing from retail establishments. About 85 percent of underage smokers in grades six through nine obtain cigarettes from social resources, whereas the majority (60 percent) of older children who are regular smokers are able to purchase them.

Canada's 2008–2009 Youth Smoking Survey divides statistics about smokers younger than age eighteen years between younger children (grades six through nine) and older children (grades ten through twelve). Three percent of younger children are regular smokers, a statistic that remains unchanged from the previous year's survey. The older children category increased from 11 percent in 2006–2007 to 13 percent in 2008–2009.

Laura J. Pinchot, BA

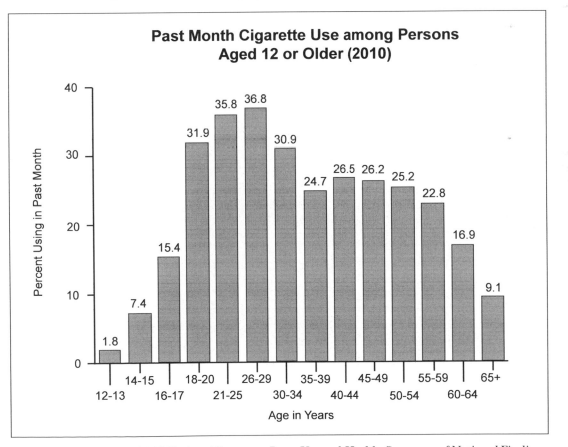

Source: Results from the 2010 National Survey on Drug Use and Health: Summary of National Findings, Substance Abuse and Mental Health Services Administration (SAMHSA)

FURTHER READING

Al-Sahab, Ban, et al. "Prevalence of Smoking during Pregnancy and Associated Risk Factors among Canadian Women: A National Survey." *BMC Pregnancy and Childbirth* 10 (2010): 24–29. Print. Discusses smoking trends during pregnancy and related risk factors among Canadian women.

Centers for Disease Control and Prevention. "Cigarette Smoking among Adults and Trends in Smoking Cessation—United States, 2008." *Morbidity and Mortality Weekly Report* 58.44 (2009): 1227–32. Print. Reports on trends in cigarette smoking and attempts to quit the habit.

---. "Vital Signs: Current Cigarette Smoking among Adults Aged ≥18 Years—United States, 2009." *Morbidity and Mortality Weekly Report* 59.35 (2010): 1135–40. Print. Provides statistics on adults and cigarette smoking.

Dresler, Carolyn. "The Tobacco Epidemic." *Principles and Practice of Lung Cancer: The Official Reference Text of the IASLC.* Eds. H. I. Pass et al. 4th ed. Philadelphia: Wolters, 2010. Provides a historical and global overview of tobacco usage and its effect on health.

WEBSITES OF INTEREST

Campaign for Tobacco-Free Kids
http://www.tobaccofreekids.org

Centers for Disease Control and Prevention
http://www.cdc.gov/tobacco

Centers for Disease Control and Prevention: Tobacco Use and Pregnancy
http://www.cdc.gov/reproductivehealth/tobaccousepregnancy

Health Canada: Canadian Tobacco Use Monitoring Survey
http://www.hc-sc.gc.ca/hc-ps/tobac-tabac/research-recherche/stat/index-eng.php

See also: Smoking; Trends and statistics: Alcohol abuse; Trends and statistics: Behavioral addictions; Trends and statistics: Illegal drug use; Trends and statistics: Prescription drug abuse

Trichotillomania

CATEGORY: Psychological issues and behaviors
ALSO KNOWN AS: Compulsive hair pulling
DEFINITION: Trichotillomania is an impulse control disorder characterized by a compulsion to pull one's hair. It is thought to be a complex neurological-behavioral disorder.

CAUSES

The cause of trichotillomania is unclear. It is likely that it is caused by both environmental (learned) and biological factors. One possibility is that hair pulling is a learned response to increasing stress and that the act relieves that stress. Biological explanations are neurological in nature and focus mainly on an imbalance of neurotransmitters.

RISK FACTORS

Some indication exists that there may be a family history of trichotillomania. The disorder begins most commonly between the ages of six and thirteen years and is more often seen in girls. It typically appears in persons who are depressed, anxious, or stressed.

SYMPTOMS

Persons with trichotillomania generally show signs of depression, anxiety, or increasing stress. The obvious symptoms of trichotillomania involve hair pulling from the head, eyelashes, eyebrows, beard, or other area of the body.

The disorder is characterized by areas of baldness or by patches of hair just starting to grow. Persons with trichotillomania may play with their pulled hair or even eat it. In cases where enough hair is ingested, an intestinal obstruction may develop.

SCREENING AND DIAGNOSIS

A person with trichotillomania presents with hair loss. Differential diagnosis involves ruling out other causes of hair loss, including both congenital and acquired causes. When hair loss cannot be attributed to any other medical condition in a person who exhibits high levels of stress or anxiety, that person is evaluated to determine if he or she exhibits hair-pulling behavior on a regular basis. Such an individual is likely to be diagnosed with trichotillomania.

TREATMENT AND THERAPY

Because the causes of trichotillomania are not clearly understood, treatment can often be complicated. All treatments generally involve attempts at decreasing or managing stress, anxiety, and depression, which can affect trichotillomania. Specific treatments for trichotillomania can be either psychological or pharmacological in nature.

Psychological treatment involving cognitive-behavioral therapy seems to be most effective, although hypnosis and biofeedback have also been used. The most common type of cognitive-behavioral therapy used is habit reversal, in which the person is taught to attend to hair-pulling desires and to engage in a behavior that prevents the hair pulling.

Most of the medications that are used to treat trichotillomania block noradrenalin and serotonin reuptake in the brain. Effexor (venlafaxine) has been found most effective in treatment. Selective serotonin reuptake inhibitors and dopamine-blocking medications also have been investigated as treatment modalities. All of these potential pharmacological treatments deal with the regulation of neurotransmitters.

PREVENTION

The only real means of prevention involves diagnosing anxiety, stress, or depression prior to the onset of hair-pulling behavior. Treating the underlying condition may prevent this physical manifestation.

Robin Kamienny Montvilo, PhD

FURTHER READING

Keuthen, Nancy J., Dan J. Stein, and Gary A. Christenson. *Help for Hair Pullers: Understanding and Coping with Trichotillomania.* Oakland, CA: New Harbinger, 2001.

Penzel, Fred. *The Hair-Pulling Problem: A Complete Guide to Trichotillomania.* New York: Oxford UP, 2003.

Walther, Michael R., et al. "Recent Advances in the Understanding and Treatment of Trichotillomania." *Journal of Cognitive Psychotherapy* 24 (2010): 46–64. Print.

WEBSITES OF INTEREST

Trichotillomania Learning Center
http://www.trich.org

Trichotillomania Support Online
http://www.trichotillomania.co.uk

See also: Anxiety; Body modification addiction; Depression; DSM-IV criteria for behavioral addictions; Impulse control disorders; Kleptomania

Twelve-step programs for addicts

CATEGORY: Substance abuse

ALSO KNOWN AS: Mutual aid programs; self-help programs; recovery groups

DEFINITION: Twelve-step programs for addicts are self-help programs that provide active assistance and support to persons who are dependent on substances such as alcohol, cocaine, heroin, marijuana, narcotics, and nicotine, and to behaviors such as excessive eating, compulsive gambling, Internet addiction, and sex addiction.

PROGRAM TYPES

Alcoholics Anonymous (AA) was the first twelve-step program, and it was designed for alcoholics wishing to recover from their alcoholism. AA was launched in 1935 in Akron, Ohio, by two alcoholics, physician Bob Smith and businessman Bill Wilson. The official launch date was the first date of sobriety for Smith.

AA has an estimated 2 million members (1.2 million in the United States) in 160 countries, and white men represent the majority of members. The average age of the AA member is forty-seven years.

Other organizations for other types of addictions have modeled themselves on the twelve steps of AA. For example, Narcotics Anonymous (NA) was created in 1953 for persons addicted to narcotics. NA has an estimated 200,000 members in the United States and 131 other countries.

In 2009, NA surveyed about twelve thousand members and found that 58 percent are male. The largest percent (34 percent) was forty-one to fifty years of age, followed by those age fifty-one to sixty years (24 percent). Nearly one-half of the surveyed members learned about the existence of NA through treatment or counseling centers. The majority of NA members surveyed were white, and the average time that members had been clean from narcotic use was 9.1 years. Most NA members (61 percent) were employed.

Cocaine Anonymous (CA) was launched in 1982 and Marijuana Anonymous was created in 1987. Crystal Meth Anonymous debuted in 1992. These organizations offer meetings throughout the United States and other countries. Pills Anonymous (PA), launched in the latter part of the twentieth century (the exact date is unknown), is an organization for persons addicted to prescription drugs. PA has meetings in Arizona, California, Colorado, Illinois, Nevada, New York, and Virginia. Heroin Anonymous began in 2004 and offers meetings in Arizona, California, Illinois, Michigan, and Texas.

Overeaters Anonymous (OA) is a twelve-step group for persons with eating problems. The majority of members are white and female. In a 2010 survey of OA members, 44 percent said that food first became a problem for them as children. For example, 44 percent said that food first became a problem for them when they were between one and ten years of age, while 24 percent developed an overeating problem when they were from eleven to fifteen years of age. Most survey participants (95 percent) said they were compulsive eaters or overeaters. The broad majority (69 percent) said they had lost weight since they joined OA.

"My Name Is Andy and I'm an Alcoholic"
Many addicts deny that they are dependent on a substance or that they engage in a problematic behavior, so twelve-step groups help members to acknowledge the severity of their problems by asking them to provide their first name along with an admission of their addiction. It can be extremely difficult for the individual, who may have denied an active addiction for many years, to openly admit that he or she is an addict. However, acknowledgement and awareness are both crucial to working toward recovery.

All alcohol- and drug-related twelve-step groups promote complete abstinence from the problematic substance. Some persons are addicted to multiple substances, such as alcohol and cocaine, and they may wish to attend both AA and CA groups. Another twelve-step group, Dual Recovery Anonymous (DRA), is focused on persons with dual diagnoses.

According to research by addictions specialist Alexandre B. Laudet, who compared reasons for attendance at meetings for both AA and NA members, the key reason for attendance by AA members is support, acceptance, and fellowship (58 percent), followed by the organization's promotion of recovery and sobriety (41 percent). Among NA members, the key reasons are reversed: The promotion of recovery and

sobriety was most important (59 percent), followed by support, acceptance, and fellowship (33 percent).

In all twelve-step groups, no attendance is taken and no fees are charged; donations are accepted, however, to cover the cost of the meeting room. To protect the privacy of the participants and to insure they to return to the group, attendees are instructed to avoid talking to others outside the room about what was said by anyone during meetings.

Meetings are usually held every day; in some cities, meetings are available several times each day. Most meetings are open to anyone but some are open only to persons with the specific "problem" of the group. The goal of groups oriented to alcohol or drugs is lifelong abstinence from the substance. This emphasis on abstinence may be the key behind the success of members who are alcoholics or drug addicts because, in their personal and family lives, they may have strong associations with others who are heavy drinkers or alcoholics. Making new connections with those who do not drink or use drugs may provide the important social network that is needed and that was absent before the addict joined a twelve-step group.

Often, persons who have been sober for years continue to participate in twelve-step meetings because they still believe they are at risk for relapse. All attendees, regardless of length of sobriety, introduce themselves at meetings as addicts.

Furthermore, the twelve-step group is not meant to be a form of therapy. To that end, mental health professionals and physicians are banned from all meetings unless they are addicts themselves.

The Steps and the Traditions
The first step of all twelve-step groups is the acknowledgement of the individual's powerlessness over controlling the substance abuse or other problem. The steps are adapted to the particular organization. For example, CA's first step is the following: "We admitted we were powerless over cocaine and all other mind-altering substances—that our lives had become unmanageable."

The second step for all twelve-step programs is the acceptance that there is a greater power than the addict and that this power can help the addict restore stability to his or her life. The third step involves surrendering individual will and one's life to this higher power. The higher power may be God or some other higher power as defined by the individual. The next few steps involve making a moral inventory of one's life and admitting faults.

These other steps include listing persons who were harmed by the addict in the past and creating a plan to make amends to those persons, if possible. In addition, the person is expected to continue to review his or her life and admit to past wrongs. The final step of AA and other twelve-step groups is to carry the message to others who suffer from the same problem. Research by Maria E. Pagano and colleagues indicates that the behavior of helping others has the effect of decreasing the depressive symptoms of alcoholics.

Each twelve-step group has its own twelve traditions in addition to the twelve steps. For example, the first tradition encompasses the welfare of the group. CA's first tradition is "Our common welfare should come first; personal recovery depends upon CA unity." Another tradition is that the only requirement to join the organization is a desire to change (stop consuming alcohol, cocaine, or other drugs, or stop the problematic behavior). Other traditions are to carry the message of the group to others with the same problem and that anonymity is a vital principle of the organization. Each twelve-step group provides its own particular twelve steps and twelve traditions.

SPONSORS

Addicts who join twelve-step groups are matched with a sponsor, who is a sober member who has completed the twelve steps. The sponsor is available to the addict who feels a craving to drink, use drugs, or to perform the problematic behavior.

In addition, if the addict cannot resist the compulsion and uses alcohol or drugs or continues to engage in other addictive behaviors, then the sponsor is to be contacted immediately. Sponsors realize that relapses are common with addictive behavior, and they also know that such setbacks do not mean that the person can never overcome an addiction. Sponsors share these insights with the addict and help the person return to recovery and sobriety.

EFFECTIVENESS OF TWELVE-STEP GROUPS

Most twelve-step groups have not been studied or analyzed, with the exception of AA. Most studies of AA have concluded that the organization is effective with those alcoholics who stay with the program.

For example, researchers Rudolf H. Moos and Bernice Moos evaluated subjects who received assistance from AA compared with those who were untreated, looking at their success at one, three, eight, and sixteen years from their initial participation in AA. Moos and Moos found that subjects who had participated in AA for twenty-seven weeks or more had a significantly better outcome sixteen years later than those who did not participate for this length of time sixteen years earlier.

In another study, researcher Keith Humphreys and Rudolf H. Moos compared successes among 887 patients in twelve-step programs with 887 patients treated only with cognitive-behavior therapy (CBT), a form of therapy that helps a person to identify and challenge irrational thoughts contributing to the addiction.

After two years, both groups had about the same level of success. For example, 33.3 percent of the CBT group reported being free of substance-abuse-related problems, compared with 32.6 percent of the twelve-step group. In addition, 80.5 percent of the CBT group reported being free of psychiatric symptoms, compared with 81.6 percent of the twelve-step group. However, the twelve-step group had a significantly higher rate of abstinence than the CBT group (49.5 percent were abstinent, compared with 37 percent of the CBT group). The researchers also found that the overall costs were significantly lower for the subjects in the twelve-step group.

Some persons do not succeed with a twelve-step group or do not join in the first place. There may be many reasons for this. For example, the addict may not be ready to admit that he or she has a problem. Also, some persons are opposed to the higher power element of twelve-step groups, citing its religious overtones. Twelve-step organizations, however, deny any religious affiliation.

Furthermore, the twelve steps are sometimes understood by local groups to mean that no psychiatric drugs should be taken by members. As a result, persons with psychiatric problems may believe that the group does not regard them as "clean" if they take prescribed medications for their emotional or psychiatric illness. One solution is to join the twelve-step group DRA, which is focused on persons with dual diagnoses. Members are encouraged with certain suggestions, such as "Today I will be free of alcohol and other intoxicating drugs" and "Today I will follow a healthy plan to manage my emotional or psychiatric illness."

Christine Adamec, BA, MBA

FURTHER READING

Brook, David W., and Henry I. Spitz. *The Group Therapy of Substance Abuse.* New York: Haworth Medical, 2002. Examines the methods of group therapy in treating substance abuse addictions.

Gold, Michael S., and Christine Adamec. *The Encyclopedia of Alcohol Abuse and Alcoholism.* New York: Facts On File, 2010. Provides comprehensive information about medical and psychiatric issues related to alcoholism and alcohol abuse.

Gross, Michael. "Alcoholics Anonymous: Still Sober after 75 Years." *American Journal of Public Health* 100.12 (2010): 2361–63. Print. This source describes the evolution of Alcoholics Anonymous from its earliest days.

Humphreys, Keith, and Rudolf H. Moos. "Encouraging Posttreatment Self-Help Group Involvement to Reduce Demand for Continuing Care Services: Two-Year Clinical and Utilization Outcomes." *Focus* 5.2 (2007): 193–98. Print. Compares and contrasts the success rate of persons treated with cognitive-behavior therapy to those who used twelve-step groups.

Laudet, Alexandre B. "The Impact of Alcoholics Anonymous on Other Substance Abuse Related Twelve Step Programs." *Recent Developments in Alcohol* 18 (2008): 71–89. Print. This source discusses the origins of alcohol and drug programs based on the twelve-step program of Alcoholics Anonymous and compares patterns of attendance between the groups.

Moos, Rudolf, and Bernice S. Moos. "Participation in Treatment and Alcoholics Anonymous: A 16-Year Follow-Up of Initially Untreated Individuals." *Journal of Clinical Psychiatry* 16.6 (2006): 735–50. Print. This source followed up on the success rates of persons who participated in Alcoholics Anonymous.

Pagano, Maria E., et al. "Predictors of Initial AA-Related Helping: Findings from Project MATCH." *Journal of Studies on Alcohol and Drugs* 70.1 (2009): 117–25. Print. This study analyzed factors predictive among members of Alcoholics Anonymous who later helped other alcoholics, such as a greater number of meetings that were attended, a higher number of steps achieved, and a longer period of abstinence.

WEBSITES OF INTEREST

Alcoholics Anonymous
http://www.aa.org

Cocaine Anonymous
http://www.ca.org

Crystal Meth Anonymous
http://www.crystalmeth.org

Dual Recovery Anonymous
http://draonline.org

Gamblers Anonymous
http://www.gamblersanonymous.org

Heroin Anonymous
http://ww.heroin-anonymous.org

Marijuana Anonymous
http://www.marijuana-anonymous.org

Narcotics Anonymous
http://www.na.org

Nicotine Anonymous
http://nicotine-anonymous.org

Overeaters Anonymous
http://www.oa.org

Pills Anonymous
http://www.pillsanonymous.org

See also: Abstinence-based treatment; Alcohol abuse and alcoholism: Treatment; Alcoholics Anonymous; Cocaine Anonymous; Debtors Anonymous; Group therapy for substance abuse; Narcotics Anonymous; Outpatient treatment; Overeaters Anonymous; Sponsors; Support groups; Treatment methods and research; Twelve-step programs for family and friends

Twelve-step programs for family and friends

CATEGORY: Treatment

DEFINITION: Al-Anon family groups (including Alateen) and similar programs, including Nar-Anon, Co-Dependents Anonymous, and Adult Children of Alcoholics, use the meeting and twelve-step format developed by Alcoholics Anonymous to provide support and recovery for relatives and friends of alcoholics and addicts. The programs emphasize repairing the psychological damage caused to the relative or partner, not implementing the addict's recovery.

INTRODUCTION

Addictions of all descriptions exact a grievous emotional and physical toll on family members and close associates of the addict. People who live in close association with an addict for any considerable time develop patterns of behavior and ways of looking at the world that are decidedly maladaptive. Spouses, partners, parents, and children become socially isolated, frustrated, and discouraged at futile efforts to bring about reform in the loved one and they have difficulty identifying their own needs and desires and in taking reasonable steps to see that their needs are met. Depression and physical illnesses with a strong psychological component are common in this demographic.

There is a definite hereditary component to addiction that appears to be a combination of anomalies in brain chemistry that influence pleasure-seeking behavior and, in the case of alcoholism, differences in metabolism that reduce adverse consequences of excessive use in the early stages of the disease. Children and siblings of addicts are at high risk of becoming addicts themselves and can benefit from any program that reduces their chances of involvement. Growing up in an addicted environment also increases the likelihood that a person will select an addicted partner and remain in a destructive relationship, perpetuating the unhappy family cycle.

The term *addict* conjures an image of a person addicted to illegal street drugs, particularly heroin. However, in terms of impact on families, alcohol is the most common and most damaging substance of abuse; thus efforts to repair the damage caused by

addiction, whether through twelve-step programs or through psychiatric intervention, concentrate on alcoholism. This focus on alcoholism occurs because the use of hard drugs typically destroys relationships and breaks up families before a chronic pattern of dysfunctionality is established.

AL-ANON

Al-Anon was founded after Alcoholics Anonymous (AA), which itself was founded in 1935. Within a few years AA had established a small network of groups meeting regularly to share stories and achieve sobriety through working a series of twelve steps. Briefly, these steps involve admission of powerlessness, reliance on a higher power, identification of and admission of shortcomings, making restitution (when possible) to persons harmed, continuing to lead a sober and spiritual life, and carrying the message to current alcoholics.

The original AA membership was overwhelmingly male. At many meetings the wives would get together informally to discuss how to be supportive of their husbands' recovery and also to share experiences about the challenges they were facing in their own lives. Lois Wilson, wife of AA cofounder Bill Wilson, was active from the start in facilitating a New York group for wives and in corresponding with similar groups in other parts of the country. The first (1939) edition of *Alcoholics Anonymous* contains the chapters "to Wives" and "the Family Afterwards," incorporating some of Lois Wilson's experience and wisdom. These chapters, however, were written by Bill Wilson and emphasize how families can reinforce and support the man's sobriety rather than how to help with the emotional recovery of the wives of alcoholics.

As these groups evolved it became apparent that the twelve-step format also could be used to benefit the spouses of alcoholics, substituting "powerless over the alcoholic" for "powerless over alcohol." A woman working the twelve steps of what later became Al-Anon was encouraged to detach from her husband's addiction, abandon efforts to reform him, and concentrate on strengthening her own connection to a higher power, on identifying and trying to eliminate undesirable patterns of thought and behavior in her own life, and on making amends to people who had been harmed by her own actions.

In 1941, Lois Wilson began collaborating with Ann B., wife of an AA member who was unable to stay sober. Over the next ten years family groups developed under the guidance of the two women. Al-Anon became a formal organization in 1951. It has its own corporate structure, parallel to AA but entirely separate from it. In 1957, Bob, a California teenager with an alcoholic father, established the first group for young people, and in 1959 the Alateen Committee was formed within Al-Anon to coordinate groups for minor children of alcoholic parents. Alateen groups have an adult Al-Anon sponsor and usually meet at the same time and location as an established Al-Anon group.

As of 2003, Al-Anon had roughly 320,000 members worldwide, and Alateen about 15,000. The average Al-Anon member has been in the program for more than ten years. Members report an average of three alcoholics in their lives, with more than one-half currently having an alcoholic spouse and nearly one-half an alcoholic parent. In many cases the spouse is in recovery in AA. A significant number of Al-Anon members also attend AA for their own alcohol problems.

How Al-Anon Works

Like AA, Al-Anon is open to anyone with a desire to recover from the adverse effects of living with an alcoholic. There are no dues or fees for membership; the organization is supported through voluntary contributions and through the sale of literature. The first step for an individual is usually to locate and attend a meeting. There are online, telephone, and correspondence resources for people in small communities without Al-Anon meetings.

It is recommended that an individual get a sponsor, a person who has some experience with the program, to guide them through the twelve steps. Unlike AA, Al-Anon publishes a twelve-step workbook and a number of pamphlets with specific guidance and advice on psychological matters.

The membership is slowly changing, but Al-Anon remains a mostly female fellowship of partners and former partners of alcoholics.

There is a common misconception that Al-Anon exists to help a spouse, sibling, or parent get an alcoholic loved one sober, and that Al-Anon will provide some "magic formula" or will help to organize an intervention. This is not the case. Al-Anon provides hope for leading a stable and happy life despite damage done by the alcoholic; it is up to the alcoholic to seek his or her own recovery.

Other Programs

There exists a plethora of twelve-step programs for addressing myriad addictions, compulsive behaviors, and miscellaneous life problems. None is as widespread or successful as AA. At one time or another most of these programs have probably spawned a few coordinating family groups of their own, but the only groups with staying power are Nar-Anon, Co-Dependents Anonymous (CODA), and Adult Children of Alcoholics (ACOA). Addictive behaviors such as gambling and pornography often have alcohol abuse as a copathology, in which case Al-Anon is a useful resource.

Nar-Anon, for family members of hard-drug addicts, filed articles of incorporation in 1971 and established a world service office in 1976. Meetings are held mainly in urban areas in the United States. Members are more likely to be parents and siblings of addicts than spouses of addicts, and the problems addressed can include extensive legal involvement.

First published in 1965, Al-Anon Faces Alcoholism *reflects the organization of* Al-Anon *itself by presenting firsthand accounts of both professionals in the treatment of alcoholism and Al-Anon members.* (Arkent Archive)

ACOA, founded in New York City in 1976, has about forty thousand members worldwide. The goal of ACOA membership is emotional sobriety. The organization publishes a variety of literature, including a "big book," collections of personal stories, and a step workbook.

CODA is a twelve-step format fellowship of people whose problems in relationships stem from being raised in dysfunctional families. Its common purpose is to develop healthy relationships; members gather to support and share with each other in a journey of self-discovery and self-love. To the extent that the dysfunctionality of the family stemmed from addictive behavior, CODA can help a person from an addictive background.

Although they still follow the twelve-step format, ACOA and CODA deemphasize the need for personal reform that characterizes AA and Al-Anon. Recovery tends to be an elusive concept, at least when compared with AA and Narcotics Anonymous. Although it may be questionable how much improvement the twelve-step approach produces in emotional health, many people find it sufficiently helpful to continue participating, and a twelve-step program has the advantage of being accessible to all at little to no cost.

Martha A. Sherwood, PhD

FURTHER READING

ACA World Services. *Adult Children: Alcoholic/Dysfunctional Families.* Torrance, CA: Author, 2006. A guide to using the twelve steps for emotional recovery, with a collection of personal narratives.

Al-Anon Family Groups. *How Al-Anon Works for Families and Friends of Alcoholics.* Virginia Beach, VA: Author, 2008. The Al-Anon "big book." Includes a description of the program and a collection of personal stories.

Borchert, William G. *The Lois Wilson Story: When Love Is Not Enough.* Center City, MN: Hazelden, 2005. Biography of Lois Wilson, the founder of Al-Anon.

Rivinus, Timothy M., ed. *Children of Chemically Dependent Parents: Multiperspectives from the Cutting Edge.* New York: Brunner, 1991. Emphasizes treatment centers and psychotherapy. Discusses ACOA and Alateen.

Zajdow, Grazna. *Al-Anon Narratives: Women, Self-Stories, and Mutual Aid.* Westport, CT: Greenwood, 2002. A feminist sociological study based on interviews with Australian Al-Anon members.

WEBSITES OF INTEREST

Adult Children of Alcoholics
http://www.adultchildren.org

Al-Anon and Alateen
http://www.al-anon.alateen.org

Co-Dependents Anonymous
http://www.coda.org

Nar-Anon
http://www.nar-anon.org

See also: Group therapy for substance abuse; Sponsors; Support groups; Treatment methods and research; Twelve-step programs for addicts;

V

Valium

CATEGORY: Substances

ALSO KNOWN AS: Diazepam

DEFINITION: Valium is a benzodiazepine derivative drug used in treating a number of nervous system disorders. The drug has a calming effect on the body.

STATUS: Legal by prescription only

CLASSIFICATION: Schedule IV controlled substance

SOURCE: Pharmaceutical preparation in the laboratory

TRANSMISSION ROUTE: Oral as tablets, capsules, or liquid; parenteral as intravenous or intramuscular solution; rectal suppositories; inhalation as an aerosolized vapor

HISTORY OF USE

Valium, the brand name of diazepam, was invented in the 1950s by Leo Sternbach of the pharmaceutical company Hoffmann-La Roche and was released for medical purposes in 1963. As a benzodiazepine drug, Valium acts on the central nervous system to enhance the effects of the neurotransmitter gamma-amino butyric acid, producing a sedative effect on the body.

Valium quickly became a popular prescription drug, as physicians prescribed it for anxiety and panic disorders, insomnia, and (as an anticonvulsant) acute seizures. It is also often used in medicating patients with anxiety prior to surgery and for procedures such as endoscopy.

Valium can be used in the short-term to treat persons exhibiting withdrawal from alcohol and hallucinogenic drugs, and for persons living with the results of spinal cord injuries and strokes. It also is sometimes used in the treatment of vertigo and in persons with Ménière's disease.

A pronounced risk of drug dependence exists with prolonged (four to six weeks) use of Valium. For this reason, its use has decreased since the 1980s, with many doctors prescribing safer alternatives for patients with conditions requiring benzodiazepine derivatives. Persons coming off long-term treatment with Valium should have their dosage gradually decreased to avoid benzodiazepine withdrawal syndrome, which can cause acute depression and cognitive deficits.

EFFECTS AND POTENTIAL RISKS

There are many potential side effects of Valium, and risk increases with its use in long-term treatment. Side effects include nervousness, irritability, panic disorder, sedation or insomnia, increased suicidal and self-harming tendencies, confusion, amnesia, dizziness, and nausea. Side effects seem to be more pronounced among children and the elderly. If taken during the third trimester of pregnancy, Valium can lead to potentially serious problems in newborns, including floppy infant syndrome, sedation, and respiratory distress.

Tolerance to and dependence on Valium are common. Withdrawal from Valium mimics that of alcohol withdrawal, with symptoms ranging from mild or severe and including seizures and psychotic episodes. There also is a risk of overdose, particularly when Valium is combined with depressant medications or with alcohol.

Lenela Glass-Godwin, MS

FURTHER READING

Ben-Porath, Denise D., and Stuart P. Taylor. "The Effects of Diazepam (Valium) and Aggressive Disposition on Human Aggression: An Experimental Investigation." *Addictive Behaviors* 27 (2002): 167–77. Print.

De Wit, H., J. Pierri, and C. E. Johanson. "Reinforcing and Subjective Effects of Diazepam in Nondrug-Abusing Volunteers." *Pharmacology, Biochemistry, and Behavior* 33 (1989): 205–13. Print.

"Drug Abuse and Addiction: Benzodiazepines." *Cleveland Clinic: Current Clinical Medicine.* 2nd ed. Cleveland, OH: Elsevier, 2010.

Martin, Elizabeth. *An A to Z of Medicinal Drugs.* New York: Oxford UP, 2010.

WEBSITES OF INTEREST

Benzo.org
http://www.benzo.org.uk/manual/bzcha01.htm

Drugs.com
http://www.drugs.com/valium

MayoClinic.com
http://www.mayoclinic.com/health/drug-information/DR602809

See also: Anxiety; Anxiety medication abuse; Benzodiazepine abuse; Panic disorders and addiction; Prescription drug addiction: Overview

Veterans and addiction

CATEGORY: Social issues
DEFINITION: Combat-related stress disorders often leave military veterans vulnerable to alcohol and drug abuse. To address this vulnerability, military and civilian mental health specialists are seeking the best practices and implementing programs to support the emotional health of veterans.

COMBAT-RELATED STRESS DISORDERS

Battle trauma symptoms and substance abuse are not unique to veterans of wars and conflicts such as Operation Enduring Freedom (OEF) and Operation Iraqi Freedom. Veterans of World Wars I and II and of the Vietnam War also presented classic symptoms of post-traumatic stress disorder (PTSD). Researchers have been studying the disorder for decades.

According to a 2010 article in the journal *Behavioral Healthcare*, since the start of OEF in 2001, a minimum of 15 percent of US and 6.1 percent of Canadian military personnel have presented symptoms of PTSD or major depressive disorder. In a 2009 *Social Work* journal article, specialists pointed out that 25 percent of the more than 100,000 veterans treated by US Veterans Administration (VA) health services received a mental health disorder diagnosis. More than one-half of these veterans were diagnosed with both PTSD and a substance abuse disorder. In addition, an estimated 70 percent of homeless veterans have a substance addiction.

In their book *After the War Zone* (2008), Laurie B. Slone and Matthew J. Friedman recommend that military personnel with PTSD and substance abuse disorders be treated for both conditions concurrently. PTSD and substance abuse disorders are underdiagnosed among military servicemembers, largely because both disorders carry a heavy stigma in the military; if either condition is reported on one's medical record, the person likely will be excluded from pursuing a career in defense or law enforcement.

SUBSTANCE ABUSE TREATMENT

With a combat-related stress disorder, the servicemember's thoughts are overwhelmed by memories of battle trauma. Symptoms include anxiety, anger, depression, and chronic nightmares.

Since the start of OEF in 2001, specialists have become increasingly convinced that addiction among veterans is directly related to the stresses of deployment and combat and that the treatment of substance abuse disorders among war veterans must occur in tandem with treatment for combat-related stress disorders like PTSD. Furthermore, specialists found that recovery strategies should involve psychological therapy, should address spiritual issues, and should focus on relaxation techniques and anger management. Because PTSD and substance abuse are chronic and dangerous disorders that are extremely difficult to treat, veterans, their family members, and care specialists should expect follow-up therapies, such as twelve-step and other support programs, to continue for several years following initial treatment.

According to a 2010 article in the journal *Addiction Professional*, more veterans are seeking treatment at the community level, rather than receiving services through the VA. Servicemembers and veterans experience a degree of distrust in relying on the government to treat their conditions, so, knowing that military personnel and veterans are more inclined to seek help outside the military structure, the VA is seeking to partner with community resources. Treatment strategies include support groups, impulse-control programs, and soldiers-helping-soldiers programs, in which soldiers are trained to help their peers in dealing with combat-related stress. According to a June 2010 poll by *Addiction Professional*, more than 90 percent of respondents believed there is a shortage of community-based assistance for combat veterans, many citing the lack of PTSD treatment.

The man pictured here, a former seal in the Navy who fought in Afghanistan and Iraq, undergoes treatment for PTSD and drug addiction, February 9, 2007 at the "Better Tomorrow" treatment center in Murrieta, California. He has struggled with mixing back into civilian life after serving six years in the navy. (Getty Images)

OUTLOOK

Knowing the potential for veterans to tap the services of community mental health providers rather than government services, the US government seeks to raise awareness of the specific mental health issues affecting veterans. In 2006, the Substance Abuse and Mental Health Services Administration and Treatment Communities of America held the National Behavioral Health Conference on Returning Veterans and Their Families to facilitate the partnership of government VA services with mental health practitioners and specialists in the private sector.

In July 2010, the US National Institutes of Health announced the approval of $6 million in federal funding to support research by institutions in eleven US states specializing in substance abuse among military personnel, veterans, and their families. The National Institute on Drug Abuse partnered with the VA to award grants earmarked for investigating the links

between deployment and combat-related trauma with the prevalence of substance abuse, mainly among veterans returning from the wars in Iraq and Afghanistan.

Melissa Walsh

FURTHER READING

Enos, Gary A. "Doing Whatever It Takes: Treatment Programs Try to Employ a Full Arsenal to Meet the Complex Needs of Veterans." *Addiction Professional* 8.4 (2010): 16. Print.

Hambley, Janice M., and Anne Pepper. "An Assault on Trauma and Addiction: Returning Military Personnel Often Carry Hidden Wounds That Need Intensive, Long-Term Addiction Treatment." *Behavioral Healthcare* 30.9 (2010).

Peters, Katherine McIntire. "Agencies Examine Combat-Related Substance Abuse." 26 Aug. 2010. Web. 10 Apr. 2012. http://www.govexec.com/

defense/2010/08/agencies-examine-combat-related-substance-abuse/32231.

Savitsky, Laura, Maria Illingworth, and Megan DuLaney. "Civilian Social Work: Serving the Military and Veteran Populations." *Social Work* (2009): 327.

Schneider, Mary Ellen. "Long Tours Put Vets at Greater Risk for PTSD, Substance Abuse." *Internal Medical News* (2009): 37.

Slone, Laurie B., and Matthew J. Friedman. *After the War Zone: A Practical Guide for Returning Troops and Their Families.* Cambridge, MA: DaCapo, 2008.

Volkow, Nora D. "Substance Abuse among Troops, Veterans, and Their Families." *NIDA Notes* 22.5 (2009). Web. 26 Mar. 2012. http://www.drugabuse.gov/news-events/nida-notes/2009/11/substance-abuse-among-troops-veterans-their-families.

WEBSITES OF INTEREST

NotAlone.com
http://www.notalone.com

National Center for PTSD
http://www.ptsd.va.gov

Substance Abuse and Mental Health Services Administration
http://www.samhsa.gov/militaryfamilies

See also: Elderly and addictions; Military and substance abuse; Post-traumatic stress disorder and addiction

Vicodin

CATEGORY: Substances

ALSO KNOWN AS: Hydrocodone bitartrate/acetaminophen; Lortab; Norco

DEFINITION: Vicodin is a prescription painkiller with a significant risk for dependence and abuse. The drug affects the central nervous system and smooth muscle through multiple actions to relieve moderate to moderately severe pain. The drug may prompt drowsiness, changes in mood, and mental clouding.

STATUS: Legal with a prescription

CLASSIFICATION: Schedule III controlled substance

SOURCE: Semisynthetic combination of hydrocodone and acetaminophen

TRANSMISSION ROUTE: Oral ingestion, sniffed as a powder form, injected intravenously when mixed with water

HISTORY OF USE

The combination of hydrocodone and acetaminophen as Vicodin was approved by the US Food and Drug Administration for use as a brand-name oral prescription marketed by Abbott in 1983. Nonmedical Vicodin use has risen and is of great concern to the medical, public health, drug abuse prevention, and law enforcement fields. Many people unintentionally become hooked on the drug after they receive a prescription for the drug to address specific pain.

Abusers without prescriptions buy painkillers illegally on the street; steal from pharmacies, doctors, or dentists; or steal from family or friends who may be taking the drug as prescribed. According to the 2009 National Survey on Drug Use and Health, 16 million persons age twelve years and older have taken a prescription painkiller for a nonmedical reason one or more times during the survey year.

EFFECTS AND POTENTIAL RISKS

In addition to providing temporary pain relief, Vicodin has the potential to produce many adverse reactions. It may prompt drowsiness, mood changes, impairment of mental and physical abilities, itchiness, lightheadedness, dizziness, sedation, nausea, vomiting, anxiety, and fear. Vicodin may be habit forming and can lead to abuse, addiction, physical dependence, and tolerance. At high doses, Vicodin can affect the respiratory, dermatological, and gastrointestinal systems.

Vicodin should not be taken concomitantly with alcohol and other central nervous system (CNS) depressants, such as antihistamines, antipsychotics, or antianxiety agents. The combination may produce an additive CNS depression.

The safety and effectiveness of Vicodin in children has yet to be determined. Pregnant women should not take Vicodin unless the potential benefit justifies the potential risk to the fetus. Regular use of opioids by pregnant women could cause the fetus to be born physically dependent on the drug. For mothers who are breastfeeding, acetaminophen is excreted in small amounts in breast milk, although it is unknown if hydrocodone is secreted also. Use of Vicodin should be avoided in these cases because of the potential for serious adverse reactions in infants, although in deciding, one should consider the importance of the drug to the mother. Dosing of Vicodin in geriatric patients should be moderated as well.

Patrice La Vigne

FURTHER READING

Gwinnell, Esther, and Christine Adamec. *The Encyclopedia of Drug Abuse.* New York: Facts On File, 2008.

Karsmeyer, Pamela, and Henry R. Kranzler. *Encyclopedia of Drugs, Alcohol, and Addictive Behavior.* 3rd ed. Detroit: Macmillan, 2009.

Katz, N., et al. "Internet-Based Survey of Nonmedical Prescription Opioid Use in the United States." *Clinical Journal of Pain* 24 (2008): 528–35. Print.

WEBSITES OF INTEREST

Drugs.com
http://www.drugs.com/vicodin

National Institute on Drug Abuse
http://www.nida.nih.gov

US Food and Drug Administration
http://www.fda.gov

See also: Codeine; Hydrocodone; Morphine; Narcotics abuse; Narcotics: Short- and long-term effects on the body; Opioid abuse; Oxycodone; Painkiller abuse; Prescription drug addiction: Overview; Soma; Tramadol

W

War on Drugs

CATEGORY: Diagnosis and prevention

DEFINITION: The War on Drugs began in 1971 as a comprehensive domestic and foreign campaign by the US government to stop the production, distribution, and use of illegal drugs. The campaign, although effective to some degree, has been criticized for its handling of foreign affairs. Since 2009, however, the government has refrained from using the term to describe its antidrug policies.

BACKGROUND

There are two early, especially potent images from the campaign of the War on Drugs: the determined US first lady Nancy Reagan in her red dress and pearls leading the charge to a drug-free America (through the Just Say No campaign) and the infamous television commercial showing two eggs frying and an ominously voiced narrator warning that the frying eggs are what the "brain looks like on drugs." These images are part of a one-hundred-year struggle between illicit drugs and the US government.

In the late nineteenth century and early twentieth century, there was no recognized drug problem in the United States. Cocaine, heroin, laudanum, opium, tobacco, and alcohol, for example, were legal. After the beginning of the twentieth century, drug addiction and alcohol abuse were seen as personal issues, not concerns for the federal government. At the core of early antidrug thinking were widespread racist beliefs about certain drugs and their potential effects on minority groups. However, there were also legitimate concerns. The drug laudanum, for example, caused increasing rates of addiction among middle-class women who were prescribed the drug for menstrual cramps. Some regulations were necessary. The government's first attempt at regulation, restriction, and revenue was the Harrison Narcotics Tax Act of 1914.

The next attempt to control substance use was the 1919 National Prohibition Act, which made it illegal to manufacture, sell, and consume alcohol. Despite the government's attempt to control the public's thirst for alcohol during Prohibition, more people began to drink, deaths from alcohol poisoning increased, and the law ushered in a golden age of crime, starting the careers of some of the most infamous gangsters. There were profits to be made in bootlegging, prostitution, and illegal gambling houses, where the choice beverage was alcohol. Finally, Prohibition was lifted in 1933.

Attention to drug use waxed and waned throughout the next few decades, as politics dictated. In 1937, marijuana became a political issue and candidates used sentiment against marijuana in their campaigns. President Franklin D. Roosevelt showed some interest in the drug issue, as did President Dwight D. Eisenhower, but it was not until the 1960s that the issue of drugs and politics become critically enmeshed.

By the 1960s, drug use had become more acceptable, especially among white, middle-class youths, and particularly among those protesting the Vietnam War. The government was ineffectual at controlling drug use. President Lyndon B. Johnson created the Bureau of Narcotics and Dangerous Drugs in 1968 to consolidate several government agencies in an attempt to get some results. In 1969, Operation Intercept was formed at the Mexican border, which involved a plan to search every car entering the United States. The goal was to disrupt the Mexican drug trade, but the operation failed and was abandoned after less than three weeks.

In 1971, US president Richard M. Nixon, inspired by the ordeal of Vietnam veterans returning to the United States addicted to drugs, launched the antidrug campaign called the War on Drugs. Nixon declared drugs "public enemy number one." One of the first steps of the War on Drugs was Operation Golden Flow, which administered urine tests to all servicemen; only 4.5 percent were positive. The operation was declared a success. Nixon then founded one of his most enduring legacies: the US Drug Enforcement Administration in 1973 to work as a "super agency" to oversee all federal-level work related to illegal drugs in the United States.

US president George H. W. Bush took the War on Drugs to a different level. He tasked the Central Intelligence Agency and the US military in foreign antidrug "missions" and created the Office of National Drug Control Policy (ONDCP) to centralize all drug-related activity. The director of the ONDCP was known colloquially as the "drug czar."

MISSION AND GOALS

The mission of the War on Drugs is to reduce the production, distribution, and usage of all illegal drugs. Domestically, this mission has been consistent. Manufacturers, dealers, and users remain targets of arrest and imprisonment.

Since the administration of US president Ronald Reagan, the War on Drugs has faced a great deal of criticism for, among other actions, its harsh sentencing of offenders who were "holding," that is, arrested and imprisoned for possession of small amounts of drugs. Of persons arrested for drug use in the United States, about one-quarter are arrested for marijuana possession, not for distribution. This is significant for several reasons.

Many opponents of this harsh sentencing policy argue that not all drugs and, hence, legal punishments, are handled equally by the law. For example, possession of small amounts of marijuana (for example, a few marijuana cigarettes, or joints) should not be considered as equally severe as possession of heroin or cocaine, which are much more potent and, many would argue, dangerous drugs. Thus, the penalties, critics argue, should be relative to the crime. Prison sentences for "hard" drugs such as heroin and cocaine should be lengthier than prison sentences for "softer" drugs such as marijuana.

Critics of the War on Drugs have also pointed to the ways in which these harsh sentencing policies have disproportionately affected African Americans and Hispanic Americans. According to 2001 data from the Substance Abuse and Mental Health Services Administration, Caucasian Americans accounted for seventy-six percent of current drug users (those who reported drug use within the past month), but made up only ten percent of those serving time for a drug-related offense. Conversely, African Americans represented only 13.5 percent of drug users and Hispanic Americans less than 9 percent. Nevertheless, black and Hispanic Americans made up more than 90 percent of all persons jailed for a drug charge. According to the

Drug Policy Alliance, although African Americans represent less than 14 percent of all drug users, they make up 37 percent of persons arrested for drug possession, 55 percent of all persons convicted for a drug-related offense, and 74 percent of all persons imprisoned for drugs.

Another issue concerns prison reform, specifically for drug offenders. Many persons involved in reforming the prison system, including those who run the prisons, do not believe drug users should be incarcerated with violent criminals. Instead, they believe that drug users should be kept separate from the general population and should receive treatment for their addictions and substance abuse. Many prisons are taking steps to work with incarcerated men and women to help them through detoxification and to find placement in an appropriate treatment center following their release.

At the international level, the antidrug actions of the United States in regard to the War on Drugs began to change in the late 1970s, when drug cartels from Central America, South America, and Mexico began to blur the lines of what action should be taken, and against whom. During the Reagan and Bush administrations the message to the public appeared to be clear: "Say nope to dope." However, the government had another agenda when it came to foreign policy, an agenda that ran counter to the domestic War on Drugs.

Major foreign drug arrests had already taken place in Marseilles, France (for example, the French connection bust in 1972), and in Colombia, with the 1975 seizure of 600 kilograms of cocaine. This Colombian bust was the largest drug seizure ever made at the time, and came to be known as the "Medellin massacre" following the brutal reprisals of the Medellin drug cartel, which murdered forty people in revenge. However, despite these major drug arrests, the rise of the Medellin cartel dominated the drug scene of the 1980s. The vast majority of those working to control the Medellin cartel worked in earnest, but the CIA had another agenda. This is where the War on Drugs and the Cold War came in direct conflict.

The battlefield where this war took place was primarily Nicaragua, where the Leftist Sandinistas were in a long-term battle with the pro-right Contras. During various operations, the CIA funded the Contras with full knowledge that the Contras had direct connections to drug traffickers such as Panamanian president Manual Noriega. In the 1980s, all of these secret connections exploded, as the Medellin cartel was in disarray and Noriega was sent to prison in Miami, Florida, for drug trafficking.

During this time too, the infamous Iran-Contra affair was uncovered. The affair was revealed to be a complicated arms-for-hostages negotiation with Iran, with the ultimate US goal of delivering profits to the known drug-running Contras. The Iran-Contra affair was a low point in public support for the War on Drugs.

Since about 1990, the tone of the War on Drugs has changed, both by the government and by society in general. Many people have come to accept the concept that drug addiction is a chronic brain disease instead of the result of moral deficits, and the majority of Americans no longer demonize drug use. The movement to legalize or decriminalize marijuana, for example, is no longer at the fringe but is a legitimate political movement that has even found a place on voting ballots in several US states. In 2009, under the administration of US president Barack Obama, the director of the ONDCP, R. Gil Kerlikowske, said that the phrase *war on drugs* will no longer be used because it is now believed to be counterproductive.

S. M. Willis, MS, MA

FURTHER READING

Duke, Steven B., and Albert C. Gross. *America's Longest War: Rethinking Our Tragic Crusade against Drugs.* New York: Putnam, 1993. A discussion of the effects antidrug policies have had financially, to the police departments, the penal system, and the health care system.

Miller, Richard Lawrence. *Drug Warriors and Their Prey.* Westport, CT: Praeger, 1996. A thorough examination of how the War on Drugs challenged the civil rights of ordinary citizens and how antidrug policies have led to the loss of civil liberties.

Rolles, Stephen. "An Alternative to the War on Drugs." *British Medical Journal* 341 (2010): 127–28. Print. Discussion of alternative methods of drug regulation.

WEBSITES OF INTEREST

Office of National Drug Control Policy
http://www.whitehousedrugpolicy.gov

United Nations Office on Drugs and Crime
http://www.unodc.org

US Drug Enforcement Administration
http://www.justice.gov/dea

See also: Education about substance abuse; Just Say No campaign; Law enforcement and drugs; Prevention methods and research

Withdrawal

Category: Physiology
Definition: Withdrawal is a physical reaction that occurs if a substance-dependent person suddenly stops using drugs or alcohol. This can occur if the person has been using drugs or alcohol regularly. Depending on the type of substance and the length of use, withdrawal can be a life-threatening condition. The sooner it is treated, the better the outcome.

CAUSES AND SYMPTOMS

Withdrawal can be caused by medicines, alcohol, or illegal drugs. The factors that increase the chances of developing withdrawal symptoms are a history of substance abuse, the sudden stopping of drugs or alcohol, and physical dependency on drugs or alcohol. Symptoms vary and are based on the substance used or abused. Symptoms may include loss of appetite, shaking, hallucinations, weight loss, sleeplessness, irritability, and abdominal pain and cramps.

TREATMENT AND THERAPY

There are several treatment options for withdrawal, such as detoxification and rehabilitation. Detoxification is the first step in treating substance abuse. Patients will be closely checked for signs of withdrawal and possibly be given medicines to reduce cravings. These medicines will also help with symptoms, which can be severe for withdrawal. Treatment is targeted to the specific symptoms and drugs used.

Rehabilitation is a form of treatment that uses behavioral therapy to prevent patients from using drugs or alcohol in the future. Behavior therapy may involve cognitive-behavioral therapy, which teaches

---

Symptoms of Withdrawal by Substance of Abuse

- Marijuana—loss of appetite, chills, weight loss, trouble sleeping or sleeping too much, irritability, feeling restless or nervous

- Alcohol—shaking, hallucinations, seizures, confusion, anxiety, sweating, nausea

- Barbiturates—weakness, tremors, hallucinations, lack of appetite, seizures

- Opioids—abdominal pain or cramps, muscle aches, panic, tremors, sweating, nausea, diarrhea, fever, chills, irritability, goose pimples, runny nose, drug craving, inability to sleep, yawning

- Benzodiazepines—abdominal pain or cramps, fast heartbeat, vomiting, tremors, seizures, anxiety

- Cocaine—anxiety, fatigue and tiredness, depression

- Amphetamine—depression, irritability, oversleeping, muscle aches, abdominal pain

---

recovering drug users how to recognize and avoid situations that may lead to drug abuse; family therapy, which helps patients and their families to understand patterns of drug abuse and teaches strategies to avoid future abuse; and motivational therapy, which uses positive reinforcement to prevent drug use.

Sometimes, residential treatment is necessary. The typical stay is between six and twelve months. Residential facilities will instruct on how to live a drug- or alcohol-free life. In addition, recovery groups offer continued support for a drug- or alcohol-free life. Some support groups are Narcotics Anonymous, Cocaine Anonymous, and Alcoholics Anonymous.

Patricia Griffin Kellicker, BSN

FURTHER READING

Giannini, James A. "An Approach to Drug Abuse, Intoxication and Withdrawal." *American Family Physician* 61.9 (2000): 2763–2774. A biopsychiatric model of the symptomatic effects of drug abuse.

Organizes symptoms around neurotransmitter activity.

National Institute on Drug Abuse. *Principles of Drug Addiction Treatment: A Research-Based Guide.* 2nd ed. Rockville, MD: US DHHS, National Institutes of Health (NIH) Publication No. 09-4180, 2009. Acknowledges that drug addiction is a disease and provides information for effective treatment.

O'Connor, Patrick G. "Methods of Detoxification and Their Role in Treating Patients with Opioid Dependence." *Journal of the American Medical Association* 294.8 (2005): 961–963. Covers detoxification and maintenance treatments for opioid-dependent patients so that they become opioid-free.

Professional Guide to Diseases. 9th ed. Ambler, PA: Lippincott Williams & Wilkins, 2008. Comprehensive clinical coverage of over six hundred disorders, including their causes, symptoms, diagnosis, and treatment.

WEBSITES OF INTEREST

National Institute on Drug Abuse
http://www.drugabuse.gov

Substance Abuse & Mental Health Services Administration
http://www.samhsa.gov/

See also: Alcohol: Short- and long-term effects on the body; Anhedonia; Baclofen; Cocaine use disorder; Methadone; Narcotics: Short- and long-term effects on the body; Physiological dependence; Symptoms of substance abuse

---

Women and behavioral addictions

CATEGORY: Social issues

DEFINITION: Behavioral addictions are addictions to activities such as gambling, shopping, eating, exercising, sex, working, or using the Internet. In the case of behavioral addictions, what was originally a pleasurable activity manifests as a compulsion and results in excessive use with negative consequences. Women and men have different risk factors, responses, and incidences for these behavioral addictions.

STUDYING BEHAVIORAL ADDICTIONS IN WOMEN

Behavioral addictions can be just as harmful to overall health and well-being as a substance addiction to drugs or alcohol. A behavioral addiction typically begins when the performance of a certain action elicits a feeling of pleasure, decreases depression, eases anxiety, or allows escape from a problem. Eventually, the person feels a loss of control and consistently repeats the behavior.

Similar to a substance addiction, a behavioral addiction also comes with periods of withdrawal, urges or cravings, and dependence. Later research literature suggests that the resulting feeling of depression from the addiction does not get better as the behavioral addict ages. A woman in her thirties or forties, for example, with a predisposition to an addiction, will usually have an increase in her depression.

Certain behavioral addictions occur more frequently in women than in men. Women are more likely to develop shopping and exercising addictions. A study of college-aged women and men revealed that men are more likely to gamble and to excessively use the Internet and to watch television. However, the incidence of these behaviors in women is rising.

Behavioral and substance addictions are not mutually exclusive: A person may have more than one behavioral or substance addiction at any given time. Women and men have gender-specific risk factors for behavioral addiction. It is thought that there are underlying biological genetic predispositions that make women and men more prone to specific addictions. Furthermore, psychological diagnoses besides anxiety and depression are often present in any addict.

Women, however, are at risk for unique medical and health-related concerns from certain behavioral addictions. A compulsive sexual addiction places women at increased risk for unintended pregnancies or sexually transmitted diseases.

SPENDING ADDICTIONS

Compulsive shopping affects more women than men, with approximately 5 percent of women having the diagnosis. The negative consequences include financial debt and an excess of unused purchases.

Risk factors for compulsive shopping include episodes of anxiety or depression. An additional risk factor is the widespread availability of the Internet, which allows for purchases to be made at any moment. Although an immediate positive feeling results with shopping, the addict eventually cycles back to the initial feelings of depression and anxiety; feelings of guilt may also arise after the purchases.

Women with a shopping addiction also commonly have other substance or behavioral addictions, or both. In particular, concurrent shopping and food addictions are common. For example, obese women who binge eat have greater rates of compulsive shopping than women who are not binge eaters.

Although pathological gambling addictions used to be considered a condition only affecting men, the number of women who pathologically gamble is on the rise: Approximately 25 percent of gambling addictions now occur in women. Women begin gambling at a later age, but the disorder progresses more rapidly in women. One-half of persons seeking treatment for gambling addictions are women.

Casino gambling activities for women typically include playing a slot machine or bingo alone rather than with others at a betting table or other game table. Also, specific websites target female gamblers, thereby increasing their access to solo gambling, and women can gamble in the home, away from casinos. Many women also find it socially acceptable to gamble with friends or colleagues in a sporting pool.

Women also have different psychological and physiological responses to gambling. While men try to attain the high positive feeling of a win, women typically gamble to achieve more of an emotionally deadened feeling and to forget about life's problems. Women also gamble because winning can help their self-esteem.

COMPULSIVE SEXUAL BEHAVIOR AND INTERNET ADDICTIONS

Compulsive sexual behavior, often termed *sex addiction* or *hypersexuality*, involves obsessive sexual thoughts, feelings, or behaviors that interfere with routine functions. Initial studies focused on men and sexual predators because of a failure of clinicians to recognize the addiction in women and because of a failure in women to admit a sex addiction themselves. Oftentimes, feelings of guilt, shame, and isolation keep women from sharing their stories of sex addiction, contributing to under-diagnosis of the disorder.

Women also have different symptoms of sex addiction than do men. The addiction for men is associated with pornography, masturbation, and meaningless sexual relationships. Women may display these behaviors but much less frequently. Instead, relationship or love addictions are much more common among women.

Women who have compulsive sex addictions frequently have a history of sexual abuse or molestation. This type of trauma can lead to the additional diagnosis of post-traumatic stress disorder (PTSD) or an eating disorder. With sex addiction, women are reliving a painful part of their childhood and searching for the security that these traumas will not recur. Many professionals, however, treat the PTSD or eating disorder only and fail to recognize or address the behavioral addiction.

With regard to Internet use, women typically use the web to create relationships with others and to establish emotional bonds that are not available in their community. They may or may not seek sexual pleasure as part of these relationships. Rather than foster relationships online, men use the Internet as a coping mechanism for stress and to view pornography to avoid intimacy while still gaining sexual pleasure. Women also use the Internet to express a wide range of emotions, such as anger or aggression. These emotions may not be socially acceptable in their home environment or community. Internet use becomes an addiction when it interferes with daily functioning and with interpersonal relationships.

TREATMENT

It is integral for psychotherapists to address the reason for the behavioral addiction and to provide methods to reduce its frequency. Cognitive-behavioral therapists and dialectical-behavioral therapists have been successful in treating these diagnoses. Some therapies involve the twelve steps modeled by Alcoholics Anonymous and other such treatment and recovery programs.

Family therapy is recommended too, especially if the woman is the primary caregiver or is being physically or emotionally abused. Addicts have a high rate of relapse because of the comorbid diagnosis of additional psychological diagnoses and other possible substance addictions.

Although specialty clinics now exist to handle specific behavioral addictions, services specializing in treating women with these disorders are lacking. Another lack is child care services for recovering addicts. Treatment centers that provide child care are crucial to allow the addict time to focus on her own recovery. It also may be necessary to combine psychotherapy with pharmacologic treatments for a comorbid psychological diagnosis.

A final barrier to treatment is the controversy over whether compulsive behaviors should actually be considered addictions and in the same category as substance addictions. Critics state that behavioral addictions are impulse control issues and not true addictions.

Treating psychologists should acknowledge and recognize these addictions nonetheless and should provide appropriate treatment. Although the *Diagnostic and Statistical Manual of Mental Disorders* (DSM) does not categorize behavioral addictions, these addictions have been proposed for the DSM's revision. Gambling might be listed as its own behavioral addiction, while other behavior types might be listed under the diagnosis of behavioral addiction not otherwise specified.

Janet Ober Berman, MS, CGC

FURTHER READING

Ferree, Marnie. "Females and Sex Addiction: Myths and Diagnostic Implications." *Sexual Addiction and Compulsivity* 8 (2001): 287–300. Print. Comprehensive review of compulsive sexual behavior in women that includes recommendations for diagnosing and treating the addiction.

Greenberg, Joshua, Stephen Lewis, and David Dodd. "Overlapping Addictions and Self-Esteem among College Men and Women." *Addictive Behaviors* 4.8 (1999): 565–71. Print. Study describes differences in the behavioral addictions between genders.

Holden, Constance. "Behavioral Addictions: Do They Exist?" *Science* 2 (2001): 980–82. Print. Discusses the scientific research behind behavioral addictions and the proposed biological mechanisms for each.

Hollen, Kathryn H. *Encyclopedia of Addictions.* 2 vols. Westport, CT: Greenwood, 2009. Covers various types of addictions, from substance abuse and eating disorders to gambling, pornography, and shopping.

Kuhn, Cynthia M., and George F. Koob, eds. *Advances in the Neuroscience of Addiction*. Boca Raton, FL: CRC, 2010. Discusses advancements in the psychological aspects of addiction at different levels, including genetics, behavioral, and psychological issues.

McVeigh, Tracy. "Britain's New Addicts: Women Who Gamble Online, at Home, and in Secret." 16 Jan. 2010. Web. 11 Apr. 2012. http://www.guardian.co.uk/uk/2010/jan/17/women-gamblers-online-addiction. Outlines the growing behavioral addiction of gambling in women and the unique reasons and risk factors in this population.

WEBSITES OF INTEREST

Emotions Anonymous
http://www.emotionsanonymous.org

Families Anonymous
http://www.familiesanonymous.org

Gamblers Anonymous
http://www.gamblersanonymous.org

Overeaters Anonymous
http://www.oa.org

Sex Addicts Anonymous
http://saa-recovery.org

See also: Behavioral addictions: Overview; Gambling addiction; Gaming addiction; Gender and addiction; Impulse control disorders; Internet addiction; Media and behavioral addictions; Sex addiction; Shopping/spending addiction; Women and smoking; Women and substance abuse; Work issues and behavioral addictions

Women and smoking

CATEGORY: Social issues

DEFINITION: Cigarette smoking in women is a growing public health concern because of the numerous unique medical implications in women and their children.

RISK FACTORS

Despite numerous media campaigns and medical efforts to educate the general population on the health hazards of smoking, the percentage of smokers remains high. In the United States, approximately one-sixth of all women are smokers, which translates into an estimated 23 million women. One report estimated that almost 30 percent of teenage girls in 2000 had smoked within the last month. Teen girls are more likely to have parents, family members, or peers who also smoke.

Most women smoke cigarettes rather than pipes, but cigar use is becoming more widespread. Women in general begin smoking for a number of reasons, many of them social and cultural. These reasons include starting smoking because of the perception that it will help them maintain a slim weight, because they are rebelling against authority figures such as parents or teachers, and because of peer pressure or depression. Men typically begin smoking to obtain status as a "cool" or popular person or to manage stress.

Educational and ethnic disparities exist among female smokers. Cigarette smoking is more common among uneducated females than among those who completed high school or college. Women in the United States and other developed countries are more likely to smoke than women in developing countries. Women of American Indian and Alaskan descent have the highest rates of smoking when compared with women of Caucasian, African American, Hispanic, and Asian backgrounds.

HEALTH CONCERNS

The original studies of the 1960s documenting the health hazards of smoking were based solely on men because they were the predominant cigarette smokers of that era. As it became more socially acceptable for women to smoke, health experts came to recognize that women were experiencing health effects, such as lung cancer, which were similar to those of men; however, women also were experiencing previously unrecognized health concerns specific to women.

The US Department of Health, Education, and Welfare (now the Department of Health and Human Services) reported on these effects in 1980, as the US surgeon general issued the first groundbreaking report on the matter. Since this report was released, a wealth of new medical and scientific research has accumulated, showing, for example, that the health effects of cigarette smoking on women differ from men because of gender differences in body physiology and genetics. It has been suggested that women and men have different genetic predispositions to both initiating cigarette smoking and to developing gender-specific, smoking-related medical problems.

The most common health concern in smokers of either gender is lung cancer. The incidence of lung cancer has now surpassed the incidence of breast cancer as the leading cancer diagnosis in women. Smoking more frequently and for a long time increases the risk for developing lung cancer. The risk also exists for other lung diseases, such as chronic obstructive pulmonary disease, emphysema, and chronic bronchitis. While once thought to be a risk factor, smoking itself is not believed to play a role in the development of breast cancer, but women smokers are at increased risk for cancer of the cervix, bladder, mouth, larynx, pharynx, pancreas, esophagus, and kidney and for acute myeloid leukemia.

The second largest health danger among female smokers is the risk for cardiovascular disease, including coronary artery disease (CAD), stroke, other aneurysms, and peripheral vascular disease. Women who smoke have twice the risk for CAD as nonsmokers. The younger the woman, the more likely CAD is related to smoking; the risk for CAD is higher for heavy, long-term smokers.

Women who smoke and who take oral hormonal birth control pills have a higher risk for CAD, including blood clots, heart attacks, and strokes. The risk with oral contraceptives is even greater if the woman is older than thirty-five years of age; therefore, smoking is a contraindication to this form of birth control after this age.

EFFECTS ON THE MENSTRUAL CYCLE AND PREGNANCY

All women who are planning on conceiving or who are pregnant should discontinue cigarette smoking because of the scientifically established consequences on fertility and the developing fetus. Even with these risks, approximately 10 percent of women, especially teens and younger women, continue to smoke during pregnancy.

On average, women smokers take longer to conceive than do nonsmokers, both because of infertility and because of irregular menstrual cycles. Menstrual cycles may be absent or abnormal. Smokers

experience a decrease in ovulation, impairment of fertilization, and reduced implantation rates of the embryo in the uterus. Smokers also tend to have more vaginal infections.

When pregnancy is achieved, smokers have an increased risk for a miscarriage, stillbirth, or ectopic pregnancy because the tobacco chemicals, including nicotine, are transmitted to the fetus. Additional adverse pregnancy outcomes include a risk for low birth weight and preterm delivery. Maternal smoking also can cause a newborn or infant to have reduced lung function; this is observed with both prenatal and postnatal exposure. If a woman smokes during pregnancy, the nicotine inhaled will be detected in a newborn's bloodstream, and the newborn may go through nicotine withdrawal after delivery.

Smoking also is discouraged during breastfeeding because of the transfer of nicotine through breast milk. A newborn exposed to nicotine also is at an increased risk of sudden infant death syndrome. Overall, a fetus exposed to cigarette smoking in utero or a newborn exposed to secondhand smoke in the household has a higher risk of developing a common cold or other illness such as asthma or ear infections. Even though many women use their pregnancy as motivation to quit, a significant percentage resumes smoking after delivery.

Smoking also affects women before and in menopause. Women smokers enter menopause at a younger age than nonsmokers and may have more symptoms. They have decreased bone density, which places them at an increased risk for fractures. Older women have a greater chance for cataract development or rheumatoid arthritis. Women who smoke also tend to develop more skin wrinkles than do nonsmokers. Finally, lower levels of estrogen are noted in smokers.

PREVENTION AND SMOKING CESSATION

As women are now smoking for longer periods of time and in greater amounts, cigarette smoking has become a well-established risk factor for increased mortality. The US Centers for Disease Control and Prevention reports that cigarette smoking contributes to the deaths of an estimated 178,000 women in the United States annually. If smoking is discontinued, especially at a younger age, this risk decreases dramatically. Additional education on the prevention or discontinuation of cigarette use is critical.

Studies indicate that a majority of women want to quit smoking but either do not know how or feel they cannot do so because of stress, anxiety, or depression. Treatments for women to help them cope with a possible underlying psychological diagnosis or stressor are necessary for optimal outcome. Nicotine replacement therapies have been more successful in women than in men.

It also is recommended that women quit smoking at a specific point of the menstrual cycle. The urge to smoke is greatest during the time of premenstrual symptoms, so discontinuing use after these symptoms have subsided shows greater success.

Specific websites and support groups for women are now abundant. As with the overall general population, continued medical, media, and school involvement is key to educating girls and women about smoking and its consequences.

Janet Ober Berman, MS, CGC

FURTHER READING

Bailey, Beth A., et al. "Infant Birth Outcomes among Substance Using Women: Why Quitting Smoking during Pregnancy Is Just as Important as Quitting Illicit Drug Use." *Maternal and Child Health Journal* 9.2 (2011): 162–69. Print. Emphasizes the importance of discontinuing cigarette smoking during pregnancy. Focuses on infant weight gain.

Hamajima, N., et al. "Alcohol, Tobacco, and Breast Cancer—Collaborative Reanalysis of Individual Data from 53 Epidemiological Studies, Including 58,515 Women with Breast Cancer and 95,067 Women Without the Disease." *British Journal of Cancer* 18 (2002): 1234–45. Print. Large study demonstrating no increased risk for breast cancer among women smokers.

US Department of Health and Human Services. *The Health Consequences of Smoking for Women: A Report of the Surgeon General*. Washington, DC: DHHS, 1980. Initial report on women smokers and their specific health concerns. This report laid the groundwork for future studies on gender influences in smoking.

---. *Women and Smoking. A Report of the Surgeon General*. Atlanta: DHHS, 2001. Comprehensive report on the health concerns for women who smoke that includes vital statistics. Update of the initial 1980 report; summarizes the explosion of literature in the field.

WEBSITES OF INTEREST

American Cancer Society
http://www.cancer.org/Cancer/CancerCauses/TobaccoCancer/WomenandSmoking

Smokefree Women
http://women.smokefree.gov

See also: Gender and addiction; Media and smoking; Pregnancy and smoking; Smoking; Smoking: Short- and long-term effects on the body; Tobacco use disorder; Women and behavioral addictions; Women and substance abuse

Women and substance abuse

CATEGORY: Social issues
DEFINITION: The risk factors for substance abuse in women are different from those in men, and women face unique barriers to receiving treatment. The health effects of substance abuse also are worse for women who abuse alcohol, illicit drugs, or prescription medication. Understanding these gender differences is of paramount importance for proper prevention and treatment.

RISK FACTORS

Men were once the only persons studied and treated for substance abuse. However, more recent studies on women show that more than 42 percent of women have used an illicit substance in the course of their lifetime, indicating a need for further studies of women and substance abuse. In addition, women account for approximately 33 percent of persons seeking treatment, making them the fastest growing population of substance abusers in the United States.

Women generally turn to substance abuse for different reasons than do men. Women often seek the comfort of a substance to help deal with a psychological diagnosis, such as anxiety, depression, post-traumatic stress disorder, or an eating disorder. Men typically abuse substances secondary to impulsive or aggressive behavior problems. Women also abuse more frequently than men to deal with social concerns and pressures, such as family stressors or a traumatic event, including physical, sexual, and emotional abuse. Women who abuse substances are more likely to be in a relationship with another substance abuser or in a relationship in which their partner is in control.

The female body reacts differently to substances than does the male body. Although less likely overall to develop an addiction, women who do become addicted do so faster and develop medical concerns more rapidly than do men. Women do not present for treatment as frequently as men because of gender-related barriers.

Women who use substances are more likely than men to have children, to be unemployed, and to receive medical assistance. Other risk factors for substance abuse are young age and lower educational status. These differences lead to unique barriers to treatment, including financial concerns, fear of being stigmatized by society as weak or helpless, feeling guilt or shame, and concerns of losing child custody.

ALCOHOL ABUSE

In comparison to men, women drink alcohol less frequently. When women drink, they are more likely to engage in binge drinking, defined as five or more drinks on one occasion, than to engage in heavy constant alcohol consumption, defined as five drinks per day over several days. Alcoholism is underdiagnosed in women because of the public perception that most alcoholics are men.

Women who abuse alcohol have more health concerns related to its use than do men because of the way a woman's body processes alcohol. A woman absorbs and metabolizes alcohol differently because she has a higher concentration of alcohol in the blood; has less of the enzyme called alcohol dehydrogenase, which metabolizes alcohol; and has larger amounts of estrogen, which may increase the risk for liver disease. These factors cause higher levels of alcoholic hepatitis after a shorter duration of drinking and a greater proportion of deaths from cirrhosis of the liver. Women alcohol abusers also have an increased risk

for heart disease, breast cancer, osteoporosis, gastric ulcers, and neurological complications.

Teenage girls are particularly sensitive to the effects of alcohol because the alcohol decreases levels of hormones, including estrogen. Normal growth and timing of puberty might be delayed by alcohol abuse during these formative years.

Another significant health issue is alcohol consumption during pregnancy, whereby the fetus becomes at risk for developing either fetal alcohol

---

True or False: Women Get Drunker than Men

Though some people think otherwise, women and men process alcohol differently. Women become more intoxicated and their blood alcohol concentration (BAC) is higher after drinking the same amount of alcohol as men, even if they are the same weight.

There are several physiological reasons why a woman will feel the effects of alcohol more quickly and strongly. Women are often smaller than men physically, and thus have a smaller volume of blood, so consuming the same amount of alcohol as a larger man will result in a higher BAC. However, even if a man and a woman are the same weight and drink the same amount of alcohol, the woman will still become more intoxicated. This is true for several reasons.

Women have less water in their bodies than men—water makes up 52 percent of a woman's body and 61 percent of a man's body. Therefore, a man's body can dilute more alcohol than can a woman's body, and more alcohol will stay in a woman's body (increasing the BAC).

Women tend to have a higher proportion of body fat than men of the same weight, and this affects how the body processes alcohol. Alcohol cannot be dissolved in fat, so more alcohol becomes concentrated in a woman's body fluids (such as blood), raising her BAC to a higher level than that of a man of similar weight who drinks the same amount of alcohol.

Compared with men, women have less alcohol dehydrogenase, an enzyme in the liver and stomach that breaks down alcohol. Because the alcohol in a woman's body is not broken down as efficiently as in a man's body, more alcohol enters a woman's bloodstream, and her BAC increases.

Hormonal differences between men and women also may affect alcohol metabolism. During a woman's menstrual cycle, changes in hormone levels affect the rate at which a woman becomes intoxicated. Alcohol metabolism slows down during the premenstrual phase of a woman's cycle (right before she gets her period), which causes more alcohol to enter the bloodstream and the woman to get drunker faster. Birth control pills and other medications with estrogen also slow the rate at which women process alcohol.

syndrome or fetal alcohol effects. No safe level of alcohol consumption has been determined for pregnancy, and all women are discouraged from drinking any form of alcohol through gestation.

Fetal alcohol syndrome compromises a constellation of symptoms, such as mental retardation and birth defects that include congenital heart problems, behavioral problems, and characteristic facial features. The greatest risk for fetal alcohol syndrome occurs when there is heavy alcohol consumption through the entire pregnancy.

Fetal alcohol effects generally occur when there have been lower levels of alcohol consumption; these effects may include some findings of fetal alcohol syndrome. Women who are older, educated, and in better economic standing are at greatest risk for increasing alcohol consumption in pregnancy. Teenagers who drink before pregnancy are most likely to continue drinking during pregnancy.

DRUG ABUSE

Female substance abusers who enter treatment are more likely to use drugs than partake in heavy alcohol consumption. Methadone, the primary abused drug for which women seek treatment, may be categorized as an illicit substance or as an abused medication (such as a psychotropic prescription). Women are more likely than men to be prescribed psychotropic medications for an underlying mental illness.

Women metabolize a drug's components at a slower rate than do men. The prolonged exposure to these toxic ingredients leads to an increased risk for health concerns. Women who abuse drugs often experience irregular menstrual cycles and decreased fertility because of the suppression of endocrine and sex hormones. Although both men and women drug users are at risk for contracting an infectious disease from shared needles, women infected with the human immunodeficiency virus show a more rapid progression to acquired immunodeficiency syndrome than do men. Drug use also suppresses the immune system and allows for more rapid viral replication.

As with alcohol abuse, drug use in pregnancy is of utmost concern because of the risk for birth defects and disorders and adverse pregnancy outcomes. The primary substances reported to be used during pregnancy include cocaine, crack cocaine, marijuana, and amphetamine. Abuse of these substances leads to pregnancy complications that include miscarriage,

low birth weight, premature delivery, intrauterine fetal demise, and stillbirth. These substances also can lead to neonatal dependence, from which the newborn must remain in the hospital for an extended time because of withdrawal. The possibility exists that social services will remove the newborn from the home because of this exposure. Newer research suggests an increased risk for the child to have developmental delays, both motor and cognitive.

PREVENTION AND TREATMENT

Women's risk factors must be addressed to successfully target the specific needs of women in treating substance abuse. Even though women and men do similarly well in completing treatment, the challenge is women's access to treatment.

Often women underestimate the role alcohol or drug abuse plays in contributing to their illness, and they overestimate the contribution of the mental illness to their medical and emotional concerns. It is important to address both the substance abuse and the additional comorbid psychological diagnoses. This may be accomplished by a combination of psychotherapy and pharmacotherapy.

Women often feel uncomfortable sharing their experiences in the company of men; therefore, many treatment centers now help women exclusively. Women are also more likely to have a negative perception of treatment, and specific centers have specially trained therapists and physicians who are sensitive to and aware of the unique challenges in treating female substance abusers. These facilities also have accommodations for increased access to care. For example, provision of childcare at the site of treatment relieves the financial burden of paying for this service and the worry of having to care for children while in recovery.

Transportation services to and from the treatment facility also increase the likelihood of arrival for routine appointments, as it alleviates the recovering addict's financial and logistical burden of travel. As part of the treatment process, education about substance abuse in pregnancy should be provided for current or future mothers, education that includes discussion of the risks for birth defects and disorders and other adverse pregnancy outcomes.

Data indicate that while the aforementioned services would benefit women in treatment, only a minority of treatment centers actually have these accommodations. Because of the psychological and emotional risk factors, the significant and life-threatening health effects, and the barriers to treatment, further research is needed to better understand the implications of substance abuse in women and the best methods for treatment and prevention.

Janet Ober Berman, MS, CGC

FURTHER READING

Ait-Daoud, Nassima, and Mudhasir Bashir. "Women and Substance Abuse: Health Considerations and Recommendations." *CNS Spectrums* 16.2 (2011). Print. Article detailing the negative health consequences of drug and alcohol abuse in women.

Brady, Thomas M., and Olivia Silber Ashley, eds. *Women in Substance Abuse Treatment: Results from the Alcohol and Drug Services Study (ADSS)*. DHHS Publication No. SMA 04-3968. Rockville, MD: SAMHSA, 2005. A comprehensive summary of the statistics on treatment modalities and facilities targeted to women who abuse drugs and alcohol.

Cormier, Renee, Colleen Anne Dell, and Nancy Poole. "Women and Substance Abuse Problems." *BMC Women's Health* 4, suppl. 1 (2004): 1–10. Print. Study documents the proportion of drug and alcohol use in women and addresses the barriers to successful treatment and prevention.

D'Arlach L., et al. "Children, Women, and Substance Abuse: A Look at Recovery in a Communal Setting." *Journal of Prevention and Intervention in the Community* 31.1–2 (2006): 121–31. Print. Research study demonstrating the importance of women having a supportive environment for treatment that includes other women and access to childcare.

Hecksher, Dorte, and Morten Hesse. "Women and Substance Use Disorders." *MSM: Mens Sana Monographs* 7.1 (2009): 50–62. Print. An overview of women and substance abuse concerns from the perspective of psychologists treating this population.

Salisbury, Amy L., et al. "Fetal Effects of Psychoactive Drugs." *Clinical Perinatology* 36 (2009): 595–619. Print. A study of the effects of cocaine, methamphetamine, and selective serotonin reuptake inhibitors on the developing brain and central nervous system of the fetus.

WEBSITES OF INTEREST

National Institute on Drug Abuse
http://drugabuse.gov

Substance Abuse and Mental Health Services Administration
http://www.samhsa.gov/samhsanewsletter/Volume_18_Number_2/TIP51.aspx

See also: Families and substance abuse; Gender and addiction; Marriage/partnership and substance abuse; Media and substance abuse; Parenting and substance abuse; Substance abuse; Women and behavioral addictions; Women and smoking

Work addiction

CATEGORY: Psychological issues and behaviors
ALSO KNOWN AS: Workaholism
DEFINITION: Work addiction, or workaholism, is a behavioral addiction defined as an intense need to work. The addiction comes with potentially severe physical, emotional, and social consequences. Work addicts can experience specific physical and psychological symptoms from working excessive hours and from neglecting other areas of their lives and the lives of family and friends.

CAUSES

Work addiction is caused by a complex constellation of factors, including family history of work addiction or other addictions, perfectionism, obsessive-compulsive traits, organizational cultures that encourage workaholic tendencies, modeling of work addiction by one's parents or other role models, enjoyment of one's work, and a lack of other meaningful identities in a person's life. Research published in 2009 found that work addiction results from a combination of personality traits, family background, and work cultures that promote or normalize work-addictive behaviors, such as regularly working long hours and taking work home.

RISK FACTORS

Persons who work in salaried, rather than hourly wage, jobs have an increased risk for work addiction. Working in an environment in which long hours, taking work home, working weekends, and a lack of self-care are normalized places people at risk for developing work addiction. Additionally, persons who are perfectionists or who have obsessive-compulsive features, such as frequent worrying or compulsively checking email, are at increased risk for developing work addiction.

SYMPTOMS

The clearest symptoms of work addiction are an excessive need for work and having one's work chronically overtake time spent for self-care and social activities. People who suffer from work addiction think constantly about work when not at work, will work significantly beyond what is required by their jobs, and experience stress-related medical conditions such as high blood pressure and migraines.

Workaholics often lose or have impaired social relationships and generally neglect nonwork aspects of their lives, such as hobbies, exercise, and friendships. Workaholics experience frequent conflicts between their work and other important aspects of their lives.

People with work addiction are more likely to have marital and family conflicts, get divorced, and have fewer close relationships than workers who are not addicted to their jobs.

SCREENING AND DIAGNOSIS

A comprehensive screening and assessment for work addiction can be performed by a therapist. The therapist will ask the client about symptoms, background information, work behaviors and hours, general functioning, family and social experiences, mental health history, and medical history. The therapist may ask the client to complete some paper-and-pencil questionnaires that assess the symptoms of work addiction and their severity. The therapist will then share the results of this comprehensive assessment with the client and discuss treatment options. Increasingly, employers and managers are conducting screenings for work addiction risk factors to identify employees who would benefit from preventive interventions or from referral to a mental health professional.

TREATMENT AND THERAPY

Treatment options for work addiction are similar to treatment options for other behavioral addictions. The choice of treatment is determined by the level of severity, the causes of the client's work addiction, the client's preferences, and the client's personal coping resources. Persons who are suffering from physical illnesses caused by workaholic behaviors will be referred to physicians for appropriate medical treatment.

Clients may attend weekly or biweekly counseling sessions with a therapist, who will help the client to explore the causes of his or her work addiction; to learn to set healthy boundaries with work; to develop healthier self-care behaviors, such as balanced diet and exercise; and to develop and maintain healthy social relationships. Couples or family therapy also may be integrated to address any family concerns and communication issues.

In addition to or instead of attending counseling sessions, a work addict may participate in a twelve-step self-help and recovery group such as Workaholics Anonymous. In this group format, the addict may develop personally supportive relationships with others who are also striving to recover from work addiction and who are hoping to progress through a series of steps to better understand and manage their behavior.

Several self-help books and workbooks for work addiction also exist. These resources offer concrete behavioral strategies for decreasing work addiction, such as setting time limits for work tasks, investing a consistent amount of time in hobbies, and using assertive communication in relationships. The length of treatment for work addiction varies by client and is affected by the client's willingness to engage in treatment, the client's other coping resources, and the client's symptom severity.

PREVENTION

Because work addiction is a family disease in which children of work addicts are themselves more likely to develop work addiction, one of the best ways to prevent work addiction in future generations is for parents to seek treatment when they have symptoms. Parents also can help to prevent future work addiction in their children by modeling involvement in a variety of important life roles not limited to work identities. Work addiction can be prevented by setting limits around work hours and personal time, prioritizing valued relationships, participating regularly in hobbies, and engaging in regular self-care through exercise and relaxation.

Employers can prevent work addiction by setting organizational norms of "working smart" and being efficient versus working excessive hours. Employers can limit the amount of work an employee can take home and can provide resources to promote positive worker health. Some innovative employers make available certain helpful resources, such as gyms, on-site medical clinics, and relaxation gardens, in the work environment so that employees may conveniently use these services for self-care during breaks, on the way to work, and after work.

Tracy Ksiazak, PhD

FURTHER READING

Aziz, Shahnaz, and Casie Tronzo. "Exploring the Relationship between Workaholism Facets and Personality Traits: A Replication in American Workers." *Psychological Record* 61 (2011): 269–86. Print. Researchers found that people who are highly conscientious, agreeable, and open to experience are likely to develop some of the more positive characteristics of work addiction. People who are highly neurotic are not likely to derive positive feelings from their work.

Aziz, Shahnaz, et al. "Workaholism and Work-Life Imbalance: Does Cultural Origin Influence the Relationship?" *International Journal of Psychology* 45 (2010): 72–79. Print. Researchers compared scores of Caucasian and black participants on scales measuring workaholism and its effects, finding that both groups had equal overall levels of workaholism and work-life imbalance.

Brady, Becca, Stephen Vodanovich, and Robert Rotunda. "The Impact of Workaholism on Work-Family Conflict, Job Satisfaction, and Perception of Leisure Activities." *Psychologist-Manager Journal* 11 (2008): 241–63. Print. Researchers explored how work addiction impacts the balance between work and family and people's perceptions of their jobs and nonwork activities. The study found that there are several different types of work addiction and that a person's type of work addiction predicts what problems he or she will experience. Also provides suggestions for managers to deal with work addiction.

Liang, Ying-Wen, and Chen-Ming Chu. "Personality Traits and Personal and Organizational Inducements: Antecedents of Workaholism." *Social Behavior and Personality* 37 (2009): 645–60. Print. This study explored the factors that contribute to the development of workaholism. Recommends specific screening criteria that employers can use to identify persons who are at risk for developing work addiction.

Robinson, Bryan. *Chained to the Desk: A Guidebook for Workaholics, Their Partners and Children, and the Clinicians Who Treat Them.* 2nd ed. New York: New York UP, 2007. Provides accessible information about symptoms of work addiction, its treatment, and recovery from work addiction.

---. "The Psychosocial and Familial Dimensions of Work Addiction: Preliminary Perspectives and Hypotheses." *Journal of Counseling and Development* 74 (1996): 447–52. Print. Reviews the existing research on work addiction and its symptoms. Provides suggestions for counselors to more effectively help clients who struggle with work addiction and its consequences.

Robinson, Bryan, and Lisa Kelley. "Adult Children of Workaholics: Self-Concept, Anxiety, Depression, and Locus of Control." *American Journal of Family Therapy* 26 (1998): 223–38. Print. This study examined the family-level effects of parents' work addictions after children of workaholics grew up. The findings indicate that workaholic parents, especially fathers, are more likely to have children who develop depression in adulthood, and to believe that much of their lives are outside their control.

Shimazu, Akihito, Wilmar Schaufeli, and Toon Taris. "How Does Workaholism Affect Worker Health and Performance? The Mediating Role of Coping." *International Journal of Behavioral Medicine* 17 (2010): 154–60. Print. Study found that workaholics are generally less healthy, both physically and emotionally, than nonworkaholics. Workaholism was not found to be related to poor job performance.

WEBSITES OF INTEREST

Addiction Treatment Magazine
http://www.addictiontreatmentmagazine.com/addiction/treatment-for-workaholics

Workaholics Anonymous
http://www.workaholics-anonymous.org

See also: Behavioral addictions: Overview; Computer addiction; Exercise addiction; Social media addiction; Stress and alcohol; Stress and drug abuse; Stress and smoking; Work issues and behavioral addictions; Work issues and substance abuse

Work issues and behavioral addictions

CATEGORY: Social issues

DEFINITION: Behavioral addictions such as Internet addiction, gambling, eating disorders, and or work addiction affect not only work performance but also employer profits.

PERSONAL WEB USE

The arrival of desktop computers in the 1980s transformed the workplace, increasing demands for mental productivity. Employees deal with increased stress by using the Internet for non-work-related activities such as shopping, gambling, and visiting social media or pornography sites. In excess, such activities mirror other behavioral addictions and cost employers billions of dollars in lost productivity and health claims.

Researchers estimated that by the year 2000, employees had been spending one hour per day on personal web use (PWU), which can be defined as any Internet activity not related to the job. PWU produced losses amounting to $35 million per year. By 2010, productivity losses were in the billions of dollars. PWU now accounts for more than one-half of all online activity at work, according to the American Management Association.

Mark Griffiths, an eminent researcher in the field of workplace addictions, claims that most employees are not "Internet addicts" but use the Internet to maintain other behavioral addictions, such as gambling, pornography, or shopping addictions. He refers to excessive PWU as a technological addiction, a subset of behavioral addictions that are not chemical in nature and that involve human–machine interaction.

Other researchers agree that like other behavioral (and chemical) addictions, misuse or overuse of the Internet is likely caused by problems of low self-esteem and self-control, obsessive-compulsion, and mood disorders. Excessive PWU follows the same progression as other addictions: mood modification, tolerance, withdrawal, conflict, and relapse.

While some researchers view PWU as a variation on dysfunctional work behaviors such as stealing and making long personal phone calls, others believe it is of value in the modern workplace. The "human resources view" states that PWU gives employees access to the knowledge needed in rapidly changing fields such as health care, where online collaboration is accelerating the adoption of best practices.

PWU also can be viewed as a way to take a break from concentrated endeavors or boring work. It allows employees to achieve a tolerable life-work balance as the work week expands beyond forty hours, often in a cubicle. A study in 2003 found that Americans spent more time online at home doing work than online at work doing personal business.

What is' needed in the workplace are clear examples of acceptable Internet use and a shared understanding among employees and managers. Rather than using monitoring tools, filters, and firewalls, for example, organizations should make PWU policies known and should partner with employees so that everyone is vigilant.

The main deterrents to PWU are time and lack of privacy, although sanctions and personal disincentives are also effective. A human resources officer, rather than a technical officer, should lead discussions to make employees aware of appropriate PWU.

PATHOLOGICAL GAMBLING

Pathological gambling is especially worrisome in conjunction with PWU. Most gambling takes place during workday hours to hide the compulsion from family members, and employees now have access to thousands of gambling websites. If the sites are blocked by the employer, employees can place bets by telephone.

Gambling problems may be recognized as an employee's work performance deteriorates. Other signs of a gambling problem include frequent absences and missed deadlines; eagerness to take part in or organize office betting pools; borrowing money and arguing about having to pay it back; not taking time off from work or asking to be compensated in cash; complaining about mounting debt; spending time on personal phone calls; receiving credit card and other bills at work instead of home; increased time spent gambling during lunch or other breaks; and making false claims on expense accounts, or otherwise stealing from the employer.

Businesses that deal in large amounts of cash or that are located near gambling venues should have a sound gambling policy. This policy should define the types of gambling that are acceptable (for example, office pools) at work and those that are prohibited at work.

EATING DISORDERS

The compulsion to overeat has gained behavioral addiction status among laypersons, likely due to the popularity of Overeater's Anonymous, a twelve-step program modeled after Alcoholics Anonymous and other such programs. Overeating can result in obesity and leads to high costs in the workplace. Overweight or obese employees have more workplace injuries and disability claims and use more sick leave than their coworkers who are not overweight.

A 2010 survey by the American College of Occupational and Environmental Medicine found that overweight men cost their companies between about $300 and $6,000 more per year. Estimates ranged from about $800 to $6,600 for overweight women per year. The survey concluded that 37 percent of the obese are responsible for 65 percent of excess employer costs. Employers who encourage physical activity with gym memberships or exercise classes, for example, can save a significant amount of money in benefits.

WORKAHOLISM

While it may seem counterintuitive, work addiction is not good for business. People who become "workaholics" are less effective team players, taking on so much work that their performance suffers. Some workaholics cannot get started on projects for fear that the end result will not be perfect; others begin working obsessively and then fail to finish when they get another assignment.

Like all behavioral addictions, workaholism happens in stages. In the first stage, a worker is constantly busy and will put in extra hours without being paid for those hours. The employee has a difficult time relaxing on days off. In the second stage, the employee becomes distant from family and friends, and when at home is distracted and emotionally is still at work. He or she may have trouble sleeping and may see a change in weight, up or down. In later stages, the workaholic experiences physical and emotional symptoms such as chronic headaches, high blood pressure, and stomach ulcers that lead to increased medical claims.

Laura B. Smith

FURTHER READING

Anandarajan, Murugan, and Claire Simmers. *Personal Web Usage in the Workplace: A Guide to Effective Human Resources Management.* Hershey, PA: Information Science, 2004. Examines two views of personal web use, constructive and dysfunctional, and provide recommendations for human resources professionals.

Griffiths, Mark. "Internet Abuse in the Workplace: Issues and Concerns for Employers and Employment Counselors." *Journal of Employment Counseling* 40.2 (2003): 87–96. Print. Outlines the most serious form of Internet addiction and other types of related workplace addictions. Concludes that Internet abuse should be taken seriously by all employers whose staff uses the Internet in their day-to-day work.

Ladouceur, Robert, and Stella Lachance. *Overcoming Pathological Gambling: Therapist Guide.* New York: Oxford UP, 2006. Useful therapeutic information, from a cognitive-behavioral therapy approach, for pathological gamblers.

Robinson, Bryan. *Chained to the Desk: A Guidebook for Workaholics, Their Partners and Children, and the Clinicians Who Treat Them.* 2nd ed. New York: New York UP, 2007. Provides accessible information about symptoms of work addiction, its treatment, and recovery from work addiction.

WEBSITES OF INTEREST

Center for Internet Addiction
http://www.netaddiction.com

Gamblers Anonymous
http://www.gamblersanonymous.org

Overeaters Anonymous
http://www.oa.org

Workaholics Anonymous
http://www.workaholics-anonymous.org

See also: Behavioral addictions: Overview; Media and behavioral addictions; Men and behavioral addictions; Women and behavioral addictions; Work addiction; Work issues and substance abuse

Work issues and substance abuse

CATEGORY: Social issues

DEFINITION: The abuse of alcohol, illegal drugs, and prescription drugs is a major economic, medical, public safety, and legal concern of public-sector and private-sector employees and employers. Work-related issues involve not only the use, possession, or sale of such drugs in the workplace but also impairment during working hours caused by substance abuse at home, or by emotional preoccupation with a family member's or friend's substance abuse.

ECONOMIC COSTS

Substance abuse is a common problem in the workplace in the United States. Contrary to popular stereotypes, more than 60 percent of adults with substance abuse problems are employed full time, and an additional 10 percent are part-time employees. About 9 percent of employed adults report heavy use of alcohol, and 5 percent admit that they occasionally work under the influence.

With regard to illegal drugs, 3 percent of workers admit to using these substances in the workplace or before reporting to work, and one in three full-time workers reports that drugs are sold in their workplace. Another 3 percent of employed adults admit to abusing prescription drugs at work, using them for mood alteration rather than for medical necessity.

The abuse of these substances imposes heavy financial burdens on businesses in the United States. According to the US Department of Health and Human Services, these costs amount to $276 billion per year. Direct costs include lost productivity from increased absenteeism and sick leave, compensation for workplace accidents and injuries, high employee turnover and the resulting cost of training new employees, higher disability payments and health care expenditures, drug testing and employee assistance programs, theft of or damage to company property, liability insurance, and involvement of law enforcement for drug-related crises in the workplace.

In addition to the direct costs of work-related substance abuse, employers must cover indirect costs. These costs include lowered employee morale, loss of competitiveness, damage to the company's reputation because of declining quality of goods and services, and poor decisions made by substance-impaired managers or supervisors.

Some industries and occupations have higher rates of alcohol and substance abuse among employees than others. Those with the highest rates of abuse include food service, hotel work, construction, mining, performing arts and entertainment, professional sports, and retail sales. Other fields with relatively high rates include financial services, information technology, transportation, and manufacturing.

Work-related factors known to increase the risk of substance abuse among employees, including managers and supervisors, include high stress levels, repetitious tasks, working in isolation, long and irregular work shifts, access to alcohol or drugs, and relative lack of supervision. Small businesses are at greater risk than large companies, as they are less likely to have prevention and treatment programs for impaired employees and are less likely to screen potential employees for substance abuse problems.

HEALTH AND PUBLIC SAFETY ISSUES

The well-being and safety of other workers and the general public was a major reason for increased research into and legislation regarding work-related substance abuse in the early 1980s. A "zero tolerance" policy that includes mandatory drug testing of all US military personnel was introduced in 1981 following a plane crash on an aircraft carrier that killed fourteen crew members.

Research conducted since the mid-1980s has shown that workers who abuse drugs and alcohol, whether on the job or at home, are a threat to the safety of others and themselves. For example, about one-half of all visits to emergency rooms in the United States for traumatic injuries are related to alcohol abuse, and employees who abuse alcohol have health care costs 100 percent higher than those of other workers. Employees who use illegal drugs are twice as likely as nonusers to call in sick and four times as likely to be involved in a workplace accident.

In addition to accidental injuries, employees who abuse substances are also at increased risk of such long-term health consequences as cancer and other diseases of the heart, liver, and pancreas. The Occupational Safety and Health Administration (OSHA) reports that 15 to 20 percent of workers who die on the job test positive for alcohol or drugs at autopsy.

Workers who abuse drugs and alcohol are also more likely to cause health problems for their co-workers by adding to workplace tensions. Violent behavior and accidents triggered by intoxication are obvious causes of injury to others; however, stress resulting from having to complete projects for impaired employees or to work extra shifts to make up for their absenteeism also can have long-term effects on the health and job satisfaction of other workers.

These drug-related problem behaviors, such as mood swings, unusually long breaks, hypersensitivity to criticism, missing deadlines, and borrowing or stealing money from colleagues to finance a drug habit lower the morale of other workers. Finally, more than one-half of workers who live with or are related to an alcoholic or drug addict report that their own productivity at work is affected by anxiety about their relative or roommate.

LEGAL ISSUES

Also associated with workplace substance abuse are specific legal issues. These issues include federal regulation of transportation and other safety-sensitive industries, mandates applied to companies that do business with the government, the response of law enforcement to drug-related workplace crime (such as possession and sale of drugs, embezzlement, property theft, and violent assault), the rights of employees regarding drug and alcohol testing, and the introduction of workplace drug policies.

The first major federal law in this field was the Drug-Free Workplace Act of 1988, which requires some federal contractors and all federal grantees to establish drug-free workplaces to receive grants or contracts from any federal agency. The precise requirements vary somewhat according to whether the contractor or grantee is an individual or an organization.

The US Department of Transportation and the Federal Motor Carrier Safety Administration have strict regulations regarding drug use and drug testing for employees whose jobs require a commercial driver's license. Similarly, the Omnibus Transportation Employee Testing Act of 1991 requires periodic testing of airline pilots for alcohol or drug abuse, including the abuse of prescription drugs.

Another legal issue related to workplace substance abuse is the rights of employees regarding drug testing, specifically involving federal and state disability laws. In general, substance abuse has not been considered a disability such that firing an addicted employee could be considered harassment or discrimination. Nonetheless, to avoid future lawsuits by former employees, employers are usually advised to seek legal advice when introducing a workplace drug policy.

DRUG-FREE WORKPLACE PROGRAMS

The high human and financial costs of work-related substance abuse have led more and more employers to introduce workplace policies intended to prevent and treat such abuse. OSHA has identified five essential features of a drug-free workplace policy: a written statement of company policy regarding drug use, testing, consequences for violations, and similar matters; training supervisors in appropriate handling of drug-related problems; educating employees; drug testing; and employee assistance programs or referral to professional counseling. To help employers draft policy statements that fit their particular workplace, the US Department of Labor offers an online, interactive drug-free workplace advisor.

One important aspect of such policies is the supervisor or manager's role. Supervisors are advised to focus on and document problems with an employee's performance or productivity when drug abuse is suspected, rather than attempting to diagnose substance use or provide informal counseling. In addition, supervisors are expected to protect employees' confidentiality. One of the most challenging tasks in maintaining a drug-free workplace policy at all levels of a company is balancing the rights of affected employees to confidentiality and access to treatment with the rights of nonusers to a safe and drug-free workplace.

Rebecca J. Frey, PhD

FURTHER READING

Bennett, Joel B., and Wayne E. K. Lehman, eds. *Preventing Workplace Substance Abuse: Beyond Drug Testing to Wellness.* Washington, DC: American Psychological Association, 2003. This book represents an attempt to lower the rate of workplace substance abuse through preventive wellness programs rather than drug testing and other forms of regulation.

Slavit, Wendy, Amy Reagin, and Ronald Finch. *An Employer's Guide to Workplace Substance Abuse: Strategies and Treatment Recommendations.* Washington, DC: Center for Prevention and Health Services, 2009. A concise guide for business owners and supervisors that includes basic information about alcohol and drugs of abuse and recommendations for a workplace prevention and treatment policy.

Stiller, Sharon P., and Scott R. Simpson. "A Guide to Dealing with Workplace Substance Abuse." *Inside* 28 (2010): 17–19. Print. A brief article from the official journal of the New York State Bar Association that summarizes the legal issues surrounding workplace drug testing and the hiring and firing of employees with histories of drug or alcohol abuse.

Substance Abuse and Mental Health Services Administration. *The Drug-Free Workplace: A Guide for Supervisors and Managers.* Rockville, MD: SAMHSA, 2002. Describes and explains supervisor responsibilities in dealing with substance-abusing employees. Includes sample interviews and conversations to illustrate appropriate ways to deal with difficult workplace situations.

WEBSITES OF INTEREST

Occupational Safety and Health Administration
http://www.osha.gov/SLTC/substanceabuse

Substance Abuse and Mental Health Services Administration
http://www.drugfreeworkplace.gov/federal.html

US Department of Labor
http://www.dol.gov/elaws/drugfree.htm

US Small Business Administration
http://www.sba.gov/content/drug-free-workplace

See also: Substance abuse; Work addiction; Work issues and behavioral addictions

APPENDIXES
REFERENCE TOOLS

Glossary

AA: Alcoholics Anonymous.

abstinence: Discontinuing a substance entirely and choosing to avoid additional use, often after treatment for and recovery from addiction.

abuse: Excessive and often harmful use of a substance in an unintended way.

acid: Slang for LSD.

acute: Short term or immediate, when measuring the effect of a substance on the body.

ADAM: Slang for ecstasy.

addict: Person with an addiction to a substance or behavior.

addiction: A chronic and relapsing disease that involves a craving for a substance or behavior, such as gambling, that causes physiological or psychological changes in the user, including tolerance and personality changes.

addictive drugs: Substances that affect changes in the brain and alter behavior and control.

addictive personality: Particular characteristics and behavioral traits that increase a person's risk of becoming addicted to a substance.

agonist: Substance that acts at a body receptor to cause an effect, similar to the effect caused by the receptor's natural use in the body.

aimies: Slang for amyl nitrite (or amphetamine).

Al-Anon: Family groups that use the twelve-step format developed by Alcoholics Anonymous to provide support for the relatives and friends of alcoholics and addicts.

alcohol: Ethanol-like solution found in fermented and distilled drinks, such as beer, wine, and liquor, which causes intoxicating changes to the central nervous system with ingestion.

Alcoholics Anonymous: Developed in 1935, one of the earliest addiction treatment programs, which developed the twelve-step model for recovery of addiction to alcohol.

alcoholism: A chronic and progressive relapsing disorder of excessive and repeated alcohol intake; complications include physical dependence and withdrawal, cirrhotic liver disease, unsafe behavioral changes such as drunk driving, and fatality if untreated.

alcohol poisoning: The condition caused by ingesting large amounts of alcohol in a short period of time, which causes life-threatening physical and psychological effects, such as unconsciousness, difficulty breathing, lowered heart rate, and dehydration.

amphetamine: Synthetic central nervous system stimulant used to control appetite or treat narcolepsy and misused illicitly by mouth, by injection, or by sniffing to increase energy and achieve a high.

amyl nitrite: A liquid ester that dilates blood vessels and can be inhaled for aphrodisiac effects.

anabolic steroids: Synthetic hormones related to testosterone that may be abused orally, topically, or by injection with particular dosing cycles to enhance muscle growth and development.

analgesic: A pain-relieving substance or effect.

angel dust: Slang for PCP.

antagonist: A substance that blocks receptors to prevent an effect; examples include caffeine and naloxone.

BAC: Blood alcohol content.

barbiturates: An older class of medications with depressant effects on the central nervous system, used to treat anxiety or sleep disturbances; examples include amobarbital and phenobarbital.

base: Slang for freebase cocaine.

baseballing: Smoking freebase cocaine.

bath salts: Slang for a synthetic powder containing an amphetamine like substance, such as mephedrone, that is inhaled, swallowed, or injected, with great risk of overdose.

behavioral addiction: Craving or compulsion toward an action rather than a substance.

belladonna: Toxic plant known as deadly nightshade that contains atropine, which affects the nervous system to cause dry mouth, dilated pupils, increased heart rate, hallucinations, and seizures when taken by mouth.

benzodiazepines: A class of medications with antianxiety and relaxation effects on the central nervous system via GABA receptor activity; benzodiazepines may be unsafely combined with other substances of abuse, such as methadone or alcohol, to enhance intoxication.

binge: Uninterrupted drug consumption for hours or days.

binge drinking: A type of alcohol misuse in which users drink uninterrupted and excessively in a single, short time period, often resulting in vomiting, loss of consciousness, and hangover.

black hash: Opium and hashish.

blackout: Loss of consciousness, especially secondary to substance abuse or overdose.

blood alcohol concentration: *See* blood alcohol content.

blood alcohol content: The level of ethanol measured in the blood, in percentage per weight, as a reflection of alcohol intake, used to determine impairment of function.

blow coke: To inhale cocaine.

blow the stick: To smoke marijuana.

blow the vein: To miss the vein while injecting a substance of abuse, so that the substance and effects are "wasted" in the skin.

blue acid: Slang for LSD.

breathalyzer: An instrument that measures the alcohol level in an exhaled breath in order to estimate the amount of alcohol in the blood, or blood alcohol content, and reflect the level of impairment in the user.

bummer trip: Unsettling and threatening experience that results from PCP intoxication.

bump: Small amount of cocaine used to obtain a rapid rush.

buprenorphine: Long-lasting, partial opiate, controlled substance analgesic used sublingually alone or in combination with naloxone for the treatment of addiction.

caffeine: An alkaloid found in coffee beans, tea leaves, and other plants that provides mild central nervous system stimulant effects with social use but is habitual and likely to cause withdrawal symptoms.

cannabinoid: A chemical compound found in the cannabis sativa, or marijuana, plant; tetrahydrocannabinol is a cannabinoid with central nervous system activity.

cannabis: Botanical name for the marijuana plant, cannabis sativa, which can be smoked or eaten to provide mild euphoria, along with decreased response times and poor judgment.

CBT: Cognitive behavioral therapy.

central nervous system: Brain and spinal cord.

central nervous system depressants: Types of drugs that slow central nervous system function, used therapeutically to increase sleep and reduce anxiety.

cereal: Slang for marijuana smoked in a bowl.

chalk: Slang for methamphetamine or amphetamine.

chalked up: Under the influence of cocaine.

chaser: Compulsive crack or inhaled heroin user; alternately, an alcoholic drink ingested immediately after another type of alcoholic drink.

chasing the dragon: Slang for popular method of heroin and cocaine misuse by inhaling vapors heated on tin foil instead of by injection; users are known as chasers.

chemical dependence: Adaptation of the body and brain to the recurrent and harmful presence of a substance; leads to tolerance and withdrawal.

China: Opium.

China cat: High-potency heroin.

China white: A synthetic, designer opiate drug related to heroin.

Chinese tobacco: Opium.

chronic: Long-term, or over a longer time period, relating to substance effects in the body.

club drugs: Chemical substances used recreationally at bars, clubs, or parties; examples include ecstasy, ketamine, and Nexus.

CNS: Central nervous system.

cocaine: A pure, potent, and addictive powder naturally extracted from coca leaves, which can be misused for its central nervous system stimulant effects, with its intense excitation and high, by injection, by mouth, by snorting into nostrils, or by applying the powder to mucous membranes.

cocaine freebase: Natural cocaine hydrochloride, also known as crack, which provides more rapid stimulatory effects.

codeine: A natural substance found in the opium poppy that is related to but less potent than morphine; relieves pain and suppresses cough at therapeutic doses.

Cognitive behavioral therapy: A type of psychotherapy that relies on using thoughts to change behavior even without a change in circumstances.

coke: Slang for cocaine.

coke bugs: Illusive sensation of bugs crawling on and under the skin after abusing cocaine.

comorbidity: The occurrence of two disease states in one person, often at the same time but possibly in sequence; drug addiction as a mental illness occurring in a person with another mental disorder, such as depression, is an example of comorbidity.

compulsion: An irrational and repeated behavior.

controlled substance: US Food and Drug Administration designation for prescription drugs that require documentation and use oversight because of their potential for abuse and dependency; regulation is differentiated by schedules.

convulsions: Involuntary muscle contractions that cause rapid and uncontrolled shaking movements; convulsions may be seen with seizure disorders or with substance misuse.

cook: To mix heroin with water and heat it.

cook down: To heat and liquefy heroin in order to inhale it.

cough medicine: *See* cough syrup.

cough syrup: Over-the-counter product with dextromethorphan, misused by drinking entire bottles to obtain stimulant effects.

crack: Slang for a variance of cocaine, also known as freebase cocaine, used to provide an immediate and inexpensive high.

crank: Slang for methamphetamine or amphetamine.

craving: Overpowering, unstoppable hunger for drugs, a result of brain changes and addiction, in order to maintain the effects of initial substance use; also known as psychological dependence.

cross dependence: An effect obtained when administering a drug to prevent withdrawal symptoms resulting from physical dependence on a different drug.

crystal: Amphetamine.

crystal meth: Slang for methamphetamine in a pure form, smoked by users.

dance drug: *See* club drug.

date rape drug: Any drug used illicitly to lower defenses and ease commission of sexual assault.

DEA: Drug Enforcement Agency.

delirium tremens: A neurological reaction occurring in people with chronic alcoholism during withdrawal; symptoms include sweating, terror, hallucinations and psychoses, and uncontrollable trembling that may be deadly.

delusion: A strong but false belief, even with evidence against the belief; or, a psychosis experienced while under the influence of a chemical substance.

denial: A defensive, nondeliberate refusal reaction of an abuser when confronted about his or her substance abuse.

dependence: A general term used to describe different types of reliance upon chemicals, whether physical or psychological; not necessarily reflective of addiction.

depressant: *See* Central nervous system depressants.

depression: A common term for major depressive disorder, an illness that changes moods, thoughts, and activity level and impairs function; depression may be diagnosed when mood changes and decreased interest in daily activity persists for more than two weeks.

designer drug: Illegally synthesized chemicals, such as China white, that are similar to parent drugs in makeup and effect.

detox: *See* detoxification.

detoxification: Supervised removal of toxic chemical substances from the body, as the first step to a drug-free state, and associated with overcoming withdrawal symptoms.

devil's dandruff: Slang for cocaine.

dex: Slang for dextroamphetamine, a central nervous system stimulant.

Dexedrine: Trade name for dextroamphetamine, a central nervous system stimulant.

dexing: To consume large amounts of dextromethorphan, the main ingredient in many over-the-counter cough syrups, to obtain a euphoric high.

dextromethorphan: The active ingredient in over-the-counter cough syrups, which has methamphetamine-like stimulatory psychoactive effects with overdose.

dirty joint: Marijuana rolled for smoking that is laced with cocaine.

diversion: Selling legal prescription drugs illegally.

dopamine: A brain chemical crucial to muscle movement and mood changes that provides euphoric and intoxicating effects when released by some drugs of abuse or when its reuptake is prevented by substances of abuse, such as cocaine.

dope: Slang for drug.

downers: Slang for barbiturates or other depressants of the central nervous system.

dronabinol: Generic name for synthetic tetrahydrocannabinol, a schedule III controlled substance similar to marijuana.

drug abuse: Also known as substance abuse; inappropriate, repeated, and high-dose drug use to alter reality, decrease stress, or increase pleasure.

drug addiction: A mental illness that involves compulsive drug use and intense cravings along with psychological and behavioral changes.

Drug Enforcement Agency: An arm of the Department of Justice that enforces the legal status of controlled substances.

DSM-IV: The fourth edition of the *Diagnostic and Statistical Manual of Mental Disorders*, issued in 1993, which describes and classifies officially recognized psychiatric disorders.

DTs: Delirium tremens.

DUI: Driving under the influence of an illicit substance.

dusting: Sprinkling cocaine powder on other smokable drugs.

DWI: Driving while intoxicated, whether by alcohol or another abusive substance.

DXM: Dextromethorphan.

dysphoria: An unwell feeling or state; opposite of euphoria.

ecstasy: A psychoactive, synthetic amphetamine, 3-4 methylenedioxymethamphetamine (MDMA), with stimulant and hallucinogenic properties.

eight-ball: 1/8 ounce (3.5 G) of cocaine.

enabler: A person who contributes to another person's drug abuse, either directly by providing the substances or indirectly, such as by financing the user's habit or lifestyle.

enabling: Contributing to another person's substance abuse directly or indirectly.

ephedra: The plant source of ephedrine and pseudoephedrine chemicals, the latter used commonly in over-the-counter medications to treat congestion, which have psychological and physical stimulant effects when abused.

ethylamine: A volatile liquid substance, with an ammonia or alcohol base that may be abused by inhaling it in vaporized form.

euphoria: Psychologic well-being or high happiness.

false negative: A negative result on a test, such as a blood or urine test, when a substance is actually present and undetected.

false positive: A positive result on a test, such as a blood or urine test, when a substance is not actually present.

FDA: US Health and Human Services agency that supervises all food, drugs, and cosmetic safety and drug efficacy.

flashback: An episode during which sensual perceptions or hallucinations experienced from substance abuse, most often from use of LSD, recurs at a later date when the substance is not in the body.

flower flipping: Using mushrooms combined with ecstasy.

formication: An illusory sensation of bugs crawling over the skin.

free base: A form of cocaine.

freebasing: Smoking crack cocaine.

gamma-hydroxybutyrate: Also known as GHB or liquid X, a common date rape drug that causes depressant and stimulatory effects on the central nervous system, causing rebounding effects.

habituation: Reduced response to a substance after continuous use, such that the body adapts to continuing to function with a steady level of the substance and its effects and can no longer function properly without that substance.

halfway house: A residence used by people recovering from an addiction to provide support and oversight during reintroduction to society.

hallucination: An extreme change or distortion of the perception of reality, manifested as a sensation of something that does not exist, or an imagined experience without external causes, as a result of neural and chemical disruptions in the brain; hallucinations affect all senses and may cause physical changes as well.

hallucinogen: A chemical substance, natural or synthesized, that causes serious alterations of perception of reality, feeling, or thought.

hard candy: Slang for heroin.

hashish: Also known as hash; the potent organic portion of flowers from cannabis sativa plants, or marijuana, that may be chewed or smoked for the intoxicating effects caused by the plant's chemicals.

hepatitis: A set of inflammatory diseases of the liver caused by bacteria, viruses, or chemical toxins, which may be acute or chronic and may lead to liver failure.

heroin: A potent, fast-acting opiate comprised of two linked morphines (diacetylmorphine) with high abuse and addiction potential; heroin may be injected, smoked, or snorted.

hoarding: Extreme collection of items, often without the ability to use or discard them, and possibly part of a larger compulsive disorder.

hot ice: Slang for smokable methamphetamine.

huffer: Slang for an inhalant abuser.

huffing: Slang for inhaling, with regards to a method of substance abuse.

hypnotic drug: A type of psychoactive drug used therapeutically to induce or maintain sleep; the benzodiazepine drug class and its Z drug derivative class are used for their hypnotic effects.

hypodermic needle: A needle used to inject substances under the skin and used illegally by injection drug abusers to self-administer substances into veins to obtain rapid intoxication.

iatrogenic: Describing an effect inadvertently caused by a procedure or treatment performed or prescribed by a physician.

ice: Slang for methamphetamine.

illegal drug: A drug that has not been determined therapeutic or generally regarded as safe by, for example, the US Food and Drug Administration; examples include marijuana and cocaine.

illicit: Illegal, regarding possession or sale of a chemical substance.

IM: Intramuscular.

impairment: Regarding substance abuse, a worsened physical or psychological state that prevents normal functioning.

impulse: A sudden, unplanned inclination for action; abusers under the influence of substances may become impulsive or lose control of directed actions.

inhalant: A volatile (vaporized) substance, often an anesthetic gas or an organic solvent, that can be breathed into the lungs to induce a psychoactive, mind-altering, effect.

inhaled: Regarding substance abuse, breathed gases or vapors containing an illicit chemical substance into the lungs to become intoxicated.

injection drug use: Abuse of legal or illegal drugs by injecting them into the body, often into an arm vein.

intensive outpatient program: A nonresidential program designed to treat a person dependent upon a chemical substance through frequent supportive group therapy.

intensive program: *See* intensive outpatient program.

intervention: The process of interrupting an addiction and persuading the user to undergo treatment.

intoxicated: Under the influence of a substance of abuse.

intoxication: The physical and psychological state of being poisoned as a result of the misuse of a psychoactive drug, whether for emotional pleasure or judgment alternation.

intramuscular: Injected directly into the muscle.

intravenous: Injected directly into a vein (thus, into the bloodstream).

IOP: Intensive outpatient program.

IV: Intravenous.

IV drug use: *See* injection drug use.

jaundice: A yellowing of the skin and eyes caused by excess bile in the body, which can occur as a result of liver disease.

joint: Slang for marijuana cigarettes rolled for smoking.

ketamine: An anesthetic drug with psychoactive properties similar to other hallucinogenic drugs, such as phencyclidine, but with a much shorter duration of activity when misused by muscular injection, inhaling through the nostrils, or smoked.

krystal: Slang for phencyclidine (PCP).

lid poppers: Slang for amphetamines, because of the stimulatory effects of these substances.

liver failure: The inability of the liver to continue its function of processing chemicals, producing bile, and regulating body systems as a result of infections or drug use (such as chronic alcoholism or acute acetaminophen overdose).

long-term: Describing an effect of repeated drug use, which lasts longer than use of the drug.

love trip: MDMA and mescaline

LSD: Lysergic acid diethylamide.

lucky charms: Slang for ecstasy.

ludes: Slang for depressants like methaqualone or any barbiturate.

luding out: Slang for misusing depressant substances, such as barbiturates or methaqualone.

lysergic acid diethylamide: A hallucinogenic drug that acts on the serotonin receptor in the central nervous system, better known as LSD.

lysergide: *See* lysergic acid diethylamide.

MADD: Mothers Against Drunk Driving.

magic dust: Slang for PCP.

magic mushrooms: Slang for psilocybin.

maintenance treatment: Prescribed administration of a low-dose or mixed-effect opiate, such as methadone, to treat opioid addiction and prevent severe withdrawal symptoms and cravings during detoxification of substance abuse.

marijuana: A recreational drug containing tetrahydrocannabinol (THC), the primary psychoactive chemical in the cannabis sativa plant; or, the name of the plant itself; vapors may be inhaled and leaves may be chewed or smoked to obtain central nervous system hallucinogenic and somewhat depressant effects.

Marinol: Trade name for dronabinol, a synthetic prescription tetrahydrocannabinol substance similar to marijuana, used therapeutically to ease chemotherapy-induced nausea and vomiting and to stimulate the appetite.

Mary Jane: Slang for marijuana.

MDMA: 3-4 methylenedioxymethamphetamine, a psychoactive stimulant known as ecstasy.

mellow yellow: Slang for LSD.

mental addiction: *See* drug addiction.

meperidine: A synthetic narcotic agent with sedative effects, used therapeutically for relief of moderate to severe pain.

mescaline: 3,4,5-trimethoxyphenethylamine, a natural psychedelic alkaloid substance found in the peyote and other cacti and dried into white salt crystals that works on serotonin receptors in the central nervous system to provide sensations of mild euphoria and heightened perception of colors and images, but not true delusions or hallucinations.

meth: Slang for methamphetamine.

methadone: A long-lasting synthetic opioid prescribed as a controlled substance to treat severe cancer pain or administered daily as a legal substitution for heroin in patients undergoing strictly monitored addiction treatment programs.

methamphetamine: A highly addictive and potent amphetamine, which may be prescribed therapeutically to treat attention disorders in children or which may be illicitly synthesized for abuse purposes to obtain stimulatory central nervous system effects of euphoria, increased energy and concentration, and heightened self esteem; it may be injected, taken by mouth, smoked, or snorted to provide an intense rush.

Methaqualone: An older prescription drug known for its central nervous system depressant effects of sedation and muscle relaxation.

meth lab: Any location in which a person uses household items to convert over-the-counter substances like pseudoephedrine into an amphetamine for abuse.

monkey dust: Slang for PCP.

moon: Slang for mescaline.

morphine: The most potent natural opiate from the opium poppy; although it is a narcotic analgesic

and sedative when prescribed therapeutically, it has high abuse potential, and chronic use may lead to psychological dependence.

Mothers Against Drunk Driving: A nonprofit organization established in 1980 with the aims of stopping drunk driving and increasing awareness about the risks of driving under the influence of alcohol.

mushrooms: Slang for psilocybin and psilocin, the chemical substances found in psychedelic mushrooms that provide hallucinogenic effects.

naloxone: Marketed as Narcan, a short-acting opioid antagonist that blocks opioid receptors in the brain and prevents the effects of receptor agonists like heroin or morphine, making it particularly useful for the treatment of opioid addiction.

naltrexone: A long-lasting opiate antagonist that blocks opioid receptors in the brain to prevent the effects of receptor agonists like heroin or morphine, thus used for the treatment of opioid addiction and potentially useful for the prevention of cravings experienced during alcohol detoxification.

narcotic: Generally, a psychoactive substance with central nervous system depressant, sedative, and sometimes pain-relieving activity; more specifically, in the United States, an illicit substance, restricted from any legal use and associated with high likelihood of abuse, dependence, or addiction.

Narcotics Anonymous: An outpatient supportive therapy group modeled on the twelve-step program of Alcoholics Anonymous for recovery of addiction to any drug.

National Institute on Alcohol Abuse and Alcoholism: A part of the US National Institutes of Health with the aims of researching and disseminating information about alcohol-related disorders, including studies into the genetics and biologic changes related to alcohol use.

National Institute on Drug Abuse: An agency within the National Institutes of Health with the twofold mission of conducting or supporting multidisciplinary, scientific studies on the effects on drug abuse and of increasing knowledge about drug abuse and addiction through information sharing.

National Institutes of Health: The primary medical research organization of the United States, comprised of twenty-seven centers or institutes, under the umbrella of the Department of Health and Human Services, which studies and reports on all forms of diseases and treatments.

needle exchange: A program that encourages drug abusers to turn in used needles in exchange for clean needles, in an effort to reduce the spread of blood-borne diseases, such as the human immuno-deficiency virus and hepatitis, within the injection drug user population.

needle sharing: Giving needles already used to inject drugs into the body of one person to another person for the same use; a risk factor for contracting blood-borne diseases such as the human immunodeficiency virus.

negative reinforcement: Encouragement of a behavior or activity, such as alcohol use or gambling, because something averse, such as stress or anxiety, ceases when the behavior or activity begins; also known as avoidance or escape.

nexus: 2-(4-Bromo-2,5 dimethoxy-phenyl)-ethylamine, or 2CB, a synthetic stimulant abused by combining use with other club drugs, such as ecstasy.

NIAAA: National Institute on Alcohol Abuse and Alcoholism.

nicotine: The primary alkaloid drug in the tobacco plant, also found in plants of the nightshade family; nicotine activates cholinergic receptors in the central nervous system to cause euphoria, alertness, and relaxation; physical effects of smoking or chewing products with nicotine include severe damage of the lungs and heart; the chemical is highly addictive, with severe withdrawal symptoms.

NIDA: National Institute on Drug Abuse.

NIH: National Institutes of Health.

nodding out: Alternating state of passing in and out of consciousness that occurs when someone takes too much depressant class drugs, at times intentionally to provide euphoria.

off label: Use of US Food and Drug Administration–approved drugs for a treatment that is not the intended or approved therapeutic use.

OJ: Slang for marijuana.

opiate receptors: Receptors in the brain that control pain sensations; neural activity is slowed when receptors are activated by endogenous opioids or synthetic opiates.

opiate replacement therapy: Replacing a full agonist with a long-acting agent such as methadone in order to safely facilitate opioid withdrawal.

opiates: Psychoactive chemicals similar to opium from the poppy plant, which work like morphine at opiate receptors in the brain.

opioids: Schedule II controlled substance prescription drugs that work at opiate receptors in the brain to reduce pain; oxycodone is one example of these synthetic opiates.

opium: A drug derived from the poppy seed that affects the central nervous system as a depressant at the opiate receptors. Drug from the bulb of the poppy flower, cultivated since before 3500 BC.

ORT: Opiate replacement therapy.

organic solvents: Class of inhalants like gasoline with neurotoxicity.

overdose: A dangerous and potentially fatal medical condition caused by the acute ingestion of an excessive amount of a drug.

painkillers: Analgesics, or drugs that relieve pain; may act at opioid receptors or have other, nonopioid, mechanisms.

paraphernalia: Items and supplies connected to drug use; an example is a hypodermic syringe or a pipe.

PCP: Phencyclidine.

pearls: Slang for amyl nitrite.

performance-enhancing drug: A substance taken to improve the user's ability, such as anabolic steroid use in a sports player.

peyote: The cactus source of mescaline, a psychoactive substance that enhances visual experiences; alternately used to refer to the chemical substance itself.

pharming: Consuming a mix of prescription substances for recreational use.

phencyclidine: Also known as PCP; first used as an anesthetic, now used as a hallucinogen, stimulant, or sedative.

physical dependence: Adaptation of the body and brain to the continuous presence of a substance; leads to tolerance and causes withdrawal symptoms upon substance removal.

pipe: Device used to smoke crack, marijuana, tobacco, or other drugs; also, slang for a vein into which a substance of abuse is injected.

pixies: Slang for amphetamine.

poor man's pot: Slang for an inhalant, such as an organic solvent.

poppers: Slang for amyl nitrite or isobutyl nitrite.

popping: Slang for inhaling cocaine.

poppy: The flowering plant source of opium, a strong central nervous system depressant; also, slang for opium.

poppy straw: Slang for opium.

positive reinforcement: A good experience that results from a behavior or activity and that encourages continued behavior or activity; an example is winning a bet while gambling.

pseudoaddiction: Drug-seeking behavior in patients receiving inadequate treatment for chronic pain, because the increasing requests for pain medications mimic the behavior of people with actual addiction to pain medications.

psilocin: A nonaddictive, psychoactive chemical found in psychedelic mushrooms or derived from a similar chemical, psilocybin, that provides hallucinogenic effects when the mushrooms are eaten.

psilocybin: A type of mushroom as well as the name of the chemical in the mushroom that provides a natural, nonaddictive hallucinogenic effect through activity at the serotonin receptor.

psychedelic: An effect of distorted perception, thoughts, and feelings, or a drug that causes these effects; an example is LSD.

psychedelic mushrooms: *See* psilocybin.

psychoactive: Describing a substance that changes the way the brain is working, whether through receptor activity or alteration of chemical levels.

psychosis: Loss of contact with reality, or a mental illness of thought disorders that interferes with daily ability by impairing the perception of reality.

psychotropic: A substance that causes psychosis, affecting mood and behavior.

purple haze: Slang for LSD.

psychological dependence: An intense and chronic craving to use a drug for its pleasurable psychoactive, not physiological, effects, leading to compulsion and misuse; users who are psychologically dependent upon a substance believe that they need the substance to function, but do not experience tolerance or withdrawal symptoms as with physiological dependence.

rainbows: Slang for depressants.

razed: Slang for being under the influence of drugs.

rave: A party designed to enhance a hallucinogenic experience, particularly through using club drugs.

recreational drug: A drug used illicitly, in an inappropriate manner, rather than therapeutically as when drugs are prescribed by a physician to treat or control a disease.

reinforcing: Repeating behavior to experience something pleasant again; may be negative or positive.

relapse: When a condition, whether a medical disorder or a substance addiction, afflicts a person again after a period of remission, causing recurrence of substance abuse and symptoms.

remission: A period of time without signs or symptoms, whether with regard to a medical disorder or the disease of addiction.

robotripping: Slang for drinking large quantities of Robitussin cough syrup, which contains dextromethorphan, to become intoxicated.

rock: Slang for crack, the solid form of cocaine.

Rohypnol: Flunitrazepam, a sedative hypnotic chemical used as a date rape drug to induce sedation.

rolling: Using ecstasy.

roofies: Slang for Rohypnol; a sedative made by Roche that amplifies the effects of alcohol; may be used generally as slang for benzodiazepine depressants.

run: A binge of uninterrupted drug use for hours or days, often with stimulants or with alcohol.

scheduled drugs: Medications assigned a schedule by the US Food and Drug Administration according to potential therapeutic use and safety and risk of dependence or abuse.

sedative: Any substance used to ease agitation and induce sleep by altering nerve and chemical signals in the central nervous system; many sedatives are addictive, especially with chronic use, and may lower the heart rate and breathing rate if misused or combined with alcohol.

seizures: Uncontrolled electrical activity in the brain, which causes physical changes and changes in thought processes, as a result of a medical disorder or an overdose of psychoactive substances.

serial speedballing: Sequencing cocaine, cough syrup with dextromethorphan, and heroin over a one- to two-day period for an additive and prolonged high.

sheets: Slang for PCP.

shrooms: Slang for psilocybin mushrooms, a fungi with psychedelic properties when ingested.

skin popping: Injecting a drug under the skin.

skittling: Slang for ingesting large quantities of dextromethorphan in cough syrup to become intoxicated.

slamming: Slang for using a stimulant like amphetamine or ecstasy.

sleeper: Slang for heroin, specifically, or for any depressant, generally.

smack: Slang for heroin.

snap: Slang for amphetamine.

softballs: Slang for depressants.

snorting: Inhaling a powdered chemical substance through the nostrils, typically to provide a rapid sensation of intoxication.

snow: Slang for cocaine.

snowballing: Using cocaine and heroin mixed together.

snow lights: Visual hallucinations after cocaine use, image of flashing bright lights.

snuff: Chewing tobacco.

solvent: An organic chemical compound, such as paint thinner, that is used to become intoxicated by inhaling it in vapor form.

Special K: Slang for ketamine.

speed: Slang for amphetamine, methamphetamine, or crack cocaine.

speedball: Slang for the combination of cocaine and heroin.

speedballing: Generally, combining a depressant and a stimulant for intense high and low psychoactive experiences; specifically, shooting up or smoking cocaine with heroin, or ecstasy with ketamine.

stardust: Slang for cocaine.

steroids: *See* anabolic steroids.

stigma: A mark of shame or embarrassment.

stimulants: Drugs that affect the central nervous system to increase mood, well-being, energy, excitation, wakefulness, and alertness and to cause euphoria when misused; examples include cocaine, methamphetamine, and methylphenidate.

substance abuse: Excessive and improper use of a substance, which is often a psychoactive drug, despite impairment or negative consequences. *See also* drug abuse.

Sudafed: Over-the-counter trade name of pseudoephedrine, a decongestant drug used to illicitly synthesize methamphetamine, a central nervous system stimulant.

supportive program: Any treatment program, typically outpatient, that provides therapy, particularly in a group setting, to aid in substance abuse treatment, detoxification, or maintenance of abstinence; an example is Alcoholics Anonymous.

syringe: *See* hypodermic needle.

syringe exchange: *See* needle exchange.

THC: Tetrahydrocannabinol, the primary psychoactive ingredient of marijuana.

therapeutic housing: A residence for substance abusers who are undergoing observed detoxification regimens.

tobacco: A plant found originally in South America that contains nicotine, a highly addictive chemical, in its leaves; tobacco leaves may be chewed or dried and smoked.

toke: To smoke, as in cocaine or marijuana.

tolerance: The physical adaptation of the body in response to continued exposure of a substance, such that the body requires increased amounts of the substance to achieve the same effect as with initial use; tolerance often leads to physical dependence and symptoms of withdrawal upon substance removal.

toxicity: The degree of poisonousness of any substance beyond the margin of its benefits.

track: To inject a substance into a vein; so called because repeated injections cause linear punctures and darkened, scarred veins under the skin.

trafficking: Selling drugs illegally for profit.

tranquillizer: A central nervous system depressant substance used to decrease anxiety.

tremor: An involuntary muscle shaking.

triple C's: Slang for dextromethorphan, as a reference to the product Coricidin C cough syrup, with that ingredient.

tripping: Experiencing a hallucinogenic experience while using LSD.

tussing: Slang for abusing dextromethorphan, a stimulant medication found in cough syrups such as Robitussin.

twelve-step program: A treatment method developed for Alcoholics Anonymous and used by related programs, such as Narcotics Anonymous, to help alcohol or drug abusers abstain from all substance use; the intensive program for treatment recovery consists of twelve steps to follow toward becoming clean.

uppers: Slang for stimulants, such as amphetamines.

urges: Temporary thoughts or feelings that, unlike cravings, can be suppressed or overpowered through effort by the user.

user: General term for a person using a drug substance, whether prescribed or illicitly, and not always reflective of addiction.

wacky dust: Slang for cocaine.

withdrawal: A group of signs and symptoms experienced from abrupt discontinuation or rapid tapering of a psychoactive substance on which the body had become dependent or habituated.

withdrawal symptoms: Abnormal physical and psychological symptoms experienced when a drug that has been used long term is stopped, typically occurring when the body has become physically dependent on the drug; common withdrawal symptoms are anxiety, vomiting, sweating, and tremor, but they can be more severe.

wolfies: Slang for rohypnol.

X-ing: Using ecstasy.

XTC: Ecstasy.

yerba mate: A South American plant source of the stimulant caffeine, for which the leaves are chewed or steeped in hot water to make tea.

General Bibliography

Ajzen, Icek. "From Intentions to Actions: A Theory of Planned Behavior." *Action-Control: From Cognition to Behavior.* Ed. Julius Kuhl and Jürgen Beckmann. New York: Springer, 1985. 11–39.

Ajzen, Icek, and Martin Fishbein. *Understanding Attitudes and Predicting Social Behavior.* Englewood Cliffs, NJ: Prentice Hall, 1980.

Akers, Ronald L., and John K. Cochran. "Adolescent Marijuana Use: A Test of Three Theories of Deviant Behavior." *Deviant Behavior* 6 (1985): 323–46.

Akers, Ronald L., et al. "Social Learning and Deviant Behavior: A Specific Test of a General Theory." *American Sociological Review* 44 (1979): 636–55.

Bachman, Jerald G., et al. "Explaining the Recent Decline in Marijuana Use: Differentiating the Effects of Perceived Risks, Disapproval, and General Lifestyle Factors." *Health and Social Behavior* 29 (1988): 92–112.

Bachman, Jerald G., Lloyd D. Johnston, and Patrick M. O'Malley. "Explaining the Recent Decline in Cocaine Use Among Young Adults: Further Evidence That Perceived Risks and Disapproval Lead to Reduced Drug Use." *Health and Social Behavior* 29 (1990): 92–112.

Bailey, Steffani R., et al. "Withdrawal Symptoms Over Time Among Adolescents in a Smoking Cessation Intervention: Do Symptoms Vary by Level of Nicotine Dependence?" *Addictive Behaviors* 34. 12 (2009):1017–22.

Bailey, Susan, and Robert L. Hubbard. "Developmental Variation in the Context of Marijuana Initiation Among Adolescents." *Health and Social Behavior* 31 (1990): 58–70.

Bailey, Susan L., Carol S. Camlin, and Susan T. Ennett. "Substance Use and Risky Sexual Behavior Among Homeless and Runaway Youth." *Adolescent Health* 23. 6 (1998): 378–88.

Bancalari, Eduardo. "Substance Abuse in Pregnancy: Effects on Cardiorespiratory Function in the Infant." *NIDA Research Monograph* 114 (1991): 117–27.

Bandura, Albert. "Self-Efficacy: Toward a Unifying Theory of Behavior Change." *Psychological Review* 84 (1977): 191–215.

---. *Social Foundations of Thought and Action: A Social Cognitive Theory.* Englewood Cliffs, NJ: Prentice Hall, 1986.

Basen-Engquist, K., and G. S. Parcel. "Attitudes, Norms, and Self-Efficacy: A Model of Adolescents' HIV-Related Sexual Risk Behavior." *Health Education Quarterly* 12 (1992): 263–77.

Bays, J. "Substance Abuse and Child Abuse. Impact of Addiction on the Child." *Pediatric Clinics of North America* 37. 4 (1990): 881–904.

Beauvais, Frederick. "Cultural Identification and Substance Use in North America: An Annotated Bibliography." *Substance Use and Misuse* 33.6 (1998): 1315–36.

---. "Research Topics for the Problem of Volatile Solvent Abuse." *Sociocultural Perspectives on Volatile Solvent Use.* Ed. Fred Trimble and Joseph Trimble. Binghamton, NY: Harrington Park P, 1997. 103–07.

---. "Volatile Solvent Abuse: Trends and Patterns." *Substance Use and Misuse* 32.12–13 (1997): 1829–34.

Behnke, Marylou, and Fonda D. Eyler. "The Consequences of Prenatal Substance Use for the Developing Fetus, Newborn, and Young Child." *International Journal of the Addictions* 28.13 (1993): 1341–91.

Bentler, Peter M., and George Speckart. "Models of Attitude-Behavior Relations." *Psychological Review* 86 (1979): 452–64.

Besharov, Douglas J. "Mandatory Reporting of Child Abuse and Research on the Effects of Prenatal Drug Exposure." *NIDA Research Monograph* 117 (1992): 366–84.

Bigelow, George E. "Behavioral Treatment of Alcohol Problems." *Nervous and Mental Disease* 168.1 (1980): 56–57.

Black, Maureen M., et al. "Parenting and Early Development Among Children of Drug-Abusing Women: Effects of Home Intervention." *Pediatrics* 94.4 (1994): 440–48.

Block, J., J. H. Block, and S. Keyes. "Longitudinally Foretelling Drug Usage in Adolescence: Early Childhood Personality and Environmental Precursors." *Child Development* 52 (1988): 336–55.

Broekhuizen, F. F., J. Utrie, and C. Van Mullem. "Drug Use or Inadequate Prenatal Care? Adverse Pregnancy Outcome in an Urban Setting." *American Journal of Obstetrics and Gynecology* 166. 6 (1992): 1747–56.

Brook, David W., et al. "Drug Use and the Risk of Major Depressive Disorder, Alcohol Dependence, and Substance Use Disorders." *Archives of General Psychiatry* 59 (2002): 1039–44.

Brook, Judith S., Patricia Cohen, and David W. Brook. "Longitudinal Study of Co-Occurring Psychiatric Disorders and Substance Abuse." *American Academy of Child and Adolescent Psychiatry* 37 (1988): 322–30.

Brook, Judith S., et al. "The Psychosocial Etiology of Adolescent Drug Use: A Family Interactional Approach." *Genetic, Social, and General Psychology Monographs* 116 (1990): 111–267.

Brook, Judith S., Martin Whiteman, and Ann S. Gordon. "Qualitative and Quantitative Aspects of Adolescent Drug Use: Interplay of Personality, Family, and Peer Correlates." *Psychological Reports* 51 (1982): 1151–63.

---. "States of Drug Use in Adolescence: Personality, Peer, and Family Correlates." *Developmental Psychology* 19 (1983): 269–77.

Caplehorn, John R. M. "A Comparison of Abstinence-Oriented and Indefinite Methadone Maintenance Treatment." *International Journal of the Addictions* 29.11 (1994): 1361–75.

Catalano, Richard F., et al. "An Experimental Intervention with Families of Substance Abusers: One-Year Follow-Up of the Focus on Families Project." *Addiction* 94. 2 (1999): 241–54.

Chassin, Laurie, et al. "Predicting the Onset of Cigarette Smoking in Adolescents: A Longitudinal Study." *Applied Social Psychology* 14 (1984): 224–43.

Clayton, Richard. R. "Transitions in Drug Use: Risk and Protective Factors." *Vulnerability to Drug Abuse.* Ed. Meyer Glantz and Roy Pickens. Washington: American Psychological Association, 1992. 15–22.

Cloninger, C. Robert. "Neurogenetic Adaptive Mechanisms in Alcoholism." *Science* 236 (1987): 410–16.

Cochin J., et al. "The Influence of the Mode of Morphine Administration on Tolerance and Dependence." *NIDA Research Monograph* 27 (1979): 36–47.

Cohen, S. "The Prescription of Controlled Substances: What's Right and What's Wrong?" *NIDA Research Monograph* 27 (1979): 11–16.

Cowan, J. D., et al. "Drug Abusers: Defeated and Joyless." *NIDA Research Monograph* 27 (1979): 170–76.

Craig, Robert J. "Effectiveness of Low-Dose Methadone Maintenance for the Treatment of Inner City Heroin Addicts." *International Journal of Addictions* 15.5 (1980): 701–10.

Davis, Shoni K. "Chemical Dependency in Women: A Description of Its Effects and Outcome on Adequate Parenting." *Substance Abuse Treatment* 7.4 (1990): 225–32.

DeKay, W. T., and D. M. Buss. "Human Nature, Individual Differences, and the Importance of Context: Perspectives from Evolutionary Psychology." *Current Directions in Psychological Science* 1.6 (1992): 184–89.

Dembo, R., et al. "A Longitudinal Study of the Relationships Among Alcohol Use, Marijuana/Hashish Use, Cocaine Use, and Emotional/Psychological Functioning Problems in a Cohort of High-Risk Youth." *International Journal of the Addictions* 25 (1990): 1341–82.

DeVries, H., M. Dijkstra, and G. Kok. "Self-Efficacy as a Determinant of the Onset of Smoking and Interventions to Prevent Smoking in Adolescents." *European Perspectives in Psychology* 2 (1990): 209–22.

DeVries, H., M. Dijkstra, and P. Kuhlman. "Self-Efficacy: The Third Factor Besides Attitude and Subjective Norm as a Predictor of Behavioral Decisions." *Health Education Research* 3 (1988): 273–82.

Donovan, John E., and Richard Jessor. "Structure of Problem Behavior in Adolescence and Young Adulthood." *Consulting and Clinical Psychology* 53 (1985): 890–904.

Donovan, John E., Richard Jessor, and Frances M. Costa. "Adolescent Health Behavior and Conventionality-Unconventionality: An Extension of Problem-Behavior Theory." *Health Psychology* 10 (1991): 52–61.

---. "Adolescent Problem Drinking: Stability of Psychosocial and Behavioral Correlates Across a Generation. *Studies on Alcohol* 60 (1999): 352–61.

---. "Structure of Health-Enhancing Behavior in Adolescence: A Latent-Variable Approach." *Health and Social Behavior* 34 (1993) 346–62.

Donovan, John E., Richard Jessor, and S. L. Jessor. "Problem Drinking in Adolescence and Young Adulthood: A Follow-Up Study." *Studies on Alcohol* 44 (1983): 109–37.

Dore, Martha M., and J. M. Doris. "Preventing Child Placement in Substance-Abusing Families: Research-Informed Practice." *Child Welfare* 77.4 (1998): 407–26.

Dore, Martha M., J. M. Doris, and P. Wright. "Identifying Substance Abuse in Maltreating Families: A Child Welfare Challenge." *Child Abuse and Neglect* 19.5 (1995): 531–43.

Dunn, M. G., et al. "Origins and Consequences of Child Neglect in Substance Abuse Families." *Clinical Psychology Review* 22.7 (2002): 1063–90.

Elliott, Delbert S., David Huizinga, and Scott Menard. *Multiple Problem Youth: Delinquency, Substance Use, and Mental Health Problems.* New York: Springer, 1989.

Eyler, F. D., and M. Behnke. "Early Development of Infants Exposed to Drugs Prenatally." *Clinics in Perinatology* 26.1 (1999): 107–50.

Famularo, Richard, Robert Kinscherff, and Terence Fenton. "Parental Substance Abuse and the Nature of Child Maltreatment." *Child Abuse and Neglect* 16.4 (1992): 475–83.

Farkas, A. G., D. L. Colbert, and K. J. Erskine. "Anonymous Testing for Drug Abuse in an Antenatal Population." *British Journal of Obstetrics and Gynaecology* 102.7 (1995): 563–65.

Farrell, M., et al. "Methadone Maintenance Treatment in Opiate Dependence: A Review." *British Medical Journal* 309.6960 (1994): 997–1001.

Farrington, D. P., et al. "Advancing Knowledge About the Onset of Delinquency and Crime." *Advances in Clinical Child Psychology* 13 (1990): 283–342.

Finnegan, Loretta. "Management of Maternal and Neonatal Substance Abuse Problems." *NIDA Research Monograph* 90 (1988): 177–82.

Finnegan, Loretta P., T. F. Metros, and L. E. Hopkins. "Management of Neonatal Narcotic Abstinence Utilizing a Phenobarbital Loading Dose Method." *NIDA Research Monograph* 27 (1979): 247–53.

Fishbein, Martin, and Icek Ajzen. *Belief, Attitude, Intention and Behavior: An Introduction to Theory and Research.* Reading, MA: Addison-Wesley, 1975.

Fisher, L. A., and K. E. Bauman. "Influence and Selection in the Friend-Adolescent Relationship: Findings from Studies of Adolescent Smoking and Drinking." *Applied Social Psychology* 18 (1988): 289–314.

Flay, Brian R., et al. "Cigarette Smoking: Why Young People Do It and Ways of Preventing It." *Pediatric and Adolescent Behavioral Medicine.* Ed. Patrick J. McGrath and Philip Firestone. New York: Springer, 1983. 132–83.

Flay, Brian R., and J. Petraitis. "The Theory of Triadic Influence: A New Theory of Health Behavior with Implications for Preventive Interventions." *Advances in Medical Sociology: A Reconsideration of Health Behavior Change Models.* Vol. 4. Ed. Gary L. Albrecht. Greenwich, CT: JAI Press, 1994. 19–44.

Frank, D. A., K. Bresnahan, and B. S. Zuckerman. "Maternal Cocaine Use: Impact on Child Health and Development." *Advances in Pediatrics* 40 (1993): 65–99.

Fraser, A. C., and S. Cavanagh. "Pregnancy and Drug Addiction—Long-Term Consequences." *Royal Society of Medicine* 84.9 (1991): 530–32.

Freedman R. R., and G. Czertko. "A Comparison of Thrice Weekly LAAM and Daily Methadone in Employed Heroin Addicts." *Drug and Alcohol Dependence* 8.3 (1981): 215–22.

Gabel, S., and R. Shindledecker. "Incarceration in Parents of Day Hospital Youth: Relationship to Parental Substance Abuse and Suspected Child Abuse/Maltreatment." *International Journal of Partial Hospitalization* 8.1 (1992): 77–87.

Gift, Thomas E., et al. "How Diagnostic Concepts of Schizophrenia Differ." *Nervous and Mental Disease* 168.1 (1980): 3–8.

Gold, M. S., A. L. C. Pottash, D. R. Sweeney, and H. D. Kleber. "Clonidine Detoxification: A Fourteen-Day Protocol for Rapid Opiate Withdrawal." *NIDA Research Monograph* 27 (1979): 226–32.

Goldman, M. S., S. A. Brown, B. A. Christiansen, and G. Smith. "Alcoholism and Memory: Broadening the Scope of Alcohol-Expectancy Research." *Psychological Bulletin* 110 (1991). 137–46.

Goldstein, P. J. "Ethnoeconomical Approach to the Relationship Between Crime and Drug Use: Preliminary Findings." *NIDA Research Monograph* 27 (1979): 156–62.

Gottfredson, Michael R., and Travis A. Hirschi. *A General Theory of Crime.* Stanford: Stanford UP, 1990.

Grönbladh, L., L. S. Ohlund, and L. M. Gunne. "Mortality in Heroin Addiction: Impact of Methadone Treatment." *Acta Psychiatrica Scandinavica* 82.3 (1990): 223–27.

Hawkins, J. David, Richard F. Catalano, and Janet Y. Miller. "Risk and Protective Factors for Alcohol and Other Drug Problems in Adolescence and Early Adulthood: Implications for Substance Abuse Prevention." *Psychological Bulletin* 112.1 (1992): 64–105.

Henderson, Allan, Sally Champlin, and William Evashwick. eds. *Promoting Teen Health: Linking Schools, Health Organizations, and Community.* Thousand Oaks, CA: Sage, 1998.

Hoffman, R. S., and L. R. Goldfrank. "The Impact of Drug Abuse and Addiction on Society." *Emergency Medicine Clinics of North America* 8.3 (1990): 467–80.

Huba, George J., and Peter M. Bentler. "A Developmental Theory of Drug Use: Derivations and Assessment of a Causal Modeling Approach." *Life-Span Development and Behavior.* Vol. 4. Ed. Paul B. Baltes, David L. Featherman, and Richard M. Lerner. New York: Academic Press, 1982. 147–203.

Huba, George J., J. A. Wingard, and Peter M. Bentler. "Longitudinal Analysis of the Role of Peer Support, Adult Models, and Peer Subcultures in Beginning Adolescent Substance Use: An Application of Set Wise Canonical Correlation Method." *Multivariate Behavioral Research* 15 (1980): 259–79.

Huestis, Marilyn A., and Robin E. Choo. "Drug Abuse's Smallest Victims: In Utero Drug Exposure." *Forensic Science International* 128.1–2 (2002): 20–30.

Jaudes, P. K., E. Ekwo, and J. Van Voorhis. "Association of Drug Abuse and Child Abuse." *Child Abuse and Neglect* 19.9 (1995): 1065–75.

Jessor, Richard. "Psychosocial Issues in Drug Policies: Implications for the Legalization Debate." *Drugs, Alcohol, and Tobacco: Making the Science and Policy Connections.* Oxford: Oxford UP, 1993. 319–25.

—. "Risk Behavior in Adolescence: A Psychosocial Framework for Understanding and Action." *Adolescent Health* 12 (1991): 597–605.

—. "Successful Adolescent Development Among Youth in High-Risk Settings." *American Psychologist* 48 (1993): 117–26.

Jessor, Richard, John E. Donovan, and Frances M. Costa. *Beyond Adolescence: Problem Behavior and Young Adult Development.* Cambridge: Cambridge UP, 1991.

Jessor, Richard, et al. "A Developmental Study of Heavy Episodic Drinking Among College Students: The Role of Psychosocial and Behavioral Protective and Risk Factors." *Studies on Alcohol* 67 (2006): 86–94.

Jessor, Richard, Mark S. Turbin, and Frances M. Costa. "Protective Factors in Adolescent Health Behavior." *Personality and Social Psychology: Personality Processes and Individual Differences* 75 (1998): 788–800.

Johnson, J. L., and M. Leff. "Children of Substance Abusers: Overview of Research Findings." *Pediatrics* 103.5 (1999): 1085–99.

Johnson, V., and R. J. Pandina. "Effects of the Family Environment on Adolescent Substance Use, Delinquency, and Coping Styles." *American Journal of Drug and Alcohol Abuse* 17 (1991): 71–88.

Johnston, Lloyd D. "Prescription Drug Use by Adolescents: What We are Learning and What We Still Need to Know." *Adolescent Health* 45.6 (2009): 539–40.

Johnston, Lloyd D., Patrick M. O'Malley, and L. Eveland. "Drugs and Delinquency: A Search for Causal Connections." *Longitudinal Research on Drug Use: Empirical Findings and Methodological Issues.* Ed. Denise Bystryn Kandel. Washington: Hemisphere, 1978. 137–56.

Kaiko, R. F., et al. "Relative Analgesic Potency of Intramuscular Heroin and Morphine in Cancer Patients with Postoperative Pain: A Preliminary Report." *NIDA Research Monograph* 27 (1979): 254–60.

Kandall, S. R. "Treatment Strategies for Drug-Exposed Neonates." *Clinics in Perinatology* 26.1 (1999): 231–43.

Kandel, Denise, O. Simcha-Fagan, and M. Davies. "Risk Factors for Delinquency and Illicit Drug Use from Adolescence to Young Adulthood." *Drug Issues* 16 (1986): 67–90.

Kandel, Denise B., Ronald. C. Kessler, and Rebecca Z. Margulies. "Antecedents of Adolescent Initiation into Stages of Drug Use: A Developmental Analysis." *Youth and Adolescence.* 7.1 (1978): 13–40.

Kaplan, Howard B., S. S. Martin, and C. Robbins. "Application of a General Theory of Deviant Behavior: Self-Derogation and Adolescent Drug Use." *Health and Social Behavior* 23 (1982): 274–94.

—. "Escalation of Marijuana Use: Application of a General Theory of Deviant Behavior." *Health and Social Behavior* 27 (1986): 44–61.

—. "Pathways to Adolescent Drug Use: Self-Derogation, Peer Influence, Weakening of Social Controls, and Early Substance Use." *Health and Social Behavior* 25 (1984): 270–89.

Karila Laurent, et al. "Pharmacological Approaches to Methamphetamine Dependence: A Focused Review." *British Journal of Clinical Pharmacology* 69.6 (2010): 578–92.

Kaymakcalan S. "Fifty Years of International Control of Dependence-Producing Drugs." *NIDA Research Monograph* 27 (1979): 74–76.

Keen, J., and L. H. Alison. "Drug Misusing Parents: Key Points for Health Professionals." *Archives of Disease in Childhood* 85.4 (2001): 296–99.

Keen, J., et al. "Can Methadone Maintenance for Heroin-Dependent Patients Retained in General Practice Reduce Criminal Conviction Rates and Time Spent in Prison?" *British Journal of General Practice* 50.450 (2000): 48–49.

Kellam, S. G., C. H. Brown, and J. P. Fleming. "The Prevention of Teenage Substance Use: Longitudinal Research and Strategy." *Promoting Adolescent Health: A Dialogue on Research and Practice*. Ed. Thomas J. Coates, Anne C. Petersen, and Cheryl Perry. New York: Academic Press, 1982. 171–200.

Kelley, S. J. "Parenting Stress and Child Maltreatment in Drug-Exposed Children." *Child Abuse and Neglect* 16.3 (1992): 317–28.

Kenner, C., and K. D'Apolito. "Outcomes for Children Exposed to Drugs in Utero." *Obstetric, Gynecologic, and Neonatal Nursing* 26.5 (1997): 595–03.

Kirby, M. L. "A Quantitative Method for Determining the Effects of Opiates on Fetal Rats in Utero." *NIDA Research Monograph* 27 (1979): 191–97.

Klee Hilary, et al. "The Sharing of Injecting Equipment Among Drug Users Attending Prescribing Clinics and Those Using Needle-Exchanges." *British Journal of Addiction* 86.2 (1991): 217–23.

Krohn, Marvin D., Ronald L. Akers, Marcia J. Radosevich, and Lonn Lanza-Kaduce. "Norm Qualities and Adolescent Drinking and Drug Behavior: The Effects of Norm Quality and Reference Group on Using and Abusing Alcohol and Marijuana." *Drug Issues* 12 (1982): 343–59.

Kumpfer, Karol L., Stephanie Griswold-Ezekoye, and Mary Frank. *Childhood and Chemical Abuse: Prevention and Intervention*. New York: Haworth Press, 1986.

Kumpfer, Karol L., and C. W. Turner. "The Social Ecology Model of Adolescent Substance Abuse: Implications for Prevention." *International Journal of the Addictions* 25 (1990–1991): 435–63.

Lasagna, L. "The Impact of Regulations on the Development of Psychoactive Drugs." *NIDA Research Monograph* 27 (1979): 29–35.

Lee, Ian, and Peter Tyrer. "Responses of Chronic Agoraphobics to Subliminal and Supraliminal Phobic Motion Pictures." *Nervous and Mental Disease* 168.1 (1980): 34–40.

Lerner, J. V., and J. R. Vicary. "Difficult Temperament and Drug Use: Analyses from the New York Longitudinal Study." *Drug Education* 14 (1984): 1–8.

Loveland-Cherry, C. J. "Family Interventions to Prevent Substance Abuse: Children and Adolescents."

Annual Review of Nursing Research 18 (2000): 195–218.

Maddux, J. E., and R. W. Rogers. "Protection Motivation and Self-Efficacy: A Revised Theory of Fear Appeals and Attitude Change." *Experimental Social Psychology* 19 (1983): 469–79.

Magnusson, David, ed. *Toward a Psychology of Situations: An Interactional Perspective*. Hillsdale, NJ: Erlbaum, 1981.

McBride, A. A., G. W. Joe, and D. D. Simpson. "Prediction of Long-Term Alcohol Use, Drug Use, and Criminality Among Inhalant Users." *Hispanic Journal of Behavioral Sciences* 13 (1991). 315–23.

McGlothlin, W. H., and M. D. Anglin. "Effects of Closing the Bakersfield Methadone Clinic." *NIDA Research Monograph* 27 (1979): 135–41.

McGuire, W. J. "Using Guiding-Idea Theories of the Person to Develop Educational Campaigns Against Drug Abuse and Other Health Threatening Behavior." *Health Education Research* 6 (1991): 173–84.

McLellan, Thomas A., George E. Woody, and Charles P. O'Brien. "Development of Psychiatric Disorders in Drug Abusers: Relation Between Primary Drug and Type of Disorder." *NIDA Research Monograph* 27 (1979): 149–55.

McLellan, Thomas A., Lester Luborsky, Charles P. O'Brien, and George E. Woody. "An Improved Evaluation Instrument for Substance Abuse Patients: The Addiction Severity Index." *NIDA Research Monograph* 27 (1979): 142–48.

—. "An Improved Diagnostic Evaluation Instrument for Substance Abuse Patients: The Addiction Severity Index." *Nervous and Mental Disease* 168.1 (1980): 26–33.

Mendelson, J. H., J. Ellingboe, J. Kuehnle, and N. K. Mello. "Heroin and Naltrexone Effects on Pituitary-Gonadal Hormones in Man: Tolerance and Supersensitivity." *NIDA Research Monograph* 27 (1979): 302–08.

Mills, Edward M., et al. "Uncoupling the Agony from the Ecstasy." *Nature* 426 (2003): 403–04.

Moncher, M. S., G. W. Holden, and S. P. Schinke. "Psychosocial Correlates of Adolescent Substance Use: A Review of Current Etiological Constructs." *International Journal of the Addictions* 26 (1991): 377–414.

Morrison, C. L., and C. Siney. "A Survey of the Management of Neonatal Opiate Withdrawal in England and Wales." *European Journal of Pediatrics* 155.4 (1996): 323–26.

Newcomb, Michael D., and Maria Felix-Ortiz. "Multiple Protective and Risk Factors for Drug Use and Abuse: Cross-Sectional and Prospective Findings." *Personality and Social Psychology* 63.2 (1992): 280–96.

Nurco, D. N., and N. Wegner. "Addicts and Drugs." *NIDA Research Monograph* 27 (1979): 184–90.

O'Brien, Charles P. "Unreinforced Self-Injections: Effects on Rituals and Outcome in Heroin Addicts." *NIDA Research Monograph* 27 (1979): 275–81.

Oetting, Eugene R., and Frederick Beauvais. "Peer Cluster Theory: Drugs and the Adolescent." *Counseling and Development* 65 (1986): 17–22.

—. "Peer Cluster Theory, Socialization Characteristics, and Adolescent Drug Use: A Path Analysis." *Counseling Psychology* 34 (1987): 205–13.

Osterling K. L., and M. L. Austin. "Substance Abuse Interventions for Parents Involved in the Child Welfare System: Evidence and Implications." *Evidenced-Based Social Work* 5.1–2, (2008): 157–89.

Peterson, L., S. Gable, and L. Saldana. "Treatment of Maternal Addiction to Prevent Child Abuse and Neglect." *Addictive Behaviors* 21.6 (1996): 789–801.

Petraitis, John, Brian R. Flay, and Todd Q. Miller. "Reviewing Theories of Adolescent Substance Use: Organizing Pieces in the Puzzle." *Psychological Bulletin* 117.1 (1995): 67–86.

Phil, R. Q., J. Peterson, and P. Finn. "An Heuristic Model of the Inherited Predisposition to Alcoholism." *Psychology of Addictive Behaviors* 4 (1990): 12–25.

Pilkonis, Paul A., et al. "Social Anxiety and Psychiatric Diagnosis." *Nervous and Mental Disease* 168.1 (1980): 13–18.

Pollard, I. "Substance Abuse and Parenthood: Biological Mechanisms-Bioethical Challenges." *Women and Health* 30.3 (2000): 1–24.

Popkin, Michael K., Thomas B. Mackenzie, and Allan L. Callies. "Consultees' Concordance with Consultants' Recommendations for Diagnostic Action." *Nervous and Mental Disease* 168.1 (1980): 9–12.

Regan, Dianne O., S. M. Ehrlich, and L. P. Finnegan. "Infants of Drug Addicts: At Risk for Child Abuse, Neglect, and Placement in Foster Care." *Neurotoxicology and Teratology* 9.4 (1987): 315–19.

Rosner, M. A., L. Keith, and I. Chasnoff. "The Northwestern University Drug Dependence Program: The Impact of Intensive Prenatal Care on Labor and Delivery Outcomes." *American Journal of Obstetrics and Gynecology* 144.1 (1982): 23–27.

Sadava, Stanley W. "Psychosocial Interactionism and Substance Use." *Drugs and Society* 2 (1987): 1–30.

Salamy, Joseph G., James R. Wright, and Louis A. Faillace. "Changes in Average Evoked Responses during Abstention in Chronic Alcoholics." *Nervous and Mental Disease* 168.1 (1980): 19–25.

Schlegel, R. P., et al. "Predicting Alcohol Use in Young Adult Males: A Comparison of the Fishbein-Ajzen Model and the Jessors' Problem-Behavior Theory." *Drugs and Society* 1 (1987): 7–24.

Schoenbaum, Ellie, et al. "Risk Factors for Human Immunodeficiency Virus Infection in Intravenous Drug Users." *New England Journal of Medicine* 321.13 (1989): 874–79.

Shankaran, S., et al. "Impact of Maternal Substance Use During Pregnancy on Childhood Outcome." *Seminars in Fetal and Neonatal Medicine* 12.2 (2007): 143–50.

Shedler, J., and J. Block. "Adolescent Drug Use and Psychological Health." *American Psychologist* 45 (1990): 612–30.

Simcha-Fagan, O., J. C. Gersten, and T. S. Langer. "Early Precursors and Concurrent Correlates of Patterns of Illicit Drug Use in Adolescents." *Drug Issues* 16 (1986): 7–28.

Smith, G. M., and C. P. Fogg. "Psychological Antecedents of Teenage Drug Use." *Research in Community and Mental Health* 1 (1979): 87–102.

Smith, Joshua P., and Sarah W. Book, "Comorbidity of Generalized Anxiety Disorder and Alcohol Use Disorders Among Individuals Seeking Outpatient Substance Abuse Treatment." *Addictive Behaviors* 35.1 (2010): 42–45.

Soepatmi, S. "Developmental Outcomes of Children of Mothers Dependent on Heroin or Heroin/Methadone During Pregnancy." *Acta Paediatrica* 404 (1994): 36–39.

Stacy, Allan W., Michael D. Newcomb, and Peter M. Bentler. "Personality, Problem Drinking, and Drunk Driving: Mediating, Moderating, and Direct-Effect Models." *Personality and Social Psychology* 60 (1991): 795–811.

Stacy, Allan W., Peter M. Bentler, and Brian R. Flay. "Attitudes and Health Behavior in Diverse Populations: Drunk Driving, Alcohol Use, Binge Eating, Marijuana Use, and Cigarette Use." *Health Psychology* 13 (1994): 73–85.

Stein, Judith A, Michael D. Newcomb, and Peter M. Bentler. "An 8-Year Study of Multiple Influences on Drug Use and Drug Use Consequences." *Personality and Social Psychology* 53.6 (1987): 1094–105.

—. "Personality and Drug Use: Reciprocal Effects Across Four Years." *Personality and Individual Differences* 8.3 (1987): 419–30.

—. "The Relationship of Gender, Social Conformity and Substance Use: A Longitudinal Study." *Society of Psychologists in Addictive Behaviors* 5.4 (1986): 125–38.

Sussman, S., et al. "The Motivation, Skills, and Decision-Making Model of Drug Abuse Prevention." *Substance Use and Misuse* 39.10–12 (2004): 1971–2016.

Teichman, M., Z. Barnea, and G. Ravav. "Personality and Substance Use Among Adolescents: A Longitudinal Study." *British Journal of Addiction* 84.2 (1989). 181–90.

Theis, J. G., et al. "Current Management of the Neonatal Abstinence Syndrome: A Critical Analysis of the Evidence." *Biology of the Neonate* 71.6 (1997): 345–56.

Tronick, E. Z., M. Beeghly, L. Fetters, and M. K. Weinberg. "New Methodologies for Evaluating Residual Brain Damage in Infants Exposed to Drugs of Abuse: Objective Methods for Describing Movements, Facial Expressions, and Communicative Behaviors." *NIDA Research Monograph* 114 (1991): 262–90.

van Baar, A. L., et al. "Development After Prenatal Exposure to Cocaine, Heroin and Methadone." *Acta Paediatrica* 404 (1994): 40–46.

Ward, J., W. Hall, and R. P. Mattick. "Role of Maintenance Treatment in Opioid Dependence." *Lancet* 353.9148 (1999): 221–26.

Washton, A. M., R. B. Resnick, and R. A .Rawson. "Clonidine Hydrochloride: A Nonopiate Treatment for Opiate Withdrawal." *NIDA Research Monograph* 27 (1979): 233–39.

Wiers, Reinout, W.H.J., and Allan W. Stacy. *Handbook of Implicit Cognition and Addiction*. Thousand Oaks, CA: Sage, 2006.

Wills, Thomas A., E. Baker, and G. J. Botvin. "Dimensions of Assertiveness: Differential Relationships to Substance Use in Early Adolescence." *Consulting and Clinical Psychology* 57, (1989): 473–78.

Wills, Thomas A., and T. J. Dishion. "Temperament and Adolescent Substance Use: A Transactional Analysis of Emerging Self-Control." *Clinical Child and Adolescent Psychology* 33.1 (2004): 69–81.

Wills, Thomas A., et al. "Family Communication and Religiosity Related to Substance Use and Sexual Behavior in Early Adolescence." *Psychology of Addictive Behaviors* 17.4 (2003): 312–23.

Wills, Thomas A., et al. "The Role of Parent and Peer Support in Adolescent Substance Use: A Test of Mediated Effects." *Psychology of Addictive Behaviors* 18.2 (2004): 122–34.

Wills, Thomas A., and Saul Shiffman, eds. *Coping and Substance Use*. Orlando: Academic Press, 1985.

Wills, Thomas A., and M. Stoolmiller. "The Role of Self-Control in Early Escalation of Substance Use: A Time-Varying Analysis." *Consulting and Clinical Psychology* 70.4 (2002): 986–97.

Wills, Thomas A., J. M. Sandy, and A. M. Yaeger. "Buffering Effect of Religiosity for Adolescent Substance Use." *Psychology of Addictive Behaviors* 17.1 (2003): 24–31.

—. "Moderators of the Relation Between Substance Use Level and Problems: Test of a Self-Regulation Model in Middle Adolescence." *Abnormal Psychology* 111.1 (2002): 3–21.

—. "Stress and Smoking in Adolescence: A Test of Directional Hypotheses with Latent Growth Analysis." *Health Psychology.* 21.2 (2002): 122–30.

Zeitlin, H. "Children with Alcohol Misusing Parents." *British Medical Bulletin* 50.1 (1994): 139–51.

Web Site Directory

This is a directory of essential, key, or useful organizations, support groups, research agencies, or databases related to addiction and substance abuse, largely collected from the Web Sites of Interest section that concludes each article. The following sites were visited by editors in 2012. Because URLs frequently change, the accuracy of these addresses cannot be guaranteed; however, long-standing sites, such as those of colleges and universities, national organizations, and government agencies, generally maintain links when sites are moved or updated.

Aboriginal Drug and Alcohol Council
http://www.adac.org.au

Academy of Nutrition and Dietetics
http://www.eatright.org

Action on Smoking and Health
http://www.ash.org

Adult Children of Alcoholics World Service Organization, Inc.
http://www.adultchildren.org

Al-Anon/Alateen
http://www.al-anon.alateen.org

Alcohol Cost Calculator
http://alcoholcostcalculator.org

Alcoholics Anonymous
http://www.aa.org

Alliance for Consumer Education. Inhalant Abuse Prevention Program
http://www.inhalant.org

American Academy of Child and Adolescent Psychiatry
http://www.aacap.org

American Academy of Pain Medicine
http://www.painmed.org

American Academy of Pediatrics
http://www.aap.org

American Association for Respiratory Care
http://www.aarc.org/

American Association of Nurse Anesthetists
http://www.aana.com

American Association of Poison Control Centers
http://www.aapcc.org

American Association of Suicidology
http://www.suicidology.org

American Board of Addiction Medicine
http://abam.net

American Cancer Society
http://cancer.org

American College of Chest Physicians
http://www.chestnet.org

American Council for Drug Education
http://www.acde.org

American Dental Association
http://www.ada.org/

American Diabetes Association
http://www.diabetes.org

American Liver Foundation
http://www.liverfoundation.org

American Lung Association
http://www.lungusa.org

American Pharmacists Association
http://www.pharmacist.com

American Psychological Association
http://www.apa.org

American Public Health Association
http://www.apha.org

American Rehabilitation Counseling Association
http://www.arcaweb.org

Americans for Nonsmokers' Rights
http://no-smoke.org

American Society of Addiction Medicine
http://www.asam.org

American Society of Clinical Hypnosis
http://asch.net

Anxiety Disorders Association of America
http://www.adaa.org

Association for Behavioral and Cognitive Therapies
http://www.abct.org

Association of Intervention Specialists
http://www.associationofinterventionspecialists.org

Beck Institute for Cognitive Behavior Therapy
http://www.beckinstitute.org

Caffeine Awareness Association
http://www.caffeineawareness.org

Campaign for Tobacco-Free Kids
http://www.tobaccofreekids.org

Canadian Cancer Society
http://www.cancer.ca

The Canadian Lung Association
http://www.lung.ca

Center for Media Literacy
http://www.medialit.org

Center for Science in the Public Interest
http://www.cspinet.org

Center on Alcohol Marketing and Youth
http://www.camy.org

Centers for Disease Control and Prevention
http://www.cdc.gov

Centre for Addiction and Mental Health
http://www.camh.net

Children of Alcoholics Foundation
http://www.coaf.org

Clinical Trials.gov
http://www.clinicaltrials.gov

Clutterers Anonymous
http://www.clutterersanonymous.net

Cocaine Anonymous
http://www.ca.org

Co-Dependents Anonymous
http://www.coda.org

College Drinking: Changing the Culture
http://www.collegedrinkingprevention.gov

COPD Foundation
http://www.copdfoundation.org

Crystal Meth Anonymous
http://www.crystalmeth.org

DanceSafe.org
http://dancesafe.org

Debtors Anonymous
http://www.debtorsanonymous.org

DruggedDriving.org
http://www.druggeddriving.org/ddp.html

Drug Policy Alliance
http://www.drugpolicy.org

Dual Recovery Anonymous
http://draonline.org

DUI/DWI Laws. Insurance Institute for Highway Safety
http://www.iihs.org/laws/dui/aspx

Emotions Anonymous
http://www.emotionsanonymous.org

European Monitoring Centre for Drugs and Drug Addiction
http://www.emcdda.europa.eu/publications/drug-profiles/fentanyl

Families Anonymous
http://www.familiesanonymous.org

Fetal Alcohol Spectrum Disorders Center
http://www.fasdcenter.samhsa.gov

Food Addicts Anonymous
http://www.foodaddictsanonymous.org

Gamblers Anonymous
http://www.gamblersanonymous.org

Gay and Lesbian Medical Health Association
http://www.glma.org

Government of Canada, National Anti-Drug Strategy
http://www.nationalantidrugstrategy.gc.ca

Harm Reduction Coalition
http://www.harmreduction.org

Health Canada, Drug Strategy and Controlled Substances Programme
http://www.hc-sc.gc.ca

Higher Education Center for Alcohol, Drug Abuse, and Violence Prevention
http://www.higheredcenter.org

Hoarding of Animals Research Consortium
http://vet.tufts.edu/hoarding

Homelessness Resource Center
http://www.nrchmi.samhsa.gov

Institute for Challenging Disorganization
http://www.nsgcd.org

International Centre for Science in Drug Policy
http://www.icsdp.org

International OCD Foundation
http://www.ocfoundation.org

KidsHealth.org
http://kidshealth.org

Men Can Stop Rape
http://www.mencanstoprape.org

Mental Health America
http://www.mentalhealthamerica.net/go/codependency

Monitoring the Future
http://monitoringthefuture.org

Mothers Against Drunk Driving
http://www.madd.org

Multidisciplinary Association for Psychedelic Research
http://www.maps.org

Nar-Anon Family Group Headquarters
http://www.nar-anon.org

Narcotics Anonymous
http://www.na.org

National Alliance on Mental Illness
http://www.nami.org

National Alliance to End Homelessness
http://www.endhomelessness.org

National Association of Addiction Treatment Providers
http://www.naatp.org

National Association of Cognitive-Behavioral Therapists
http://www.nacbt.org

National Association of EMS Physicians
http://www.naemsp.org

National Cancer Institute
http://www.cancer.gov

National Center for Victims of Crime
http://www.ncvc.org

National Center on Birth Defects and Developmental Disabilities
http://www.cdc.gov/ncbddd

National Child Traumatic Stress Network
http://www.nctsnet.org

National Coalition for the Homeless
http://www.nationalhomeless.org

National Commission Against Drunk Driving
http://www.ncadd.com

National Conference of State Legislatures
http://www.ncsl.org

National Council on Alcoholism and Drug Dependence
http://www.ncadd.org

National Council on Problem Gambling
http://www.ncpgambling.org

National Eating Disorders Association
http://www.edap.org

National Families in Action
http://www.nationalfamilies.org

National Health Care for the Homeless Council
http://www.nhchc.org

National Highway Traffic Safety Administration
http://www.nhtsa.gov

National Institute of Corrections
http://www.nicic.gov

National Institute of Mental Health
http://www.nimh.nih.gov

National Institute on Alcohol Abuse and Alcoholism
http://www.niaaa.nih.gov

National Institute on Drug Abuse
http://www.drugabuse.gov

National Organization on Fetal Alcohol Syndrome (NOFAS)
http://www.nofas.org/

National Partnership on Alcohol Misuse and Crime
http://www.alcoholandcrime.org/npamc/issues/alcohol-and-crime

National Registry of Evidence-based Programs and Practices
http:///www.nrepp.samhsa.gov

Nicotine Anonymous
http://nicotine-anonymous.org

NORML
http://norml.org

OCDCenter.org
http://www.ocdcenter.org

Office of National Drug Control Policy
http://www.whitehouse.gov/ondcp

Online Gamers Anonymous
http://www.olganon.org

Overeaters Anonymous
http://www.oa.org

Pew Internet and American Life Project
http://www.pewinternet.org

Pills Anonymous
http://www.pillsanonymous.org

Porn Addicts Anonymous
http://www.pornaddictsanonymous.org

Pregnancy.org
http://www.pregnancy.org/

Rape, Abuse, and Incest National Network
http://www.rainn.org

Resources for Medical and Health Professionals. National Institute on Drug Abuse
http://www.drugabuse.gov/nidamed

Sex Addicts Anonymous
http://saa-recovery.org

Sex and Love Addicts Anonymous
http://www.slaafws.org

Shopaholics Anonymous
http://www.shopaholicsanonymous.org

Smokefree.gov
http://www.smokefree.gov/

Spotlight on Poverty and Opportunity
http://www.spotlightonpoverty.org

Stanford Research into the Impact of Tobacco Advertising. Stanford School of Medicine
http://tobacco.stanford.edu

Students Against Destructive Decisions
http://www.sadd.org

Substance Abuse and Mental Health Services Administration
http://www.oas.samhsa.gov

Suicide Awareness Voices of Education
http://www.save.org

Suicide Prevention Resource Center
http://www.sprc.org

Task Force on College Drinking
http://www.collegedrinkingprevention.gov

Urgent Care Association of America
http://www.ucaoa.org

US Bureau of Alcohol, Tobacco, Firearms and Explosives
http://www.atf.gov

US Drug Enforcement Administration
http://www.justice.gov/dea

US Fire Administration
http://www.usfa.fema.gov

US Food and Drug Administration
http://www.fda.gov

US Office of the Surgeon General
http://www.surgeongeneral.gov

Veterans for Medical Cannabis Access
http://www.veteransformedicalmarijuana.org

Viagraholics Anonymous
http://www.viagraholics.com

VideoGameAddiction.Org
http://www.video-game-addiction.org

Substances of Abuse List and Cross References

2CB: See club drugs, designer drugs, hallucinogens

2,5-dimethoxy-4-methylamphetamine: See designer drugs, hallucinogens

2-(4-bromo-2,5-dimethoxyphenyl)-ethylamine: See club drugs, hallucinogens

3,4-methylenedioxymethamphetamine: See MDMA/ecstasy

3,4-methylenedioxypyrovalerone (MDPV): See designer drugs, stimulants

3,4,5-trimethoxyphenethylamine: See mescaline

4-MTA: See amphetamine, designer drugs

4-methylthioamphetamine: See amphetamine, designer drugs

5-methoxy-diisopropyltryptamine ("foxy"): See hallucinogens, stimulants

5-MeO-DIPT: See hallucinogens, stimulants

714s: See barbiturates, depressants, sedative-hypnotics

11-50: See heroin

AAS: See anabolic steroids

A-bomb: See marijuana and heroin

Acapulco gold: See marijuana

Acid: See LSD, hallucinogens

Adam: See club drugs, MDMA/ecstasy

Aimies: See inhalants, poppers

Air blast: See aerosols, inhalants

Air freshener: See aerosols, inhalants

Alley juice: See alcohol

Alpha-methyltryptamine: See hallucinogens

Alprazolam: See benzodiazepines, depressants, sedatives

Amobarbital: See barbiturates, depressants, sedatives

AMT: See hallucinogens

Amyl nitrite: See inhalants, poppers

Amytal: See barbiturates, depressants, sedatives

Anabolic-androgenic steroids: See anabolic steroids

Anadrol: See anabolic steroids

Analgesics: See painkillers

Androstenedione: See anabolic steroids

Anesthetics: See anesthesia

Angel dust: See hallucinogens, PCP

Antianxiety agents: See anxiety medication

Antidepressants: See bupropion

Anxiolytics: See anxiety medication

Atom bomb: See marijuana and heroin

Atropine: See anticholinergics

Base: See cocaine

Bath salts: See amphetamine, designer drugs

Beans: See club drugs, MDMA/ecstasy

Belladonna: See anticholinergics

Bennies: See amphetamine, stimulants

Benzene: See inhalants, gasoline, solvents

Benzodiazepines: See anxiety medications, depressants

Bhang: See marijuana

Billy: See amphetamine, stimulants

Black beauties: See amphetamine

Black hash: See opium, hashish

Black tar: See heroin

Block: See opium

Blotter: See LSD, hallucinogens

Blue acid: See LSD

Bluebirds: See barbiturates, depressants, sedatives

Blue bottle: See inhalants, nitrous oxide

Blue heaven: See LSD

Blue nitro: See GHB

Blues: See barbiturates, depressants, sedatives

Boat: See PCP, hallucinogens

Bombitas: See heroin and amphetamine

Booze: See alcohol

Brew: See alcohol

Brown sugar: See heroin

Bullets: See inhalants, poppers

Bump: See crack, ketamine, methamphetamine

Buprenex: See opioids, painkillers

Buprenorphine: See opioids, painkillers

Burgers: See MDMA/ecstasy

Business man's lunch: See DMT, hallucinogens

Butane: See inhalants

Butobarbital: See barbiturates, sedatives, depressants

Butorphanol: See opioids, painkillers

Buttons: See mushrooms/psilocybin, peyote

Butts: See cigarettes and cigars, nicotine, tobacco

Butyl nitrite: See inhalants, poppers

Cactus: See hallucinogens, peyote

Caffeine: See stimulants

Camellia sinensis: See caffeine, stimulants

Cancer sticks: See cigarettes and cigars, nicotine, tobacco

Candy flip: See LSD and MDMA/ecstasy

Cane: See cocaine

Cannabinoids: See marijuana

Cannabinol: See marijuana

Cannabis: See marijuana

Cannabis sativa: See marijuana

Cat valium: See ketamine, sedative-hypnotics

Cereal: See marijuana

Chalk: See amphetamine, methamphetamine

Charlie: See cocaine

Cherry meth: See GHB

China: See opium

China cat: See heroin

China white: See heroin

Chinese tobacco: See opium

Chlordiazepoxide: See anxiety medication, benzodiazepines, sedatives

Chloroform: See anesthesia

Cigarettes: See nicotine, tobacco

Club drugs: See GHB, ketamine, MDMA/ecstasy, Rohypnol

Coca plant: See cocaine

Cocaine freebase: See cocaine

Cocoa: See caffeine, stimulants

Coca scrub: See cocaine

Coffee: See caffeine

Coke: See cocaine

Cola: See caffeine, stimulants

Copilots: See amphetamine, stimulants

Correction fluid: See inhalants, solvents

Cough medicine: See cough and cold medications, dextromethorphan

Cough syrup: See cough and cold medications, dextromethorphan

Crack: See cocaine

Crank: See amphetamine, methamphetamine

Crystal: See amphetamine, methamphetamine

Crystal meth: See methamphetamine

Cubes: See mushrooms/psilocybin

Cyclohexyl nitrite: See inhalants, poppers

Dance drug: See club drugs

Date rape drug: See GHB, Rohypnol

Datura: See hallucinogens

De-greaser: See inhalants

Delta-9-tetrahydrocannabinol: See marijuana

Demerol: See narcotics, painkillers

Deodorant: See aerosols, inhalants

Depo-testosterone: See anabolic steroids

Depressants: See barbiturates, sedatives

Designer drug: See China white, club drugs, opiates

Desoxyn: See amphetamine, stimulants

Devil's dandruff: See cocaine

Dex: See dextroamphetamine

Dexedrine: See dextroamphetamine

Dexies: See amphetamine, dextroamphetamine, stimulants

Dextroamphetamine: See amphetamine, stimulants

Diacetyl morphine: See heroin, opioids

Diazepam: See anxiety medication, benzodiazepines, depressants, sedatives

Diet pills: See amphetamine, dextroamphetamine, ephedrine, stimulants

Dimethyltryptamine: See DMT, hallucinogens

Dirty joint: See cocaine and marijuana

Disco biscuits: See MDMA/ecstasy

Dissociatives: See hallucinogens

Dolly: See methadone

DOM: See designer drugs, hallucinogens

Dome: See methadone

Dope: See heroin, marijuana

Dots: See LSD, hallucinogens

Doves: See MDMA/ecstasy

Downers: See barbiturates, depressants, sedatives

Dummy dust: See PCP

Dust: See heroin

DXM: See dextromethorphan

Dynamite: See cocaine and heroin

E: See MDMA/ecstasy

Easy lay: See GHB

Eccies: See MDMA/ecstasy

Echoes: See MDMA/ecstasy

Ecstasy: See MDMA/ecstasy

Eight ball: See cocaine

Embalming fluid: See PCP

Ephedra: See ephedrine, stimulants

Erox: See club drugs, designer drugs, hallucinogens

Ether: See anesthesia

Ethyl alcohol: See alcohol, depressants, ethanol

Ethylamines: See solvents

Eye openers: See amphetamine, stimulants

Fantasy: See MDMA/ecstasy, GHB

Flake: See cocaine

Flurazepam: See benzodiazepines, sedatives, depressants

Forget me pill: See date rape drugs, Rohypnol

Foxy: See hallucinogens, stimulants

Free base: See cocaine

French fries: See crack, cocaine

Gamma 10: See GHB

Gamma-hydroxybutyrate: See GHB

Gasoline: See inhalants, solvents
Georgia homeboy: See GHB
Glass: See methamphetamine
Glue: See inhalants
Goofballs: See barbiturates, depressants
Gook: See GHB
Grass: See marijuana
Guarana: See caffeine, stimulants
Gym candy: See anabolic steroids
Hallucinogens: See LSD, MDMA/ecstasy, mescaline, mushrooms/psilocybin, PCP
Hair spray: See aerosols, inhalants
Hard candy: See heroin
Hash: See hashish, marijuana
Hearts: See amphetamine
Helium: See inhalants
Hemp: See marijuana
Hog: See PCP
Homegrown: See marijuana
Honey oil: See ketamine
Hop: See opium
Horse: See heroin
Hot ice: See methamphetamine
Hug drug: See MDMA/ecstasy
Hydrocarbons: See inhalants, solvents
Hydromorphone: See morphine, opioids, painkillers
Hypnotic drug: See benzodiazepines, sedative-hypnotics
Ibogaine: See hallucinogens
Ice: See methamphetamine
Inhalant: See poppers, solvents
Isoamyl nitrite: See inhalants, poppers
Isobutyl nitrite: See inhalants, poppers
Jamaican: See marijuana
Jet: See ketamine
Jimsonweed: See anticholinergics, hallucinogens
Jive: See heroin, marijuana
Joint: See marijuana
Juice: See alcohol, anabolic steroids, PCP
Junk: See heroin
Kava: See sedatives
Ketalar: See ketamine
Killer weed: See marijuana and PCP
Kit kat: See ketamine
KJ: See PCP
K jet: See ketamine
Kola nut: See caffeine, stimulants
Krystal: See PCP
Laughing gas: See inhalants, nitrous oxide

Librium: See anxiety medications, benzodiazepines, sedatives
Lid poppers: See amphetamine, poppers
Lidocaine: See anesthesia
Lighter fluid: See inhalants, solvents
Liquid ecstasy: See GHB
Liquid incense: See inhalants, poppers
Liquid X: See GHB
Little smoke: See marijuana, mushrooms/psilocybin
Locker room: See inhalants, poppers
Lorazepam: See benzodiazepines, depressants, sedatives
Love drug: See MDMA/ecstasy
Love boat: See PCP
Love drug: See MDMA/ecstasy
Love trip: See MDMA/ecstasy and mescaline
Lucky charms: See MDMA/ecstasy
Ludes: See barbiturates, depressants, sedative-hypnotics
Lysergic acid diethylamide: See LSD
Magic dust: See PCP, phencyclidine, hallucinogens
Magic mint: See salvia divinorum, dissociatives, hallucinogens
Magic mushrooms: See PCP, hallucinogens
Marching powder: See cocaine
Maria Pastora: See salvia, hallucinogens
Mary Jane: See marijuana
MDA: See amphetamine, hallucinogens, stimulants
MDEA: See amphetamine, designer drug, stimulants
Mellow yellow: See LSD
Meperidine: See narcotics, painkillers
Mephedrone: See amphetamine, stimulants
Meth: See methamphetamine
Methaqualone: See depressants, sedative-hypnotics
Methylene chloride: See inhalants, solvents
Methylmorphine: See codeine
Methylphenidate: See stimulants
Mexican mud: See heroin
Mexican valium: See date rape drugs, Rohypnol
Microdots: See LSD
Midazolam: See benzodiazepines, depressants, sedatives
Monkey: morphine
Monkey dust: See PCP
Moon: See mescaline
Morning glory: See hallucinogens
Mouthwash: See alcohol
MDPV: See designer drugs, stimulants
Musk: See mushrooms/psilocybin

Nail polish remover: See inhalants
Nature's quaalude: See GHB
Nazi speed: See methamphetamine, stimulants
Nembutal: See barbiturates, depressants, sedatives
Nexus: See amphetamine, club drugs, designer drugs, hallucinogens
Nightshade: See anticholinergics
Nimetazepam: See benzodiazepines, sedatives
Nitrites: See inhalants, poppers
Nose candy: See cocaine
OC: See oxycodone
OJ: See marijuana
Opiates: See narcotics, opioids, painkillers
Organic quaalude: See GHB, sedatives
Organic solvents: See inhalants, solvents
Oxazepam: See benzodiazepines, sedatives, depressants
Oxycontin: See oxycodone, narcotics, opioids
Ozone: See PCP, poppers
Paint thinner: See inhalants, solvents
Panama gold: See marijuana
Pane: See LSD
Paper acid: See LSD
Peace: See LSD, PCP
Pearl flake: See cocaine
Pearls: See inhalants, poppers
Pentazocine: See narcotics, opioids, painkillers
Pentobarbital: See barbiturates
Pep pills: See amphetamine, stimulants
Percocet: See oxycodone, painkillers
Percodan: See oxycodone, painkillers
Performance-enhancing drug: See anabolic steroids
Peyote: See mescaline
Peyote buttons: See mescaline
Phencyclidine: See PCP
Phenobarbital: See barbiturates
Phenylpropanolamine: See stimulants
Phenethylamine: See hallucinogens, club drugs
Phentermine: See ephedrine, stimulants
Pixies: See amphetamine
PMA (paramethoxyamphetamine): See amphetamine, stimulants
Poor man's pot: See inhalants, solvents
Poppy: See opium
Poppy straw: See opium
Pot: See marijuana
PPA: See amphetamine, stimulants
Procaine: See anesthesia
Propoxyphene: See painkillers

Pseudoephedrine: See stimulants
Psilocin: See mushrooms/psilocybin
Psilocybin: See mushrooms/psilocybin
Psychedelic mushrooms: See mushrooms/psilocybin
Psychedelics: See hallucinogens, LSD, MDMA/ecstasy, dextromethorphan, nitrous oxide
Pumpers: See anabolic steroids
Purple: See ketamine
Purple haze: See LSD
Purple passion: See mushrooms/psilocybin
R2: See date rape drug, Rohypnol
Rainbows: See LSD
Readyrock: See cocaine
Reefer: See marijuana
Rib: See date rape drug, Rohypnol
Roaches: See date rape drugs, Rohypnol
Roapies: See date rape drug, Rohypnol
Robo: dextromethorphan
Robutal: See date rape drug, Rohypnol
Roche: See date rape drug, Rohypnol
Rock: See cocaine
Rocket fuel: See PCP
Roids: See anabolic steroids
Roofies: See date rape drugs, Rohypnol
Room deodorizer: See inhalants
Rope: See date rape drugs, Rohypnol
Rophies: See date rape drugs, Rohypnol
Ro-shay: See date rape drugs, Rohypnol
Rubber cement: See inhalants
Ruffles: See date rape drugs, Rohypnol
Rush: See inhalants, poppers
Sally-D: See salvia
Salty water: See GHB
Sauce: See alcohol
Scag: See heroin
Schoolboy: See cocaine
Scopolamine: See anticholinergics
Scoop: See GHB, sedatives
Secobarbital: See barbiturates
Serial speedball: See cocaine, dextromethorphan, and heroin
Sheets: See LSD
Shepherdess's herb: See salvia
Shrooms: See mushrooms/psilocybin
Sinsemilla: See marijuana
Skittles: See dextromethorphan
Skunk: See heroin, marijuana
Sleeper: See heroin, depressants
Smack: See heroin

Smokes: See cigarettes and cigars, nicotine, tobacco
Snap: See amphetamine
Snappers: See inhalants, poppers
Sniff: See inhalants
Snow: See cocaine
Snuff: See tobacco, nicotine
Soap: See GHB, methamphetamine
Softballs: See barbiturates, depressants
Solvent: See inhalants
Somatomax: See GHB, sedatives
Sopor: See sedatives, sedative-hypnotics
Special K: See ketamine
Spectrum: See club drugs, designer drugs, hallucinogens
Speed: See amphetamine, methamphetamine, cocaine
Speedball: See cocaine, heroin
Spoor: See sedatives, barbiturates
Spot cleaner: See solvents, inhalants
Spray paint: Inhalants, aerosols
Stadol: See narcotics, painkillers
Stardust: See cocaine
Steroids: See anabolic steroids
Sticks: See marijuana
Stiva: See marijuana
STP: See club drugs, designer drugs
Subutex: See opioids, painkillers
Sugar: See LSD
Sugar cubes: See LSD
Super acid: See ketamine
Super C: See ketamine
Supergrass: See marijuana and PCP
Superweed: See marijuana and PCP
Tabs: See LSD
Tea: See caffeine, stimulants
Temazepam: See benzodiazepines, sedatives, depressants
Testosterone: See anabolic steroids
Tetrahydrocannabinol: See marijuana
THC: See marijuana
Thiopental: See anesthesia
Three-inch sticks: See cocaine
Tic tacs: See PCP
Tina: See methamphetamine

Toot: See cocaine
Tooties: See barbiturates, depressants
Tranquilizer: See depressants
Transmission fluid: See inhalants, solvents
Triazolam: See benzodiazepines, sedatives, depressants
Trichloroethylene: See inhalants, solvents
Trip: See LSD, hallucinogens
Triple C: See dextromethorphan
Tryptamines: See hallucinogens
Ultram: See tramadol
Uppers: See stimulants, amphetamine
Vicodin: See codeine, narcotics, opioids, painkillers
Vino: See alcohol, depressants
Vitamin K: See ketamine
Wacky dust: See cocaine
Weed: See marijuana
Weed oil: See marijuana
Whack: See PCP
Whippets: See inhalants, nitrous oxide, solvents
White horse: See heroin
White lady: See cocaine
White lightning: See LSD
Whiz-bang: See cocaine and heroin
Whizz: See amphetamine, stimulants
Window glass: See LSD
Window pane: See LSD
Wiper fluid: See inhalants, solvents
Wolfies: See date rape drugs, Rohypnol
X: See MDMA/ecstasy
XTC: See MDMA/ecstasy
Yaba: See club drugs, methamphetamine, stimulants
Yellow jackets: See barbiturates, depressants, sedatives
Yellow sunshine: See LSD
Yerba mate: See caffeine, stimulants
Zalepon: See sedatives, sedative-hypnotics
Z drugs: See benzodiazepine, sedatives
Zen: See LSD
Zolpidem: See depressants, sedatives
Zombie: See PCP
Zonked: See GHB
Zoom: See PCP
Zopiclone: See sedatives, sedative-hypnotics

Pharmaceutical Treatments

ALCOHOL WITHDRAWAL MEDICATIONS

BRAND NAME: Ambien, Ambien CR
GENERIC NAME: zolpidem
ROUTE OF ADMINISTRATION: oral
POSSIBLE SIDE EFFECTS: Daytime drowsiness, dizziness, weakness, light-headedness, lack of coordination, forgetfulness, vivid or abnormal dreams, nausea, constipation, stuffy nose, sore throat, headache, muscle pain, and blurred vision.
PRINCIPAL USES: Treatment of insomnia.

BRAND NAME: Antabuse
GENERIC NAME: disulfiram
ROUTE OF ADMINISTRATION: oral
POSSIBLE SIDE EFFECTS: Skin rash, acne, mild headache, mild drowsiness, tiredness, impotence, metallic taste in the mouth, and swollen or sore tongue.
PRINCIPAL USES: To treat alcohol addiction.

BRAND NAME: Calphron
GENERIC NAME: calcium acetate
ROUTE OF ADMINISTRATION: oral
POSSIBLE SIDE EFFECTS: Nausea, vomiting, loss of appetite, constipation, dry mouth, and increased urination.
PRINCIPAL USES: For patients with severe kidney disease.

BRAND NAME: Campral
GENERIC NAME: acamprosate
ROUTE OF ADMINISTRATION: oral
POSSIBLE SIDE EFFECTS: Nausea, vomiting, stomach pain, loss of appetite, constipation, diarrhea, headache, dizziness, drowsiness, vision problems, forgetfulness, weakness, flu-like symptoms, back pain, joint or muscle pain, dry mouth, decreased or distorted sense of taste, insomnia, impotence, sweating, mild skin rash, and numbness.
PRINCIPAL USES: To help alcohol-dependent patients who have recently quit drinking.

BRAND NAME: Edluar
GENERIC NAME: zolpidem
ROUTE OF ADMINISTRATION: oral (sublingual)
POSSIBLE SIDE EFFECTS: Daytime drowsiness, dizziness, weakness, light-headedness, lack of coordination, forgetfulness, vivid or abnormal dreams, nausea, constipation, stuffy nose, sore throat, headache, muscle pain, and blurred vision.
PRINCIPAL USES: Short-term treatment of insomnia, one to two weeks or less.

BRAND NAME: Eliphos
GENERIC NAME: calcium acetate
ROUTE OF ADMINISTRATION: oral
POSSIBLE SIDE EFFECTS: Nausea, vomiting, loss of appetite, constipation, dry mouth, and increased urination.
PRINCIPAL USES: To prevent high blood phosphate levels in patients with severe kidney disease.

BRAND NAME: Gabarone
GENERIC NAME: gabapentin
ROUTE OF ADMINISTRATION: oral
POSSIBLE SIDE EFFECTS: Dizziness, drowsiness, weakness, lack of coordination, blurred vision, nausea, vomiting, stomach pain, loss of appetite, diarrhea, constipation, dry mouth, runny nose, sore throat, headache, insomnia, unusual dreams, and skin rashes.
PRINCIPAL USES: To treat seizures in children three to twelve years old, and to treat alcohol withdrawal symptoms.

BRAND NAME: Gablofen
GENERIC NAME: baclofen
ROUTE OF ADMINISTRATION: intrathecal injection
POSSIBLE SIDE EFFECTS: Drowsiness, dizziness, weakness, agitation, low blood pressure, headache, confusion, insomnia, nausea, constipation, and changes in urinary frequency.
PRINCIPAL USES: For severe spasticity, cerebral palsy, spinal cord injury, brain trauma, stroke, and to treat alcohol withdrawal symptoms.

BRAND NAME: H-Tran
GENERIC NAME: Chlordiazepoxide
ROUTE OF ADMINISTRATION: oral
POSSIBLE SIDE EFFECTS: Drowsiness, dizziness, tiredness, weakness, dry mouth, diarrhea, upset stomach, changes in appetite, clumsiness, confusion, drowsiness, headache, lack of coordination, light-headedness, and unsteadiness.

PRINCIPAL USES: To treat anxiety and acute alcohol withdrawal symptoms.

BRAND NAME: Libritabs
GENERIC NAME: chlordiazepoxide
ROUTE OF ADMINISTRATION: oral
POSSIBLE SIDE EFFECTS: Drowsiness, dizziness, nausea, constipation, blurred vision, and headache.
PRINCIPAL USES: To treat anxiety disorders and alcohol withdrawal symptoms.

BRAND NAME: Librium
GENERIC NAME: chlordiazepoxide
ROUTE OF ADMINISTRATION: oral
POSSIBLE SIDE EFFECTS: Drowsiness, tiredness, swelling, skin rash, nausea, vomiting, constipation, and irregular menstrual periods.
PRINCIPAL USES: To treat anxiety disorders and alcohol withdrawal symptoms.

BRAND NAME: Lioresal
GENERIC NAME: baclofen
ROUTE OF ADMINISTRATION: oral
POSSIBLE SIDE EFFECTS: Back pain, constipation, diarrhea, dizziness, drowsiness, upset stomach, headache, increased salivation, muscle weakness, nausea, and vomiting.
PRINCIPAL USES: To treat muscle tightness and cramping due to multiple sclerosis or spinal cord injury or disease, and to treat alcohol withdrawal symptoms.

BRAND NAME: Luminal
GENERIC NAME: phenobarbital
ROUTE OF ADMINISTRATION: intravenous
POSSIBLE SIDE EFFECTS: Agitated mood, clumsiness, confusion, dizziness, daytime drowsiness, headache, injection site reactions, lightheadedness, low blood pressure, nausea, vomiting, slow heartbeat, and slow breathing.
PRINCIPAL USES: A short-term treatment of insomnia and alcohol withdrawal symptoms.

BRAND NAME: Mitran
GENERIC NAME: chlordiazepoxide
ROUTE OF ADMINISTRATION: oral
POSSIBLE SIDE EFFECTS: Drowsiness, tiredness, swelling, skin rash, nausea, vomiting, constipation, irregular menstrual periods, and blurred vision.
PRINCIPAL USES: To treat anxiety disorders and alcohol withdrawal symptoms.

BRAND NAME: Neurontin
GENERIC NAME: gabapentin
ROUTE OF ADMINISTRATION: oral
POSSIBLE SIDE EFFECTS: Dizziness, drowsiness, weakness, feeling tired, lack of coordination, blurred vision, nausea, vomiting, stomach pain, loss of appetite, diarrhea, constipation, dry mouth, runny nose, sore throat, headache, insomnia, unusual dreams, acne, and mild skin rash.
PRINCIPAL USES: Used alone or in combination with other medications to treat epilepsy and to treat alcohol withdrawal symptoms.

BRAND NAME: PhosLo Gelcap
GENERIC NAME: calcium acetate
ROUTE OF ADMINISTRATION: oral
POSSIBLE SIDE EFFECTS: Nausea, vomiting, loss of appetite, constipation, dry mouth, and increased urination.
PRINCIPAL USES: To treat renal osteodystrophy with hyperphosphatemia. Also used for patients with severe kidney disease.

BRAND NAME: Poxi
GENERIC NAME: chlordiazepoxide
ROUTE OF ADMINISTRATION: oral
POSSIBLE SIDE EFFECTS: Dizziness, nausea, constipation, blurred vision, and headache.
PRINCIPAL USES: To treat anxiety disorders and alcohol withdrawal symptoms.

BRAND NAME: ReVia
GENERIC NAME: naltrexone
ROUTE OF ADMINISTRATION: oral
POSSIBLE SIDE EFFECTS: Feeling anxious, nervous, restless, irritable, light-headed, having increased thirst, muscle or joint aches, weakness, insomnia, decreased sex drive, impotence, and difficulty having an orgasm.
PRINCIPAL USES: Treatment of drugs and alcohol addiction.

BRAND NAME: Serax
GENERIC NAME: oxazepam
ROUTE OF ADMINISTRATION: oral
POSSIBLE SIDE EFFECTS: Drowsiness, dizziness, vertigo, nausea, lethargy, swelling or water retention, slurred speech, tremors, and changes in sex drive.
PRINCIPAL USES: To treat anxiety disorders and alcohol withdrawal symptoms.

BRAND NAME: Tenormin
GENERIC NAME: atenolol
ROUTE OF ADMINISTRATION: oral
POSSIBLE SIDE EFFECTS: Decreased sex drive, impotence or difficulty having an orgasm, insomnia, tiredness, anxiety, and nervousness.
PRINCIPAL USES: To treat angina, hypertension, and alcohol withdrawal symptoms.

BRAND NAME: Topiragen
GENERIC NAME: topiramate
ROUTE OF ADMINISTRATION: oral
POSSIBLE SIDE EFFECTS: Eyesight problems including double vision and involuntary eye movement, painful or irregular menstrual periods, drowsiness, loss of memory, dizziness, lack of coordination, difficulty speaking, nervousness, numbness, weakness, confusion, breast tenderness, trouble sleeping, involuntary quivering, nausea, and diarrhea.
PRINCIPAL USES: A seizure medication used to prevent migraine headaches and reduce the number of migraine attacks.

BRAND NAME: Topomax, Topamax Sprinkle
GENERIC NAME: topiramate
ROUTE OF ADMINISTRATION: oral
POSSIBLE SIDE EFFECTS: Mild dizziness, numbness, diarrhea, weight loss, nervousness, cold symptoms, stuffy nose, sneezing, and sore throat.
PRINCIPAL USES: To treat seizures in adults and children, and to prevent migraine headaches in adults.

BRAND NAME: Tranxene SD
GENERIC NAME: clorazepate

ROUTE OF ADMINISTRATION: oral
POSSIBLE SIDE EFFECTS: Blurred or double vision, diarrhea, discouragement, dizziness, dry mouth, sadness, headache, indigestion, irritability, loss of appetite, loss of interest or pleasure, mental confusion, nausea, vomiting, nervousness, skin rash, insomnia, trouble concentrating, tiredness, and weakness.
PRINCIPAL USES: To treat anxiety disorders, partial seizures, and alcohol withdrawal symptoms.

BRAND NAME: Valium
GENERIC NAME: diazepam
ROUTE OF ADMINISTRATION: oral
POSSIBLE SIDE EFFECTS: Drowsiness, tiredness, dizziness, spinning sensation, blurred vision, insomnia, nightmares, muscle weakness, lack of coordination, slurred speech, nausea vomiting, constipation, headache, memory problems, drooling, skin rash, and loss of interest in sex.
PRINCIPAL USES: For anxiety disorders and to treat alcohol withdrawal symptoms.

BRAND NAME: Vivitrol
GENERIC NAME: naltrexone (injection)
ROUTE OF ADMINISTRATION: intravenous
POSSIBLE SIDE EFFECTS: Feeling anxious, nervous, restless, irritable, light-headed, faint, having increased thirst, muscle or joint aches, weakness, insomnia, decreased sex drive, impotence, and difficulty having an orgasm.
PRINCIPAL USES: Treatment of drug and alcohol addiction, and to prevent narcotic addiction relapse after opioid detoxification.

BARBITURATE WITHDRAWAL MEDICATIONS

BRAND NAME: Butisol Sodium
GENERIC NAME: butabarbital
ROUTE OF ADMINISTRATION: oral
POSSIBLE SIDE EFFECTS: Drowsiness, dizziness, problems with memory and concentration, excitement (especially in children and older adults), joint or muscle pain, nausea, vomiting, upset stomach, constipation, nightmares, and unusual dreams.
PRINCIPAL USES: For the short-term treatment of insomnia, as a sedative before surgery, and in the treatment of barbiturate withdrawal symptoms.

BRAND NAME: Luminal
GENERIC NAME: phenobarbital
ROUTE OF ADMINISTRATION: oral or injection
POSSIBLE SIDE EFFECTS: Agitated mood, clumsiness, confusion, dizziness, excessive daytime drowsiness, headache, injection site reactions, lightheadedness, low blood pressure, nausea, slow heartbeat, slowed breathing, and vomiting.
PRINCIPAL USES: Short-term treatment of insomnia, relief for anxiety tension and fear, treatment of seizures, and treatment of barbiturate withdrawal symptoms.

BRAND NAME: Mebaral
GENERIC NAME: mephobarbital
ROUTE OF ADMINISTRATION: oral
POSSIBLE SIDE EFFECTS: Dizziness, forgetfulness, confusion, nervousness, agitation, nausea, vomiting, and headache.
PRINCIPAL USES: A sedative to treat anxiety and tension. Also used to treat barbiturate withdrawal symptoms.

BRAND NAME: Nembutal Sodium
GENERIC NAME: pentobarbital
ROUTE OF ADMINISTRATION: intravenous
POSSIBLE SIDE EFFECTS: Drowsiness, dizziness, problems with memory and concentration, excitement (especially in children or older adults), upset stomach, constipation, loss of balance and coordination, nightmares, headache, and "hangover" effect (drowsiness the day after a dose).
PRINCIPAL USES: A short-term treatment of insomnia, treatment for seizures, and treatment for barbiturate withdrawal symptoms.

BRAND NAME: Seconal Sodium
GENERIC NAME: seccorbital

ROUTE OF ADMINISTRATION: oral
POSSIBLE SIDE EFFECTS: Drowsiness, dizziness, problems with memory or concentration, excitement (especially in children or older adults), upset stomach, constipation, headache, and "hangover" effect (drowsiness the day after a dose).
PRINCIPAL USES: For the short-term treatment of insomnia, as a sedative before surgery, and to treat some barbiturate withdrawal symptoms.

BRAND NAME: Solfoton
GENERIC NAME: phenobarbital
ROUTE OF ADMINISTRATION: oral
POSSIBLE SIDE EFFECTS: Drowsiness, dizziness, problems with memory and concentration, excitement (especially in children and older adults), upset stomach, constipation, loss of balance or coordination, nightmares, headache, and "hangover" effect (drowsiness the day after a dose).
PRINCIPAL USES: To treat or prevent seizures, short-term treatment of insomnia, a relaxation sedative before surgery, and for the treatment of barbiturate withdrawal symptoms.

OPIATE WITHDRAWAL MEDICATIONS

BRAND NAME: Butrans
GENERIC NAME: buprenorphine
ROUTE OF ADMINISTRATION: transdermal patch
POSSIBLE SIDE EFFECTS: Headache, vomiting, dry mouth, upset stomach, constipation, mild dizziness or drowsiness, skin redness, itching, and mild skin rash where the patch was worn.
PRINCIPAL USES: To treat moderate to severe chronic pain when treatment is needed around the clock. Also used to treat opiate withdrawal symptoms.

BRAND NAME: Dolophine
GENERIC NAME: methadone
ROUTE OF ADMINISTRATION: oral
POSSIBLE SIDE EFFECTS: Constipation, dizziness, drowsiness, dry mouth, headache, increased sweating, itching, lightheadedness, nausea, vomiting, and weakness.
PRINCIPAL USES: For pain relief and as part of drug addiction detoxification and maintenance programs.

BRAND NAME: Methadone Diskets
GENERIC NAME: methadone

ROUTE OF ADMINISTRATION: oral
POSSIBLE SIDE EFFECTS: Constipation, dizziness, drowsiness, dry mouth, headache, increased sweating, itching, lightheadedness, nausea, vomiting, and general weakness.
PRINCIPAL USES: Used in the treatment of narcotic addiction as part of a controlled program.

BRAND NAME: Methadose
GENERIC NAME: methadone
ROUTE OF ADMINISTRATION: oral
POSSIBLE SIDE EFFECTS: Feeling anxious, nervousness, restlessness, insomnia, weakness, drowsiness, dry mouth, nausea, vomiting, diarrhea, constipation, loss of appetite, decreased sex drive, impotence, and difficulty having an orgasm.
PRINCIPAL USES: For pain relief and as part of drug addiction detoxification and maintenance programs.

BRAND NAME: Provigil
GENERIC NAME: modafinil
ROUTE OF ADMINISTRATION: oral
POSSIBLE SIDE EFFECTS: Headache, dizziness, feeling

nervous or agitated, nausea, diarrhea, insomnia, and dry mouth.

PRINCIPAL USES: Used in the treatment of excessive sleepiness caused by sleep apnea, narcolepsy, or shift work disorder. Also used to treat opiate withdrawal symptoms.

BRAND NAME: Robaxin, Robaxin-750
GENERIC NAME: methocarbamol

ROUTE OF ADMINISTRATION: oral
POSSIBLE SIDE EFFECTS: Dizziness, drowsiness, nausea, vomiting, skin redness, tingly feeling under the skin, fever, headache, memory problems, blurred vision, insomnia, stuffy nose, mild skin rash, and itching.
PRINCIPAL USES: For the treatment of skeletal muscle conditions combined with rest and physical therapy. Also used to treat opiate withdrawal symptoms.

TOBACCO DEPENDENCE

BRAND NAME: Aplenzin
GENERIC NAME: bupropion
ROUTE OF ADMINISTRATION: oral
POSSIBLE SIDE EFFECTS: Headache, migraine, insomnia, nausea, vomiting, constipation, dry mouth, dizziness, tremors, appetite changes (weight loss or gain), mild itching, skin rash, increased sweating, and loss of interest in sex.
PRINCIPAL USES: An antidepressant used to treat smoking cessation.

BRAND NAME: Budeprion
GENERIC NAME: bupropion
ROUTE OF ADMINISTRATION: oral
POSSIBLE SIDE EFFECTS: Headache, migraine, insomnia, nausea, vomiting, constipation, dry mouth, dizziness, tremors, appetite changes (weight loss or gain), mild itching, skin rash, and increased sweating.
PRINCIPAL USES: An antidepressant used to treat major depressive disorders, seasonal affective disorders, and smoking withdrawal cravings.

BRAND NAME: Catapres
GENERIC NAME: clonidine
ROUTE OF ADMINISTRATION: oral or transdermal patch
POSSIBLE SIDE EFFECTS: Dizziness, drowsiness, feeling tired, dry mouth, dry or burning eyes, blurred vision, headache, muscle or joint pain, nausea, vomiting, constipation, loss of appetite, insomnia, urinating more at night, mild skin rash, itching, decreased sex drive, and impotence.
PRINCIPAL USES: Approved by the US Food and Drug Administration to treat hypertension and is used "off-label" as a smoking cessation medicine.

BRAND NAME: Chantix
GENERIC NAME: verenicline
ROUTE OF ADMINISTRATION: oral

POSSIBLE SIDE EFFECTS: Nausea (may persist for several months), stomach pain, indigestion, vomiting, constipation, gas, weakness, tired feeling, increased appetite, unpleasant taste in the mouth, headache, and insomnia.
PRINCIPAL USES: A smoking cessation medicine used in combination with a stop-smoking program.

BRAND NAME: Commit, Habitrol
GENERIC NAME: nicotine (gum, lozenge)
ROUTE OF ADMINISTRATION: oral
POSSIBLE SIDE EFFECTS: Mild dizziness, dry mouth, upset stomach, burping, hiccups, muscle or joint pain, mouth or throat soreness, changes in taste, and headache.
PRINCIPAL USES: A smoking cessation aid that helps reduce nicotine withdrawal symptoms.

BRAND NAME: Nicoderm CQ
GENERIC NAME: nicotine patch
ROUTE OF ADMINISTRATION: transdermal patch
POSSIBLE SIDE EFFECTS: Mild dizziness, dry mouth, upset stomach, burping, hiccups, muscle or joint pain, mouth or throat soreness, changes in taste, and headache.
PRINCIPAL USES: A smoking cessation aid that helps reduce nicotine withdrawal symptoms.

BRAND NAME: Nicorelief, Nicorette Plus, Thrive
GENERIC NAME: nicotine gum
ROUTE OF ADMINISTRATION: oral
POSSIBLE SIDE EFFECTS: Dizziness, belching or hiccups, stomach upset or nausea, mouth or throat soreness, dry or watering mouth, watering eye, headache, runny or stuffy nose, white patches or sores inside the mouth or lips, constipation, sneezing, coughing, changes in taste, and itchiness.
PRINCIPAL USES: A smoking cessation aid that helps reduce nicotine withdrawal symptoms.

BRAND NAME: Wellbutrin
GENERIC NAME: bupropion
ROUTE OF ADMINISTRATION: oral
POSSIBLE SIDE EFFECTS: Headache, migraine, insomnia, nausea, vomiting, constipation, dry mouth, dizziness, tremors, appetite changes (weight loss or gain), mild itching, skin rash, increased sweating, and loss of interest in sex.
PRINCIPAL USES: To treat major depressive disorder, seasonal affective disorders, and smoking withdrawal cravings.

BRAND NAME: Zyban
GENERIC NAME: bupropion
ROUTE OF ADMINISTRATION: oral
POSSIBLE SIDE EFFECTS: Hcadache, migraine, insomnia, nausea, vomiting, constipation, dry mouth, dizziness, tremors, appetite changes (weight loss or gain), mild itching, skin rash, increased sweating, and loss of interest in sex.
PRINCIPAL USES: An antidepressant used to help people stop smoking by reducing cravings and other withdrawal effects.

Treatment Centers and Programs

According to the Substance Abuse and Mental Health Services Administration (SAMHSA), there are more than 11,000 addiction treatment centers throughout the United States, the majority of which are publicly funded and apply the twelve-step program methodology. The industry is expected to experience growing revenue. In fact, a 2011 article in *DailyFinance* suggested that industry revenues for addiction treatment in the United States will reach $34 billion by 2014, a soaring increase seemingly validated by the job outlook for substance abuse and behavioral disorder counselors estimated by the Bureau of Labor Statistics, which predicts a faster than average growth of 27 percent between 2010–20. (According to the business research company Hoovers, the American substance abuse and mental health services industry has combined revenue of $20 million annually.)

Below represents a small sampling of the treatment centers and programs available nationwide, both for-profit and nonprofit and private or public, categorized either nationally or geographically by Census-designated regions. For a comprehensive list searchable by state, please consult the Substance Abuse Treatment Facility Locator:

http://findtreatment.samhsa.gov/TreatmentLocator/faces/quickSearch.jspx

NATIONAL

CRC Health Group
www.CRCHealth.com

Headquartered in California, CRC operates 145 facilities nationwide, offering comprehensive treatment options and services for addiction, disorders, and weight loss. Services including boarding programs for teenagers, programs for trauma and anger management, programs for behavioral addictions such as sex addiction, Internet addiction, and problem gambling, and specialized treatment programs for teenagers who experience anxiety or depression, or have addictions such as a video game addiction. A range of therapies are also offered, including Gestalt therapy, canine therapy, psychodrama, culinary therapy, and equine therapy.

Hazelden
www.Hazelden.org

The nonprofit Hazelden Foundation, in operation since the mid-twentieth century, maintains treatment facilities across the country, including in the states of Minnesota, New York, Illinois, and Florida. Based in Minnesota, where the foundation began a publishing operation in 1954, Hazelden bases its treatment on the twelve-step program and treats both drug and alcohol dependency in adults and youth. It also offers specialized treatment programs for legal and healthcare professionals and for those suffering from post-traumatic stress disorder, as well as family-oriented programs.

Phoenix House
www.PhoenixHouse.org

The nonprofit Phoenix House operates over 120 programs nationwide, offering the most locations in the state of New York (where Phoenix House originated in the late 1960s). Treatment services vary, with some locations offering only outpatient treatment, while others are dedicated to youth and teen recovery or for families. Phoenix also offers specialized services for expectant mothers and women with children, as well as programs for individuals with mental health issues.

Valley Hope
ValleyHope.com

The nonprofit Valley Hope Association operates nine treatment centers in seven states, most of which are located in the Midwest, including five in the state of Kansas. With an emphasis on affordability, Valley Hope offers both residential and outpatient treatment services based on the twelve-step program, as well as a family program. A Fly to Recovery service allows the association to coordinate flights for patients, at an extra cost.

WESTERN

Azure Acres Recovery Center
2264 Green Hill Road
Sebastopol, CA 95472
AzureAcres.CRCHealth.com

The redwoods of California's northern coast provide the setting for this small treatment center, housed in a lodge, that uses the twelve-step program for both alcohol and drug treatment. A weekend family program is offered, and online treatment is also available. According to the treatment center, approximately 99 percent of the staff is also in recovery.

Betty Ford Center
39000 Bob Hope Drive
Rancho Mirage, CA 92270
www.BettyFordCenter.org

Famous for its cofounding by former First Lady Betty Ford, the nonprofit Betty Ford Center in California treats both alcoholism and chemical dependency at its twenty-acre, gated hospital facility in the resort city of Rancho Mirage, California. In addition to programs for adults, the center offers programs for families, children, and young adults, and patients are separated by gender. Extended treatment offering housing is also available.

Camp Recovery Center
3192 Glen Canyon Road
Mailing: PO Box 66569
Scotts Valley, CA 95067
www.CampRecovery.com

Similar to many California-based treatment facilities and programs, this twenty-five-acre Northern California treatment center combines a pristine and peaceful natural setting—in this case, California's northern redwood forests—with an assortment of specialized and standard treatments for drug and alcohol addiction. Services are available for both adolescents and adults, and family programs are also offered.

Hawaii Natural Drug Rehabilitation and Raw
    Detoxification Center
885 Kilauea Avenue
Hilo
Hawaii 96720
www.RawDetox.org

This center takes a naturopathic approach to drug and alcohol addiction treatment, focusing on holistic medicine and diet, specifically raw foods. Utilized therapies include hydrotherapy and psychotherapy, with treatment services designed to address the needs of each individual. Rehabilitation is also offered for salt addiction, steroids abuse, white sugar addiction, and caffeine addiction.

Promises Treatment Centers
20729 Rockcroft Drive
Malibu, CA 90265
www.Promises.com

With two California locations—West Los Angeles and Malibu, the former being more affordable—Promises is a high-end treatment center that has received attention in the past for its celebrity clientele. Programs are based on the twelve-step program. Promises is also the originator of the registered "Malibu Model," and treats clients individually, and is known as one of the first centers to offer therapeutic methods such as yoga, equine therapy, and counseling for nutrition and diet, among other methods. At Promises Malibu, a specific program for executives and business leaders was enhanced in 2011.

Sierra Tucson
39580 S. Lago del Oro Parkway
Tucson, AZ 85739
www.SierraTucson.com

Situated on a 160-acre campus in Arizona's Santa Catalina Mountains, Sierra Tucson utilizes a trademarked approach built from the twelve-step philosophy to offer treatment services for alcohol and chemical dependency and other trauma or disorders. Functioning as both a psychiatric hospital and residential treatment center, Sierra Tucson emphasizes family participation, self-help practices, and psychological and other therapies, such as equine or adventure therapies, at the core of its treatment model.

Sober Living by the Sea
2811 Villa Way
Newport Beach, CA 92663
www.SoberLiving.com

Designed as a treatment community and located in an idyllic beach setting, Sober Living by the Sea advertises a combination of serene settings and proven methods (twelve-step program) for the specialized treatment of alcohol and drug abuse, as well as eating disorders. A program encouraging family participation is also offered, while a college program offers patients the opportunity to earn academic credits.

The Meadows
1655 North Tegner Street

Wickenburg, AZ 85390
www.TheMeadows.com

Self-described as "America's leading treatment center for addiction and psychological trauma," The Meadows is a fourteen-acre treatment facility located in Arizona. The center is open to those suffering from a wide range of traumas and addictions, including alcohol and drug addiction, work addiction, sexual addiction and love addiction, and eating and other disorders.

MIDWESTERN

Eagle Ridge Institute
601 N.E. 63rd Street
Oklahoma City, OK 73105
www.EagleRidgeInstitute.com

The not-for-profit Eagle Ridge Institute focuses on improving the lives of families and children affected by substance and drug abuse. They also offer educational programs for societal issues such as gang affiliation and offer like skills and alternative recreation programs for youth. A residential treatment center, which maintains preference for pregnant women, offers long-term treatment and residency for women and their children. In addition, the institute offers juvenile counseling, court advocacy for youth and families, and numerous community services.

Gateway Foundation
www.RecoverGateway.org

Gateway Foundation is a substance treatment provider that operates nine locations in the state of Illinois, and is considered the largest provider of treatment for substance abuse in the state. They offer gender-specific treatment plans, both residential and outpatient programs, aftercare programs, and programs customized for dual diagnosis and adolescents and teens. Gateway also provides alcohol and drug treatment in correctional settings, operating twenty-one such programs. Gateway also has a campus in the state of Delaware.

Harbor Hall
704 Emmet Street
Petoskey, Michigan 49770
www.HarborHall.com

Billed as "Michigan's Affordable Drug Rehab Center," Harbor Hall is a non-profit provider of drug, alcohol, and gambling addiction treatment. Located in northern Michigan along a bay of Lake Michigan, Harbor Hall offers a treatment model established by the American Society of Addiction Medicine, and offers both outpatient and residential services. Other services include cognitive behavioral therapy, motivational interviewing, moral recognition therapy, and dialectical behavioral therapy.

PRIDE Institute
14400 Martin Drive
Eden Prairie, MN 55344
www.Pride-Institute.com

PRIDE Institute, founded in the mid-1980s, specializes in treating mental health issues and addiction and chemical dependencies in the lesbian, gay, bisexual, and transgender (LGBT) community. Both residential and outpatient treatment programs are offered for various addictions, disorders, and afflictions, including body image issues, bipolar disorder, anxiety and sexual anorexia; specialized programs include a Sexual Health Program and the Kindred Program, which focuses on family and friend participation. A sister program, PRIDE Institute Florida, is located in Fort Lauderdale.

Timberline Knolls
40 Timberline Drive
Lemont, Illinois 60439
www.TimberlineKnolls.com

Situated on 43 acres in the northeastern corner of the state of Illinois, the Timberline Knolls residential treatment center offers a holistic approach in treating a range of addictions and disorders, from eating and mood disorders to alcoholism and addiction to cocaine and heroin. It was founded in 2005, and admits both adolescent and adult females; as of 2012, the treatment center offers four separate lodging areas as well as an education program for adolescents and teenagers. The campus has earned recognition from the American Institute of Landscape Architects.

NORTHEASTERN

Arms Acres
75 Seminary Hill Road
Carmel, NY 10512
www.ArmsAcres.com

Located approximately ninety miles outside of New York City, Arms Acres is a residential facility that uses the twelve-step philosophy to treat alcohol and drug addiction. Arms Acres also maintains five outpatient clinics throughout New York, including in Queens and the Bronx. Certain clinics offer a wide range of specialized services, including gay, lesbian, and transgendered programs, a Latino program, and family counseling.

Caron Pennsylvania
243 North Galen Hall Road
Wernersville, PA 19565
www.Caron.org

Servicing the state of Pennsylvania since the mid-twentieth century, Caron, a nonprofit operation, provides both alcohol and drug addiction treatment that is based on the twelve-step program and its philosophy. Family programs and treatment options for young adults and adolescents are offered, and the nonprofit provides rehabilitation programs for compulsive gambling. Operating under the Caron Treatment Centers umbrella, the nonprofit has established facilities in both Florida and Texas, as well as numerous regional offices, including an office in Bermuda.

Mountainside Addiction Treatment Center
187 South Canaan Road
Canaan, CT 06018
www.Mountainside.com

Located in seclusion in the Berkshires on sixty acres, Mountainside Addiction Treatment center offers a number of therapies, including adventure-based therapy and the twelve-step program for alcohol and drug rehabilitation. Treatment plans are designed to treat the individual, and unique elements of the treatment services offered include an on-site maze and sweat lodge, artistically-focused workshops, acupuncture, and gender-specific approaches.

Samaritan Village, Inc.
138-02 Queens Boulevard
Briarwood, NY 11435
www.SamVill.org

Samaritan Village, with locations throughout the New York metropolitan area, offers substance abuse treatment programs based on the self-help Therapeutic Community model, which emphasizes environment and social learning. In addition to residential treatment services, Samaritan Village maintains a residential methadone-to-abstinence program and services for veterans and the homeless. Treatment services focusing on basic education and work skills training are also offered.

SOUTHERN

Austin Recovery
8402 Cross Park Drive Austin, TX 78754
www.AustinRecovery.org

Based in and around Austin, Texas, Austin Recovery, which operates separate men's and women's facilities as well as a ranch, emphasizes affordability and life skills needed in recovery. Utilizing the twelve-step program in conjunction with a spiritual approach, Austin Recovery also offers a family-based program where women can recover from addiction in a residential setting alongside their children. Austin Recovery is completely tobacco-free.

Behavioral Health of the Palm Beaches
509 Federal Highway
Lake Park, FL 33403
www.BHPalmBeach.com

The primary facility for this residential treatment center is located in Lake Worth, Florida, and offers a range of treatment programs concerning behavioral health and addiction, including treatment for pain medication addiction, eating disorders, anger management, and depression. A separate facility in Palm Beach County offers luxury accommodations for patients and an executive rehabilitation program. The center also offers professional programs for athletes, pilots, and healthcare professionals, as well as traditional treatment focused on the Christian or Jewish faith.

Father Martin's Ashley
800 Tydings Lane
Havre de Grace, MD 21078
www.FatherMartinsAshley.org

Located on Maryland's Chesapeake Bay, the private, nonprofit Father Martin's Ashley offers a range of treatment options for men, women, and young adults, as well family programs and youth workshops. Integrating both holistic and twelve-step practices with the science of addiction medicine, Father Martin's Ashley also offers therapeutic services such as yoga, arts and crafts, and music workshops. The facility is situated on 147 acres that feature an abundance of wildlife.

La Hacienda Treatment Center
PO Box 1
145 La Hacienda Way
Hunt, TX 78024
www.LaHacienda.com

A sister facility of the Ajijic, Mexico-based Hacienda del Lago, a Spanish-speaking treatment center, La Hacienda Treatment Center in Texas treats both alcoholism and chemical dependency. The center works with referring professionals, including physicians, and offers certain targeted treatment programs, including a Recovering Professionals Program, a Collegiate Program, and a Christian focus program. Outreach offices are also located in four other state destinations.

New Life Lodge
999 Girl Scout Road
Burns, TN 37029
www.NewLifeLodge.com

Situated on approximately 120 acres of woodlands, this centrally-located treatment center in Tennessee treats both adolescents and adults for drug and alcohol abuse. Offering an assortment of programs based on the twelve-step program, from inpatient and outpatient treatment to programs set up for transitional living, the facility also offers an onsite school for younger clients and onsite medical staff, including both an addictionologist and psychiatrist.

Right Step
The Right Step Corporate Offices 902 W. Alabama
Houston, TX 77006
www.RightStep.com

Advertised as the largest alcohol and drug treatment provider in the southwestern region of the United States, The Right Step offers numerous treatment options at its numerous locations, including a holistic and luxurious facility near Austin, Texas, (Spirit Lodge) and a treatment center for men between the ages of eighteen and twenty-six in New Mexico. The majority of Right Step treatment centers and residential facilities are located throughout Texas, with programs varying based on location.

Santé Center for Healing
914 Country Club Road
Argyle, TX 76226
www.SanteCenter.com

Offering varying levels of rehabilitation, the rural Santé Center for Healing treats not only alcohol and drug dependency and addiction, but eating disorders, compulsive gambling, sex addiction, and other behavioral addictions and disorders. Programs emphasizing familial therapy and transitional living are also offered. The treatment offered is built upon the twelve-step program, and incorporates holistic approaches and therapies, both experimental and traditional, such as stress reduction and cognitive-behavioral therapies.

The Treatment Center
4905 Lantana Road
Lake Worth, FL 33463
www.TheTreatmentCenter.com

The Treatment Center, based in Florida, offers a variety of treatment options for alcohol and drug addiction, including specialized or personalized treatment for crack cocaine, crystal meth, heroin, and other opiates, as well as both drug and alcohol therapy and treatment for couples using cognitive-behavior therapy. Dual diagnosis treatment is also offered at the Florida-based facility.

Starlite Recovery Center
230 Mesa Verde Drive EMailing: PO Box 317
Center Point, TX 78010
www.StarliteRecovery.com

This fifty-five-acre Texas facility treats both alcoholism and drug addiction among adults and adolescent males. The center touts an "innovative" treatment program for chemical dependency that therapeutically treats the patient both physically and metaphysically, with treatment also

CANADA

Ledgehill Treatment and Recovery Centre
7608 Hwy 201 RR #1
Lawrencetown, Nova Scotia B0S 1M0
www.LedgeHill.com

Nova Scotia's Ledgehill Treatment and Recovery Centre offers drug and alcohol treatment services based on the twelve-step program while also incorporating therapeutic practices such as yoga, exercise, and meditation into the recovery process. Standard treatment lasts forty-five days minimum, and the facility emphasizes the beautiful locale as beneficial to the rehabilitation process.

Orchard Recovery and Addiction Treatment Center
811 Grafton Road
Bowen Island, BC V0N 1G2
www.OrchardRecovery.com

Located in British Columbia, Canada, on Bowen Island, the residential Orchard Recover Center offers a wide array of treatment services with a treatment philosophy that combines holistic, medical, and psychological approaches and practices, with the twelve-step program cited as a foundation. The center is situated on four acres on the former site of a four-star resort.

Pickerel Lake Recovery Center
2159 Pickerel & Jack Lake Road
Burks Falls, Ontario, P0A 1C0
www.PickerelLakeRecovery.com

This 100-plus-acre residential treatment center, located in Ontario, Canada, offers a resort setting for the treatment of alcohol and drug addiction. Services used include holistic and therapeutic approaches such as massage therapy, psychotherapy, and Reiki. The treatment center is also one of the few centers in Canada to treat methadone addiction.

Serenity Ranch
Box 51
Tees, Alberta T0C 2N0
www.SerenityRanch.ca

The private and residential Serenity Ranch, situated in Alberta, Canada, utilizes the twelve-step program to treat alcohol and drug dependency and abuse. Several programs are offered, including a one-week family program. The treatment center also offers local pick-up options in locations throughout Central Alberta, as well as at major airports in the region.

Addictions Support Groups and Organizations

Drug and Alcohol Support Groups

Al-Anon and Alateen
Contact information in the United States:
1600 Corporate Landing Parkway
Virginia Beach, VA 23454-5617
www.al-anon.alateen.org/

Al-Anon is a support group for family and friends of alcoholics. Alateen is a support group for children of alcoholics. No membership fees. Worldwide services are provided.

Alcoholics Anonymous World Services, Inc. (AA)
475 Riverside Drive at West 120th Street, 11th Floor
New York, NY 10115
www.aa.org/

This is a support group for men and women who want to recover from alcoholism. Meetings are available worldwide. Review the website for meeting locations. No membership fees.

Christians in Recovery
P.O. Box 4422
Tequesta, FL 33469
christians-in-recovery.org/

This support group is available to individuals who are looking to recover from their addiction using biblical principles.

Cocaine Anonymous (CA)
21720 S. Wilmington Avenue, Suite 304
Long Beach, CA 90810-1641
www.ca.org/

This is a support group for men and women who want to recover from cocaine addiction. Worldwide support is available. Review the website for meeting locations. No membership fees.

Jewish Alcoholics, Chemically Dependent Persons, and Significant Others.
135 West 50th Street, 6th Floor
New York, NY 10020
www.jbfcs.org/programs-services/jewish-community-services-2/jacs/

This program is sponsored by the Jewish Board of Family and Children Services. The website, dedicated to Jewish people suffering from drug and alcohol dependencies, offers multiple resources exclusive to the Jewish community. Meetings are available worldwide. See the website for details.

Making a Difference Junction
www.mdjunction.com/drug-addiction

This website has multiple online support groups maintained by recovering addicts and family members.

Nar-Anon
22527 Crenshaw Boulevard, Suite 200 B
Torrance, CA 90505
nar-anon.org/

This is a support group for people affected by someone else's drug addiction. Worldwide services are provided. Review the website for meeting locations. No membership fees.

Narcotics Anonymous (NA)
www.na.org/

This is a nonprofit organization designed for men and women who want to recover from any narcotic addiction. Groups are available worldwide. Review the website for meeting locations. No membership fees.

One Step at a Time
www.12step.com/

This website offers multiple different twelve-step addiction support groups including: alcohol, prescription drug, smoking, cocaine, crack, heroin, marijuana, and many others. These are faith-based support groups with meetings available nationwide. Review the website for meeting locations.

Recoveries Anonymous
RA Universal Services
PO Box 1212
East Northport, NY 11731
www.r-a.org/

This is a support group that offers alternatives to the traditional twelve-step programs. See website for additional details and meeting locations.

Recovery Connection
www.recoveryconnection.org/support_groups/drug-
　alcohol-addiction-support-groups.php
This websites offers information on multiple local addiction support groups. See website and enter your location information for support groups near you.

Secular Organizations for Sobriety (SOS)
Council for Secular Humanism
4773 Hollywood Boulevard
Hollywood, CA 90027
www.cfiwest.org/sos/
This is an alternative support group for individuals suffering from alcohol or drug addiction. The support group does not include the spiritual content of the twelve-step programs. Meetings are available worldwide. See website for more details.

SMART Recovery
7304 Mentor Avenue, Suite F
Mentor, OH 44060
www.smartrecovery.org/
This is a self-help website that teaches individuals how to take the first few steps towards recovery. It also offers online support groups (both text meetings and voice meetings) as well as face-to-face support groups worldwide for multiple addictions. Review website for meeting information.

Sober Recovery
www.soberrecovery.com/
This website offers online self-help forums to drug addicts and alcoholics as well as family members. Printed materials are available for those who would like to take the first few steps towards recovering from addiction. Chat meetings and discussion groups are available seven days a week.

Transformations
www.transformations.com/
This is an online support group for recovering alcoholics and drug addicts.

OTHER ADDICTIONS SUPPORT GROUPS

Co-Dependents Anonymous (CoDA)
CoDA, Fellowship Services Office
PO Box 33577
Phoenix, AZ 85067 3577
www.coda.org/
This is a support group for men and women trying to recover from dysfunctional relationships. Groups are available nationwide. Review the website for meeting locations. No membership fees.

Cyber Recovery Community
www.cyberrecovery.net/
This is a resource website that provides information, guidance, and help to individuals already involved in a program for drug addiction.

DailyStrength
3280 Peachtree Road, Suite 600
Atlanta, GA 30305 USA
www.dailystrength.org
This is an organization that offers online support to family and friends of individuals suffering from any addiction, including but not limited to alcohol and nicotine addictions.

Gamblers Anonymous
P.O. Box 17173
Los Angeles, CA 90017
www.gamblersanonymous.org/
This is an international support group for men and women trying to recover from a gambling problem. Review the website for meeting locations. No membership fees.

Marijuana Anonymous
P.O. Box 7807
Torrance, CA 90504
www.marijuana-anonymous.org/
This is a website dedicated to people looking to overcome their marijuana addiction. There are online and worldwide meetings available. See the website for additional meeting details.

Nicotine Anonymous
Nicotine Anonymous World Services
6333 E. Mockingbird # 147-817
Dallas, TX 75214
www.nicotine-anonymous.org/
This website offers support to individuals who

would like to cease using tobacco and nicotine products. Groups are available nationwide. Review the website for meeting locations. No membership fees.

Online Addiction and Recovery Resource
www.myaddiction.com

This website offers advice on different treatment options. It also has online support groups for multiple addictions and links to different treatment centers.

Overeaters Anonymous
6075 Zenith Court NE
Rio Rancho, New Mexico 87144-6424
Mailing address:
PO Box 44020
Rio Rancho, New Mexico 87174-4020
www.oa.org/

This is a support group for compulsive eaters. Support for family and friends is available. Groups are available worldwide. Review the website for meeting locations. No membership fees.

Project Know
www.projectknow.com/

This website provides general information and online support groups on multiple addictions. A twenty-four-hour hotline is available to help individuals and interested family members find local support. Nationwide services are provided.

Provident Living
providentliving.org/content/list/0,11664,4177-1,00.
html

This is a faith-based support group sponsored by the Church of Jesus Christ of Latter Day Saints (Mormon). Counseling services are available to all individuals regardless of race or religious background. Worldwide locations available. See website for further information.

Rational Recovery
PO Box 800
Lotus, CA 95651
rational.org/

This is a non-religious and non-spiritual recovery group. The website contains information on how to achieve addiction recovery independently from group participation.

Ready to Quit Smoking
www.readytoquit.com/

This website offers an online support group for people looking to quit their nicotine addiction.

Sex and Love Addicts Anonymous (SLAA)
Fellowship-Wide Services
1550 NE Loop 410, Suite 118
San Antonio, TX 78209
www.slaafws.org/

This is a fellowship of men and women who help each other stay sober and recover from sexual addiction.

Sexual Compulsives Anonymous (SCA)
P.O. Box 1585, Old Chelsea Station
New York, NY 10011
www.sca-recovery.org

This is a support group for men and women trying to recover from sexual compulsion. Members develop their own recovery plan.

Smoking Cessation
www.smoking-cessation.org/

This website provides self-help tools for smokers looking to kick the addiction. Support groups are also available.

Stop Smoking Center
sg.stopsmokingcenter.net/support/

Free online forum for individuals looking for resources to quit smoking. The forum is moderated by health educators.

Support Groups
www.supportgroups.com

This website offers over two hundred different online support groups, among them alcohol, cocaine, caffeine, gambling, prescription drugs, shopping addiction, smoking, and others. The site also has a large list of treatment centers and online resources.

Women for Sobriety, Inc.
PO Box 618
Quakertown, PA 18951
womenforsobriety.org/

This is a nonprofit group dedicated to helping women overcome alcoholism and drug abuse. Online chat groups are available.

ORGANIZATIONS

Above the Influence
www.abovetheinfluence.com/

This website is sponsored by the National Youth Anti-Drug Media Campaign. It provides drug fact information and provides videos and advertisements. Additionally, the campaign lets anyone send drug-related questions to qualified doctors.

American Cancer Society
www.cancer.org/

This is a nonprofit organization. It offers information on the relationship between smoking and lung cancer. Information is available in several languages.

American Public Health Association (APHA)
800 I Street, NW
Washington, DC 20001
www.apha.org/

This organization provides information on legislative initiatives and advocacy groups for all aspects of health related issues.

American Society of Addiction Medicine (ASAM)
4601 N. Park Avenue, Upper Arcade, Suite 101
Chevy Chase, MD 20815
www.asam.org/

This organization provides addiction and substance abuse information to the medical community.

Association for Medical Education and Research in Substance Abuse (AMERSA)
Street address:
201 Hillside Road, Suite 102
Cranston, RI 02920
Mailing address:
PO Box 20160
Cranston, RI 02920
www.amersa.org/

This organization publishes its own peer-reviewed journal on substance abuse. Copies are available on the website.

Behavioral Health Research Center of the Southwest
612 Encino Place NE
Albuquerque, NM 87102
www.bhrcs.org/

This organization is part of the Center of Pacific Institute for Research Evaluation. They conduct clinical trials related to drug abuse.

Building Blocks for a Healthy Future
1 Choke Cherry Road
Rockville, MD 20857
bblocks.samhsa.gov/

This organization is sponsored by the Substance Abuse and Mental Health Services Admin-istration (SAMHSA). It is designed to train parents and caregivers on early childhood substance abuse prevention.

California Wellness Foundation
Main office:
6320 Canoga Avenue, Suite 1700
Woodland Hills, CA 91367
Branch Office:
575 Market Street, Suite 1850
San Francisco, CA 94105
www.calwellness.org/

This foundation provides funding for health-related issues that affect the people of the state of California.

Center for Alcohol and Addiction Studies (CAAS)
121 South Main Street
Providence, RI 02903
Mailing address:
PO Box G-S121-5
Brown University
Providence RI 02912
www.caas.brown.edu/

This website is sponsored by Brown University. It includes their research information on identification, prevention, and treatment of substance abuse.

Center for Substance Abuse Research (CESAR)
4321 Hartwick Road, Suite 501
College Park, MD 20740
www.cesar.umd.edu/

This center is supported by the University of Maryland College of Behavioral and Social Services. It provides information on drug and alcohol abuse for the citizens of Maryland.

Center on Alcoholism, Substance Abuse, and
    Addictions (CASAA)
2650 Yale SE, MSC11-6280
Albuquerque, NM 87106
casaa.unm.edu/
This organization is sponsored by the University
of New Mexico. It is dedicated to prevention and
treatment research, as well as to teaching family and
friends of drug abusers to accept treatment.

Club Drugs
6001 Executive Boulevard
Bethesda, MD 20892-9561
www.clubdrugs.gov/
This website is sponsored by the National Institute
on Drug Abuse. It offers medical and research information on different drugs.

Corporation for National and Community Service
1201 New York Avenue, NW
Washington, DC 20525
www.nationalservice.gov/
For specific state information, see: nationalservice.
gov/about/role_impact/state_profiles.asp
This is a federal agency dedicated to serving local
communities.

Dual Diagnosis and Addiction Treatment
www.dual-diagnosis.net/
This organization provides information on mental
health conditions and how they relate to drug
addictions.

Elks Drug Awareness Program
Director's contact information
67597 550th Street
Griswold, IA 51535-6005
www.elks.org/dap/
This is a volunteer drug awareness program spon-
sored by the Elks. Programs are available nationwide.
See the website for details.

Find Youth Info
findyouthinfo.gov/
This organization was created by the Interagency
Working Group on Youth Programs (IWGYP). It promotes positive and healthy youth development by
promoting the collaboration of government agencies,
private organizations, and nonprofit organizations.

Fundación Azteca America
1139 Grand Central Avenue
Glendale, CA 91720
www.fundacionaztecaamerica.org/
This is a nonprofit organization designed to promote the well-being of the Latino community in the
United States. They sponsor multiple antidrug projects throughout the country.

GLOBALink
www.globalink.org
This website is geared towards communities and
organizations looking for tobacco control information. The website information is available in multiple
languages.

Hands Net
www.handsnet.org/
This is a nonprofit organization that offers information on drug policies and government funding.

Health Finder
P.O. Box 1133
Washington, DC 20013-1133
www.healthfinder.gov/
This is a government website that offers online in-
formation on multiple health and addiction issues.
Search the database for specific health and addiction
information.

Intervention
www.intervention.com/
This is an organization that provides drug and
addiction intervention services and training in the
United States and worldwide.

Join Together
The Partnership at Drugfree.org
352 Park Avenue South, 9th Floor
New York, NY 10010
www.drugfree.org/join-together
This website provides information for communities. It contains drug policy information and federal
funding news.

Just Think Twice
www.justthinktwice.com/
This website is sponsored by the Drug Enforcement Agency (DEA). It outlines scientific facts for

multiple different drugs and consequences for drug use. This website is geared toward teenagers.

Marijuana Information
6001 Executive Boulevard
Bethesda, MD 20892-9561
www.drugabuse.gov/drugs-abuse/marijuana/
This website is sponsored by the National Institute of Health. It contains fact sheets on marijuana, plus research and statistics for teenagers and parents to use as reference.

Medline Plus
8600 Rockville Pike
Bethesda, MD 20894
http://www.nlm.nih.gov/medlineplus/
This website is sponsored by the National Library of Science and the National Institute of Health. It provides medical information on a variety of drug abuse problems. Videos and multiple printed aids are available.

Metro Council for Teen Potential
585 Joseph Avenue
Rochester NY 14605
www.metrocouncil.us/
This is a local organization that promotes the well-being of children. This group sponsors multiple youth programs. See the website for additional details.

Mothers Against Drunk Driving (MADD)
MADD National Office
511 E. John Carpenter Freeway, Suite 700
Irving, TX 75062
www.madd.org/
This organization is devoted to the prevention of underage drinking and to stop drunk driving. Additionally, they offer support to victims of drunk driving. Local offices are always looking for volunteers. See website for details.

National Families in Action (NFIA)
P.O. Box 133136
Atlanta, Georgia 30333-3136
www.nationalfamilies.org/
This organization provides information to parents and children regarding drug abuse.

National Inhalant Prevention Coalition (NIPC)
318 Lindsay Street

Chattanooga, TN 37403
www.inhalants.org/
This website contains inhalant statistics as well as signs and effects of inhalant drug abuse. A detailed description of state laws is included. Information is also available in Spanish.

National Institute for Drug Abuse – for Teens
teens.drugabuse.gov/
This website is sponsored by NIDA and it is dedicated to teaching children the science behind drug abuse. Multiple downloads, worksheets, and videos are available through the site.

National Institute on Alcohol Abuse and
   Alcoholism (NIAAA)
5635 Fishers Lane, MSC 9304
Bethesda, MD 20892-9304
www.niaaa.nih.gov/
This organization is part of the National Institutes of Health. It conducts research on alcohol abuse and the prevention of alcoholism.

National Institutes of Health – National Institute on
   Drug Abuse (NIDA)
6001 Executive Boulevard, Room 5213
Bethesda, MD 20892-9561
www.drugabuse.gov
This is a government agency charged with the dissemination of information regarding drug abuse and prevention, as well as treatment and relevant government policies. This agency sponsors multiple anti-drug campaign initiatives including:
   Anabolic steroid abuse: steroidabuse.gov/
   Drugs and HIV learn the link: hiv.drugabuse.gov/

National Meth Center – Meth Resources
http://www.nationalmethcenter.org/RESOURCES.
   html
This anti-methamphetamine website provides updated links to numerous resources for prevention and recovery.

National Opinion Research Center (NORC)
Bethesda, MD Office:
4350 East-West Highway, Suite 800
Bethesda, MD 20814
Chicago Offices:
University of Chicago

1155 East 60th Street
Chicago, IL 60637
Loop Offices:
55 East Monroe Street
Chicago, IL 60603
One North State Street
Chicago, IL 60602
www.norc.uchicago.edu/

This is a nonprofit organization that gathers information and conducts research on multiple fields, including drugs and alcohol. They are sponsored by the University of Chicago.

Northwest Regional Education Laboratory
    (REL Northwest)
Education Northwest
101 SW Main Street, Suite 500
Portland, OR 97204-3213
educationnorthwest.org/

This website contains information for schools and communities on how to educate children and young adults regarding drug abuse.

No Smoke Software
www.smokefreekids.com/smoke.htm

This is a computer program designed to help children stop smoking. It is available free for individual use in English and German.

Office of National Drug Control Policy (ONDCP)
Drug Policy Information Clearinghouse
P.O. Box 6000
Rockville, MD 20849-6000
whitehousedrugpolicy.gov/

This organization is dedicated to help solve the national drug control problems, including the reduction of drug use and the crime and violence associated with it. Additionally, part of their goal is to help families with drug-related health consequences.

Recovery Resources
www.recoveryresources.org/

This website provides links to different treatment centers and organizations.

Research Institute on Addictions
1021 Main Street
Buffalo, NY 14203-1016

www.ria.buffalo.edu/

This organization has information on current research involving addictions and substance abuse. It is associated with the State University of New York at Buffalo. They also offer treatment services through their clinical research center.

Robert Wood Johnson Foundation – Substance Abuse
    Policy Research Program
SAPRP
One Leadership Place
Greensboro, NC 27410
www.saprp.org/
Main Office:
Route 1 and College Road East
PO Box 2316
Princeton, NJ 08543
www.rwjf.org/

This organization identifies, analyzes, and evaluates policies on tobacco, alcohol, and drug abuse.

Safe Schools, Healthy Students
www.sshs.samhsa.gov/

This is a federal initiative for violence and substance abuse prevention in communities across the nation. Schools and communities are encouraged to apply for a federal grant to help with their fight against drugs.

Santa Barbara Alcohol, Drug, and Mental Health
    Services
315 Camino del Remedio
Santa Barbara, CA 93110-1316
www.countyofsb.org/admhs/

This website is dedicated to providing early drug addiction intervention for the citizens of Santa Barbara, California.

Smoke Free Network
1711 18th Street NW, Basement
Washington, DC 20008
www.smokefree.net/

Advocate organization dedicated to obtaining a smoke-free environment nationwide.

Smoke Free Washington Workers
www.smokefreedc.org/

This organization was formed by citizens of Washington, DC, to fight for a smoke-free environment.

Society for Prevention Research
11240 Waples Mill Road, Suite 200
Fairfax, VA 22030
www.preventionresearch.org/
  This organization is focused on the prevention of drug and alcohol abuse, in addition to associated crimes and behavior disorders.

Society for Research on Nicotine and Tobacco
2424 American Lane
Madison, WI 53704
www.srnt.org/
  This website contains international research information on tobacco and nicotine addiction.

Stop Underage Drinking
www.stopalcoholabuse.gov/
  This is a government-sponsored organization dedicated to the prevention of underage drinking. Many resource materials are available for download. The site contains information sections geared toward communities, parents, businesses, educators, and teenagers.

Substance Abuse and Mental Health Services Administration (SAMHSA)
1 Choke Cherry Road
Rockville, MD 20857
Mailing address:
PO Box 2345
Rockville, MD 20847-2345
www.samhsa.gov/prevention/spf.aspx
  This is a government agency that works together with states, territories, federally recognized tribes, and communities to build effective evidence based drug prevention programs.

The Annie E. Casey Foundation
701 St. Paul Street
Baltimore, MD 21202
www.aecf.org/
  This is a nonprofit organization that provides funding for health-related issues that affect the welfare of children.

The Center for Social Gerontology
2307 Shelby Avenue
Ann Harbor, MI 48103
www.tcsg.org/tobacco.htm

This website has information on tobacco and how it affects senior citizens.

The Ford Foundation
Headquarters:
320 East 43rd Street
New York, NY 10017 USA
www.fordfoundation.org/
  This is a nonprofit organization that provides funding for health-related issues that affect the welfare of children worldwide.

The Henry J. Kaiser Family Foundation
Headquarters:
2400 Sand Hill Road
Menlo Park, CA 94025
Washington, DC Office/Public Affairs Center:
1330 G Street, NW
Washington, DC 20005
www.kff.org/
  This is a nonprofit organization that provides funding for public health information campaigns in the United States and around the world.

The John D. and Catherine T. MacArthur Foundation
Headquarters:
Office of Grants Management
140 S. Dearborn Street
Chicago, IL 60603-5285
www.macfound.org
  This is a nonprofit organization that provides funding for health-related issues that affect the welfare of children worldwide.

The Pew Charitable Trusts
Philadelphia Office:
One Commerce Square
2005 Market Street, Suite 1700
Philadelphia, PA 19103-7077
Washington, DC Office:
901 E. Street NW
Washington, DC 20004-2008
www.pewtrusts.org/
  This is a nonprofit organization that provides information on multiple issues and trends.

Tobacco.org
PO Box 359
Village Station

New York, NY 10014-0359
www.tobacco.org/

This organization focuses on tobacco-related issues and offers assistance to smokers trying to quit the habit.

Tobacco Documents
tobaccodocuments.org/

This organization searches and provides multiple tobacco research documents as part of the settlement between the United States and the tobacco industry.

Too Smart to Start
1 Choke Cherry Road
Rockville, MD 20857
www.toosmarttostart.samhsa.gov/

This website is part of the national initiative to prevent underage drinking. It is designed to help and inform families, educators, pre-teens, and teenagers on underage drinking.

United States Department of State – International

Narcotics Control Strategy Report
2201 C Street NW
Washington, DC 20520
www.state.gov/j/inl/rls/nrcrpt/2012/index.htm/

This is a government organization that reports on the international drug trade and progress against it made by the United States government.

Web of Addictions
www.well.com/user/woa/

This website provides multiple links to drug addiction information.

W. K. Kellogg Foundation
One Michigan Avenue East
Battle Creek, MI 49017-4012
www.wkkf.org/

This organization provides funding for health-related issues that affect the welfare of children worldwide.

INTERNATIONAL SUPPORT GROUPS AND ORGANIZATIONS

Al-Anon and Alateen
Contact information outside the United States:
Capital Corporate Centre
9 Antares Drive, Suite 245
Ottawa, ON K2E 7V5
www.al-anon.alateen.org/

Al-Anon is a support group for family and friends of alcoholics. Alateen is a support group for children of alcoholics. No membership fees. Worldwide services are provided.

Canadian Centre on Substance Abuse (CCSA)
75 Albert Street, Suite 500
Ottawa, ON K1P 5E7
Canada
www.ccsa.ca/

This website provides information and links to drug policy and drug treatments available in Canada. Information is available in English and French.

Canadian Foundation for Drug Policy
70 MacDonald Street

Ottawa, ON K2P 1H6
Canada
www.cfdp.ca/

This website offers information on drug policy and resources specific to Canada.

Drug Policy and Human Rights Foundation
Koninginneweg 189
1075 CP Amsterdam
The Netherlands
www.drugtext.org/

This website offers information on drug policies worldwide. Information is available in multiple languages.

DrugScope
Prince Consort House
Suite 204 (2nd Floor)
109/111 Farringdon Road
London EC1R 3BW
www.drugscope.org.uk/

This website provides information on drug policies in the United Kingdom.

United Nations Office on Drugs and Crime (UNODC)
UNODC
PO Box 500
A 1400
Vienna, Austria
www.unodc.org/

This international organization provides information on drug-related topics from around the world.

World Health Organization (WHO), Department of Mental Health and Substance Abuse
20, Avenue Appia
CH-1211 Geneva 27
Switzerland
www.who.int/substance_abuse/en/

This organization works toward the management and reduction of the health and social effects of drug abuse worldwide. Information is available in various languages.

Timeline of Major Developments in Addictions and Substance Abuse

YEAR	EVENT
10,000 BCE	Earliest evidence for brewing and consumption of beer.
8000 BCE	Earliest record of wine production and consumption, in present-day Georgia (country) and Armenia.
6000 BCE	Earliest archaeological evidence for the chewing of coca leaves, in Peru.
3400 BCE	Opium poppies are cultivated in Mesopotamia for the treatment of asthma as well as for pain relief.
3000 BCE	Reign of the legendary Emperor Shennong, credited by later Chinese writers with the discovery of coffee.
c. 1500 BCE	Beginnings of the Greek cult of Dionysus (Roman name Bacchus), the god of wine, ritual intoxication, and madness.
c. 700 BCE	The book of Proverbs contains the earliest warnings against drunkenness in the Old Testament.
650 BCE	Early Chinese medical texts warn about the moral as well as the physical dangers of drunkenness.
400 BCE	The Sushruta Samhita, an ancient Indian text on surgery and Ayurvedic medicine, recommends alcohol as an anesthetic during surgery.
c. 800 CE	The Maya of Central America invent an early form of the cigarette, using plant wrappers instead of paper to hold the tobacco.
c. 1000	Medieval European law deals with public drunkenness as a minor offense handled at the local level; it is not yet considered a disease or a danger to the general public.
c. 1300	Earliest documentation of the distillation of alcohol, at the medical school of the University of Salerno.
c. 1400	Europeans in various countries discover how to distill alcohol from wheat, barley, rye, and various fruits or berries, leading to the production of gin (England), schnapps (Germany), vodka (Russia), akvavit (Scandinavia), and grappa (Italy).
c. 1450	Earliest documented evidence of drinking coffee as a stimulant, in the Sufi monasteries of southern Arabia.
1540	German botanist and chemist Valerius Cordus (1515–1544) first synthesizes ether, although he is unaware of its anesthetic or intoxicating properties.

YEAR	EVENT
1560	Jean Nicot (1530–1600), the French ambassador to Portugal, brings tobacco plants to France, introduces snuff to the French court, and recommends tobacco as a medicine. His name will be given to the addictive chemical in tobacco.
1604	King James I of England (1566–1625) publishes the first antismoking pamphlet: A Counterblaste to Tobacco, which attacks "the manifold abuses of this vile custom of tobacco taking."
1647	A Greek monk named Agapios is the first to document the long-term effects of alcohol abuse on the digestive tract and central nervous system.
1652	Opening of the first coffee house in London, in St. Michael's Alley. Coffee houses quickly become popular across Western Europe.
1657	The General Court of Massachusetts declares the sale of rum, brandy, and other "strong liquors" illegal.
1660	Thomas Sydenham (1624–1689), an eminent English physician, formulates a tincture of opium that he calls laudanum, and recommends it to treat a wide range of diseases. By the nineteenth century, Sydenham's mixture of opium and alcohol is widely used in patent medicines as a pain reliever and sleeping aid. Its potential for addiction goes unrecognized until the early twentieth century.
1774	Anthony Benezet (1713–1784), a Philadelphia Quaker, publishes the first American essay on alcoholism, titled "The Mighty Destroyer Displayed."
1804	Friedrich Sertürner (1783–1841), a German pharmacist, is the first to extract morphine from the juice of the opium poppy. Advances in organic chemistry in the nineteenth century will contribute to a widespread increase in substance abuse.
1820	Friedlieb Ferdinand Runge (1795–1867), a German chemist, isolates and identifies caffeine, the psychoactive compound found in coffee beans.
1821	Thomas De Quincey (1785–1859), an English journalist and writer, publishes his Confessions of an English Opium-Eater, a personal account of his addiction to opium and alcohol.
1828	Wilhelm Posselt and Karl Reimann, two students at the University of Heidelberg, isolate nicotine from the leaves of the tobacco plant. They identify it as a poison and recommend its use as a pesticide.
1830s	American medical students hold ether frolics—gatherings in which they "get high" by inhaling ether or nitrous oxide. In some cases, fellow students paid admission to watch the foolish behavior of those intoxicated by the gas.
1832	The French chemist Pierre Jean Robiquet (1780–1840) isolates the alkaloid codeine from the juice of the opium poppy. Codeine will become the most frequently prescribed opiate worldwide.

YEAR	EVENT
1839–1842	The First Opium War is fought between the United Kingdom and the Qing Dynasty of China when the Chinese government attempts to stop British traders from selling opium in Canton in order to slow the spread of opium addiction.
1849	Magnus Huss (1807–1890), a Swedish physician, coins the term alcoholism to refer to what he considers a chronic disease with frequent relapses. He is credited with introducing the concept of alcoholism as a disease.
1853	The hypodermic syringe is invented independently by Charles Pravaz (1791–1853), a French surgeon, and Alexander Wood (1817–1884), a Scottish physician. The new device will help to spread the abuse of morphine and other injectable drugs.
1856–1860	The Second Opium War, involving the French as well as the British, ends in the legalization of the opium trade in China.
1858	Construction begins on the New York State Inebriate Asylum in Binghamton; the institution is the first in the United States to treat alcoholism as a mental disorder. Other inebriate asylums quickly follow, offering treatment for addiction to such other drugs as opium, morphine, cocaine, ether, and chloroform. Most of these institutions will close between 1910 and 1925.
1859	Albert Niemann (1834–1861), a graduate student in chemistry at the University of Göttingen, successfully isolates cocaine from coca leaves.
1874	C. R. Alder Wright, an English chemist, first synthesizes a semi-synthetic narcotic from morphine called diacetylmorphine. In 1895 Bayer begins selling diacetylmorphine as an over-the-counter cough suppressant under the trade name Heroin.

The Women's Christian Temperance Union (WCTU) is founded in Cleveland, Ohio, to combat alcohol as a source of social and family problems. The group supports women's suffrage as well as the prohibition of alcohol. |
1875	San Francisco becomes the first city in the United States to ban opium dens.
1881	Kansas becomes the first state to ban alcoholic beverages in its constitution.
1884	Sigmund Freud (1856–1939) publishes a paper recommending cocaine as a cure for a number of physical and mental disorders, including morphine addiction. He does not stop his own cocaine use until 1896.
1893	The Japanese chemist Nagai Nagayoshi (1844–1929) first synthesizes methamphetamine from ephedrine.

YEAR	EVENT
1899	Carrie Nation (1846–1911) begins her career of hatchet attacks on bars and saloons across the Midwest.
1906	President Theodore Roosevelt (1858–1919) signs the Pure Food and Drug Act into law on June 30. The US Department of Agriculture's Bureau of Chemistry (the forerunner of the FDA) is given the authority to regulate the labeling and purity of certain specific drugs, including alcohol, cocaine, heroin, morphine, and cannabis.
1910	New York becomes the first state to pass legislation against drunk driving. Substance abuse is increasingly recognized as a danger to the general public.
1914	Congress passes the Harrison Narcotics Tax Act to regulate the distribution of opiates in the United States and to collect taxes on them. It is estimated that one American adult in every 400—two-thirds of them women—were addicted to opiates in 1914.
1915	Emil Kraepelin (1856–1926), a German psychiatrist, first identifies compulsive shopping as a behavioral addiction. He calls it oniomania, from the Greek words for "for sale" and "insanity."
1916	Two German chemists at the University of Frankfurt synthesize oxycodone from thebaine, a derivative of opium. The drug is first used in Europe in 1917 but is not approved for use in the United States until 1939.
1919	The Eighteenth Amendment to the US Constitution (Prohibition) is ratified on January 16. It goes into effect on January 17, 1920.
1924	Formation of the US Border Patrol to detect and arrest persons involved in the illegal drug trade as well as illegal immigrants from Canada or Mexico.
1927	The Bureau of Chemistry is reorganized into the Food, Drug, and Insecticide Administration (FDIA) and the Bureau of Chemistry and Soils.
1929	The National Academy of Sciences (NAS) forms the Committee on Problems of Drug Dependence (CPDD), the first professional group in the United States to address problems of drug dependence and abuse.
1930	The FDIA is renamed the Food and Drug Administration (FDA).
1933	The Twenty-first Amendment to the Constitution repeals the Eighteenth; Prohibition ends on December 5.
1935	Bill Wilson (1895–1971) and Dr. Bob Smith (1879–1950) open the first meeting of Alcoholics Anonymous (AA) in Akron, Ohio.
1936	Florence Rankin becomes the first female member of AA.

YEAR	EVENT
1937	Methadone is developed as a synthetic opioid for pain relief by German chemists working for the I. G. Farben Company.
1938	Temmler Pharmaceuticals introduces a form of methamphetamine called Pervitin to the German market. By 1940 the German military is shipping millions of tablets to its soldiers, sailors, and pilots. Albert Hofmann (1906–2008), a Swiss chemist, synthesizes LSD from lysergic acid. He discovers its hallucinogenic properties in 1943 when he accidentally absorbs a small quantity through his fingertips.
1939	Publication of the first edition of the book *Alcoholics Anonymous* (the "Big Book").
1944	The Yale Center of Alcohol Studies in New Haven opens the Yale Plan Clinics, the first outpatient facilities for the treatment of alcoholism. The center also starts the Yale Plan for Business and Industry, an early version of contemporary employee-assistance programs. Marty Mann (1904–1980), an early pioneer in outreach to women alcoholics, founds the National Council on Alcoholism (NCA).
1948	A Danish pharmaceutical company accidentally discovers the effectiveness of disulfiram in treating alcohol abuse while testing the drug as a treatment for intestinal parasites.
1949	The Hazelden Foundation begins in Center City, Minnesota, as a simple farmhouse retreat called the Old Lodge for alcoholic men.
1950	Sir Richard Doll (1912–2005), an English physiologist, publishes a landmark article in the *British Medical Journal* linking tobacco use to lung cancer and heart disease.
1951	Lois Wilson (1891–1988), wife of AA co-founder Bill Wilson, forms Al-Anon/Alateen as an organization for family members affected by a spouse's or parent's alcoholism.
1953	Jimmy Kinnon (1911–1985) founds Narcotics Anonymous and adopts the twelve-step model of AA with permission from the parent organization.
1954	Aldous Huxley (1894–1963), the author of *Brave New World* (1932), publishes "The Doors of Perception," an essay in which he recommends experimenting with mescaline, LSD, and other mind-altering drugs. Hazelden begins its publication ventures with *Twenty-Four Hours a Day,* a collection of meditations and prayers for those struggling with addictions. The book will sell more than eight million copies worldwide by 2011. Formation of the American Society of Addiction Medicine (ASAM)
1957	Gamblers Anonymous (GA) is started in Los Angeles.

YEAR	EVENT
1958	The FDA approves dextromethorphan for over-the-counter sale as a cough suppressant.
1960	Overeaters Anonymous (OA) is started in Rio Rancho, New Mexico.
	E. Morton Jellinek (1890–1963), an addiction researcher, publishes *The Disease Concept of Alcoholism*, a landmark book that advanced the movement to medicalize alcohol abuse rather than define it as a moral failing.
1964	Vincent Dole (1913–2006) and Marie Nyswander (1919–1986) pioneer the use of methadone maintenance therapy in treating heroin addiction.
1970	Establishment of the National Institute on Alcohol Abuse and Alcoholism (NIAAA).
	The Controlled Substances Act (CSA) is signed into law on October 27 by President Richard Nixon (1913–1994).
1971	Nixon becomes the first US president to use the phrase "War on Drugs."
	The Public Health Cigarette Smoking Act of 1970 goes into effect, forbidding cigarette advertising on television and radio, and requiring warning labels on cigarette packages.
	Debtors Anonymous (DA) is started in Needham, Massachusetts.
1972	The Bureau of Alcohol, Tobacco, Firearms, and Explosives (ATF) is detached from the Internal Revenue Service (IRS) and becomes a separate bureau within the Treasury Department. It will be transferred to the Department of Justice in 2002.
1973	The National Institute on Drug Abuse (NIDA) is founded.
	President Nixon signs into law a reorganization plan that forms the Drug Enforcement Administration (DEA) out of several older federal bureaus tasked with enforcing laws against drug abuse.
1975	Stanton Peele (1946–), a psychologist in New Jersey, publishes *Love and Addiction*, a book in which he introduces the life process model of addiction—the view that people abuse alcohol and other drugs to cope with life. His opposition to the disease model of alcoholism and his rejection of twelve-step programs make him a controversial figure.
1977	The American Cancer Society holds its first Great American Smokeout, in which smokers are invited to quit for twenty-four hours in the hope that they can give up smoking permanently.
1980	Candace Lightner founds Mothers Against Drunk Driving (MADD) after her daughter is killed in a hit-and-run accident by an intoxicated cannery worker.

YEAR	EVENT
1982	First Lady Nancy Reagan (1921–) coins the slogan "Just Say No" when asked by a schoolgirl in Oakland, California, what she should do if offered drugs. The phrase is adopted by an NIH substance abuse prevention program that began in the late 1970s.
	Cocaine Anonymous (CA) opens its first meeting in Los Angeles.
1986	Two Australians, Kevin Barlow and Brian Chambers, are hanged in Malaysia for drug trafficking. They are the first Westerners to be executed under Malaysia's newly stiffened drug laws.
1988	The Anti-Drug Abuse Act of 1988 establishes the Office of National Drug Control Policy (ONDCP).
1990	The NCA changes its name to the National Council on Alcoholism and Drug Dependence (NCADD).
1991	The CPDD, now independent of the NAS, reorganizes itself as a membership organization with a new name—the College on Problems of Drug Dependence. It has 700 members as of 2011.
1992	The Substance Abuse and Mental Health Services Administration (SAMHSA) is formed as part of the Department of Health and Human Services.
1995	The FDA approves a time-release version of oxycodone known as OxyContin. OxyContin will become the best-selling non-generic narcotic pain reliever in the United States by 2001.
1996	Publication of first studies of compulsive hoarding as a behavioral addiction.
1997	The Hoarding of Animals Research Consortium (HARC) is established at Tufts University to study and treat animal hoarding as a distinctive form of hoarding behavior.
1999	The Hazelden Foundation opens the Hazelden Graduate School of Addiction Studies in Center City, Minnesota. The school offers a master's degree in addiction counseling.
2001	The World Health Organization (WHO) estimates that there are at least 140 million active alcoholics worldwide.
2005	The National Institutes of Health estimates that alcohol abuse costs the United States $220 billion each year—more than cancer or obesity.
2006	The Combat Methamphetamine Epidemic Act (CMEA) goes into effect, limiting the sales of over-the-counter cold and allergy medications containing ephedrine, phenylpropanolamine, or pseudoephedrine because of their use in the illegal production of crystal meth.

YEAR	EVENT
2008	The St. Gregory Retreat Center in Iowa introduces its Life Process Program, developed by Stanton Peele, for the treatment of drug and alcohol abuse. The program is based on Peele's life process model of addiction together with cognitive-behavioral therapy (CBT).
2009	Gil Kerlikowske becomes the newest director of the ONDCP.
2010	The FDA votes against placing dextromethorphan on a drug schedule even though it is known that the drug is widely abused by teenagers.
	The Mexican newspaper *Reforma* reports in December that over 10,000 murders related to drug cartels have occurred during the calendar year. The total death toll since 2006 is estimated at 28,000.

INDEXES

Categorical Index

Subject Index